Nature's Conscience

The life and legacy of Derek Ratcliffe

Derek Ratcliffe in the field, Ben Armine, Sutherland. Painting by Will Williams from a photograph by Des Thompson, June 1989

Nature's Conscience

The life and legacy of Derek Ratcliffe

Edited by
Des B.A. Thompson, Hilary H. Birks
and H. John B. Birks

Foreword by
Professor Sir John Lawton CBE FRS

LANGFORD PRESS 2015

Langford Press, 32 Eastfield,
Narborough, Kings Lynn, Norfolk PE32 1SS

www.langford-press.co.uk

Email sales@langford-press.co.uk

ISBN 978-1-904078-59-3 (paperback)
ISBN 978-1-904078-60-9 (hardback)

A CIP Record for this book is available from the British Library

Design origination and typeset by
MRM Graphics Ltd, Winslow, Bucks.
Printed in Spain

To the memory of Derek Ratcliffe,

always true to himself, friends and colleagues,

and

to those striving to continue his immense legacy of nature well protected, and committed to passing on his passion for nature and wild places to future generations

Contents

Contributors

Dick Balharry Naturalist

Dick has spent a lifetime passionately advocating the conservation of wild land and nature. Early days were spent in the Nature Conservancy, with 1962 being especially significant when Dick became the Reserve Warden of Britain's first National Nature Reserve, Beinn Eighe. Here, Dick met Derek Ratcliffe, and they remained in contact for decades afterwards.

On leaving Scottish Natural Heritage, where he worked closely with the late Sir Magnus Magnusson to communicate the wider importance of wildlife and nature reserves, Dick was appointed to several positions in public and charitable bodies. He has been Chairman of the John Muir Trust, National Trust for Scotland, Hebridean Whale & Dolphin Trust, and Local Access Group for the Cairngorms National Park, as well as President of Ramblers Scotland until 2013. Currently, he is a Director Trustee of a relatively new charity, The West Highland Coastal Trust, which has natural and cultural objectives. Awarded an MBE for services to nature conservation, Honorary Masters (Aberdeen) and DSc (Abertay) degrees, and elected an Honorary Fellow of the Royal Zoological Society, Dick thrives on being in the field with colleagues and friends – and challenging scientific ideas on conservation and management.

Rick Battarbee Professor Emeritus, Environmental Change Research Centre, University College London

Rick is an environmental scientist and former Director of the Environmental Change Research Centre at University College London. His research is concerned with the use of diatoms preserved in lake sediments as indicators of environmental change with respect especially to problems of eutrophication, acidification, and climate change. His recent work focuses on the recovery of upland lakes from the effects of 'acid rain' using a combination of sediment-core data and long-term chemical and biological records from the UK's Upland Waters Monitoring Network.

Rick is a Foreign Member of the Norwegian Academy of Science and Letters (1991), a Fellow of the Royal Society (2006), an Honorary Fellow of University College London (2011), and an Einstein Professor of the Chinese Academy of Sciences (2012). He is also Editor-in-Chief of the Royal Society journal *Biology Letters*.

David Bellamy Landscape Artist

David is a self-taught landscape artist specialising in mountain, desert, and Arctic scenery, and other wild places, including the coastline. He has written seventeen books illustrated with his paintings and sketches, and produced eight films on painting in watercolour with APV Films of Chipping Norton. He runs occasional courses on watercolour painting, and has presented a television series, *Painting Wild Wales*, for HTV Wales. Through his work he is keen to highlight the many threats to the natural environment. See www.davidbellamy.co.uk.

Hilary Birks Professor Emerita , Department of Biology, University of Bergen, Norway

Hilary is a botanist and palaeoecologist at the University of Bergen. Her research is centred on the use of plant remains (seeds, fruits, leaves, etc.) preserved in lake sediments to reconstruct the flora and vegetation of the past, particularly at the transition from the last glacial period to the present Holocene warm period. She is especially interested in how plants and ecosystems responded to climate changes in the past, which is a historical analogue for our present situation of climate warming. She has a great love of mountains and alpine plants and their ecology. Her husband, John Birks, relates in his biosketch how they met Derek Ratcliffe in 1966. They thoroughly enjoyed many subsequent memorable outings in the field with him and some rather wild expeditions together, especially searching for Atlantic bryophytes and the Killarney Fern. Their son's interest in natural history was stimulated by Derek and he is currently passing it on to Norwegian school children.

Hilary is a Foreign Member of the Norwegian Academy of Science and Letters (2003) and a Fellow of the American Association for the Advancement of Science (2014).

John Birks Professor Emeritus, Department of Biology, University of Bergen, Norway
John is a botanist and palaeoecologist at the University of Bergen where he currently researches on vegetation history and biotic responses to environmental change in Scandinavia and Tibet. He holds an emeritus position at University College London. Although primarily a pollen analyst and quantitative palaeoecologist, he has strong interests in alpine plants and ecology world-wide, and in bryophytes and pteridophytes of western Europe.

His interests in alpine botany, bryophytes, and pteridophytes were greatly stimulated by Derek Ratcliffe. They first met in a wooded valley in Borrowdale in 1966 when John and Hilary were on their honeymoon in the Lake District. From this chance encounter, they became close friends and together they explored many wild parts of northern and western Britain and of Ireland in search of mountain plants and Atlantic bryophytes and ferns, in particular the Killarney Fern between 1967 and 1982. Derek inspired John to take up vegetation surveys which led to John's study of the present vegetation of the Isle of Skye as a basis for studying its past vegetation. John and Derek were part of the National Vegetation Classification team 1974-1981. John and Des Thompson were recently involved in a PhD project by Louise Ross at the University of Aberdeen on re-surveying the vegetation of the North-West Highlands 50 years after Derek's pioneering vegetation survey in the 1950s. Hilary and John moved to Bergen in 1985 and live outside Bergen in Ravnestølen ('the summer home of the Raven'). The large cliff behind their house is a constant reminder of past adventures with Derek in search of wildlife, including his beloved Ravens.

John is a Foreign Member of the Norwegian Academy of Science and Letters (1987) and the Royal Swedish Academy of Science (2014), and an Honorary Fellow of University College London (2010). He received a Lifetime Achievement Award from the International Paleolimnological Association in 2012.

Peter Bridgewater Professor, Visitor, School of Archaeology and Anthropology, Australian National University, Canberra, and Visiting Professor, Beijing Forestry University
Peter was the immediate past Chair of the UK Joint Nature Conservation Committee serving from 2007 to 2014 and Visiting Professor at United Nations University – Institute of Advanced Studies. He held the posts of Secretary Gen-

eral of the Ramsar Convention (2003–2007); Director, Division of Ecological Sciences in UNESCO 1999-2000; and prior to that held senior level posts in the Australian Government, after a spell in Academia. In 1989 Peter took up the post of Chief Scientist at the Nature Conservancy Council, following Derek Ratcliffe's retirement. Following an offer from the Minister of the Environment in Australia, and the uncertainty surrounding future conservation arrangements in the UK, Peter returned to Australia in early 1990 as Director of the Australian National Parks and Wildlife Service.

Among a range of appointments he has served as a Member of the Science and Technology Advisory Panel to the Global Environment Facility, UN Environment Programme (1998-2000); as Chairman of the International Whaling Commission (1995-1997); and as Commissioner of the Independent World Commission on the Oceans (1995-1998). Peter has more than 200 publications on nature conservation, sustainable development, vegetation science, biodiversity, and science-policy links.

Ingvar Byrkjedal Associate Professor, Curator of Vertebrates at University Museum of Bergen, Norway

Ingvar is responsible for the care and management of the scientific collections of vertebrates at the University Museum of Bergen. The collections currently have a focus on fish taxonomy, a field in which Ingvar carries out research. His main interest, however, has been the study of breeding behaviour of shorebirds in Norwegian uplands and mountains, as well as on arctic tundra in Canada and Siberia. His special focus has been on the three species of golden plovers and Grey Plover, but studies have extended to Eurasian Dotterel, Bar-tailed Godwit, Spotted Redshank, and Pintail Snipe. He has also studied mating systems of Northern Lapwings on farmland in southern Norway.

The vertebrate collections at the University Museum of Bergen run a nest-record scheme, to which Derek and Jeannette Ratcliffe contributed substantially following their summer visits to Lapland. Through this activity Ingvar had the pleasure of being in regular contact with Derek over many years.

Roderick Corner Botanist and retired General Practitioner

Roderick was born in Edinburgh in 1937 and spent his childhood at St Boswells in Roxburghshire. As a student he reported the considerable botanical interest of the Whitlaw Mosses to the Nature Conservancy Council. Derek Ratcliffe was one of the botanists to visit the site and recommended it as a National Nature Reserve. Roderick graduated in Medicine at Edinburgh University in 1961 and after hospital appointments, he spent several months in the Falkland Islands where he made plant collections before heading south to the Argentine Islands on the Antarctic Peninsula where he over-wintered. He studied the plant life there paying special attention to *Deschampsia antarctica* and *Colobanthus quitensis*, the only two higher plants native to the Antarctic, as well as making collections of bryophytes and lichens. In 1968 he joined a medical practice in Penrith, Cumbria and at the same time became the Botanical Society of the British Isles Recorder for Roxburgh and Selkirkshire, a post he still holds. He was much involved in collecting records for Geoffrey Halliday's *Flora of Cumbria* and the challenge of refinding some of Derek's montane records. He has made several botanical trips to north-east Greenland. He was elected an Honorary Member of the Botanical Society of the British Isles (now Botanical Society of Britain and Ireland) in 2012.

Humphrey Crick Ornithologist and Ecologist, Natural England

Humphrey spent his pre-fledging period becoming a bird ringer on the experimental wildfowl reserve in Sevenoaks, inspired by Jeffery Harrison – a pioneering and amateur scientific naturalist. Post-fledging, he studied the social behaviour of Bee-eaters, and then spent a spell up on Deeside and Sutherland working on the side-effects of aerial pesticide spraying on forestry. This led to similar work in Zimbabwe, before landing a dream job at the British Trust for Ornithology as Head of the Nest Record Scheme.

One of the best ways to monitor raptors is through nest recording and so Humphrey became drawn into a range of raptor work. This culminated in coordinating the national Peregrine surveys in 1991 and 2002, enabling him to work closely with Derek Ratcliffe. Particularly enjoyable were the occasions when he would visit Derek at his home in Cambridge and pore over the data, including some magical spreadsheets, which were literally that – massive A1-sized squared paper that listed every known Peregrine site in the UK and showed their breeding occupancy and success for each year since 1961 – amazing. Talk, over lunch, was wonderful and was often very forthright about conservation policy and practice! Humphrey has since moved on to working at Natural England, first in the Chief Scientist Team on climate change, and now as its Principal Specialist in Conservation Ecology.

Lynne Farrell Botanist and Ecologist

From 1965-68 Lynne was a botanical assistant at Monks Wood Experimental Station, near Huntingdon, to where she returned in 1973 after taking a degree in Biology at Coleraine University, Northern Ireland. She worked in the Biological Records Centre producing the first Red Data Book for vascular plants published in 1977. She then became a member of Derek Ratcliffe's Chief Scientist Team in the Nature Conservancy Council, and later in English Nature, being responsible for plant ecology, lowland heaths, and the Species Recovery Project. She relocated to Scotland working in Edinburgh on the Natura 2000 project, followed by 5 years in the Argyll and Stirling area, and finally as the senior plant ecologist based in Perthshire prior to her retirement in 2007. She was the Honorary General Secretary of the Botanical Society of Britain and Ireland until 2014 and is now a Trustee of the Society and its recorder for Mull, Coll, and Tiree.

Jeremy Greenwood Honorary Professor, Centre for Research into Ecological and Environmental Modelling, University of St Andrews, Scotland

Drawn into ecology through teenage bird-watching, Jeremy's earliest published work was on seabirds, studied mainly on Handa – where he fell in love with the Highlands. In his twenty years lecturing at Dundee University he continued his doctoral interest in the population genetics of snails, with work in the Hebrides and west Highlands, but increasingly worked on the foraging behaviour and ecology of birds, including three expeditions to east Greenland. Mainly through committee-work, he became involved in various conservation issues.

During 1988-2007 he was Director of the British Trust for Ornithology (BTO). This fed his interest in the role of collaborative work by volunteers. He became particularly interested in how programmes should be designed to provide both rewarding fulfilment for the participants and high-quality results. Working for the BTO also allowed him to meet Derek Ratcliffe on various occasions and to have conversations that always deepened his respect for that remarkable man. After retiring from the BTO, he returned to eastern Scotland, to a home with a Peregrine eyrie within 2 miles. The effective analysis of broad-scale survey data remains an active area of his research, but most of his time is spent on trying to write a history of the work of the BTO – of which the Peregrine surveys have been a significant element.

Stuart Housden Director of Royal Society for the Protection of Birds (RSPB) Scotland
Stuart joined the RSPB more than 30 years ago as a Zoology graduate of Royal Holloway College, London, where he was President of its Student Union. His early jobs involved protected species issues, including combating wildlife crime and losses of wetland habitats, and devising better measures for protecting special sites for nature. This culminated in the passage of the Wildlife and Countryside Act 1981, during which Stuart was steeped in Parliamentary lobbying to improve the Act.

In 1994 Stuart was appointed Director of RSPB Scotland, and a Member of the RSPB's UK Board. He now leads an important part of the RSPB with some 80,000 members in Scotland and a staff of 300. Stuart is passionate about good and effective land- and water-conservation management. RSPB Scotland is, after all, Scotland's eighth largest land manager with over 65,000 hectares of nature reserves. Stuart and his team have been particularly active in devising and promoting environmental gains secured through the Common Agricultural Policy, and coined the term 'Cross Compliance' which is now enshrined in the EU principle that farmers should undertake conservation management in return for public subsidies.

Stuart sits on a number of bodies to advise Government, statutory bodies, and corporate interests in the conduct of land-use policy, biodiversity, and rural development. He is an avid bird-watcher and co-author of the bestselling *RSPB Handbook of Scottish Birds* (2009). In December 2013, on behalf of RSPB Scotland, Stuart lodged a petition with the Scottish Parliament urging the Government to declare the Golden Eagle as the national bird of Scotland. He is indefatigable in fighting for the protection of the nation's best sites for wildlife, and relishes taking on powerful interests to achieve this. In 2005 he was awarded an OBE for services to the conservation of biodiversity, and in 2009 was awarded an Honorary Fellowship by the Scottish Agricultural College.

Cathy Jenks Personal Assistant and Research Assistant, Department of Biology, University of Bergen
Cathy first trained as a secretary and took a diploma in Public Administration before moving on to a more enjoyable subject and gaining a degree in Earth Sciences. She has always had an interest in natural history, learning bird identification with her brother who became an ornithologist and has increased her botany knowledge

after working closely with John and Hilary Birks since 2003. She has always endeavoured to live in places close to nature and has spent time in Shropshire, South Wales, the Lake District, and now western Norway, exploring the countryside. Although she never met Derek, working on this book has given her a great insight into Derek's character and remarkable achievements.

Keith Kirby Woodland Ecologist and Visiting Researcher, Department of Plant Sciences, University of Oxford
In 1979 Keith was taken on as a woodland ecologist in the Chief Scientist Team with the Nature Conservancy Council and survived in that role through English Nature and Natural England until 2012. This involved increasing amounts of time on forestry policy and strategy reviews, so having retired he has taken up research again, revisiting old vegetation plots in Wytham Woods where he did his DPhil.

John Lawton Ecologist
John was Chairman of the Royal Commission on Environmental Pollution (2005-2011), Chief Executive of the Natural Environment Research Council (1999-2005), and Director of the Centre for Population Biology at Imperial College (1989-1999). He trained as a zoologist at the University of Durham, and subsequently held posts at Oxford and York Universities. His scientific interests have focussed on bird and insect population dynamics and biodiversity, with emphasis over the last three decades on the impacts of global environmental change. He was chair of the *Making Space for Nature* report to the Department for Environment, Food, and Rural Affairs (2010) that led to the establishment of Nature Improvement Areas in England.
John is a past President of the British Ecological Society, a former Chairman of the Royal Society for the Protection of Birds (RSPB) Council (and currently a Vice-president of RSPB), and immediate past Chairman of the Yorkshire Wildlife Trust (and now President) and Chairman of the York Museums Trust. He is also a non-executive Board member of the Food and Environment Research Agency.
Elected a Fellow of the Royal Society in 1989, and awarded a CBE in 1997, John was knighted in 2005 for his contributions to ecological science. He has been awarded numerous national and international prizes, including the Japan Prize 2004, and was elected as a Foreign Member of both the US National Academy of Sciences and the American Academy of Arts and Sciences in 2008. John has been an obsessive birder since he was a child, and also enjoys botanising and bug-hunting. A keen walker, gardener, and cook, John is married to Dot, with two grown-up children and five grandchildren.

Richard Lindsay Head of Environmental Research Group, University of East London
Richard worked for almost 20 years as the Nature Conservancy Council's, and successor nature conservation agencies', Senior Peatlands Specialist. Within the NCC Chief Scientist Team he played a leading role in several high-profile peatland casework issues, notably involving Duich Moss on Islay, the Flow Country in Caithness and Sutherland, and the NGO Peatland Campaign. For 15 years Richard was Chairman of the International Mire Conservation Group, the global network of specialist peatland conservation advisers. He led the production of guidelines

for Sites of Special Scientific Interest for Britain's peatlands, and was the principal architect of the UK network of peatland Special Areas of Conservation, classified under the EC Habitats Directive.

On leaving Scottish Natural Heritage in 1996, Richard joined the University of East London (UEL) and established a suite of degree programmes in conservation science on which he taught for 12 years. He now works for UEL's Sustainability Research Institute and continues to be actively involved in peatland conservation issues, both in the UK and abroad, most recently leading the production of the technical report underpinning the IUCN UK Peatland Conservation Programme. He has spent some time in Japan as a Visiting Professor based at the University of Tokyo and the University of Hokkaido.

David Long Research Associate in Bryology, Royal Botanic Garden Edinburgh

David is a native of Berwickshire in the Scottish Borders and became an all-round naturalist at an early age. He graduated in Botany at Edinburgh University in 1966 and obtained his PhD at Trinity College, Dublin in 2001. From joining the Royal Botanic Garden Edinburgh (RBGE) in 1975 until 1995 he was co-author and editor of the *Flora of Bhutan*. Following its completion, his research transferred to bryophytes and from 2003 until his retirement in 2013 he was head of the newly-created Cryptogamic Plants and Fungi Section. His main research focus has been on floristics, systematics, and evolution of bryophytes, particularly liverworts, publishing a new classification of liverworts in 2009 with colleagues in the USA, and supervising PhD and MSc students in several countries on bryophyte research projects. His work has involved numerous botanical expeditions, particularly to Bhutan and other parts of the Himalaya and western China, collecting material for research, most recently collaborating with researchers from China and the USA on a major 5-year biological survey of the Gaoligongshan Range in the western Yunnan mountains. He has also worked on bryophyte surveys and expeditions in Europe, Macaronesia, the Arctic, the Middle East, tropical Africa, Central and South America.

In 2002 and 2003 he served as President of the British Bryological Society and is active in bryophyte recording in Scotland, particularly the Scottish Borders, and in training bryophyte apprentices in identification and site surveying. In 1996 he published a bryophyte checklist for St Kilda with Derek Ratcliffe. In addition to co-authoring several volumes of the *Flora of Bhutan*, he has published over 250 botanical papers and has described many new species and several new genera of bryophytes, mostly from Asia. Recently the expanding application of DNA barcoding to bryophyte taxonomy, with colleagues at RBGE, led to the discovery and description of a new species of liverwort *Herbertus norenus* from Norway and Shetland, where it was first collected by Derek in 1968. His main outside interest is in restoration of native woodland in the Scottish Borders where he is a Trustee of the Borders Forest Trust.

Peter Marren Writer and Naturalist

Peter was a former colleague of Derek Ratcliffe in the Nature Conservancy Council between 1977 and 1989, serving as Assistant Regional Officer in North-east Scotland and Oxfordshire before becoming the in-house 'author-editor'. Derek

Ratcliffe was his editor for two New Naturalist volumes, *The New Naturalists* and *Nature Conservation*, while Peter reciprocated with some minor help over Derek's own New Naturalist, *Lakeland*, and his unpublished book on nature conservation and politics. Peter Marren is the author of twenty books on natural history (*sensu lato*), military history, and bibliography. His latest book, *Rainbow Dust*, to be published in 2014, is a personal look at butterflies and moths.

John Mitchell Naturalist

John is a self-taught naturalist who, during his military service in the early 1950s, joined the Catterick Field Club led by Derek Ratcliffe. On returning to civilian life, John worked as a jazz musician until 1966 when he swapped hobby and profession around and became Reserve Warden for the Nature Conservancy with responsibility for the Ben Lui, Glen Diomhan, and Loch Lomondside National Nature Reserves, and was subsequently Area Officer for Scottish Natural Heritage until his retirement in 1994. He played a crucial role in the establishment of Scotland's first National Park at Loch Lomond and the Trossachs. He has also been a lecturer and summer tutor for further education courses on nature conservation and local history at Glasgow and Strathclyde Universities. He has published on a wide range of topics including Loch Lomond's shielings and drove ways, folk-lore, cornstone workings and their flora, fern collecting, birds of prey, and *Loch Lomondside* (2001) in the New Naturalist series.

Ian Newton Professor, Centre for Ecology and Hydrology, Wallingford

Ian is a population ecologist with a love of birds, having worked in the field on finches, waterfowl, and raptors. He is perhaps best known for his research on birds of prey, including a long-term population study of the European Sparrowhawk, and for his work on pesticide impacts on birds. He gained a BSc from Bristol University, followed by DPhil and DSc degrees from the University of Oxford, and worked from 1967 until his retirement for the Natural Environmental Research Council in Great Britain, latterly at Monks Wood Research Station.

He first met Derek Ratcliffe in the 1960s when Derek came to Oxford to lecture on Golden Eagles. Through a mutual interest in birds, they became close friends, corresponded frequently, and over the years spent many days together in the field. Ian has authored around 300 papers in the scientific literature, and several books, including *Finches* (1972), *Population Ecology of Raptors* (1979), *The Sparrowhawk* (1986), *Population Limitation in Birds* (1998), *The Speciation and Biogeography of Birds* (2003), *The Migration Ecology of Birds* (2008), *Bird Migration* (2010), and *Bird Populations* (2013). He has served as President of the British Ornithologists' Union (BOU) and the British Ecological Society (BES), and is an Honorary Fellow of the North American Ornithologists' Union. He has also served as Chairman of the Royal Society for the Protection of Birds (RSPB), the British Trust for Ornithology, and the Peregrine Fund in the United States. He is now Vice-President of the RSPB.

He is a Fellow of the Royal Society (1993) and Royal Society of Edinburgh (1994). He received the North American Ornithologist's Union Elliot Coutes Award in 1985, BOU's Union Medal in 1987 and Godman-Salvin Medal in 2010, BES's Gold Medal in 1989, RSPB's Gold Medal in 1991, and an OBE in 1999.

Mike Pienkowski Honorary Executive Director, UK Overseas Territories Conservation
Forum
Mike joined the Nature Conservancy Council Chief Scientist Directorate (CSD) in
1984 as Head of the Ornithology Branch – just in time for the Flow Country issue,
as well as several other controversial issues, such as on Islay. Derek Ratcliffe's
CSD was responsible for specialist advice to NCC personnel, government, and
others, and for commissioning research to fill gaps in the science-base for this.
He inherited Tim Reed's Upland Bird Survey and commissioned David Stroud's
successor Moorland Bird Study. As the senior officer directly managing some of
the relevant research and informing policy development, it fell to him to lead
most of the briefings and presentations on Flow Country issues to government
and other interested parties and to participate in negotiations with them. In this,
he worked closely with Derek. Mike managed the Seabirds at Sea Team, and the
major contracts with the British Trust for Ornithology and the Wildfowl & Wetlands Trust, and initiated the programmes of work on the re-introduction of the
Red Kite, and on what became known as high-nature-value traditionally managed farmland.
Prior to working for NCC, Mike led a research team on shorebird ecology and
behaviour at Durham University, and ran the international Wader Study Group,
after earlier organising overseas research expeditions on wader migration behaviour and ecology. After the Flow Country work, he became NCC's Assistant Chief
Scientist and then the first Director of the successor body, the Joint Nature Conservation Committee. Later, he became senior editor of the *Journal of Applied Ecology* and ran various non-governmental conservation organisations, continuing
in his present role in helping UK Overseas Territories in conservation matters.

Chris Preston Botanist, Centre for Ecology and Hydrology, Wallingford
Chris's childhood interest in plants was rekindled during his student years in
Cambridge, and it was then that John Birks introduced him to Derek Ratcliffe's
paper 'An ecological account of Atlantic bryophytes in the British Isles'. Since
1980 he has worked at the Biological Records Centre, collating and analysing
records of British and Irish plants in collaboration with the Botanical Society of
Britain and Ireland and the British Bryological Society. Much of this work seeks
to identify recurrent distribution patterns, historic changes in plant ranges, and
current trends. His other interests include aquatic plants, the bryophytes of Cambridgeshire, and the work of 17th-century botanist John Ray. He was awarded
the 2012 John Thackray Medal, along with Philip Oswald, for work on John Ray's
(1660) *Cambridge Catalogue* and the 2012 Jane Smart Plantlife Award for Outstanding Contributions to Plant Conservation.

David Rae Director of the Stanley Smith (UK) Horticultural Trust, Royal Botanic
Garden Edinburgh
David was Director of Horticulture and Learning at the Royal Botanic Garden
Edinburgh, from 2000 to 2014. He joined the Garden in 1978 as a lecturer in the
School of Horticulture and, from 1989, was also the Garden's Conservation Co-
ordinator. In 1985 and 1995 he completed a MSc and PhD, respectively, both by
part-time research. From 1996-2006 he was the UK representative on the Euro-

pean Botanic Garden Consortium. He is currently Honorary President of Plant Network – the Plant Collections Network of Britain and Ireland and on the Board of the National Tropical Botanical Garden, Hawaii. In 2003 he launched *Sibbaldia*, a journal on botanic garden horticulture. He has undertaken fieldwork in more than 15 countries, spoken at numerous conferences, initiated two major Darwin Initiative projects, and published more than 50 papers. He is, or has been, a member of eight horticulture-related trusts, is a Fellow of the Institute of Horticulture, was awarded the Scottish Horticultural Medal in 2008, and was elected a Fellow of the Royal Society of Edinburgh in 2014.

Tim Reed Ecologist, Tim Reed Ecological Consultants Ltd

After completing a DPhil at Oxford University on birds in the largely treeless Hebrides, Tim joined the Chief Scientist Team of the Nature Conservancy Council (NCC) under Derek Ratcliffe in 1981 to lead the upland bird surveys in the equally treeless uplands of Wales, the Pennines, and, most critically, the Flow Country. Focusing predominantly on waders, the initial emphasis was on making sure that survey methodologies were robust: in the expectation that as more areas with important wader, and raptor, populations were discovered, then the data had to be able to withstand the inevitable negative criticism and scrutiny that would undoubtedly come.

Over the course of several years of daily car journeys to NCC Headquarters, Tim and Derek shared many details of the birds, people, and sites in the uplands of the UK.

After the Flow Country work, Tim led the revision of management planning for National Nature Reserves and other conservation sites in the NCC and the non-governmental organisation sector. In the Joint Nature Conservation Committee (JNCC) he developed conservation planning and recording systems that are still in use in the statutory and voluntary sector. Since 1998 he has worked in ecological consultancy around the world, from the Tropics to the Arctic, but retains a soft spot for waders and Peregrines – developed from fieldwork with Derek Ratcliffe.

With over 100 papers, and several books, he works increasingly in landscape change processes and the use of credible field methods, and providing robust datasets for assessing potential development impacts. Current interests include long-term monitoring sites in Amazonian Ecuador and Sri Lanka, bird monitoring, and Nightingales at the bottom of the garden.

Chris Rollie Area Manager, Royal Society for the Protection of Birds (RSPB), Scotland

Chris is Area Manager with RSPB Scotland in Dumfries & Galloway, where he manages the area office team and is the Society's strategic conservation lead across the region. Originally from Ayrshire, where he was a Biology teacher in secondary schools for ten years, Chris moved to Galloway to become Conservation Officer with the RSPB in 1991, and Area Manager in 2000. He is also Chairman of the Dumfries & Galloway Raptor Study Group and the UK Ring Ouzel Study Group.

Although interested in all birds from an early age, hill birds, and raptors in particular, are a special passion. He first met Derek Ratcliffe in the 1980s and they became close friends and field companions in south-west Scotland from the early 1990s, making annual pilgrimages to favourite Raven, Peregrine, and wader haunts. Chris lives in St John's Town of Dalry, which was also the home of the late Donald Watson, renowned bird artist, author, ornithologist, and dear friend. Chris has many fond memories of evenings with Derek at Donald's house, listening to the stories of these master craftsmen and being inspired.

Gordon Rothero Consultant Bryologist

Gordon's primary interest in and passion for mountains and wild places gradually came to include an enthusiasm for alpine plants which, by some inexplicable process, became an obsession with bryophytes. This process started in North Wales and has developed over the past 30 years in Scotland where a particular interest in oceanic bryophytes, partly inspired by Derek Ratcliffe's seminal 1968 paper, and snowbed vegetation, informed by Donald McVean and Derek's survey work in the Highlands, has provided both intellectual stimulus and lots of fun. This interest has produced numerous papers and reports and a series of long-term monitoring plots in Scottish snowbeds. Having retired from the City of Edinburgh's Outdoor Education Centre at Benmore in Argyll, he is now a consultant botanist, mainly dealing with bryophytes. He is the Botanical Society of Britain and Ireland Joint-Recorder for Main Argyll and is President and Conservation Officer of the British Bryological Society.

David Stroud Senior Ornithologist, Joint Nature Conservation Committee (JNCC)

David is Senior Ornithologist with the JNCC, where he led a large amount of national and international activity related to ornithological and wetland conservation. He leads within the country conservation agencies for the UK's implementation of the Ramsar Convention and its international linkages, and has been a member of the Convention's Scientific and Technical Review Panel (STRP) in various capacities since 2003, including as STRP's thematic expert for Ramsar site designation and management. He has been a member of and/or chaired the UK's Ramsar Committee in its various incarnations since 1989. Working with Wetlands International since the early 1990s, David has contributed to processes supporting the regular preparation of global waterbird population estimates used for the identification of wetlands of international importance and other conservation purposes.

David was a member of NCC's Chief Scientist Directorate, where, taking over from Tim Reed in 1985, he led the Moorland Bird Survey (MBS) team in the Flow Country and elsewhere for four years. Together the MBS team produced many publications documenting the distribution and abundance of UK's important upland bird communities including *Birds, Bogs and Forestry* (1987). Joining JNCC in 1991, David has been involved in the management of many UK ornithological surveillance programmes co-supported by JNCC as well as, in recent years, contributing to a number of national and international advisory groups relating to the spread of highly pathogenic avian influenza. He has co-ordinated three national reviews of the UK's network of Special Protection Areas established under the EU Birds Directive.

William Sutherland Professor, Conservation Science Group, University of Cambridge

Bill is an ornithologist, ecologist, and conservation biologist. He holds the Miriam Rothschild Chair in Conservation Biology in the Department of Zoology, University of Cambridge. Much of his current interest is in improving conservation practice and policy making, for example by better use of evidence.

Possessing many of his books and having regularly used the encyclopaedic *A Nature Conservation Review* as a site guide, Bill was delighted to join Derek Ratcliffe on the National Trust's Nature Conservation Panel. Bill found Derek an inspiration in his ability to stand to his principles and ensure practice followed the science, so providing the best for conservation, and found him a joy to be in the field with as he shared his astonishing knowledge of everything.

Bill is currently President of the British Ecological Society.

Des Thompson Professor, Scottish Natural Heritage

Des is a Principal Adviser with Scottish Natural Heritage, where he manages policy and advisory work on biodiversity and climate change. He has specialist interests in upland and bird ecology, and has published widely, with seven of his books having strong associations with Derek Ratcliffe as co-author, foreword author, photographer, or dedicatee.

As a schoolboy, Des joined Derek in the field to study nesting Greenshanks, Golden Plovers, and other birds researched by his father, Desmond Nethersole-Thompson. Out of this grew a close friendship, and some twenty years after they met, in autumn 1985, Des joined the Nature Conservancy Council as Mountains and Moorland Ecologist in the Chief Scientist Directorate, headed by Derek. Thereafter, Des worked closely with Derek, and is now one of only three members of the Directorate's Board still working in the UK conservation agencies. In 2014 he became Chairman of the Field Studies Council, and was recently elected Chairman of the UN Convention on Migratory Species Technical Advisory Group developing an action plan for the conservation of African and Eurasian migratory raptors. He lives with Dawn in Penicuik, where most mornings they see the Moorfoots that were searched so extensively for Golden Plover by Derek in his youth.

Will Williams Watercolour Artist

Will had a career in the UK conservation agencies and finally as Director of Natural Economy Northwest. His love of natural beauty came from childhood years on his parents' farm near Llandeilo, Carmarthenshire followed by studying geology and ecology at Aberdeen University, before researching for his PhD with John Birks at the University of Cambridge on the vegetation history of the Isle of Skye and Morar Peninsula. He is a self-taught watercolour artist, see his website www.watercolourjazz.co.uk. Now retired, he is a Trustee of the John Muir Trust, a member of the National Trust Advisory Board for NW England, Chair of the Cumbria Third Sector Executive, and Chair of the Cumbria Leaders Board.

Preface

Derek Almey Ratcliffe (9 July 1929–23 May 2005) was an outstanding British field biologist and nature conservationist. He was Deputy Director (Science) of the Nature Conservancy from 1970 to 1973, and then Chief Scientist of the Nature Conservancy Council from 1 January 1974 until his retirement on 8 July 1989. Derek's influence extended over a very wide field with many seminal contributions to our knowledge, understanding, and conservation of Britain's flora and fauna and their habitats. He was the first person to link the decline of birds of prey with organochlorine pesticide use and he had a deep knowledge of birds of prey and corvids, which, with other birds, he monitored over decades. He was the chief architect of Britain's post-war nature conservation policy, culminating in the two volume *A Nature Conservation Review* (1977). Sometimes referred to as Britain's modern Doomsday book, this review identified the country's most important wildlife localities. It was based on a range of criteria that Derek largely devised and that are now adopted internationally. He tackled the powerful forestry lobby in the 1980s and played a major role in persuading the UK Government to halt the tax-benefit scheme that made possible the massive afforestation of the unique peatlands of the Flow Country of Caithness and Sutherland. He had a remarkable mastery of a huge range of topics – he was one of the great ornithologists of his time and the authority on the Peregrine Falcon; he was a skilled plant ecologist and did pioneering work on the description, classification, and interpretation of mountain vegetation and peat bogs; and he was an expert on Atlantic mosses, liverworts, and ferns. He led the first rigorous science-based survey of British habitats for the statutory nature conservation movement in Britain, provided leadership in the designation of hundreds of Sites of Special Scientific Interest, and spearheaded opposition to the many assaults on the British uplands.

Derek received national and international awards including the Bernard Tucker Medal of the British Trust for Ornithology (1964), a commemorative Bronze from the Peregrine Fund and the Raptor Research Foundation of North America for services to the conservation of the Peregrine Falcon (1985), the Royal Society for the Protection of Birds (RSPB) medal (1989), the Godman-Salvin Medal of the British Ornithologists' Union (1991), and Life Membership of the British Ecological Society (2003). In 1983 he was appointed to the Most Excellent Order of the Golden Ark by HRH Prince Bernhard of The Netherlands, as Grand Master of the Order, for "his pioneering work on the effect of pesticides on birds of prey and his major contribution to the science of nature conservation in the UK". Surprisingly, Derek was never honoured by the British State or the British scientific establishment. *The Sunday Times* did, however, include him in their list of the 20th century's most influential people, mainly on the basis of his work on pesticides and conservation evaluation.

We have tried to draw together contributions that give a sense of what Derek did, and how he did it. We hope it will appeal not just to people who knew Derek, but to young naturalists and conservationists who want to make a difference. Derek had an extraordinarily enriching time as a schoolboy and student studying wildlife, and we would love to think that this could inspire others to follow his example. The book contains 30 chapters reflecting Derek's wide interests and contributions to plant ecology, ornithology, pesticide research, and nature conservation, together with personal recollections of his diverse life and his major legacies, and the opinions of Derek himself.

The book is divided into five parts on the:

- young naturalist in pursuit of nature;

- botanist understanding vegetation in mountain landscapes and discovering rarities in remote areas;

- ornithologist searching for and saving birds in wild places;

- conservationist protecting nature; and

- communicator through writing and photography.

Each part ends with an article written by Derek ranging from his first article in *The Carliol*, the Carlisle Grammar School's magazine, on 'Personal observations on some local birds' (1947), to his seminal 'Thoughts towards a philosophy of nature conservation' (1976), published in the international journal *Biological Conservation*, and his reminiscence from the Introduction to his classic book *The Peregrine Falcon* (1980).

Derek is not just remembered but revered, as much for his deeds as for his words. Quietly and determinedly plotting his course in the field, his simple motivation was to see nature flourish and untamed. He loathed injustice, and argued persistently that wildlife deserved a footing at least equal to other countryside interests. He was kind, modest, and unfailingly loyal and generous with his time to friends and colleagues. Versatile, indefatigable, with a deep knowledge and high moral principles, uncompromising, sceptical, latterly outraged, and with an exceptional intellect, he galvanised the nature conservation movement in the latter part of 20th century Britain. But for many of us he was first and foremost a field companion of incomparable measure, who loved searching out nature in the spacious wilds of the north and west. Rarely alone, but often isolated, it was in the field that Derek was happiest. He was nature's conscience.

Acknowledgements

All of the contributors, many of whom were friends and colleagues of Derek Ratcliffe, have enthusiastically provided a unique collection of chapters about many aspects of his life and legacies. Everyone has patiently worked with us as we pulled the book together, and for this we are immensely grateful.

Sir John Lawton kindly wrote the Foreword, and encouraged us with his enthusiasm and wisdom. Some of our contributors have provided additional advice and support, and for this we thank Rick Battarbee, Ingvar Byrkjedal, Lynne Farrell, Jeremy Greenwood, Stuart Housden, Richard Lindsay, David Long, Peter Marren, John Mitchell, Ian Newton, Chris Preston, Chris Rollie, Gordon Rothero, David Stroud, and Bill Sutherland. We have benefitted greatly from additional contributions, advice, help, and/or comments from many friends, associates, and colleagues, including Björn Backman, Patrick Barkham, Phil Boon, Andrew Branson, Arild Breistøl, Steve Brooks, Terry Burke, Mike Clarke, Roger Crofts, Alan Crowden, Susan Davies, Debra Dawson, Roy Dennis, Roddy Fairley, Alan Fielding, Colin Galbraith, Paul Haworth, John Hopkins, Geoff Horne, Ian Jardine, Peter Lindberg, Ron Macdonald, Lord Peter Melchett, Peter Moore, Philip Oswald, Robin Payne, George Peterken, Steve Redpath, Peter Schofield, Dick Seamons, John Sheail, Rob Soutar, Patrick Stirling-Aird, Pam Taylor, L.B. Tettenborn, Peter Tilbrook, Pat Thompson, Martin Tither, Alan Vittery, Paul Walton, Phil Whitfield, and Kate Wilkinson.

Jeannette, Derek's widow, took a keen interest in the book and provided access to Derek's correspondence, field notes, and photographic collection.

At an early stage in this book's development, we received invaluable advice from Mark Cocker, John Krebs (Lord Krebs of Wytham), Peter Marren, Ian Newton, and the late Magnus Magnusson.

Our publisher, Ian Langford, has encouraged and helped us beyond normal expectations. We have had wonderful and invaluable assistance from Cathy Jenks in Bergen, who helped in a hundred and one ways. We thank the following for supplying images: Dick Balharry, Arild Breistøl, Ann Brooks, Laurie Campbell, Tim Caroen, Rod Corner, Tony Cross, Lynne Farrell, Maurice Gordon, Paul Harris, Kristian Henriksen, Neil Hulme, David Knott, Kåre Kyllingstad, Richard Lindsay, Terje Lislevand, David Long, Heather McHaffie, Chris Miles, John Mitchell, Norman Moore, Peter Moore, Steve Moore, Caroline Pannell, Mike Pienkowski, David Rae, Derek Ratcliffe, John Riggall, Jeremy Roberts, Chris Rollie, Gordon Rothero, Dick Seamons, Paul Waring, and Kate Wilkinson. Will Williams painted the superb portrait of Derek, and Will and David Bellamy have donated some enchanting landscape paintings; we are grateful to them both for allowing us to reproduce these here. We thank the publishers of the periodicals *Biological Conservation*, *British Wildlife*, and *Punch*, and Bloomsbury (Poyser), for allowing us to reproduce Derek's articles and other materials.

In his many books and papers Derek took considerable trouble to acknowledge each person who had helped him; the total runs to several hundred names. We feel it is appropriate that we should pay tribute to those of whom Derek spoke most frequently and warmly, and regarded as his most influential mentors. Ernest Blezard was described by Derek as a 'naturalist extraordinaire', and he inspired, taught, and instilled in Derek a spiritual love of nature and a deep sense of public duty. It was from Ernest that Derek acquired what was to become his hallmark – a highly disciplined and beautifully communicated scientific approach. Roy Clapham's inspired botanical teaching resulted in Derek abandoning his zoological studies at Sheffield University, with all their anatomy and dissection, and becoming a botanist. Roy was an outstanding, broad-minded, and unassuming plant scientist, who greatly encouraged and stimulated Derek's many interests as a field biologist, analytical ecologist, and devoted conservationist throughout his professional career. The ornithologist Desmond Nethersole-Thompson was in almost every regard a polar opposite to Derek – exuberant, physically imposing, rebellious, and 'with some of the extrovert confidence of the public schoolboy'. He became a close and loyal friend, a stimulating influence, and a close adviser. His prodigious memory and exceptional nest-finding abilities appealed to Derek, but it was his observations of people and birds that Derek appreciated most. Donald Watson, naturalist and extraordinarily gifted landscape and bird artist, was a dear friend, confidante, and outstanding ornithologist. Derek enjoyed many special days in the field with him, particularly in their beloved Galloway. Four of Derek's Nature Conservancy Council (NCC) colleagues massively influenced his working life – Sir William Wilkinson, Ian Prestt, Norman Moore, and Max Nicholson; each had defining impacts on Derek's career within the NCC and far beyond. Sadly, only one of these intellectual giants is still with us, but we have been touched by their many and very different roles in influencing Derek's life and legacy.

Our families have been a huge support. Dawn, John Matthew, and James Thompson have critically read parts of the manuscript. John Matthew had the good fortune to spend time in the field with Derek at around the same infant age as his father was when Derek led him un-roped down the precipitous Clo Mor cliffs near Cape Wrath. Maimie Nethersole-Thompson has provided vivid recollections of being with Derek. Christopher Birks has shared his memories as a school-boy and young naturalist in the field with Derek and being driven at speed through East Anglia.

We were fortunate to have known and worked with Derek. Talking with others who also had this privilege and reading the chapters in this book highlight just how much Derek is missed and the huge role he played in ornithology, botany, ecology, conservation, and scientific communication. He inspired us all. The chapters have greatly expanded our appreciation of his meticulous, devoted, and determined approach to all that he did in discovering, understanding, and conserving Britain's nature. We thank Derek for his loyal friendship, and for being so true to himself – and nature.

Nomenclature

Nomenclature (scientific and where appropriate English names) follows as far as possible the following authorities:

British and Irish vascular plants – Stace, C.A. (2010) *New Flora of the British Isles* (3rd edition). Cambridge University Press, Cambridge.

Scandinavian vascular plants – Grey-Wilson, C. & Blamey, M. (1995) *Alpine Flowers of Britain and Europe*. HarperCollins, London.

Mosses, liverworts, and hornworts – Hill, M.O., Blockeel, T.H., Long, D.G. & Rothero, G.P. (2008) *A Checklist and Census Catalogue of British and Irish Bryophytes*. British Bryological Society, Middlewich.

Lichens – Smith, C.W., Aptroot, A., Coppins, B.J., Fletcher, A., Gilbert, O.L., James, P.W., Wolseley, P.A. & Orange, A. (eds.) (2009) *The Lichens of Great Britain and Ireland*. British Lichen Society, London.

Diatoms – Stevenson, A.C., Juggins, S., Birks, H.J.B., Anderson, D.S., Anderson, N.J., Battarbee, R.W., Berge, F., Davis, R.B., Flower, R.J., Haworth, E.Y., Jones, V.J., Kingston, J.C., Kreiser, A.M., Line, J.M., Munro, M.A.R. & Renberg, I. (1991) *The Surface Water Acidification Project Palaeolimnology Programme: Modern diatom/lake-water chemistry data-set*. Ensis Publications, London.

Mammals – Harris, S. & Yalden, D. (2008) *Mammals of the British Isles: Handbook*. Mammal Society, London.

Birds – British Ornithologists Union Records Centre (BOURC) (2012) The British List. http://www.bou.org.uk/british-list/

Butterflies – Thomas, J. & Lewington, R. (2010) *The Butterflies of Britain and Ireland*. British Wildlife Publishing, Rotherwick.

Moths – Skinner, B. (2009) *Colour Identification Guide to Moths of the British Isles*. Harley Books, Colchester.

Dragonflies – Brooks, S.J. (ed.) (2004) *Field Guide to the Dragonflies and Damselflies of Great Britain and Ireland* (4th edition). British Wildlife Publishing, Rotherwick.

Des Thompson, Hilary Birks, and John Birks

December 2014

Foreword

I started to get *British Birds* in November 1957 when I was 14. It was delivered by the local news agent to my parents' house in Leyland, and cost three shillings a month. I still remember the excitement created by those green covers; they opened up a whole new world for a boy-birder long before the age of instant communication. I remember the impact of some of the earliest articles; indeed, I remember them better than many of those I have read much more recently (I still get *British Birds*). The January 1958 edition had a Short-eared Owl on the cover, and the lead article was about the almost mythical Coto Doñana. Starting on page 23, there was a short note just over three pages long on 'Broken eggs in Peregrine eyries' by a man I had never heard of – D.A. Ratcliffe. It was rather strange, for he had recorded cracked and broken Peregrine eggs in the UK in unprecedented numbers, and provided compelling evidence that the birds were eating their own eggs. But he had no idea why. By 1958 I had only ever seen one Peregrine (in 1954), and I remember thinking: "How on earth can one man find so many nests of these magical birds? He must be a genius." The rest, as they say, is history.

In 1964 I began to find out who Derek Ratcliffe was. I was an undergraduate reading Zoology at Durham University. In the period between his *British Birds* paper and the early 1960s, Derek had almost single-handedly documented the catastrophic collapse of the UK Peregrine population from the mid-1950s, and begun to piece together the link between the birds eating their own eggs and the population collapse. The ornithologist John Coulson was one of my teachers, and I remember him telling me about the Peregrine's collapse (of which I knew nothing), and how a "scientist called Ratcliffe" suspected that it was being driven by organochlorine insecticides such as DDT accumulating in the birds' bodies. Three-years later, in 1967, and now a research student in Durham, I read Derek's classic *Nature* paper on egg-shell thinning not only in Peregrines, but also other raptors – and he entered my mental list of the all-time greats. It was at the time, and rightly remains, a brilliant, painstakingly careful piece of ecological research, combining deep intuition with clever biology and enormous hard work.

I finally got to meet the man at an Edward Grey Institute conference in Oxford, organised, as always in those days, by David Lack. I have lost my diaries from this period, but it must have been after his 1967 paper (and so possibly 1968 or 1969, by which time I had moved to Oxford), because Derek talked about his work on egg-shell thinning, and the detective work involved. It was inspiring stuff. And, as I recall, he then said absolutely nothing of substance for the rest of the conference, and conversing with him was an effort. It was, to put it mildly, rather deflating. Yet, as we now know, from several of the chapters in this book, this was hall-mark Derek Ratcliffe – though of course I did not realise it at the time – and simply assumed it was me he did not want to talk to.

Time passed, and I bought *The Peregrine Falcon* as soon as it was published (by Poyser) in 1980. I had moved to York in 1971, and by now was a senior lecturer, pegging away at my own research. In York I had helped to found the York Royal Society for the Protection of Birds (RSPB) Members' Group, and was aware, rather passively, of looming environmental threats. My own research and environmental concerns were in largely separate mental compartments. Science was science and, frankly, emotion did not have a lot to offer. But, Derek Ratcliffe astonished me – *The Peregrine Falcon* is by any measure a piece of scientific writing of the highest order, assembling facts and figures with astonishing clarity and giving a compelling account of these wonderful birds. One cannot say that of all the books in Trevor Poyser's classic series, a few of which read like telephone directories. Derek's 'Introduction: a reminiscence' (reprinted as Chapter 30 in this book) took me by surprise. Here was a scientist writing from the heart about a subject he loved. Science and emotion can mix, without losing either scientific objectivity or emotional clout. And indeed his love of Peregrines and wild places permeates the whole text. It literally changed my life. From that moment on I would use my science to the best of my ability to promote my own love of wild places, and their fragile inhabitants.

E.O. Wilson calls it *Biophilia*. He makes a strong case that most (if not all) children are fascinated by the natural world. For many (fortunate) adults it stays with us into adulthood; others just loose it, and their world is in my view infinitely the poorer for it. Derek's penultimate book, *Lapland: A Natural History* (again in the Poyser series, and definitely not a telephone directory), was published in 2005. Combining scientific insight with brilliant natural history, Derek's love of birds and plants, bogs and boreal forests pours forth. Here we have *Biophilia* in buckets through the eyes of a great ecological scientist.

In my view, during his lifetime, Derek Ratcliffe never really received the recognition he deserved from the ranks of the 'great and the good'; his quiet, unassuming, even retiring, nature may have had something to do with it. Yet he came alive in the written word, combining the precision of his science with a deep appreciation and understanding of the natural world. I hope this book will bring his life and many achievements to the attention of a much wider audience – he was, indeed, nature's conscience. He deserves no less, and if still with us, would take quiet satisfaction in his greatest legacy (not that he would have said much about it). The UK Peregrine population is in rude health compared with when Derek first worked on them, though of course we still have concerns about illegal persecution. In a world where too often nature struggles to survive, the Peregrine is emblematic of recovery and improving fortunes – and we have Derek Ratcliffe to thank for that.

Professor Sir John Lawton CBE FRS

York, December 2014

THE YOUNG
NATURALIST –
early days and influences

1. Derek Ratcliffe – early days in pursuit of nature

John Birks, Des Thompson, and Hilary Birks

Wood Green and Norfolk 1929-1938 – the first nine years

Derek Ratcliffe (9 July 1929 – 23 May 2005) was born in London and lived in its suburb of Wood Green until 1938. It was an inauspicious beginning for one who went on to develop a deep and unparalleled fascination for virtually all of Britain's landscapes and wildlife – except those in urban areas. Although Wood Green was not the most promising of environments for a budding young field naturalist, the eight-year-old Ratcliffe quickly acquired an interest in butterflies and moths from sightings in the small garden of his home, in the local park, around Alexandra Palace[1], and, perhaps most significantly, on Jarvis Farm, in his mother's family, between Felbrigg and Roughton just south of Cromer on the Norfolk coast[1]. The north Norfolk countryside in the late 1930s and early 1940s must have been a wonderful place for butterflies, dragonflies, and moths, with many exciting species including High-brown Fritillary (*Argynnis adippe*) and Dark-green Fritillary (*Argynnis aglaja*) butterflies (Fig. 1.1), Migrant Hawker (*Aeshna mixta*), Broad-bodied Chaser (*Libellula depressa*), and Common Darter (*Sympetrum striolatum*) dragonflies (Fig. 1.2), and Hummingbird (*Macroglossum stellatarum*) and Broad-bordered Bee (*Hemaris fuciformis*) hawk-moths (Fig. 1.3)[1].

Here, Derek became captivated by wildlife during holidays spent carefree and utterly curious in all that he saw and heard. An intense interest began during his Easter holiday in 1938, when just a nine-year-old, he learnt from his uncle how to find birds' nests. His list of finds between 1938 and 1949 is impressive – Red-legged Partridge (*Alectoris rufa*), Grey Partridge (*Perdix perdix*), Pheasant (*Phasianus colchicus*), Sparrowhawk (*Accipiter nisus*), Kestrel (*Falco tinnunculus*), Moorhen (*Gallinula chloropus*), Lapwing (*Vanellus vanellus*), Snipe (*Gallinago gallinago*), Stock Dove (*Columba oenas*), Wood Pigeon (*Columba palumbus*), Turtle Dove (*Streptopelia turtur*), Nightjar (*Caprimulgus europaeus*), Little Owl (*Athene noctua*), Jay (*Garrulus glandarius*), Jackdaw (*Corvus monedula*), Crow (*Corvus corone*), Swallow (*Hirundo rustica*), Blackcap (*Sylvia atricapilla*), Wren (*Troglodytes troglodytes*), Starling (*Sturnus vulgaris*), Blackbird (*Turdus merula*), Song Thrush (*Turdus philomelos*), Mistle Thrush (*Turdus viscivorus*), Robin (*Erithacus rubecula*), House Sparrow (*Passer domesticus*), Dunnock (*Prunella modularis*), Chaffinch (*Fringilla coelebs*), Greenfinch (*Chloris chloris*), and Yellowhammer (*Emberiza citrinella*)[1].

Figure 1.1. Butterflies. High-brown Fritillary (*Argynnis adippe*), Cumbria, 2012 (*top left*). Dark-green Fritillary (*Argynnis aglaja*), Sussex, 2011 (*top right*). Large Heath (*Coenonympha tullia*), Shropshire, 2010 (*lower left*). Mountain Ringlet (*Erebia epiphron*), Cumbria, 2012 (*lower right*). Photos: Neil Hulme, copyright Neil Hulme 2013

Figure 1.2. Dragonflies. Migrant Hawker (*Aeshna mixta*), Kent, 2012 (*top*), photo: Tim Caroen (copyright Tim Caroen). Broad-bodied Chaser (*Libellula depressa*), immature female, Essex, 1995 (*middle*), photo: Ann Brooks. Common Darter (*Sympetrum striolatum*), male, Lower Saxony, 2008 (*bottom*), photo: L. B. Tettenborn (*Creative Commons License*)

Figure 1.3. Moths. Beautiful Yellow Underwing (*Anarta myrtilli*), Yorkshire, 2012 (*top left*), photo: Maurice Gordon, copyright Maurice Gordon Photography. Broad-bordered Bee Hawk-moth (*Hemaris fuciformis*), Dorset, 1983 (*top right*), photo: Paul Harris (http://ukmoths.org.uk/show.php?id=1054). True Lover's Knot (*Lycophotia porphyrea*) (*bottom*), photo: Paul Waring

Carlisle and Cumbria 1938 onwards

In 1938 the Ratcliffe family moved to Carlisle, where Derek's father Frank Bernard Ratcliffe was a cinema organist (to whom Derek owed his love of classical music) and his mother Kathleen Marie Ratcliffe a teacher of English and French (from whom Derek acquired an elegant style of handwriting, which did not change throughout his life, and a mastery of descriptive prose – concise, accurate, and captivating). Derek attended Carlisle Grammar School from 1940 to 1947. Aged 18, he published his first essay in the

School magazine *The Carliol*[2] (dated as written in September, 1947 and reprinted as Chapter 3 in this book). This was no simple scribbling by a young boy, but rather a presciently measured and insightful collection of personal observations of Ravens (*Corvus corax*) (Fig. 13.4) and Peregrine Falcons (*Falco peregrinus*) (Fig. 14.5)[2]. Awarded a school prize[3], it ended thus[2],

> "Many are the days I have spent in search of all kinds of birds throughout various types of country – wood, plain, marsh, river, estuary and moor – yet it is the mountains which make the strongest appeal. Not for one moment has this lure of the wild diminished or abated, rather it has strengthened throughout the years, and may the birds always exist to lend additional charm and attraction to the hills of home."

The themes of wildness, charm, and appeal of mountain wildlife recurred in his writing over the next six decades, not least in his monumental monographs on these two birds[4,5], and in his masterly books on the bird life of mountains and uplands[6], the flora of the Scottish Highlands[7], and the natural history of Lakeland[8] and Galloway and the Borders[9].

His schoolboy days in Carlisle were probably the most formative. He had easy access to the wonderful countryside of the Solway Plain and Cumberland lowlands and the Solway Firth, and, less easily, the Lakeland fells, the vast Border Moors of Bewcastle, Kielder, and Cheviot, the unspoilt Northern Pennines, and even the vast wilderness of the remote Galloway Hills (Figs. 1.4 & 1.5) and the Langholm Hills

Figure 1.4. The Merrick, the highest hill (2766 feet; 843 m) in Galloway, March 1979. Photo: Derek Ratcliffe

Figure 1.5. Craigdews Gairy and Paltnure Burn near Talnotry, Galloway, March 1981. It is described by Derek Ratcliffe[9] as "A Galloway scene that has hardly changed since I first knew it". Photo: Derek Ratcliffe

(Fig. 1.6) and Moffatdale (Fig. 5.1) in the Southern Uplands of south-west Scotland[1]. These explorations were only possible by 1940's public transport, especially trains. Derek knew many of the head engines by name, relished the odd chance to ride on the foot-plate, and could recite the histories of many of the stations he passed through. Through-out his life he would wave to train drivers in rural settings, and be delighted when one waved back! Well, he would of course, for trains took him to places where he could connect with nature – each station was his 'wardrobe' of C.S. Lewis's *The Lion, the Witch and the Wardrobe*[10]. With his bicycle in tow, and his untiring ability to tramp great distances over moor and hill, always at the same steady pace up or down slopes, early or late in the day (and often into the night!), Derek was absorbed by the wild country-side. In these areas he found for himself Buzzard (*Buteo buteo*), Raven, Merlin (*Falco columbarius*), Golden Eagle (*Aquila chrysaetos*) (Fig. 12.4), and Peregrine. April 21 1945 is described by Derek in his memoirs[1] as a 'red-letter day', the day he realised his boyhood dream of finding and climbing to the eyrie of a Peregrine. This he did himself in the Northern Pennines at some considerable personal risk as it involved difficult rock-climb-ing and jumping off the lowermost 4 m of the holdless pitch at the base of a fearsome precipice. His 'rope' was a sash-window cord that he 'borrowed' from the window in his bedroom in Carlisle. Whilst racing back to reach the train, one of the rubber soles of his shoes peeled back, and having cut it off he hobbled back across the fell to the station[1]. A month later, he was in the Lakeland fells where he located three Peregrine nests[1]. After much searching in the field and scouring the scattered literature, Derek concluded that the Lake District had, in the late 1940s, about 30 pairs as well as 70 pairs of Ravens[1].

Later, his love of searching for difficult and elusive birds and their nests in Lakeland turned to Merlins, Golden Plover (*Pluvialis apricaria*) (Fig. 11.10), scarce Dotterel (*Charadrius morinellus*) (Figs. 11.3-11.5, 13.8 & 13.9) and, tantalisingly, Purple Sandpiper (*Calidris maritima*) – a bird very rarely recorded in Britain outwith the Cairngorms[1,8]. He retained his keen interest in butterflies, moths, and dragonflies and found some rare and local species such as the Large Heath (*Coenonympha tullia*) (Fig. 1.1) and Mountain Ringlet (*Erebia epiphron*) (Fig. 1.1) butterflies and the Beautiful Yellow Underwing (*Anarta myrtilli*) (Fig. 1.3) and True Lover's Knot (*Lycophotia porphyrea*) (Fig. 1.3) day-flying moths[1].

In his explorations of the Solway Plain and, later, of the Galloway Hills, he discovered several raised bogs and other mires and acquired his life-long interest in peatlands and their surface patterns, and subsequently their flora and vegetation[11]. And it was here, on

Figure 1.6. A deep ravine cut into Old Red Sandstone in the Langholm Hills, Dumfriesshire where both Ravens (*Corvus corax*) and Peregrines (*Falco peregrinus*) nest, March 1971. This site was regularly visited by Derek Ratcliffe[1,4,5,9]. Photo: Derek Ratcliffe

the Silver Flowe bogs in Galloway (Fig. 1.7), that he discovered the first breeding record of the Azure Hawker (*Aeshna caerulea*) dragonfly (Fig. 1.8) south of the Scottish Highlands, which featured in his first 11-line scientific publication[12] (characteristic of Derek, the Silver Flowe was not named, with the location instead described as "an area of desolate peat bogs in the north of Kirkcudbrightshire"[12]). Derek developed a comprehensive knowledge of *Sphagnum* and other mire bryophytes, an interest that must have been stimulated by one of his teachers at Sheffield, Verona Conway, a distinguished mire ecologist[11]. Whilst an undergraduate at Sheffield and subsequently as a PhD student at Bangor, Derek also became fascinated by mountain plants[11] and in 1952 he and his mentor, Ernest Blezard, refound two patches of Mountain Avens (*Dryas octopetala*) (Fig 4.10) on Helvellyn. One additional colony of Mountain Avens was subsequently found on the Helvellyn range by Derek, and in 1957 he found an inaccessible patch on Wasdale Screes. Two further colonies have been found in the same locality, bringing the total Lakeland

Figure 1.7. The Silver Flowe National Nature Reserve, Galloway, a series of patterned bogs discovered by Derek Ratcliffe in 1946[1]. Top: the northern end of the Silver Flowe before afforestation of the slopes behind, October 1956. Below: the southern end of the Silver Flowe after afforestation of the slopes beyond Snibe and Craigeazle Bogs. Photos: Derek Ratcliffe

population of this iconic mountain plant to six patches[1]. In 1947, he acquired his first camera and quickly became a gifted photographer of landscapes, of the plants and animals that occurred in these areas, of habitats, and of nests and nesting sites. He had already made a habit of writing careful field notes and documenting his findings about local Carlisle birds[2] in 1947 and his observations on Magpies (*Pica pica*)[13] in 1949.

Figure 1.8. Azure Hawker (*Aeshna caerulea*) dragonfly; male (*top*) and female (*below*). Photos: Tim Caroen, copyright Tim Caroen 2013. www.british-dragonflies.org.uk

Tullie House Museum, Carlisle 1940 onwards – falling under the spell of Ernest Blezard

Looking back at Derek's early activities, the single greatest influence on him was Ernest Blezard (Fig 1.9), the Curator of the Tullie House Museum in Carlisle and Secretary of the Carlisle Natural History Society[1]. Derek revered Ernest as a mentor and second father figure, and fell under his spell when he first attended a meeting of the Society aged 11. Although "shyness forbade enquiry about actual membership of the Society"[1], in 1942 it was suggested that aged 13 he should be formally enrolled; duly proposed and seconded, Derek paid his annual subscription of half-a-crown (12½ pence)[1]. Of the various international and national awards and prizes that Derek received later in his life for his work on raptors, pesticides, and wider conservation matters, we suspect that he was most delighted and proud to have been elected an Honorary Life Member of the Society in 1997[14], as the Society and its Secretary meant so very much to him in fostering his youthful interests in natural history.

Figure 1.9. Ernest Blezard (1902-1970), Curator and Keeper of Natural History and Post-Medieval Antiquities, Tullie House Museum, Carlisle, described by Derek Ratcliffe[1] as "my mentor in chief". The photograph was taken in 1947, reproduced with permission of the Tullie House Museum, Carlisle and Stephen Hewitt.

Ernest was a superb self-taught naturalist with a vast knowledge of birds, insects, other animals, plants, landscapes, geology, archaeology, and local history[1,15]. He was, as Derek wrote[1],

> "a man of iron principle, with a strong sense of duty to the public who provided his job, and a relentless insistence on accuracy and honesty in all matters of natural history and its recording. He had little time for those who gave themselves the benefit of the doubt over what they saw, and even less for those who reported other peoples' finds as their own, or had too large a sense of their own importance. I acquired from him an ethic as well as factual knowledge. In the field his erudition flowed naturally and without any desire to impress. He knew so much about the ways of birds and other animals, and had a sound knowledge of the local flora. Yet it was not just his lore and fieldcraft that made an outing with Ernest so enjoyable, but also his fund of reminiscences, humorous asides, discerning comments and inimitable turn of phrase. He was always keen to learn still more, and found great delight in fresh insights and discoveries, especially over the realising of particular ambitions. A seeker after knowledge until the very end, his last field trip was with Geoff Horne to view the returned Lakeland Golden Eagle, only four days before his death."

This description of Ernest is as apt of Derek in the field and at home, and he instilled these principles into the three of us at around the same time (though we were quite unaware of this until much later). John and Hilary Birks, as PhD students in the late 1960s, came under Derek's tutelage and learnt much about field botany, plant hunting, mountain ecology, bryology, scientific method, meticulous observations and field notes, loyalty, work ethic, and responsibility[11]. Des was a young schoolboy then, but through many visits to his parents' home and field study area in Sutherland, Derek took Des and his father (Desmond Nethersole-Thompson) and brothers (Patrick and Richard) into the field to study birds[16]. Aged just eleven in 1969, Des has vivid memories of dangling from the end of a rope held by Derek to check if a Golden Eagle's eyrie was occupied (it was not), and the next day inching his way along a sea-cliff ledge close to Cape Wrath, this time unroped, to collect Kittiwake (*Rissa tridactyla*) eggs for Derek to take to Monks Wood for toxic residue analyses[16].

Derek taught us by example how to write detailed field notes about localities, habitats, plants found, birds seen, etc. Derek's notes are an outstanding example of '*Field Notes on Science and Nature*'[17], in which E.O. Wilson writes,

> "If there is a heaven, and I am allowed entrance, I will ask for no more than an endless living world to walk through and explore. I will carry with me an inexhaustible supply of notebooks, from which I can send back reports to the more sedentary spirits (mostly molecular and cell biologists). Along the way I would expect to meet kindred spirits."

Derek and his meticulous notebooks would be one such kindred spirit. When asked about how he had learnt to write such amazingly thorough notes, Derek's answer was simple – "Ernest Blezard".

Although we never met Ernest, he was clearly a remarkable person and a great source of inspiration to those who had the good fortune to have known him. Donald Walker, a Sheffield student colleague and life-long friend of Derek, wrote in his monograph[18] on the vegetational history of the Cumberland Lowland "my greatest debt is undoubtedly to Mr. E. Blezard, Curator of Tullie House Museum, Carlisle, whose depth of understanding of Cumberland natural history has been an inspiration to many and whose personal interest in this work has so often revitalized the author when his enthusiasm has flagged."

Galloway 1946 onwards

A major event in Derek's formative years was his first expedition in 1946[1] to the then unspoilt and remote Galloway hills of south-west Scotland (Figs. 1.4 & 1.5) with their intriguing and evocative place names such as Deil's Booling Green, Nick of Curleywee, Loch Dungeon, Clints of Dromore, Cooran Lane, Cauldron of the Dungeon, Corserine, Craignaw, Clatteringshaws Loch, Kells, The Silver Flowe, The Round Loch of Glenhead, Mullwharchar, Rig of the Jarkness, Benyellary (hill of the eagle) and/or The Lum of the Black Gitter (Merrick; Fig. 1.4), and The Backhill of the Bush (Fig. 1.10). After Hilary Birks started her PhD research on the vegetational history of Galloway in 1965, she asked Derek why he had first visited Galloway in 1946 and regularly returned there – the answer was "Ernest Blezard suggested it". Ernest thought it was an area with a fauna and flora that would quickly change in response to environmental change. How right he

Figure 1.10. The deserted shepherd's cottage at Backhill of the Bush, Galloway, June 1988. The scenery has changed greatly since Derek Ratcliffe first stayed there in 1949[1,9] when no trees could be seen anywhere, unlike the extensive afforestation seen here. More recently, the forest road now extends to the cottage[9]. Photo: Derek Ratcliffe

was with the massive afforestation and its ecological impacts on the Galloway hills[9], the impact of acid-rain on its freshwaters[19], recent changes in water quality[20], the possible impacts of recent climate change[16,21], and other recent land-use impacts[22].

Being so close to Carlisle, the Galloway hills and Ernest's suggestions attracted young Derek. Galloway was soon to become a 'magic place' for him[1,9]. Fired by tales of large crags with nesting raptors from Ernest, Peter Day, Ray Laidler, and Sandy Bannister[1], the sixteen-year-old planned to visit this desolate and remote area in the spring of 1946. Galloway then must have been a very different place from what it is today – no blanket afforestation, no forestry roads, no footpaths, just endless open moorland, bog, cliffs, crags, and boulder fields[9]. The Galloway landscape is so rough and rugged that Charlie Park[23] said that "a mile walked in the Galloway hills equals three miles anywhere else". It was real wilderness to Derek in 1946; he had just acquired a copy of Rev. C.H. Dick's *Highways and Byways in Galloway and Carrick*[24], and was so inspired by this remarkable book that he later included a passage from it in both *The Raven*[4] and his memoirs[1],

> "If, when you reach The Dungeon, the shepherd at The Backhill of The Bush is able to give you lodging, it is an immense advantage. One cannot, by any route, visit and return from The Dungeon in a single day with any satisfaction. One needs to live beside it, fish the lochs and streams, scramble on the crags with a camera, watch The Fingers of The Awful Hand creep across the moor as the evening sun throws the shadows of the hills eastwards, talk with the shepherd over a peat-fire

at night, and rise in the morning to see the mist floating along the faces of The Dungeon and Craignaw. You are here in the heart of the great Cauldron, on an expanse of moor and bog drained by many streams. Although it is almost completely encircled by hills, it gives a wonderful sense of spaciousness. The loneliness is profound, for the house is distant some six miles from any road-end. If you wander about casting into the burns, you have a feeling of constraint that prevents you from becoming absorbed in your sport. You are here on a precarious sufferance. Something in the wilderness is uneasy and resentful at your presence. You are glad to hear the croak of the raven that tells you that you are not quite alone. This is the effect of the place in fine weather. On a sunless day, when the clouds are low, you feel like a lost soul committed to some chill reach of eternity."

Derek's parents would only allow him to go to these remote hills if he could find a companion. At a late stage his friend backed out, but his parents, sensing Derek's intense disappointment if his 1946 Galloway trip fell through, agreed to let him go alone, provided he took great care. His mother's concern for her son's safety continued through her life. Derek, John and Hilary Birks stayed with her in Carlisle in August 1967 after the three of them had been on a plant-hunting trip (mainly for the Killarney Fern (*Trichomanes speciosum*) in Ireland)[1,11]. As Derek loaded two 30 m climbing ropes into the car (they were planning to continue fern-hunting in Lakeland), she sweetly said "Derek, you are not doing anything dangerous?" – little did she know what situations her son regularly got into on crags and in ravines!

For his 1946 lone ten-day reconnaissance trip to Galloway, Derek obtained lodgings with the McColms, a shepherd and his wife, at the remote cottage of Caldons Farm in Glen Trool. After taking the train to Dumfries and then to Newton Stewart and a bus to Bargrennan, young Derek trudged the last 4–5 miles (6.5–8 km) to Caldons with his rucksack and recently acquired small telescope. For the next nine days, he averaged some 16 miles (26 km) a day on foot as he trekked his way alone through the remote and virtually trackless terrain (Figs. 1.4, 1.5 & 1.7). He sought out the breeding crags of Peregrines, Ravens, and Golden Eagles, climbing to ledges in some of the wildest and most inhospitable parts of the UK. Perhaps Derek's greatest find on his first trip to Galloway was a Golden Eagle eyrie that had been occupied in 1945[1]. This was the first Golden Eagle nest found in modern times in Galloway[23].

Derek was so enthralled by the Galloway area that he returned year after year, missing only one year in the next 59[12,25]! He stayed with various shepherds, where he was fed "like a fighting cock"[1], and where he grew to admire and respect the ways and lore of the hill folk[1]. In this way over the years he came to know just about every significant crag in Galloway, together with those in Dumfriesshire[9], the Borders[9], Lakeland[8], the Pennines[1], Snowdonia[1], and Northumberland[1]. It is unlikely that any other person has ever had such a comprehensive knowledge of these upland areas and their crags and ravines. Just short of sixty years after his first Galloway visit, and only a few days before he died, Derek lodged with Collins the manuscript for his New Naturalist series book *Galloway and the Borders*[9].

After Derek's reconnaissance trip to Galloway in 1946[1], he began in 1947 his annual spring visit there and to the Lake District to assess the status of Peregrine Falcons and Ravens[1]. As a result he developed his interest in bird population biology based on his simple but meticulously thorough field observations[16]. From these he was able to deduce reasons for the decline of the Raven and the Golden Eagle in Galloway as a result of afforestation. His annual observations on Peregrines were crucial in his interpretation of the national Peregrine decline[1,4,26,27]. He first found broken eggs in a Peregrine eyrie in Galloway in 1949 and then in Lakeland in 1952. These early finds, together with additional observations by other ornithologists on broken eggs, were critical in Derek's subsequent work on understanding the underlying causes of the Peregrine decline since 1945[4,26].

Having won a Carlisle City Corporation Major Scholarship to the University of Sheffield, Derek matriculated in late September 1947 and graduated three years later. The dullness of the Sheffield zoology courses and the brilliance of the botanical teachings of Roy Clapham, Verona Conway, and others resulted in Derek becoming a botanist. His contributions as a botanist are discussed in a later chapter[11].

Although no longer living in Carlisle after 1947, Derek continued to visit regularly his favourite haunts in Cumbria (Fig. 1.11), the Northern Pennines, Galloway (Figs. 1.4 & 1.5) and the Southern Uplands (Fig. 1.6), and the Borders for the rest of his life[1,9,28]. In 1997, fifty years after his first systematic Peregrine and Raven monitoring trip to Galloway, Derek, who was like a second father to John and Hilary Birks' son Christopher, found himself in a very difficult position. Christopher's wedding was in April 1997, exactly at the time of Derek's spring monitoring trip! After much letter writing and telephone conservations, Derek was convinced by the Birks family that he should be amongst his Peregrines and Ravens (Fig. 11.17) for the 50th year. Christopher Birks is now the very proud owner of Derek's favourite binoculars.

Figure 1.11. Ullswater in the English Lake District, April 2004. Derek Ratcliffe found many interesting and rare animals and plants in the catchment of this lake. Photo: Derek Ratcliffe

Norfolk – the return 1963–2005

It was only after Derek came to live in Cambridge in 1963, having moved to the newly opened Monks Wood Experimental Station of the then Nature Conservancy near Huntingdon, that he was able to visit regularly his early stamping ground of north Norfolk[1]. What changes he must have seen in the landscape in the 25 years since he first visited Roughton Heath, where he had found in 1937 High-brown and Dark-green Fritillaries, along with Graylings (*Hipparchia semele*) and Green Hairstreaks (*Callophrys rubi*). Today the Heath is no more as it was converted into arable farmland in the 1950s[1]. In April 1994 Derek did, however, see a Kestrel at Felbrigg Hall, now owned by the National Trust, 51 years after finding his first Kestrel nest there[1]. As Derek noted of north Norfolk[1], "some things have changed greatly but others are much the same, and so, I hope, they will remain".

Hilary and John Birks, and later their son Christopher, would join Derek on weekend trips in the 1970s and early 1980s to the East Anglian Breckland in search of the Breckland flora 'rarities' and Stone Curlews (*Burhinus oedicnemus*), and to Norfolk and Suffolk and their interesting wet heaths, valley mires, fens, and other wetlands. They found several interesting local but declining bryophytes such as *Sphagnum molle* and *Dicranum spurium*, and the very rare liverwort *Leiocolea rutheana* var. *laxa*. Despite many searches they never managed to refind some of the rarer plants once recorded in the Waveney-Ouse fens on the Norfolk-Suffolk border such as Fen Orchid (*Liparis loeselii*), and the mosses *Tomentypnum nitens*, *Splachnum ampullaceum*, and *Hamatocaulis vernicosus*[29]. These are probably extinct there because of local drainage and land-use changes, including the overall regional lowering of the ground-water table in East Anglia, and increased supply of nitrogen, phosphorus, and potassium from fertilisers that has enhanced the growth of tall reeds, such as Common Reed (*Phragmites australis*) and plants such as Stinging Nettle (*Urtica dioca*).

Shaped by his early life

By 1947, when Derek began his university studies, many parts of his subsequent career and scientific research were already fully active in the 18-year-old – his fascination with the Peregrine Falcon, Raven, and other birds of prey; his great love of Galloway and the Borders, the Solway Plain and Solway Firth, Lakeland, and the Northern Pennines; his never-ending dogged determination to find particular nests or species; his meticulous field observations and thorough notes; his ability to read the landscape and to understand the natural history and population biology of species such as the Raven and Peregrine; and his remarkable memory for species, habitats, and localities. Further extraordinary abilities not yet developed in 1947 came later – great skills as a field botanist, plant hunter, and vegetation ecologist, broad-scale analytical and descriptive strengths, insights to the perils befalling wildlife, a grasp of the fragmentation of habitats, and an unerring awareness of human nature and foibles. We shall see these emerge later in the book. But on train journeys, cycle runs, and then long hauls in the field, young Derek developed an acutely sharp sense of nature – its beauty, complexity, what was happening to it, and what needed to be done. As only happens in youth, Derek developed an uncanny attachment to wild nature as if it was a parental surrogate. Later, he would be chastened, frustrated, stimulated, and sometimes rewarded by this relationship.

Figure 1.12. Storm over Scafell Pike, Cumbria, an area that Derek Ratcliffe intensively searched for birds and rare mountain plants. Painting by David Bellamy

References

(1)   Ratcliffe, D.A. (2000) *In Search of Nature*. Peregrine Books, Leeds.

(2)   Ratcliffe, D.A. (1947) Personal observations on some local birds. *The Carliol*, **XXII** (No. 221, December), 428-437. Reprinted in this volume as Chapter 3.

(3)   Geoff Horne and John Mitchell, personal communication 2006.

(4)   Ratcliffe, D.A. (1980) *The Peregrine Falcon* (1st edition). Poyser, Calton.
       Ratcliffe, D.A. (1993) *The Peregrine Falcon* (2nd edition). Poyser, London.

(5)   Ratcliffe, D.A. (1997) *The Raven*. Poyser, London.

(6)   Ratcliffe, D.A. (1990) *Bird Life of Mountain and Upland*. Cambridge University Press, Cambridge.

(7)   Ratcliffe, D.A. (1977) *Highland Flora*. Highlands and Islands Development Board, Inverness.

(8)   Ratcliffe, D.A. (2002) *Lakeland*. HarperCollins, London.

(9)   Ratcliffe, D.A. (2007) *Galloway and the Borders*. Collins, London.

(10)   Lewis, C.S. (1950) *The Lion, The Witch, and The Wardrobe*. Geoffrey Bles.

(11)   Birks, H.J.B. & Birks, H.H. (2015) Derek Ratcliffe – botanist and plant ecologist. In: *Nature's Conscience – The Life and Legacy of Derek Ratcliffe* (eds. D.B.A. Thompson, H.H. Birks & H.J.B. Birks). This volume, Chapter 4.

(12)   Ratcliffe, D.A. (1949) *Aeshna caerulea* in Kirkcubrightshire. *The Scottish Naturalist,* **61**, 175.

(13)   Ratcliffe, D.A. (1949) Magpies nesting in Rocks. *North Western Naturalist,* **3**, 129.

(14)   Hewitt, S.M. (1997) Honorary Membership Award to Derek Ratcliffe. *The Carlisle Naturalist,* **5**, 24.

(15)   Ratcliffe, D.A. (1996) Ernest Blezard, 1902-1970. *Transactions of the Carlisle Natural History Society,* **12**, 89-106.

(16)   Thompson, D.B.A. (2015) In search of nesting birds. In: *Nature's Conscience – The Life and Legacy of Derek Ratcliffe* (eds. D.B.A. Thompson, H.H. Birks & H.J.B. Birks). This volume, Chapter 11.

(17)   Canfield, M.R. (ed.) (2011) *Field Notes on Science and Nature*. Harvard University Press, Cambridge, Massachusetts.

(18)   Walker, D. (1966) The late Quaternary history of the Cumberland Lowland. *Philosophical Transactions of the Royal Society of London B,* **251**, 1-210.

(19)   Battarbee, R.W., Stevenson, A.C., Rippey, B., Fletcher, C., Natkanski, J., Wik, M. & Flower, R.J. (1989) Causes of lake acidification in Galloway, south-west Scotland: a palaeoecological evaluation of the relative roles of atmospheric contamination and catchment change for two acidified sites with non-afforested catchments. *Journal of Ecology,* **77**, 651-672

(20)   Battarbee, R.W. (2010) Are our acidified upland waters recovering? *Freshwater Biology Association News,* **52**, 4-5.
       Battarbee, R.W. (2015) Forestry, 'acid rain', and the acidification of lakes. In: *Nature's Conscience – The Life and Legacy of Derek Ratcliffe* (eds. D.B.A. Thompson, H.H. Birks & H.J.B. Birks). This volume, Chapter 22.

(21)   Battarbee, R.W., Curtis, C. & Shilland, E.M. (2011) The Round Loch of Glenhead: Recovery from acidification, climate change monitoring and future threats. *Scottish Natural Heritage Commissioned Report 469*, pp. 35. Inverness.

(22)   Stevenson, A.C., Jones, V.J. & Battarbee, R.W. (1990) The cause of peat erosion: a palaeolimnological approach. *New Phytologist,* **114**, 727-735.

(23)   Watson, D. (2010) *In Search of Harriers*. Langford Press, Peterborough.

(24)   Dick, C.H. (1916) *Highways and Byways in Galloway and Carrick*. Macmillan, London.

(25)   Rollie, C.J. (2015) In Galloway and the Borders – in search of an enduring youth. In: *Nature's Conscience – The Life and Legacy of Derek Ratcliffe* (eds. D.B.A. Thompson, H.H. Birks & H.J.B. Birks). This volume, Chapter 13.

(26)   Newton, I. (2015) Pesticides and birds of prey – the breakthrough. In: *Nature's Conscience – The Life and Legacy of Derek Ratcliffe* (eds. D.B.A. Thompson, H.H. Birks & H.J.B. Birks). This volume, Chapter 15.

(27) Greenwood, J. & Crick, H.Q.P. (2015) "It seemed like a dream come true": Derek Ratcliffe and the Peregrine surveys. In: *Nature's Conscience – The Life and Legacy of Derek Ratcliffe* (eds. D.B.A. Thompson, H.H. Birks & H.J.B. Birks). This volume, Chapter 14.

(28) Corner, R.W.M. (2015) Derek Ratcliffe and plant-hunting in southern Scotland and northern England. In: *Nature's Conscience – The Life and Legacy of Derek Ratcliffe* (eds. D.B.A. Thompson, H.H. Birks & H.J.B. Birks). This volume, Chapter 5.

(29) Bellamy, D.J. & Rose, F. (1960) The Waveney-Ouse Valley Fens of the Suffolk-Norfolk border. *Transactions of the Suffolk Naturalists Society,* **11**, 367-385.

2. National Service and beyond

John Mitchell

My first meeting with Derek Ratcliffe—which came about during a time of military service at Catterick Camp in North Yorkshire during the early 1950s—was quite by chance. Although supposedly at peace after the end of the Second World War, Britain still maintained its army at full strength through compulsory conscription, with well over 25,000 of these two-year-stint National Servicemen attached to various regiments at Catterick alone. Having been a fair trombonist in those far-off days, I was fortunate in being accepted into the Staff Band of the Royal Corps of Signals. My comfortable life in the band was threatened, however, when the Director of Music decreed that all the newer recruits should undergo once-a-week physical training. After just one taste of what proved to be a very unpleasant experience, on those particular afternoons I took to hiding in the last place they would think of looking for me – the Education Building. Had it not been for this I would never have seen a card pinned-up on the notice board there, inviting anyone with an interest in natural history to a meeting with the aim of forming the Catterick Field Club. The invitation was signed by a Sergeant Education Instructor by the name of Derek Ratcliffe.

Derek, as it turned out, was several years older than the mixed bag of budding ornithologists, botanists, and entomologists who turned up on the appointed evening, the reason being that his military service had been deferred until he had completed his university studies. Right from the start it was a field club in its purest form: no set meeting place, no elected officer bearers, and definitely no subscription as none of us had any money – just informal excursions on a Sunday during the spring and summer months. Looking back, I rather suspect that Derek's main reason for taking a bunch of novice naturalists under his wing was not entirely altruistic. An army vehicle could be made available for weekend educational purposes *only* if there were at least six participants, and forming a club ensured Derek of regular access to a set of wheels and driver. He invariably took the decision on the destination for the day, but as the rest of us were rather in awe of this young man's breadth of knowledge – be it of flowering plants or cryptogams, butterflies or birds – we were content just to hang on to his coat-tails.

The very first club outing (by courtesy of Northern Command and the tax-payer, as Derek later wrote in his memoirs[1]) was in mid-March 1954 to Raven Scar at the foot of Ingleborough, one of North Yorkshire's notable Three Peaks. Winter had not yet lost its grip and snow still thickly blanketed the upper slopes. The occupied Ravens' (*Corvus corax*) nest was soon found and, despite the covering of ice over the rock face, Derek deftly scrambled up and called down that there was a clutch of six eggs. At this point he produced from his pocket an indelible pencil and proceeded to scribble lightly over the surface of the eggs, in no way damaging the shells but making them useless as a prize for the oologist's cabinet. Throughout his life Derek held very ambivalent views about 'eggers'. While undoubtedly admiring the high level of field craft and climbing ability of many of yesteryear's egg collectors, he strongly disapproved of the amassing of large private collections. Yet it was these very same egg collections – particularly of Peregrine (*Falco peregrinus*) – which were later to provide him with the base-line evidence to prove that critical eggshell thinning had followed the post-war widespread use of the insecticide DDT[2–5]. The journey from Raven Scar back to barracks set the pattern for other Sundays to follow. As the other excursionists chatted amongst themselves or finished off the last of their sandwiches, Derek sat quietly writing down the details of the day's findings, only joining in the general conversation when his note book was safely tucked away.

Further ornithological trips followed in fairly quick succession. On an exploratory expedition looking for Peregrine in the Ravenseat area of Upper Swaledale, all we found were a few cast feathers at one potential nesting site, and to our dismay a female bird long dead in a gin trap at another. On the next outing we followed an old drove road up to Tan Hill, the inn at the summit said to be the highest in England. Leaving the army vehicle at the inn, the club members struck out across the moor in a westerly direction, eventually coming across a pair of nesting Merlins (*Falco columbarius*) on the slopes of Nine Standards Rigg. Derek fired us with tales of Dotterel (*Charadrius morinellus*) formerly nesting on some of the high tops of Lakeland and one or two other places in northern England, but with the exception of Wild Boar Fell overlooking the famous Settle to Carlisle Railway, all of the other old sites worth another look were beyond our reach. As the season progressed the forays took on more of a botanical flavour, with visits to the superb limestone pavements which outcrop near Ingleborough and Malham Cove. Because of musical engagements at the weekend, I still regret having missed out on club visits to Upper Teesdale and Little Fell, the latter hill never easy to get to at the best of times, but in those days one had to pass through a tank firing range in almost constant use.

Whereas the rest of us took our allocated number of days leave from army service at the first opportunity – frittering away our time on all the usual things off-duty soldiers get up to – Derek saved up most of his leave to take in the spring, thus enabling him to undertake complete coverage of his already established study areas for Peregrine and Raven in Southern Scotland's Galloway Hills[1,4–6].

Our time up serving Queen and Country, one by one the members of the club went their separate ways to pick up the threads of civilian life, and it was to be almost 10 years before my own and Derek's paths crossed again. Idly thumbing through an old copy of *Scottish Field* in my dentist's waiting room in Glasgow, I unexpectedly came across a short piece which he had written for the first National Nature Week in May 1963. Importantly, the article told me that Derek was also living in Scotland, having been working as a research officer for the Nature Conservancy since leaving the army. Contact was made, Sandra (my wife-to-be) and I travelling through to Edinburgh to meet up with him at the Nature Conservancy's Scottish Headquarters at 12 Hope Terrace. There I found myself talked into taking on the annual monitoring of Peregrines and Ravens during the breeding season in the Loch Lomond and Trossachs area, little realising that as the depleted populations of both species slowly recovered their numbers, this was going to occupy all of my spare time every April to June for the next 25 years.

Before leaving his Edinburgh office that winter's afternoon, Derek casually enquired if I would also be interested in a few joint outings in the months to come, suggesting picking up where we left off in the Catterick Field Club days on the North Yorkshire / Westmorland border. I must have agreed, for the following spring saw the two of us at his Golden Plover (*Pluvialis apricaria*) study site at Tailbridge near Kirkby Stephen (which featured in his classic paper on the Golden Plover[7]). The Ratcliffe way of intensive bird study meant living on site in tents, so that every daylight hour could be utilised to good effect. It was the same when we moved up to Cross Fell to tackle the Golden Plovers of the Northern Pennines. An initial failure in pinning-down a particular pair meant returning to their territory in the evening to walk over the ground towards the setting sun, intensely scanning the skyline for that first tell-tale 'flash' from a sitting bird's light under-parts as she rises from her eggs. With Derek the nest and eggs *had* to be found. A few weeks later the pair of us were under canvas again, this time having set up camp just below the 3504 ft (1068 m) summit of Glas Maol on the eastern fringe of the Cairngorms to seek out nesting Dotterel. It was also to be my introduction to the rich arctic-alpine flora of the corrie at the head of Caenlochan Glen[8]. Dotterels' nests and mountain flowers aside, still etched on my memory of that trip is how incredibly cold it was on the plateau at night despite the time of year. While brewing up the late evening tea (from snow stuffed into the kettle as every rivulet was frozen) the conversation ranged over all manner of topics including our family backgrounds. We were intrigued to discover that both of our fathers as young men had played in a cinema orchestra pit during the last days of silent films, before having to move on to other careers.

A new phase in our joint excursion calendar came when Sandra and I began taking our two small boys every year for a short stay with my parents at Peterborough on the edge of the East Anglian Fens. By then Derek and his wife Jeannette (Fig. 17.2) were living not all that far away at Girton near Cambridge, well within strike of 'the Brecks' (Breckland) which to this day still retain a surprising amount of good birding country. Over the next few summers we successfully notched-up nest-finding encounters with Stone Curlew (*Burhinus oedicnemus*) and Nightjar (*Caprimulgus europaeus*), but had to settle for just tantalising glimpses of Red-backed Shrike (*Lanius collurio*). As always there were some choice plants to be found and photographed. When carrying around a flower identification book in the rucksack, for myself I find that a small pocket guide with nice colour pictures will usually do. But on the rare occasions Derek thought one

Figure 2.1. Derek consulting his copy of 'CTW'[9] on the finer points of Spanish Catchfly (*Silene otites*) in the East Anglian Breckland. Photo: John Mitchell

might be useful he insisted on lugging around the unabridged Clapham, Tutin, and Warburg's *Flora of the British Isles*[9], which must weigh the best part of three pounds (Fig. 2.1). A couple of times we ventured deep into Norfolk, tracking down several of the county specialities such as the Swallowtail (*Papilio machaon*) butterfly and the Norfolk Hawker (*Aeshna isoceles*) dragonfly.

The last outing we had together was in April 1996 back in Scotland once more. Our objective was to search for possible new localities for the Killarney Fern (*Trichomanes speciosum*), a blue riband species with all botanists, but with Derek this delicate filmy fern had taken on the status of the Holy Grail[8]. The Killarney Fern is not only extremely sensitive to desiccation and frost, its rarity in the British Isles especially attracted the attentions of the Victorian fern hunters, who succeeded in bringing the species to the verge of extinction[10]. Derek once took me to a secret location for the fern in the Lake District, where a remnant colony he had come across grew hidden behind one of the region's many waterfalls[1]. If I wished to see and photograph the Killarney Fern *in situ* there was nothing for it but to take off all my clothes but for the boots, retaining a modicum of propriety with a plastic raincoat. Pretty obvious writing about it now, but at the time I never foresaw the painful consequence of discharging the external electric flash to my camera in the highly saturated atmosphere behind the curtain of water. I still have the picture he took of this bedraggled figure staggering out from behind the falls. But back to our 1996 fern expedition north of the border. After consulting his motley collection of vintage one-inch-to-the-mile OS maps, Derek reckoned a likely area to prospect was the Loch Riddon area of Argyll. No mature fronds were seen on this occasion, but his day was made when we came across a mat of slender filaments of the Killarney Fern's gametophyte stage in the dark recesses of a cave[8].

During the course of drawing together these personal recollections, I went through again some of the correspondence I received from Derek over the years. Even when electronic mail seemed to completely take over all communications, he never lost the art of writing a good letter (Fig. 27.1)[11]. I cannot think of a single occasion when he neglected to respond with several hand-written pages of constructive comments on receipt of my Peregrine and Raven data for the season, or to offer his congratulations on a good plant 'find'. Without his constant encouragement and support, it is unlikely my contribution to the New Naturalist Series – *Loch Lomondside*[12] – would have ever seen the light of day. I can say no more than it was a privilege to have known him, and to have enjoyed both a long friendship and his companionship in the field.

References

(1)   Ratcliffe, D.A. (2000) *In Search of Nature*. Peregrine Books, Leeds.

(2)   Ratcliffe, D.A. (1967) Decrease in eggshell weight in certain birds of prey. *Nature*, **215**, 208-210.

(3)   Ratcliffe, D.A. (1970) Changes attributable to pesticides in egg breakage frequency and eggshell thickness in some British birds. *Journal of Applied Ecology*, 7, 67-115.

(4)   Newton, I. (2015) Pesticides and birds of prey – the breakthrough. In: *Nature's Conscience – The Life and Legacy of Derek Ratcliffe* (eds D.B.A. Thompson, H.H. Birks & H.J.B. Birks). This volume, Chapter 15.

(5)   Rollie, C.J. (2015) In Galloway and the Borders – in search of an enduring youth. In: *Nature's Conscience – The Life and Legacy of Derek Ratcliffe* (eds D.B.A. Thompson, H.H. Birks & H.J.B. Birks). This volume, Chapter 13.

(6)   Ratcliffe, D.A. (1962). Breeding density in the peregrine *Falco peregrinus* and raven *Corvus corax*. *Ibis*, **104,** 13-39.

(7)   Ratcliffe, D.A. (1976). Observations on the breeding of the golden plover in Great Britain. *Bird Study*, **23**, 63-116.

(8)   Birks, H.J.B. & Birks, H.H. (2015) Derek Ratcliffe – botanist and plant ecologist. In: *Nature's Conscience – The Life and Legacy of Derek Ratcliffe* (eds D.B.A. Thompson, H.H. Birks & H.J.B. Birks). This volume, Chapter 4.

(9)   Clapham, A.R., Tutin, T.G. & Warburg, E.F. (1952) *Flora of the British Isles* (1st edition). Cambridge University Press, Cambridge.

(10) Ratcliffe, D.A., Birks, H.J.B. & Birks, H.H. (1993) The ecology and conservation of the Killarney Fern (*Trichomanes speciosum* Willd.) in Britain and Ireland. *Biological Conservation*, **66**, 231-247.

(11) Marren, P. (2015) Derek and I: A correspondence. In: *Nature's Conscience – The Life and Legacy of Derek Ratcliffe* (eds. D.B.A. Thompson, H.H. Birks & H.J.B. Birks). This volume, Chapter 27.

(12) Mitchell, J. (2001) *Loch Lomondside*. HarperCollins, London

3. Personal observations on some local birds

Derek Ratcliffe

Reprint of Ratcliffe, D.A. (1947) Personal
observations on some local birds.
The Carliol, **XXII**, 428-437.

The Carlisle Grammar School Magazine

VOL. XXII   No. 221   DECEMBER, 1947

The Carliol

THE
CARLISLE
GRAMMAR
SCHOOL
MAGAZINE

The Peregrine Falcon, Raven and Buzzard are three of the finest birds to be found in the British Isles, and it is indeed fortunate that all three occur in reasonable numbers among the local fells. Without these birds the remote dales and crags would lose much of their charm, at least as far as the ardent bird lover is concerned. However, there is little cause for anxiety in this direction, for in spite of persecution in various ways during bygone years, the birds are present in numbers which maintain a fairly constant level. During the war period, owing to a considerable decrease in persecution, the Buzzard most certainly showed a relative increase in numbers and the same is probably true of the Raven.

Unfortunately the Peregrine was condemned for killing carrier pigeons and in some localities was persistently harried. Nevertheless, it is doubtful if this resulted in a serious depletion of their numbers—at least there is no such evidence in the areas with which I am familiar.

These notes are entirely the result of my own experience, and have been collected during the past four years.

The areas covered include:
(1)   The central fells of Cumberland and Westmorland.
(2)   The Cumberland and Westmorland Pennines.
(3)   Parts of the Border Hills, including the counties of
          Dumfriesshire, Roxburghshire, and Northumberland.
(4)   Part of Southern Scotland.

These areas are dissimilar and show great diversity of physical features. Area (1) comprises the tourists "Lakeland" and is far the best known of the four. This district is remarkable for its magnificent, spectacular scenery. The numerous precipices afford many suitable nesting sites for the crag-nesting birds of prey. It is partly the occurrence of suitable crags in any district that determines the numbers of these birds to be found there. For instance, in Areas (2) and (3) large outcrops of rock are less common and the predatory birds are correspondingly scattered.

The fourth and last area is, perhaps, the least known, but in some ways is the finest. Here, as in the Pennines and the Borders, one may walk for many days without seeing another human soul, but it differs from those regions considerably. The Scottish area has many remote lochs and lonely mountain valleys. Crags are numerous, being mainly composed of granite, or other volcanic rock and the hills are higher, several peaks rising to two thousand five hundred feet above sea level.

THE RAVEN

The popularly named 'Bird of ill omen' is found in all four areas, being most common in the Lake District and Galloway.

I do not intend to deal with descriptions of the birds mentioned previously, as these may be consulted in any textbook upon birds, but reference will be made to characteristic features.

In general appearance the Raven resembles a carrion crow—which abounds on the fells—but may be distinguished from that bird by the larger size; rounded, wedge-shaped tail and relatively larger beak. The most certain method of identifying the bird in the field is by the deep croak, which may be represented as "crok-crok". This call has innumerable variations, one of which is a distinct "glonk-glonk".

Another remarkable habit, most frequently performed during the breeding season, is the Raven's dive, when the bird drops like a stone, while at the same time rolling over so that it falls backwards.

As stated previously, the number of Ravens in any district is dependent upon the number of suitable nesting sites occurring in that region.

Obviously the Lake District, with all its crags, could be expected to have a fairly high Raven population, whereas in the Borders many miles may separate two pairs of birds.

Each pair has its own territory and any intruders, such as another Raven or Buzzard, usually receive a 'warm welcome'. The Raven will attack even an intruding Peregrine.

It must be understood that these three birds—Peregrine, Raven and Buzzard—very often share the same crag range, and on many occasions use each other's deserted eyries.

Owing to the fact that each pair has a definite territory, there is a limit set to the numbers of Ravens in a district, and even if there are other suitable nesting sites the birds could not increase beyond this number. In this case the district could be said to be 'saturated' with Ravens.

This is certainly the case in at least two of the areas with which I am familiar.

The territory of each pair usually amounts to several square miles of fell country, but in some cases a single pair presides over a vast area. In Lakeland the average distance between occupied nesting sites in any one breeding season is from three to five miles, there being at least three instances where two occupied sites are only one mile apart—in one case in the same dale.

A district in the South of Scotland, however, holds the record, for at one place there are three nests each year lying within a mile radius. At another place in this district, two pairs nest less than a mile apart, on different aspects of the same hill. This is exceptional, but in every instance each pair hunts a large territory. The pairs of Ravens in the Pennines and the Borders are much more scattered.

Where precipices abound a pair may have one or more alternative nesting crags, these being used irregularly and in no definite order. Most usually the Raven is constant to its nesting haunt and returns every year to the same crags—or the alternative—to breed. Some sites have been occupied for many years without once being deserted.

One pair, in the Dumfriesshire hills, have only one suitable site in their territory—there are no more crags for many miles—and, I have been told, have occupied the place for over ninety years without a break. They have certainly been present every season since I first visited their haunt.

The two nearest sites to this pair are both tree nests.

It seems probable that during the recent war the Raven increased, and in areas where very little rock occurs the new birds were driven to nesting in trees. In the South of England the Raven commonly nests in trees, but in the North 'tree-nests' were previously rare. The inference that tree-nests are now more frequent than formerly is evident, for during the past three years I have seen three such nests.

The first tree-nest was in the Cumberland Pennines in a rock ravine, where the

Raven sometimes nests on a crag. The birds had decided on this occasion to erect their domicile in a small birch tree growing out of a steep rocky slope near a waterfall. The following, season they returned to a rock face and thereon built their eyrie.

The second tree-nest was in Dumfriesshire, being only three miles from the 'regular' rock nest already described. A tiny burn flowing through a ravine deep in the hills held a spreading rowan, and at a height of seven feet above the ground in this tree was a large Raven's nest containing three eggs. The bottom of the nest could be touched by standing at the base of the tree.

The third was in an aged alder growing in a wooded burn of the Roxburghshire hills. The farmer on whose land the nest was situated told me that never before during his lifetime had a Raven nested there.

After the breeding season, the Raven roosts communally, the roosting site very often being a remote and high-lying crag or outcrop. The birds to be found at any roost are usually gathered from a fairly large area.

When the nesting season returns the pairs disperse, each returning to its own haunt. The Raven very seldom deserts the high ground, even under the severest weather conditions, so that, at any time during the year, it may be seen ranging the fells far and wide.

Among the hill farmers the Raven has gained a bad name as a lamb and sheep killer. Personally, I have never seen any living creature attacked by a Raven, but have often flushed a bird feeding on an already defunct sheep. Indeed it appears that this 'braxy' mutton forms a considerable part of the Raven's food throughout the year.

During a severe winter, when the death-rate among the fell sheep is high, the Ravens, Buzzards, and Foxes are provided with food in abundance. In the case of the two birds, it is probable that a plentiful supply of dead sheep results in the production of larger clutches of eggs.

The Raven normally starts nest-building during the latter part of February, but may be delayed by very severe weather, such as was the case this year (1947). It must be remembered that at this time of year the mountains are often deep in snow and temperatures may be considerably below freezing point. These factors do not deter the hardy birds, provided that the actual nesting ledges are not deep in snow or ice-bound. The eggs are often laid under the same Arctic conditions.

Egg-laying usually commences during the early part of March, but varies with different individuals.

The earliest nesting instance was that of a Galloway bird, which had fully fledged young on the 19th April; this meant that egg laying began about 20th February.

The actual nesting haunt is a precipitous rock face, either inland or above the sea— I have no experience of sea-cliff Ravens, Peregrines or Buzzards. The crag may be situated on the open mountainside or else in a ravine, and may range from thirty to five hundred feet or more in height. Many of the highest and most precipitous crags in Lakeland are tenanted by Ravens, but in the Border and the Pennines, where large crags are exceedingly scarce, the birds often have to be content with a small, broken face of rock, and in such a situation the nest is sometimes very easy of access.

The most elevated site in Lakeland lies at about 2,300 feet above sea level and it is a secluded, craggy combe facing North—a situation where snow often lies until late in the year. Many nests lie below 1,000 feet above sea level, but the majority are situated between the altitudes of 1,200 and 2,000 feet.

It is noticeable that in Lakeland the majority of nesting sites face North, North-East, or East. Various suggestions have been made by various writers about this fact, but I believe that it is simply because many of the suitable crags happen to face in those directions.

Many sites, especially those in the remoter districts, lie at a considerable distance from human habitation, whereas some others are situated in close proximity to main roads, and one is within a few hundred yards of a railway.

The number of nesting sites is always greater than the number of breeding pairs, due to the fact that each pair may have one or more alternative sites.

The choice of a nesting ledge often shows great cunning and foresight on the part of the old birds, for on many occasions the nest may only be reached by the process of being lowered down the crag face on a rope. As I usually work alone, such nests are completely inaccessible, at least, as far as I am concerned.

However, a fair number of nests is accessible without having to resort to these measures. Sometimes, even on a large crag, the eyrie may be fairly easy of access.

The actual nesting places include overhung ledges, corners, clefts and columns—the overhang is seldom absent, for the wily Raven fully appreciates the danger of falling stones and ice.

When trying to climb to Ravens' eyries, one frequently discovers that it is a case of 'so near and yet so far', for a bulging slab or narrow gulf may spell failure.

At one nest, with which I am familiar, the absence of a single hand-hold renders the climb impossible, although the nest appears to be within arm's reach.

The nest itself appears externally to be a rough pile of sticks, but is actually of very sound construction. The outer part is composed mainly of dead heather stems and rowan twigs, while the cup of the nest is lined first with earth, moss, grass and coarse vegetation and then finally with sheep's wool, of which a considerable amount is present. The wool is packed in firmly to form a very warm and soft lining.

The average height of a nest is from one to two feet, but in some instances where the same eyrie is used annually the height grows accordingly until a great mass of sticks is present. Such accumulations may be five or six feet high, with an equal width throughout its height.

Another site in the Lakeland Fells appeared to have a similar column, which I judged to be about eight feet high, but I was uncertain, for the nest was examined through the telescope at a distance of about two hundred yards and not closely approached.

On an extensive crag range a pair of Ravens may have several alternative nesting places, which they use irregularly. One local pair has at least ten alternative nests on their home crags.

The birds will often begin to repair two or three nests, and then leave these in favour of another old eyrie. One pair or Ravens has occupied the identical eyrie for the past four years, although they have at least four alternatives in their territory.

The clutch of eggs is commonly four or five, but may be only three, while on three occasions I have found sets of six. In appearance they are eggs typical of the crow family. The ground colour ranges from various shades of light blue to light green, with varying amounts of greyish olive, brown, or black, markings, freckles and botches.

A distinct type occasionally encountered has a blue ground with a few nearly black blotches and spots—in appearance similar to gigantic eggs of the Song Thrush. I have never seen the very rare erythristic or red type of egg.

Relative to the size of the bird the eggs are very small—average dimensions are: Length, 2 inches; breadth, 1.35 inches.

The eggs are deposited on successive days until the clutch is completed, and the incubation period is approximately three weeks. If the first set of eggs is taken the female usually lays again—about three weeks later—in a different nest. Sometimes the birds will utilise an alternative nesting crag for their second attempt. Under no circumstances is more than one brood reared in a season.

The young are quite naked when hatched and remain in the nest for five or six weeks. At the end of this time the eyrie is flattened and much bedaubed with their droppings. To visit such a nest on a hot day may scarcely be described as a pleasant experience—indeed one well-known writer once remarked that the best guide to a Raven's nest containing large young was one's nose.

As with other large crag-nesting birds, the amount of staining and 'whitewash' on the rocks rarely fails to reveal the precise location of a Raven's nest, especially if the nest happens to be frequently used and is situated on bare rock.

Some eyries on extensive cliff ranges are exceedingly difficult to locate, for the birds themselves are not exactly helpful in this respect. While the hen is sitting, the cock bird, unless he is away foraging, usually remains perched upon a jutting part of the crag and maintains a careful watch over his domain. As soon as intruders are seen approaching he utters his warning croak, whereupon the hen quietly slips from the nest and glides away, keeping close to the crag front. This may occur even when the intruders are half a mile or more distant, so that it requires keen perception on the part of the Raven hunter to discern the bird leaving the nest.

Some Scottish granite crags are composed of a very light grey, and even white, rock, thus rendering the 'whitewash' almost invisible, though the birds themselves are more conspicuous than against a background of black rock.

The hen Raven then joins her mate, and both circle around, croaking at intervals. The croaking becomes more furious as the nest is approached. Individual birds may sometimes be recognised in successive years by their behaviour at the nest, and also by the type of egg they produce, for the same bird produces similar eggs throughout its life.

The parents are most demonstrative when they have young. When visiting an eyrie containing young it is a common occurrence for the parents to perch on the ground within a short distance, and start tearing up tufts of grass, or else to settle on a small tree and hammer at the branches and twigs in their rage. Other observers have even seen an irate Raven alight upon a sheep and start ripping the wool from the poor animal's back— for the Raven has an extremely powerful bill.

On the other hand, at places where the parents have been shot at they are very shy and maintain a respectful distance from human intruders. This is more noticeable at some Scottish sites and in the Borders, where gamekeepers are more active. There is comparatively little of this type of persecution in Lakeland. At one site in the Border Hills it is pleasing to know that the keeper would not shoot or harm a Raven in any way, because he evidently feared an old local superstition.

A well-known local Naturalist has commented on the strange effect of Ravens upon other members of their family, such as Rooks. While sitting by a Raven tree-nest containing eggs, as I watched, the parent birds happened to fly over a hill slope about half a mile distant, where a large party of Rooks was feeding. Immediately the Rooks rose in a body and with loud 'caws' of alarm, flew at top speed down the valley in the direction of their home trees some two miles away.

Other birds to be found nesting in the Ravens' haunts include Ring Ousel, Wheatear, Dipper (in the becks), Stock Dove, Common Wren, Carrion Crow, Kestrel, Merlin, and, of course, Peregrine and Buzzard.

Early during the previous March I visited a Raven haunt situated in a remote ravine of the Border Hills, which were at that time thick with snow, while the ravine itself was blocked by huge drifts and the waterfalls there were completely frozen and covered with snow.

Such were the conditions as I ploughed through the snow alongside the hill burn, where numerous hawthorn bushes grew. Presently the hillsides steepened about the burn to form a small gorge. At this place I encountered a small party of Waxwings which were feeding upon the haws. The past Winter was notable for the great Waxwing visitation, but I was amazed to see the bird at this remote spot. The Ravens on this occasion were still building their eyrie under a huge projecting block which effectively sheltered it from the blizzards.

Such was a typical, yet none the less memorable day in quest of that grand old bird of the hills, the Raven.

THE PEREGRINE FALCON

This magnificent bird occurs in all four districts, but is present in smaller numbers (about half) than the Raven, for on the grouse moors it is subject to considerable persecution.

The most noticeable field characters are the long, sharply cut wings and tail which, together with the extremely powerful flight, afford a means of identifying the bird. Care must be taken not to confuse this falcon with its smaller relative, the Kestrel, which has a relatively longer tail and weaker flight.

The normal flight consists of a series of rapid wing beats, alternating with short periods of gliding. The most famous feature of the bird's flight is the terrific downward 'stoop' when the Peregrine strikes at prey. This is effected by the bird almost closing its wings and diving headlong for a considerable distance. If the 'stoop' occurs fairly close to an observer a tremendous roaring sound is heard, which seems out of all proportion to the bird's size. The cry, usually heard only during the breeding season, is a raucous chattering scream – "Lek-ek-ek-ek-ek".

As previously mentioned in the account of the Raven, the occurrence of suitable nesting sites affects the distribution of crag nesting birds and therefore Peregrines. These birds are less common than Ravens and the minimum distance separating two nesting pairs is usually about three miles and is often considerably more. Many of the Raven's habits already referred to apply equally well to the Peregrine and only passing mention will be made of these.

Such habits include the occupation of similar and often the same nesting sites— I have seen a Raven's eyrie with four large young within thirty yards of a Peregrine with eggs, and this is quite a common occurrence—use of alternative sites and alternative nesting places on the same crag range, and also recognition of individuals by their behaviour and type of egg.

The Raven, Buzzard, and Peregrine frequently share the same crags, but although they are such close neighbours, continual warfare rages amongst them and many are the aerial battles which take place in the vicinity of the nesting haunts. Similarly, any intruders of their own species are attacked and driven away.

The Peregrine is the lord of the air and neither Raven nor Buzzard are able to hold their own with him. In spite of this, neither or the two latter birds will hesitate to attack the Falcon, should he or she venture too close to their nest. The battles are accompanied by the various calls of the birds, but are not of a really serious nature and it is only rarely that one of the combatants is injured.

Throughout the Autumn and Winter the Peregrine ranges far and wide over both the plains and the elevated ground, though in some cases the nesting crags are used as roosts throughout the year.

The prey, which is struck down on the wing, invariably consists of other birds, varying in size from the smaller species to larger types, such as Grouse.

In this country the Peregrine has never been known to breed in a tree. No nest is built, for the eyrie normally consists of a shallow scraping in a soily or grassy ledge, although frequently an old Raven's eyrie is utilised. Most authorities assert that when a Raven's eyrie containing wool is used the female always scratches out this lining, the eggs being laid on the bare mud and sticks. However, this was not so at one eyrie, since the eggs reposed on the intact wool lining of a new Raven's nest, which had probably been robbed earlier in the year.

In one case the requisitioned nest had belonged to a Buzzard. The Kestrel also occupies disused Raven nests and one such nest in the Border Hills at the site in the ravine previously mentioned, contained six eggs of the former bird.

The Peregrine does not exhibit the same degree of cunning as the Raven in the choice of a nesting ledge, with the result that this is frequently accessible. Two eyries visited were in such simple positions that a child could have reached them without the slightest risk—one was in heather just at the summit of a crag buttress. Many other nests are only accessible by the use of ropes.

The eggs are usually laid during the second and third weeks of April, but at one eyrie the eggs were hatching on 28th April, which indicates that laying commenced before the end of March. The eggs are laid on alternate days, the full clutch numbering three or four, and the incubation period extends over four weeks,

The Peregrine is renowned for the beauty of its eggs, which range from plain orange brown to various shades of rust and brick red, blotched and marked with similar or darker markings. Some eggs show a considerable amount of light ground colour, and occasionally lilac grey, or grey, shell markings, while others are very plain. Indeed it would scarcely be an exaggeration to say that no two eggs of this species are exactly alike. It is usual to find dissimilarity among the eggs laid by the same bird.

A powdery bloom is sometimes present on the shell, but is soon worn away by the sitting bird. The average size of the eggs is 2 inches by 1.6 inches, but one eyrie held three normal sized eggs and a fourth which was a dwarf, being smaller than the smallest Sparrow-Hawk's egg, and in appearance rather similar to an egg of that species.

If the eggs are taken when fresh the Falcon will lay again after a lapse of about a month, but if the eggs have hatched, or are even 'hard sat', a second laying is seldom attempted. Only one brood is reared in a season.

Both sexes incubate, although the female undertakes the greater part of this duty. Once when I was searching for an eyrie on some extensive crags, the male suddenly flew down to a ledge, and thus, by his careless action, revealed the position of the nest, which contained three eggs.

The Falcon usually makes two or three scrapes and in one of these the eggs are deposited. It is not usual for the same eyrie to be occupied in successive years, but at one Galloway site the same ledge has been used for many years—at least this appears to be the case, for the soil of the ledge is inches deep in the bones of the long deceased prey.

The eyrie is often revealed by the amount of 'whitewash' on the rocks in its immediate vicinity but, unlike the Raven, the Falcon is a fairly close sitter and may usually be flushed from the nest. I have stood on a crag ledge and gazed down to where, on another ledge only seven feet below, a Peregrine was sitting her eggs, completely oblivious to my presence—this was the extremely early nest alluded to above.

On another occasion, when climbing up a crag face to an eyrie situated on a broad ledge, I put my hand over the ledge to obtain a hold and almost touched the sitting bird, which promptly left its four eggs in a great hurry. It would be difficult to say which of us was the more surprised.

Some birds are exceedingly demonstrative when the nest is being investigated, particularly when the eggs are hatched, and very bold birds may 'stoop' close to one's head, while their harsh screams continuously ring across the precipices.

The young when hatched are covered with white down, which is gradually replaced by feathers as they mature. At the age of three weeks or more they show flight, and if an attempt is made to handle them the youngsters promptly throw themselves on to their backs and strike viciously with their talons.

The fledglings remain in the nest for about six weeks. The young stay with their parents until about August, when the family scatters and the offspring are left to fend for themselves. The parents usually continue to roost on or near the home crags.

The Falcon, flushed from the eyrie in heather, disappeared for a short while, only to return with two tiercels, or male birds.

This following account serves as an example of the attachment of the Peregrine to its nesting haunt.

A pair of these birds has bred for many years without a break on some large crags in Northern Lakeland, and each year every egg they have laid has been taken by a nearby gamekeeper, who probably sold his booty for a fair price.

The determined birds still attempt to breed there, although it must be many years since they reared a brood successfully. If the stupid birds would change their quarters and move to some smaller crags three or four miles away they would have a greater chance of rearing a brood.

Other sites have been deserted for no apparent reason, but as a local Naturalist said: "Once a site, always a site". The birds may return again some day.

Many are the days I have spent in search of all kinds of birds throughout various types of country—wood, plain, marsh, river, estuary and moor—yet it is the mountains which make the strongest appeal. Not for one moment has this lure of the wild diminished or abated, rather has it strengthened throughout the years, and may the birds always exist to lend additional charm and attraction to the hills of home.

September, 1947.   D. A. RATCLIFFE

THE BOTANIST –
a quest for rarities and understanding plants in the landscape

4. Derek Ratcliffe – botanist and plant ecologist

John Birks and Hilary Birks

"By chance I became a botanist and specialised in the study of mountain vegetation" [1]

Introduction

If anyone unfamiliar with the scientific work of Derek Ratcliffe consults Google Scholar, they will be surprised to discover someone with over 750 citations to his publications on each of several very different topics – nature conservation, the Peregrine Falcon (*Falco peregrinus*), eggshell thinning and pesticides, and plant ecology and vegetation. A 'wordle' or word cloud (Fig. 4.1) based on the titles of his 1996–2005 publications that are stored in the Scopus database similarly highlights Derek's great breadth of work through his later publications on the Peregrine Falcon, conservation, mountain ecology, vegetation, and the Killarney Fern (*Trichomanes speciosum*). Even today, many ecologists do not realise that the 'bird' Ratcliffe, the 'conservation' Ratcliffe, and the 'botanist' Ratcliffe are all the same person!

Throughout his life Derek Ratcliffe was an active and talented natural historian, field biologist, and ecologist. As a young boy, his interests centred on butterflies and moths[1,2]. Later, as a teenager, he developed his life-long passion for birds[1-3]. It was only when he was an undergraduate at the University of Sheffield that he became interested in plants and became a botanist[1].

This chapter is about Derek's work as a botanist and plant ecologist and is divided into six parts, the first four of which follow the major phases in Derek's botanical career. These are (1) Sheffield 1947-1950, (2) Bangor 1950-1953, (3) Edinburgh 1956-1963, and (4) Monks Wood, London, Huntingdon, Peterborough, and Cambridge 1963-2005. The last two parts are (5) our personal recollections of adventures with Derek 1966-2005 and (6) some final comments about Derek's major botanical achievements, long-lasting contributions, and legacies to the conservation of the British flora and our understanding of British upland vegetation.

Figure 4.1. A word cloud or 'wordle' based on titles from Derek Ratcliffe's 1996-2005 publications in the Scopus database.

Sheffield 1947-1950: a change from zoology to botany

In 1947 Derek Ratcliffe went to the University of Sheffield to study zoology but he found the course with its endless animal anatomy, morphology, and dissection disappointing and very boring[1,2]. Fortunately he was so impressed by the wonderfully inspiring and balanced teaching of A. Roy Clapham (Fig. 4.2), Verona M. Conway, and others at Sheffield that he changed to botany in which he gained a First Class degree in 1950. Roy Clapham was a major influence on Derek and on his future career. In his autobiography[1], Derek wrote of Roy Clapham

> "He was an inspired teacher, but communicated his knowledge in a modest and unaffected way, precise with his words and clear in his information. The course he ran was a model of balance and liveliness across the diverse field of what is now termed plant science. He took a broad-minded view of his role, and once said that he was concerned to turn out scientists who had been trained in the medium of Botany, than purely Botanists."

Figure 4.2. Roy Clapham (1904-1990), Professor of Botany at the University of Sheffield 1944-1969. It was Roy's inspiring and balanced teaching that led Derek Ratcliffe to change from zoology to botany and become a botanist. Roy followed Derek's career and work with interest and was immensely proud of Derek's achievements as a botanist, ornithologist, and conservationist.

Roy was an all-round plant taxonomist and ecologist who coined the term 'ecosystem' popularised by Sir Arthur Tansley[1]. Roy had a wide range of biological interests and always encouraged young scientists to study organisms in the field. He excused Derek from his Easter 1949 botany field course to Malham so that Derek could go on his annual Peregrine trip to Galloway – "That's all right", said Roy, "you'll probably get more out of it than if you came with us"[1]. How right Roy was, because on that 1949 Galloway trip Derek found his first broken Peregrine egg beneath an eyrie, a find that led to Derek's ground-breaking and globally important work on eggshell thinning in raptors[1,4-8].

Before becoming a student at Sheffield[1,2], Derek had discovered in 1947 the amazing series of patterned bogs called The Silver Flowe (Fig. 1.7) along the Cooran Lane in the Cauldron of the Dungeon in Galloway. The bogs got their name from the light reflected off the masses of pools on the surface of the bogs. Whilst at Sheffield, Derek told Verona Conway who was a specialist on peat bogs about The Silver Flowe bogs and she encouraged him to survey the bogs and to document their amazing surface patterns, as nothing like these bogs had ever been studied in the British Isles. This Derek did in 1951 (see below). He regularly visited these bogs during his annual Galloway trips[1,2] and in the summer 1949 he found there the Azure Hawker (*Aeshna caerulea*) dragonfly (Fig. 1.8), not previously known outside the Scottish Highlands[1,2].

Bangor 1950-1953: mountain plant ecology, bryophytes, and ferns

In 1950 Derek moved to the then University College of Wales at Bangor (now the University of Bangor) to begin his Ph.D. research under the supervision of Paul W. Richards on the vegetation and ecology of the Carneddau (Carnedd Llewellyn and Carnedd Dafydd) mountain range adjoining the Conway valley. Derek's Ph.D. work involved detailed vegetation surveys and mapping and a critical analysis of the factors determining the different plant communities on the Carneddau, such as climate, soils, grazing, burning, and other types of management. He completed his Ph.D. thesis late in 1953 and it was an outstandingly thorough study[9]. His results are now being used to assess the recent impacts of atmospheric nitrogen deposition and grazing on mountain vegetation, particularly *Racomitrium lanuginosum* summit heath, over the last 50 years[10].

Whilst at Bangor, Derek developed a life-long interest in bryophytes (mosses, hornworts, liverworts) through his close friendship with Reg Parker. Reg and Derek travelled around North Wales in search of plants on Reg's motorbike, with Reg shouting details of their destination, what plants to look out for, what their distinguishing characteristics were, and so on over his shoulder to Derek who was clinging on in the pillion seat. They made many new botanical discoveries, particularly of mountain bryophytes and vascular plants and found several new localities for the very rare and elusive Snowdon Lily (*Lloydia serotina*). From Evan Roberts and Paul Richards, Derek also acquired a keen interest in rare flowering plants and ferns, particularly filmy ferns (Fig. 4.3). His life-long passion for the Killarney Fern (*Trichomanes speciosum*) started on a student botanical excursion in Merioneth in the autumn of 1950 when Paul Richards announced to all the participants that Paul and his teaching assistant Stanley Greene were leaving the party for a short time to go to a 'secret' locality to see the 'special' *Trichomanes speciosum*. The inquisitive Derek looked out to see where Paul and Stanley alighted (Talsarnau) and asked Reg "what is *Trichomanes speciosum*?" Reg replied it was some rare fern. Later that autumn Derek visited his former Sheffield colleague Donald Walker who was now based in the then Cambridge Botany School starting research on Quaternary pollen analysis and vegetation history of north-west England. Derek looked at the folder of Killarney Fern specimens in the Cambridge Herbarium and was bowled over to see various collections of large fronds of the Killarney Fern (Fig. 4.3) from a "damp ravine in northern part of Snowdon range" and "part of the Snowdon range" made by James Backhouse Jr. and Sr. and J.F. Rowbotham in 1863 and "from the mountains of Merionethshire" made by the Backhouse family and friends in the 1860s and 1870s. He returned to Bangor determined to refind without delay the Killarney Fern. By the time Derek left Bangor late in 1953, he had searched by himself every ravine or stream of any size around the northern part of the Snowdon range and also many places to the south for the Killarney Fern but with no success. He failed to find any Killarney Fern but in the process he found many new localities in North Wales for nationally rare Atlantic bryophytes (Figs. 4.4-4.6) such as *Fissidens polyphyllus* (Fig. 4.4), *Hageniella micans* (Fig. 4.4), *Radula voluta* (Fig. 4.4), *R. aquilegia* (Fig. 4.5), *Lepidozia cupressina* (Fig. 4.5), *Plagiochila exigua* (Fig. 4.5), *Sematophyllum demissum*, *Metzgeria leptoneura* (Fig. 4.6), *Isothecium holtii* (Fig. 4.6), *Adelanthus decipiens* (Fig. 7.6), *Jubula hutchinsiae* (Fig. 7.6), and *Fissidens bryoides* var. *caespitans*.

During his Bangor years Derek also developed an interest in photography after he acquired a small plate camera with a Zeiss lens made in 1947[1,2]. He always used a tripod for his photographs and he became an outstanding photographer in both black-

Figure 4.3. The filmy ferns that so fascinated Derek Ratcliffe whilst he was at Bangor and subsequently throughout his career. Killarney Fern (*Trichomanes speciosum*) specimens from North Wales collected in the 1860s by James Backhouse Jr. and Sr. and family and friends housed in the Herbaria of Royal Botanic Gadens Kew (*top left*) and the University of Cambridge (*top right*). Wilson's Filmy-fern (*Hymenophyllum wilsonii*), Isle of Skye, 1966 (*lower left*) and Tunbridge Filmy-fern (*Hymenophyllum tunbrigense*), Sussex, 1967 (*lower right*) Photos: John Birks

Figure 4.4. Southern Atlantic bryophytes that mainly occur in humid and shaded habitats. Derek Ratcliffe found several new localities for these species, including finding *Fossombronia angulosa* and *Dumortiera hirsuta* new to Scotland. *Radula voluta*, Cumbria, 1966 (*top left*); *Dumortiera hirsuta*, Kerry, 1965 (*top centre*); *Fissidens polyphyllus*, Caernarvonshire, 1965 (*top right*); *Marchesinia mackaii*, Cornwall, 1966 (*lower left*); Hageniella micans, Cumbria, 1966 (*lower centre*); and *Fossombronia angulosa*, Cornwall, 1966 (*lower right*). Photos: John Birks

and-white and colour media of plants, vegetation, and landscapes. His favourite cameras were a Pentax single lens reflex for plant portraits and a Hasselblad for large format pictures of habitats and landscapes.

In his second year at Bangor, Derek returned to Galloway in the summer of 1951 to study The Silver Flowe bogs with his friend from his Sheffield undergraduate days Donald Walker[1]. They spent a very wet two weeks surveying in detail the seven main bogs and lived in the deserted Backhill of the Bush cottage (Fig. 1.10) near the northern end of The Silver Flowe[1,2] (Fig. 1.7). In this work, Derek mastered the taxonomy and the considerable intra-specific variation in the many *Sphagnum* species on these bogs. Donald and Derek estimated the vertical range of the major vascular plants and bryophytes on the bogs in relation to the water-table. Together they developed new ideas on the development of the pool and hummock patterns on bogs, ideas that were later supported by detailed peat-stratigraphical studies by Donald and Pat Walker[11]. As a result of their work, The Silver Flowe was designated a National Nature Reserve in 1955. Derek and Donald published a major paper about The Silver Flowe in 1958[12]. Their work formed the basis for Hilary Birks' detailed pollen-stratigraphical studies on the history and development of Snibe Bog[13], and subsequent ecological studies by Derrick Boatman[14] and David Goode[15] on the patterned pool features, *Sphagnum* growth, and water chemistry of The Silver Flowe bogs.

Figure 4.5. Widespread Atlantic bryophytes that occur in varying frequency in western Britain and/or Ireland. Derek Ratcliffe found several new localities for these species. *Daltonia splachnoides*, Argyll, 1966 (*top left*); *Hedwigia integrifolia*, Isle of Skye, 1966 (*top right*); *Radula aquilegia*, Wester Ross, 1966 (*middle left*); *Plagiochila exigua*, Argyll, 1966 (*middle right*); *Lepidozia cupressina*, Devon, 1966 (*lower left*); and *Ulota calvescens*, West Sutherland, 1966 (*lower right*). Photos: John Birks

Figure 4.6. Widespread Atlantic bryophytes that occur locally in western Britain and/or Ireland. Derek Ratcliffe found several new localities for these species. *Isothecium holtii*, Waterford, 1967 (*top left*); *Colura calyptrifolia*, Wester Ross, 1966 (*top right*); *Metzgeria leptoneura*, Argyll, 1968 (*middle*); *Aphanolejeunea microscopica*, Glencoe, 1966 (*lower left*); and *Drepanolejeunea hamatifolia*, Yorkshire, 1965 (*lower right*). Photos: John Birks

Edinburgh 1956-1963: mountain plant ecology, plant recording, bryophytes, and mire ecology

After his National Service in 1954-1955[16], Derek joined the Nature Conservancy in Edinburgh in January 1956 to participate in the 'Highland Vegetation Survey', an important and demanding project on the description and classification of Scottish Highland vegetation in collaboration with Donald McVean (Fig. 4.7). During 1956-1959, Donald and Derek, almost always working independently, surveyed much of the vegetation of the Highlands. Derek concentrated on the remote and poorly known mountains of the North-West Highlands and the botanically rich areas of the western, central, and eastern Highlands (Fig. 4.8) because of his interests in bryophytes and rare mountain plants, whereas Donald surveyed the Cairngorms and other acid areas in the eastern and central Highlands where lichens form a prominent component of the vegetation. Between

Figure 4.7. The 'Highland Vegetation Survey' team of Derek Ratcliffe (left) and Donald McVean (right) near Oban, 1990. Photo: Des Thompson

them they recorded over 1,100 vegetation quadrats in which all species of vascular plant, bryophyte, and lichen were identified and their cover-abundances estimated (Fig. 4.9). They defined about 100 vegetation types on the basis of their quadrat data and of Duncan Poore's early survey in the Breadalbane area. Nearly all these vegetation types have stood the test of time and form the basis of many of the vegetation units in the *Illustrated Guide to British Upland Vegetation*[17].

For the first two seasons (1956, 1957) of the Highland Vegetation Survey, Derek had to rely almost entirely on bicycle and public transport to get around. He explored several remote areas where botanists had never been before and he made many exciting vascular plant and bryophyte discoveries in the North-West Highlands[18,19], on the Seana

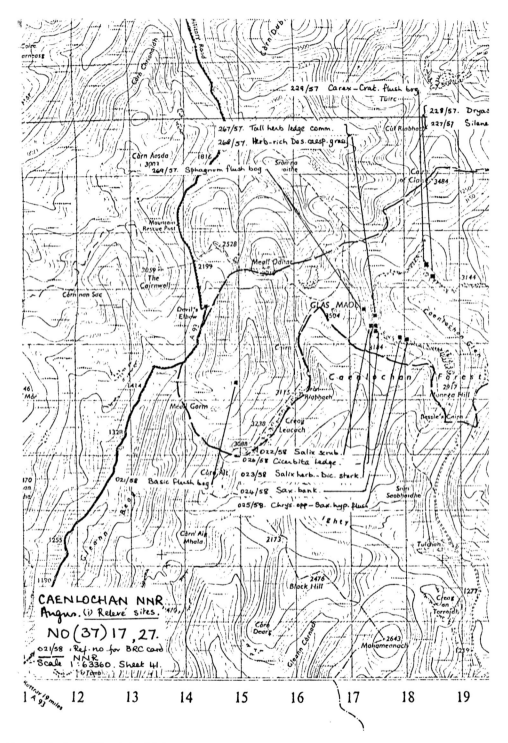

Figure 4.8a. Copy of Derek Ratcliffe's map marking his 1957 survey quadrats in the western part of Caenlochan Glen (formerly a National Nature Reserve (NNR)) in the Grampian Highlands. The area shown is part of the Caenlochan Glen Site of Special Scientific Interest (SSSI), Special Protected Area (SPA), and Special Area for Conservation (SAC). Reproduced from the archive of Derek Ratcliffe's vegetation records and site maps donated to the National Vegetation Classification project in 1974

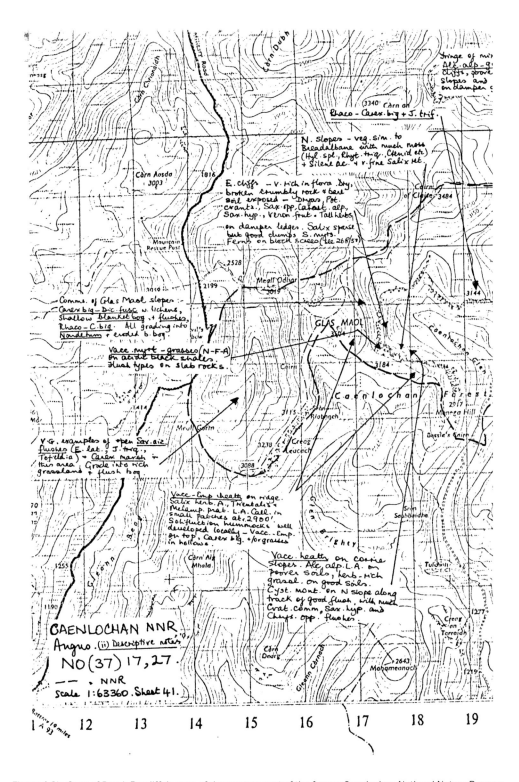

Figure 4.8b. Copy of Derek Ratcliffe's map of the western part of the former Caenlochan National Nature Reserve (NNR) with his general vegetation notes marked on

Alt.	Asp.	Slope
2800 ft	South	av. 45°

Cover	Height	
Complete.		Plot size = 4 m²

Soil profile and other data.

Broken foot of calcareous mica-schist crags. A rather drier bank than Sp. 227 (Silene intermittent flush) Accessible to sheep and deer and with a rather open, soily appearance, though the cover of vegetation is fairly complete. Dryas grows more densely on the rock ledges, often with Vacc. uliginosum.

Soil
0 - 1½" Dark brown, grey-tinged, humus rich loam

1½ - 8" Rich medium brown crumbly loam, full of micaceous fragments.

McVean + Ratcliffe, 1962.
Table 23, List 6.

Figure 4.9a. Part of Derek Ratcliffe's notes on his recording card for a quadrat from *Dryas* vegetation in Caenlochan Glen in the Grampian Highlands. Reproduced from the archive of Derek Ratcliffe's vegetation records and site maps donated to the National Vegetation Classification project in 1974

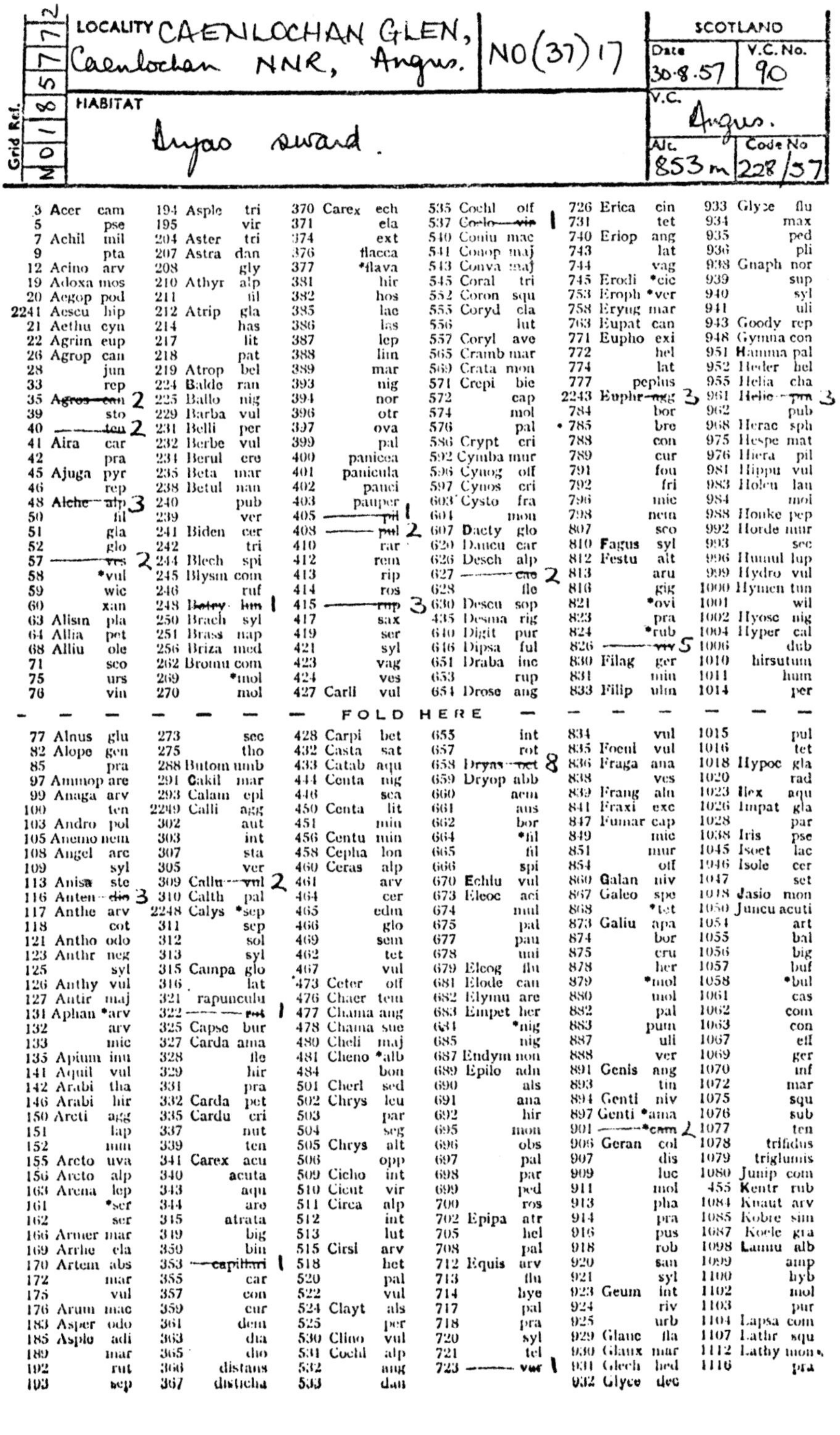

LOCALITY CAENLOCHAN GLEN, Caenlochan NNR, Angus. NO(37)17

Grid Ref.

HABITAT Dryas sward.

SCOTLAND
Date 30·8·57 V.C. No. 90
V.C. Angus.
Alt. 853 m   Code No 228/57

3	Acer	cam	194	Asplc	tri	370	Carex	ech	535	Cochl	olf	726	Erica	cin	933	Glyce	flu

3 Acer cam
5 pse
7 Achill mil
9 pta
12 Acino arv
19 Adoxa mos
20 Aegop pod
2241 Aescu hip
21 Aethu cyn
22 Agrim eup
26 Agrop can
28 jun
33 rep
35 Agros-com 2
39 sto
40 -tcu 2
41 Aira car
42 pra
45 Ajuga pyr
46 rep
48 Alche alp 3
50 fil
51 gla
52 glo
57 -res 2
58 •vul
59 wic
60 xan
63 Alisin pla
64 Allia pet
68 Alliu ole
71 sco
75 urs
76 vin

77 Alnus glu
82 Alope gen
85 pra
97 Ammop are
99 Anaga arv
100 ten
103 Andro pol
105 Anemo nem
108 Angel arc
109 syl
113 Anisa ste
116 Anten din 3
117 Anthe arv
118 cot
121 Antho odo
123 Anthr neg
125 syl
126 Anthy vul
127 Antir maj
131 Aphan •arv
132 arv
133 mic
135 Apium inu
141 Aquil vul
142 Arabi tha
146 Arabi hir
150 Arcti agg
151 lap
152 min
155 Arcto uva
156 Arcto alp
161 Arena lep
161 •ser
162 ser
166 Armer mar
169 Arrhe ela
170 Artem abs
172 mar
175 vul
176 Arum mac
183 Asper odo
185 Asplo adi
189 mar
192 rut
193 sep

194 Asplc tri
195 vir
204 Aster tri
974 ext
376 flacca
377 •flava
208 gly
210 Athyr alp
211 fil
212 Atrip gla
214 has
217 lit
218 pat
219 Atrop bel
224 Balde ran
225 Ballo nig
229 Barba vul
231 Belli per
232 Berbe vul
234 Berul ere
235 Beta mar
238 Betul nan
240 pub
239 ver
241 Biden cer
242 tri
244 Blech spi
245 Blysm com
246 wic
248 Botry hm
250 Brach syl
251 Brass nap
256 Briza med
262 Bromu com
269 •mol
270 mol

273 sec
275 tho
288 Butom umb
291 Cakil mar
293 Calam epl
2249 Calli agg
302 aut
303 int
307 sta
305 ver
309 Callu vul 2
310 Calth pal
2248 Calys •sep
311 sep
312 sol
313 syl
315 Campa glo
316 lat
321 rapunculu
322 rot
325 Capse bur
327 Carda ama
328 fle
329 hir
331 pra
332 Carda pet
335 Cardu cri
337 nut
339 ten
341 Carex acu
340 acuta
343 aqu
344 arc
345 atrata
349 big
350 bin
353 capillari
355 car
357 con
359 cur
361 dem
363 dia
365 dio
366 distans
367 disticha

370 Carex ech
371 ela
974 ext
376 flacca
377 •flava
381 hir
382 hos
385 lac
386 las
387 lep
388 lin
389 mar
393 nig
394 nor
397 otr
397 ova
399 pal
400 panicea
401 panicula
402 panci
403 pauper
405 pil
408 pul 2
410 rar
412 rem
413 rip
414 ros
415 rup 3
417 sax
419 ser
421 syl
423 vag
424 ves
427 Carli vul

FOLD HERE

428 Carpi bet
432 Casta sat
433 Catab aqu
444 Centa nig
450 Centa lit
451 min
456 Centu min
458 Cepha lon
460 Ceras alp
461 arv
464 cer
465 edm
466 glo
469 sem
462 tet
467 vul
473 Ceter olf
476 Chaer tem
477 Chama ang
478 Chama suc
480 Cheli maj
481 Cheno •alb
484 bon
501 Cherl sed
502 Chrys leu
503 par
504 seg
505 Chrys alt
506 opp
509 Cicho int
510 Cicut vir
511 Circa alp
512 int
513 lut
515 Cirsl arv
518 het
520 pal
522 vul
524 Clayt als
525 per
530 Clino vul
531 Cochl alp
532 ang
533 dan

535 Cochl olf
537 Cœlo vir
540 Coniu mac
541 Conop maj
543 Conva maj
545 Coral tri
552 Coron squ
555 Coryd cla
556 lut
557 Coryl ave
565 Cramb mar
569 Crata mon
571 Crepi bie
572 cap
574 mol
576 pal
586 Crypt cri
592 Cymba mur
596 Cynog off
597 Cynos cri
603 Cysto fra
604 mon
607 Dacty glo
620 Dancu car
626 Desch alp
627 cœs 2
628 fle
630 Descu sop
635 Desma fig
640 Digit pur
646 Dipsa ful
651 Draba inc
653 rup
654 Drose ang

655 int
657 rot
658 Dryas oct 8
659 Dryop abb
660 acm
661 aus
662 bor
664 •fil
665 fil
666 spi
670 Echlu vul
673 Eleoc aci
674 mul
675 pal
677 pau
678 uni
679 Eleog flu
681 Elode can
682 Elymu are
683 Empet her
684 •nig
685 nig
687 Endym non
689 Epilo adn
690 als
691 ana
692 hir
695 mon
696 obs
697 pal
698 par
699 ped
700 ros
702 Epipa atr
705 hel
708 pal
712 Equis arv
713 flu
714 hye
717 pal
718 pra
720 syl
721 tel
723 var

726 Erica cin
731 tet
740 Eriop ang
743 lat
744 vag
745 Erodi •cic
753 Eroph •ver
758 Eryng mar
763 Eupat can
771 Eupho exi
772 hel
774 lat
777 peplus
2243 Euphr nng 2
784 bor
785 bre
788 con
789 cur
791 fou
792 fri
796 mic
798 nem
807 sco
810 Fagus syl
812 Festu alt
813 aru
816 gig
821 •ovi
823 pra
824 •rub
826 vw 5
830 Filag ger
831 min
833 Filip ulm

834 vul
835 Foenl vul
836 Fraga ana
838 ves
839 Frang aln
841 Fraxi exc
847 Fumar cap
849 mic
851 mur
854 off
860 Galan niv
867 Galeo spe
868 •tet
873 Galiu apa
874 bor
875 cru
878 her
879 •mol
880 mol
882 pal
883 pum
887 uli
888 ver
891 Genis ang
893 tin
894 Genti niv
897 Genti •ama
901 •cam 2
906 Geran col
907 dis
909 luc
911 mol
913 pha
914 pra
916 pus
918 rob
920 san
921 syl
923 Geum int
924 riv
925 urb
929 Glauc fla
930 Glaux mar
931 Glech hed
932 Glyce dec

933 Glyce flu
934 max
935 ped
936 pli
938 Gnaph nor
939 sup
940 syl
941 uli
943 Goody rep
948 Gymna con
951 Hamma pal
952 Heder hel
955 Helia cha
961 Helie pm 3
962 pub
968 Herac sph
975 Hespe mat
976 Hiera pil
981 Hippu vul
983 Holeu lan
984 mol
988 Honke pep
992 Horde mur
993 sec
996 Humul lup
999 Hydro vul
1000 Hymen tun
1001 wil
1002 Hyose nig
1004 Hyper cal
1006 dub
1010 hirsutum
1011 hum
1014 per

1015 pul
1016 tet
1018 Hypoc gla
1020 rad
1023 Ilex aqu
1026 Impat gla
1028 par
1038 Iris pse
1045 Isoet lac
1046 Isole cer
1047 set
1048 Jasio mon
1050 Juncu acuti
1054 art
1055 bal
1056 big
1057 buf
1058 •bul
1061 cas
1062 com
1063 con
1067 eff
1069 ger
1070 inf
1072 mar
1075 squ
1076 sub
1077 ten
1078 trifidus
1079 triglumis
1080 Junip com
455 Kentr rub
1084 Knaut arv
1085 Kobre sim
1087 Kœle gra
1098 Lamiu alb
1099 amp
1100 hyb
1102 mol
1103 pur
1104 Lapsa com
1107 Lathr squ
1112 Lathy mons
1116 pra

Figure 4.9b. Part of Derek Ratcliffe's recording card for a quadrat from *Dryas* vegetation in Caenlochan Glen. The numbers written in are his estimated Domin cover-abundance values for the species in the quadrat

51

Bhraigh massif near Ullapool[18,19], on Rum[1], and in the Ben Alder range[20]. For his exploration of these remote areas, Derek would often sleep 'out on the hill' for one or two nights using his heavy black government-issue raincoat as a groundsheet and existing on Mars Bars! In the case of Seana Bhraigh, the weather was very unsettled so Derek returned each evening to near Ullapool and walked in on four consecutive days to reach remote areas east of Seana Bhraigh itself. He found many interesting plants on his 1956 visits[1,18,19], and in 1957 he found Norwegian Mugwort (*Artemisia norvegica*) (Fig. 4.10) in its second Scottish locality. Derek later discovered that Humphrey Milne-Redhead, a hardy Galloway medical doctor, had found it there two weeks earlier[1]. Humphrey had spent a rough night bivouacking near the head of Glen Douchary before awakening soaked to the skin, to find Norwegian Mugwort near the summit. He left a note for Derek at Fasagrianach Cottage near Corrieshalloch Gorge telling him of his find but the note never reached Derek.

Derek made many other important discoveries in his botanical explorations of remote areas in 1956 and 1957 including Net-leaved Willow (*Salix reticulata*) (Fig. 4.10), Mountain Bladder-fern (*Cystopteris montana*) (Fig. 4.10), Highland Saxifrage (*Saxifraga rivularis*) (Fig. 4.10), Tufted Saxifrage (*S. cespitosa*), Alpine Saxifrage (*S. nivalis*) (Fig. 4.11), Alpine Woodsia (*Woodsia alpina*) (Fig. 4.11), Highland Cudweed (*Gnaphalium norvegicum*) (Fig. 4.11), Scorched Alpine-sedge (*Carex atrofusca*) (Fig. 4.10), Rock Sedge (*C. rupestris*), Hair Sedge (*C. capillaris*), Holly Fern (*Polystichum lonchitis*) (Fig. 4.12), and Alpine Cinque-foil (*Potentilla crantzii*) (Fig. 4.12), and the bryophytes *Hypnum bambergeri* (Fig. 4.13), *Ptychodium plicatum*, *Encalypta alpina* (Fig. 4.13), *Campylophyllum halleri*, *Rhytidium rugosum* (Fig. 4.13), and *Pseudoleskeella catenulata*. In the North-West Highlands he found many new localities for a range of Northern Atlantic bryophytes[21] such as the liver-worts *Anastrophyllum donnianum* (Fig. 4.14), *A. joergensenii*, *A. alpinum* (Fig. 4.14), *Bazzania pearsonii* (Fig. 4.14), *Scapania nimbosa* (Fig. 4.14), *S. ornithopodioides* (Fig. 4.15), *Plagiochila carringtonii* (Fig. 4.15), *Mastigophora woodsii* (Fig. 7.7), *Herbertus borealis* (Figs. 6.7 & 7.11)[22], and the mosses *Paraleptodontium recurvifolium* (Fig. 4.15), *Campylopus setifolius* (Fig. 4.15), *C. shawii* (Fig. 6.4), *C. atrovirens* var. *falcatus*, *Myurium hochstetteri* (Fig. 6.4), and *Sphagnum strictum* (Fig. 7.8). Many of the large liverworts are part of a distinct vegetation type, the so-called 'mixed hepatic mat', a community that Derek made a special study of (see below) (Figs. 6.13 & 7.12)[21,23,24].

The Survey continued in 1958 and 1959 and Derek, now mobile in a land-rover and later a small estate-car, travelled around much of the Highlands making further vegetational analyses, collecting samples for soil analysis, taking photographs of different vegetation types, and mapping ecological patterns. He refound the very rare Alpine Blue-sow-thistle (*Cicerbita alpina*) on a near inaccessible ledge in Corrie Kander[25]. He visited the St. Kilda archipelago in 1959 and, to his surprise, found the Southern Atlantic liverwort *Fossombronia angulosa* (Figs. 4.4 & 6.9) growing on Hirta[21,23]. It was previously known only as far north as North Wales[21]. This discovery prompted Derek to wonder if other Southern Atlantic species[21,23,24] might be found in western Scotland. He also found on Hirta what was subsequently identified as *Sanionia orthothecioides* (Fig. 6.10), an arctic moss new to Britain[26,27]. Derek devoted much of his vacation-time to exploring intensively the Southern Uplands, especially the Moffat Hills (Fig. 5.1), the Northern Pennines, and the Lakeland fells (Fig. 1.11) for mountain plants[28-30]. Patiently he re-found almost all the rarities of these areas, including Mountain Avens (*Dryas*

Figure 4.10. Some of the mountain plants that Derek Ratcliffe found in new localities in Scotland. Mountain Avens (*Dryas octopetala*), West Sutherland, 1969 (*top left*); Net-leaved Willow (*Salix reticulata*), Perthshire, 1967 (*top right*); Scorched Alpine-sedge (*Carex atrofusca*), Norway, 1986 (*middle left*); Norwegian Mugwort (*Artemisia norvegica*), Wester Ross, 1967 (*middle right*); Highland Saxifrage (*Saxifraga rivularis*), Cairngorms, 1967 (*lower left*); and Mountain Bladder-fern (*Cystopteris montana*), Aberdeenshire, 1967 (*lower right*). Photos: John Birks

Figure 4.11. Some of the rare plants that Derek Ratcliffe excelled at finding in new localities. Pyramidal Bugle (*Ajuga pyramidalis*), Austria, 1969 (*top left*) and Alpine Saxifrage (*Saxifraga nivalis*), Perthshire, 1966 (*top right*). Photos: John Birks. Highland Cudweed (*Gnaphalium norvegicum*), Norway, 1962 (*lower left*) and Alpine Woodsia (*Woodsia alpina*), Perthshire, 1958 (*lower right*). Photos: Derek Ratcliffe

Figure 4.12. Some of the rare plants of the Moffat Hills and the northern Pennines that Derek Ratcliffe refound, often after much searching. Alpine Cinquefoil (*Potentilla crantzii*), Perthshire, 1966 (*top left*); Dwarf Cornel (*Cornus suecica*), Norway, 1999 (*top right*); Oblong Woodsia (*Woodsia ilvensis*), Norway, 1986 (*middle left*); Holly Fern (*Polystichum lonchitis*), West Sutherland, 1966 (*middle right*); *Aplodon wormskioldii*, a very rare Arctic coprophilous moss (*lower left*) growing on a sheep carcass (*lower right*) in Cumbria, 1968. *Aplodon* has not been seen in Britain since 1981 (Chris Preston personal communication). Photos: John Birks

octopetala) (Fig. 4.10)[1,2], Pyramidal Bugle (*Ajuga pyramidalis*) (Fig. 4.11), Alpine Saxifrage (Figs. 4.11 & 5.3)[31], Marsh Saxifrage (*Saxifraga hirculus*) (Fig. 5.6)[31], Holly Fern (Fig. 4.12)[31], Oblong Woodsia (*Woodsia ilvensis*) (Figs. 4.12 & 9.4)[32], Dwarf Cornel (*Cornus suecica*) (Fig. 4.12), Alpine Cinquefoil (Fig. 4.12), and the very rare coprophilous moss *Aplodon wormskioldii* growing on a sheep carcass (Fig. 4.12). He also made many new vascular plant and bryophyte records[28,29,31], including Alpine Foxtail (*Alopecurus magellanicus*) (Fig. 5.4) new to England[31,33].

The full results of the 'Highland Vegetation Survey' were published in 1962 as *Plant Communities of the Scottish Highlands*[34] despite strong opposition from the then in-

Figure 4.13. Some of the rare or local mountain calcicolous bryophytes that Derek Ratcliffe discovered in the Ben Alder range in 1957, some of which had been thought to be confined to the mountains of Breadalbane or Glencoe[20]. *Encalypta alpina*, Aberdeenshire, 1966 (*top left*); *Orthothecium rufescens*, Yorkshire, 1965 (*top right*); *Hypnum bambergeri*, Aberdeenshire, 1966 (*lower left*); and *Rhytidium rugosum*, Suffolk, 1965 (*lower right*). Photos: John Birks

fluential plant ecologist W.H. Pearsall[35]. It was the first detailed and extensive plant sociological and ecological study of its kind in Britain. In addition, the last three chapters cover "Climate and Vegetation", "Soils", and "Plant Geographical Factors" and are masterpieces of ecological and phytogeographical synthesis. The book remains an ecological 'classic' of great interest not only to British botanists but also to everyone concerned with alpine and arctic flora, vegetation, and ecology. It is a monument to meticulous field botanical descriptions and it remains an invaluable source of information about plant associations, species occurrences, elevational ranges, distributions, and ecological preferences of species. It laid the foundation for John Birks' work on the present vegetation of the Isle of Skye[36] and for the National Vegetation Classification (NVC) project initiated, commissioned, and funded by the Nature Conservancy Council (NCC) in 1975 involving several plant ecologists, including Derek, Donald Pigott, Michael Proctor, Andrew Malloch, Dave Shimwell, Bryan Wheeler, Paul Adam, and ourselves, with John Rodwell as co-ordinator. When completed in 2000, the NVC project resulted in the monumental five-volume *British Plant Communities*[37]. The original idea of the NVC project came jointly from Donald Pigott and Derek Ratcliffe who both recognised in the late 1960s the urgent need for a unified up-to-date account of British vegetation types that could provide a much-needed basis for the design, preparation, and writing of *A Nature Conservation Review* (NCR)[38,39] (see below). In the absence of such an account, Derek and the Chief Scientist Team[40] in the NCC along with other ecologists including Paul Adam, Andrew Malloch, Donald Pigott, Bryan Wheeler, and ourselves developed provisional working-schemes of British vegetation types solely for the purposes of the NCR and for conservation surveys[e.g. 41]. The NVC has provided an essential and useful vegetational framework for British plant ecologists, conservationists, applied ecologists, and field biologists[17,42,43] and it owes much to the pioneering studies of Donald McVean and Derek Ratcliffe in their 'Highland Vegetation Survey'[34].

Thanks to Derek's meticulous field notes (Fig. 4.9) and his detailed site-maps (Fig. 4.8) for the 'Highland Vegetation Survey', it was possible for Louise Ross, as part of her Ph.D. research at the University of Aberdeen, to re-locate and re-sample in 2007 and 2008 126 plots in the North-West Highlands[44,45] (86% of the original plots surveyed by McVean and Ratcliffe[34] in this area). Louise showed that species richness of grasslands and heathlands has declined over the last 50 years, whereas mires showed little change in their richness. Previously distinct vegetation types[34] have become more similar in composition, characterised by an increased dominance of upland graminoids and reduced dwarf-shrub, forb, and lichen cover[44,45]. This biotic homogenisation[46] may be the result of climate change, acidification, over-grazing, and interactions between these drivers. The original[34] and re-survey[44,45] data from the North-West Highlands were also used as part of an analysis of recent floristic change in 16 areas of Fennoscandia, Spitsbergen, Greenland, and Scotland in terms of changes in species co-occurrences[47]. This analysis shows that changes in species co-occurrences in the last 20-90 years are greater than expected by chance but are not related to major gradients in richness or productivity. These analyses suggest that site- and habitat-specific factors (e.g. land-use and species interactions) may be important in influencing recent compositional shifts in arctic, alpine, and boreal vegetation in northern Europe and they emphasise the need for further re-survey studies and long-term monitoring projects. Maren Flagmeier, Louise Ross, and colleagues[48] have recently re-analysed many of Derek's plots of 'mixed hepatic mats' growing under tall heather in the western and north-western Scottish Highlands (Figs. 4.14, 4.15, 6.13 & 7.12). In the 50 years since Derek's original survey, dwarf shrubs and the large leafy hepatics have decreased whereas Mat-grass (*Nardus stricta*) and Fescues (*Festuca* spp.) have increased, possibly in response to changes in grazing, climate, and nitrogen deposition.

Although modelling studies[49] can provide interesting predictions about the impacts of future climate change on Scottish mountain vegetation, the field-based re-survey studies of Louise Ross[44,45,47], Andrea Britton[46], and Maren Flagmeier[48] in the Scottish Highlands clearly demonstrate the role of multiple ecological drivers such as land-use, climate change, and atmospheric contamination on recent changes in vegetation composition.

Besides mountain plant ecology and floristics, Derek made major contributions to mire ecology, particularly of bogs. These include the vegetation and an improved understanding of the formation of surface pool patterns in The Silver Flowe system of bogs in Galloway (Fig. 1.7)[12], of the floristics, water chemistry, and ecology of mires in Scotland[50,51], and of the vegetation and ecology of the vast Flow Country in Caithness and Sutherland (Figs. 23.1, 24.3 & 24.4)[52,53]. Derek had a remarkable grasp of mire ecology and the many factors that determine the flora, vegetation, and hydrology of mires and an exceptional eye for rare species of *Sphagnum* (Fig. 4.16), other rare mire bryophytes including *Dicranum undulatum* (Fig. 24.2), *Hamatocaulis vernicosus*, and

Figure 4.14. Northern Atlantic liverworts that mainly occur in the internationally unique 'mixed hepatic mat' on steep, block-strewn shaded slopes in the mountains of north-west Scotland and western Ireland[21,23,24]. Derek Ratcliffe found several new localities for these species. *Anastrophyllum alpinum*, Wester Ross, 1966 (*top left*); *A. donnianum*, Wester Ross, 1966 (*top right*); *Bazzania pearsonii*, Isle of Skye, 1967 (*middle left*); *Scapania nimbosa*, Wester Ross, 1966 (*middle right*); *Herbertus stramineus*, Wester Ross, 1966 (*lower left*); and *Adelanthus lindenbergianus*, Mayo, 1967 (*lower right*). Photos: John Birks

Tomentypnum nitens, and easily-overlooked mire sedges such as Few-flowered Sedge (*Carex pauciflora*), Tall Bog-sedge (*C. magellanica*), Bog-sedge (*C. limosa*), Mountain Bog-sedge (*C. rariflora*), and Brown Beak-sedge (*Rhynchospora fusca*). He made a detailed eco-logical study of the rare mountain *Sphagnum lindbergii* (Fig. 6.6)[19] and found it in many new localities, sometimes growing with *S. riparium* (Fig. 4.16).

In the late 1950s and early 1960s Derek Ratcliffe had become the leading field botanist in the Scottish Highlands. Besides contributing many new vascular plant and bryophyte records and mapping the distribution of several Atlantic species in the British Isles[21], he discovered that there was a very special vegetation type virtually confined to the North-West Highlands[21,23,34]. This vegetation type occurred on shaded north- or east-facing block-strewn slopes (Fig. 7.12) with tall heather and with a 'mixed hepatic mat' of large liverworts (Fig. 6.13) (e.g. *Bazzania pearsonii* (Fig. 4.14), *Scapania nimbosa* (Fig. 4.14), *S. ornithopodioides* (Fig. 4.15), *Herbertus hutchinsiae* (= *H. aduncus* ssp. *hutchinsiae*)[21] (Fig. 7.8), *Pleurozia purpurea* (Fig. 7.7), and *Mastigophora woodsii* (Fig. 7.7)) that have spectacular disjunct distributions between the British Isles and the Faeroes and Nepal, Bhutan, Sikkim, Yunnan, Tibet, Kamchatka, and north-west North America[21,23,48]. It is largely due to Derek's work that these oceanic-montane liverwort heaths have now been recognised for their global importance[21,23,48]. David Long and Gordon Rothero[23] discuss Derek's considerable bryological work in Scotland in the context of the history of bryological exploration and study in Scotland.

Derek Ratcliffe led the first British Trust for Ornithology (BTO) National Peregrine Enquiry in 1961 and 1962 to assess the status of the Peregrine Falcon (*Falco peregrinus*) (Fig.14.5) and its population declines[1,54]. During the two years of this Peregrine survey, Derek, living mainly in a dormobile, visited a huge number of remote cliff locations as he travelled the length and breadth of Britain assessing the status of the Peregrine population. He made many important and exciting plant records during this survey, including finding Rock Cinquefoil (*Potentilla rupestris*) (Fig. 4.17) new to Scotland[55], several new localities for local chasmophytes on igneous or ultramafic cliffs such as Rock Whitebeam (*Sorbus rupicola*), Wood Bitter-vetch (*Vicia orobus*), Wood Vetch (*V. sylvatica*), Forked Spleenwort (*Asplenium septentrionale*), Serrated Wintergreen (*Orthilia secunda*) (all Fig. 4.17), and Pyramidal Bugle (Fig. 4.11), and several records of rare *Grimmia* species, *Frullania teneriffae*, *Dicranum scottianum* (Fig. 7.9), and *Glyphomitrium daviesii* (Fig. 7.10). As the Peregrine survey involved visiting many of the sea-cliffs on which Peregrines once nested (Fig. 14.1), Derek found many new localities for mountain plants growing near sea-level on or near sea-cliffs (e.g. Moss Campion (*Silene acaulis*) (Fig. 4.24), Mountain Avens (Fig. 4.10), Hoary Whitlowgrass (*Draba incana*), Alpine Saw-wort (*Saussurea alpina*), Mountain Sorrel (*Oxyria digyna*), Alpine Meadow-rue (*Thalictrum alpinum*), Mountain Crowberry (*Empetrum hermaphroditum*), and Roseroot (*Rhodiola rosea*)[34]). He also made many records of the Southern Atlantic liverwort *Adelanthus decipiens* (Fig. 7.6)[21], the Atlantic Hay-scented Buckler Fern (*Dryopteris aemula*), and the two *Hymenophyllum* Filmy-ferns (Fig. 4.3) in western woodlands, scrub, and rivulets as he travelled to the next Peregrine cliff.

Although he moved to live permanently in the south of England in 1963[1], Derek continued to visit the Scottish Highlands, the Border Country, Lakeland, the Northern Pennines, and North Wales almost every year until his death in search of plants, birds, wilderness, and solitude, to visit his close friends[3,5,16,31], and to inspect and monitor the populations of some of his most special species such as Killarney Fern (Figs. 4.3 & 4.27), Oblong Woodsia (Figs. 4.12 & 9.4), and Marsh Saxifrage (Fig. 5.6).

Monks Wood, London, Huntingdon, Peterborough, Cambridge 1963-2005: bryophytes, ferns, conservation, books, and photography

In 1963 Derek moved to the Nature Conservancy's Monks Wood Experimental Station near Huntingdon to continue work on Peregrine Falcons, other birds of prey, and the

Figure 4.15. Northern Atlantic bryophytes that mainly occur in the mountains or, more rarely, in the spray zone of waterfalls in ravines of western Britain and western Ireland. Derek Ratcliffe found several new localities for these species. *Plagiochila carringtonii*, West Sutherland, 1966 (*top left*); *Paraleptodontium recurvifolium*, Wester Ross, 1966 (*top right*); *Scapania ornithopodioides*, Wester Ross, 1966 (*lower left*); and *Campylopus setifolius*, Merioneth, 1965 (*lower right*). Photos: John Birks

Figure 4.16. Some of the rare or local *Sphagnum* species that Derek Ratcliffe found in several new localities and studied their ecology. *Sphagnum riparium*, Aberdeenshire, 1967 (*top left*); *S. austinii*, Cumbria, 1968 (*top right*); *S. warnstorfii*, Perthshire, 1968 (*lower left*); and *S. squarrosum*, Yorkshire, 1968 (*lower right*). Photos: John Birks

effects of pesticides on raptors[4]. Whilst at Monks Wood he completed his major monograph on the ecology and phytogeography of Atlantic bryophytes in the British Isles[21,24] based on his extensive and unique field observations in Scotland, north-west England, Wales, and Ireland. He visited Ireland twice by himself in 1961 and 1963 to study Irish mountain vegetation and bryophytes and to hunt for the Killarney Fern. In the process he found *Plagiochila carringtonii* (Fig. 4.15) in Mayo, new to Ireland and *Adelanthus lindenbergianus* (Fig. 4.14) in a second Irish locality on the Twelve Bens of Connemara[56]. Chris Preston[21] discusses more fully the importance of Derek's monograph on Atlantic bryophytes[24] in highlighting the unique international importance of the British and Irish Atlantic bryophyte flora and in stimulating further ecological, palaeoecological, conservation, taxonomic, and phytogeographical studies of this flora[21,23,48].

In 1965 Derek was given the demanding task by Max Nicholson (Fig. 19.2), then Director General of the Nature Conservancy, of surveying the flora and vegetation of the Cow Green site in Upper Teesdale in north-east England where Imperial Chemical Industries (ICI) planned to construct a large reservoir to serve its Bellingham works[57,58]. Derek concluded that the western slopes of Widdybank Fell, a famous botanical locality, were of very special scientific interest and "the loss of even twenty acres would be a very serious matter, for each part of this highly diversified complex of species was almost totally dissimilar from the rest"[57]. On the basis of Derek's survey report, the Nature Conservancy informed the Tees Valley and Cleveland Water Board on 22 July 1965 that it would object to the Cow Green site[57,58]. The resulting hearings by the House

Figure 4.17. Some chasmophyte plants that Derek Ratcliffe found on cliffs during the National Peregrine Enquiry in 1961 and 1962. Rock Cinquefoil (*Potentilla rupestris*), Sutherland, 1969 (*top left*); Rock Whitebeam (*Sorbus rupicola*), Isle of Skye, 1968 (*top right*); Serrated Wintergreen (*Orthilia secunda*), Norway, 1985 (*middle left*); Forked Spleenwort (*Asplenium septentrionale*), Caernarvonshire, 1966 (*middle right*); Wood Bitter-vetch (*Vicia orobus*), Merioneth, 1976 (*lower left*); Wood Vetch (*V. sylvatica*), Isle of Skye, 1967 (*lower right*). Photos: John Birks

of Commons and the House of Lords Select Committees became a major controversial case for nature conservation in Britain[57]. On 22 March 1967 the Tees Valley and Cleveland Water Bill received Royal Assent, and the fate of Cow Green and its flora and vegetation was finally sealed. Today the reservoir remains but its water is not used by ICI. Derek subsequently wrote a detailed account of the flora and vegetation of Upper Teesdale[59] in a book about the area and its natural history edited by his Sheffield teacher Roy Clapham (Fig. 4.2).

In 1969 Derek was appointed Deputy Director (Science) of the Nature Conservancy (from 1973, the Nature Conservancy Council (NCC)), becoming Chief Scientist of NCC in 1973. He held this position until his retirement in 1989. His first major task was to mastermind the publication of *A Nature Conservation Review*[38,39], a project that he initiated in 1966 and had completed by 1970[1,39]. The *Review* (Fig. 19.4) is an amazing distillation of Derek's and his colleagues' enormous field knowledge of the flora, fauna, vegetation, and conservation importance of sites in Britain. The *Review* has served as the foundation of modern nature conservation policy in Britain and is probably one of Derek's most important contributions to conservation and ecology[39]. He was deeply involved in the "Battle of the Bogs" over the conservation of the vast patterned peatlands of Caithness and Sutherland, the so-called Flow Country[52,53,60,61]. This unique area of patterned mires[52] was being rapidly drained and afforested for commercial forestry[53,60]. Derek spearheaded conservation attempts to prevent further afforestation. The resulting bitter environmental conflict between the NCC, land-owners, and government departments contributed, to a large extent, to the dismemberment of the NCC by the Conservative Secretaries of State for the Environment (Nicholas Ridley) and for Scotland (Malcolm Rifkind) within a week of Derek's retirement[61,62].

Although Derek's work between 1963 and 1989 was primarily scientific administration and conservation policy and he was largely office-bound, he retained a strong interest in plant ecology and botany. He organised with Eric Smith and Roy Clapham a meeting at the Royal Society entitled 'Discussion on the Scientific Aspects of Nature Conservation in Great Britain'[63]. Derek contributed a thoughtful and important paper on nature conservation and its aims, methods, and achievements[64]. Derek gained great pleasure in writing a magnificent review paper on Post-Medieval and Recent Changes in British Vegetation: The Culmination of Human Influence[65] for a special issue of *The New Phytologist* in honour of the 80th birthday of Roy Clapham (Fig. 4.2). Derek played a major role in the initiation, implementation, and completion of the National Vegetation Classification Project from 1975 until its final publication between 1991 and 2000[37].

Throughout his time in 'the south' he continued to visit his favourite haunts in the north and west of Britain and to search for plants in unexplored areas. He made many interesting records including *Dumortiera hirsuta* (Fig. 4.4) and *Cyclodictyon laetevirens* (Fig. 7.5)[21,23] on Jura, both new to Scotland, confirming his hunch that more Southern Atlantic[21,24] species could be found growing in western Scotland; he found *Adelanthus decipiens* (Fig. 7.6) in south-west England exactly where he predicted it should be growing on the basis of present-day climate[21,24]; he discovered new colonies of Killarney Fern in North Wales and western Scotland (Figs. 4.3 & 4.27); and he found an undescribed species of *Herbertus* on Ronas Hill, Shetland, now described and named *H. norenus* (Fig. 6.11)[21,23].

Besides being an outstanding field botanist, ornithologist, and ecologist, Derek

Figure 4.18. Some of the photographs taken by Derek Ratcliffe specially for *A Nature Conservation Review*[38]. Sheep-scombe Wood, Gloucestershire (*top left*); Lodore Falls, Cumbria (*top right*); Abernethy Forest, Inverness-shire (*lower left*); and Beinn a'Bhuird, Aberdeenshire (*lower right*). Photos: Derek Ratcliffe

was a very eloquent author and gifted and skilful photographer. In addition to the McVean and Ratcliffe monograph[34] and his many scientific papers on plants, mountain vegetation, and mire ecology, he published a popular book *Highland Flora*[66] which gives a wonderfully vivid account of the plant life of the Scottish Highlands and Islands and is illustrated by many of Derek's magnificent photographs of plants and landscapes. The high quality of the colour and black-and-white plates in *A Nature Conservation Review*[38] is a credit to Derek's skill and patience as a photographer (Figs. 4.18 & 19.8). He often took landscape photographs from the same place over several years to provide a valuable record of habitat change. Examples of such repeat photography can be seen in his *Galloway and the Borders* book[67] that was published posthumously in 2007 and as

Figure 4.19. Ecological landscapes in southern Scotland. Fence-line effect showing the conversion of heather moor to acidic grassland on the more heavily grazed and burned side of the wall, White Hill, Langholm, Dumfriesshire, 1976 (*top*); management of moorland for Red Grouse (*Lagopus lagopus scoticus*), showing the pattern of rotational burning of Heather (*Calluna*), Tarras Water, Langholm, Dumfriesshire, 1985 (*middle*); contrasting upland pastures with and without fertiliser, Laghead, Galloway, 1990 (*lower*). Photos: Derek Ratcliffe

Figure 4.20. Coastal sea-cliffs, a favourite habitat for Derek Ratcliffe in his search for birds, coastal plants, and alpine plants growing near sea-level. Mull of Galloway, Wigtownshire, 1986 (*left*) and nesting place of Chough (*Pyrrhocorax pyrrhocorax*) in a cave on the Wigtownshire sea-cliffs, 1989 (*right*). Photos: Derek Ratcliffe

Figure 22.2 in the chapter by Rick Battarbee[68]. He also wrote several detailed book chapters on the flora and vegetation of the Cairngorms[69], on the vegetation of Upper Teesdale[59], and on the ecology of the habitats of Snow Buntings (*Plectrophenax nivalis*) (Fig. 11.25)[70], Dotterel (*Charadrius morinellus*) (Figs. 11.3–11.5, 13.8 & 13.9)[71], and Greenshank (*Tringa nebularia*) (Figs. 11.21, 11.22 & 17.7)[72]. He also contributed sections to the New Naturalist book *The Lake District – A Landscape History*[73]. All these accounts are a treasure-trove of uniquely detailed ecological insights. Derek excelled at photographing ecological aspects of landscapes, a notoriously difficult challenge. Some examples are shown in Figures 4.18–4.20. Given his life-long interests in bogs, coasts, upland areas, and mountains[1,66,67,74-77], he took many wonderful images of common and rare plants in these habitats (Figs. 4.21–4.26).

After we moved to Norway in 1985, we saw less of Derek and his wife Jeannette (née Chan-Mo) but Derek maintained an extensive correspondence with us[35]. About every four weeks a thick envelope would arrive containing 2-4 double-sided A4 pages of neatly hand-written text (Fig. 27.1) with news of recent visits, for example, to Rod and Jean Corner, Geoff Horne, and Jean Roger in the Borders[31], to Chris Rollie and Donald and Joan Watson in Galloway[5], and to John Mitchell in southern Scotland[16]; to Norfolk, western Ireland, Lakeland, or Lapland; of his latest writing projects; of the status of 'his' populations of special plants such as Oblong Woodsia and Killarney Fern; and of frustrations with the state of the world, British politics, the British Establishment, the

Figure 4.21. Bog or mire plants of northern Britain or Scandinavia that Derek Ratcliffe always enjoyed finding. Bog-rosemary (*Andromeda polifolia*), Cumbria, 1986 (*top left*); Labrador-tea (*Rhododendron tomentosum* (=*Ledum palustre*)), Finnish Lapland, 1998 (*top right*); Bog Asphodel (*Narthecium ossifragum*), Galloway, 1975 (*lower left*); and Arctic Cottongrass (*Eriophorum scheuchzeri*), northern Norway, 2002 (*lower right*). Photos: Derek Ratcliffe

demise of effective nature conservation in Britain, and of other matters such as queries about acid rain, Fennoscandian plants and vegetation, or vegetation history that had arisen in his current writing projects, or requests for photographs of particular plants. We greatly value this correspondence as it is a wonderful record of Derek's activities and interests during the last 20 years of his life.

Derek primarily returned in his active and productive retirement to his first love of birds[3,74], but he continued to revisit the colonies of the rarest plants that meant so much to him – Oblong Woodsia (Figs. 4.12 & 9.4), Marsh Saxifrage (Fig. 5.6), Killarney Fern (Fig. 4.27), etc. – and his favourite habitats in the Highlands (Fig. 4.18), Lakeland (Figs. 4.28 & 1.11), Southern Uplands (Figs. 1.4, 1.5, 5.1, & 13.2)[31], Northern Pennines[1], and North Wales (Fig. 4.28). He was staggered by the floristic changes in the Northern Pennines that followed the Foot and Mouth outbreak in 2001 when sheep were removed from the fells[31]. Suddenly Alpine Foxtail grass (Fig. 5.4) and the rare and elusive Marsh Saxifrage (Fig. 5.6), two plants that Derek had a particular interest in[1], flourished[31]. These rapid changes confirmed Derek's early ideas of the overriding importance of over-grazing in Britain and Ireland on mountain flora and vegetation[9,29,31,76]. He also visited Ireland (1983, 1999) in search of further colonies of Killarney Fern[1]. Derek was struck by the marked changes in recent land-use and the so-called 'improved' areas in Ireland resulting in serious habitat loss as has occurred in Britain[1].

Derek wrote two masterly New Naturalist volumes, one on *Lakeland*[75] and one on

Figure 4.22. 'Tall herbs' growing in meadows or damp forests in Scotland or Fennoscandia. Derek Ratcliffe was particularly interested in 'tall-herb' dominated vegetation, especially on near-inaccessible ungrazed cliff ledges. Globeflower (*Trollius europaeus*), Galloway, 1975 (*top left*); Lady's-slipper (*Cypripedium calceolus*), northern Sweden, 1997 (*top right*); White False Helleborine (*Veratrum album*), northern Norway, 1994 (*lower left*); and Giant Bellflower (*Campanula latifolia*), East Lothian, 1966 (*lower right*). Photos: Derek Ratcliffe

Galloway and the Borders[67], and a scholarly overview of the British Isles and Irish mountain flora[76]. He also wrote his autobiography as a field biologist in Britain and Ireland[1] in which he relates many of his botanical adventures in Wales, northern England, Scotland, and Ireland. In retirement, he rekindled his strong spirit of adventure, exploration, and discovery, and fulfilled his life-long dream of annual expeditions with his wife Jeannette (Fig 17.2) to arctic Fennoscandia to study rare waders and other birds in near pristine conditions[78]. Derek's dream of exploring the wilds of arctic Fennoscandia may have been stimulated in part by Lakeland ornithologist Marjory Garnett (1896-1977) who visited arctic Norway from 1932 to 1970. Her records and diaries are in the Tullie House Museum, Carlisle[75], where Derek studied them. Derek went on to write a wide-ranging and superbly illustrated book on many aspects of the natural history, ornithology, botany, and ecology of Lapland based on his fourteen expeditions to the far north (Fig. 11.18)[77]. Some of Derek's striking images of Lapland landscapes are reproduced as Figures 29.1-29.29 in a photo-essay in this book[79] and of Lapland plants in Figures 4.21-4.26 in this chapter.

As Peter Marren discusses in his chapter[35], Derek served as an editor of the New Naturalist series for twelve years. Besides writing his own two volumes[67,75], Derek played a major editorial role for several volumes[80] including *The New Naturalists, Ireland, Lichens, Loch Lomondside, Nature Conservation, Northumberland, Mosses & Liverworts*, and

Figure 4.23. Locally common ferns growing in their natural habitats in northern Britain or Fennoscandia. Derek Ratcliffe had a particular interest in ferns of northern and western Britain, especially rare and endangered species. Parsley Fern (*Cryptogramma crispa*), Cumbria, 1965 (*top left*); Scaly Male-fern (*Dryopteris borreri*), Galloway, 1982 (*top right*); Oak Fern (*Gymnocarpium dryopteris*), northern Sweden, 1997 (*lower left*); and Green Spleenwort (*Asplenium trichomanes-ramosum*), Roxburghshire, 1977 (*lower right*). Photos: Derek Ratcliffe

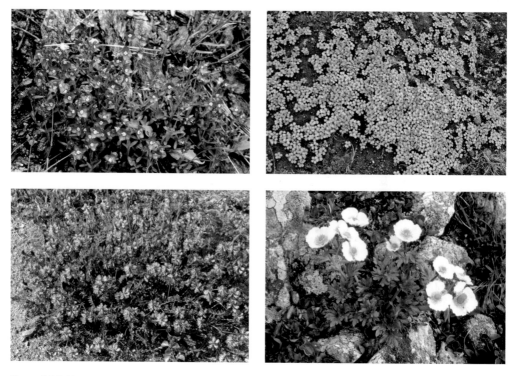

Figure 4.24. Alpine plants growing in Fennoscandia. Mountain 'arctic-alpine' plants were a keen interest of Derek Ratcliffe since he began his Ph.D. research on North Wales mountain vegetation in 1950. Rock Speedwell (*Veronica fruticans*), central Norway, 1984 (*top left*); Moss Campion (*Silene acaulis*), northern Norway, 1991 (*top right*); Northern Alpine Milk-vetch (*Astragalus alpinus* ssp. *arcticus*), northern Norway, 1997 (*lower left*); Glacier Buttercup (*Ranunculus* (*Beckwithia*) *glacialis*), central Norway, 1984 (*lower right*). Photos: Derek Ratcliffe

A History of Ornithology. With the creation of the journal *British Wildlife* by Andrew and Anne Branson in 1989, Derek wrote two important articles for *British Wildlife* on mountain flora[76] and upland birds[81]. He also greatly encouraged *British Wildlife* to be an independent commentary on conservation after the break-up of the Nature Conservancy Council in 1989[82].

Personal recollections 1966-2005

We first met Derek Ratcliffe by chance in September 1966 in Borrowdale, Cumbria. We were on our honeymoon and we had been looking for bryophytes in the Lake District. We were descending a wooded glen and Derek was ascending the same glen. We stopped and exchanged a few words. He realised that we had been looking for bryophytes as we had hand lenses around our necks. Derek asked us if we had found anything of interest. We replied yes, but we did not tell him at that stage that we had found *Radula voluta* (Fig. 4.4) in one of his special 'secret' localities! Derek then drove us, at great speed[39], around the Borrowdale area to show us some of the rare bryophytes that we had not found for ourselves, such as *Lophocolea fragrans*. We returned very late to our hotel at Buttermere to discover that by mistake we had not booked for that night so after a rapid supper, we had to drive to John's parents in Manchester! So began a

Figure 4.25. Four local Fennoscandian plants not known to occur in Britain today. Norwegian Wintergreen (*Pyrola norvegica*), northern Norway, 1990 (*top left*), Upright Primrose (*Primula stricta*), northern Norway, 1997 (*top right*), Arctic Bramble (*Rubus arcticus*), northern Norway, 1990 (*lower left*), and Matted Cassiope (*Cassiope* (*Harrimanella*) *hypnoides*), central Norway, 2003 (*lower right*). Photos: Derek Ratcliffe

Figure 4.26. Coastal shingle plants in Scotland and northern Norway. Derek Ratcliffe greatly enjoyed examining coastal shingle habitats for birds and plants. Two of his favourite shingle plants were Oysterplant (*Mertensia maritima*), Orkney, 1963 (*left*) and Sea Pea (*Lathyrus japonicus*), northern Norway, 2002 (*right*). Photos: Derek Ratcliffe

Figure 4.27. Killarney Fern (*Trichomanes speciosum*) growing in North Wales, 1967 (*top*) and western Scotland, 1979 (*right*). Photos: John Birks. Derek Ratcliffe[1] wrote of this North Wales find "No other botanical discovery has given me such pleasure and satisfaction".

life-long friendship with Derek, during which we spent many fine (and wet) field days together searching woods, ravines, crags, and mountain cliffs for plants across Britain and Ireland and many winter evenings in Cambridge poring over maps and planning our next field explorations and adventures together.

About a month after our meeting in Borrowdale, the door-bell of our small house in Cambridge rang late one evening. It was Derek armed with packets of bryophytes and maps and full of questions about Atlantic bryophytes. He was at that stage working on his monograph about Atlantic bryophytes in Britain and Ireland[24]. We came to expect weekly late-evening visits from Derek whilst he was completing this monograph. From bryophytes and mountain plants, our discussion turned to the Killarney Fern and its early records from North Wales (Fig. 4.3). Derek enthralled us with tales of his hunting Killarney Fern in North Wales without success[1], in Lakeland with limited success[1,31], in western Scotland without success, and in western Ireland with some

Figure 4.28. Two of Derek Ratcliffe's favourite botanical habitats (*left*) – wooded gorges rich in Atlantic species, North Wales, 1976 and steep rocky slopes, screes, and gullies supporting rare mountain plants, Cumbria, 1977 and two of his favourite botanical activities (*right*) – intensive and meticulous plant hunting in difficult terrain, North Wales, 1967 and careful field observations and measurements, Kerry, 1967. Photos: John Birks

Figure 4.29. Discovering Killarney Fern (*Trichomanes speciosum*) in a cave (*top left*) behind a waterfall in the mountains of North Wales in December 1966 and subsequently in March 1967. Photo: John Birks. The figures under the water are John Dransfield, (*bottom*; photo: John Birks) and John Birks (*top right*; photo: Derek Ratcliffe)

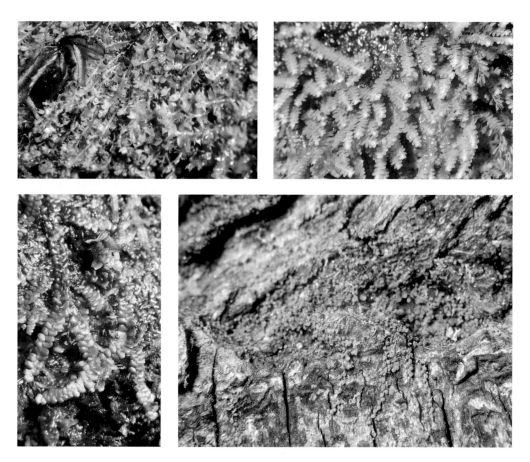

Figure 4.30. South Atlantic liverworts that, with the exception of *Cololejeunea minutissima*[16], occur only in humid and shaded habitats in western Scotland and western Ireland. Derek Ratcliffe found new localities for some of these species. *Acrobolbus wilsonii*, Isle of Skye, 1966 (*top left*); *Lejeunea flava* ssp. *moorei*, Kerry, 1967 (*top right*); *Radula carringtonii*, Kerry, 1967 (*lower left*); and *Cololejeunea minutissima*, Cornwall, 1966 (*lower right*). Photos: John Birks

success[1]. In December 1966, the two of us and our botanical friend and colleague John Dransfield set off to North Wales to see if we could find Killarney Fern for ourselves. Much to our surprise, and to Derek's, we did (Fig. 4.29)! All four of us returned in March 1967 to admire our colony and to see if we could find any more Killarney Fern colonies. We did and found two colonies in another locality (Fig. 4.27). As Derek wrote "No other botanical discovery has given me such pleasure and satisfaction"[1]. We subsequently revisited North and central Wales 13 times for a total of 24 weeks, and despite searching almost all accessible and near-inaccessible ravines, cascading streams, and sea-caves and finding several interesting bryophytes (e.g. *Fissidens polyphyllus* (Fig. 4.4), *F. serrulatus*, *Radula voluta* (Fig. 4.4), *Sematophyllum demissum*, *Plagiochila heterophylla* (Fig. 6.5), *P. exigua* (Fig. 4.5), *Ulota calvescens* (Fig. 4.5), *Leptoscyphus cuneifolius*), we never found any further new Killarney Fern colonies in Wales[83] although Derek found for himself one additional colony in North Wales in the late 1990s that he subsequently showed us.

We also hunted extensively for Killarney Fern in northern England, southern Scotland, and western Scotland as far north as Skye and Lochalsh but failed to find any more populations, only many interesting bryophytes such as *Jubula hutchinsiae* (Fig. 7.6), *Dumortiera hirsuta* (Fig. 4.4), *Fissidens polyphyllus* (Fig. 4.4), *Radula carringtonii* (Fig. 4.30), *Acrobolbus wilsonii* (Fig. 4.30), *Cyclodictyon laetevirens* (Fig. 7.5), *Lejeunea eckloniana*, and *Plagiochila heterophylla* (Fig. 6.5). By 1993 we had searched 159 suitable-looking streams or ravines in Wales, 132 in north-west England, 39 in southern Scotland, 151 in the western Highlands, and 68 in Ireland. We had also searched many of the 'raised beaches' and their gullies and caves along the coast of western Scotland. Between the three of us, we found a total of 45 Killarney Fern populations (sporophyte generation), 30 of which were in Ireland, 3 in England, 7 in Wales, and 5 in Scotland[83]. Killarney Fern, at least in its sporophyte generation, is certainly one of Britain's rarest and most elusive plants!

An interesting twist in the search for Killarney Fern was the discovery in 1989 by the American fern expert Don Farrer of its gametophyte in the Lake District. Fred Rumsey, Clive Jermy, and others then found the gametophyte to be widespread in western Britain and Ireland, almost wherever suitable shady gorges, woodland ravines, and sandstone rocks occur. Vastly more localities are now known for the gametophyte than for the very rare mature sporophyte Killarney Fern plant[1,16,31,84]. In recent years there have been reports of young sporophyte plants growing out of the gametophyte patches[31,85], raising the exciting possibility that with continuing climate change there may be an increase in the number of Killarney Fern sporophyte populations in Britain and Ireland[83], something that Derek Ratcliffe could never have envisaged.

In 1969 we searched a long stretch of very inaccessible rocky coast in western Scotland that had many suitable-looking habitats for Killarney Fern. All we found were several rare and interesting bryophytes and an abundance of Atlantic Hay-scented Buckler Fern and both Filmy-fern (*Hymenophyllum*) species (Fig. 4.3). However, we had only managed to search one half of the stretch of coast. In 1978 Derek and Peter Wormell returned by boat to the other half that we had not searched and together they found three colonies of Killarney Fern! They returned the next year and generously showed John these magnificent colonies (Fig. 4.27). Two additional patches of the fern were found that day by Derek and John, bringing the total to five colonies in one locality – a record for us other than on Brandon Mountain in Kerry (Fig. 7.2).

We visited western Ireland together in 1967, primarily to look for bryophytes and Killarney Fern. We had a very successful and memorable trip, including finding *Geocalyx graveolens*[86], refinding a rich set of mountain plants on Slieve League[87], and discovering several new localities for Killarney Fern and for many Southern Atlantic bryophytes such as *Dumortiera hirsuta* (Fig. 4.4), *Cyclodictyon laetivirens* (Fig. 7.5), *Lejeunea flava* ssp. *moorei* (Fig. 4.30), *L. eckloniana*, *L. hibernica*, *Radula carringtonii* (Fig. 4.30), *R. holtii*, and *Cololejeunea minutissima* (Fig. 4.30).

We had many other botanical adventures together in the Scottish Highlands, in Lakeland, on Skye, in Galloway, in central Wales, and in south-west England. We found new localities for several mountain plants, including Mountain Bladder-fern (Fig. 4.10), Rock Sedge, Hair Sedge, Net-leaved Willow (Fig. 4.10), Whortle-leaved Willow (*Salix myrsinites*), and Holly Fern (Fig. 4.12), and we made many interesting bryophyte records. Some of these trips were enlightened by the company of J. Grant Roger whose humour and turn of phrase could brighten us all up, even on the coldest and wettest days imaginable.

Derek had a keen interest in Quaternary vegetation history, perhaps because of his early botanical training by Roy Clapham and Verona Conway, both of whom had published papers on pollen analysis, and because of his close friendship with Donald Walker who became a leading authority on Quaternary vegetation history. Derek had a 'good eye' for potentially suitable sites for pollen analytical investigations and he suggested several important sites that we subsequently studied – Abernethy Forest, Inverness-shire[88], An Druim, near Eriboll, west Sutherland[89], and Johnny's Wood, Cumbria[90]. When Hilary was researching the palaeoecology of fossil pine stumps preserved in Scottish peats (Fig. 4.31), Derek provided many records for her distribution map of pine stumps[91]. He also collected fossil wood remains from peats in the northern Pennines, Southern Uplands, and Lakeland for identification – many were Willow (*Salix*), Juniper (*Juniperus*), and Birch (*Betula*). Pine was very rare in these areas.

Figure 4.31. Rannoch Moor, Argyll/Perthshire, 1969. This large complex of blanket and valley mires contains many remains ('pine stumps') of Scots Pine (*Pinus sylvestris*) that are being exposed as a result of peat erosion. These remains are about 4500–6200 years old[91] and their history and palaeoecology were studied by Hilary Birks[88]. Photo: Derek Ratcliffe

Derek was a great field companion and we have many memories of adventures together, often ending up climbing out of deep ravines in poor light or even darkness at the end of a long day's plant hunting. He was a most remarkable field botanist, with an amazingly perceptive eye for plants and their habitats. He would patiently search a likely area with binoculars (Fig. 4.28) and then decide where to climb and search. He was a fearless climber on crags and cliffs, and in ravines. He would never give up searching a promising locality until almost every crevice, crag, ledge, overhang, or cave had been examined or until darkness set in. Darkness usually set in first! He had a prodigious memory for species, localities, and old records. Field days with Derek were inevitably long and usually physically demanding as he never wanted to turn back and return[5,40], even after continuous rain on a dark December day in Merioneth. His company in the field and in the evenings was always a wonderful tonic, with his characteristically clear, concise, and crisp comments on a wide range of topics such as the Forestry Commission, afforestation, agriculture, farming interests, lobbyists, Conservatism, Margaret Thatcher, sleaze, wealthy land-owners, the British Establishment, plant nomenclatural changes, pomposity, overly influential figures in British ecology and conservation, academic honours and accolades, the 'old-boy' network, Nicholas Ridley, Malcolm Rifkind, plant collecting, the global environment, and the House of Lords. He was a wonderfully generous teacher and we learnt an immense amount from him about field botany (Fig. 4.28), plant hunting (Fig. 4.28), field recording (Fig. 4.28), field notes[2], community ecology, plant photography, birds, butterflies, general field natural history, plant geography, plant sociology, climbing crags, abseiling into ravines, exploring waterfall gorges (Figs. 4.28 & 4.29), loyalty, and never giving up[2]. Besides being a wonderful teacher and mentor and a magnificent field companion, he was a truly loyal and supportive friend to us both.

Derek Ratcliffe was a meticulous field botanist and careful recorder[2] and his botanical specimens (mainly bryophytes) are now housed at the Royal Botanic Garden, Edinburgh[23], where they can be consulted. Many of his Cumbrian vascular-plant specimens are housed in the Tullie House Museum, Carlisle (Stephen Hewitt, personal communication) where they can also be consulted.

Final comments

In this section we try to summarise the major long-lasting contributions and legacies made by Derek Ratcliffe to botany and plant ecology. These can be grouped into eight broad categories.

Plant Communities of the Scottish Highlands[34] was the first extensive and consistent application of the philosophy and working methods of descriptive plant sociology in Britain. Besides providing a detailed account of Highland vegetation, it laid the foundation for the National Vegetation Classification[37] that attempted to cover all vegetation types throughout Britain and it has provided the basis of many subsequent important studies[e.g. 36,44,45,47,48].

Through *A Nature Conservation Review*[38,39] and the National Vegetation Classification[37], we now have a detailed account of British vegetation and ecosystems as they were in the 1970s, thanks to Derek's unique knowledge, determination, and insights[39].

Derek Ratcliffe provided many basic, accurate, and unrivalled records of mountain vegetation in North Wales[9] and the Scottish Highlands[34]. His data are being used in vegetation resurveys[44,45,47,48] and ecological impact studies[10].

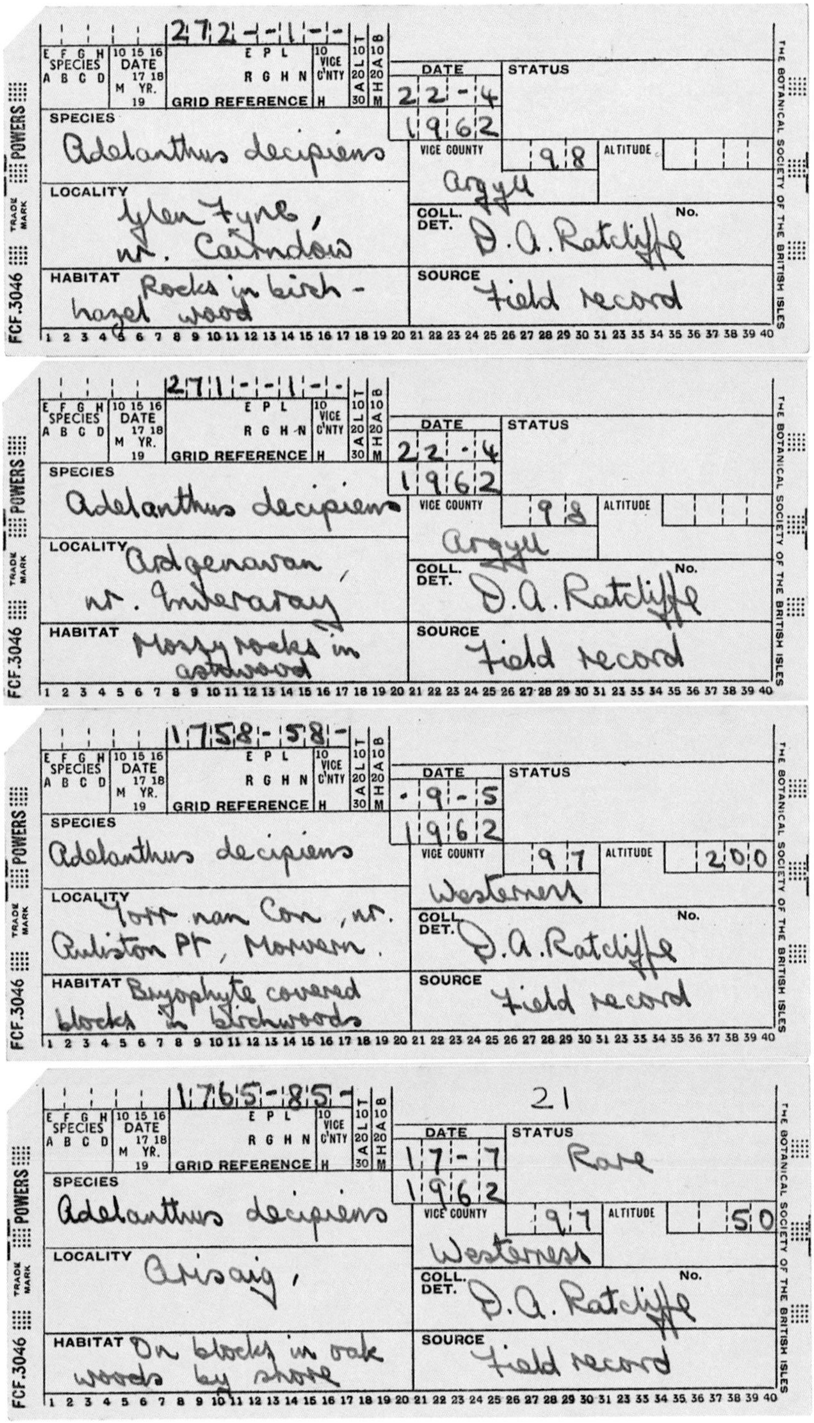
272 - 1 - 1 -
SPECIES: Adelanthus decipiens
DATE: 22 - 4 - 1962
VICE COUNTY: 98 Argyll
LOCALITY: Glen Fyne, nr. Cairndow
COLL. DET.: D.A. Ratcliffe
HABITAT: Rocks in birch-hazel wood
SOURCE: Field record

271 - 1 - 1 -
SPECIES: Adelanthus decipiens
DATE: 22 - 4 - 1962
VICE COUNTY: 98 Argyll
LOCALITY: Ardgenavan, nr. Inveraray
COLL. DET.: D.A. Ratcliffe
HABITAT: Mossy rocks in ashwood
SOURCE: Field record

1758 - 58 -
SPECIES: Adelanthus decipiens
DATE: 19 - 5 - 1962
VICE COUNTY: 97 Westerness
ALTITUDE: 200
LOCALITY: Torr nan Con, nr. Rubiston Pt, Morvern.
COLL. DET.: D.A. Ratcliffe
HABITAT: Bryophyte covered blocks in birchwoods
SOURCE: Field record

1765 - 85 -
21
SPECIES: Adelanthus decipiens
DATE: 17 - 7 - 1962
STATUS: Rare
VICE COUNTY: 97 Westerness
ALTITUDE: 50
LOCALITY: Arisaig,
COLL. DET.: D.A. Ratcliffe
HABITAT: On blocks in oak woods by shore
SOURCE: Field record

FCF.3046 TRADE MARK POWERS
THE BOTANICAL SOCIETY OF THE BRITISH ISLES

Figure 4.32. British Bryological Society species recording cards completed by Derek Ratcliffe for the Southern Atlantic liverwort *Adelanthus decipiens* (Fig. 7.6) in four 10-km grid squares in western Scotland. Derek had a particular interest in this species(21,24) and he made many new records of it during his travels during the Peregrine surveys of 1961 and 1962(54). Reproduced with permission from the Biological Records Centre, Centre for Ecology and Hydrology, Wallingford

LOCALITY **Helvellyn and Fairfield Ranges and Thirlmere**

NORTH

Date 1953 –1955 V.C. No. 69 + 70

HABITAT **Meadows, woodland, acidic grassland + heath, scree, acidic + basic crags, blanket + flush bogs, streams, tarns + lakes.**

V.C. Westmorland Cumberland

Alt. 500' 3100' Code No. 531

Grid Ref. 3 5 3

3	Acer cam	194	Asple tri	366	Carex distan	530	Clino vul	740	Eriop ang	934	Glyce max
5	pse	195	vir	367	disticha	532	Cochl ang	743	lat	935	ped
7	Achil mil	204	Aster tri	368	divisa	533	dan	744	vag	936	pli
9	pta	207	Astra dan	370	ech	535	off	745	Erodi *cic	940	Gnaph syl
12	Acino arv	208	gly	371	ela	537	Coelo vir	748	mar	941	uli
19	Adoxa mos	211	Athyr fil	374	ext	540	Coniu mac	753	Eroph *ver	948	Gymna con
20	Aegop pod	212	Atrip gla	376	flacca	541	Conop maj	758	Eryng mar	952	Heder hel
2241	Aescu hip	214	has	377	*flava	543	Conva maj	762	Euony eur	955	Helia cha
21	Aethu cyn	217	lit	381	hir	544	Convo arv	763	Eupat alb	961	Helic pra
22	Agrim eup	218	pat	382	hos	551	Coron did	771	Eupho exi	962	pub
23	odo	219	Atrop bel	385	lae	552	squ	772	hel	968	Herac sph
26	Agrop can	224	Balde ran	386	las	555	Coryd cla	775	par	975	Hespe mat
28	jun	225	Ballo nig	387	lep	556	lut	777	peplus	976	Hiera pil
33	rep	229	Barba vul	388	lim	557	Coryl ave	780	por	981	Hippu vul
34	Agros git	231	Belli per	393	nig	565	Cramb mar	2243	Euphr agg	983	Holcu lan
35	Agros can	232	Berbe vul	396	otr	569	Crata mon	784	bor	984	mol
39	sto	234	Berul ere	397	ova	571	Crepi bie	785	bre	988	Honke pep
40	ten	235	Beta mar	399	pal	572	cap	788	con	992	Horde mur
41	Aira car	240	Betul pub	400	panicea	576	pal	789	cur	993	sec
42	pra	239	ver	401	panicula	579	Crith mar	796	mic	996	Humul lup
46	Ajuga rep	241	Biden cer	402	pauci	586	Crypt cri	798	nem	999	Hydro vul
48	Alche alp	242	tri	404	pen	592	Cymba mur	803	riv	1001	Hymen wil
51	gla	244	Blech spi	405	pil	596	Cynog off	804	ros	1002	Hyosc nig
57	ves	245	Blysm com	407	pse	597	Cynos cri	807	sco	1003	Hyper and
58	*vul	246	ruf	408	pul	603	Cysto fra	810	Fagus syl	1004	cal
60	xan	247	Borag off	412	rem	607	Dacty glo	812	Festu alt	1006	dub
63	Alism pla	248	Botry lun	413	rip	617	Daphn lau	813	aru	1008	elo
64	Allia pet	250	Brach syl	414	ros	620	Daucu car	816	gig	1010	hirsutum
68	Alliu ole	251	Brass nap	419	ser	627	Desch cae	821	*ovi	1011	hum
71	sco	252	nig	420	str	628	fle	823	pra	1013	mon
75	urs	254	rap	421	syl	630	Descu sop	824	rub	1014	per
76	vin	256	Briza med	424	ves	434	Desma mar	830	Filag ger	1015	pul
77	Alnus glu	262	Bromu com	427	Carli vul	435	rig	831	min	1016	tet
82	Alope gen	269	*mol	428	Carpi bet	640	Digit pur	833	Filip ulm	1020	Hypoc rad

— — — F O L D H E R E — — —

85	pra	270	mol	431	Carum ver	645	Diplo ten	834	vul	1023	Ilex aqu
87	Altha off	271	rac	432	Casta sat	646	Dipsa ful	836	Fraga ana	1026	Impat gla
97	Ammop are	273	sec	433	Catab aqu	648	Doron par	838	ves	1027	nol
99	Anaga arv	275	tho	436	Cauca lap	654	Drose ang	839	Frang aln	1028	par
100	ten	276	Bryon dio	440	Centa cya	655	int	841	Fraxi exc	1038	Iris pse
103	Andro pol	288	Butom umb	444	nig	657	rot	845	Fumar bas	1045	Isoet lac
105	Anemo nem	291	Cakil mar	446	sca	658	Dryas oct	847	cap	1047	Isole set
109	Angel syl	293	Calam epi	450	Centa lit	660	Dryop aem	854	off	1048	Jasio mon
113	Anisa ste	302	Calli aut	451	min	661	aus	859	Gagea lut	1050	Juncu acuti
116	Anten dio	303	int	453	pul	662	bor	860	Galan niv	1054	art
117	Anthe arv	307	sta	456	Centu min	664	*fil	867	Galeo spe	1057	buf
118	cot	305	ver	457	Cepha dam	665	fil	868	*tet	1058	*bul
121	Antho odo	309	Callu vul	460	Ceras alp	666	spi	873	Galiu apa	1062	com
123	Anthr neg	310	Calth pal	461	arv	667	vil	874	bor	1063	con
125	syl	2248	Calys *sep	466	glo	670	Echiu vul	875	cru	1067	eff
126	Anthy vul	311	sep	469	sem	673	Eleoc aci	878	her	1069	ger
128	Antir oro	312	sol	462	tet	674	mul	879	*mol	1070	inf
131	Aphan *arv	313	syl	467	vul	675	pal	880	mol	1072	mar
132	arv	315	Campa glo	473	Ceter off	677	pau	882	pal	1075	squ
133	mic	316	lat	474	Chaen min	679	Eleog flu	883	pum	1076	sub
134	Apium gra	320	rapunculo	476	Chaer tem	681	Elode can	887	uli	1077	ten
135	inu	322	rot	477	Chama ang	685	Elymu are	888	ver	1080	Junip com
137	nod	325	Capse bur	480	Cheli maj	685	Empet nig	891	Genis ang	455	Kentr rub
141	Aquil vul	327	Carda ama	481	Cheno *alb	687	Endym non	893	tin	1082	Kickx ela
142	Arabi tha	328	fle	484	bon	689	Epilo adn	897	Genti *ama	1083	spu
146	Arabi hir	329	hir	493	pol	690	als	901	*cam	1084	Knaut arv
150	Arcti agg	330	imp	496	rub	691	ana	906	Geran col	1087	Koele gra
151	lap	331	pra	502	Chrys leu	692	hir	907	dis	1098	Lamiu alb
152	min	333	Carda dra	503	par	695	mon	909	luc	1099	amp
153	vul	335	Cardu cri	504	seg	696	obs	911	mol	1100	hyb
155	Arcto uva	337	nut	505	Chrys alt	697	pal	913	pha	1102	mol
163	Arena lep	339	ten	506	opp	698	par	914	pra	1103	pur
161	*ser	341	Carex acu	509	Cicho int	699	ped	916	pus	1104	Lapsa com
162	ser	340	acuta	510	Cicut vir	700	ros	918	rob	1107	Lathr squ
166	Armer mar	344	are	511	Circa alp	705	Epipa hel	920	san	1112	Lathy mon
167	Armor rus	345	ata	512	lut	708	pal	923	Geum int	1116	pra
169	Arrhe ela	349	big	513	lut	712	Equis arv	924	riv	1117	syl
170	Artem abs	350	bin	515	Cirsi arv	713	flu	925	urb	1126	Lemna min
172	mar	353	capillari	518	het	714	hye	929	Glauc fla	1128	tri
175	vul	355	car	520	pal	717	pal	930	Glaux mar	1129	Leont aut
176	Arum mac	357	con	522	vul	720	syl	931	Glech hed	1130	his
183	Asper odo	359	cur	523	Cladi mar	721	tel	932	Glyce dec	1131	ley
185	Asple adi	361	dem	524	Clayt als	726	Erica cin	933	flu	1133	Lepid cam
189	mar	363	dia	525	per	731	tet			1139	smi
192	rut	365	dio								

Figure 4.33. Botanical Society of the British Isles (now Botanical Society of Britain and Ireland) grid-square recording cards completed by Derek Ratcliffe for a wide range of habitats in the Helvellyn and Fairfield Ranges and around Thirlmere, Cumbria (grid square 35/31) based on his discoveries there between 1953 and 1955 (*above*) and from salt marshes, roadside verges, fields, and a raised bog[53] at Bowness on Solway, Cumbria (grid square 35/26) recorded on 17 July 1957 (*right*). Both areas were favourite haunts of Derek Ratcliffe[1]. Reproduced with permission from the Biological Records Centre, Centre for Ecology and Hydrology, Wallingford

Grid Ref.	LOCALITY		NORTH	
16/1 352	Bowness on Solway, Cumberland.		Date 17/7/57	V.C. No. 70
	HABITAT Salt marsh, roadside verges and fields. Raised bog.		V.C. Cumb. Alt.	Code No. 531

Upper half (left to right columns):

3 Acer cam / 5 pse / 7 Achil mil / 9 pta / 12 Acino arv / 19 Adoxa mos / 20 Aegop pod / 2241 Aescu hip / 21 Aethu cyn / 22 Agrim eup / 23 odo / 26 Agrop can / 28 jun / 33 rep / 34 Agros git / 35 Agros can / 39 sto / 40 ten / 41 Aira car / 42 pra / 46 Ajuga rep / 48 Alche alp / 51 gla / 57 ves / 58 *vul / 60 xan / 63 Alism pla / 64 Allia pet / 68 Alliu ole / 71 sco / 75 urs / 76 vin / 77 Alnus glu / 82 Alope gen

194 Asple tri / 195 vir / 204 Aster tri / 207 Astra dan / 208 gly / 211 Athyr fil / 212 Atrip gla / 214 has / 217 lit / 218 pat / 219 Atrop bel / 224 Balde ran / 225 Ballo nig / 229 Barba vul / 231 Belli per / 232 Berbe vul / 234 Berul ere / 235 Beta mar / 240 Betul pub / 239 ver / 241 Biden cer / 242 tri / 244 Blech spi / 245 Blysm com / 246 ruf / 247 Borag off / 248 Botry lun / 250 Brach syl / 251 Brass nap / 252 nig / 254 rap / 256 Briza med / 262 Bromu com / 269 *mol

366 Carex distan / 367 disticha / 368 divisa / 370 ech / 371 ela / 374 ext / 376 flacca / 377 *flava / 381 hir / 382 hos / 385 lae / 386 las / 387 lep / 388 lim / 393 nig / 396 otr / 397 ova / 399 pal / 400 panicea / 401 panicula / 402 pauci / 404 pen / 405 pil / 407 pse / 408 pul / 412 rem / 413 rip / 414 ros / 419 ser / 420 str / 421 syl / 424 ves / 427 Carli vul / 428 Carpi bet

530 Clino vul / 532 Cochl ang / 533 dan / 535 off / 537 Coelo vir / 540 Coniu mac / 541 Conop maj / 543 Conva maj / 544 Convo arv / 551 Coron did / 552 squ / 555 Coryd cla / 556 lut / 557 Coryl ave / 565 Cramb mar / 569 Crata mon / 571 Crepi bie / 572 cap / 576 pal / 579 Crith mar / 586 Crypt cri / 592 Cymba mur / 596 Cynog off / 597 Cynos cri / 603 Cysto fra / 607 Dacty glo / 617 Daphn lau / 620 Daucu car / 627 Desch cae / 628 fle / 630 Descu sop / 434 Desma mar / 435 rig / 640 Digit pur

740 Eriop ang / 743 lat / 744 vag / 745 Erodi *cic / 748 mar / 753 Eroph *ver / 758 Eryng mar / 762 Euony eur / 763 Eupat can / 771 Eupho exi / 772 hel / 775 par / 777 peplus / 780 por / 2243 Euphr agg / 784 bor / 785 bre / 788 con / 789 cur / 796 mic / 798 nem / 803 riv / 804 ros / 807 sco / 810 Fagus syl / 812 Festu alt / 813 aru / 816 gig / 821 *ovi / 823 pra / 824 *rub / 830 Filag ger / 831 min / 833 Filip ulm

934 Glyce m / 935 p / 936 / 940 Gnaph s / 941 / 948 Gymna c / 952 Heder h / 955 Helia cl / 961 Helic p / 962 pu / 968 Herac s / 975 Hespe m / 976 Hiera l / 981 Hippu v / 983 Holcu l / 984 m / 988 Honke pe / 992 Horde m / 993 s / 999 Humul lu / 999 Hydro l / 1001 Hymen v / 1002 Hyosc n / 1003 Hyper ar / 1004 c / 1006 du / 1008 e / 1010 hirsutu / 1011 hu / 1013 mo / 1014 p / 1015 p / 1016 t / 1020 Hypoc r

FOLD HERE

Lower half (left to right columns):

85 pra / 87 Altha off / 97 Ammop are / 99 Anaga arv / 100 ten / 103 Andro pol / 105 Anemo nem / 109 Angel syl / 113 Anisa ste / 116 Anten dio / 117 Anthe arv / 118 cot / 121 Antho odo / 123 Anthr neg / 125 syl / 126 Anthy vul / 128 Antir oro / 131 Aphan *arv / 132 arv / 133 mic / 134 Apium gra / 135 inu / 137 nod / 141 Aquil vul / 142 Arabi tha / 146 Arabi hir / 150 Arcti agg / 151 lap / 152 min / 153 vul / 155 Arcto uva / 163 Arena lep / 161 *ser / 162 ser / 166 Armer mar / 167 Armor rus / 169 Arrhe ela / 170 Artem abs / 172 mar / 175 vul / 176 Arum mac / 183 Asper odo / 185 Asple adi / 189 mar / 192 rut

270 mol / 271 rac / 273 sec / 275 tho / 276 Bryon dio / 288 Butom umb / 291 Cakil mar / 293 Calam epi / 302 Calli aut / 303 int / 307 sta / 305 ver / 309 Callu vul / 310 Calth pal / 2248 Calys *sep / 311 sep / 312 sol / 313 syl / 315 Campa glo / 316 lat / 320 rapunculo / 322 rot / 325 Capse bur / 327 Carda ama / 328 fle / 329 hir / 330 imp / 331 pra / 333 Carda dra / 335 Gardu cri / 337 nut / 339 ten / 341 Carex acu / 340 acuta / 344 are / 345 atr / 349 big / 350 bin / 353 capillari / 355 car / 357 con / 359 cur / 361 dem / 363 dia / 365 dio

431 Carum ver / 432 Casta sat / 433 Catab aqu / 436 Cauca lap / 440 Centa cya / 444 nig / 446 sca / 450 Centa lit / 451 min / 453 pul / 456 Centu min / 457 Cepha dam / 460 Ceras alp / 461 arv / 466 glo / 469 sem / 462 tet / 467 vul / 473 Ceter off / 474 Chaen min / 476 Chaer tem / 477 Chama ang / 480 Cheli maj / 481 Cheno *alb / 484 bon / 493 pol / 496 rub / 502 Chrys leu / 503 par / 504 seg / 505 Chrys alt / 506 opp / 509 Cicho int / 510 Cicut vir / 511 Circa alp / 512 int / 513 lut / 515 Cirsi arv / 518 het / 520 pal / 522 vul / 523 Cladi mar / 524 Clayt als / 525 per

645 Diplo ten / 646 Dipsa ful / 648 Doron par / 654 Drose ang / 655 int / 657 rot / 658 Dryas oct / 660 Dryop aem / 661 aus / 662 bor / 664 *fil / 665 fil / 666 spi / 667 vil / 670 Echiu vul / 673 Eleoc aci / 674 mul / 675 pal / 677 pau / 679 Eleog flu / 681 Elode can / 682 Elymu are / 685 Empet nig / 687 Endym non / 689 Epilo adn / 690 als / 691 ana / 692 hir / 695 luc / 696 obs / 697 par / 698 par / 699 ped / 700 ros / 705 Epipa hel / 708 pal / 712 Equis arv / 713 flu / 714 hye / 717 pal / 720 syl / 721 tel / 731 Erica cin / 731 tet

834 vul / 836 Fraga ana / 838 ves / 839 Frang aln / 841 Fraxi exc / 845 Fumar bas / 847 cap / 854 off / 859 Gagea lut / 860 Galan niv / 867 Galeo spe / 868 *tet / 873 Galiu apa / 874 bor / 875 cru / 878 her / 879 *mol / 880 mol / 882 pal / 883 pum / 887 uli / 888 ver / 891 Genis ang / 893 tin / 897 Genti *ama / 901 *cam / 906 Geran col / 907 dis / 909 luc / 911 mol / 913 pha / 914 pra / 916 pus / 918 rob / 920 san / 921 syl / 923 Geum int / 924 riv / 925 urb / 929 Glauc fla / 930 Glaux mar / 931 Glech hed / 932 Glyce dec / 933 flu

1023 Ilex ac / 1026 Impat g / 1027 n / 1028 n / 1038 Iris p / 1045 Isoet la / 1047 Isole s / 1048 Jasio m / 1050 Juncu acu / 1054 a / 1057 b / 1058 *bu / 1062 co / 1063 cc / 1067 e / 1069 ge / 1070 li / 1072 ma / 1075 sq / 1077 su / 1080 Junip co / 455 Kentr ru / 1112 Kickx el / 1082 sp / 1083 / 1084 Knaut ar / 1087 Koele gr / 1098 Lamiu al / 1099 am / 1100 hy / 1102 mo / 1103 pu / 1104 Lapsa co / 1107 Lathr sq / 1112 Lathy mo / 1116 pr / 1116 sy / 1126 Lemna mi / 1128 t / 1129 Leont au / 1130 h / 1131 le / 1133 Lepid ca / 1139 sm

Derek Ratcliffe unravelled the history and development of surface pattern features on bogs such as The Silver Flowe[12] and put the floristic and vegetational variation in Scottish mires into a rigorous ecological framework[50,51]. Again his pioneering studies on bog ecology have led to further studies[e.g. 11,13,14].

Derek Ratcliffe provided the first detailed ecological account of Atlantic bryophytes in Britain and Ireland[24]. These bryophytes are one of the internationally unique components of British and Irish plant biodiversity[21,23]. Since Derek's monograph[24] on this flora, there has been renewed interest in its history, phytogeography, taxonomy, ecology, and conservation[21,23,48].

Derek Ratcliffe contributed greatly to knowledge about the distribution, ecology, and population status of rare mountain plants[28,29], cliff plants[55], and bryophytes[19,23,24,27] in Britain and Ireland and he freely gave his records to the Botanical Society of the British Isles (now the Botanical Society of Britain and Ireland) and British Bryological Society recording schemes[21]. His botanical notes and records were used extensively in the redesignation of existing mountain Sites of Special Scientific Interest (SSSIs) and in the designation of several new SSSIs[92].

Derek Ratcliffe searched over many years for very rare and much persecuted and over-collected plants, especially ferns, to assess their current conservation status[28,29,83]. As a result of his detailed searching and monitoring of population changes of Oblong Woodsia, *ex-situ* conservation and reintroduction are being undertaken by the Royal Botanic Garden Edinburgh to ensure the survival of this fern in Britain (Fig. 9.4)[32].

Through his unrivalled field knowledge and experience, Derek Ratcliffe was able to develop informed and sound major nature conservation policies for Britain. Such policies continue to play critically important roles in nature conservation in the 21st century[21,23,39,43,53,92].

Through his writings, field recording cards and maps (Figs. 4.8 & 4.9), plant records (Figs. 4.32 & 4.33), collections, and photographs, Derek has left a truly exceptional documentation and understanding of the flora and vegetation of Britain and Ireland, particularly of northern and western parts of Britain. Through his example[2] he greatly inspired us and our students such as Paul Adam, Will Williams, and Chris Preston, by his knowledge, scholarship, courage, integrity, modesty, loyalty, and dogged determination. Derek's many contributions to botany, to mountain and mire ecology, and to bryology were outstanding and equalled the contributions made by many leading full-time plant ecologists. In addition to all his botanical work, Derek excelled in ornithology, pesticide research, and nature conservation and made major international contributions in all these fields (Fig. 4.1). He was, without doubt, the greatest field ecologist of his generation. His botanical studies are a vitally important part of Derek Ratcliffe's immense legacy to our understanding and conservation of Britain's nature and its fauna and flora.

Acknowledgements

We are grateful to Rod Corner, Lynne Farrell, Stephen Hewitt, David Long, Chris Preston, Gordon Rothero, and Des Thompson for information or comments and to Cathy Jenks for her considerable editorial help.

References

(1)   Ratcliffe, D.A. (2000) *In Search of Nature*. Peregrine Books, Leeds.

(2)   Birks, H.J.B., Thompson, D.B.A. & Birks, H.H. (2015) Derek Ratcliffe – early days in pursuit of nature. In: *Nature's Conscience – The Life and Legacy of Derek Ratcliffe* (eds. D.B.A. Thompson, H.H. Birks & H.J.B. Birks). This volume, Chapter 1.

(3)   Thompson, D.B.A. (2015) Contributions to field ornithology – in search of nesting birds. In: *Nature's Conscience – The Life and Legacy of Derek Ratcliffe* (eds. D.B.A. Thompson, H.H. Birks & H.J.B. Birks). This volume, Chapter 11.

(4)   Newton, I. (2015) Pesticides and birds of prey – the breakthrough. In: *Nature's Conscience – The Life and Legacy of Derek Ratcliffe* (eds. D.B.A. Thompson, H.H. Birks & H.J.B. Birks). This volume, Chapter 15.

(5)   Rollie, C. (2015) In Galloway and the Borders – in search of an enduring youth. In: *Nature's Conscience – The Life and Legacy of Derek Ratcliffe* (eds. D.B.A. Thompson, H.H. Birks & H.J.B. Birks). This volume, Chapter 13.

(6)   Ratcliffe, D.A. (1967) Decrease in eggshell weight in certain birds of prey. *Nature*, **215**, 208-210.

(7)   Ratcliffe, D.A. (1980) *The Peregrine Falcon*. Poyser, Calton.

(8)   Ratcliffe, D.A. (1970) Changes attributable to pesticides in egg breakage frequency and eggshell thickness in some British birds. *Journal of Applied Ecology*, **7**, 67-115.

(9)   Ratcliffe, D.A. (1959) The vegetation of the Carneddau, North Wales. 1. Grasslands, heaths and bogs. *Journal of Ecology*, **47**, 371-413.

(10)   Armitage, H.F. (2010) Assessing the influence of environmental drivers on the current condition and recovery potential of *Racomitrium* heath. Ph.D. Thesis, University of Aberdeen.
        Armitage, H.F., Britton, A.J., van der Wal, R., Pearce, I.S.K., Thompson, D.B.A. & Woodin, S.J. (2012) Nitrogen deposition enhances moss growth, but leads to an overall decline in habitat condition of mountain moss-sedge heath. *Global Change Biology*, **18**, 290-300.
        Averis, A. (2002) Vegetation survey of the western part of the Carneddau SSI and cSAC, Conway, summer 2001/2. Unpublished report, Countryside Council for Wales.
        Britton, A.J., Pearce, I.S.K. & Jones, B. (2005) Impacts of grazing on montane heath vegetation in Wales and implications for the restoration of montane areas. *Biological Conservation*, **125**, 515-524.
        Pearce, I.S.K. & van der Wal, R. (2002) Effects of nitrogen deposition on growth and survival of montane *Racomitrium lanuginosum* heath. *Biological Conservation*, **104**, 83-89.

Pearce, I.S.K., Britton, A.J., Armitage, H.F. & Jones, B. (2010) Additive impacts of nitrogen deposition and grazing on a mountain moss-sedge heath. *Botanica Helvetica*, **120**, 129-137.

van der Wal, R., Pearce, I.S.K., Brooker, R., Scott, D., Welch, D. & Woodin, S.J. (2003) Interplay between nitrogen deposition and grazing causes habitat degradation. *Ecology Letters*, **6**, 141-146.

(11)　Walker, D. (1961) Peat stratigraphy and bog regeneration. *Proceedings of the Linnean Society of London*, **172**, 29-33.

Walker, D. & Walker, P.M. (1961) Stratigraphic evidence of regeneration in some Irish bogs. *Journal of Ecology*, **49**, 169-185.

(12)　Ratcliffe, D.A. & Walker, D. (1958) The Silver Flowe, Galloway, Scotland. *Journal of Ecology*, **46**, 407-445.

(13)　Birks, H.H. (1972) Studies in the vegetational history of Scotland II. Two pollen diagrams from the Galloway Hills, Kirkcudbrightshire. *Journal of Ecology*, **60**, 183-217.

(14)　Boatman, D.J. (1977) Observations on the growth of *Sphagnum cuspidatum* in a bog pool on the Silver Flowe National Nature Reserve. *Journal of Ecology*, **65**, 119-126.

Boatman, D.J. & Tomlinson, R.W. (1973) The Silver Flowe. I. Some structural and hydrological features of Brishie bog and their bearing on pool formation. *Journal of Ecology*, **61**, 653-666.

Boatman, D.J. & Tomlinson, R.W. (1977) The Silver Flowe. II. Features of the vegetation and stratigraphy of Brishie bog, and their bearing on pool formation. *Journal of Ecology*, **65**, 531-546.

Boatman, D.J., Hulme, P.D. & Tomlinson, R.W. (1975) Monthly determinations of the concentrations of sodium, potassium, magnesium, and calcium in the rain and in pools on the Silver Flowe National Nature Reserve. *Journal of Ecology*, **63**, 903-912.

(15)　Goode, D.A. (1970) Ecological studies on the Silver Flowe Nature Reserve. Ph.D. Thesis, University of Hull.

(16)　Mitchell, J. (2015) National Service and beyond. In: *Nature's Conscience – The Life and Legacy of Derek Ratcliffe* (eds. D.B.A. Thompson, H.H. Birks & H.J.B. Birks). This volume, Chapter 2.

(17)　Averis, A.M., Averis, A.B.G., Birks, H.J.B., Horsfield, D., Thompson, D.B.A. & Yeo, M.J.M. (2004) *An Illustrated Guide to British Upland Vegetation*. Joint Nature Conservation Committee, Peterborough.

(18)　Ratcliffe, D.A. (1960) Montane plants in Ross-shire and Sutherland. *Transactions of the Botanical Society of Edinburgh*, **39**, 107-113.

(19)　Ratcliffe, D.A. (1958) The range and habitats of *Sphagnum lindbergii* Schp. in Scotland. *Transactions of the British Bryological Society*, **3**, 386-391.

(20)　Ratcliffe, D.A. (1959) A limestone flora in the Ben Alder group. *Transactions of the Botanical Society of Edinburgh*, **37**, 217-219.

(21)　Preston, C.D. (2015) Derek Ratcliffe and the Atlantic bryophytes of Britain and Ireland. In: *Nature's Conscience – The Life and Legacy of Derek Ratcliffe* (eds. D.B.A. Thompson, H.H. Birks & H.J.B. Birks). This volume, Chapter 7.

(22) Crundwell, A.C. (1970) *Herberta borealis*, a new species from Scotland and Norway. *Transactions of the British Bryological Society, 6*, 41-49.

(23) Long, D.G. & Rothero, G.P. (2015) Bryology in the Highlands and Islands of Scotland. In: *Nature's Conscience – The Life and Legacy of Derek Ratcliffe* (eds. D.B.A. Thompson, H.H. Birks & H.J.B. Birks). This volume, Chapter 6.

(24) Ratcliffe, D.A. (1968) An ecological account of Atlantic bryophytes in the British Isles. *New Phytologist, 67,* 365-439.

(25) Ratcliffe, D.A. (1959) *Cicerbita alpina* (L.) Wallr. in Glen Callater. *Transactions of the Botanical Society of Edinburgh, 38,* 287-288.

(26) Long, D.G. (1992) *Sanionia orthothecioides* (Lindb.) Loeske in Scotland, new to the British Isles. *Journal of Bryology, 17,* 111-117.

(27) Long, D.G. & Ratcliffe, D.A. (1996) Bryophytes of Hirta, St Kilda. *Journal of Bryology, 19,* 89-111.

(28) Ratcliffe, D.A. (1959) The mountain plants of the Moffat Hills. *Transactions of the Botanical Society of Edinburgh, 37,* 257-271.

(29) Ratcliffe, D.A. (1960) The mountain flora of Lakeland. *Proceedings of the Botanical Society of the British Isles, 4,* 1-25.

(30) Ratcliffe, D.A. (1961) Mountain plants in Peeblesshire (v.c. 78) and Selkirkshire (v.c. 79). *Transactions of the Botanical Society of Edinburgh, 39,* 233-234.

(31) Corner, R.W.M. (2015) Derek Ratcliffe and plant-hunting in southern Scotland and northern England. In: *Nature's Conscience – The Life and Legacy of Derek Ratcliffe* (eds. D.B.A. Thompson, H.H. Birks & H.J.B. Birks). This volume, Chapter 5.

(32) Rae, D. (2015) Royal Botanic Garden Edinburgh (RBGE) and caring for Scotland's flora. In: *Nature's Conscience – The Life and Legacy of Derek Ratcliffe* (eds. D.B.A. Thompson, H.H. Birks & H.J.B. Birks). This volume, Chapter 9.

(33) Ratcliffe, D.A. & Eddy, A. (1960) *Alopecurus alpinus* Sm. in Britain. *Proceedings of the Botanical Society of the British Isles, 3,* 389-391.

(34) McVean, D.N. & Ratcliffe, D.A. (1962) *Plant Communities of the Scottish Highlands.* Her Majesty's Stationery Office, London.

(35) Marren, P. (2015) Derek and I: A correspondence. In: *Nature's Conscience – The Life and Legacy of Derek Ratcliffe* (eds. D.B.A. Thompson, H.H. Birks & H.J.B. Birks). This volume, Chapter 27.

(36) Birks, H.J.B. (1973) *Past and Present Vegetation of the Isle of Skye - A Palaeoecological Study.* Cambridge University Press, Cambridge.

(37) Rodwell, J.S. (ed.) (1991-2000) *British Plant Communities Volumes 1-5.* Cambridge University Press, Cambridge.

(38) Ratcliffe, D.A. (ed.) (1977) *A Nature Conservation Review, Volumes 1 and 2.* Cambridge University Press, Cambridge.

(39) Thompson, D.B.A., Sutherland, W. & Birks, H.J.B. (2015) Nature conservation and the Nature Conservation Review – a novel philosophical framework. In: *Nature's Conscience – The Life and Legacy of Derek Ratcliffe* (eds. D.B.A. Thompson, H.H. Birks & H.J.B. Birks). This volume, Chapter 19

(40) Farrell, L. (2015) In the field with Derek Ratcliffe: long days and driving at speed. In: *Nature's Conscience – The Life and Legacy of Derek Ratcliffe* (eds. D.B.A. Thompson, H.H. Birks & H.J.B. Birks). This volume, Chapter 8.

(41) Birks, H.J.B. & Ratcliffe, D.A. (1980) *Classification of upland vegetation types in Britain*. Nature Conservancy Council, Edinburgh.

(42) Proctor, M.C.F. (2013) *Vegetation of Britain and Ireland*. Collins, London.

(43) Kirby, K.J. (2015) Battling forestry and building consensus: woodland conservation post-1949. In: *Nature's Conscience – The Life and Legacy of Derek Ratcliffe* (eds. D.B.A. Thompson, H.H. Birks & H.J.B. Birks). This volume, Chapter 21.

(44) Ross, L.C., Woodin, S.A., Hester, A.J., Thompson, D.B.A. & Birks, H.J.B. (2012) Biotic homogenisation of upland vegetation: patterns and drivers at multiple spatial scales over five decades. *Journal of Vegetation Science*, **23**, 755-770.

(45) Ross, L. C., Woodin, S.A., Hester, A.J., Thompson, D.B.A. & Birks, H.J.B. (2011) Is the vegetation of the North-West Highlands changing? Results from a 50-year re-visitation study of major upland vegetation types. In: *The Changing Nature of Scotland* (eds. S.J. Marrs *et al.*), pp. 429-436. Scottish Natural Heritage.

(46) Britton, A.J., Beale, C.M., Towers, W. & Hewison, R.L. (2009) Biodiversity gains and losses: Evidence for homogenisation of Scottish alpine vegetation. *Biological Conservation*, **142**, 1728-1739.

(47) Kapfer, J., Birks, H.J.B., Felde, V.A., Klanderud, K., Martinessen, T., Ross, L.C., Høistad Schei, F., Virtanen, R. & Grytnes, J.-A. (2013) Long-term vegetation stability in northern Europe as assessed by changes in species co-occurrences. *Plant Ecology and Diversity*, **6**, 289-302.

(48) Flagmeier, M., Long, D.G., Genney, D.R., Hollingsworth, P.M., Ross, L.C. & Woodin, S.J. (2013) Fifty years of vegetation change in oceanic-montane liverwort-rich heath in Scotland. *Plant Ecology & Diversity*, **7**, 457-470.

(49) Trivedi, M.R., Browne, M.K., Berry, P.M., Dawson, T.P. & Morecroft, M.D. (2007) Projecting climate change impacts on mountain snow cover in central Scotland from historical patterns. *Arctic, Antarctic, and Alpine Research*, **39**, 488-499.
Trivedi, M.R., Berry, P.M., Morecroft, M.D. & Dawson, T.P. (2008) Spatial scale affects bioclimate model projections of climate change impacts on mountain plants. *Global Change Biology*, **14**, 1089-1103.
Trivedi, M.R., Morecroft, M.D., Berry, P.M. & Dawson., T.P. (2008) Potential effects of climate change on plant communities in three montane nature reserves in Scotland. *Biological Conservation*, **141**, 1665-1675.

(50) Ratcliffe, D.A. (1964) Mires and bogs. In: *The Vegetation of Scotland* (ed. J.H. Burnett), pp. 426-478. Oliver and Boyd, Edinburgh.

(51) Ratcliffe, D.A. (1964) Montane mires and bogs. In: *The Vegetation of Scotland* (ed. J.H. Burnett), pp. 536-558. Oliver and Boyd, Edinburgh.

(52) Lindsay, R.A., Charman, D.J., Everingham, F., O'Reilly, R.M., Palmer, M.A., Rowell, T.A., Stroud, D.A. (eds. D.A. Ratcliffe & P.H. Oswald) (1988) *The Flow Country – The Peatlands of Caithness and Sutherland*. 174 pp. Nature Conservancy Council, Peterborough.

(53) Lindsay, R. (2015) A letter to Derek Ratcliffe. In: *Nature's Conscience – The Life and Legacy of Derek Ratcliffe* (eds. D.B.A. Thompson, H.H. Birks & H.J.B. Birks). This volume, Chapter 24.

(54) Greenwood, J.J.D. & Crick, H.Q.P. (2015) "It seemed like a dream come true"– Derek Ratcliffe and the Peregrine surveys. In: *Nature's Conscience – The Life and Legacy of Derek Ratcliffe* (eds. D.B.A. Thompson, H.H. Birks & H.J.B. Birks). This volume, Chapter 14.

(55) Ratcliffe, D.A. (1962) *Potentilla rupestris* in East Sutherland. *Proceedings of the Botanical Society of the British Isles*, **4**, 501.

(56) Ratcliffe, D.A. (1962) The habitat of *Adelanthus unciformis* (Tayl.) Mitt. and *Jamesoniella carringtonii* (Balf.) Spr. in Ireland. *Irish Naturalists' Journal*, **14**, 38-40.

(57) Gregory, R. (1971) *The Price of Amenity. Five Studies in Conservation and Government*. Macmillan, London.

(58) Smith, P.J. (ed.) (1975) *The Politics of Physical Resources*. Penguin Education and The Open University Press.

(59) Ratcliffe, D.A. (1978) Plant communities. In: *Upper Teesdale – The Area and its Natural History* (ed. A. R. Clapham), pp. 64-87. Collins, London.

(60) Stroud, D., Reed, T., Pienkowski, M. & Lindsay, R. (2015) The Flow Country: battles fought, war won, organisation lost. In: *Nature's Conscience – The Life and Legacy of Derek Ratcliffe* (eds. D.B.A. Thompson, H.H. Birks & H.J.B. Birks). This volume, Chapter 23.

(61) Marren, P. (2002) *Nature Conservation*. Harper Collins, London.

(62) Radcliffe (sic), D. (1989) The end of British nature conservation? *New Scientist*, **9 September**, 75-76.

(63) Smith, J.E., Clapham, A.R. & Ratcliffe, D.A. (eds.) (1977) Scientific Aspects of Nature Conservation in Great Britain. *Proceedings of the Royal Society of London B-Biological Sciences*, **197**, 3-103.

(64) Ratcliffe, D.A. (1977) Nature conservation - aims, methods and achievements. *Proceedings of the Royal Society of London B-Biological Sciences*, **197**, 11-29.

(65) Ratcliffe, D.A. (1984) Post-medieval and recent changes in British vegetation - the culmination of human influence. *New Phytologist*, **98,** 73-100.

(66) Ratcliffe, D.A. (1977) *Highland Flora*. Highlands and Islands Development Board, Inverness.

(67) Ratcliffe, D.A. (2007) *Galloway and the Borders*. Collins, London.

(68) Battarbee, R.W. (2015) Forestry, 'acid rain', and the acidification of lakes in Galloway, south-west Scotland. In: *Nature's Conscience – The Life and Legacy of Derek Ratcliffe* (eds. D.B.A. Thompson, H.H. Birks & H.J.B. Birks). This volume, Chapter 22.

(69) Ratcliffe, D.A. (1974) The Vegetation. In: *The Cairngorms – their natural history and scenery* (eds. D. Nethersole-Thompson & A. Watson), pp. 42-76. Collins, London.

(70) Ratcliffe, D.A. (1966) The habitat of the snow bunting in Scotland. In: *The Snow Bunting* (by D. Nethersole-Thompson), pp. 153-165. Oliver and Boyd, Edinburgh.

(71)   Ratcliffe, D.A. (1973) Breeding habitat of the dotterel in Britain. In: *The Dotterel* (by D. Nethersole-Thompson), pp. 153-173. Collins, London.

(72)   Ratcliffe, D.A. (1979) The breeding habitat of the greenshank in Scotland. In: *Greenshanks* (by D. Nethersole-Thompson & M. Nethersole-Thompson), pp. 185-192. Poyser, Berkhamsted.

(73)   Pearsall, W.H. & Pennington, W. (1973) *The Lake District – A Landscape History*. Collins, London.

(74)   Ratcliffe, D.A. (1990) *Bird Life of Mountain and Upland*. Cambridge University Press, Cambridge.

(75)   Ratcliffe, D.A. (2002) *Lakeland*. HarperCollins, London.

(76)   Ratcliffe, D.A. (1991) The mountain flora of Britain and Ireland. *British Wildlife*, **3**, 10-21. (Reprinted in this volume as Chapter 10)

(77)   Ratcliffe, D.A. (2005) *Lapland: A Natural History*. Poyser, London.

(78)   Byrkjedal, I. (2015). A thousand nest cards – from Derek Ratcliffe to the University of Bergen. In: *Nature's Conscience – The Life and Legacy of Derek Ratcliffe* (eds. D.B.A. Thompson, H.H. Birks & H.J.B. Birks). This volume, Chapter 17.

(79)   Ratcliffe, D.A. (2015) Lapland images. In: *Nature's Conscience – The Life and Legacy of Derek Ratcliffe* (eds. D.B.A. Thompson, H.H. Birks & H.J.B. Birks). This volume, Chapter 29.

(80)   Marren, P. (2002) *The New Naturalists*. HarperCollins, London.
Cabot, D. (1999) *Ireland*. HarperCollins, London.
Gilbert, O. (2000) *Lichens*. HarperCollins, London.
Mitchell, J. (2001) *Loch Lomondside*. HarperCollins, London.
Marren, P. (2002) *Nature Conservation*. HarperCollins, London.
Lunn, A. (2004) *Northumberland*. Collins, London.
Porley, R. & Hodgetts, N. (2005) *Mosses & Liverworts*. Collins, London.
Bircham, P. (2007) *A History of Ornithology*. Collins, London.

(81)   Ratcliffe, D.A. (1990) Upland birds and their conservation. *British Wildlife*, **2**, 1-12. (Reprinted in this volume as Chapter 18)

(82)   Branson, A. (2014) Passing on the baton. *British Wildlife*, **25**, 153.

(83)   Ratcliffe, D.A., Birks, H.J.B. & Birks, H.H. (1993) The ecology and conservation of the Killarney Fern *Trichomanes speciosum* Willd. in Britain and Ireland. *Biological Conservation*, **66**, 231-247.

(84)   Rumsey, F.J., Jermy, A.C. & Sheffield, E. (1998) The independent gametophyte stage of *Trichomanes speciosum* Willd. (Hymenophyllaceae), the Killarney Fern and its distribution in the British Isles. *Watsonia*, **22**, 1-19.

(85)   Forbes, R.S. & Northridge, R.H. (2012) *The Flora of Fermanagh*. National Museum of Northern Ireland, Hollywood.
Porter, M. & Halliday, G. (2014) *Cumbrian Rare Plant Register*. Trollius Publications, Milnthorpe.

(86)   Birks, H.H., Birks, H.J.B. & Ratcliffe, D.A. (1969) *Geocalyx graveolens* (Schrad.) Nees in Kerry, a hepatic new to Ireland. *Irish Naturalists' Journal*, **16**, 204-205.

(87) Birks, H.J.B., Birks, H.H. & Ratcliffe, D.A. (1969) Mountain plants on Slieve League, Co. Donegal. *Irish Naturalists' Journal*, **16**, 203-204.

(88) Birks, H.H. (1970) Studies in the vegetational history of Scotland I. A pollen diagram from Abernethy Forest, Inverness-shire. *Journal of Ecology*, **58**, 827-846. Birks, H.H. & Mathewes, R.W. (1978) Studies in the vegetational history of Scotland V. Late Devensian and Early Flandrian pollen and macrofossil stratigraphy at Abernethy Forest, Inverness-shire. *New Phytologist*, **80**, 455-484.

(89) Birks, H.H. (1984) Late-Quaternary pollen and plant macrofossil stratigraphy at Lochan an Druim, north-west Scotland. In: *Lake Sediments and Environmental History* (eds. E.Y. Haworth & J.W.G. Lund), pp. 377-405. University of Leicester Press, Leicester.

(90) Birks, H.J.B. (1993) Quaternary palaeoecology and vegetation science - current contributions and possible future developments. *Review of Palaeobotany and Palynology*, **79**, 153-177.

(91) Birks, H.H. (1975) Studies in the vegetational history of Scotland IV. Pine stumps in Scottish blanket peats. *Philosophical Transactions of the Royal Society of London B*, **170**, 181-226.

(92) Sydes, C. (2008) Can we protect threatened Scottish arctic-alpine higher plants? *Plant Ecology & Diversity*, **1**, 339-349.

5. Derek Ratcliffe and plant-hunting in southern Scotland and northern England

Roderick W.M. Corner

Introduction

I first met Derek Ratcliffe in the lecture hall of the Royal Botanic Garden Edinburgh at a talk by Professor Sir Harry Godwin in the 1950s. I was a medical student, and had written to the Nature Conservancy about the considerable botanical interest of the Whitlaw Mosses. Derek and I spoke briefly about his visit to the area, as a result of my letter, which eventually led to the area being notified as a Site of Special Scientific Interest (in 1962) and declared a National Nature Reserve (in 1974, and extended in 1980). Twenty or so years passed before I contacted Derek again to ask for his advice about a note I was writing on Sheathed Sedge (*Carex vaginata*) in Selkirkshire[1]. Twenty years after that in 1992 when I was President of the Carlisle Medical Society, I asked him to give a lecture on Nature Conservation in Cumbria. And so, forty years after we first met, Derek started his annual spring and autumn visits to Penrith where he stayed with my wife Jean and me for a few days, as well as with Geoff Horne, his great ornithological friend[2,3]. These visits continued up until his untimely death in 2005. He and I visited many varied sites in Cumbria and Dumfriesshire which he had known intimately in the past and which he used in the write-up and photography for his two New Naturalist books on these areas[3,4]. Each evening Derek would write up the day's observations in his note book. It was disappointing to learn that so many of the sites he had known for nearly 50 years had changed for the worse but also rewarding to refind some of his discoveries from the 1950s and early 1960s.

Southern Scotland

The Moffat Hills (Fig. 5.1) of the Southern Uplands were one of Derek's favourite areas[2] and his paper[5] is the definitive botanical work on these hills which have the best sites for alpine species in southern Scotland. One such plant is Alpine Saxifrage (*Saxifraga nivalis*) (Fig. 5.2) which we attempted to refind at his site on Hart Crag by ascending the Blackhope Valley in 2004 but the weather closed in and we were unsuccessful. He had another solo attempt later by descending the steep ground from above but again failed to refind it. It remains a prize for the future. He took especial pleasure in refinding Bearberry (*Arctostaphylos uva-ursi*) (Fig. 5.3), a rare plant of the Southern Uplands, by scrambling up the rocky slopes above the Tail Burn above the Grey Mare's Tail (Fig. 5.1) during a quick visit with Jean Roger whose late husband Grant was a great friend and colleague. The first record of the grass Alpine Foxtail (*Alopecurus megellanicus*) (Fig. 5.4) from southern Scotland was made by Derek on White Coomb (vice-county (v.c.) 72) in 1956 and again on Cramalt Craig in the Tweedsmuir Hills (v.c. 78) in 1960 and since then it has been found to be more widespread. Pyramidal Bugle (*Ajuga pyramidalis*) (Fig. 4.11) is still extant having been seen by Jeff Waddell recently and the rare Oblong Woodsia (*Woodsia ilvensis*) (Figs. 4.12 & 9.4), monitored by the late Hugh Lang, has now been reintroduced from native stock to several sites by the Royal Botanic Garden Edinburgh[6]. Hoary Whitlowgrass (*Draba incana*), not on Derek's Moffat Hills list[5], has recently been reported from the Scottish Borders Forest Trust's valley of Carrifran where great work is being done on afforestation with native species[7]. Within the last two years, the hybrid forget-me-not (Pale x Creeping Forget-me-not: *Myosotis stolonifera* x *secunda*) new to Scotland, has been found in the same valley. The discovery of Holly Fern (*Polystichum*

Figure 5.1. Two rich areas in the Moffat Hills for alpine species – Devil's Beef Tub, Annanhead, Dumfriesshire, 1993 (*left*) and Grey Mare's Tail, Moffatdale, Dumfriesshire, 1967 (*right*). Photos: Derek Ratcliffe (*left*), John Birks (*right*)

lonchitis) (Fig. 4.12) in the Talla area to the north in a new site by Jeff Waddell in 2009 would have interested Derek greatly and David Long has added several montane species to the bryophyte list from Polmood Craigs on Broad Law which Derek visited in 1959/60[8]. All these records are in fact from v.c. 78, showing how confusing vice-county boundaries can be.

Figure 5.2. Alpine Saxifrage (*Saxifraga nivalis*) in the Moffat Hills, 1962. Described by Derek Ratcliffe[4] as "probably the rarest plant in southern Scotland" and last seen in 1973. Photo: Derek Ratcliffe

Figure 5.3. Bearberry (*Arctostaphylos uva-ursi*), a plant Derek Ratcliffe was proud of refinding above the Tail Burn above the Grey Mare's Tail in Moffatdale (Fig. 5.1). Here in northern Sweden, 1965. Photo: John Birks

I have no real experience of the Galloway hills (Figs. 1.4 & 1.5) which were a great study area for Derek as a young man especially from the ornithological point of view[2,4,9,10]. It grieved him to see the massive march of commercial forestry over the landscape which he was unable to stem (Figs. 13.10 & 22.1)[4,10]. Humphrey Milne-Redhead as a single handed General Practitioner (GP) from Mainsriddle was the Botanical Society of the British Isles (BSBI) (now the Botanical Society of Britain and Ireland) recorder for the area and was a very energetic field botanist and expert bryologist, much admired by Derek[11,12]. He had a great love for the hills and other remote places. They were rarely in the field together but they kept in good contact, especially about plant records in Galloway and Dumfriesshire. Hugh Lang, another GP from Newton Stewart, also covered the hill country and was rewarded by discovering Purple Saxifrage (*Saxifraga oppositifolia*) on the Merrick (Fig. 1.4), new to the area and the third record for southern Scotland. Recently Chris Miles has extended the range of Northern Spike-rush (*Eleocharis mamillata* ssp. *austriaca*) into Eskdale, Dumfriesshire from its only known Scottish sites in Selkirkshire.

The south-east of Scotland was part of Derek's areas of particular interest but apart from the Moffat, Langholm, Moorfoot, and Tweedsmuir Hills he did not know this area as well, perhaps because he concentrated on the wilder parts of the country. However over the years some exciting records have been made there. It was Humphrey Milne-Redhead who made the first records for Alpine Rush (*Juncus alpino-articulatus*), Holy-grass (*Hierochloe odorata*), and Narrow Small-reed (*Calamagrostis stricta*) in the 1960s and additional sites for them have been found by myself over the years. However in common with other areas of blanket afforestation to which Derek was so opposed, many of the habitats of Alpine Rush have now been destroyed.

Figure 5.4. Alpine Foxtail (*Alopecurus megallanicus*) at Cross Fell, 2002 (*left*) and at Great Dun Fell, 2008 (*right*). Photos: Rod Corner (*left*), Jeremy Roberts (*right*)

The Small-reed genus *Calamagrostis* is a difficult one and my write-up[13] of the putative hybrid *Calamagrostis stricta* x *canescens* (*C.* x *gracilescens*) as *C. scotica* (Scottish Small-reed) has continued to cause confusion. It is a strongly growing hybrid with its British headquarters in the area. Interestingly I turned up Narrow Small-reed new to Peeblesshire with Mike Porter and Luke Gaskell near West Linton in 2012 which shows that intensive searching of good sites can be rewarding. Two hepatics new to Scotland namely *Leiocolea rutheana* var. *rutheana* by me and *Scapania paludicola* by David Long were recently recorded from the Hawick and Alemoor areas and the richer Border mires continue to add new habitats for the local moss *Hamatocaulis vernicosus* and some rare hepatics.

Northern England

The Northern Pennines were a favourite stamping ground of Derek's from an early age[2,9] and he greatly enjoyed finding and refinding attractive plants such as Alpine

Figure 5.5. A plant that Derek always enjoyed finding in the Northern Pennines – Cloudberry (*Rubus chamaemorus*) (this photo was taken in Lapland, 1997). Photo: Derek Ratcliffe

Forget-me-not (*Myosotis alpestris*) and Cloudberry (*Rubus chaemomorus*) (Fig. 5.5). He repeatedly tried to refind Mountain Avens (*Dryas octopetala*) (Fig. 4.10) on Melmerby Scar without success but found a good colony of Holly Fern (Fig. 4.12) and protected it from grazing by surrounding it with rocks which has ensured its survival. Alpine Foxtail was new to England when he and Alan Eddy recorded it independently from the Cross Fell range in 1959[14]. During the *Flora of Cumbria*[15] years of recording organised by Geoffrey Halliday, we tried to refind it in some of Derek's sites without success. However in 2002, the year after the Foot and Mouth disaster when the sheep had been removed from the fells, a group of us including Linda Robinson, Jeremy Roberts, and myself were rewarded by a magnificent floral display which is unlikely to be seen again for a considerable time[16]. The Alpine Foxtail (Fig. 5.4) was luxuriant in places and in sites where it was previously unknown. Not only was this remarkable but the occurrence of Sheathed Sedge new to England was especially rewarding[17,18]. Species that Derek was not aware of here have continued to be found. Jeremy Robert's Lady's-mantle (*Alchemilla glomerulans*) and the Water Whorl-grass (*Catabrosa aquatica*) were new and his discovery of Water Sedge (*Carex aquatilis*) near the summit of Little Dun Fell was noteworthy. Since then Sheathed Sedge and Alpine Foxtail have been found by Linda Robinson to extend south to the Yorkshire Dales[19] and a new site for Marsh Saxifrage (*Saxifraga hirculus*) (Fig. 5.6) has recently been added to the flora of North West Yorks (v.c. 65) in 2012, Derek having discovered it many years ago on Great Shunner Fell[2]. It is however, a species that is declining in the Northern Pennines[20] possibly because of changes in grazing and other land-use practices or because of nitrogen enrichment. Another species which Jeremy Roberts has worked on and added to the Teesdale flora is Northern Deergrass

(*Trichophorum cespitosum*). He has shown that it is able to tolerate the highly acid ombrogenous peat of Butterburn Flow and the lowland peat mosses of the Solway Plain whereas previously it was thought to require a degree of mineral enrichment for survival. It was the late George Swan who first showed convincingly that it occurred in the British Isles with confirmation by isozyme work carried out by Peter Hollingsworth.

Derek had recorded Wilson's Filmy-fern (*Hymenophyllum wilsonii*) (Fig. 4.3) from above The Flatt on the Bewcastle Fells in north Cumbria, with Mike Porter recently adding Tunbridge Filmy-fern (*H. tunbrigense*) (Fig. 4.3). In 2012, Jeremy Roberts, after painstaking and prolonged searches in the deep cavities in the gritstone outcrops, found some subtly different plants which he considered to be a possible hybrid. This was confirmed by Fred Rumsey and described formally as *H.* x *scopulorum*, new to science[21]. This was a remarkable discovery from a superficially rather dull and unremarkable botanical area. Derek would have been delighted and surprised to have known of this.

The Lake District was the area that Derek knew intimately from his early years[2,3,9,11] being drawn there originally by his ornithological interests. Similar to his account on the botany of the Moffat Hills[5], his *Mountain Flora of Lakeland*[22] is a must for anyone interested in its montane flora. It gives a lucid and easily assimilated account of the flora with the elevational range of the species. Those of us who participated in Geoffrey Halliday's *Flora of Cumbria*[15] project found it a challenge to search for species from a list of Ratcliffe desiderata as many were from difficult ground which most of us were unwillingly to risk. A recent search I made for his record of Mountain Crowberry (*Empetrum hermaphroditum*) below a scree slope in Riggindale, and which I came across independently, was unsuccessful and I am sure it is now extinct from over grazing by sheep and deer. Conversely his Pyramidal Bugle (Fig. 4.11) from Kentmere has been

Figure 5.6. Marsh Saxifrage (*Saxifraga hirculus*) at Knock Ore Gill, 2008 and (inset) Yad Moss, 2011 in the Northern Pennines. The inset highlights the distinctive spotting on the petals. Photos: Jeremy Roberts

refound in good quantity at its only English site by assiduous searching by Jeremy Roberts helped by Mike Porter and Peter Bullard. The recent impressive discoveries of Dwarf Cornel (Fig. 4.12) on Broad Stand by Simon Webb in 2005 and by Bill Burleton from near the summit of Helvellyn in 2011 are noteworthy for a very rare English species with a predominantly eastern distribution. Simon Webb of Natural England and colleagues are making determined efforts to propagate and reintroduce some of last remaining members of the Lake District alpine flora, especially Downy Willow (*Salix lapponum*).

Tomentypnum nitens, the very attractive relict fen moss, has gone from several of the sites in the eastern Lake District where Derek knew it but I have turned it up in new ones. I was able to get my eye in for the montane hepatic *Scapania paludosa* which I refound at his site on Skiddaw and then added a second English record to the south in Matterdale. At the same site, the coprophilous moss *Splachnum vasculosum* (Fig. 5.7) was new to the Lake

Figure 5.7. *Splachnum vasculosum* in Perthshire, 1967. Photo: John Birks

District bryophyte flora and also the lichen *Platismatia norvegica*, which was new to England when I first found it there in the 1980s.

Over-grazing has become a real problem and I have noted local extinctions of the terricolous lichens *Alectoria nigricans*, *Cetraria islandica*, and *Cladonia rangiferina* from the eastern Lake District fells, but recently, lack of grazing has resulted in some flushes and springs being overwhelmed by Sharp-flowered Rush (*Juncus acutiflorus*) with the loss of the locally rare mosses *Cinclidium stygium* and *Bryum weigelii*. The pressures put on the rare flora of the Lakes were demonstrated in 2008 when the small population of *Splachnum vasculosum* appeared to be extinct. There had been two years of the Antler Moth (*Cerapteryx graminis*) plague, the caterpillars of which decimated the grazing, and hungry sheep combined with a dry spell meant that the trampled flush had been grazed bare and the moss gone. Luckily another small colony nearby in wetter conditions had survived.

At Barons Wood on the River Eden, Derek found in late 1956 the very rare Killarney Fern (*Trichomanes speciosum*) (Fig. 4.27) and collected a frond for the Tullie House Museum, Carlisle. We went to look for it at his site in 2000 but there was no trace of it. He had feelings of guilt about collecting the frond but it was probably the severe winter of 1962/3 that finished it off[2,23,24]. More recently, the late Ken Trewren, during intensive searches in the same area of steep sandstone rocks of the Eden gorge, found tiny immature fronds of this fern in several places but there is no evidence that these fronds will ever produce the large mature plant that Derek found. In 2008 in the flood zone of the river there, Mark Lawley made the exciting discovery of two mosses *Thamnium angustifolium* and *Anomodon attenuatus* previously only known from single sites in the British Isles showing that this is indeed a very special section of the River Eden[25].

I am very conscious that botany and his love of the native flora, especially in the wilder places, were only a small part Derek's wide-ranging Natural History repertoire[2]. I feel privileged to have accompanied him on these days in the field and to have shared our common interest in the plants of southern Scotland and northern England.

References

(1) Corner, R.W.M. (1981) *Carex vaginata* Tausch in southern Scotland. *Watsonia*, **13**, 317-318.

(2) Ratcliffe, D.A. (2000) *In Search of Nature*. Peregrine Books, Leeds.

(3) Ratcliffe, D.A. (2002) *Lakeland*. HarperCollins, London.

(4) Ratcliffe, D.A. (2007) *Galloway and the Borders*. Collins, London.

(5) Ratcliffe, D.A. (1959) The mountain plants of the Moffat Hills. *Transactions of the Botanical Society of Edinburgh*, **37**, 257-271.

(6) Rae, D. (2015) Royal Botanic Garden Edinburgh and caring for Scotland's flora. In: *Nature's Conscience – The Life and Legacy of Derek Ratcliffe* (eds. D.B.A. Thompson, H.H. Birks & H.J.B. Birks). This volume, Chapter 9.

(7) Ashmole, M. & Ashmole, P. (2009) *The Carrifran Wildwood Story*. Borders Forest Trust, Jedbergh & Galashiels.

(8) Ratcliffe, D.A. (1961) Mountain plants in Peeblesshire (v.c. 78) and Selkirkshire (v.c. 79) in Notes on the Scottish Flora. *Transactions of the Botanical Society of Edinburgh*, **39**, 233-234.

(9) Birks, H.J.B., Thompson, D.B.A. & Birks, H.H. (2015) Derek Ratcliffe – early days in pursuit of nature. In: *Nature's Conscience – The Life and Legacy of Derek Ratcliffe* (eds. D.B.A. Thompson, H.H. Birks & H.J.B. Birks). This volume, Chapter 1.

(10) Rollie, C.J. (2015) In Galloway and the Borders – in search of an enduring youth. In: *Nature's Conscience – The Life and Legacy of Derek Ratcliffe* (eds. D.B.A. Thompson, H.H. Birks & H.J.B. Birks). This volume, Chapter 13.

(11) Birks, H.J.B. & Birks, H.H. (2015) Derek Ratcliffe – botanist and plant ecologist. In: *Nature's Conscience – The Life and Legacy of Derek Ratcliffe* (eds. D.B.A. Thompson, H.H. Birks & H.J.B. Birks). This volume, Chapter 4.

(12) Ratcliffe, D.A. (1975) Humphrey Milne-Redhead 1906-1974. *Journal of Bryology*, **8**, 415-416.

(13) Corner, R.W.M. (1967) *Calamagrostis scotica* in Southern Scotland. *Transactions of the Botanical Society of Edinburgh*, **40**, 336-337.

(14) Ratcliffe, D.A. & Eddy, A. (1960) *Alopecurus alpinus* Sm. in Britain. *Proceedings of the Botanical Society of the British Isles*, **3**, 389-391.

(15) Halliday, G. (1997) *A Flora of Cumbria*. University of Lancaster, Lancaster.

(16)   Robinson, L. (2003) Observations on *Alopecurus borealis* at Green Fell in the Northern Pennines, Cumbria after Foot and Mouth. *Botanical Society of the British Isles News*, **93**, 11-12.

Roberts, F.J. (2010) The flowering of Cross Fell: montane vegetation and Foot and Mouth. *British Wildlife*, **21**, 160-167

(17)   Corner, R.W.M. (2004) *Carex vaginata* Tausch (Cyperaceae): a sedge new to England. *Watsonia*, **25**, 127-130.

(18)   Corner, R.W.M., Roberts, J. & Robinson, L. (2006) Sheathed sedge (*Carex vaginata*): an update on its status in the Northern Pennines. *Botanical Society of the British Isles News*, **101**, 6-8.

(19)   Robinson, L. (2008) The discovery of *Alopecurus borealis* and *Carex vaginata* in the Yorkshire Dales (v.c. 65) with observations on *Saxifraga hirculus*. *Botanical Society of the British Isles News*, **107**, 6-7.

(20)   Robinson, L. (2012). Observations on the decline of *Saxifraga hirculus* in the north Pennines. *Botanical Society of the British Isles News*, **121**, 53-56.

(21)   Rumsey, F.J. & Roberts, F.J. (2011) A new *Hymenophyllum* hybrid from the British Isles: *Hymenophyllum* x *scopulorum* F.J. Rumsey & F.J. Roberts (*Hymenophyllum tunbrigense* (L.) Sm. x *H. wilsonii* Hook.), Hymenophyllaceae. *New Journal of Botany*, **1**, 93-97.

(22)   Ratcliffe, D.A. (1960) The mountain flora of Lakeland. *Proceedings of the Botanical Society of the British Isles*, **4**, 1-25.

(23)   Ratcliffe, D.A., Birks, H.J.B. & Birks, H.H. (1993) The ecology and conservation of the Killarney Fern *Trichomanes speciosum* Willd. in Britain and Ireland. *Biological Conservation*, **66**, 231-247.

(24)   Ratcliffe, D.A. (1968) An ecological account of Atlantic bryophytes in the British Isles. *New Phytologist*, **67**, 365-439.

(25)   Lawley, M. (2008) Mossing about in Eden. *Field Bryology*, **96**, 10-13.

6. Bryology in the Highlands and Islands of Scotland

David G. Long and Gordon P. Rothero

Scotland's national bryophyte herbarium

The Royal Botanic Garden Edinburgh (RBGE) was founded in 1670[1]. From the time of Professor John Hope, Regius Keeper from 1761 to 1786[2], the great importance of the herbarium as a repository of dried plant specimens has been recognised in Scotland. Unfortunately, Hope's private herbarium has not survived. An important force behind the early development of the modern Edinburgh herbarium was the Botanical Society of Edinburgh[1] from its foundation in 1836, led by Professor Robert Graham (Regius Keeper from 1820 to 1845). Indeed, in only four years the specimens acquired by the Society had reached 150,000[3]. In those early years the focus was primarily on vascular plants but around 1845 the important cryptogamic herbarium of Robert Kaye Greville was united with the substantial herbarium of the University of Edinburgh, and transferred to RBGE in 1863. From that time on, collections from home and abroad, including cryptogams, steadily accumulated and grew into what effectively became Scotland's national herbarium.

But a herbarium is much more than just a collection of dried plants[4]. The specimens themselves, when carefully dried and stored, retain most of the features of the living plants, and in the case of bryophytes (mosses, liverworts, hornworts), soaking in water can quickly restore their natural habit and morphology, for study of their characters and for use in preparing taxonomic descriptions, identification keys, and illustrations. In the 18th century the data associated with specimens (locality, habitat, elevation, etc.) were often scanty or almost non-existent. In contrast, collectors now record with greater precision and detail, but, nevertheless, specimens from the early botanists are still very important in recording changes in plant distributions, working out itineraries of collectors, and helping to understand early taxonomic concepts. Modern collectors now use sophisticated tools in the field such as global positioning system (GPS) hand-sets to record precise locations, and collect plant material in silica gel for

DNA extraction for molecular research, but the basic method of herbarium vouchering has changed little in over two centuries.

Since 1863 many important public and private bryophyte herbaria have been added to the national collection which now totals several hundred thousand specimens. Important recent acquisitions include the bryophyte herbaria from the University of Lancaster and non-British specimens from the University of Glasgow, and the private herbaria of important bryologists such as H.H. Birks and H.J.B. Birks, M.F.V. Corley, A.C. Crundwell, U.K. Duncan, E.W. Jones, A.G. Kenneth, J.A. Paton, D.A. Ratcliffe, C.C. Townsend, and E.V. Watson, to add to the many historic collections accumulated since Greville's time, as well as large numbers of specimens collected by RBGE bryologists. Scottish material is extremely well represented in the collection, from the first dated specimens collected by Archibald Menzies in 1778 until the present day, as are specimens from many other parts of the world, particularly Europe, the Middle East, and eastern Asia. The herbarium is rich in historic 'type specimens', many of these acquired by Menzies, George Walker Arnott, and Greville from leading European bryologists, for example Palisot Beauvois, Nees von Esenbeck, J.C. Schleicher, W.J. Hooker, and others. These types are vitally important for taxonomic research – they are the voucher specimens for new bryophyte names.

The 18th century - the pioneers

Without voucher specimens, it is often difficult to interpret early literature reports of bryophytes but a combination of the two, when possible, gives a highly informative history of bryological exploration of the Highlands and Islands. In the 18th century, only a few botanists, notably Johannes Jacobus Dillenius (1684-1747) with his *Historia Muscorum*[5], had opened the eyes of British botanists to cryptogams, but the bryophytes of the Highlands and Islands of Scotland were completely unknown. During the period known as the 'Scottish Enlightenment', Professor John Hope (1725-1786) emerged in Edinburgh as the leading researcher and first teacher of botany in Scotland[2]. He corresponded with Linnaeus and several of his students became pioneers of botanical exploration in Scotland and overseas[1]. One of these, James Robertson (died 1796) was a gardener in Hope's Royal Botanic Garden and became the first naturalist to conduct a botanical and zoological survey in the Scottish Islands, between 1767 and 1771. Robertson listed 42 relatively common species of bryophytes from Bute, Arran, Mull, Skye, Orkney, Shetland, and the Long Island (Lewis and Harris) as well as 18 from Ben More [?Assynt] and Ben Hope[6,7]. Amongst the mosses he listed were *Climacium dendroides*, *Fontinalis antipyretica*, *Homalothecium sericeum*, and *Rhizomnium punctatum*. Most remarkable is his mention of *Lunularia cruciata*, from Bute and Arran. According to Macvicar[8] this did not arrive in Scotland until around 1900 as an accidental introduction from the south, growing almost exclusively in gardens and near habitations. This puts its date of introduction into Scotland back by over a century, though it was recorded in Essex by John Ray in 1686[9]. However, none of Robertson's reports were of montane or Atlantic bryophytes, and none of his specimens has survived.

Not until the pioneering tour of the English cleric John Lightfoot and Welsh zoologist Thomas Pennant in 1772[10] did the first of the more esoteric bryophytes of the

Scottish Highlands and Islands become known to the world. In their remarkable four-month journey by boat and on horseback they explored the Inner Hebrides, Ben Lomond, Kintyre, Torridon, Knoydart, Loch Tay (but not Ben Lawers), Blair Atholl, Perth, and lowland Angus. Lightfoot reported his finds in his *Flora Scotica*[11], the first exclusively Scottish flora[1]. His discoveries included *Targionia hypophylla* 'on the Tarbet of Cantire', *Anthelia julacea* on Goat Fell on Arran, and *Pleurozia purpurea*[12] (Fig. 7.7) probably from Skye or Torridon. Lightfoot also collected *Gymnomitrion corallioides*, *G. crenulatum*, and *G. obtusum*, but not *G. concinnatum* which he later described, probably based on material of *G. crenulatum*[13]. Lightfoot's herbarium survives at Kew, but few specimens are accurately labelled, and they still await careful study.

On their return south, Lightfoot and Pennant called on the nurseryman James Dickson in Kelso[10]. Dickson (1738-1822) was the most important 18th century bryological explorer of the Highlands, adding species such as *Blasia pusilla* from Loch Tay, *Oligotrichum hercynicum* from Ben Nevis, and *Tetraplodon angustatus* by 'Loch Awen' [Loch Avon]. His Highland tours took place from 1785 up to 1789, in which year he was accompanied by his second wife's brother, the explorer Mungo Park from Selkirk[14,15]. In his *Plantarum Cryptogamicarum Britanniae*[16] he described several new Atlantic and montane species from Scotland such as *Plagiochila spinulosa*, *Tayloria lingulata*, and *Zygodon conoideus*, and others of his pre-1801 moss names were validated by Hedwig[17] such as *Conostomum tetragonum*, *Hygrohypnum molle*, *Isopterygiopsis pulchella*, and *Plagiobryum zieri*. The last commemorated John Zier, who apparently wrote many of Dickson's descriptions, but was unacknowledged[14]. Unfortunately, Dickson was careless with his specimen data and erroneously reported *Tayloria froelichiana* and *Herbertus aduncus* from Scotland, where his specimens were later thought to have originated from overseas. Dickson was the first to issue a *'Hortus Siccus'*—a collection of dried specimens, including Scottish bryophytes, with printed labels[18,19,20]. As with Lightfoot, Dickson's specimens require more study, but the labels are mostly uninformative. More meticulous in his collecting and record-keeping was another of John Hope's students, Archibald Menzies (1754-1842), who in 1778 made a tour of the Highlands, discovering *Andreaea alpina* and *Herbertus hutchinsiae* (Fig. 7.8) on Ben Lomond, *Anthelia julacea* and *Grimmia ramondii* on Ben Nevis, and *Porella arboris-vitae* (Fig. 6.1) on the north side of Loch Ness. Menzies was generous with his specimens, sharing the *Herbertus* and *Porella*, and probably many others, with Dickson and other contemporaries.

George Don (1764-1814), a native of Angus, was the first botanist to reveal the riches of the Cairngorm and Clova mountains[1,21,22], where he found many species new to Scotland from 1795 onwards, such as the montane mosses *Hygrohypnum duriusculum*, *Oncophorus virens*, *Saelania glaucescens*, and *Splachnum vasculosum* (Fig. 5.7) in the Clova mountains, *Oedipodium griffithianum* in Glen Callater, *Kiaeria blyttii* on Lochnagar, *Ptilium crista-castrensis* near Braemar, and perhaps most significantly, the first of the large oceanic-montane or Northern Atlantic[23,24] liverworts in the Cairngorms, *Anastrophyllum donnianum* (Fig. 4.14) and *Scapania ornithopodioides* (Fig. 4.15). Don also issued exsiccatae of specimens of Scottish bryophytes[25,26] and some of his finds were new to science and described by James Edward Smith and William Jackson Hooker.

Figure 6.1. Specimen of the liverwort *Porella arboris-vitae* collected from near Loch Ness in 1778 by Archibald Menzies and housed in the RGBE herbarium.

The 19ᵗʰ century – Hooker to Dixon and Macvicar

The appointment of W.J. Hooker (1785-1865) as Professor of Botany in Glasgow in 1820 was a momentous event for cryptogamic botany in Scotland. Even before this date, as early as 1807 he was exploring the Highlands with his father-in-law Dawson Turner, when they discovered *Neckera pumila* at Inverary. The following year, with his friend William Borrer, Hooker discovered *Andreaea nivalis*, *Kiaeria glacialis*, *Polytrichastrum sexangulare* (Fig. 6.2), and *Pleurocladula albescens* on Ben Nevis, *Andreaea megistospora* at Ballachulish (but not described until 1987), *Herbertus stramineus* (Fig. 4.14) on Ben Lawers, *Herzogiella striatella* on Ben Loyal, and *Tetralophozia setiformis* on Cairngorm. He superbly described and illustrated new Scottish liverworts such as *Anastrophyllum donnianum* (Fig. 4.14) (discovered by George Don) and *Anastrepta orcadensis* (which he discovered in 1808 on Ward Hill, Orkney) in his *British Jungermanniae*[27]. His botanical lectures in Glasgow received wide acclaim, "never was such a lecturer known at Glasgow University"[28] and his *Flora Scotica*[29], including cryptogams, was published for his devoted students.

Until his departure to Kew in 1841, Hooker and his Scottish contemporaries George Walker Arnott (1799-1868) and Robert Kaye Greville (1794-1866), formed a truly formidable cryptogamic team, based in Glasgow and Edinburgh, exploring together many parts of the Highlands between 1823 and 1830, along with Hooker's students and botanists from overseas. One of their field encampments by Loch Lomond was illustrated by Greville[30]. Already classic localities such as Ben Lomond, Ben Nevis, and

Figure 6.2. The snow-bed moss *Polytrichastrum sexangulare* on Ben MacDui, Cairngorms, 2007.
Photo: David Long

Clova were re-visited but they were the first bryologists to explore thoroughly the Breadalbane hills and other places such as Glen Tilt, Ben Vorlich by Loch Lomond, and other mountains as far north as Sutherland. Many of their specimens survive in herbaria and from these and various publications their activities can be envisaged. On the Lawers range they made numerous new finds, for example *Anomodon longifolius*, *Blindia caespiticia*, *Brachytheciastrum trachypodium*, *Brachythecium cirrosum*, *Campylophyllum halleri*, *Heterocladium dimorphum*, *Hygrohypnum smithii* (Fig. 6.3), *Plagiobryum demissum*, *Pseudoleskea incurvata*, *P. patens*, and *Rhytidium rugosum* (Fig. 4.13), all new to Scotland and many new to Britain. In Glen Tilt they discovered *Dicranella grevilleana* in 1823 and in Glen Clova *Cynodontium strumiferum*. Greville was the first to explore the metalliferous outcrops in Glen Callater, discovering in 1830 the 'copper mosses' *Grimmia atrata* and *Mielichhoferia elongata*. Significantly, they all but ignored the west coast woodlands and islands, though Greville found a few Atlantic species new to Scotland, such as *Bazzania tricrenata* on Ben Lomond in 1820, *Dicranum scottianum* (Fig. 7.9) by Loch Lomond, *Dicranodontium uncinatum* on Ben Voirlich and, on the Sutherland mountains in 1824 and 1840, *Plagiochila carringtonii* (Fig. 4.15) and *Mastigophora woodsii* (Fig. 7.7). Some of these were beautifully illustrated by Greville in his *Scottish Cryptogamic Flora*[31], which included finds made by another contemporary, Thomas Drummond (c. 1793-1835), notably *Ulota drummondii*. Between 1823 and 1828 Drummond also discovered, in his native Angus, *Grimmia funalis*, *G. torquata*, *G. unicolor*, *Stegonia latifolia*, *Timmia austriaca*, and *Ulota coarctata*. He also issued two volumes of exsiccatae, under the title *Musci Scotici*[20,32].

With a few notable exceptions, much of the bryological focus prior to 1840 had been on mosses, particularly those of the mountains. The oakwoods with their humid ravines on the western seaboard had been almost completely neglected, with the

Figure 6.3. The moss *Hygrohypnum smithii* collected on Ben Challum in 1824 by Robert Kaye Greville, with his herbarium sketch, housed in the RGBE herbarium.

remarkable result that many of Scotland's Atlantic liverworts[24] were first discovered in Ireland rather than Scotland. These had been described and illustrated by Hooker[27] from Irish collections made by Ellen Hutchins (1785-1815) and others, notably *Adelanthus decipiens* (Fig. 7.6), *Colura calyptrifolia* (Fig. 4.6), *Jubula hutchinsiae* (Fig. 7.6), *Leptoscyphus cuneifolius*, *Mastigophora woodsii* (Fig. 7.7), *Moerckia hibernica*, and *Mylia taylorii*. This emphasis on mosses was set to gradually change over the next sixty years until the arrival of Symers Macvicar, when the focus spectacularly jumped to liverworts. Indeed, no fewer than forty-two different bryologists made impor-

tant new records between 1835 and 1900 from many parts of the Highlands and Islands. Geographically, however, the focus did not change much, with Perth and Angus attracting the greatest attention, particularly from two of the leading bryologists of the period.

The first was John Fergusson (1834-1907), a clergyman in Angus who followed in Drummond's footsteps but took more interest in liverworts, with notable discoveries such as *Anthelia juratzkana*, *Cephalozia pleniceps*, *Hygrobiella laxifolia*, *Jamesoniella autumnalis*, *Leiocolea bantriensis*, *Marsupella funckii*, and *M. sprucei*, all in Angus. However, he did add a few mosses, particularly *Anomodon attenuatus* in 1867 in the Den of Airlie, where it survives to the present day, and *Grimmia elatior* and *G. elongata* in Glen Clova in 1868. The second, James Stirton (1833-1917) was a prominent Glasgow physician, with a highly individual approach to his hobbies of mountaineering and moss taxonomy, and as pointed out by Porley and Hodgetts[33] he was perhaps the first to show concerns for bryophyte conservation. He had a critical taxonomic eye and narrow species concept, resulting in the description of many new taxa which have since sunk into synonymy. A few, such as *Bryoerythrophyllum ferruginascens* discovered on Orkney in 1887, and *Tortella limosella* from Arisaig in 1906 have been maintained although the latter is considered extinct. Stirton visted Ben Lawers many times, adding *Ctenidium procerrimum*, *Paraleucobryum longifolium*, *Pseudoleskeella nervosa*, and *Timmia norvegica* to the Scottish flora.

Between 1840 and 1900 other Scottish bryologists pushed the exploration of mountain bryophytes into new and more remote regions, particularly Alexander Croall (1809-1885) from Stirling, William Gardiner (1808-1852) from Dundee, and John Sim (1824-1901) from Aberdeen. Croall was the first to discover *Andreaea frigida*, on Ben MacDhui in 1835. Gardiner's many finds included *Philonotis seriata* on Beinn a'Bhuird in 1844, and Sim found *Molendoa warburgii* near Banchory in 1871 (but not described until

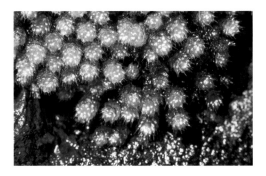

Figure 6.4. Two large and distinctive mosses that mainly occur in north-west Scotland, Skye, and the Outer Hebrides. *Myurium hochstetteri*, Isle of Skye, 1966 (*left*), and *Campylopus shawii*, Harris, 1972 (*right*). Photos: John Birks

1977) and *Marsupella adusta* and *M. sparsifolia* on Lochnagar. For the first time, the farthest parts of the Hebrides were explored for bryophytes. The most spectacular find, perhaps, was of the subtropical moss *Myurium hochstetteri* (Fig. 6.4) on North Uist by Rev. Colin Smith in 1851, and on the same island *Campylopus shawii* (Fig. 6.4) by John Shaw (1837-1890) in 1866 and long thought to be an endemic. Another rare *Campylopus*, *C. setifolius* (Fig. 4.15), was first detected in 1863 by George Edward Hunt (c. 1841-1873) on Skye. Peter Ewing, (1849-1913), encouraged by James Stirton in Glasgow, was rewarded with two new records on Mull in 1887: *Drepanolejeunea hamatifolia* (Fig. 4.6) and *Plagiochila bifaria*. Other rare species were found during this period on western mountains – *Paraleptodontium recurvifolium* (Fig. 4.15) on the western Ben Vorlich by A. McKinlay in 1863, *Marsupella boeckii* on Ben Nevis in 1875 by John Whitehead, and *Scapania nimbosa* (Fig. 4.14) on Ben Laoigh by James Murray in 1895. Close to sea level, two Atlantic liverworts were added, *Jubula hutchinsiae* (Fig. 7.6) in a cave near Dunoon in 1839 by G.J. Lyon, and *Harpalejeunea molleri* (Fig. 7.10) by Loch Maree in 1889 by Benjamin Carrington.

At the end of the 19th century, two bryological 'giants' came on the Scottish scene, Hugh Neville Dixon (1861-1944), the foremost British moss taxonomist of the day, and Symers Macdonald Macvicar (1857-1932), the same for liverworts. Both wrote the standard floras for their groups which served bryologists at home and abroad for almost a century, a testament to their outstanding quality. Both also made major contributions to bryological exploration. Dixon visited Scotland in 1893, 1898, and 1899, adding mosses such as *Didymodon icmadophilus*, *Mnium lycopodioides*, and *Plagiomnium medium* on Ben Lawers and *Bryum dixonii* and *B. riparium* on Ben Narnain in Argyll. He also reached the far north where *Conardia compacta* was detected in Smoo Cave at Durness and *Schistidium robustum* was found at Inchnadamph.

The contribution of Symers Macdonald Macvicar to the discovery of Scotland's Atlantic liverwort flora was enormous. After serving briefly as a doctor, he married and settled on Eilean Shona in Moidart and for the rest of his life made the study of liverworts his main pursuit. The previous neglect of the native western woodlands and their humid ravines, and his ideal location in the oceanic west, meant that he could advance greatly knowledge of the tiny leafy liverworts so characteristic of those habitats[24]. Between 1898 and 1904 he added no fewer than 16 new Atlantic liverworts to the Scottish flora, several of these new to Britain such as *Geocalyx graveolens* which he found on the Plock of Kyle in 1902. As well as discovering species such as *Acrobolbus wilsonii* (Fig. 4.30), *Adelanthus decipiens* (Fig. 7.6), *Lejeunea mandonii*, *Leptoscyphus cuneifolius*, *Radula carringtonii* (Fig. 4.30), and *Sphenolobopsis pearsonii* around his home, he added others on the Lawers range such as *Barbilophozia quadriloba*, *Scapania calcicola*, and *S. degenii*. Another major contribution he made was checking and reviewing almost all the liverwort records made until then in Scotland, and summarizing these in his *Distribution of Hepaticae in Scotland*[8].

The 20th Century

In 1896 Dixon and Macvicar were two of the founding members of the Moss Exchange Club[34] that developed in 1923 into the British Bryological Society (BBS)[35]. A few early BBS members, C.H. Binstead, E. Cleminshaw, J.B. Duncan, H.H. Knight, and W.E. Nicholson made their own visits to Scotland from the south, adding species such as *Anastrophyllum alpinum* in Sutherland, *Plagiothecium piliferum* on Ben Lawers, and *Bazzania pearsonii* (Fig. 4.14) in Glen Nevis. In 1902 Binstead made the remarkable discovery of *Pseudocalliergon turgescens* on Ben Lawers, surprisingly missed by the numerous earlier visitors and refound there by John Birks and John Dransfield in 1969[36].

After its founding in 1923, the BBS became the driving force behind bryological exploration throughout the British Isles. The first BBS meeting in the Scottish Highlands was in 1929, held at Killin and Crianlarich, attracting no less than forty participants[37], and relocating many of the Ben Lawers rarities. Ten years later they met in Fort William and since then Scottish meetings have been held at increasingly frequent intervals, becoming less focussed on rarities but more on improving the coverage of general bryological recording and mapping. It was during the early years of this new era that E.C. ('Ted') Wallace (1909-1986) from London began his regular summer visits to Scotland, often exploring remote and little known sites. His many significant records contributed greatly to a better understanding of the distribution of many more uncommon species and also some new plants for Scotland and the British Isles. Out west in 1950 on the shores of Loch Moidart he discovered *Plagiochila atlantica* (Fig. 6.5) (then new to science but now united with the South American *P. heterophylla*) and at Kinlochourn in 1971 he found *Campylopus subporodictyon*, one of only a few mosses disjunct with the Sino-Himalaya. In the mountains, Ted found *Hygrohypnum polare*, an arctic-montane species, on the shore of a lochan on Beinn Dearg in

Figure 6.5. The Atlantic liverwort *Plagiochila heterophylla* (*P. atlantica*), Argyll, 1976, discovered by Ted Wallace in Scotland in 1950. Photo: John Birks

1952, but it took another 20 years before it was identified and published as a new addition to the Scottish mountain flora. Up in the hills on the rather dull ground of Sgurr nan Conbhairean he collected a *Pohlia* in 1968 which turned out to be *P. crudoides*, a cryptic boreal species yet to be seen again in Scotland, but few if any bryologists visit seemingly dull hills like this. His record of *Dicranum elongatum* from Creag an Dail Bheag in 1954 is one of the last for that species which now seems to have been lost from the Scottish flora. His visits extended well into the 1970s, one of his last discoveries being the Southern Hemisphere liverwort *Lophocolea bispinosa* found on Colonsay in 1978.

This was also the era of Derek Ratcliffe[38], who, during extensive vegetational survey work for what was to become *Plant Communities of the Scottish Highlands*[39] made bryophyte records from many areas in the Highlands which had had few botanical visitors. In 1957 these surveys first revealed the ecology and distribution of *Sphagnum lindbergii* (Fig. 6.6) on several eastern hills[40]. The same year he was the first to discover the rich bryophyte flora on Geal-charn in the Ben Alder Forest which included a number of the Ben Lawers rarities such as *Blindia caespiticia* and *Campylophyllum halleri*[38,41]. The following year, on Beinn Eighe, he collected material of a distinctive *Herbertus*, later described as *H. borealis* (Figs. 6.7 & 7.11) by Crundwell[42] and now shown to be endemic to Scotland[43]. As part of the same survey, Ratcliffe studied the bryoflora of the remote

Figure 6.6. The moss *Sphagnum lindbergii* on Ben Wyvis, Easter Ross, 2010. Photo: David Long

Figure 6.7. The liverwort *Herbertus borealis*, in its original British site in the Beinn Eighe National Nature Reserve, Wester Ross, 1966, discovered by Derek Ratcliffe in 1959. Photo: John Birks

Figure 6.8. Southern peninsula of Hirta, St Kilda, 2010, explored for bryophytes by Derek Ratcliffe in 1959. Photo: David Long

Figure 6.9. The Southern Atlantic liverwort *Fossombronia angulosa* on Hirta, St Kilda, 2010. Photo: David Long

Figure 6.10. The Arctic moss *Sanionia orthothecioides* on Hirta, St Kilda, 2010. Photo: David Long

but bryologically rich St Kilda (Outer Hebrides) in 1959[38] (Fig. 6.8) and made two remarkable but contrasting discoveries – the Southern Atlantic liverwort *Fossombronia angulosa* (Figs. 6.9 & 7.5) new to Scotland, and an Arctic moss *Sanionia orthothecioides* (Fig. 6.10), new to the British Isles but not identified until 1990[44,45]. Closer to the mainland, another major discovery by Derek was the rich Southern Atlantic flora of Jura, turning up the first Scottish sites for *Cyclodictyon laetevirens* (Fig. 7.5) and *Dumortiera hirsuta* (Fig. 4.4)[24,38].

Derek Ratcliffe's interest in the Atlantic flora of Britain and Ireland produced not only a large number of species records[24], improving our knowledge of the distribution of the plants, but also a more refined understanding of their biogeography and ecology through his seminal paper *An ecological account of Atlantic bryophytes in the British Isles*[23], published in 1968[24]. In that same year came yet another remarkable find, again in the genus *Herbertus*, on

Figure 6.11. The liverwort *Herbertus norenus*, in its original British site on Ronas Hill, Shetland, 2009, discovered by Derek Ratcliffe in 1968. Photo: David Long

Ronas Hill in Shetland from where his collection lay unrecognised for 44 years until it was described as a second new species *H. norenus* (Fig. 6.11)[43]. In the latter half of the 1960s and in the 1970s John and Hilary Birks continued Ratcliffe's search for Atlantic species such as *Lejeunea mandonii*, *L. eckloniana*, *Radula carringtonii* (Fig. 4.30), and *R. voluta* (Fig. 4.4) in new sites, and also made important records of montane calcicole species in the North-West Highlands and Skye and from the Ben Lawers area including the first UK record of *Schistidium agassizii* in 1966[46]. They published a bryophyte flora of the Isle of Skye[47], an area rich in Atlantic species. During this same period Martin Corley spent a lot of time in the west of Argyll improving the coverage of this area's excellent Atlantic flora and making many notable discoveries, including a new site for *Jamesoniella undulifolia* and the first find of *Grimmia tergestina* for the British Isles in 1965. His work extended to the islands of the Inner Hebrides producing a paper on the ecology and phytogeography of their rich bryophyte flora[48].

From the 1970s onwards, encouraged by the success of the Botanical Society of the British Isles (now the Botanical Society of Britain and Ireland) vascular plant atlas, the British Bryological Society's Atlas project[24] was getting underway and some effort was made to visit areas of Scotland with few records, although most visits on Society meetings were still to areas thought to have a good flora. The BBS effort was supplemented in the 1980s by the Cryptogamic section of the then Botanical Society of Edinburgh which made a series of 'bothy trips' in remote areas notably to Letterewe Forest and to Seana Bhraigh, places that are not possible to explore without staying overnight in a bothy or bivouac[38]. These trips were notable for the exploration of little visited areas and the number of interesting lichen and bryophyte records as well as for the consumption of malt whisky.

Survey and Monitoring

Apart from Derek Ratcliffe's unrivalled field knowledge of Scottish sites important for conservation and the use he made of it in *A Nature Conservation Review*[49], lower plants were fairly low on the radar in the then Nature Conservancy Council (NCC), but, thanks to the enthusiasm of Peter Pitkin, in the summers of 1989 and 1990, Gordon Rothero was employed to survey the bryophytes of montane areas of late snow-lie[50-52]. This survey confirmed the pre-eminence of the Cairngorms (Fig. 6.12) and the Ben Nevis area for chionophilous bryophytes (Fig. 6.2) and also showed that there were important sites elsewhere, particularly on Ben Alder and the Aonachs, east of Ben Nevis. Accompanying Gordon Rothero on the trek to the Garbh Choire snowbeds on Braeriach in 1989, David Long found a very distinctive liverwort by the Pools of Dee and this proved to be *Marsupella arctica*, a species which now has two sites in the Cairngorms, the only other European sites being on Svalbard and a recent find in Norway. The same year, while descending into the Northern Corries, Gordon Rothero found a nondescript pleurocarpous moss growing on the wet granite which was later identified by Martin Corley as *Hygrohypnum styriacum*, another species that is rare in Europe.

This was the start of the current era of 'Bryological Contract Surveys' in Scotland, at last a formal recognition of the global importance of the bryophytes of Scotland's oceanic woodlands and mountains. In addition to Gordon Rothero's snow-bed surveys, Ben and Alison Averis began their remarkable survey of Scottish woodlands, funded by NCC, again through Peter Pitkin. Building on the work by Derek Ratcliffe, this survey concentrated on Atlantic broadleaf woodlands in the west of Scotland, and finally

Figure 6.12. The mountains around Loch Avon, Cairngorms, 2007, home of Northern Atlantic liverworts and snow beds with arctic bryophyte communities. Photo: David Long

reached a tally of over 400 woodlands, giving a much clearer idea of the distribution of our important Atlantic flora[24]. This level of coverage also means that woodlands can be compared with each other to give an idea of where the richest sites are and also facilitate community analysis. This very large data source has been invaluable in revealing both the distribution of the core areas of woodland and also in establishing which species are genuinely rare. Research by Alison Averis on Scotland's oceanic-montane liverwort heath (Figs. 6.13, 7.11 & 7.12) greatly increased knowledge of this enigmatic and spectacular bryophyte community[24], and led to another remarkable addition to the British Flora, of *Adelanthus lindenbergianus* (Fig. 4.14) on Islay in 1990, and more recently extended to Jura by Gordon Rothero. This work on this community has now been continued by Maren Flagmeier at the University of Aberdeen[53].

The increase of paid survey work has been the source of more detailed information on the status of some of our rare bryophytes but has also revealed a trickle of species new to Britain. Bryologists are often the target of sums of money left in the conservation agency coffers at the end of the financial year as "bryophytes can be surveyed at any time of the year". Such a winter survey near Braemar led to the discovery of *Athalamia hyalina*[54], a thalloid liverwort which becomes necrotic and almost invisible later in the year, presumably the reason it had been overlooked during a BBS summer visit in 1964. As part of the process of site condition monitoring (SCM), a six-year programme of assessment of the state of all notified features of interest on designated sites funded by Scottish Natural Heritage, a number of interesting records have been made. While monitoring the condition of the vascular plant interest on the Ben Hope Site of Special Scientific Interest (SSSI) in the far north, Gordon Rothero allowed his concentration on

Figure 6.13. Northern Atlantic liverworts *Bazzania pearsonii* and *Pleurozia purpurea* forming a 'mixed hepatic mat' on Twelve Bens, Connemara, 2004. Photo: David Long

vascular plants to stray far enough to record a third British site for *Mielichhoferia elongata* and to find a small population of *Arctoa anderssonii*, adding another arctic species to the British flora. More recently, similar SCM work on bryophytes has produced two records of *Dicranum spadiceum*, new to Britain, from Creag an Dail Bheag in the Cairngorms and from Glen Callater[55]. Survey work connected with the development of small-scale hydro schemes has very recently led to the remarkable discovery of the Southern Atlantic *Radula holtii* in Scotland by Nick Hodgetts in 2012, a species previously known from south-west Ireland and west Mayo.

Taxonomic research on Scottish bryophytes

As exemplified by workers such as William Hooker and Symers Macvicar to Alan Crundwell and Jean Paton, diligent fieldwork combined with critical herbarium research has repeatedly brought about significant advances in knowledge of our bryophyte flora. In both Glasgow and Edinburgh the Scottish tradition of taxonomic research, founded by Hooker, Arnott, and Greville, was rekindled in 1949 when Alan Crundwell, one of the leading bryophyte taxonomists of his day, took up a lectureship at the University of Glasgow where he remained until 1983. Crundwell devoted his research to taxonomically difficult groups such as *Bryum*, *Cynodontium*, *Pohlia*, and *Weissia*[56], and described the above-mentioned liverwort *Herbertus borealis* (Figs. 6.7 & 7.11) from collections by Derek Ratcliffe in 1958[42], as well as the endemic *Pohlia scotica* from Argyll. In Edinburgh, collaboration with Barbara Murray from Alaska led to a milestone revision of *Andreaea* which added several species new to Britain[57], and diligent taxonomic study revealed yet another Breadalbane rarity, *Bryoerythrophyllum caledonicum* described by David Long[58].

Although working far from Scotland in Cornwall, Jean Paton's work for *The Liverwort Flora of the British Isles*[59] dramatically increased our knowledge of the taxonomy, ecology, and distribution of Scottish liverworts. In the 1960s and 1970s her numerous trips to Scotland made a major contribution to our knowledge of the more cryptic liverworts in the Highlands, and gave her the material for the thorough taxonomic revision which is the hallmark of her internationally-renowned *Flora*. Her discoveries and thorough reporting of species such as *Fossombronia fimbriata*, *Jungermannia borealis*, *Liochlaena lanceolata*, and *Scapania praetervisa* were a product of her meticulous work in the field, often in collaboration with other bryologists including Ursula Duncan and Jeff Duckett, and her subsequent detailed work at the microscope.

More recently, RBGE has become one of the leading centres for molecular research on bryophytes and amongst the projects under way is the application of the technique known as 'DNA Barcoding' to selected British liverworts and mosses[60]. This is a technique which can be used to help to resolve taxonomic problems in 'difficult' groups – it adds a whole suite of molecular characters to more traditional morphological features of the plants. Results from its application to a number of problem groups has shown that in some cases it supports the traditional taxonomic *status quo*, and in others it has revealed the presence of previously undetected species.

Two ground-breaking studies have succeeded in resolving taxonomic problems in two important Scottish liverwort genera – *Anastrophyllum* (Fig. 6.14) and *Herbertus*. The traditional concept of *Anastrophyllum joergensenii* was shown to encompass two genetically and morphologically distinct species, both with disjunct global distributions

Figure 6.14. The RBGE *Anastrophyllum* survey on Foinaven, West Sutherland in 2004. Photo: David Long

between NW Europe and Asia[61]. Similarly, in the genus *Herbertus*, study of the four 'accepted' European members of the genus, showed that in fact five distinct species are involved, leading to the description of *H. norenus* (Fig. 6.11) from western Norway and Shetland[43]. This encouraging start to the molecular era will undoubtedly lead to advances in taxonomy of other troublesome genera such as *Bryum* and *Dicranum*.

Conservation and the future

So where does this latest surge in activity leave Scotland's magnificent bryophyte flora and what of its future? There are no more rich, unexplored areas to be found, no new Ben Alders, St Kildas, Skyes, or Juras but there are still large areas in the hills that have had only scant attention and, as described above, there is still a trickle of new species, but mostly from well-known sites. However, even the richest sites still receive very few visits from bryologists and this is unlikely to change. In terms of species protection, we now know much more about the extent and abundance of our more interesting species and this is at least in part due to the addition of bryophyte species to Schedule 8 of the *Wildlife and Countryside Act* and to the *Biodiversity Action Plan* process[1]. The effective protection provided was limited but at least the process raised the profile of lower plants and stimulated the gathering of some basic data so that some degree of surveillance became possible if budgets allowed.

Habitat protection is still the most important single measure to safeguard Scotland's internationally important bryophyte flora and this is mostly provided through the Site of Special Scientific Interest (SSSI) system. There are some 70 SSSIs in Scotland where bryophytes are a 'notified feature', mostly for a 'bryophyte assemblage' but a few are notified for species protected by European legislation such as *Buxbaumia viridis*, *Petalophyllum ralfsii*, and *Hamatocaulis vernicosus*. This is important because only those sites with bryophytes as a notified feature will be considered for Site Condition Monitoring for that feature, but increasingly, budgets will only allow monitoring of a small selection of these sites in each six-year cycle of monitoring. There should be more sites notified for their bryophytes but the respectable list that we have is due in no small part to the magnificent efforts of Derek Ratcliffe and his *A Nature Conservation Review*[49].

There are still management practices which threaten bryophyte communities, even on SSSIs. The internationally important Scottish liverwort heath (Figs. 6.13 & 7.12) first described by McVean and Ratcliffe[39] has a patchy distribution and is absent from many seemingly suitable sites[62]. There is a strong case[23,62] to be made for the proposition that this distribution is due to muirburn (Fig. 6.15), as practised in the north and west of Scotland, where burns are often large and uncontrolled. The liverwort heath grows on thin organic soils where there is little buffering from the heat and the plants are destroyed (Figs. 6.13, 7.11 & 7.12). None of the species produces sporophytes in Scotland and they have limited means of vegetative spread, and re-colonisation from the fragmented metapopulation will be slow or may not happen.

Inevitably, one source of concern for bryophyte communities is climate change. It is not easy to predict the general response of bryophytes to changes in weather patterns

Figure 6.15. The widespread practice of muirburn, highly destructive to Northern Atlantic liverwort-rich heaths, Wicklow Mountains, Ireland, 2010. Photo: Gordon Rothero

Figure 6.16. Gordon Rothero setting up permanent bryophyte quadrats on Ben MacDui, Cairngorms to monitor effects of future climate change on snow-bed vegetation, 2007. Photo: David Long

but at least one important bryophyte community is clearly under threat. Observations over the last 30 years indicate that snow accumulation and persistence in the Scottish mountains is decreasing; long-lasting snow patches are smaller and are melting away earlier. A re-survey in 2007 (Fig. 6.16) of some of the snow-bed areas visited by Gordon Rothero in 1989[50-52] indicated that, although the snow-bed bryophyte communities showed only small changes in floristics, site photographs suggested a loss of area covered by bryophyte-dominated ground on at least some sites on the Cairngorm plateau[63]. Permanent transects have been set up across the snow-bed vegetation on a number of sites so that future changes can be monitored.

Warmer and wetter weather as a result of climate change may benefit the Atlantic bryophyte flora but it may also exacerbate the threat presented by invasive Rhododendron (Fig. 6.17). In some woodlands and ravines, Rhododendron already forms a complete understorey and the low light levels and persistent litter eventually reduce the bryophyte flora to a few species tolerant of deep shade. Once Rhododendron has become established and starts to engulf rocks and crags, stands of important Atlantic species such as *Plagiochila heterophylla* (Fig. 6.5) and *Adelanthus decipiens* (Fig. 7.6) can quickly disappear[23]. Rhododendron can be defeated but it is very expensive, particularly where crags and ravines require rope access, and the problem is increasing exponentially. The threat posed by Rhododendron is generally accepted now and grants are available for its eradication but it is a problem which needs to be tackled on a regional scale rather than by piecemeal projects, so just treating SSSIs is not sufficient. While not yet on the same scale, the spread of Beech (*Fagus sylvatica*) from policy woodland into

Figure 6.17. Invasive Rhododendron in an Atlantic Oakwood, Ardtilligan, Knapdale, 2007. Photo: Gordon Rothero

native Oak (*Quercus* spp.) woodland and especially into ravines poses some of the same threats of low light levels and copious and persistent leaf litter.

On a more cheerful note, a number of species listed as extinct in the floras have been refound. *Paraleucobryum longifolium* is a large, distinctive moss that a whole generation of bryologists 'lost sight of', and a renewed familiarity has meant that it has gone from presumed extinction to having at least 12 sites, including such well-bryologised areas as Ben Lawers and the Cairngorms. *Anomodon attenuatus* has a similar story; long thought to be lost from Scotland, all it really needed was for someone to go and look hard at one of its old sites on the River Isla to reinstate it. The single cushion of *Orthotrichum gymnostomum* found in Rothiemurchus in 1966 by John Dransfield[64] was long considered to be a casual occurrence, a short-lived and one-off colonisation from Scandinavia, but in 2003, targeted surveying of Aspen (*Populus tremula*) in the Cairngorms National Park area produced three more scattered populations, one of which, on the Muir of Dinnet National Nature Reserve, is very large.

There is less cheerful news of the one remaining population of *Bryum schleicheri* var. *latifolium* in the hills near Stirling. The spring containing the moss is being rapidly invaded by Sharp-flowered Rush (*Juncus acutiflorus*), much reducing the available habitat; the invader is being repelled by aggressive gardening at present, but this sort of conservation is not sustainable in the long term and this large and attractive moss is probably doomed. The stand of *Hygrohypnum styriacum* in the Northern Corries has disappeared and targeted searching has failed to find other patches but hope must remain that it is hanging on somewhere in the Cairngorms. *Plagiothecium piliferum* has proved elusive in its Lawers and Caenlochan sites since 1939, but tiny populations of other rare, montane species such as *Timmia austriaca* and *Hypnum revolutum* seem to be hanging on with little apparent change. However, no new sites have been found for many years.

References

(1)   Rae, D. (2015) Royal Botanic Garden Edinburgh (RBGE) and caring for Scotland's flora. In: *Nature's Conscience – The Life and Legacy of Derek Ratcliffe* (eds. D.B.A. Thompson, H.H. Birks & H.J.B. Birks). This volume, Chapter 9.

(2)   Noltie, H. (2011) *John Hope (1725-1786). Alan G. Morton's Memoir of a Scottish Botanist. A new and revised edition.* Royal Botanic Garden, Edinburgh.

(3)   Hedge, I.C. & Lamond, J.M. (1970) *Index of Collectors in the Edinburgh Herbarium.* HMSO, Edinburgh.

(4)   Bridson, D. & Forman, L. (1998) *The Herbarium Handbook* (3rd edition). Royal Botanic Gardens, Kew.

(5)   Dillenius, J.J. (1742) *Historia Muscorum* (1st edition). Theatro Sheldoniana, Oxford.

(6)   Dickson, J.H. (1985) Bryophytes, lichens and seaweeds of Bute 1768. *Transactions of the Buteshire Natural History Society,* **22**, 71-74.

(7)   Henderson, D.M. & Dickson, J.H. (1994) *A Naturalist in the Highlands. James Robertson. His life and travels in Scotland 1767-1771.* Scottish Academic Press, Edinburgh.

(8)   Macvicar, S.M. (1910) The distribution of Hepaticae in Scotland. *Transactions and Proceedings of the Botanical Society of Edinburgh,* **25**, 1-336.

(9)   Hill, M.O., Preston, C.D. & Smith, A.J.E. (1991) *Atlas of the Bryophytes of Britain and Ireland. Volume 1. Liverworts.* Harley Books, Colchester.

(10)   Bowden, J.K. (1989) *John Lightfoot. His Work and Travels.* Royal Botanic Gardens, Kew and Carnegie Mellon University, Pittsburgh.

(11)   Lightfoot. J. (1778) *Flora Scotica*. Two volumes. White, London.

(12)   Grolle, R., Long, D.G. & McNeill, J. (2005) Nomenclatural problems in *Pleurozia* (Pleuroziaceae): the lectotypification of *Pleurozia* Dumort., *Jungermannia sphagnoides* Schwägr., *Pleurozia sphagnoides* Dumort., *P. purpurea* Lindb., *Mnium jungermannia* L. and *Jungermannia undulata* L. (Hepaticae). *Taxon,* **54**, 503–508.

(13)   Long, D.G. (2004) (1608) Proposal to conserve the name *Jungermannia concinnata* (Hepaticae) with a conserved type. *Taxon,* **53**, 195.

(14)   Simmonds, A. (1943) The Founders. James Dickson (1738? - 1822). *Journal of the Royal Horticultural Society,* **68**, 66-72.

(15)   Coats, A.M. (1964) James Dickson and Mungo Park. *Gardeners Chronicle,* **156**, 229.

(16)   Dickson, J. (1785-1801) *Plantarum Cryptogamicarum Britanniae.* 4 Fascicles. London.

(17)   Hedwig, J. (1801) *Species Muscorum Frondosorum*. Leipzig.

(18)   Dickson, J. (1789-1791) *A Collection of Dried Plants, named on the authority of the Linnean herbarium and other original collections*. Fascicles I-IV, numbers 1-100. London.

(19)   Dickson, J. (1793-1802) *Hortus Siccus Britannicus, being a collection of dried British plants, named on the authority of the Linnean herbarium and other original collections*. Fascicles I-XIX, 475 numbers. London.

(20)   Sayre, G. (1971) Cryptogamae Exsiccatae. An annotated bibliography of published exsiccatae of Algae, Lichenes, Hepaticae, and Musci. Introduction, IV. Bryophyta. *Memoirs of the New York Botanical Garden*, **19**, 175-276.

(21)   Duncan, U.K. (1966) A bryophyte flora of Angus. *Transactions of the British Bryological Society*, **5**, 1-82.

(22)   Roger, J.G. (1986) George Don, 1764-1814. *Scottish Naturalist*, **1986**, 97-108.

(23)   Ratcliffe, D.A. (1968) An ecological account of Atlantic bryophytes in the British Isles. *New Phytologist*, **67**, 365-439.

(24)   Preston, C.D. (2015) Derek Ratcliffe and the Atlantic bryophytes of Britain and Ireland. In: *Nature's Conscience – The Life and Legacy of Derek Ratcliffe* (eds. D.B.A. Thompson, H.H. Birks & H.J.B. Birks). This volume, Chapter 7.

(25)   Don, G. (1804-1812) *Herbarium Britannicum, consisting of fasciculi of dried British plants, with their appropriate names and particular habits annexed*. Fascicles I-IX, number 1-225. Neill, Johnstone, Edinburgh.

(26)   Sayre, G. (1969) Cryptogamae Exsiccatae. An annotated bibliography of published exsiccatae of Algae, Lichenes, Hepaticae, and Musci. Introduction, I. General Cryptogams, II. Algae, III. Lichenes. *Memoirs of the New York Botanical Garden*, **19**, 1-174.

(27)   Hooker, W.J. (1812-1816) *British Jungermanniae*. Longman and co., London.

(28)   Allen, M. (1967) *The Hookers of Kew*. Michael Joseph, London.

(29)   Hooker, W.J. (1821) *Flora Scotica or A Description of Scottish Plants*. Constable & co., Edinburgh and Hurst, Robinson & co., London.

(30)   Nelson, E.C. (2011) "A botanical encampment at the foot of Ben Voirlich June 22[d]. 1821" by Robert Kaye Greville, and a Scottish beetle. *Archives of Natural History*, **38**, 96-103.

(31)   Greville, R.K. (1823-1828) *Scottish Cryptogamic Flora*. Six volumes. Edinburgh.

(32)   Drummond, T. (1824-1825) *Musci Scotici or, Dried Specimens of the Mosses that Have Been Discovered in Scotland*. Two Volumes.

(33)   Porley, R.D. & Hodgetts, N.G. (2009) *Mosses and Liverworts*. Collins, London.

(34)   Foster, R.D. (1979) The history of the Moss Exchange Club. *Bulletin of the British Bryological Society*, **33**, 19-26.

(35)   Richards, P.W. (1985). The British Bryological Society 1923-1983. *British Bryological Society Special Volume*, **1**, 3-10.

(36)   Birks, H.J.B. & Dransfield, J. (1970) A note on the habitat of *Scorpidium turgescens* (T. Jens). Loeske in Scotland. *Transactions of the British Bryological Society*, **6**, 129-132.

(37) Armitage, E. (1930) British Bryological Society. *Journal of Botany London,* **68,** 26-27.

(38) Birks, H.J.B. & Birks, H.H. (2015) Derek Ratcliffe – botanist and plant ecologist. In: *Nature's Conscience – The Life and Legacy of Derek Ratcliffe* (eds. D.B.A. Thompson, H.H. Birks & H.J.B. Birks). This volume, Chapter 4.

(39) McVean, D.N. & Ratcliffe, D.A. (1962) *Plant Communities of the Scottish Highlands.* HMSO, London.

(40) Ratcliffe, D.A. (1958) The range and habitats of *Sphagnum lindbergii* Schp. in Scotland. *Transactions of the British Bryological Society,* **3,** 386-391.

(41) Ratcliffe, D.A. (1959) A limestone flora in the Ben Alder group. *Transactions of the Botanical Society of Edinburgh,* **37,** 217-220.

(42) Crundwell, A.C. (1970) *Herberta borealis,* a new species from Scotland and Norway. *Transactions of the British Bryological Society,* **6,** 41-49.

(43 Bell, D. & Long, D.G. (2012) European *Herbertus* and the 'Viking Prongwort'. *Field Bryology,* **106,** 3-14.

(44) Long, D.G. (1992) *Sanionia orthothecioides* (Lindb.) Loeske in Scotland, new to the British Isles. *Journal of Bryology,* **17,** 111-117.

(45) Long, D.G. & Ratcliffe, D.A. 1996. Bryophytes of Hirta, St Kilda. *Journal of Bryology,* **19,** 89-111.

(46) Birks, H.H. & Birks, H.J.B. (1967) *Grimmia agassizii* (Sull. & Lesq.) Jaeg. in Britain. *Transactions of the British Bryological Society,* **5,** 215-217.

(47) Birks, H.J.B. & Birks, H.H. (1974) Studies on the bryophyte flora and vegetation of the Isle of Skye. I. Flora (Hepatics and *Sphagnum). Journal of Bryology,* **8,** 19-64.
Birks, H.J.B. & Birks, H.H. (1974) Studies on the bryophyte flora and vegetation of the Isle of Skye. I. Flora (Mosses). *Journal of Bryology,* **8,** 197-254.

(48) Corley, M.F.V. (1983) Ecology and phytogeographical affinities of the bryophytes in the Inner Hebrides. *Proceedings of the Royal Society of Edinburgh,* **83B,** 373-401.

(49) Ratcliffe, D.A. (ed.) (1977) *A Nature Conservation Review, Volumes 1 and 2.* Cambridge University Press, Cambridge.

(50) Rothero, G.P. (1990) *Survey of bryophyte-dominated snow-beds Part I. Cairngorms and Aonach Mor.* Scottish Field Unit Survey Report 41.

(51) Rothero, G.P. (1991) *Survey of bryophyte-dominated snow-beds Part II. The Highlands other than the main Cairngorms.* Scottish Field Unit Survey Report 51.

(52) Rothero, G.P. (1991) *Bryophyte-dominated snow-beds in the Scottish Highlands.* M.Sc. thesis, University of Glasgow.

(53) Flagmeier, M., Long. D.G., Genney, D.R., Hollingsworth, P.M. & Woodin, S.J. (2013) Regneration capacity of oceanic-montane liverworts: implications for community distribution and conservation. *Journal of Bryology,* **35,** 12-19.

(54) Long, D.G., Rothero, G.P. & Paton, J.A. (2003) *Athalamia hyalina* (Sommerf.) S. Hatt. in Scotland, new to the British Isles. *Journal of Bryology,* **25,** 253-257.

(55) Rothero, G.P. (2014) *Dicranum spadiceum* J.E. Zetterst. in Scotland, new to the British Isles. *Journal of Bryology,* **36,** 75-77.

(56) Perry, A.R. & Long, D.G. (2001) Alan Cyril Crundwell, B.Sc. (1923-2000). *Journal of Bryology*, **23**, 267-272.

(57) Murray, B. (1988) The genus *Andreaea* in Britain and Ireland. *Journal of Bryology*, **15**, 17-82.

(58) Long, D.G. (1982) *Bryoerythrophyllum caledonicum*, a new moss from Scotland. *Journal of Bryology*, **17**, 141-157.

(59) Paton, J.A. (1999) *The Liverwort Flora of the British Isles*. Harley Books, Colchester.

(60) Long, D.G., Forrest, L.L. & Hollingsworth, P.M. (2007) Barcoding Britain's liverworts and hornworts: a new project and request for material. *Field Bryology*, **93**, 11-13.

(61) Long, D.G., Paton, J.A., Squirrell, J., Woodhead, M. & Hollingsworth, P.M. (2006) Morphological, ecological and genetic evidence for distinguishing *Anastrophyllum joergensenii* Schiffn. and *A. alpinum* Steph. (Jungermanniopsida: Lophoziaceae). *Journal of Bryology*, **28**, 108-117.

(62) Averis, A.M., Averis, A.B.G., Birks, H.J.B., Horsfield, D., Thompson, D.B.A. & Yeo, M.J.M. (2004) *An Illustrated Guide to British Upland Vegetation*. Joint Nature Conservation Committee, Peterborough.

(63) Rothero, G.P., Birks, H.J.B., Genney, D., Grytnes, J.-A. & Long, D.G. (2011) Climate change and its consequences on bryophyte-dominated snowbed vegetation. In: *The Changing Nature of Scotland* (eds. S.J. Marrs *et al.*), pp. 436-440. Scottish Natural Heritage.

(64) Perry, A.R. & Dransfield, J. (1967) *Orthotrichum gymnostomum* in Scotland. *Journal of Bryology*, **5**, 218-221.

7. Derek Ratcliffe and the Atlantic bryophytes of Britain and Ireland

Chris D. Preston

Introduction

Most British and Irish naturalists are sadly aware that the flora and fauna of their island archipelago are less diverse than those of many other parts of Europe, and are especially poor when compared to the great mountain ranges of central Europe and the intimate mix of montane and lowland habitats in the Mediterranean region. However, there are some species groups which do not conform to this trend, and which are richly represented in the Atlantic fringe of Europe. The bryophytes (mosses, liverworts, hornworts) and ferns are notable examples of such groups. The wetter parts of Britain and Ireland not only have more bryophyte species than the drier areas (Fig. 7.1), but they also support a number of species of outstanding phytogeographical interest (Fig. 7.2). Derek Ratcliffe did more than any other 20th century botanist to investigate the factors affecting the distribution of the Atlantic bryophyte species in Britain and Ireland. He was also able to ensure that many of the key British sites for these species were taken into account in the development of conservation policy and in the choice of sites for statutory designation. In addition to Atlantic bryophytes, he was passionately interested in the Atlantic filmy ferns, especially Killarney Fern (*Trichomanes speciosum*)[1-3]. The aim of this chapter is to outline Derek's contributions to the study of the Atlantic bryophyte flora, to summarise his main conclusions, and finally to review some of the recent advances in our knowledge of these species since he finished his intensive studies in 1970.

This chapter concentrates on the strictly Atlantic bryophytes recognised by Ratcliffe[4], the 75 species and one variety listed in his Northern Atlantic, Southern Atlantic, and Widespread Atlantic groups. Nomenclature has been updated to follow Hill *et al*.[5], with the exception of *Herbertus aduncus* ssp. *hutchinsiae* and *H. delavayi* as it is appropriate to revert to the earlier names *H. hutchinsiae* and *H. borealis*[6].

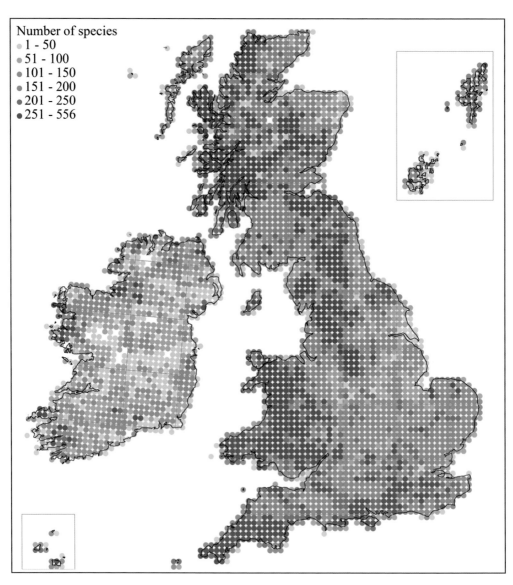

Figure 7.1. Number of bryophyte taxa recorded from each 10-km square from 1950 onwards. All taxa (*left*) and strictly Atlantic taxa (*right*) (see text for definition). The map of strictly Atlantic taxa excludes *Grimmia retracta*, which is now regarded as a synonym of the more widespread *G. lisae*. Many of the south-eastern dots on this map represent records of *Cololejeunea minutissima* (Fig. 4.30), which has spread eastwards in recent years.

Derek Ratcliffe's studies of the Atlantic bryophytes

Fieldwork in the Atlantic zone

Derek Ratcliffe became interested in the Atlantic flora when he moved to Bangor in 1950 to begin work on his PhD thesis[(1,7)]. His supervisor, Paul Richards, was one of the leading academic bryologists of his generation. Derek teamed up with his fellow research student Reg Parker, a more experienced bryologist, to explore the rich bryophyte flora of

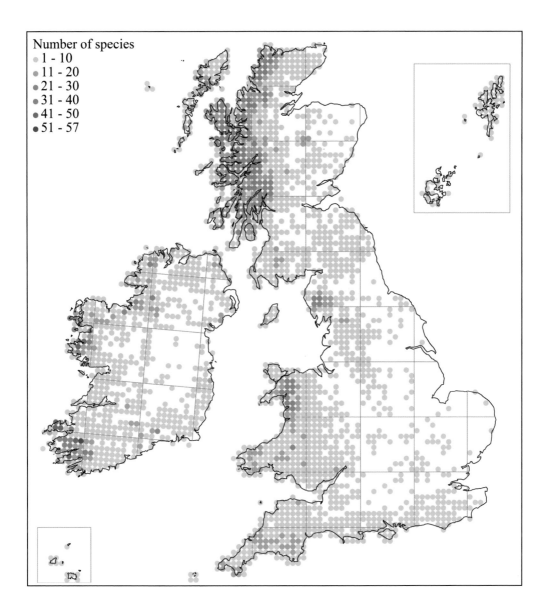

North Wales, travelling around on Reg's motorbike[1,3]. The Atlantic bryophyte flora was already well-known[8-12], but hitherto the species had been approached primarily from a taxonomic and biogeographical standpoint. Derek brought to his fieldwork an increasingly acute ecological eye. In North Wales, and later in northern England, Scotland, and Ireland, he combined his skills as a field naturalist[1] and his analytical abilities as an ecologist[1] to develop our understanding of the factors controlling the national, regional, and local distribution of Atlantic species.

Derek joined the British Bryological Society (BBS) in 1952 and the progress and geographical coverage of his fieldwork can be followed by his new vice-county records published in the Society's journals (Figs. 7.3 & 7.4). His first published record was *Orthothecium intricatum*, a species of upland, base-rich crags and ravines which he found on the bank of Mosspeeble Burn, Ewes Water, Langholm in August 1951, new

Figure 7.2. Brandon Mountain, Kerry, 2009. This site, visited by Derek Ratcliffe in 1961, 1963, 1967, and 1983, supports a very rich assemblage of Atlantic bryophyte species with contrasting geographical affinities. They include Southern Atlantic bryophytes at their highest recorded elevations in Britain or Ireland (e.g. *Adelanthus decipiens* (Fig. 7.6), *Cyclodictyon laetevirens* (Fig. 7.5)) and some of the rarest Northern Atlantic species (e.g. *Adelanthus lindenbergianus* (Fig. 4.14), *Scapania nimbosa* (Fig. 4.14)). Photo: Caroline Pannell

to Dumfriesshire[13]. This was followed by almost 400 more records documenting his own discoveries or joint finds with other botanists (particularly, from 1966 onwards, Hilary and John Birks). Most were from the Lake District, the Southern Uplands, or the Scottish Highlands, with significant batches of records from his first two visits to Ireland, in 1961 and 1963[3], and from a further visit with John and Hilary in 1967. Amongst these records are some notable discoveries of Atlantic species. These include *Fossombronia angulosa* (Figs. 7.5 & 6.9) on St Kilda, Outer Hebrides, in 1959, its first Scottish site and still its northernmost world locality, *Plagiochila carringtonii* (Fig. 4.15) on Slievemore, Mayo, in 1961, new to Ireland[14], records of *Adelanthus lindenbergianus* (Fig. 4.14) from the Twelve Bens of Connemara in the same year[14], and *Cyclodictyon laetevirens* (Fig. 7.5) and *Dumortiera hirsuta* (Fig. 4.4), both new to Scotland and found with J. Grant Roger on the coast of the Isle of Jura in 1967. Later in 1967, the 'Birks, Birks & Ratcliffe' team found *Geocalyx graveolens*, new to Ireland, near Waterville, Kerry[15]; this has a more widespread range in Europe than an Atlantic species but a very westerly range in the British Isles. These records are of course only the tip of the iceberg, the most notable discoveries in a period of sustained fieldwork in which he found many new sites for the scarcer Atlantic species including *Radula voluta* (Fig. 4.4), *Sematophyllum demissum*, *Hageniella micans*

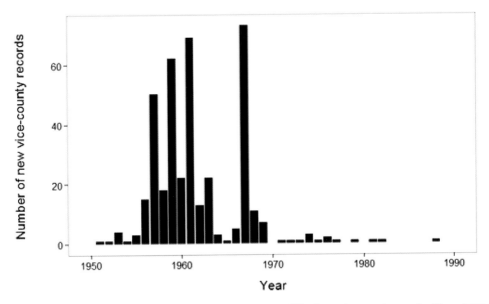

Figure 7.3. Histogram showing annual contributions by Derek Ratcliffe of new vice-county records of bryophytes to the British Bryological Society.

(Fig. 4.4), *Hedwigia integrifolia* (Fig. 4.5), and *Daltonia splachnoides* (Fig. 4.5), and the small filmy-ferns *Hymenophyllum wilsonii* and *H. tunbrigense* (Fig. 4.3). He discovered *Sphagnum strictum* (Fig. 7.8) in 10 new vice-counties, *Jubula hutchinsiae* (Fig. 7.6) in 9, and *Adelanthus decipiens* (Fig. 7.6) in 7, but these records of Atlantic species were exceeded by the number of new vice-county records he made of the non-Atlantic *Sphagnum* species *S. warnstorfii* (Fig. 4.16) (12 vice-counties) and *S. austinii* (Fig. 4.16) (8 vice-counties). However, in 1970 Derek, "after much agonising", exchanged his job as a field biologist for an administrative role[3] and after this his intensive and exploratory fieldwork came to an end. One of his few notable finds after this, and his last published record, was *Adelanthus decipiens* (Fig. 7.6), which he found with his wife Jeannette at Dewerstone Woods, south Devon, in 1988, new to south-west England, growing exactly where he had predicted it should occur from its climatic requirements[4].

Almost as revealing as the localities where Derek found new vice-county records are those where he did not. Few

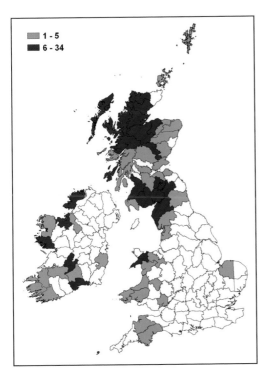

Figure 7.4. Map of new vice-county records contributed by Derek Ratcliffe, 1951-1988.

127

bryologists had a more focused approach to the subject; he was interested in the species of semi-natural habitats in the north and west but showed no interest in urban or arable bryophytes or those of the lowland south and east. With the exception of three *Sphagnum* species, recorded with Hilary and John Birks from the valley bogs and wet heaths of west Norfolk (Fig. 7.4), he made no new vice-county records in south-eastern England. His feat of living in a county (Cambridgeshire) for over 40 years without ever making a single bryophyte record there is surely unmatched by any other leading bryologist in any era!

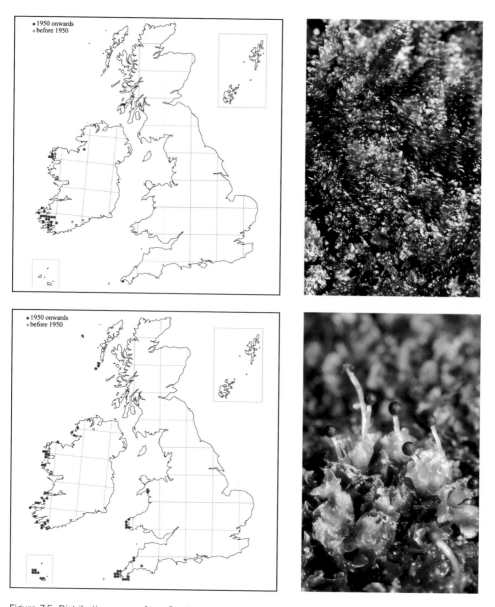

Figure 7.5. Distribution maps of two Southern Atlantic species in 10-km grid squares in Britain and Ireland. *Cyclodictyon laetevirens*, Sligo, 1967 (*top*) and *Fossombronia angulosa*, Cornwall, 1966 (*bottom*). Photos: John Birks

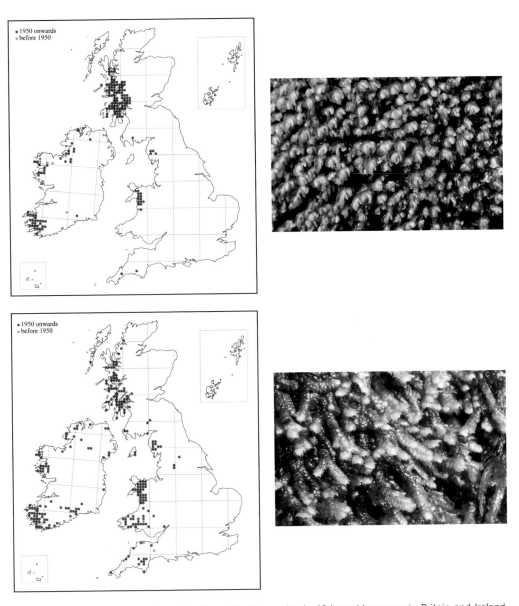

Figure 7.6. Distribution maps of two Southern Atlantic species in 10-km grid squares in Britain and Ireland. *Adelanthus decipiens*, Kerry, 1967 (*top*) and *Jubula hutchinsiae*, Kerry, 1965 (*bottom*). Photos: John Birks

Mapping the Atlantic species

In 1960 the BBS started a scheme to map the bryophytes of Britain and Ireland at the 10-km square scale. From 1963 until 1978, an annual batch of maps of the less common species was published in the *Transactions of the British Bryological Society* (later renamed *Journal of Bryology*). Individual members of the society compiled the maps and contributed accompanying ecological notes. The first map in the 1963 batch was *Adelanthus decipiens* (Fig. 7.6), compiled by Derek, and he also contributed maps of *Bazzania pearsonii*

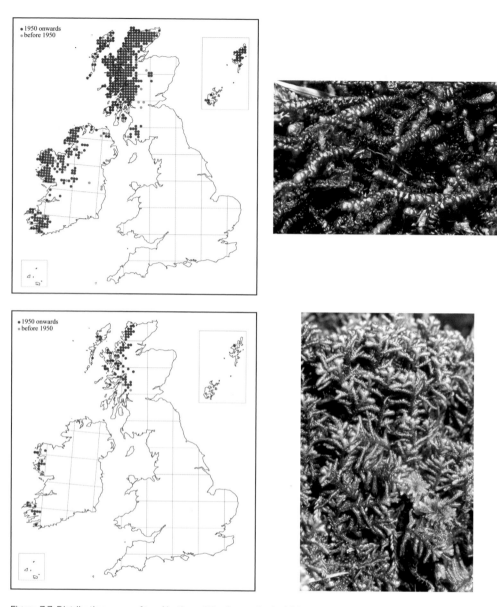

Figure 7.7. Distribution maps of two Northern Atlantic species in 10-km grid squares in Britain and Ireland. *Pleurozia purpurea*, Wester Ross, 1966 (*top*) and *Mastigophora woodsii*, Isle of Skye, 1967 (*bottom*). Photos: John Birks

(Fig. 4.14), *Mastigophora woodsii* (Fig. 7.7), *Plagiochila carringtonii* (Fig. 4.15), *Hedwigia integrifolia* (Fig. 4.5), *Paraleptodontium recurvifolium* (Fig. 4.15), and †*Sphagnum lindbergii* (Fig. 6.6) to the initial set of maps. In later years he compiled maps of *Anastrophyllum donnianum* (Fig. 4.14), *A. joergensenii* s.l., *Fossombronia angulosa* (Figs. 7.5 & 6.9), *Herbertus hutchinsiae* (Fig. 7.8), *H. stramineus* (Fig. 4.14), *Scapania nimbosa* (Fig. 4.14), and *S. ornithopodioides* (Fig. 4.15) (in 1965), †*Coscinodon cribrosus* (in 1966), *Lepidozia cupressina* (Fig. 4.5), *Pleurozia purpurea* (Fig. 7.7), and †*Hylocomiastrum umbratum* (in 1969) and finally, with John Birks in 1976, *Frullania teneriffae* (Fig. 7.9), *Radula aquilegia* (Fig. 4.4), †*Sphagnum fuscum* (Fig. 24.1), *S. strictum* (Fig. 7.8), †*S. warnstorfii* (Fig. 4.16), and (with John Birks and David Goode) †*S. imbricatum* s.l. (Fig. 4.16). All of these are strictly Atlantic species, as defined by Ratcliffe[4] (see above), except for those marked with a dagger. Many other Atlantic species (e.g. *Dicranum scottianum* (Fig. 7.9), *Glyphomitrium daviesii* (Fig. 7.10)) were mapped by other bryologists including John Birks and Humphrey Milne-Redhead[1], a country doctor from Galloway whose botanical interests, approach to field-work, and love of unexplored wild areas were remarkably similar to Derek's and who was described by Derek as one of bryology's "most colourful and kindly characters"[16].

Herbertus borealis – *a new species discovered in Scotland*

Herbertus is a very distinctive and attractive genus of large liverworts, but separating and finding the correct name for the British species has proved to be very troublesome. *Herbertus* species have highly disjunct distributions and are rarely fertile (no fruits have ever been found in Europe). They therefore need to be defined on rather subtle leaf characters which are difficult to quantify[17]. Two species have long been recognised in Britain; they are now called *H. hutchinsiae* (Fig. 7.8) and *H. stramineus* (Fig. 4.14) and both were regarded as Northern Atlantic species by Ratcliffe[4], although the plant he called *Herberta adunca* is now known as *Herbertus stramineus*[6], a symptom of the nomenclatural confusion to which the genus is subject.

In August 1958 Derek, while surveying the vegetation of the North-West Highlands, encountered a population of *Herbertus* on Beinn Eighe, Wester Ross, "that he immediately recognised as belonging to a third species". Subsequently it turned out to have been collected from this locality, but not recognised as distinct, by C. Howie and C. Jenner in 1868 and by several later bryologists. The Beinn Eighe plant was described by Alan Crundwell[18] as the new species *Herbertus borealis*, although because of the difficulty of the genus he admitted that "while *H. borealis* is certainly new to Europe, it is much less certain that it is new to science". Ratcliffe[19] described its characteristic habitat, in patches of dwarf-shrub heath on a quartzite slope (Fig. 7.11). It grows amongst a semi-prostrate carpet of Common Juniper (*Juniperus communis* ssp. *nana*) mixed with Bearberry (*Arctostaphylos uva-ursi*) (Fig. 5.3) and Heather (*Calluna vulgaris*), and in taller vegetation where Heather is dominant. In addition to the plants from Beinn Eighe, Crundwell[18] recognised specimens of *H. borealis* from three localities in Norway (but see below).

'An ecological account of the Atlantic bryophytes in the British Isles' - 1968

Derek drew on his rich field experience for his monographic paper 'An ecological account of the Atlantic bryophytes in the British Isles'[4]. Writing with an expansiveness which would probably be frowned upon by editors today, he reviewed in detail the ecology of the species, discussed the factors controlling their distributions, and presented hypotheses to explain some of the unusual features of their British and Irish ranges.

Derek began by defining six phytogeographical groups, based on the distribution of their component species in Europe as a whole. The species in the *Northern Atlantic* group (25 species) are found in the northern and mountainous parts of Britain and Ireland (Figs. 7.7 & 7.8), and often in the Faeroes and western Norway, but are rare in Europe south of the Baltic and absent from Macaronesia. They include several famously

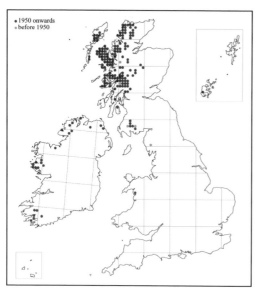

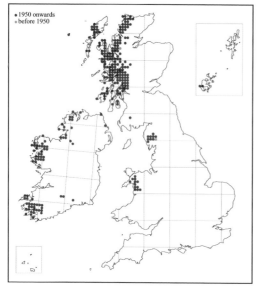

Figure 7.8. Distribution maps of two Northern Atlantic species in 10-km grid squares in Britain and Ireland. *Sphagnum strictum*, Galloway, 1966 (*top*) and *Herbertus hutchinsiae*, Kerry, 1965 (*bottom*). Photos: John Birks

disjunct liverworts, such as *Plagiochila carringtonii* (Fig. 4.15), known elsewhere only in the Faeroes and the Himalaya (Nepal, Sikkim, Bhutan, Yunnan), and *Mastigophora woodsii* (Fig. 7.7), found in the Faeroes, British Columbia, and central and eastern Asia (especially the Himalaya). Many are present in our area as a single sex (*P. carringtonii* is male in Europe, female in Nepal) or, like *M. woodsii*, are not known to produce sex organs. The 27 *Southern Atlantic* species are concentrated in the south-west, especially Cork and Kerry (Figs. 7.5 & 7.6), and often occur in Macaronesia and in the Atlantic zone of Spain and France, but very rarely extend north to Norway; many also occur in the Tropics

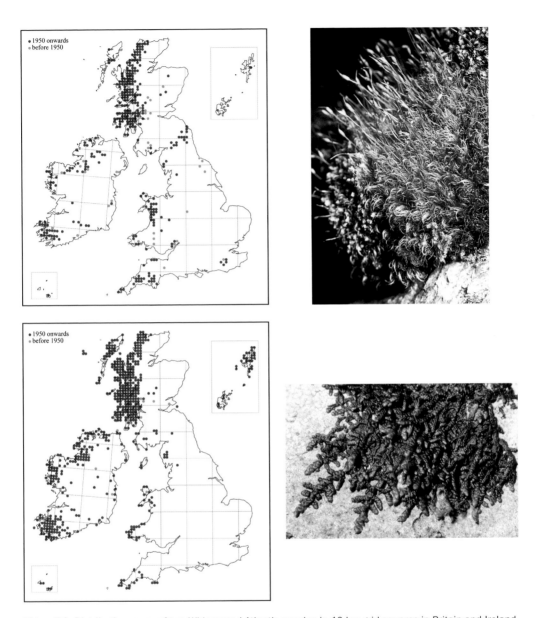

Figure 7.9. Distribution maps of two Widespread Atlantic species in 10-km grid squares in Britain and Ireland. *Dicranum scottianum*, Isle of Skye, 1968 (*top*) and *Frullania teneriffae*, Isle of Skye, 1966 (*bottom*). Photos: John Birks

(e.g. *Dumortiera hirsuta* (Fig. 4.4), *Jubula hutchinsiae* (Fig. 7.6)). *Widespread Atlantic* taxa (24 species) are more widely distributed in the Atlantic zones of Britain (Figs. 7.9 & 7.10) and Europe. These three groups comprise the strictly Atlantic species. In addition, there are Sub-Atlantic (45 species), Mediterranean-Atlantic (42), and Western British (35) groups; the last includes species which are markedly western in the British Isles but not in continental Europe.

Derek's paper[4] went on to describe the habitats of the Atlantic bryophytes, highlighting the importance of damp, shaded habitats, both below and above the tree-line.

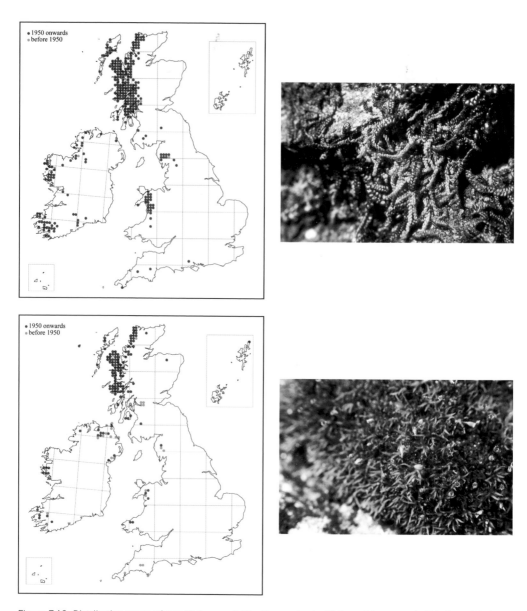

Figure 7.10. Distribution maps of two Widespread Atlantic species in 10-km grid squares in Britain and Ireland. *Harpalejeunea molleri*, Cumbria, 1966 (*top*) and *Glyphomitrium daviesii*, Isle of Skye, 1966 (*bottom*). Photos: John Birks

Within the forest zone, stream gorges are particularly rich because of the different microhabitats they offer. Above the tree-line, in particularly favourable sites at higher elevations in western Scotland and Ireland (Figs. 7.2 & 7.12), up to 10 species of large Atlantic liverworts "may be found growing together, in great luxuriance and profusion, forming dense, soft cushions" in a "mixed hepatic mat". This community "locally replaces the typical moss layer of dwarf shrub heaths" and "reaches its finest development on steep, rocky slopes facing between north-west and east, especially in deep and dark, sheltered corries" ([4] pp. 379-380). This community was first recognised by McVean

Figure 7.11. Habitat of *Herbertus borealis* growing amidst prostrate Common Juniper (*Juniperus communis* ssp. *nana*) on a quartzite slope, Beinn Eighe, Wester Ross, 1966. Photo: John Birks

and Ratcliffe[20] in their monograph *Plant Communities of the Scottish Highlands* as Vaccineto-Callunetum hepaticosum, but it was in the 1968 paper[4] that it was described so eloquently and given the memorable name "mixed hepatic mat" (Figs. 6.13 & 7.12). This fixed the concept in the minds of bryologists and ecologists, and ensured that its international importance was appreciated[21-24].

The factors affecting the regional distribution of the Atlantic species were discussed in the next part of the paper[4], which highlighted the importance of humidity. Derek considered that drought was the most important factor limiting the distribution of many species, so that the number of 'wet days' (with >1 mm rain) provides a better correlation with distribution patterns than total rainfall. He mapped the distribution of the 'mixed hepatic mat' community, showing that it was found only where there were more than 220 wet days a year. Species dependent on groundwater, such as *Jubula hutchinsiae* (Fig. 7.6) which grows on dripping rocks in streams and caves and by waterfalls, are less restricted in their ranges than those which are exposed to the prevailing atmospheric humidity. Temperature may also be important in controlling the distribution of some species. The liverwort *Adelanthus decipiens* (Fig. 7.6), for example, requires both high humidity (>190 wet days) and freedom from low winter temperatures[4].

Derek then discussed the recent history of Atlantic bryophytes, suggesting that their ranges had been fragmented by the felling of woodland and by the burning and grazing of heathland in open habitats[4]. He drew attention to the fact that apparently similar woodlands in the same region can differ greatly in the richness of their Atlantic

Figure 7.12. The habitat of the 'mixed hepatic mat' on steep, heather-dominated, north- or east-facing block-strewn slopes in western Scotland and western Ireland. The general view of the habitat (*top*) is on Beinn Dearg, Wester Ross, 1966 and the closer view (*bottom*) is on Muckish Mountain, Donegal, 1967. Photos: John Birks

flora, and suggested that many species have survived only in areas where there has been a continuous history of woodland cover. Throughout the paper he emphasised that "the importance of chance in affecting plant distribution is greatly under-estimated, and the closer a species is to limiting conditions, the more important does it become" ([4] p. 403). The chances of dispersal for species which often do not reproduce sexually and lack vegetative propagules, and the chances of surviving habitat disturbance and recolonising sites following local extinction, have affected observed patterns of distribution. "Over much of western Britain it would appear that the quality of the Atlantic bryophyte flora of a woodland or wooded gorge depends on some historical accident of management" ([4] p. 407). Only where the climate is exceptionally favourable to Atlantic species, in western Ireland and the western Highlands, are relatively disturbed woodlands rich in Atlantic species.

Conservation of the key British sites for Atlantic bryophytes

Although Atlantic bryophytes are concentrated in the thinly populated areas of Britain and Ireland (Figs. 7.1, 7.5–7.10), they are vulnerable to the effects of habitat change. Derek recorded[4] how, on his first visit to Ireland in 1961, he visited woods at Blackstones Bridge, Kerry, a site where a BBS party had recorded a rich selection of Atlantic species ten years before. By 1961 the native woodland had been felled and replanted by conifers, and although he found "some of the more sensitive plants surviving down crevices", other species "were just recognisable as dead or moribund vestiges, scorched out by exposure to the sun". In preparing *A Nature Conservation Review*[25,26], he was able to ensure that many of the known British sites for Atlantic species were listed. Characteristically, bryophytes which "have their main or only occurrences in man-made habitats, such as arable or much disturbed land, banks and ditches, walls and buildings" are given short shrift, and "these are the groups least well represented in the series of key sites". By contrast, as "Britain is the European headquarters for many Atlantic bryophytes … the choice of key sites has deliberately included a good selection of habitats and localities important for these plants, especially woodlands, coastlands and uplands in western Britain" ([25] p. 353). In Wales, for example, Atlantic bryophytes are prominently mentioned in the description of the nationally (Grade 1) and internationally (Grade 1*) important woodland sites of Coed Rheidol, Cardiganshire; Cothi Tywi, Carmarthenshire; Coedydd Dyffryn Maentwrog, Coed Ganllwyd and Coed Crafnant, all in Merioneth; and Coedydd Aber, Caernarvonshire; as well as the upland sites Cader Idris and Rhinog, both in Merioneth, and the Eryri Mountains of Snowdonia, Caernarvonshire[26]. Of these nine sites, no less than six are now National Nature Reserves (NNR) (Cader Idris, Coed Ganllwyd, Coed Rheidol, Coedydd Aber, Coedydd Dyffryn Maentwrog (as Coedydd Maentwrog), and Rhinog), and part of Eryri is included in the Yr Wyddfa NNR. All the really noteworthy sites for oceanic[27] bryophytes in Wales now have statutory protection, at least as Sites of Special Scientific Interest[28]. However, the problem of identifying rich sites in Scotland (Fig. 7.12) and Ireland (Fig. 7.2) is much greater than in Wales and work is still needed to ensure that all the important sites are protected.

Advances in our knowledge of the Atlantic flora since 1968

Taxonomic and molecular studies

In the years since 1968, a few new species have been added to the Atlantic flora as a result of taxonomic revisions, and the relationships of others have been clarified. The taxonomy of a distinctive *Plagiochila*, first collected by Ellen Hutchins in the early 19th century, was clarified by Jones and Rose[29] who described it as a new species, *P. atlantica* (Fig. 6.5). Jean Paton, working systematically through the genus for her great work *The Liverwort Flora of the British Isles*[30], realised that the Sub-Atlantic *Plagiochila spinulosa* consisted of two species, *P. spinulosa* and *P. killarniensis*. Molecular methods have proved to be a most effective tool to unravel the complexities of the genus *Herbertus*. *Herbertus borealis* (Fig. 6.7)[31] has been confirmed to be a distinct species, and it is apparently endemic to Beinn Eighe in Wester Ross (Fig. 7.11) and nearby Slioch. There is a fourth British species, first collected in Britain by Derek on Ronas Hill, Shetland, in 1968, but not at that time recognised as a new species. This has recently been described as *H. norenus* (Fig. 6.11), and the Norwegian plants hitherto thought to be *H. borealis* are in fact this species[6,17,31]. *Anastrophyllum joergensenii*, a Northern Atlantic species, has also proved (like *Plagiochila spinulosa*) to consist of two species. Most of the British material is *A. alpinum* (Fig. 4.14) but Derek had also collected the rarer of the two species, the true *A. joergensenii*, on Foinaven, West Sutherland[31], in 1957, and noted it as "a small form ... in shallow high level blanket bog"[30,32,33].

When Derek wrote his paper in 1968 ([4] p. 380), bryologists had only recently realised that the liverwort which had been described as an Irish endemic *Adelanthus dugortiensis* was actually a species (now called *A. lindenbergianus* (Fig. 4.14)) which is widespread in the Southern Hemisphere. Further work has shown that several more species with Atlantic distributions in Europe are tropical species at the northern edge of their world ranges. *Plagiochila atlantica* (Fig. 6.5) and *P. killarniensis*, which were described from Ireland and not initially known outside Europe, have turned out to be synonymous with the Neotropical species *P. heterophylla* (Fig. 6.5) and *P. bifaria*, respectively[34-36]. *Plagiochila bifaria*, for example, is widespread in mountains from Mexico and Cuba south to Bolivia and south-east Brazil. *Plagiochila punctata*, another species first described from Ireland, has recently been shown to be widespread in Central and South America and in tropical Africa, with northern outliers in Tennessee and the Atlantic fringe of Europe[37,38]. In other genera, too, familiar names based on Irish types have been replaced recently by those of tropical taxa. The Southern Atlantic *Cephalozia hibernica* is conspecific with the Neotropical *C. crassifolia*[39], and *Lejeunea holtii*, another Southern Atlantic species, is conspecific with the widespread African *L. eckloniana*[40]. However, in stark contrast to these examples, the one native British and Irish *Telaranea* species is now regarded as a European endemic, *T. europaea*, following taxonomic revision, rather than the Neotropical *T. nematodes*[41].

Molecular techniques have been used in recent years to compare the British and Irish populations of the Atlantic species with those from further afield. Although it is not itself an Atlantic species, a study of the variation of *Radula lindenbergiana* perhaps throws some light on the possible history of the more Widespread Atlantic bryophytes. Laenen *et al.*[42] found that the greatest genetic diversity was in Macaronesia, suggesting that these islands may have served as refugia during the Quaternary glaciations. The populations in north-west Africa and western Europe were also moderately diverse, and many of these could have had a Macaronesian ancestor; however, there was a marked decrease in diversity eastwards from western Europe to central Europe and western Asia. The temperate (European and North American) subspecies of *Jubula hutchinsiae* (Fig. 7.6), an Atlantic species, have been shown to be less variable than the tropical subspecies[43]. The molecular similarity of tropical and European populations of species such as *Plagiochila bifaria* has led contemporary bryologists to favour the hypothesis that the European populations of Atlantic species may be the result of relatively recent, rare long-distance dispersal rather than the survival of ancient, relict populations[22,36,37,44].

Recording distributions

The work of mapping the bryophyte flora of Britain and Ireland, started by Derek with the first published map in 1963, has continued to be a major activity for members of the BBS. The *Atlas of the Bryophytes of Britain and Ireland*[45] included maps of all British and Irish bryophyte species and some varieties – 1038 taxa in all. Derek contributed the Foreword to the first volume, noting its importance "in expanding our knowledge of one of the richest moss and liverwort floras in Europe, and one of the internationally important features of Britain and Ireland". A revised atlas is now available[46]. Whereas fieldwork since 1970 has sometimes simply filled out the known distribution of some species, such as the very conspicuous *Herbertus hutchinsiae* (Fig. 7.8) and *Mastigophora woodsii* (Fig. 7.7), there have also been some notable extensions of range. *Campylopus subporodictyon* was added to the British flora by Corley and Wallace[47] and represents a remarkable addition to the bryophytes of western Scotland which have disjunct distributions in high rainfall localities elsewhere (Himalaya, Yunnan, western Canada). Range extensions within the British Isles include the discovery in western Scotland of two species hitherto known only from Ireland, the Northern Atlantic *Adelanthus lindenbergianus* (Fig. 4.14) and the Southern Atlantic *Radula holtii*[31]. Three Southern Atlantic species, *Dendrocryphaea lamyana*, *Lejeunea mandonii*, and *Telaranea europaea*, have been added to the Welsh flora. *Dendrocryphaea lamyana* was previously known from Cornwall and Devon. *Telaranea europaea*, known from one site in Cornwall, has recently been found in Caernarvonshire, growing in the dense shade of Rhododendron. *Lejeunea mandonii*, a very rare species in western Ireland, Cornwall, and western Scotland[48], might have been expected in Wales although not in the area in which it has been discovered, the Wye Valley, Monmouthshire[49]. There have also been significant rediscoveries of species in sites where they had long been feared extinct. *Cyclodictyon laetevirens* (Fig. 7.5), thought to have been exterminated deliberately by a ruthless collector at its only English locality in Cornwall, was refound there in 1996. *Glyphomitrium daviesii* (Fig. 7.10) was rediscovered in North Wales in 2003 and discovered in South Wales in 2003, almost a century after the last Welsh record. South Wales, a region where Ratcliffe ([4] p. 412) recognised that the Atlantic bryophytes were under-recorded, has now been much more thoroughly worked, particularly by S.D.S. Bosanquet and G.S. Motley[50,51]. Many additional sites for Atlantic species have been documented in Scotland as a result of Ben Averis' monumental study of 448 woodlands[52] (see also [31]).

The addition of new species, and the discovery of known species in new localities, is an expected result of further intensive fieldwork. Indeed, Ratcliffe ([4] p. 380) had suggested that *Adelanthus lindenbergianus* "may yet be found in western Scotland". However, the range expansions of a few of the strictly Atlantic species are much less expected. The rare moss *Daltonia splachnoides* (Fig. 4.5) and the tiny liverwort *Colura calyptrifolia* (Fig. 4.6), both Widespread Atlantic species, have spread out of their highly oceanic redoubts. In many cases the new sites are in humid conifer plantations, where both species may grow epiphytically on conifers and also on other hosts such as streamside willows. *Colura calyptrifolia* (Fig. 4.6) has a wider habitat range, and also grows as an epiphyll on conifers and on substrates such as dwarf shrubs, brambles, fern fronds, bracket fungi, and even on dumped plastic and polystyrene rubbish[53-56]. The Southern Atlantic *Cololejeunea minutissima* (Fig. 4.30) has spread even more widely, moving eastwards in Britain from its south-westerly range to colonise most of southern England; it is now well established even in Cambridgeshire. Ratcliffe[4] had noted that this is a species with affinities to the Mediterranean-Atlantic group. Although it is difficult in Britain and Ireland to deduce the causes of such range changes, as habitats, air quality, and climate have all changed in recent decades, it seems likely that climate as well as habitat change may have played some part in the expansion of these species[57]. In contrast to these expanding species, the elusive Northern Atlantic moss *Philonotis cernua*, which grows on burnt areas and open soil in heathland, apparently hovers on the verge of extinction: it was last seen in Britain in 1961 and in Ireland in 1987[24]. It is a species that Derek never found in his many years of botanising in the north and west.

Classifications of species into elements based on geographic ranges

The Atlantic bryophytes have been included in more general studies of the ranges of British and Irish bryophytes. Hill and Preston[27] classified species on the basis of their distribution in Eurasia. When classified by these wider criteria, the strictly Atlantic species proved to be relatively homogeneous, with the Northern Atlantic species corresponding with the Oceanic Boreal-montane element and both Widespread and Southern Atlantic groups with the Hyperoceanic Southern-temperate element in the new system. The Mediterranean-Atlantic group was recognised in both systems. However, Ratcliffe's Subatlantic and Western British groups are much more heterogeneous when classified in a system which considers their wider ranges.

A numerical classification of the British and Irish ranges of species on the basis of their distributions at the 10-km square scale has only recently become possible, with advances in computer technology. Liverwort distributions have been classified into 10 groups[58]. Groups characterised by *Pellia epiphylla*, *Scapania undulata*, and *Harpalejeunea molleri* (Fig. 7.10) form one nested series of distributions which are increasingly restricted to westerly, high rainfall areas, and *Pellia epiphylla*, *Scapania undulata*, *Anastrepta orcadensis*, *Moerckia blyttii*, and *Marsupella condensata* another series with increasingly upland, high rainfall ranges. The 32 Southern and Widespread Atlantic liverworts are almost all found in the *Harpalejeunea molleri* group, with only five exceptions. The 15 Northern Atlantic liverworts are found in the *Anastrepta orcadensis* (8 species), *Moerckia blyttii* (3), and *Harpalejeunea molleri* groups (4), again suggesting that the Northern Atlantic liverworts are rather distinct from the other strictly Atlantic species. In a similar analysis of moss distributions[59], the Northern Atlantic mosses are evenly split between the widespread, western *Amphidium mougeotii* group and the more restricted *Hylocomiastrum umbratum* group of mosses (broadly equivalent to the *Anastrepta orcadensis* and *Harpalejeunea molleri* groups of liverworts). Most Widespread and Southern Atlantic species are members of the *Amphidium mougeotii* or the *Fontinalis squamosa* groups of mosses, the latter being a group concentrated in south-west England and Wales with no equivalent in the liverwort classification.

Ecological studies

Alison Averis[21] re-examined the distribution of the components of the mixed hepatic mat in Scotland (Fig. 7.12) in relation to environmental factors, concluding that "high numbers of these species are in [10-km] squares which have a low annual temperature range, high rainfall distributed evenly throughout the year and irregular topography with a lot of north-facing slopes".

Mary Edwards[60] tested Derek's hypothesis[4] that woods which are rich in Atlantic species in North Wales have a different disturbance history to species-poor woods. With John Birks, she surveyed the vegetation and bryophyte flora of four contrasting woods[61] and examined their history by pollen analysis[60]. All four woods prove to have been disturbed in the last 300–400 years, but the history of disturbances such as felling and coppicing is often complex and patchy. However, Coed-y-Rhygen (Fig. 21.2), one of the two species-rich woods, "probably once had an open, park-like appearance"[60]. There is, therefore, no simple relationship between disturbance history and the richness of the Atlantic flora. The richness and abundance of Atlantic species was largely correlated with the availability of suitable habitat. The richest sites possessed extremely moist and shaded rocks where species would have been able to persist during periods of clearance, and from which they could then expand. Similarly, John Birks[62] showed that the bryophyte-rich Johnny's Wood in Borrowdale, Cumbria[26] had been extensively disturbed in Norse times, according to pollen-analytical studies of a small mire within the Wood.

In his 1968 paper[4], Derek suggested that even though species may not reproduce sexually, "the capacity for spread by vegetative propagules – even by simple fragmentation of the mature plant – may be greater than is realised" (p. 402), but that "these problems will never be solved by theoretical argument, and evidence of actual powers of spread is needed" (p. 403). It is only recently that experimental studies have begun to test this hypothesis. Flagmeier et al.[63] macerated material of *Herbertus hutchinsiae* (Fig. 7.8) in a blender and poured the resulting soup onto plots on a heathery slope. After two years there was visible regeneration of *Herbertus* amongst bryophyte-dominated vegetation, less regeneration in graminoid-dominated vegetation, and much less on bare soil under dwarf shrubs. They also studied the regeneration capacity in laboratory cultures of eight species of liverwort which characteristically grow in the 'mixed hepatic mat' (which they prefer to call "Oceanic-montane liverwort-rich heath").

In recent years both Rory Hodd (Ireland) and Maren Flagmeier (Scotland) have been studying Atlantic bryophytes; the results of their work are beginning to appear[22,23,63,64] and we can anticipate major contributions to our understanding of these species in the next few years.

Derek's 'Ecological account'[4] concluded by discussing the conservation of the Atlantic bryophytes in the light of their national and international importance. He identified collecting by bryologists and habitat destruction as the major threats. The degradation of habitats by ploughing, burning, grazing, the felling of woods, and their conversion to commercial forestry plantations "have in the past caused depletion of the Atlantic bryophyte flora, and will continue to do so … Another serious local problem, as in some of the fine oakwoods around Killarney, is the rapid spread of non-indigenous rhododendron … The tapping of streams and lakes or the flooding of ground by reservoir construction is likely to continue .. The most irrevocable … destruction is that caused by extension of urban and industrial development, with its inevitable corollary, atmospheric pollution" ([4] pp. 425-426).

Several studies have examined changes in the mixed hepatic mat vegetation in recent decades. In Scotland, a Nature Conservancy Council team revisited ten sites surveyed by McVean & Ratcliffe[20] and found that the 'mixed hepatic mat' vegetation remained intact in only four; in four cases it had disappeared and in two there was evidence for recent destruction of the hepatic community by grazing and burning[65]. Flagmeier *et al.*[64] re-recorded 17 of the McVean & Ratcliffe quadrats in the North-West Highlands. The quadrats had become more heterogeneous; dwarf shrubs (e.g. Heather, (*Calluna vulgaris*), Crowberry (*Empetrum nigrum*)) and specialist liverworts (e.g. *Herbertus hutchinsiae, Mastigophora woodsii*) had decreased whereas large mosses (e.g. *Hylocomium splendens, Rhytidiadelphus loreus*) and graminoids (e.g. Bent Grass (*Agrostis* spp.), Tufted Hair-grass (*Deschampsia cespitosa*), Greater Woodrush (*Luzula sylvatica*), Purple Moor-grass (*Molinia caerulea*), Deergrass *Trichophorum germanicum*)) had increased. As a result, the vegetation had changed to a more open, grassy community. Flagmeier *et al.*[64] suggest that these changes may have been driven by increased grazing, by eutrophication, or by warmer and drier conditions.

A particularly tragic case has been the recent destruction of the 'mixed hepatic mat' communities on the Twelve Bens of Connemara (Fig. 6.13), by subsidised overgrazing[66]. Of the populations of *Adelanthus lindenbergianus* (Fig. 4.14) discovered there by Derek in 1961[14], growing "quite abundantly", only a small fragment survives[67].

One response to the overgrazing of heathland communities has been the promotion of tree regeneration by the fencing of areas to exclude large grazing animals. Moore *et al.*[68] were able to examine the effect of the exclusion of Red Deer (*Cervus elaphus*) from the rich mixed hepatic mat vegetation at Coire Dhorrcail, Knoydart, by recording paired quadrats, one inside an exclosure which had been erected 20 years previously and the other outside. The vegetation within the exclosure now consists of thickets of Heather with dense Downy Birch (*Betula pubescens*) regeneration, a stark contrast to the heavily grazed grassland outside. Seven liverwort species associated with the mixed hepatic mat were recorded in the quadrats, and the cover of two, *Bazzania tricrenata* and the most abundant of the seven, *Herbertus hutchinsiae*, was significantly less in the exclosures. The others were too scarce for any difference between the two treatments to be detectable. Bulky pleurocarpous mosses and *Sphagnum* species had increased in the area protected from grazing. There is clearly an optimal level of grazing for the liverwort species at Coire Dhorrcail, where under-grazing has been more destructive to *Herbertus hutchinsiae* than over-grazing.

Rhododendron (Fig. 6.17) now threatens important sites in Scotland as well as in Ireland[31,69,70] and there are currently numerous proposals to exploit ravines in western Britain for hydroelectricity[71], with impacts on the Atlantic bryophyte species which are impossible to predict. To set against these reverses, air quality has improved, resulting in the dramatic range expansion of many epiphytic bryophytes. British and Irish bryologists are much more responsible in their behaviour than they were, and the collection of specimens is no longer a significant threat to the Atlantic species. Finally, in considering the future of the Atlantic species, there are the imponderables of climate change. It is salutary to read that in 1968, "the overall trend at the present seems to be towards lower temperatures" ([4] p. 386). With increasing rather than decreasing temperatures, the Northern Atlantic species would appear to be the most vulnerable, and, as Hodd and Sheehy Skeffington[22] conclude, "the future of the mixed northern hepatic mat is currently unclear".

Acknowledgements

I am grateful to John and Hilary Birks for providing me with their draft chapter on 'Derek Ratcliffe – botanist and plant ecologist', on which I have drawn freely. I thank Mark Hill for a list of Derek's published vice-county records, Björn Beckmann for help in converting this into a map, Oliver Moore for an advance copy of his paper on the impact of red deer management on hepatic mat species, and Sam Bosanquet for information about the conservation of bryophyte sites in Wales. The other maps are based on records collected by members of the British Bryological Society and were plotted by Stephanie Rorke of the Biological Records Centre using the DMAP program written by Dr A.J. Morton. I also thank Sam Bosanquet and Gordon Rothero for generously sharing their expertise on a few memorable days when I have had the privilege of joining them in the field on visits to sites rich in Atlantic species. I am grateful to Sam Bosanquet, Mark Hill, and David Long for comments, to Caroline Pannell for the picture of Brandon Mountain, and to John Birks for providing the other photographs.

References

(1)   Birks, H.J.B. & Birks, H.H. (2015) Derek Ratcliffe – botanist and plant ecologist. In: *Nature's Conscience – The Life and Legacy of Derek Ratcliffe* (eds. D.B.A. Thompson, H.H. Birks & H.J.B. Birks). This volume, Chapter 4.

(2)   Ratcliffe, D.A., Birks, H.J.B. & Birks, H.H. (1993) The ecology and conservation of the Killarney Fern (*Trichomanes speciosum* Willd.) in Britain and Ireland. *Biological Conservation*, **66**, 231-247.

(3)   Ratcliffe, D.A. (2000) *In Search of Nature.* Peregrine Books, Leeds.

(4)   Ratcliffe, D.A. (1968) An ecological account of Atlantic bryophytes in the British Isles. *New Phytologist*, **67**, 365-439.

(5)   Hill, M.O., Blackstock, T.H., Long, D.G. & Rothero, G.P. (2008) *A Checklist and Census Catalogue of British and Irish Bryophytes: Updated 2008.* British Bryological Society, Middlewich.

(6)   Bell, D., Long, D.G., Forrest, A.D., Hollingsworth, M.L., Blom, H.H. & Hollingsworth, P.M. (2012) DNA barcoding of European *Herbertus* (Marchantiopsida, Herbertaceae) and the description of a new species. *Molecular Ecology Resources*, **12**, 36-47.

(7)   Birks, H.J.B. & Birks, H.H. (2006) Obituary. Derek Almey Ratcliffe, B.Sc., Ph.D., D.Sc. (1929-2005). *Journal of Bryology*, **28**, 71-75.

(8)   Spruce, R. (1887) *Lejeunea holtii*, a new hepatic from Killarney. *Journal of Botany*, **25**, 33-39, 72-82.

(9)   Herzog, T. (1926) *Geographie der Moose*. Gustav Fischer, Jena.

(10)   Amann, J. (1929) L'hygrothermie du climat, facteur déterminant la répartition des espèces atlantiques. *Revue Bryologique*, n.s., **2**, 126-133.

(11)   Nicholson, W.E. (1930) 'Atlantic' hepatics in Yunnan. *Annales Bryologici*, **3**, 151-153.

(12)   Greig-Smith, P. (1950) Evidence from hepatics on the history of the British flora. *Journal of Ecology*, **38**, 320-344.

(13)   Warburg, E.F. (1952) New vice-county records. Musci. *Transactions of the British Bryological Society*, **2**, 97-108.

(14)   Ratcliffe, D.A. (1962) The habitat of *Adelanthus unciformis* (Tayl.) Mitt., and *Jamesoniella carringtonii* (Balf.) Spr. in Ireland. *Irish Naturalists' Journal*, **16**, 38-40.

(15)   Birks, H.H., Birks, H.J.B. & Ratcliffe, D.A. (1969) *Geocalyx graveolens* (Schrad.) Nees in Kerry, a hepatic new to Ireland. *Irish Naturalists' Journal*, **16**, 204-205.

(16)   Ratcliffe, D.A. (1975) Obituary. Humphrey Milne-Redhead 1906-1974. *Journal of Bryology*, **8**, 415-416.

(17)   Bell, D. & Long, D.G. (2012) European *Herbertus* and the 'Viking prongwort'. *Field Bryology*, **106**, 3-14.

(18)   Crundwell, A.C. (1970) *Herberta borealis*, a new species from Scotland and Norway. *Transactions of the British Bryological Society*, **6**, 41-49.

(19)   Ratcliffe, D.A. (1970) *Herberta borealis* in Scotland. pp. 44-46. In: Crundwell, A.C. (1970) *Herberta borealis*, a new species from Scotland and Norway. *Transactions of the British Bryological Society*, **6**, 41-49.

(20)   McVean, D.N. & Ratcliffe, D.A. (1962) *Plant Communities of the Scottish Highlands*. Her Majesty's Stationery Office, London.

(21)   Averis, A.M. (1992) Where are all the hepatic mat liverworts in Scotland? *Botanical Journal of Scotland*, **46**, 191-198.

(22)   Hodd, R.L. & Sheehy Skeffington, M.J. (2011) Mixed northern hepatic mat: a threatened and unique community. *Field Bryology*, **104**, 2-11.

(23)   Hodd, R.L. & Sheehy Skeffington, M.J. (2011) Climate change and oceanic mountain vegetation: a case study of the montane heath and associated plant communities in western Irish mountains. In: *Climate Change, Ecology and*

Systematics (eds. T.R. Hodkinson, M.B. Jones, S. Waldren & J.A.N. Parnell). pp. 490-515. Cambridge University Press, Cambridge.

Hodd, R.L., Bourke, D. & Sheehy Skeffington, M. (2014) Projected range contractions of European protected oceanic montane plant communities: Focus on climate change impacts is essential for their future conservation. *PLoS ONE*, **9**, e95147.

(24) Lockhart, N., Hodgetts, N. & Holyoak, D. (2012) *Rare and Threatened Bryophytes of Ireland*. National Museums Northern Ireland, Holywood.

(25) Ratcliffe, D.A. (ed.) (1977) *A Nature Conservation Review. Volume 1.* Cambridge University Press, Cambridge.

(26) Ratcliffe, D.A. (ed.) (1977) *A Nature Conservation Review. Volume 2. Site accounts.* Cambridge University Press, Cambridge.

(27) Hill, M.O. & Preston, C.D. (1998) The geographical relationships of British and Irish bryophytes. *Journal of Bryology*, **20**, 127-226.

(28) Bosanquet, S.D.S. personal communication

(29) Jones, E.W. & Rose, F. (1975) *Plagiochila atlantica* F. Rose, sp. nov. – *P. ambagiosa* auct. *Journal of Bryology*, **8**, 417-422.

(30) Paton, J.A. (1999) *The Liverwort Flora of the British Isles*. Harley Books, Colchester.

(31) Long, D.G. & Rothero, G.P. (2015) Bryology in the Highlands and Islands of Scotland. In: *Nature's Conscience – The Life and Legacy of Derek Ratcliffe* (eds. D.B.A. Thompson, H.H. Birks & H.J.B. Birks). This volume, Chapter 6.

(32) Ratcliffe, D.A. (1965) Distribution maps of bryophytes in Britain. *Anastrophyllum joergensenii* Schiffn. *Transactions of the British Bryological Society*, **4**, 875.

(33) Long, D.G., Paton, J.A., Squirrell, J., Woodhead, M. & Hollingsworth, P.M. (2006) Morphological, ecological and genetic evidence for distinguishing *Anastrophyllum joergensenii* Schiffn. and *A. alpinum* Steph. (Jungermanniopsida: Lophoziaceae). *Journal of Bryology*, **28**, 108-117.

(34) Groth, H., Lindner, M., Wilson, R., Hartmann, F.A., Schmull, M., Gradstein, S.R. & Heinrichs, J. (2003) Biogeography of *Plagiochila* (Hepaticae): natural species groups span several floristic kingdoms. *Journal of Biogeography*, **30**, 965-978.

(35) Heinrichs, J. Grolle, R. & Drehwald, U. (1998) The conspecificity of *Plagiochila killarniensis* Pearson and *P. bifaria* (Sw.) Lindenb. (Hepaticae). *Journal of Bryology*, **20**, 495-497.

(36) Heinrichs, J., Groth, H., Lindner, M., Feldberg, K. & Rycroft, D.S. (2004) Molecular, morphological, and phytochemical evidence for a broad species concept of *Plagiochila bifaria* (Hepaticae). *The Bryologist*, **107**, 28-40.

(37) Davison, P.G., Smith, D.K., Feldberg, K., Lindner, M. & Heinrichs, J. (2006) *Plagiochila punctata* (Plagiochilaceae) in Tennessee, new to North America. *The Bryologist*, **109**, 242-246.

(38) Heinrichs, J., Lindner, M., Groth, H. & Renker, C. (2005) Distribution and synonymy of *Plagiochila punctata* (Taylor) Taylor, with hypotheses on the evolutionary history of *Plagiochila* sect. *Arrectae* (Plagiochilaceae, Hepaticae). *Plant Systematics and Evolution*, **250**, 105-117.

(39) Váňa, J. (1990) *Cephalozia* (Dum.) Dum. in Africa, with notes on the genus (Notes on some African Hepatic Genera 10). *Beihefte zur Nova Hedwigia*, **90**, 179-198.

(40) Dirkse, G.M., Bouman, A.C. & Losada-Lima, A. (1993) Bryophytes of the Canary Islands, an annotated checklist. *Cryptogamie, Bryologie Lichénologie*, **14**, 1-47.

(41) Engell, J.J. & Merrill, G.J.S. (2004) Austral Hepaticae. 35. A taxonomic and phylogenetic study of *Telaranea* (Lepidoziaceae), with a monograph of the genus in temperate Australasia, and a commentary on extra-Australasian taxa. *Fieldiana, Botany* n.s., **46**, 1-265.

(42) Laenen, B., Désamoré, A., Devos, N., Shaw, A.J., González-Mancebo, J.-M., Carine, M.A. & Vanderpoorten, A. (2011) Macaronesia: a source of hidden genetic diversity for post-glacial recolonization of western Europe in the leafy liverwort *Radula lindenbergiana*. *Journal of Biogeography*, **38**, 631–639.

(43) Pätsch, R., Hentschel, J., Linares-Palomino, R., Zhu, R.-L. & Heinrichs, J. (2010) Diversification and taxonomy of the liverwort *Jubula* Dumort. (Jungermanniopsida: Porellales) inferred from nuclear and chloroplast DNA sequences. *Systematic Botany*, **35**, 6-12.

(44) Heinrichs, J., Lindner, M., Groth, H., Hentschel, J., Feldberg, K., Renker, C., Engel, J.J., Konrat, M. von, Long, D.G. & Schneider, H. (2006) Goodbye or welcome Gondwana? – insights into the phylogenetic biogeography of the leafy liverwort *Plagiochila* with a description of *Proskauera*, gen. nov. (Plagiochilaceae, Jungermanniales). *Plant Systematics and Evolution*, **258**, 227-250.

(45) Hill, M.O., Preston, C.D. & Smith, A.J.E. (1991-94) *Atlas of the Bryophytes of Britain and Ireland*. 3 vols. Harley Books, Colchester.

(46) Blockeel, T.L., Bosanquet, S.D.S., Hill, M.O. & Preston, C.D. (2014) *Atlas of British and Irish Bryophytes: The Distribution and Habitat of Mosses and Liverworts in Britain and Ireland*. 2 volumes. Pisces Publications, Newbury.

(47) Corley, M.F.V. & Wallace, E.C. (1974) *Dicranodontium subporodictyon* Broth. in Scotland. *Journal of Bryology*, **8**, 185-189.

(48) Moore, O. (2011) Current status of the known populations of *Lejeunea mandonii* in Scotland. *Field Bryology*, **103**, 2-8.

(49) Bosanquet, S.D.S. (2013) Wildlife reports. Bryophytes. *British Wildlife*, **24**, 212-214.

(50) Bosanquet, S.D.S. (2010). *The Mosses and Liverworts of Pembrokeshire*. Privately published.

(51) Bosanquet, S.D.S., Graham, J.G. & Motley, G.S. (2005) *The Mosses and Liverworts of Carmarthenshire*. Privately published.

(52) Averis, A.B.G. (1991) *A survey of the bryophytes of 448 woods in the Scottish Highlands*. Scottish Field Unit Survey Report no. 54. Nature Conservancy Council, Edinburgh.

(53) Averis, A.B.G. (2007) Habitats of *Colura calyptrifolia* in north-western Britain. *Field Bryology*, **91**, 17-21.

(54) Averis, A.B.G. (2009) *Colura calyptrifolia* growing on rubbish in a Scottish conifer plantation. *Field Bryology*, **99**, 19-21.

(55) Bosanquet, S.D.S. (2004) *Colura calyptrifolia* in Wales. *Field Bryology*, **82**, 3-5.

(56) Bosanquet, S.D.S., Coote, L., Kelly, D.L., Long, D.G. & Preston, C.D. (2010) *Daltonia splachnoides* in Irish conifer plantations – another epiphyte on the move. *Field Bryology*, **100**, 16-21.

(57) Bates, J.W. & Preston, C.D. (2011) Can the effects of climate change on British bryophytes be distinguished from those resulting from other environmental changes? In: *Bryophyte Ecology and Climate Change* (eds. Z. Tuba, N.G., Slack & L.R. Stark). pp. 371-407. Cambridge University Press, Cambridge.

(58) Preston, C.D., Harrower, C.A. & Hill, M.O. (2011) Distribution patterns in British and Irish liverworts and hornworts. *Journal of Bryology*, **33**, 3-16.

(59) Preston, C.D., Harrower, C.A. & Hill, M.O. (2013) A comparison of distribution patterns in British and Irish mosses and liverworts. *Journal of Bryology*, **35**, 71-87.

(60) Edwards, M.E. (1986) Disturbance histories of four Snowdonian woodlands and their relation to Atlantic bryophyte distributions. *Biological Conservation*, **37**, 301-320.

(61) Edwards, M.E. & Birks, H.J.B. (1986) Vegetation and ecology of four western oakwoods (Blechno-Quercetum petraeae Br.-Bl. et Tx. 1952) in North Wales. *Phytocoenologia*, **14**, 237-262.

(62) Birks, H.J.B. (1993) Quaternary palaeoecology and vegetation science - current contributions and possible future developments. *Review of Palaeobotany and Palynology*, **79**, 153-177.

(63) Flagmeier, M., Long. D.G., Genney, D.R., Hollingsworth, P.M. & Woodin, S.J. (2013) Regneration capacity of oceanic-montane liverworts: implications for community distribution and conservation. *Journal of Bryology*, **35**, 12-19.

(64) Flagmeier, M., Long. D.G., Genney, D.R., Hollingsworth, P.M., Ross, L.C. & Woodin, S.J. (2014) Fifty years of vegetation change in oceanic-montane liverwort-rich heath in Scotland. *Plant Ecology & Diversity, 7,* 457-470.

(65) Hobbs, A.M. (1988) Conservation of leafy liverwort-rich *Calluna vulgaris* heath in Scotland. In: *Ecological Change in the Uplands* (eds. M.B. Usher & D.B.A. Thompson). pp. 339-343. Blackwell Scientific Publications, Oxford.

(66) Holyoak, D.T. (2006) Progress towards a species inventory for conservation of bryophytes in Ireland. *Proceedings of the Royal Irish Academy*, **106B**, 225-236.

(67) Long, D.G. (2010) The tragedy of the Twelve Bens of Connemara: is there a future for *Adelanthus lindenbergianus*? *Field Bryology*, **100**, 2-8.

(68) Moore, O., Standen, L. & Crawley, M.J. (2014) The impact of red deer management on liverworts associated with the mixed hepatic mat community and other terrestrial cryptogams. *Plant Ecology and Diversity* (in press). DOI: 10.1080/17550874.2013.815664.

(69) Rothero, G.P. (2003) Bryophyte conservation in Scotland. *Botanical Journal of Scotland*, **55**, 17-26.

(70)   Preston, C.D. (2010) Alien plants in Scotland - is there a problem? In: *Species Management: Challenges and Solutions for the 21ˢᵗ Century* (eds. J.M. Baxter & C.A. Galbraith). pp. 193-208. The Stationery Office, Edinburgh.

(71)   Averis, A.B.G., Hodgetts, N.G., Rothero, G.P. & Genny, D. (2011) *Bryological Assessment for Hydroelectric Schemes in the West Highlands*. SNH Commissioned Report 449, Inverness.

8. In the field with Derek Ratcliffe: long days and driving at speed

Lynne Farrell

In my first job in 1965, as a botanical assistant in the Conservation Research Section of the Nature Conservancy's Monks Wood Experimental Station in Huntingdonshire, I heard about an elusive but very knowledgeable person called Derek Ratcliffe. From all accounts, he was the one to talk to about natural history, conservation, and most importantly to me at that time, fieldwork. If you wanted to learn a lot, discuss your findings and their implications, then this was who you needed to speak to. But where was he, and how and when could I find him? Although nominally based at Monks Wood, he rarely appeared, and when he did it was quite difficult for a junior member of staff simply to ask for a meeting with such a senior scientist. Such things were not done; you had to wait in line, and hope for a chance meeting before he was off into the wilds again!

Well, eventually I did meet him, but only after he came to discuss the defence of Upper Teesdale with my boss, Terry Wells. He seemed very approachable, quite normal really, and with a tremendous knowledge and fervour for all aspects of nature. Informal chats in the canteen confirmed my suspicions – this was indeed 'the man for all seasons'. His quiet, rather shy, authoritative manner allowed you to listen intently to him, and he was always willing to look at specimens, even if they were common, and then to pronounce on the species and their significance.

During this time at Monks Wood, we were suddenly dispatched to help with a major project entitled the Nature Conservation Review (NCR), which Derek would edit and bring together[1]. The chalk grassland section at Monks Wood had to spend most weeks over the next two summers in the field travelling throughout much of England, surveying potential sites. This was a delightful period, dashing around in a long-wheel-base landrover (no power steering then) visiting sites, recording quadrats, and taking detailed notes and photographs. In the evenings we would go through the information, deciding on the best sites and ranking them. All this information was synthesised by my bosses, and ultimately rationalised by Derek in the publication of *A Nature Conservation Review*[2].

Enthused by all this, I went off to the New University of Ulster at Coleraine (now the University of Ulster) for three years, and then worked surveying sites in southern Ireland, before returning to Monks Wood to research a report on the Chequered Skipper (*Carterocephalus palaemon*) butterfly. I then obtained a permanent job as Franklyn Perring's botanical assistant in the Biological Records Centre (BRC), which is where I again met Derek. My job was mainly dealing with plant records, recorders, and plant distribution, so I would often be asked for information and summaries of the relevance and importance of various species. Even Derek needed to check things occasionally. One of the species he enquired about was one of his favourite plants, Killarney Fern (*Trichomanes speciosum*) (Fig. 4.3)[3–5], and we discovered that the records for this species were totally inadequate and out-of-date. So, we set about sorting them. Needless to say, the Ratcliffe records were so much more informative than previous ones[5]. This developed into Derek approaching Franklyn Perring about updating and surveying many of Britain's rarer species, especially timely as the first British Red Data Book on vascular plants[6] was in progress. Gigi Crompton was known to Derek, and was taken on to help with this work, and the Rare Plant Surveys for all English and Welsh counties came to be based on her initial formats and reports.

Figure 8.1. Military Orchid (*Orchis militaris*), an extremely rare orchid in Britain. Suffolk, 1978. Photo: John Birks

Whilst at BRC, I met Joanna Robertson (Martin), who was then an area officer in Dumfries and Galloway, where she had met Derek through his interest in the Silver Flowe bogs[4]. She later moved to Banbury, working in Berkshire, Buckinghamshire, and Oxfordshire, where we worked together on the Military Orchid (*Orchis militaris*) (Fig. 8.1). All Monks Wood, colleagues—including Derek—were pressed into helping monitor the populations of this rare orchid over the next 20 years, which I had the joy of coordinating (Fig. 8.2). Derek, of course, asked many pertinent questions about its population ecology and biology, which helped me in the preparation of its Biological Flora[7,8]. But, it was the Purple Emperor (*Apatura iris*) which gave us all an exciting day out. Derek really wanted to see this butterfly, and so I discovered from Joanna where we might find it. Derek was delighted, and we set off early one summer's morning from Needingworth, where I was living. Derek was at the wheel of his splendid dark blue Triumph Stag, which he drove at great speed. Yes, fast sports cars do have an appeal for most young ladies! And driving at speed like a racing-driver was one of Derek's passions! We collected Joanna at Banbury, squashed her in the back of the Stag, and proceeded to Bernwood Forest. Now into the late morning (the Purple Emperor is an early day flier), we spent several hours searching, peering into the oak canopy through binoculars, and flashing pieces of silvery-blue foil in the sunlight to attract the males. But to no avail; we were even bold enough to mention its attraction to urine. Derek was contemplating this remark when suddenly an Emperor swooped down and alighted on the bonnet of the Triumph Stag, glinting in the sunshine in the car park. I have to say, we were triumphant!

Figure 8.2. Derek Ratcliffe at the Rex Graham nature reserve, Suffolk (1984). Photo: Lynne Farrell

In 1973 the Nature Conservancy was split into the Nature Conservancy Council (NCC) and the Institute of Terrestrial Ecology[1], the former concentrating mainly on nature conservation management and policy, and the latter on research aspects: both working together in a cohesive way. Staff had to decide for which organisation they wished to work and to apply for a post. I opted for the NCC, but it was a difficult choice, as I was interested in all aspects of ecology and conservation. One of the deciding factors was that Derek was setting up the Chief Scientist Team (CST) and looking for botanists. Dare I hope I would be considered? I went along to a sort of interview with Derek, not very formal, and discussed various botanical and conservation topics. Some months later I heard I had been successful and so began a truly rewarding time as a botanist and lowland heathland specialist in the CST. This job occupied me for many years and taught me the most about nature conservation.

Derek was the ultimate field teacher, and anyone who was fortunate to accompany him in the field was simply amazed by his instant empathy for the plants and animals, and their niches (Fig. 8.3). As I had become an overnight specialist on lowland heaths (literally), Derek invited me to accompany him to Lazonby and Wan Fells in Cumbria. There was some doubt about their current management and grading in the NCR. However, before we reached this area, we detoured to another one at the request of the regional staff, where a major landowner was unsure of the nature conservation value of his land. What he had in mind was pheasant rearing and shooting. The local staff thought Derek might be able to help, particularly as he had served in the Army[9] and the owner had an Army back-

Figure 8.3. Derek Ratcliffe at Waldridge Fell, Durham (1969).
Photo: Lynne Farrell

ground. So, we wandered around the site slowly walking through mixed woodland and heath. Derek chatted with the owner, pointing out Green Hairstreaks (*Callophrys rubi*), which the owner had never seen before, identifying the birds by their calls, then turning to the different species of trees and plants, and finally bringing it all together in a summary of the overall interest. He also touched on aspects of site management, and asked why the owner was so interested in pheasants. Would he not be interested in putting some cattle on his land to help graze it? After three hours the owner was convinced, the regional staff had a positive solution to a future management agreement, and I had a fantastic example of how to tackle a potentially difficult problem using a gentle approach combined with tremendous knowledge of the environment and people's backgrounds and interests.

After that, we were off to Lazonby and Wan Fells. They are extensive and slightly separate sites, each with their own characteristics. Were they really lowland heaths at 247 m (810 ft) elevation? The entry in the NCR[2] records the eventual decision – "the affinities with upland heather moorland are strong". But it was only by walking across much of the rough terrain discussing lowland and upland characteristics, and looking at the variety of habitats, that we reached this conclusion. There is no substitute for seeing a site at first hand.

Was that the end of the day? Oh no! We then stopped off and ambled along a wooded river valley with no apparent purpose. I was getting rather tired after a further hour or so. Eventually I sat down on a shaded rock, whilst Derek said he would just go on a bit further. Fifteen minutes later he returned and I enquired whether he had found anything special. "No", he replied, there was just some good habitat. Later, I learnt he had been to an old Killarney Fern site[5], which he hoped to re-find, but did not on this occasion. That was an opportunity missed by me! Always make the most of the whole day – another lesson learned.

When the NCC relocated its headquarters to Peterborough, there were small sections of surrounding land which were initially planted out with the usual non-native shrubs and other plants. It was suggested that we could do better and show the attractiveness of native plants. So Marney Hall, who had worked at Monks Wood as an entomological assistant, and was now into a new career as a native plant garden designer, was engaged to design and plant out these beds. I asked for a small plot to be left, as I wanted somewhere for a surplus of rare plants from East Anglia, successfully grown from native seed by Cambridge Botanic Gardens, as part of the Species Recovery Project. So, I toiled in front of the office at lunchtimes, planting out various species –some of which looked much more attractive than others. Everyone was of the opinion that they would not last long and would be removed overnight by persons unknown. However, they were not, and once an explanatory and illustrated board accompanied them, people would stop to admire and enjoy them. Whenever I was out weeding, passers-by would stop and ask me about the plot's plants. It was easy to explain, and it was a simple way to get the message across about how interesting plants can be. None was removed without permission!

When I had initially planted it up, I needed someone to admire my handy work. Who better than Derek, who was writing assiduously in his office on a lovely summer's day, and obviously needed a quick break? Not many Chief Scientists would put down the pen at short notice, come down in their shirt sleeves, christen a new flower-bed with a watering can, and then stand to have their photograph taken in full view of the whole office and the local people (Fig. 8.4). Well, Derek did! That was typical of Derek – a very down-to-earth, yet quite exceptional person.

Figure 8.4. Derek Ratcliffe at Northminster House, Peterborough watering Lynne Farrell's newly planted East Anglian rare plants, 1988. Photo: Lynne Farrell

References

(1)   Thompson, D.B.A., Sutherland, W.J. & Birks, H.J.B. (2015) Nature conservation and the Nature Conservation Review – a novel philosophical framework. In: *Nature's Conscience – The Life and Legacy of Derek Ratcliffe* (eds. D.B.A. Thompson, H.H. Birks & H.J.B. Birks). This volume, Chapter 19.

(2)   Ratcliffe, D.A. (ed.) (1977) *A Nature Conservation Review, Volumes 1 and 2*. Cambridge University Press, Cambridge.

(3)   Ratcliffe, D.A. (2000) *In Search of Nature*. Peregrine Books, Leeds.

(4)   Birks, H.J.B. & Birks, H.H. (2015) Derek Ratcliffe – botanist and plant ecologist. In: *Nature's Conscience: Life and Legacy of Derek Ratcliffe* (eds. D.B.A. Thompson, H.H. Birks & H.J.B. Birks). This volume, Chapter 4.

(5)   Ratcliffe, D.A., Birks, H.J.B. & Birks, H.H. (1993) The ecology and conservation of the Killarney Fern *Trichomanes speciosum* Willd. in Britain and Ireland. *Biological Conservation*, **66**, 231-247.

(6)   Perring, F.H. & Farrell, L. (1977) *British Red Data Books, 1. Vascular Plants*. Royal Society for Nature Conservation, London.
        Perring, F.H. & Farrell, L. (1983) *British Red Data Books, 1. Vascular Plants* (Second edition). Royal Society for Nature Conservation, London.

(7)   Farrell, L. (1985) Biological flora of the British Isles: *Orchis militaris* L. *Journal of Ecology*, **73**, 1041-1053.

(8)   Farrell, L. (1991) Population changes and management of *Orchis militaris* at two sites in England. In: *Population Ecology of Terrestrial Orchids* (eds. T.C.E. Wells & J.H. Willems). pp. 63-68. SPB Academic Publishing, The Hague.

(9)   Mitchell, J. (2015) National Service and beyond. In: *Nature's Conscience: Life and Legacy of Derek Ratcliffe* (eds. D.B.A. Thompson, H.H. Birks & H.J.B. Birks). This volume, Chapter 2.

9. Royal Botanic Garden Edinburgh (RBGE) and caring for Scotland's flora

David Rae

Introduction

The Royal Botanic Garden Edinburgh (RBGE) can be traced back to 1670 when two physicians, Andrew Balfour and Robert Sibbald established a small garden adjacent to the Royal Palace of Holyrood House. Its purpose was to cultivate medicinal herbs for supply and for teaching apothecaries. It soon became too small and in 1675 a new site was found on what is now Waverley railway station. This site was prone to flooding from Nor' Loch (now Princes Street Gardens) which, along with its restricted size, forced another move, in 1763, to a greenfield site in north Edinburgh. A fourth and final move to the current site in the Inverleith district of Edinburgh (Figs. 9.1 & 9.2) was made in 1820-1823. The Garden has thus moved, grown, and developed within Edinburgh, but it has also grown across Scotland with the addition of its three Regional Gardens at Benmore in Argyll (1928), Logan, south of Stranraer (1969), and Dawyck, near Peebles (1979).

Initially, RBGE's focus was purely on medicinal plants, and as many of those used were native species it is therefore unsurprising to see many listed in the Garden's first Catalogue of Plants, Sutherland's *Hortus Medicus Edinburghensis* of 1683. A study[1] of this Catalogue reveals that of the 2000 items listed, 383 plants (about 20%) were considered 'officinal', in other words were used medicinally, with the rest being either ornamental or Scottish natives. By the latter half of the 18th century, the 4th Regius Keeper, John Hope, began an interest in physiology and classification (he was one of the first British advocates of the Linnaean classification system). Hence botany, as a discipline independent of medicine, began to emerge in RBGE in Hope's day.

In the early 20th century, with plants new to science arriving from China and the Himalaya, expertise centred on important genera such as *Rhododendron* and *Primula*. Plant systematics, biodiversity studies, evolution, and development, along with horticulture, conservation, and education are the main activities of RBGE today, with partic-

155

ular expertise in several plant families and geographical regions including Scotland. The recording, study, description, and now conservation, of native plants has been a constant thread running through RBGE's history with activity on Scottish plants stronger now than for many years, despite the very international scope of RBGE's research.

Figure 9.1. Azaleas in full bloom at the Royal Botanic Garden Edinburgh, with Display Glasshouses and Temperate and Tropical Palmhouses behind, 2009. Photo: David Knott

History of early recording and collecting of Scottish plants by RBGE staff

Robert Sibbald was commissioned by Charles II to prepare a general botanical description of Scotland. The result was *Scotia Illustrata*[2], published in 1684, followed by a 1696 edition. Its second part lists nearly 500 species although some are not really Scottish natives. Only two species are recorded for the first time as British, Alpine Sibbaldia (*Sibbaldia procumbens*) and Scots Lovage (*Ligusticum scoticum*). Many references to plants in the neighbourhood of Edinburgh are noted, including the rare Sticky Catchfly (*Lychnis viscaria*) (Fig. 9.3) and Forked Spleenwort (*Asplenium septentrionale*) (Fig. 4.17), both discovered on Arthur's Seat where they still grow.

In 1762, the London apothecary, William Hudson published *Flora Anglica*[3], but it contained only a few Scottish records. The next major advance was Rev. John Lightfoot's *Flora Scotica*[4] of 1778 which marked a major advance in knowledge about Scotland's plants, with 1,250 species listed.

Despite Lightfoot's *Flora*[4], John Hope (Regius Keeper 1761-1786) and his students

Figure 9.2. Alpine House surrounded by alpine plant troughs with the Temperate Palmhouse in the background at the Royal Botanic Garden Edinburgh, 2010. Photo David Knott

were the pioneer investigators of the Scottish flora for, from Hope's notebooks, it is clear that his students recorded and collected widely in Scotland. Hope helped Lightfoot with the itinerary for his visit to Scotland in 1772. In the preface to *Flora Scotica*, Lightfoot records that Hope "not only favoured me with the sight of his copious Herbarium, but permitted me the use of his notes and observations, the result of a long enquiry." The whereabouts of the "copious Herbarium" is not known but from Hope's notebooks it is clear that he and his students had collected many Scottish plants long before they had been found by others and published as new records for the Scottish or British flora. An example is Alpine Speedwell (*Veronica alpina*), collected on Ben Nevis in 1768. Lightfoot, during his 1772 tour, is generally considered to have discovered Alpine Meadow-grass (*Poa alpina*), Trailing Azalea (*Loiseleuria procumbens*), Leafy Spurge (*Euphorbia esula*), Creeping Spearwort (*Ranunculus reptans*), Pyramidal Bugle (*Ajuga pyramidalis*) (Fig. 4.11), Creeping Lady's-tresses (*Goodyera repens*), and Dwarf Birch (*Betula nana*), and yet all are listed by Hope in his herbarium in 1768 (while the whereabouts of his herbarium is unknown, its contents are listed in one of his notebooks held in RBGE's library).

John Hope's Head Gardeners not only managed the daily work of the botanic garden but were also responsible for helping with practical classes and taking field trips. Many were very proficient field botanists. John Williamson is probably the best remembered due to the memorial tablet erected by Hope in his memory. James Robertson, though not so closely linked to the Garden, deserves mention too for recording plants (as well as geology, agriculture, people, and ruins) on his travels through Scotland in 1761-1771[5]. John Rutherford's (Regius Keeper 1786-1819) teaching followed the same general pattern of Hope's, but he did not appear to have encouraged field botany among his students as Hope had done. Even so, the exploration of the Scottish flora expanded, but only because of the enthusiasm and ability of Rutherford's Principal Gardeners. John McKay was Principal Gardener from 1800-1802 when field botany flourished. In the summers of 1800 and 1801, for instance, McKay led some of the keenest students on botanical excursions around Edinburgh and to the Highlands and Islands.

In 1804 George Don (Principal Gardener 1802-1806) began to publish his *Herbarium Britannicum*[6]. During his frequent visits to Ben Lawers he collected Mountain Sandwort (*Minuartia rubella*), Alpine Forget-me-not (*Myosotis alpestris*), and Scorched Alpine-sedge (*Carex atrofusca*) (Fig. 4.10), all new to the British flora, also Alpine Woodsia (*Woodsia alpina*) (Fig. 4.11) and the three rushes Two-flowered Rush (*Juncus biglumis*), Bulbous Rush (*J. bulbosus*), and Chestnut Rush (*J. castaneus*). Other new discoveries and new locations included Alpine Bartsia (*Bartsia alpina*), Alpine Pearlwort (*Sagina saginoides*), and Sheathed Sedge (*Carex vaginata*). He discovered Curved Wood-rush (*Luzula arcuata*), Mountain Bog-sedge (*Carex rariflora*), Oblong-leaved Hawkweed (*Hieracium lingulatum*), Yellow Oxytropis (*Oxytropis campestris*), Sticky Catchfly (Fig 9.3), Sea Pearlwort (*Sagina maritima*), Russet Sedge (*Carex saxatilis*), Bladder-sedge (*Carex versicaria*), Alpine Mouse-ear (*Cerastium alpinum*), Purple Saxifrage (*Saxifraga oppositifolia*), Highland Saxifrage (*Saxifraga rivularis*) (Fig. 4.10), Alpine Meadow-rue (*Thalictrum alpinum*), Pyrenean Scurvygrass (*Cochlearia pyrenaica* ssp. *alpina*), Alpine Blue-sow-thistle (*Cicerbita alpina*), and the grasses Alpine Tufted Hair-grass (*Deschampsia cespitosa* ssp. *alpina*), Alpine Foxtail (*Alopecurus magellanicus*; previously *A. borealis*) (Fig. 5.4), Wavy Meadow-grass (*Poa flexuosa*), and Swedish Meadow-grass (*Poa x jemtlandica*). Localities included Ben Nevis, Cairngorm, Schiehallion, Ben Vorlich, and Lochnagar. Don's most important paper was *An account of the native plants in the county of Forfar, and the animals to be found there*[7]. This formed Appendix B to the *General View of the Agriculture of the County of Angus, or Forfarshire* and lists 90 species of flowering plant, 100 bryophytes, and 120 lichens.

Annually in August and September, accompanied by William McNab (Head Gardener 1810-1838), and some students and friends, Robert Graham (Regius Keeper 1819-1845) would travel through various parts of Scotland, England, and Ireland, searching and studying the native flora. As a result several additions to the British flora were made, including Small Restharrow (*Ononis reclinata*) and Alpine Milk-vetch (*Astragalus alpinus*) which he, with one of his students, William Brand, and Robert Kaye Greville, author of the *Scottish Cryptogamic Flora*[8] discovered in Glen Doll, Clova, in 1831.

Despite his ability and hard work, Graham was greatly overshadowed as a Scottish botanist by William Jackson Hooker (Joseph Hooker's father) who was appointed to the University of Glasgow Regius Chair of Botany in 1820, publishing *Flora Scotica*[9] in 1821 and *British Flora*[10] in 1830.

Graham is also remembered for helping to establish the Botanical Society of Edinburgh (now Botanical Society of Scotland (BSS)), founded on 8 February 1836. This was devoted exclusively to advancing botanical science and Graham was elected its first President. As well as meetings and excursions, a main activity was collecting and exchanging herbarium specimens. Initially all specimens were housed in the University but in 1863 the foreign and then the British specimens were gifted to RBGE. So too, in 1872, was the Society's extensive library.

Early volumes of the Society's *Transactions* show how closely its members were in touch with advances in knowledge of the British flora. It was the practice for botany classes to hold regular excursions to study plants in the field and throughout the pages of the first dozen volumes of the *Transactions* there are records of the species observed. Likewise, especially from 1885-1925, there are numerous papers by botanists noted for their work on various aspects of the British flora.

John Hutton Balfour succeeded Graham in 1845 (with his son, Isaac Bayley Balfour, who was Regius Keeper from 1888-1922, the Balfours ruled the Garden for a total of 68 years, 34 years each, but with a seven year gap in the middle, 1880-1887 while Alexander Dickson was Regius Keeper) and during his tenure the Garden flourished. As well as stimulating lectures, he continued the tradition of field work, introducing generations of students to Scottish plants and documenting their occurrence and localities. However, as well as simply identifying and recording the plants seen, Balfour was keen to add extra value and used the excursions to describe the plants' biology and ecology.

The excursion accounts that Balfour wrote are remarkable not only for the number of plants recorded but also for the picture they give of the attitude of those undertaking the excursions. For instance, in the *Edinburgh New Philosophical Journal* for July 1848[11], Balfour prefaces his account of a three-week excursion in 1847 to the richest alpine districts in Britain – the mountains of Braemar, Glen Isla, Clova, and Ben Lawers with these remarks:

> "Excursions may be truly said to be the *life* of the botanist. They enable him to study the science practically, by the examination of plants in their living state, and in their native localities; they impress upon the mind the structural and physiological lessons he has received; they exhibit to him the geographical range of species, both as regards latitude and altitude; and with the pursuit of scientific knowledge, they combine that healthful and spirit-stirring recreation which tends materially to aid mental efforts. The companionship too of those who are prosecuting with zeal and enthusiasm the same path of science, is not the least delightful feature of such excursions…"

In 1854 Balfour was given an assistant, John Sadler, to help him with his increasingly heavy workload. Sadler was an enthusiastic walker who botanised extensively. He gained a great knowledge of the Scottish flora, especially Perthshire. In 1879 he was appointed Curator on the death of James McNab. Sadler was an active member of the Botanical Society and the Scottish Alpine Botanical Club. He had an almost unrivalled knowledge of Scottish plants, and discovered many new locations. His name is perpetuated by the small willow, *Salix* x *sadleri*, a hybrid between Woolly Willow (*Salix lanata*) and Dwarf Willow (*S. herbacea*).

While all this botanising, recording, and collecting was building up a picture of what native species existed in Scotland, there was no comprehensive account of the geographic distribution of the species. However, this changed in 1832 when Hewett Cottrell Watson published *Outlines of the Geographical Distribution of British Plants*[12]. Watson had been a student in Edinburgh and knew Graham and William Hooker. His writings on the geographical distribution of the British flora covered a period of over 40 years. After the *Outlines*, Watson started compiling what was to be his most important publication – *Cybele Britannica*[13], or *British Plants and their Geographical Relations*, a work of four volumes published between 1847 and 1859.

Robert Lindsay succeeded Sadler as Curator and he was also an excellent field botanist. He had a deep knowledge of alpine plants and cultivated them expertly. In his Scottish explorations he made several exciting finds; his most notable was discovering a white form of Alpine Milk-vetch on Ben Vrackie, near Pitlochry.

In 1903, Balfour appointed Robert Moyes Adam as an assistant gardener but Adam soon proved that he was much more than a gardener. He had a flair for drawing and a deep interest in Scotland's native plants. He was also a talented photographer and in his spare time photographed wild plants, especially alpines[14]. In his official working time he photographed vast numbers of new Sino-Himalayan introductions to the Garden. Adam was appointed RBGE's Photographer and Artist, and in 1915 became assistant in the Studio. Adam held this post until retiring in 1949, by which time he had earned an unrivalled reputation as a photographer of Scottish landscapes and plants[14]. His photographic archives are now held in University of St Andrews' Library.

A 460 page entry in the Garden's *Notes from the Royal Botanic Garden Edinburgh*[15] (now the *Edinburgh Journal of Botany*) gives a fascinating insight into the number of botanical excursions made and places visited. Titled *History of the RBGE, Botanical excursions made by Prof John Hutton Balfour in the years 1846-1878 inclusive*, the entry lists every excursion undertaken, the number in each party, destination, and plants seen or collected. Excursions took place most Saturdays from mid-May to September, averaging about 12 excursions each year but rising to 17 in 1864. In addition there was a two-week excursion further afield.

In the later part of the 19th century and early part of the 20th century botanical excursions and work on British and Scottish native plants did not decrease, but work on the new influx of Sino-Himalayan plants increased, giving the impression that that was the main focus of the Garden's work. Whilst Balfour concentrated mainly on the two great genera of *Rhododendron* and *Primula*, Wright Smith (Regius Keeper 1922-1956) endeavoured to encompass the rest. Between 1912 and 1921 he published descriptions of over 550 species, including species of Saxifrage (*Saxifraga*), Rock-jasmine (*Androsace*), Larkspur (*Delphinium*), Gentian (*Gentiana*), Bonnet Bellflower (*Codonopsis*), Ragwort (*Senecio*), Michaelmas Daisy (*Aster*), Magnolia (*Magnolia*), and Cotoneaster (*Cotoneaster*) in *Notes from the Royal Botanic Garden Edinburgh*.

Mention should be made of the influence of J.R. Matthews on Scottish botany and teaching at this time. In 1920 he was appointed a lecturer in Botany at Edinburgh University under Professor Isaac Bailey Balfour and in 1934 he was appointed Regius Professor of Botany at Aberdeen University. He was a major influence on the Botanical Society of Edinburgh, an excellent teacher, and enthusiastic field botanist[16].

Fletcher and Brown[17] provide more detail of RBGE's early involvement in Scottish plant recording, collecting, and discovery and Burnett[18] provides a detailed account of Scotland's vegetation.

RBGE's contribution to Scottish plant surveying and documentation in the second half of the 20th century

Details of the Garden's involvement in native plant research and recording for the first half of the 20th century are sketchy, but the two wars meant that staff numbers were limited. In the second half of the century, various staff were involved curating the British herbarium and handling enquiries: Ian Hedge (who is best known for his work on Lamiaceae, Brassicaceae, and plants of SW Asia), Peter Green, Bill Burtt (better known for his work on Gesneriaceae and the flora of southern Africa), and Andrew Grierson, before the move to the new herbarium in 1964 took place, then later on Win Muirhead. About this time, H.H. (David) Davidian, of *Rhododendron* fame, lectured to students on British botany and took them on local excursions.

In the 1970s Paul Harrold joined the staff and was assigned to work on the British herbarium. He was contacted by Lynne Farrell and Franklyn Perring from the Nature Conservancy's Monks Wood Experimental Station and asked if he would be prepared to take on the ownership of the Scottish Rare Plant records. At that time rare plants were considered to be species which occurred in less than fifteen 10-km grid squares in Great Britain. He went to Monks Wood and, with Farrell and Perring, extracted the Scottish records which were all held on paper sheets, sometimes with additional notes attached. This coincided with the disbanding of the Committee for the Study of the Scottish Flora (CSSF) and the creation of a Scottish sub-group of the Botanical Society of the British Isles (BSBI) (now the Botanical Society of Britain and Ireland). In 1975 he spent some months carrying out a survey of many of the Scottish rare-species sites which was made difficult by the inaccuracy of locations given (well before modern technology and GPS). This was funded by the then Nature Conservancy and a report was written containing accurate localities, assessments of populations, and obvious conservation risks. In 1976 Harrold visited one of the Rannoch Moor sites of Rannoch-rush (*Scheuchzeria palustris*) and collected, under permit, a small quantity of live material for cultivation at Benmore Botanic Garden. Regrettably, this species proved to be irresistible to Rabbits (*Oryctolagus cuniculus*) and is no longer growing at Benmore.

When Harrold moved in 1980, Douglas McKean took over, holding the post until 2008. During this time the job involved curating the British Herbarium, recording new locations for Scottish plants, answering public enquiries about native species, and liaising with what is now Scottish Natural Heritage (SNH).

In the 1970s RBGE started undertaking detailed vegetation surveys of plants occurring in Sites of Special Scientific Interest (SSSI) for what was then the Nature Conservancy Council and these became an annual tradition lasting for up to three weeks each year. Surveys frequently also included bryophytes and lichens and often focussed on particular habitats such as aquatic or alpine habitats. These surveys were also used for training purposes and many new recruits to the herbarium found themselves on these trips which were usually remembered in hindsight with fondness, even if they appeared an ordeal at the time because of midges and wet weather.

While not so much involved in documenting the occurrence of Scottish native plants the *Flora Celtica* project, co-ordinated by RBGE, has been involved in documenting and promoting the knowledge and sustainable use of native plants in the Celtic countries and regions of Europe, focusing initially on Scotland. Achievements to date include the Millennium-funded Flora Celtica – Scotland 2000 (1999-2001), whose products include a database, a touring exhibition, a schools roadshow, and various publications[19].

A major output in 2002 was *Plantlife of Edinburgh and the Lothians*[20], the most extensive and authoritative account of the plants of Edinburgh and the Lothians to be published since 1927. Prior to its publication, however, there was an extensive period (1981-2001) of survey work. This work, under guidance from the BSS, had a large input from McKean with numerous staff and other volunteers undertaking surveys of 1-km grid squares.

The UK Biodiversity Action Plan

Biodiversity: the UK Action Plan (UK BAP)[21] was published in January 1994 in response to article 6A of the Convention on Biological Diversity (CBD)[22]. The Plan, which RBGE had input into, was presented in three sections. The first was mostly devoted to describing UK's biodiversity, the second considered conservation within and outside natural habitats, and the third concentrated on targets and monitoring.

Following publication of the Action Plan, the Biodiversity Action Plan Steering Group was established to take forward the recommendations made in the third section and, in particular, to develop action plans for the most threatened species and habitats. The Group had a wide membership, including myself. Criteria for identifying key species for priority action were developed to produce a list of 1,250 species. From this 'long list' 400 species were selected as being either globally threatened or rapidly declining in the UK, and from this a short-list of 116 species which contained species for which action plans had been developed was published. These Species Action Plans (SAPs) followed a defined structure including current status, factors causing loss or decline, current action, action plan objectives and targets, and proposed action with lead agencies. Action plans were also developed for habitats (Habitat Action Plans or HAPs). The process for developing these plans was published in *Biodiversity; the UK Steering Group Report, Volume 1: Meeting the Rio Challenge*[23]. *Volume 2: Action Plans*[24], covered the initial 116 SAPs and 37 HAPs.

RBGE was actively involved in the whole SAP process becoming the 'Lead Partner' for 17 species and chairing the '*Woodsia ilvensis* Partnership'. RBGE was the first Lead Partner to submit the required annual reports. RBGE was also given specific responsibility for individual actions, for example, the SAP for Eyebrights (*Euphrasia* species endemic to the UK). These included six species stated under 'Future research and monitoring' that required morphological and genetic investigations to clarify the taxonomic status of the species (see below).

Since the creation of the UK BAP, devolution led the four countries of the UK to produce their own biodiversity strategies and, again, RBGE has been fully involved, first through myself, followed in 2000 by Mary Gibby. Other staff members have been involved in various sub-committees and Local Biodiversity Action Plans and this work and involvement continue today.

The *Euphrasia* Project

Of the 19 named species of Eyebright considered for the British Red Data List, seven are endemic, five are in the IUCN category of 'endangered', three 'vulnerable', and eight 'data deficient'[25]. However, a major problem in implementing Biodiversity Action Plans for these Eyebright species is taxonomic uncertainty and RBGE investigated the problem through Graham French's PhD project, supervised by Peter Hollingsworth. It was unclear whether the currently recognised species represented genetically coherent and distinct groups or not, and it was difficult to identify some of the local, endemic species that had been given the highest conservation status. Detailed genetical and morphological investigations identified two distinct diploid endemic species, widespread outcrossing tetraploids, and widespread inbreeding tetraploids, with the outbreeders having a distinctly different gene-pool from the inbreeders. Although species-based action plans were appropriate for the diploid endemics, this approach needed modification to conserve the complex and dynamic diversity found within the tetraploids. As a solution, French *et al.*[26] and Ennos *et al.*[27] proposed the adoption of 'taxonomic' action plans, designed to protect the evolutionary processes generating Eyebright diversity.

The Scottish Rare Plants Project

The Scottish Rare Plants Project (SRPP) was launched in 1991 as a partnership project with SNH to concentrate on threatened species in Scotland. The initial focus, led by Phil

Figure 9.3. Planting Sticky Catchfly (*Lychnis viscaria*) on Arthur's Seat, Edinburgh with Jo Muir, Roland Whiteman, and Phil Lusby, 1994. Photo: David Rae. Inset: Sticky Catchfly, Perthshire, 1975. Photo: John Birks

Figure 9.4. RBGE staff Daniela Weber and Andy Ensoll reintroducing Oblong Woodsia (*Woodsia ilvensis*) in the eastern Highlands, 2005 (*top*), photo: Heather McHaffie. Oblong Woodsia in its only known extant native locality in the Moffat Hills, 1968 (*bottom*), photo: John Birks

Lusby, was to compile species dossiers, population monitoring, and surveys of selected priority species including Sticky Catchfly (Fig. 9.3), One-flowered Wintergreen (*Moneses uniflora*), and Whorled Solomon's-seal (*Polygonatum verticillatum*)[28]. Information from this research was used to provide advice and training on habitat management and to prioritise early species restoration projects. Two such projects were the augmentation of the critically reduced population of Sticky Catchfly on Authur's Seat in Edinburgh in 1994 (Fig. 9.3) and the re-introduction of the rare fern Oblong Woodsia (*Woodsia ilvensis*) (Fig. 9.4), at two former sites in County Durham in 1999. The latter work was carried out in association with a Leverhulme-funded research project on the conservation biology and autecology of Oblong Woodsia, led by Stuart Lindsay.

The type locality in Britain for Sticky Catchfly is Arthur's Seat, an igneous outcrop within Edinburgh. In 1991 only four plants remained there due to grazing, encroachment from Gorse (*Ulex europaeus*), and occasional fires caused by the public. Seeds were collected from each plant in 1993, grown on in RBGE's Nursery, and in 1994 twenty plants were replaced close to, but slightly separated from, the original site (Fig. 9.3). Eighty per cent of the plants established into mature plants and a healthy reproducing population continues to thrive today.

Oblong Woodsia was subject to over-collecting during the so-called 'Victorian Fern Craze' and populations have failed to regain their former numbers and distribution since that time, to the extent that only five localities remained in the UK with small numbers found at all but one site. It is a fern that Derek Ratcliffe searched for intensively and refound in Lakeland[29] and the Moffat Hills near the Grey Mare's Tail[30]. Its spores were gathered under licence from each population in 1997 and by 1998 a conservation collection of 2,500 individuals representing each population had been established at RBGE. Since then reintroductions or reinforcements have taken place at five sites with a success rate of 43% to 92% establishment (Fig. 9.4).

Other species, such as Whorled Solomon's-seal and Woolly Willow (Fig. 9.5), were collected and propagated as part of the Project's programme and have gone on to form the basis of further species restoration work, developed and expanded under the Target 8 project, described below.

During 1998-2000, SRPP was responsible for collecting samples of seed of the rarest and most threatened Scottish species for the Kew Millennium Seed Bank based at Wakehurst Place, Sussex.

The Partnership for Plants in Scotland

The Partnership for Plants in Scotland evolved from the SRPP, changing its focus to include more education and training but still retaining a strong fieldwork programme. Education and training on Scottish plant conservation are delivered through formal courses at the MSc, BSc, and HND level, specialist workshops and short courses on plant identification, talks to natural history groups, and engagement with the general public through Edinburgh Science Festival/Biodiversity Week events. Students on all the courses are given the opportunity to contribute to a range of *in situ* and *ex situ* conservation projects and the Partnership has provided an excellent opportunity for staff in the Science and Horticulture Divisions of RBGE to work together. Heather McHaffie, the Partnership Officer, has botanical, horticultural, and educational experience and is ideally suited to provide the projects with the scientific, practical, and communication elements required. Horticultural staff members accompany her on fieldwork and, in return, Heather contributes her practical knowledge on the cultivation requirements of the various species. Together this has proved to be an excellent combination to develop work on Target 8 of the Global Strategy for Plant Conservation (GSPC).

The Target 8 Project

History

Target 8 of the Global Strategy for Plant Conservation requires the most horticultural input to achieve and is most obviously aligned to the work of botanic gardens, although RBGE contributes to at least eight of the 16 targets. The updated target[1] seeks to conserve "75% of threatened plant species in accessible *ex situ* collections, preferably in their country of origin, and 20% of them available for recovery and restoration programmes"[31]. In response to Target 8, a project was initiated in 2005 by PlantNetwork[32] (the plant collections network of Britain and Ireland) to encourage botanic gardens to develop and maintain conservation collections of nationally threatened species from their own region. The initial feasibility study for PlantNetwork at RBGE was undertaken by Natacha Frachon who went on to coordinate RBGE's contribution. A key feature was to grow threatened plants as well as storing their seed in seed banks. In line with these objectives, in 2005 RBGE decided to respond to the target and take responsibility for cultivating the threatened species in Scotland. RBGE's strategies and actions with respect to the conservation of Scotland's biodiversity are specified in *Collection Policy for the Living Collection*[33].

Selecting and sampling the species

The starting point of this project was to identify all vascular plants, including ferns and fern allies, designated as nationally threatened and occurring in Scotland using *The Vascular Plant Red Data List*[25] and *The Scottish Biodiversity List*[34]. Once the initial list of all threatened species was compiled, the selection of species proposed for *ex situ* conservation was examined based on conservation priorities and the feasibility of growing and producing seed of the species. The selection focused on the most threatened of the red-listed species and the species prioritised by SNH which includes species listed in the UK Biodiversity Action Plan[21]. Finally, a list of 170 taxa was drawn up to determine which seed or vegetative material had to be collected for propagation at RBGE.

---

[1] The *Global Strategy for Plant Conservation* was updated at the tenth meeting of the Conference of the Parties to the Convention on Biological Diversity. This was adopted as the *Global Strategy for Plant Conservation 2011–2020* (Convention on Biological Diversity, 2011)[31].

A survey of the Living Collection showed that 36 species on the proposed list for *ex situ* conservation were already in RBGE. This also revealed a low level of genetic diversity, a shortage of basic collection information, and a lack of propagation history records. In the past, species had been collected on an *ad hoc* basis and as a result they were represented by a single accession or single-specimen accession which is inadequate for conservation purposes. These findings influenced the strict sampling strategy which also highlighted the importance of recording full collection details from the actual site where the species grows as well as recording data on subsequent cultivation.

In order to raise stock for a recovery programme, it was agreed that care had to be taken to gather a genetically representative sample of the species. This should be from more than one population and from at least three individuals, preferably ten or more if the population was large enough. In some of the most endangered populations there were fewer than three plants, causing a potential difficulty in ensuring adequate genetic representation in re-introductions. For some re-introductions, plants from other populations were considered after careful consideration by all stakeholders.

Collecting the species

Collecting for this project started in 2005 and by the end of September 2012, 142 species had been sampled from the wild with permission from SNH and agreement from landowners. Many people have been involved in this effort including SNH area officers, BSBI vice-county recorders, the National Trust for Scotland (NTS), a few private individuals, and RBGE staff.

Most species were collected as seed (68%), while hybrids that are infertile or taxa with complex biological relationships such as the Wintergreens *Pyrola* and *Moneses* were received as plants (26%). A small number of species (6%) were propagated from wild-collected cuttings. Alpine Blue-sow-thistle is now at risk because of loss of habitat coupled with the dangers of sheep and deer grazing and is only found on near-inaccessible ledges at four sites in the eastern Highlands, one of which was discovered by Derek Ratcliffe[35]. The species does not appear to set viable seed in the wild and the only opportunity to propagate it is from rhizomes which were collected from two different sites. Plants from both populations are now growing and flowering in the Living Collection and are providing a source of material with which to experiment with seed propagation.

As a general rule, care is taken not to collect material in quantity and certainly not without knowledge of reliable methods of propagation. For very rare species such as Diapensia (*Diapensia lapponica*), which is known to be difficult to grow from stem cuttings, propagation trials were carried out for two years prior to collection using material bought from a commercial nursery.

Re-introduction programmes

The Target 8 project has also made progress towards the second recommendation of Target 8, to make "20% of them available for recovery and restoration programmes". Nine of the threatened species cultivated at RBGE are now included in restoration programmes. In addition to Sticky Catchfly and Oblong Woodsia these include Woolly

Willow, Downy Willow (*Salix lapponum*), Northern Hawk's-beard (*Crepis mollis*), Rock Whitebeam (*Sorbus rupicola*), Whorled Solomon's-seal, Pyramidal Bugle (which is yet to yield successful results), and Purple Oxytropis (*Oxytropis halleri*) (which has not yet started).

As a grassland species, Northern Hawk's-beard has suffered from loss of habitat and is only found in northern England and southern Scotland. Seed was collected by the Borders Forest Trust and propagated at RBGE, and a year later plants were translocated to a site near the original population.

The Whorled Solomon's-seal is only found at eight sites in Scotland. Over ten years ago it was discovered that a small population in Glen Tilt was being washed out of the steep bank and might disappear altogether. After applying for a licence, a piece of rhizome was collected and propagated at RBGE for several years by which time the original population had disappeared. Plants were re-introduced further up the bank with a second batch of plants added in autumn 2010.

Other rare plants that are not included in recovery programmes are raised as an insurance against unexpected losses in the wild. This is the case for the three endemic Whitebeams on the Isle of Arran: Arran Whitebeam (*Sorbus arranensis*), Arran Service-tree (*S. pseudofennica*), and Catacol Whitebeam (*S. pseudomeinichii*). *In situ* management is preferred for these species to ensure the long-term survival of the wild populations but seed and vegetative material from known clones have been collected and propagated and will be maintained in RBGE as a backup.

Capacity building and sharing resources

The Target 8 Project has grown steadily since its launch and has developed a network of interested people and organisations committed to plant conservation. A wide range of species has been grown for the John Hutton Institute at Invergowrie for their research into Water Moulds (*Phytophthora*). Plant material was shared with the Shetland Amenity Trust for trials in micropropagation of rare species and a number of plants have been distributed to other botanical collections in Glasgow, Dundee, and St Andrews.

Some rare taxa are grown from seed to provide experimental material for staff working on conservation genetics at RBGE. Scottish dock (*Rumex aquaticus*)—now restricted to the banks of Loch Lomond—is known to hybridise with the commoner Broad-leaved Dock (*R. obtusifolius*). Plants were raised in cultivation to study the extent of introgressive hybridisation in the field. The taxonomy, ecology, and genetics of Scottish Small-reed (*Calamagrostis scotica*) are now under investigation too[36]. To further this work a genetically representative collection of the species has been grown to provide fresh plant material for DNA and other analyses, and to allow garden experimentation.

The project provides substantial material for tertiary education. Most of the rare species grow in distant, often remote, parts of Scotland. By bringing them together in one easily accessible location, the plants can be used for education programmes, particularly for species identification. The collection also offers the opportunity for horticulture students to be trained in practical plant conservation.

All four Gardens of RBGE are used as an interface between the world of wild plants and the public to promote awareness of biodiversity and conservation. The Target 8 plants have featured in 'Behind the Scenes' events, and the collection has been

Figure 9.5. RBGE staff Heather McHaffie, Richard Marriott, and Caroline Mullen assessing the maturity of Woolly Willow (*Salix lanata*) and Downy Willow (*Salix lapponum*) seed in Coire Sharrock, Clova, 2007 (*top*), photo: Natacha Frachon. Woolly Willow, Coire Sharrock, Clova, 1967 (*bottom*), photo: John Birks

visited by groups ranging from botanical societies to the International Plant Propagators Society. Many of the targeted species are on display in the garden at Edinburgh. Dawyck Botanic Garden has a rare plants trail in which they feature. Benmore Botanic Garden can accommodate plants that require a higher level of rainfall. Logan Botanic Garden has a collection of locally rare plants and is especially useful for growing species that only occur in south-west Scotland.

Partnership working

The Sub-arctic Willow Project

Sub-arctic willow scrub is one of the rarest and most endangered habitats in the UK (on Annex I of the European Habitats Directive), being largely restricted to the Scottish mountains where it forms a component of the montane scrub occurring above the natural tree-line[37,38]. The surviving fragments are of considerable conservation concern and, without intervention, many populations are in danger of terminal decline[39]. One of the species in this vegetation type, Woolly Willow, is listed in the British Red Data Book of Vascular Plants and is the subject of a Species Action Plan that sets out targets for its conservation.

A research consortium led by RBGE has studied the taxonomy and natural hybridisation of montane willows in this habitat, their genetics, the associated ectomycorrhizal fungal diversity, ecology, and herbivory to produce recommendations for conservation action[39]. Despite small population sizes and fragmented populations, the genetic diversity of the remaining willow populations was found to be high. However, low frequencies of seed production and poor dispersal during this research suggest that any regeneration from seed is likely to require collection and translocation of seed to new sites or close to existing sites. In recommending restoration, the consortium highlighted the need to (1) avoid the possibility of introducing hybridised material, (2) ensure that introduced material comes from a wide genetic background, ideally propagated from appropriate local seed, and (3) protect the restoration site from heavy grazing to facilitate sexual reproduction and seedling recruitment.

Again, for Woolly Willow, as for Eyebrights, conservation success depends upon understanding the autecology of the target species. Botanic gardens have the staff skills to undertake the essential underpinning research work, given sufficient resources and priority focus.

Woolly Willow (Salix lanata)

Research on Woolly Willow was undertaken as part of the above project (Fig. 9.5). There are only a few large populations of this species in the wild and some are represented by a single individual. Given that the species is dioecious, solitary individuals represent what Dan Janzen calls "the living dead"[40]. Initial research has now translated into conservation action through a project to restore montane willows in Scotland, following the recommendations derived from research on this habitat by Stamati et al.[41]. This has involved collecting seeds and cuttings for propagation in RBGE's nursery to achieve at least 30 accessions from each site to ensure appropriate levels of genetic diversity in the stock. Working with SNH area officers, the first site for augmentation was selected and in 2009 816 young plants were planted by a team of RBGE staff together with SNH and BSBI volunteers.

Conclusions

Staff at RBGE have been involved with Scottish plants since the Garden was founded in 1670. The initial focus was on exploration of the Scottish countryside, looking for species new to Scotland and recording new localities. In more recent years, and especially since the 1992 Rio 'Earth Summit'[42], the focus has increasingly been on conservation. RBGE continues to play a major role in studying and caring for Scotland's internationally important flora, including bryophytes[43] and lichens.

RGBE was a place where Derek Ratcliffe, when he lived in Edinburgh 1956-1963 and was not away in the field, would find peace and tranquillity within the busy city. He enjoyed sitting, watching the garden's wildlife, and thinking of the great plant hunters who brought many wonderful Sino-Himalayan plants into cultivation (Fig. 9.1). Although the concept of *ex situ* conservation had hardly developed during his career as a conservationist, he actively encouraged RBGE's Oblong Woodsia reintroduction project and viewed such projects as essential for the long-term conservation of Scotland's native flora. His botanical collections from Scotland, mainly bryophytes, are housed in RBGE and are used in on-going research by RBGE staff[43].

References

(1)   Robertson, F.W. (2000) *Early Scottish Gardeners and their Plants, 1650-1750*. Tuckwell Press, Edinburgh

(2)   Sibbald, R. (1684) *Scotia Illustrata*. Ex Officina Typographica, Edinburgh.

(3)   Hudson, W. (1762) *Flora Anglica*. London.

(4)   Lightfoot, J. (1778) *Flora Scotica*. London.

(5)   Henderson, D.M. & Dickson, J.H. (eds.) (1994) *A Naturalist in the Highlands: James Robertson - His Life and Travels in Scotland, 1767-71*. Scottish Academic Press.

(6)   Donn, G. (1804) *Herbaricum Britannicum, consisting of fasciculi of dried British plants, with their appropriate names and particular habits annexed*. Fascicles I-IX, number 1-225. Neill, Johnstone, Edinburgh.

(7)   Don, G. (1813) An account of the native plants in the county of Forfar, and the animals to be found there. In: *General View of the Agriculture of the County of Angus, or Forfarshire* (ed. J. Headrock). Edinburgh

(8)   Greville, R.K. (1823-1828) *Scottish Cryptogamic Flora*. Six volumes. Edinburgh.

(9)   Hooker, W.J. (1821) *Flora Scotica*. London.

(10)   Hooker, W.J. (1830) *British Flora*. London.

(11)   Balfour, J.H. (1848) Account of excursions to Clova, Glen Isla, Braemar, and Ben Lawers. *Edinburgh New Philosophical Journal*, **45**, 122.

(12) Watson, H.C. (1832) *Outlines of the Geographical Distribution of British Plants.* Edinburgh.

(13) Watson, H.C. (1847-59) *Cybele Britannica, Volumes 1-4.* London.

(14) Holden, A.E. & Adam, R.M. (1952) *Plant Life in the Scottish Highlands.* Oliver & Boyd, Edinburgh.

(15) Anon. (1902) History of the RBGE, Botanical excursions made by Prof John Hutton Balfour in the years 1846-1878 inclusive. *Notes from the Royal Botanic Garden Edinburgh,* **2**, 1-460.

(16) Roger, J.G. (1980) Obituary, James Robert Matthews. *Transactions of the Botanical Society of Edinburgh,* **43**, 247-249.

(17) Fletcher, H.R. & Brown, W.H. (1970) *The Royal Botanic Garden Edinburgh, 1670-1970.* HMSO, Edinburgh.

(18) Burnett, J.H. (1964) *The Vegetation of Scotland.* Oliver & Boyd, Edinburgh.

(19) Milliken, W. & Bridgewater, S. (2004) *Flora Celtica.* Birlinn and Royal Botanic Garden Edinburgh, Edinburgh.

(20) Smith, P.M., Dixon, R.O.D. & Cochrane, P.M. (eds.) (2002) *Plantlife of Edinburgh and the Lothians.* Edinburgh University Press, Edinburgh.

(21) Anon. (1994) *Biodiversity: the UK Action Plan.* HMSO, London. Available at http://jncc.defra.gov.uk/page-1817 (Accessed February 2012).

(22) http://www.cbd.int/ (accessed February 2013)

(23) Anon. (1995) *Biodiversity; the UK Steering Group Report, Volume 1: Meeting the Rio Challenge.* HMSO, London.

(24) Anon. (1995) *Biodiversity; the UK Steering Group Report, Volume 2: Action Plans.* HMSO, London.

(25) Cheffings, C.M. & Farrell, L. (2005) *Species Status: No.7 The Vascular Plant Red Data List 2005.* Joint Nature Conservation Committee. Available at http://jncc.defra.gov.uk/pdf/pub05_speciesstatusvpredlist3_web.pdf (accessed February 2012).

(26) French, G.C., Ennos, R.A., Silverside, A.J. & Hollingsworth, P.M. (2005) The relationship between flower size, inbreeding coefficient and inferred selfing rate in British *Euphrasia* species. *Heredity.* **94**, 44-51.

(27) Ennos, R.A., French. G.C. & Hollingsworth, P.M. (2005) Conserving taxonomic complexity. *Trends in Ecology and Evolution,* **20**, 164-168.

(28) Holden, A.E. & Adam, R.M. (1952) *Plant Life in the Scottish Highlands.* Oliver & Boyd, Edinburgh.

(29) Ratcliffe, D.A. (1960) The mountain flora of Lakeland. *Proceedings of the Botanical Society of the British Isles,* **4,** 1-25.
       Ratcliffe, D.A. (2002) *Lakeland.* HarperCollins, London.

(30) Ratcliffe, D.A. (1959) The mountain plants of the Moffat Hills. *Transactions of the Botanical Society of Edinburgh,* **37,** 257-271.

(31) Convention on Biological Diversity (2011) Available at http://www.cbd.int/gspc/targets.shtml (accessed January 2012).

(32) PlantNetwork. http://plantnetwork.org (accessed January 2013).

(33)   Rae, D., Baxter, P., Knott, D., Mitchell, D., Paterson, D. & Unwin, B. (2006) *Collection Policy for the Living Collection.* Royal Botanic Garden Edinburgh, Edinburgh.

(34)   Scottish Natural Heritage (2005) *The Scottish Biodiversity List.* Available at http://www.snh.gov.uk/protecting-scotlands-nature/biodiversity-scotland/scottish-biodiversity-list/ (accessed February 2012).

(35)   Ratcliffe, D.A. (1959) *Cicerbita alpina* (L.) Wallr. in Glen Callater. *Transactions of the Botanical Society of Edinburgh,* **38,** 287-289.

(36)   Corner, R.W.M. (2015) Derek Ratcliffe and plant-hunting in southern Scotland and northern England. In: *Nature's Conscience – The Life and Legacy of Derek Ratcliffe* (eds. D.B.A. Thompson, H.H. Birks & H.J.B. Birks). This volume, Chapter 5

(37)   McVean, D.N. & Ratcliffe, D.A. (1962) *Plant Communities of the Scottish Highlands.* Her Majesty's Stationery Office, London.

(38)   Averis, A.M., Averis, A.B.G., Birks, H.J.B., Horsfield, D., Thompson, D.B.A. & Yeo, M.J.M. (2004) *An Illustrated Guide to British Upland Vegetation.* Joint Nature Conservation Committee, Peterborough.

(39)   Scottish Montane Willow Research Group (2005) *Biodiversity: Taxonomy, Genetics and Ecology of Sub-Arctic Willow Scrub.* Royal Botanic Garden Edinburgh.

(40)   Janzen, D.H. (2001) Saving fractured oases of biodiversity. *Quarterly Review of Biology,* 76, 327-330.

(41)   Stamati, K., Hollingsworth, P.M. & Russell, J. (2007) Patterns of clonal diversity in three species of sub-arctic willow (*Salix lanata, Salix lapponum* and *Salix herbacea*). *Plant Systematics and Evolution,* **269,** 75-88.

(42)   Bridgewater, P. (2015) National and global biodiversity politics and legalities – some reflections. In: *Nature's Conscience – The Life and Legacy of Derek Ratcliffe* (eds. D.B.A. Thompson, H.H. Birks & H.J.B. Birks). This volume, Chapter 25.

(43)   Long, D.G. & Rothero, G.P. (2015) Bryology in the Highlands and Islands of Scotland. In: *Nature's Conscience – The Life and Legacy of Derek Ratcliffe* (eds. D.B.A. Thompson, H.H. Birks & H.J.B. Birks). This volume, Chapter 6.

10. The mountain flora of Britain and Ireland

Derek Ratcliffe

Reprint of Ratcliffe, D.A. (1991) The mountain flora of Britain and Ireland. *British Wildlife,* **3**, 10-21.

THE MOUNTAIN FLORA OF BRITAIN AND IRELAND

D A Ratcliffe

The term 'mountain plant' is a somewhat arbitrary category for species which belong entirely or largely to the hill country, and are predominantly northern. They represent a flora associated especially with low temperatures, and evolved in the colder regions of the World. Their wider European or World distribution is in far northern and/or mountainous regions, and their geographical distribution is accordingly characterised as arctic, alpine or arctic-alpine (Matthews 1955). A few species of continental northern or northern montane distribution occur mainly on mountains in Britain and Ireland. This article deals only with flowering plants and ferns, but these are accompanied by a rich assemblage of mosses, liverworts, lichens and fungi adapted to montane conditions.

The interaction between present climate, topography, geology and soils

The overriding influence of high altitude is to reduce temperature. In Britain, mean temperature falls by 1°C for every 150m increase in elevation. Windspeed, precipitation and cloud cover also increase, and are especially important factors in our generally oceanic climate. This local altitudinal gradient of climate produces zonation of vegetation, from woodland through scrub to alpine heaths and grasslands, as the response to increasingly harsh conditions for plant growth. Such zonation is, however, mediated by the larger-scale regional gradients of climate within our islands – the tendencies for mean temperature to fall from south to north, and for oceanicity (high rainfall, windiness and cloudiness; small temperature range) to increase from east to west. The result is to cause an altitudinal descent of vegetation zones in a north-westerly direction, so that alpine communities with species such as Least Willow, *Salix herbacea*, Dwarf Azalea, *Loiseleuria procumbens*, and Alpine Bearberry, *Arctous alpinus*, occur in

10

Dryas heaths on Durness limestone near sea-level, Sutherland.

Sutherland, Orkney and Shetland 300m or more below their lower limits in the central Highlands. The climatic 'tree-line' now lies at about 640m in the Brecon Beacons and the Cairngorms, but is lower on many western mountain ranges (probably 535m in Snowdonia and Lakeland), and disappears on exposed western and northern coasts. Its position is taken as a convenient separation between the sub-alpine and alpine (or sub-montane and montane) zones.

Some alpines, such as Roseroot, *Sedum rosea*, Moss Campion, *Silene acaulis*, and Purple Saxifrage, *Saxifraga oppositifolia*, have secondary habitats on northern sea cliffs, and on the Sutherland coast Mountain Avens, *Dryas octopetala*, grows in spectacular abundance on limestone and blown shell sand down to sea level. Purple Oxytropis, *Oxytropis halleri*, is more a coastal than a mountain plant with us, and Scottish Primrose, *Primula scotica*, is distinctly maritime. True coastal plants such as Thrift, *Armeria maritima*, Scurvygrass, *Cochlearia officinalis*, and Sea Plantain, *Plantago maritima*, are abundant on many Scottish mountains, though they appear there to be different physiological strains. Many

of our mountain plants are nevertheless confined to high elevations. Some appear intolerant of the warmer conditions below the potential tree-line, but for many the competition from taller life-forms is the major limitation. They occur in greatest variety and abundance on the coldest and highest mountains where snow lies longest, in the central Scottish Highlands. The mountain flora decreases in importance with distance south, and in south-west England is represented by only a few sub-alpine species.

Snow-lie is a most significant factor in determining the pattern of vegetation at higher levels. Its influence is either slight or difficult to detect in the more southerly hill regions, but in the Highlands it becomes extremely important. Variable snow-cover is largely a matter of topography in relation to wind exposure. As snow-cover increases beyond average in sheltered places within the dwarf-shrub zone there is a change from dominance of heather to that of Bilberry, *Vaccinium myrtillus* (often with much Northern Crowberry, *Empetrum hermaphroditum*), and then to Mat Grass, *Nardus stricta* (with Deer Grass, *Scirpus cespitosus*, in the Cairngorms). At the higher altitudes there is an increasing contrast between ground where snow

11

Table 1 Montane species, found mainly above potential tree-line

Fir Clubmoss *Huperzia selago* NM
Interrupted Clubmoss *Lycopodium annotinum* **R** NM
Alpine Clubmoss *Diphasiastrum alpinum* NM
Parsley Fern *Cryptogramma crispa* NM
Green Spleenwort *Asplenium viride* Ca AA
Alpine Lady Fern *Athyrium alpestre* H Hi AA
Flexile Lady Fern *A. flexile* H Hi E
Mountain Bladder Fern *Cystopteris montana* H Ca **S C+** AA
Alpine Woodsia *Woodsia alpina* H Ca **R* C+** AA
Oblong Woodsia *W. ilvensis* Ba **R* C+** NM
Mountain Male Fern *Dryopteris oreades* NM
Northern Buckler Fern *D. expansa* AA
Holly Fern *Polystichum lonchitis* CA C+ AA
Dwarf Juniper *Juniperus communis* ssp. *nana* NM

Alpine Meadow-rue *Thalictrum alpinum* Ba AA
Alpine Penny-cress *Thlaspi alpestre* Ca(U) **S** A
Alpine Scurvygrass *Cochlearia officinalis* ssp.*alpina* Ba AA
Scottish Scurvygrass *C. micacea* H Ba Hi **R** E
Norwegian Whitlowgrass *Draba norvegica* H Ca Hi **S** AS
Hoary Whitlowgrass *D. incana* Ca **S** AA
Northern Rockcress *Cardaminopsis petraea* Ba **S** AA
Alpine Rockcress *Arabis alpina* H Ba Hi **R*** AA
Rock Violet *Viola rupestris* Ca Ne **R** + NM
Dwarf Milkwort *Polygala amara* Ca Ne **R** + CN
Moss Campion *Silene acaulis* AA
Alpine Catchfly *Lychnis alpina* H U **R*** AA
Starwort Mouse-ear *Cerastium cerastoides* H Hi **S** AA
Arctic Mouse-ear *C. arcticum* H Ba **S** AS
Edmonston's Mouse-ear *C. arcticum* ssp. *edmonstonii* U Hi
R + AA
Alpine Mouse-ear *C. alpinum* H Ca **S** AA
Alpine Pearlwort *Sagina saginoides* H Ba Hi **S** AA
Scottish Pearlwort *S. normaniana* H Ba Hi **R** AA

Snow Pearlwort *S. intermedia* H Ba Hi **R** AS
Spring Sandwort *Minuartia verna* Ca(U) **S** AA
Bog Sandwort *M. stricta* Ca Ne **R* C+** AA
Alpine Sandwort *M. rubella* H Ca Hi **R** AS
Mossy Cyphel *Cherleria sedoides* Hi **S** A
Arctic Sandwort *Arenaria norvegica* ssp. *norvegica* Ba Hi
R* AS
Alpine Milk-vetch *Astragalus alpinus* H Ca Hi **R C+** AA
Yellow Oxytropis *Oxytropis campestris* Ca Hi **R** AA
Cloudberry *Rubus chamaemorus* AS
Shrubby Cinquefoil *Potentilla fruticosa* Ba Ne **R C+** NM
Alpine Cinquefoil *P. crantzii* Ca **S** AA
Sibbaldia *Sibbaldia procumbens* H Hi **S** AA
Mountain Avens *Dryas octopetala* Ca **S** AA
Alpine Lady's-mantle *Alchemilla alpina* AA
Roseroot *Sedum rosea* Ba AA
Hairy Stonecrop *S. villosum* Ca **S** CN
Alpine Saxifrage *Saxifraga nivalis* H Ca **S C+** AA
Starry Saxifrage *S. stellaris* AA
Marsh Saxifrage *S. hirculus* Ca **R** + AA
Drooping Saxifrage *S. cernua* H Ba Hi **R* C+** AA
Highland Saxifrage *S. rivularis* H Ba Hi **R C+** AS
Tufted Saxifrage *S. cespitosa* H Ca **R* C+** AS
Irish Saxifrage *S. rosacea* Ca I **R** AA
Mossy Saxifrage *S. hypnoides* Ca NM
Yellow Saxifrage *S. aizoides* Ba AA

Purple Saxifrage *S. oppositifolia* Ca AA

Alpine Willow-herb *Epilobium anagallidifolium* AA
Chickweed Willowherb *E. alsinifolium* Ba **S** AA
Dwarf Cornel *Cornus suecica* AS
Viviparous Bistort *Polygonum viviparum* Ba AA
Iceland Purslane *Koenigia islandica* H U Hi **R** AS
Mountain Sorrel *Oxyria digyna* Ba AA
Dwarf Birch *Betula nana* **S** + AA
Downy Willow *Salix lapponum* H Ba **S** AA
Woolly Willow *S. lanata* H Ba Hi AS
Plum-leaved Willow *S. arbuscula* H Ba Hi **S** AA
Whortle-leaved Willow *S. myrsinites* Ca **S** AA
Net-leaved Willow *S. reticulata* H Ca Hi **S** AA
Least Willow *S. herbacea* H AA
Dwarf Azalea *Loiseleuria procumbens* H Hi AA
Blue Heath *Phyllodoce caerulea* H Hi **R* C+** AA
Bearberry *Arctostaphylos uva-ursi* AA
Alpine Bearberry *Arctous alpinus* Hi N AA
Bog Whortleberry *Vaccinium uliginosum* AA
Lesser Cranberry *V. microcarpum* Hi **S** NM
Diapensia *Diapensia lapponica* H Hi **R*** AS
Northern Crowberry *Empetrum hermaphroditum* AA
Spring Gentian *Gentiana verna* Ca Ne **R* C+** A
Snow Gentian *G. nivalis* H Ca Hi **R* C+** AA
Alpine Forget-me-not *Myosotis alpestris* H Ca A
Rock Speedwell *Veronica fruticans* H Ca Hi **R C+** AA
Alpine Speedwell *V. alpina* H Ba Hi AA
Alpine Bartsia *Bartsia alpina* Ca **R** + AA
Purple Coltsfoot *Homogyne alpina* Ca Hi **R*** A
Norwegian Cudweed *Gnaphalium norvegicum* H Hi **R** AA
Least Cudweed *G. supinum* H AA
Alpine Fleabane *Erigeron borealis* H Ca Hi **R* C+** AS
Norwegian Mugwort *Artemisia norvegica* H Hi **R** AS
Alpine Saw-wort *Saussurea alpina* Ba AA
Alpine Sow-thistle *Cicerbita alpina* H Ba Hi **R*** AA
Scottish Asphodel *Tofieldia pusilla* Ca **S** AA
Snowdon Lily *Lloydia serotina* H Ca W **R* C+** AA
Three-pointed Rush *Juncus trifidus* H Hi AA
Alpine Rush *J. alpinoarticulatus* Ca **S** NM
Chestnut Rush *J. castaneus* H Ba Hi **S** AA
Two-flowered Rush *J. biglumis* H Ca Hi **S** AA
Three-flowered Rush *J. triglumis* Ba AA

Spiked Woodrush *Luzula spicata* Hi AA
Curved Woodrush *L. arcuata* H Hi **S** AS
False Sedge *Kobresia simpliciuscula* Ca **R** + AA
Hair Sedge *Carex capillaris* Ca **S** AA
Russet Sedge *C. saxatilis* H Ba Hi **S** AS
Sheathing Sedge *C. vaginata* H Ba **S** AA
Mountain Bog Sedge *C. rariflora* H Hi **R** AS
Alpine Sedge *C. norvegica* H Ba Hi **R C+** AA
Black Sedge *C. atrata* H Ca **S** AA
Small Jet Sedge *C. atrofusca* H Ca Hi **R C+** AA
Mountain Sedge *C. bigelowii* AA
Hare's-foot Sedge *C. lachenalii* H Hi **R** AA
Rock Sedge *C. rupestris* Ca Hi **S** AA
Bristle Sedge *C. microglochin* H Ca Hi **R** AA
Viviparous Fescue *Festuca vivipara* AA
Alpine Meadow Grass *Poa alpina* H Ca **S C+** AA
Wavy Meadow Grass *P. flexuosa* H H **R** AS
Glaucous Meadow Grass *P. glauca* H Ca **S** AA
Don's Couch Grass *Agropyron donianum* Ca Hi AS
Alpine Hair Grass *Deschampsia alpina* H **S** AS
Alpine Timothy Grass *Phleum alpinum* H Ba **S C+** AA
Alpine Foxtail Grass *Alopecurus alpinus* H **S** AS

12

Table 2 Sub-montane and northern species, found mainly below potential tree-line

Dutch Rush *Equisetum hyemale* Ca C
Variegated Horsetail *E. variegatum* Ca **S** NM
Shady Horsetail *E. pratense* Ba **S** NM
Forked Spleenwort *Asplenium septentrionale* U **S** **C+** NM
Rigid Buckler Fern *Dryopteris villarii* Ca **S** A
Limestone Polypody *Gymnocarpium robertianum* Ca NM
Globeflower *Trollius europaeus* Ba + NM
Mountain Pansy *Viola lutea* (U) + A
Sticky Catchfly *Lychnis viscaria* U **R** CN
English Sandwort *Arenaria norvegica* ssp. *anglica* Ca Ne **R*** E
Wood Cranesbill *Geranium sylvaticum* Ba + CN
Purple Oxytropis *Oxytropis halleri* Ba(U) **R** A
Upright Bitter Vetch *Vicia orobus* **S** + NM
Stone Bramble *Rubus saxatilis* Ba NM
Rock Cinquefoil *Potentilla rupestris* Ba(U) **R*** **C+** NM
Alpine Enchanter's Nightshade *Circaea alpina* Ba CN
Spignel *Meum athamanticum* **S** CN
Dark Willow *Salix nigricans* Ba **S** CN
Tea-leaved Willow *S. phylicifolia* Ba NM
Labrador Tea *Ledum groenlandicum* **R** CN
Bog Rosemary *Andromeda polifolia* **S** + CN

Cowberry *Vaccinium vitis-idaea* AA
Serrate Wintergreen *Orthilia secunda* **S** CN
Intermediate Wintergreen *Pyrola media* **S** CN
Crowberry *Empetrum nigrum* AA
Bird's-eye Primrose *Primula farinosa* Ca **S** + NM
Scottish Primrose *P. scotica* (U) Hi **S** E
Chickweed Wintergreen *Trientalis europaea* NM
Jacob's Ladder *Polemonium caeruleum* Ca Ne **R** NM
Pale Forget-me-not *Myosotis stolonifera* Ba **S** CN
Wood Cow-wheat *Melampyrum sylvaticum* **S** CN
Northern Bugle *Ajuga pyramidalis* NM
Northern Bedstraw *Galium boreale* Ba CN

Mountain Everlasting *Antennaria dioica* NM
Melancholy Thistle *Cirsium helenioides* Ba + CN
Small White Orchid *Leucorchis albida* + NM
Lesser Twayblade *Listera cordata* NM
Brown Bogrush *Schoenus ferrugineus* Ca Hi **R** + CN
Rannoch Rush *Scheuchzeria palustris* Hi **R** + CN
Tall Bog Sedge *Carex paupercula* **S** + NM
Bird's Foot Sedge *C. ornithopoda* Ca **R** CN
Northern Sedge *C. aquatilis* **S** AS
String Sedge *C. chordorrhiza* Hi **R** NM
Few-flowered Sedge *C. pauciflora* NM
Mountain Melick Grass *Melica nutans* Ba NM
Blue Moor-grass *Sesleria albicans* Ca **S** A

Notes to Tables 1 & 2

Assignment to the categories montane and sub-montane is based on subjective choice, and follows Ratcliffe(1977a). Some species classed as montane have significant occurrences below the potential tree-line, though mostly in open habitats. *Rubus arcticus* and *Pinguicula alpina* are regarded as extinct in Britain. Lusitanian species which occur on mountains in Ireland are not included. Micro-species in the genus *Hieracium*, *Alchemilla vulgaris* agg. and *Euphrasia officinalis* agg. include some notable mountain taxa, but are also omitted.

Symbols

Altitude H=High montane, only above tree-line

Substrate needs Ca=Calcareous, Ba=Base-enriched, U=Unusual soils, including heavy metal concentration (other species are calcifuge or base-tolerant in some degree)

Geographical restriction W=Wales only, Ne=Northern England only, Hi=Highlands only, I=Ireland only

Rarity class **R**=Red data species (Perring & Farrell 1983), *=Schedule 8 (specially protected) species, **S**=nationally scarce species (in 16-100 10km grid squares)

Status +=declined through human impact during last 100

lies until late in the year and that which tends to be blown clear of snow and so has only a thin and short cover. The latest snow patches are mostly dominated by carpets of mosses, liverworts and lichens, with sparse growths of vascular plants, including high montane species such as Starwort Mouse-ear, *Cerastium cerastoides*, and Hare's-foot Sedge, *Carex lachenalii*.

High-level areas with minimal snow-cover are much subject to frost-thaw movements, and often show a variety of patterned ground, including stone nets and stripes, soil hummocks and ridges, wind-rows, terraces and lobes. Ablation and re-deposition help to maintain instability and there is often much bare rock and soil, though some summits have extensive closed moss and lichen heaths. Certain plants benefit equally from the openness and lack of competition in both late snow beds and wind-blasted fell

fields, e.g. Dwarf Cudweed, *Gnaphalium supinum*, Sibbaldia, *Sibbaldia procumbens*, and Least Willow.

Interacting with these climatic influences, the occurrence of calcareous rocks and soils is a modifying factor of tremendous importance. Although some mountain plants show quite wide tolerance in soil-nutrient requirements, a much greater number is adapted to base-rich, and especially calcareous, substrates than to base-poor, acidic kinds. Upland limestone areas thus have by far the richest floras in terms of species number, especially since they nearly always have examples of non-calcareous habitat as well. Spreads of acidic glacial drift and the propensity of the oceanic climate to soil-leaching ensure this. Indeed, in the wettest regions, acidic peat has tended to form even over strongly calcareous substrates, wherever there is no replacement of

13

D A Ratcliffe

Sugar limestone outcrop at White Well, Cronkley Fell, Upper Teesdale and prevailing acidic moorland.

nutrients by water seepage or physical instability.

Through geological chance there is a predominance of hard, non-calcareous rocks and podsolised, acidic soils in the British and Irish mountains, so that the flora of many upland areas is quite limited and composed mainly of calcifuge or tolerant species. The prominence of 'peat alpines' in our mountain flora is a distinctive feature. The occurrence of massive exposures of Carboniferous limestone in the Pennines and parts of western Ireland accounts for the botanical richness of these areas, at only low to moderate elevations. The richest areas of all for mountain plants are, however, where there is the vital combination of high altitude and calcareous substrates – notably in certain ranges of the central to eastern Highlands, with their extensive occurrence of Dalradian limestones and mica-schists. The Cairngorms are the most important massif of all for montane habitats and have the largest number of species, but the spectacular richness of the other mountains is approached only where the sterility of the prevailing granite is interrupted by localised outcrops of basic rock.

Since cliffs and steep, unstable ground have assumed a particular importance for British and Irish mountain plants, in providing open and ungrazed habitats, the craggier massifs tend to be the most productive. The springs, rills and flushes where drainage water flows at or just below the ground are important plant habitats, but these are plentiful in most uplands under the generally wet climate. A special habitat created by past human activity is the weathered spoil from old lead mines. In calcareous areas this supports a distinctive flora with Spring Sandwort, *Minuartia verna*, Alpine Penny-cress, *Thlaspi alpestre*, Alpine Scurvygrass, *Cochlearia officinalis* ssp. *alpina*, Thrift and Mountain Pansy, *Viola lutea*.

This ecological summary has dealt with the influence of present physical conditions. The occurrence and distribution of mountain plants in our islands can, however, be properly understood only by examining historical processes of vegetation migration and modification caused by long-term change in climate and increasing human activity.

Quaternary climatic change

The successive advance and retreat of glaciation during the Quaternary period pushed the major zones of tundra, steppe, scrub and forest back and forth across Europe, and down and up its mountain systems. At the height of the last main advance of the ice sheets, most of the lowlands of England and the extreme south of Wales and Ireland were ice-free but covered with tundra and

14

steppe. The flora included elements derived by movements southwards from the Arctic regions and north-westwards from the Alps, which had migrated into Britain and Ireland across the land-bridges linking them with mainland Europe and with each other. Some species may also have survived in unglaciated refuges closer to the ice sheets. When the ice retreated, the tundra and steppe moved northwards and, under the influence of warming climate, were followed and replaced by scrub and forest. At the time of greatest warmth, around 6000-7000BC, forest occupied most lower ground, except where it was too wet or rocky, and advanced up the mountain sides to at least 760m in places.

The tundra zone thus came to occupy the upper levels of the higher mountains, and on lower hills became excluded altogether by the more vigorous and competitive taller shrubs and trees. Only in some northern and western coastal areas did cooler conditions and extreme windiness confine scrub and forest to lower elevations, or exclude them. This post-glacial restriction of the tundra complex of fell-fields, moss and lichen

heaths, late snow-patch communities, dwarf shrub heaths, peat bogs and sedge marshes, resulted in the loss of many species from some regions, and the total extinction of some in these islands. We know from the sub-fossil remains in late-glacial deposits, such as those of the Lea Valley, not only that plants such as Mountain Avens and Dwarf Birch, *Betula nana*, were widespread in the English lowlands, but also that there were species unknown in Britain or Ireland in recent times – *Salix polaris, Ranunculus hyperboreus, Pedicularis hirsuta* and *Stellaria crassifolia* (Godwin 1975).

This climatic displacement of vegetation zones also explains why the highest and coldest mountains – in the Scottish Highlands – have remained the richest for the tundra-type flora. They gave the best chances for survival of such plants when conditions became least favourable for them. Subsequent cooling caused an estimated drop in mean temperatures by 2°C, evidently matched by a downwards shift in the upper limits of scrub and forest, and re-expansion of the mountain tundra zone above. Increases in rainfall during the post-glacial period heralded the extensive growth of blanket bogs on poorly drained

Ungrazed tall herb ledge with Roseroot, Angelica, Melancholy Thistle and Holly Fern – Caenlochan Glen, Angus.

D A Ratcliffe

15

ground at all elevations, and this peat-tundra habitat favoured some moisture-loving mountain plants.

Human influence

The other main historical factor that became increasingly important with passage of time was the activities of people, beginning with Neolithic clearance of forest. The human onslaught on the forests and their expanding conversion to agricultural land has had profound effects on the mountain flora. In the hill country, the forests were extensively replaced by grazing range for sheep, goats and cattle, first mainly with ericaceous dwarf-shrub heath, and then, as grazing and repeated burning disadvantaged the woody species, with grasslands and Bracken, *Pteridium aquilinum*. Soil erosion often resulted in scree formation, and nutrient depletion may have amplified natural leaching, which has given a prevalence of acidic, base-poor soils under our cool oceanic climate and mainly acidic parent rock formations.

This allowed an increase of mountain plants which need treeless conditions or the reduced competition of close-grazed swards, open soils and bare rock debris. Some small shrubs became more abundant as upland heaths expanded. Yet still other species declined as human impact built up. The original natural altitudinal zonation of vegetation formations was gradually obscured or lost. Patchy remnants of woodland have survived, but mostly as heavily grazed and grassy derivatives, re-planted on the sites of original forest, and lacking a natural upper limit. The zone of medium shrubs, especially willows, *Salix* spp., and Juniper, *Juniperus communis*, that once lay between the upper forest fringe and the alpine heaths above, has been almost totally lost. The merest fragments, with some of the mountain willows (Table 1), survive on ungrazed ledges in the Highlands.

The mountain dwarf shrubs lost ground as the ericaceous heaths retreated, and some also became restricted to rocky or peaty ground. Herbaceous plants in general became reduced through grazing, the taller species especially so. Some which were characteristic field-layer herbs of the northern woods thrived and became notable plants of the upland hay meadows. Exam-

ples include Globeflower, *Trollius europaeus*, Melancholy Thistle, *Cirsium helenioides*, and Wood Cranesbill, *Geranium sylvaticum*. However, on the close-cropped open hill they became limited to the ungrazed ledges of steep crags. Alpine Lettuce, *Cicerbita alpina*, became an extreme rarity of high-lying cliffs. Some mountain herbs flourished under grazing, such as Alpine Ladies' Mantle, *Alchemilla alpina*, Mountain Pansy, Spring Gentian, *Gentiana verna*, and Alpine Forget-me-not, *Myosotis alpestris*. Yet there appears to be a limit, and under excessive grazing few of the true mountain plants seem able to hold their ground indefinitely. Ferns show variable tolerance, from Bracken, *Pteridium aquilinum*, which expands under heavy grazing, to Holly Fern, *Polystichum lonchitis*, and Mountain Bladder Fern, *Cystopteris montana*, which are rapidly destroyed.

Hill-land improvement and reclamation during the last half century have affected mainly the already modified sub-alpine grasslands and dwarf-shrub heaths, but many notable species have been reduced. Bird's-eye Primrose, *Primula farinosa*, Alpine Bistort, *Polygonum viviparum*, and Hair Sedge, *Carex capillaris*, are plants of the hill pastures that have declined through the addition of nitrogenous and phosphatic fertilisers. Draining has reduced many wet-ground species, especially in small marshes and flushes. And as the enclosed hay meadows of the hill farms have been improved by ploughing, fertilising and re-seeding, the taller herbs, that survived from the sub-alpine woods, have also declined. Coniferous afforestation has likewise transformed sub-alpine communities on a large scale, and has had an especially serious effect on the upland bog flora.

The best impression of what our mountain vegetation once looked like can be gained by visiting the mountains of Norway, particularly the oceanic south-west, where climatic similarity to Britain and Ireland is greatest. There is a huge extent of natural vegetation, with hill farms (saeters) forming only small enclaves within great sweeps of pine, spruce and birch forest, passing above into extensive medium scrub of Juniper, Dwarf Birch and willows. Within the low and middle alpine zones of the Norwegian mountains there is the closest resemblance to the

16

vegetation of the Scottish mountains, with quite similar communities of both exposed fell-fields and late snow beds. The true mountain flora is in vastly greater abundance in the Norwegian mountains, and the component of ascending lowland plants is much less than in Britain. It is a revelation to find many of our rarest species so abundant, and in a much wider range of habitats than here.

The recreational use of the mountains has begun to affect the vegetation. Ski developments have caused extensive erosion and other disturbance in some high corries. Hiking has caused a widespread problem of trampling damage and especially footpath erosion. Showy plants such as the clubmosses have been reduced by collecting. These impacts have all tended to fall mainly on the more widespread species. A more serious problem has been the collecting of rarer plants by botanists and gardeners, which has greatly reduced some, especially ferns.

REGIONAL HIGHLIGHTS

This brief scan is amplified by the detailed data in Tables 1 and 2. A selected list of titles is appended for further reading.

England, Wales and Southern Scotland

All uplands in these regions are predominantly sub-alpine, with vegetation dominated by widespread species and mountain plants contributing only a tiny fraction of the total cover. They mostly show general, and often extreme, modification of original communities by centuries of heavy grazing and burning, and many hills are little but dull mounds of impoverished, Bracken-infested acidic grasslands. Even high summits have shown a progressive loss of Fringe Moss, *Racomitrium lanuginosum*, heath and species such as Least Willow. Grouse moors have remained heathery, with more floristic variety, but they are often too low to support alpine vegetation, though some have good blanket bogs with abundance of Cloudberry, *Rubus chamaemorus*. Botanical interest is highly dependent on the occurrence of rock habitats and calcareous substrates. The following are the more notable areas.

Brecon Beacons: the most southerly location for an assemblage of mountain plants, on cliffs of Old Red Sandstone, with Purple and Mossy Sax-

Mountain cliffs and blocks of calcareous pumice tuff above Llyn Idwal, Snowdonia. Note also the severe footpath erosion.

ifrages, *Saxifraga hypnoides*, Roseroot, Lesser Meadow-rue, *Thalictrum minus*, Northern Bedstraw, *Galium boreale*, and Green Spleenwort, *Asplenium viride*; native populations of Welsh Poppy, *Meconopsis cambrica*, and Rock Stonecrop, *Sedum forsteranum*, grow on cliffs and Least Willow in high summits.

Snowdonia: the extensive outcrops of calcareous pumice tuff on Snowdon, the Glyders and Moel Hebog have the best ledge communities south of the Highlands. The adjoining Carneddau and the more southerly Cader Idris range are rather less rich. Snowdon Lily, *Lloydia serotina*, is confined in Britain to a few cliffs of the area, while Tufted Saxifrage, *Saxifraga cespitosa*, Arctic Mouse-ear, *Cerastium arcticum*, Northern Rockcress, *Cardaminopsis petraea*, and Alpine Woodsia, *Woodsia alpina*, are not otherwise found south of the Highlands. Many species reach their southern British limit here and though some are in small quantity, others are abundant within their localised habitats.

Craven Pennines: the massive exposures of tabular limestone around Malham, and on the flanks of Ingleborough, Whernside and Penyghent, and the associated grasslands, marshes and flushes,

17

D A Ratcliffe

Limestone grassland, screes and outcrops girdling the summit of Mickle Fell, Yorkshire: the habitat of Alpine Forget-me-not, Spring Gentian and Spring Sandwort.

are an important area for sub-alpine and northern plants. Species such as Rigid Buckler Fern, *Dryopteris villarii*, Limestone Polypody, *Gymnocarpium robertianum*, Bird's-eye Primrose, Jacob's Ladder, *Polemonium caeruleum*, Globeflower, Wood Cranesbill, Melancholy Thistle, Mountain Melick, *Melica nutans*, and Blue Moor-grass, *Sesleria albicans*, are well represented. The extensive limestone scars at higher levels also have alpines such as Mountain Avens, Purple Saxifrage and Hoary Whitlowgrass, *Draba incana*.

Upper Teesdale: the friable metamorphosed 'sugar' limestone bedrock on Cronkley and Widdybank Fells has afforded a classic refuge for an alpine flora. By resisting the development of closed woodland it provided open niches where small species hung on and eventually expanded again when deforestation gave the opportunity. Bog Sandwort, *Minuartia stricta*, occurs nowhere else in Britain and several species of highly restricted distribution occur, though some also grow on unaltered limestone of the adjoining hills (e.g. Spring Gentian, Rock Violet, *Viola rupestris*) and others are confined to this (e.g.

Alpine Forget-me-not, Marsh Saxifrage, *Saxifraga hirculus*). Northern hay meadow communities are well developed.

Lakeland: there is a creditable total list of species, but some are present in minute amounts and illustrate well the concept of relict status. Calcareous beds of Borrowdale Igneous rock on the Helvellyn and Fairfield ranges are the best for cliff calcicoles, but many hills are acidic and unproductive. Downy Willow, *Salix lapponum*, Mountain Bladder Fern, Interrupted Clubmoss, *Lycopodium annotinum*, Alpine Timothy Grass, *Phleum alpinum*, and Alpine Lady's-mantle are at their southern limits. The last species and Yellow Saxifrage, *Saxifraga aizoides*, are abundant, in contrast to their unaccountable absence from identical habitats in Snowdonia.

Moffat Hills: the most productive area of the Southern Uplands, from the extensive occurrence of basic rock and flush habitats, on calcareous Silurian greywackes and shales. Many species are in very small amounts, and many northern England species are absent. Whortle-leaved Willow, *Salix myrsinites*, and Sheathing Sedge, *Carex vaginata*, reach their southern limits. Oblong Woodsia, *Woodsia ilvensis*, was once abundant but has been brought almost to extinction by collecting.

High granite block litters,fell-fields, corries and snowbeds at Braeriach from Ben Macdhui in the Cairngorms at midsummer.

The Highlands and Islands

This large region is by far the richest for mountain plants in our islands, and even the less productive areas can often muster a longer species list than the best uplands south of the Highland Line. Of 167 taxa in Tables 1 and 2, 54 are confined to the Highlands. Calcifuge species and dwarf shrubs are well represented, and some species are widespread. The vegetation of some higher and remoter summits approaches a truly natural condition. Only the most important areas will be mentioned.

The Ben Lawers range: the high Breadalbane mountains of Perth and Argyll from Ben Lawers to Ben Lui are our most celebrated area for alpines. Nowhere else do calcareous rocks outcrop so massively at high altitudes, and the soft Dalradian limestones and mica-schists give a particularly fertile substrate. Several hills are almost equally rich, though no two are identical. Many species occur abundantly on all, but some (e.g. Mountain Avens) vary greatly in abundance between one hill and the next, and several are in only a few places. Ben Lawers itself has the greatest variety, probably because it is the highest and the good rocks go right to the summit.

Caenlochan, Glen Doll, Corrie Fee and Corrie Kander: this equally famous area explored by Victorian botanists is more restricted, and consists of the corries at the head of Glens Isla, Clova and Callater, and the adjoining plateau-land, in Angus and Aberdeen. Calcareous Dalradian rocks again outcrop extensively, and Caenlochan probably has a larger number of alpine species than any other single corrie in Britain, though some are on acidic substrates. Many of the rare Breadalbane plants are here, plus a few unknown there. Mountain willows are especially well represented, and lush herbaceous ledge communities are again finely developed.

The Cairngorms and Lochnagar: these mountains of Inverness, Aberdeen and Banff are by far the largest area of really high plateau, with the most extensive occurrence of alpine communities, both of the open fell-field and late snow-bed types. The prevailing bedrock is acidic granite, so that calcifuge alpines are especially prominent, but localised occurrences of calcareous Moine schist and other basic rock towards the edges of the massif give a long list of additional species, including some rarities of the two previous areas. In total species number this is our richest mountain area, and important new discoveries have been made in recent years.

19

Beinn Dearg and Seana Bhraigh: this Ross-shire massif is the richest of the many ranges of high mountains north of the Great Glen. In places, the Moine rocks have strongly calcareous schists which give northern outposts for some Breadal-bane rarities on the extensive cliffs, and the peat alpines are especially well represented. The high tops have great amounts of cushion herbs (Moss Campion, Mossy Cyphel, *Cherleria sedoides*, and Thrift) in Fringe Moss heath, and there is much open fell-field with abundance of other small alpines, and good snow-bed communities. **Inchnadamph:** this relatively low-lying Suther-land area is composed largely of Durness lime-stone, massively exposed as crag and scree. Mountain Avens and Whortle-leaved Willow are in great abundance, and calcicolous com-munities are finely represented.

Many other Highland mountain areas are im-portant for their alpine flora, and I have given details elsewhere (Ratcliffe 1977a & b). The Islands show the phenomenon of island impover-ishment in species, though Skye, Rum and Hoy are quite productive.

Ireland

The climate of Ireland is too mild to have allowed the survival of a large alpine flora, and the highest mountains, from Kerry to Wicklow, have a rather limited variety of these plants. In the far west, however, the limestone hills of Sligo and Leitrim have a good relict flora which includes Alpine Saxifrage, *Saxifraga nivalis*, and Nor-wegian Sandwort, *Arenaria norvegica*. The most famous area is the Burren of Co. Clare, where extensive heaths of Mountain Avens and Bear-berry, *Arctostaphylos uva-ursi*, with Spring Gen-tian and Pyramidal Bugle, *Ajuga pyramidalis*, on limestone pavements are in company with Me-diterranean species such as Maidenhair Fern, *Adiantum capillus-veneris*, and Dense-flowered Orchid, *Neotinea maculata*. This side-by-side survival of northern and southern elements is explained by the combination of cool summers and mild winters, which also accounts for the overlap of the Killarney Fern, *Trichomanes spe-ciosum*, and Holly Fern on Brandon Mountain, Co. Kerry. The Irish Saxifrage, *Saxifraga rosa-cea*, is now confined to the mountains and sea cliffs in Ireland.

Conservation

Although the British and Irish mountain flora is a minor and depleted remnant, compared with those of other European mountain regions, it has considerable historical, ecological and biogeo-graphical interest. The relict status of many species bears witness to the long period of Ho-locene change in climate, soil development and human influence. They belong to a southern and oceanic outlier of a northern and montane eco-system complex. The combination of different phytogeographical elements is unique, and many of the distinctive plant communities are either peculiar to our islands or variants of Continental types. There is very little endemism, but some species have evolved distinct insular races. Be-yond this, the mountain flora includes some es-pecially attractive plants which add to the beauty and fascination of the hill country, our last refuge of wild nature, which we cherish accordingly. And some communities, such as heaths of Moun-tain Avens, are as fine as anything to be seen in the Arctic.

Conservation measures consist largely of trying to arrest, ameliorate or reverse those pro-cesses that have caused decline and loss of species in the past. Only human activities are amenable to such intervention but they have been the most serious of the adverse influences in recent times. Appropriate control of land-use practices can best be achieved within protected areas, and so the establishment of National Nature Reserves and notification of Sites of Special Scientific In-terest in mountain areas by the Nature Conser-vancy Council has been a key part of the pro-gramme. The two National Trusts own a number of important upland properties and the Royal Society for the Protection of Birds has acquired hill reserves. Important reserves include the Cairngorms, Ben Lawers-Meall nan Tarmachan, Clova-Caenlochan, Inchnadamph, Bettyhill Links, Upper Teesdale, Moor House and Snow-don-Cwm Idwal. These protected areas should be enlarged and increased.

Remedial management is nevertheless diffi-cult. In many areas, grazing by sheep and deer needs to be greatly reduced and moor-burning stopped or drastically curtailed. The heather re-covery programmes now in hand may help other dwarf shrubs or herbs. Yet many depleted or lost

20

species will not readily increase or return, and some will do so only if directly assisted. Where human agency has caused decline, and especially by deliberate collecting, there is a strong case for trying to re-stock populations. This has been done with some initial success in the case of Tufted Saxifrage in Snowdonia. Fragments of the last wild remnant were propagated vegetatively in the Liverpool Botanic Garden and then transferred back to the original site. A reduced Pennine population of Holly Fern has also been expanded. Each case must be decided on its own merits, but many other species would appear to qualify for similar treatment.

Some communities, such as montane willow scrub, have so completely disappeared that only a more heroic scale of restoration would be meaningful. Fencing against sheep and deer is a first requirement, followed by re-introduction of the right species. Successful pilot experiments on some reserves point the way, but only the complete removal of grazing over large areas would give any chance of recovering the vegetational appearance that our mountains must have once had. Tree-planting is problematical: restoration should aim to re-establish woodland up to the climatic tree-line, but with typical native species, leaving open spaces where they would naturally occur and avoiding the planting of peat bogs in particular.

Plant-collecting remains a serious threat to the rarer species, despite legal protection against picking and uprooting in general, and with special penalties for taking scheduled rarities. Only change in attitudes could remove this problem, and it is vital that educational work be continued, or increased, to instil a sense of respect for wildlife more widely, and a wish to enjoy the native flora as an essential part of the countryside scene, whether upland or elsewhere.

The cloud now casting shadows on our conservation efforts is the threat of global warming with its especially serious portents for the plants and animals that have survived only in the coldest parts of our islands. Many of our mountain plants would be greatly at risk from any appreciable rise in temperatures, and concern for their survival gives particular reason for campaigning vigorously against this most ominous of environmental hazards.

Plant collecting has threatened some alpine species such as the Snowdon Lily here on a remote Welsh cliff.

References

Clapham, A R (ed) 1978 *Upper Teesdale: the area and its natural history*. Collins, London

Condry, W M 1966 *The Snowdonia National Park*. New Naturalist 47 Collins, London

Condry, W M 1981 *The Natural History of Wales*. New Naturalist 66, Collins, London

Godwin, H 1975 *History of the British Flora*. Cambridge University Press, Cambridge

Matthews, J R 1955 *Origin and Distribution of the British Flora*. Hutchinson's University Library, London

McVean, D N, & Ratcliffe, D A 1962 *Plant Communities of the Scottish Highlands*. Nature Conservancy Monograph No 1, HMSO, London

Nethersole-Thompson, D, & Watson, A 1981 *The Cairngorms: their natural history and scenery*. The Melven Press, Perth

Pearsall, W H 1950 *Mountains and Moorlands*. New Naturalist 11, Collins, London

Perring, F H, & Farrell, L 1983 *British Red Data Books, 1 Vascular Plants*, second edition. RSNC, Nettleham

Ratcliffe, D A 1959 The mountain plants of the Moffat Hills. *Trans and Proc Bot Soc Edinb* 37:257-271

Ratcliffe, D A 1960 The mountain flora of Lakeland. *Proc Bot Soc Br Isl* 4:1-25

Ratcliffe, D A 1977a (ed.) *A Nature Conservation Review*, 2 Vols, Cambridge University Press, Cambridge

Ratcliffe, D A 1977b *Highland Flora*. Highlands and Islands Development Board, Inverness

Raven, J, & Walters, S M 1956 *Mountain Flowers*. New Naturalist 33, Collins, London

Usher, M B & Thompson, D B A (ed.) 1988 *Ecological change in the Uplands*. Blackwell Scientific Publications, Oxford

County floras covering the upland regions are the main source of information on distribution of mountain plants.

Dr Derek Ratcliffe was the NCC's Chief Scientist before his retirement in 1989. His PhD thesis was on the mountain vegetation of Snowdonia.

21

THE ORNITHOLOGIST –
searching for and saving birds in wild places

11. Contributions to field ornithology - in search of nesting birds

Des Thompson

"I have always been drawn to the mountains and moorlands above all other types of country. Their birds gain in charm and fascination from the wild and beautiful places in which they live, and seeking them here has a special appeal."

Bird Life of Mountain and Upland (p.ix) Derek Ratcliffe[1]

Introduction

Of the three principal disciplines for which Derek Ratcliffe is best known[2]—field botany, nature conservation, and ornithology—it is arguably for the last that we know most about his work and results, but least about his field methods and approaches. His contributions to field ornithology were numerous and exceptional, and some have been summarised very well elsewhere in this book[3-6] and previously[7,8]. Several aspects of Derek's bird work have been covered in detail, such as his pioneering work on raptors and pesticides[4,5] and his exceptionally detailed work on some parts of Britain, notably Galloway and the Borders[6] and the Flow Country of Caithness and Sutherland[9]. Having spent many memorable spells in the field with Derek, spread over four decades, I want to provide an insight into how he worked, and what he was like to be with in the field. I begin with nest finding, and end with the personal recollections of an eleven-year-old in the field with him.

Nest hunting and nest hunters

"My uncle gave me a little book with attractive paintings of 72 different kinds of birds' nests and eggs in their natural habitats, as well as quite good life-size illustrations of the eggs themselves. I pored over the pictures and descriptions and resolved to find as many of them as possible." From *In Search of Nature* by Derek Ratcliffe[10], writing about T.A. Coward's *The Birds of the British Isles and their Eggs*[11].

Unless you have watched birds with an insatiable hunger for finding their nests you can have no idea of what drives people to do so. Patrick Barkham[12] captured well the mania of egg collecting: "An obsessive-compulsive attention to detail can obscure reality… Others seem addicted, gripped by an obsession they can no longer master." The Jourdain Society, named after the Reverend F.C.R. Jourdain following his death in 1940 (and formed out of the British Oological Association, established in 1922 by Walter Rothschild—the second Baron Rothschild—and Jourdain), is dedicated to the advancement of the science of oology. Many of its members were egg collectors, and some still are, with the discipline of oology beginning in the 19th century. Unfortunately, the illegality of egg collecting (from 1954 onwards) and the absurd lengths some collectors have gone to acquire hauls of literally thousands of clutches of eggs in the time since then has besmirched its image[e.g. 12,13]. Oology is the scientific study of eggs (especially birds' eggs) and their size, shape, colouration, and number. Lloyd Kiff[14] provides a fascinating account of advances in this ornithological field and the many uses now being made of egg collections, and Kevin Winkler[15] gives an overview of research making use of bird collections. And for the sheer beauty of eggs, Hauber's *The Book of Eggs*[16] is sumptuous with its 656 pages adorned by 2,400 colour plates. Birds' eggs are fascinating, and the quest to find nests can be one of nature's purest and most rewarding pursuits.

A hunger for nests

Derek and I talked a lot about nest hunting – about eggs, the tell-tale signs of nest locations, and the extraordinary lengths parent birds go to in concealing their whereabouts. Just as he loved searching for rare plants, particularly rare and persecuted ferns such as the Killarney Fern (*Trichomanes speciosum*) (Fig. 4.27)[2], and seeking out special places for wildlife[10], Derek was equally obsessive when it came to finding nests. If a nest was in a cliff or tree, he had to get to it to see the eggs (and photograph them in later years) (Figs. 11.1 & 11.2). What is it that drives us to such lengths that several days may be spent hunting down a nest, with life being put at risk, to get at a precariously placed clutch? We often mused on this, sometimes after sweaty descents down a crag to a Peregrine's (*Falco peregrinus*), Golden Eagle's (*Aquila chrysaetos*) or, if we were lucky, a near-impossibly placed Raven's (*Corvus corax*) nest. It is not just the hunt evolved from ancestral days of finding food. It is not even related to a particular bird being rare, for some of the commoner ones have the hardest nests to find. No, there is something utterly predatory about nest hunting, pitting your wits and observational skills against the parent birds in order to feast your eyes on their eggs. It is a strangely primitive pursuit, and it is the eggs that matter, for few people go to such lengths to see the chicks.

There is special joy to watching a bird back to its nest—flitting, running, often lost and out of sight or earshot—but finally settling down on eggs. You either sense a warm glow of satisfaction on seeing this, or you do not. Birds ranging in scarcity from Lapwing (*Vanellus vanellus*), Curlew (*Numenius arquata*), and Ringed Plover (*Charadrius hiaticulata*) to Greenshank (*Tringa nebularia*), Dotterel (*Charadrius morinellus*) (Fig. 11.3), Snow Bunting (*Plectrophenax nivalis*), and Purple Sandpiper (*Calidris maritima*) gave us thrilling

Figure 11.1. Derek Ratcliffe scaling a Birch (*Betula*) tree to inspect a Merlin's (*Falco columbarius*) brood of two 3–4-day-old chicks in an old Carrion Crow's (*Corvus corone*) nest in the foothills of Skiddaw in the Lake District. The picture was taken on 9 June 1989, a month before Derek's retirement. Photo: Des Thompson

enjoyment. Part of this is drawing on earlier experiences and lessons learnt from books, papers, and conversations.

Figure 11.2. Derek Ratcliffe in 1959 preparing to descend one of the steep cliffs on Boreray (St Kilda archipelago) in order to ring Guillemots (*Uria aalge*) and Fulmars (*Fulmarus glacialis*) that throng the sea-cliff ledges. Photograph reproduced by permission of Dick Seamons

Anticipation, honed through years of graft, and rewarded when the bird nestles down, is an addiction. As you get older you get more, not fewer, rewards from the chase. The many disappointments, when nests are missed and the sequences of behaviour

Figure 11.3. Dotterel (*Charadrius morinellus*) in central Norway, 1995. The Dotterel is one of a few species where the male typically incubates the eggs. Photos: Derek Ratcliffe

woefully misinterpreted, add to the almost intellectual allure of learning from your mistakes and hoping the next quest will be successful. Oddly though, we thought there was far more to it than that. We often discussed the antics and habits of nest hunters and egg collectors so vividly described by my father, Desmond Nethersole-Thompson, in his monographs[17-19]. In *The Dotterel*[18], he refers to an 'Acquisitive Society' of people who use every means to trap, kill, and acquire specimens, including eggs.

The egg collectors described by Cole and Trobe[20] are a curious cornucopia of Government ministers, judges, solicitors, civil servants, schoolmasters, clergymen, and all manner of other professions, but rarely businessmen. Predominantly male, and elderly, they are some of the oddest people you might encounter, united by a predilection for collecting eggs. For many of them, their collections were at the centre of their lives, invariably housed in one or more beautiful wooden cabinets of great craftsmanship, with the clutches within the drawers nestling on a pristine cotton-wool base, and protected by a glass cover. Derek and others taking measurements[5] from these have remarked how, as a drawer was carefully withdrawn, the collector would eagerly reminisce over each clutch – where it was from, the position of the nest, the difficulty of the climb, and all manner of other associations. The cabinets were boxes of precious memories, many of which extended back over decades, and were perhaps substitutes for diaries covering the highlights of a lifetime in the field. We could never come to terms with what they did, but agreed that something deeply psychological must have excited, or at least enticed them, for the risks of being caught and punished were, and are, significant.

Birds' eggs are bewilderingly varied in size, shape, colour, pattern, and even texture. That there is so little variation between eggs in a clutch, compared with that between clutches, is down to the personalised 'number plates' of the females laying the eggs. Some long-lived hens have been tracked over decades by the familiar and consistent physiognomy of their eggs, and in a few cases uniquely distinctive eggs mark out particular birds. In 1974 I had the privilege of seeing a Herring Gull's (*Larus argentatus*) clutch of erythrthistic (red pigmented) eggs on Handa Island, north-west Sutherland, and for decades afterwards Derek asked me to describe their detail and setting. I only realised much later why he was so interested, for on p.94 of the second (green) edition of *Highland Birds*[21] by my father, there was a lovely picture of three erythristic Herring Gulls' eggs alongside a normal greenish egg, and below it to the left was a fabulous picture of the Clo Mor sea-cliffs (Fig. 14.1), taken by Derek, just 18 miles (28 km) away! Such eggs are rare[e.g. 22], and all the more alluring. Reading the draft manuscript of Derek's book on *The Raven*[23] made me realise the high importance of pink and red eggs laid by these birds, with the first known record of a clutch of four in Unst, Shetland, in 1854, described by Sir Alfred Newton. Several erythristic clutches[6] have been recorded in the Highlands, Southern Uplands, Lakeland, and Wales, with one female Raven laying a clutch in each of at least seven years.

'Dottereling'

One of the most important features of Derek's writing is the immense tribute he pays to nest hunters. In his classic *The Peregrine Falcon*[24] (Fig. 14.6) he devotes Chapter 1 to 'The Peregrine and Man', and in the space of 23 pages provides a fascinating account of people working on the birds, with four pages devoted to egg collectors (with a full page colour plate showing a varied series of twelve clutches from Edgar Chance's Collection, photographed by Derek), two pages to falconers, and three to 'the ornithologists'. In his last book, *Galloway and the Borders*[25], literally tapped out on his computer weeks before he died, Derek devoted twenty pages to 'The naturalists', with ten pages given over to the birdwatchers, including three of his closest friends (with photographs of them taken by him).

Figure 11.4. Desmond Nethersole-Thompson's monograph on *The Dotterel*[18] in which Derek Ratcliffe wrote two outstanding chapters, one on the breeding status of Dotterel in England[26] and one on its breeding habitat in Britain[28], both based on years of patient 'dottereling' and field observations in upland Britain.

My own favourite is a work of scholarship much read, but little quoted – Chapter 19[26] in *The Dotterel* (Fig. 11.4)[18] – 'The Dotterel as a Breeding Bird in England'. In just eight pages, drawing heavily on the experiences of his great mentor, Ernest Blezard, and other workers, Derek tantalises us with his views on the changing fortunes of Dotterel – not just in England, but across Britain[26]. He explores a number of reasons for Dotterel having largely abandoned their southern breeding ranges since the late 19th century, citing acidic deposition, grazing pressures, and recreational disturbance as principal factors; climate change, now being examined as a possible cause, was not a contender then. Derek wrote fine accounts on the habitats of upland birds in Nethersole-Thompson's monographs[27-29], but his essay on the occurrence of Dotterel in parts of southern Britain[26] is now all the more important given the changes we are seeing today[e.g. 30].

Special finds in northern England

Finding nests of some birds requires extraordinary

patience and skill, and the rewards are special. On 29 May 1959, Derek found the first authenticated post-War nest of Dotterel in northern England (Fig. 11.5), on a hill that best remains nameless. His field notes[31] give a sense of the occasion, when he comments after watching a bird near its nest:

> "With the certainty that this was the nest, I rose and made for the place, only about 30 yards distance. I was delighted to see two eggs lying there on one of the solifluction hummocks [...] This was the first authentic Dotterel nest in the north of England that we have heard of since Dr E.S. Stewart found one on Raise, Helvellyn Range, about 1944, though there was a rumour of one robbed on Crossfell in 1957 and birds have been seen there occasionally."

On 31 May Derek and Ernest Blezard (Fig. 1.9) returned to photograph the nesting Dotterel, and next year they found them nesting in the same place, and nine years later Derek alone found nesters there again, on 30 May 1968 (Fig. 11.5).

Figure 11.5. Incubating Dotterel (*Charadrius morinellus*) on a hill in northern England, 1968 (*left*) and a Dotterel's nest in northern Norway, 1999 (*right*). Derek found the first authenticated post-War Dotterel nest in England in 1959. Photos: Derek Ratcliffe

Precisely two years later to the day, Derek records in his notes[31]:

> "With Geoff Horne, Ritson Graham, Ralph Stokoe and the Blezard family. Dotterel found... numerous photos taken. It would not quite submit to being touched, and ran off to disclose three eggs, of an ordinary type....125 yards north of the summit cairn. Found another nest just 200 yards from the other, with eggs somewhat similar to those of the other nest. With two nests so close it is always possible that a polyandrous female was involved. It was remarkable that these two nests, so close to the Pennine Way ... and constantly passed by hikers, should have been successful in hatching, and says much for the ability of Dotterel to tolerate casual disturbance."

Figure 11.6. Desmond Nethersole-Thompson on a Ross-shire mountain summit heath frequented by nesting Dotterel (*Charadrius morinellus*), posing for the photographer. August 1967. Photo: Derek Ratcliffe

Looking for Dotterel in the Highlands and beyond

Much later Derek and I spent weeks on the high tops of North Wales, Lakeland, and the Highlands 'dottereling', as he liked to call it. Our record day's haul was of six nests on a Ross-shire fellfield where, 23 years earlier, my father had posed for Derek on his last full ascent of a high mountain (Fig. 11.6). By then, not short of 20 stone (125 kg) in weight, he toiled to the summit, all the more remarkable for it was in August when Dotterel and Snow Bunting would have been scarce.

In 1992, Phil Whitfield and I returned to where this photo (Fig. 11.6) was taken to re-take it and see how the vegetation had changed – it had become grassier, part of the phenomenon of 'homogenisation' we are learning about through revisiting the earlier vegetation plots sampled by Derek, Donald McVean, and other botanists[see 2].

These were magical times in search of Dotterel[see also 6]. Walking on what felt like the roof of the world, you spend hours meander-searching for the mossfool, as the Gaelic vernacular refers to it (*Amadan Mointeach*), on account of its extreme tameness. Typically walking 100 m apart, we would cover 100-200 m, scan the horizon through binoculars hoping to see a bobbing bird off the nest, or perhaps even the dark cap and white stripe above the eye of the incubating male (for he alone attends to virtually all parental care), and then keep going. We would peer in all directions, and especially behind us, for it was easy to miss a bird sitting tightly or who ran back to its nest after we passed. For hours, walking many miles over the high tops, and always keeping to the plateaux and upper, smoother slopes, we would cover some of Britain's most extensive natural heaths. The variety of textures and colours was remarkable, and we rapidly developed a search image for the preferred habitats – the mossy *Racomitrium lanuginosum–Carex bigelowii* (Stiff Sedge) heaths, especially where broken up by solifluction hummocks and myriad ablation surfaces, and the wind clipped heaths of Bilberry (*Vaccinium myrtillus*), Crowberry (*Empetrum nigrum*), *Cladonia arbuscula*, and *Racomitrium*, and sometimes the uppermost reaches of wind-pruned dwarf Heather (*Calluna vulgaris*). It could be foggy, raining and sleeting periodically, and invariably windy, but on we went coming together every half hour or so to compare notes and jot down grid references and sightings (or lack of them). With wild abandon and the hungry hunter's urge, the prized find of a nest or sighting of a brood was celebrated always with a handshake, followed by the shutter click of Derek's camera mounted on a tripod. Some birds were so tame they would return to the nest whilst we were weighing the eggs, and some of Derek's pictures of incubating males have become classic images capturing superbly their brilliant camouflage (Figs. 11.5 & 13.8). What hardy birds these are, sometimes enduring days of snow lie, and hunkering down against the harshest spring and summer weather in the temperate world.

We did most of this work in the mid 1980s through to the late 1990s, during a time when the scarce Dotterel population in Britain numbered between around 500 and 800 nesting males. We were working some areas previously studied by my father during 1933-1951, and it was thrilling to find sometimes double the nests recorded in his time. The population had been much smaller then, although some have debated this, and now numbers have fallen back except on the highest hills where there appears to be little overall change. Well into the evening we would search, before reluctantly calling it a day and beginning our silent descent.

Most of our days on the tops drew blanks, and sometimes we were fortunate even to see Ptarmigan (*Lagopus muta*). But 26 May 1975 in Skiddaw Forest, was especially exciting, for on the blanket bogs of Knott beyond the head of Burdle Gill, Derek and friends were 'rope dragging'[6] when they flushed:

> "A Purple Sandpiper in breeding plumage, with breast heavily spotted like a Song Thrush, a heavily flecked and freckled face, and black feathers with fawn-brown edging... It was evidently attached to the area, but we could not rouse a second bird. Its behaviour was reminiscent of the Dotterel I saw on Knott in 1954, and perhaps like that bird it was a lone straggler which had chanced to stop awhile on the hill."[31]

Derek and I returned there in 1989 but did not see Purple Sandpiper. This is a blue riband nesting bird, with no more than a handful nesting in Britain, and seen by us on three tops. The reference to rope dragging[6] reminds me of the field method about which we disagreed intently. After hours of fruitless searching Derek would announce it was time for 'the rope'. This infernal object was a neatly coiled washing line some 30 m long. On Ben Hee and Ben Hope, on the ethereal Am Faochagach plateau, over the vast mossy *Racomitrium lanuginosum–Carex bigelowii* plains of Ben Wyvis, on Skiddaw, and the stony Carneddau, to name just a few, we dragged this damned line in the hope of flushing a bird off its nest. It worked, of course, but was misery – each time I lifted my binoculars to look ahead there would be a whacking tug of the rope as Derek marched on, oblivious and eager only to put up a bird. When it did, and God knows we would probably have overlooked the sitting gem now fluttering in front of the rope, Derek would delight in saying "How about that!" I hated the rope, and so rancorous were some of our arguments over its use that Derek occasionally attached one end to a cairn or protruding rock and walked in circles whilst I headed off to scan ahead.

Working with my boss

In the mid to late 1980s Derek was my 'boss', the Nature Conservancy Council's (NCC) Chief Scientist until his retirement in 1989, training up a youthful Mountains and Moorland Ecologist. That was how we got away each year for two weeks of early June fieldwork. 'Training in the field' was part of my loosely termed 'personal development plan', with Derek insisting on overseeing it. We were mostly out of office contact, though on alternate days we met up with regional staff who relished the chance of being out with Derek and bending his ear on a multitude of problems. Some of them were enlisted as rope partners, and instead of wise counsel and sage advice, they got commands to walk faster and keep flicking the rope. Several times they would be confronted by hillwalkers asking them what on earth they were doing. Once, a sheepish Derek and a senior NCC colleague were confronted by a recently recruited NCC officer walking his new beat, who demanded to see their licences for the use of the rope. No parchment was forthcoming, and the rope was tucked away, but deployed shortly afterwards when, as Derek called him, 'the new-boy' had gone out of sight!

Each evening we ate late, with Derek always changing for dinner and sporting a tie no matter how informal the setting (he often wore a tie in the field; see Figure 11.2). Conversation topics could run for days, punctuated by mimicked mischievous remarks and asides. Derek had a great memory for anecdotes and tales of compatriots' deeds and exploits, and an armoury of quotes from his favourite author – George Orwell. As John and Hilary Birks[2], Chris Rollie[6], John Mitchell[32], Ian Newton[5], and other friends remark, Derek was wonderful company – convivial, challenging, judicious, erudite, deeply sceptical, sensitive, warm, and, in bouts, and I have to say more so towards the end of his life, outraged and frustrated over the injustice of nature's poor standing in society's and the political pecking order.

Late into the night we would write up field notes and work on papers. During the 1987 sortie we assembled parts of our overview of the international importance of the British uplands[33], the following spring we worked on drafts of *The Flow Country*[34] [see 9,35] (Fig. 23.9), and in 1989 debated and modified the large summary tables in *Bird Life of Mountain and Upland*[1] (Fig. 11.7).

Derek always composed his text carefully before committing to paper in beautiful handwriting, almost always in blue ink, which needed only the most modest of editing. He began word-processing

Figure 11.7. Derek Ratcliffe's masterpiece on *Bird Life of Mountain and Upland*[1] in which he synthesised over 45 years of his personal field observations as well as data from others to provide an overview of upland and mountain birds, and their habitats and ecology in Great Britain.

in 1989, and made an easy transition to the keyboard. In meetings Derek was not any-where near his best and often came out of them seething and reeling off what he should have said, and wanted to say, during hours of silent anger. Frankly, I think a lot of this was down to the way he thought and wrote – carefully marshalling the facts, linking the evidence, and assembling words to best effect. But in stiffly formal gatherings his moments passed too quickly. He would often say "it is not what you say, but how you say it that matters", but Derek's trouble was that his best moment for an interjection had often long passed. How he hated meetings, and in particular being flanked by "smart Alecs and ruddy jobsworths", as he called them. He admired effective and well versed committee men on his side, and Derek Langslow, his able Assistant Chief Scientist, Max Nicholson (Figs. 19.2 & 19.7), as Director General of the Nature Conservancy (1952-66), and Sir William Wilkinson (Figs. 19.6 & 19.7), the NCC's Chair at the end of Derek's tenure as Chief Scientist, were standouts – and fine ornithologists (e.g. Fig. 11.8).

Figure 11.8. Sir William Wilkinson (1912-1996) (second from left), delighting in seeing nesting Dotterel (*Charadrius morinellus*) for the first time on an east Drumochter top in the Cairngorm area of central Scotland, 1992. He is ac-companied by his wife Kate (centre), Dick Balharry (second from right), the late John Drysdale (far right), and Sue Holt (far left with the telescope) who found the nest. The telescope is trained on an incubating male. A Ptarmigan (*Lagopus muta*) sitting tightly on its nest was viewed 15 minutes later. Photo: Des Thompson

The Golden Plover – spirit of moorlands in spring

In 1976 Derek published a paper on the Golden Plover (*Pluvialis apricaria*) (Fig. 11.9) in *Bird Study*[36]. He had not published anything previously on this bird, and out of the blue came a 53-page distillation of research by him and others on this most elusive of nest-ing birds (Fig. 11.10). It is a *tour de force*[3]. It transpired that Derek had developed an in-tensive study of populations on the area loosely between Tailbridge Hill and Rollinson

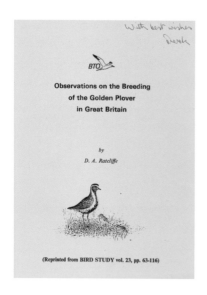

Figure 11.9. Derek Ratcliffe's *tour de force* on the breeding and behaviour of Golden Plover (*Pluvialis apricaria*) in Britain[36]. It is one of the most elegantly written and well researched papers published on birds.

Figure 11.10. Golden Plover (*Pluvialis apricaria*) on the Færoe Islands, 2008. Photo: Arild Breistøl

Haggs in Cumbria, and in the Moorfoot Hills south of Edinburgh. There, he searched out nests and built up a remarkable picture of timing of nesting, breeding success, habitat use, and other facets of their population ecology.

When Ingvar Byrkjedal and I worked on our monograph on the Golden Plover and the three other tundra plovers[37] we often spoke about Derek's unstinting work on the bird[3]. Derek was our natural choice to write the book's Foreword, which he opened with[38]:

> "As a youngster, I was charmed by the Eurasian Golden Plover of our northern uplands, having encountered my first on a grouse moor in the foothills of the Lake District of northern England. It was a bird I came to regard as the spirit of the moorlands in spring, and I loved to hear its evocative territorial song as the plover floated with slow wing beats high above its nesting grounds."

We dedicated the book (Fig. 11.11) to my father, and when I mentioned our intention to Derek he told me how he had "got a shove" having read my father's two volume, handwritten account on the Golden Plover[39], which had formed the basis of the essay in Bannerman's *Birds of the British Isles* published three decades later[40]. That blue fountain-pen inked manuscript[39] ended thus:

> "In this story our diaries have spoken and we have not attempted to write up or embroider the facts. That there is also another kind of story will be obvious when one understands that in its making five long years, summer and winter, have been spent in a Highland shieling. Not for a moment however do we suggest that this biology is all we would wish it to be. But in that it gives a cross-section in the life of a hitherto apparently neglected bird, its telling may possibly justify its birth-pangs."

Derek liked that.

TUNDRA PLOVERS

The Eurasian, Pacific and American
Golden Plovers and Grey Plover

INGVAR BYRKJEDAL and DES THOMPSON

Figure 11.11. Ingvar Byrkjedal and Des Thompson's monograph on *Tundra Plovers*[37] in which they detail the ecology, breeding behaviour, and distribution of Golden Plover (*Pluvialis apricaria*) and three other tundra plovers. Derek Ratcliffe wrote the Foreword[38] to this book.

The plumage of the Golden Plover varies greatly in terms of the darkness of its face, breast, and belly, with vividly black-fronted birds found further north and at higher elevation where they nest later in spring. It was only when Derek spent his later years in spring studying birds in the far north[3] that he came to appreciate the marked plumage differences. As Derek wrote in the Foreword to *Tundra Plovers*[38]:

> "In Fennoscandia, I was intrigued to find Eurasian Golden Plovers breeding on bogs within the great pine and spruce forests of the Boreal zone, and more constantly on lichen heaths amongst open birch scrub on the Lapland fells – nesting habitats they have lost or forsaken in Britain. Very widely they were birds of tundra and fell-field, from the high mountain barrens of the Jotunheim and Hardangervidda at 1,500 m to sea-level on the bleak Finnmark shore. And what handsome birds were most of these Fennoscandian goldies, compared with many of our paler birds at home."

Its cryptic behaviour during incubation renders its nest immensely difficult to find. Often leaving the nest stealthily at a great distance and being out of sight to the approaching observer, some will sit tight, superbly camouflaged, and rise at just one or two metres. What is worse, the sitting bird's mate may be several miles away off duty, betraying no sense of where the nest might be. For Derek, this added to the allure of discovering more about these enchanting and elusive birds (Fig. 11.12).

A record find

In the Moorfoots, on 12 May 1969, Derek remarked on the sixth day of fieldwork[31] that "I had, for the first time, found the nests of all 16 pairs of Golden Plovers in my study group." Four years later, his entry for 3 May 1973 is[31]:

"Chris Durell, Sandy Kerr and DAR ascended Dewar Hill by Gill Cleugh. Found nest there and on summit of Eastside Height found another two nests. At Ladyside Height… the rope jumped a bird from its nest. Later, half a mile further on, Sandy, at the end of the line, almost stepped on a sitting plover, which flew off hurriedly… After another 250 yards, Chris in the middle of the line, flushed another sitting plover at about 3 yards, again from 4 eggs."

Figure 11.12. Derek Ratcliffe examining a Golden Plover (*Pluvialis apricaria*) nest on Alston Moor, Cumbria, 1962. Photo: Derek Ratcliffe

Later still, as they ascended Rawburn Head, Derek flushed a Golden Plover at five yards. That made seven nests found in a day. He concluded[31]:

"The score of Golden Plover nests equals my previous best, and was due in part to the severe conditions, which made an unusual number of birds sit tight… The following day, in mist and pouring rain, we went over the Plover grounds, but had no success. Birds were getting off their nests unseen, and called through the mist."

They returned for another two days, and by the end had a tally of 15 nests – a remarkable feat for a moor within 20 miles of the centre of Edinburgh. His field method was simple (beyond the use of his infernal rope) – walking fast across the moor and looking far ahead for birds flushing off the nest. In his *Bird Study* paper[36], Derek notes that:

"There is a special technique which has to be diligently cultivated; the impulse to look at the ground at one's feet has to be resisted, and the gaze concentrated as far ahead as possible, not in one place, but scanning continuously over a wide arc from one side to the other and back. This has to be kept up whilst walking over the moor, and it is astonishing how often a bird chooses to fly at the moment the gaze falters or the mind wanders."

Figure 11.13. Golden Plover (*Pluvialis apricaria*) clutch, northern Norway, 1993. Photo: Derek Ratcliffe

Only recently have Ingvar Byrkjedal and I appreciated how remarkably well Derek fared in finding nests (Fig. 11.13), for the above extracts from his notebooks reveal what we think is a world record tally of Golden Plover nests found in a day. Derek was rightly very proud of his nest record finds[6].

Understanding nest spacing

Derek had one important weapon in his armoury of field methods, and its use defined his greatest breakthrough in understanding the fate of the Peregrine and other raptor populations[5]. A simple clue is found in Figure 3 of his *Bird Study* paper[36], reproduced here as Figure 11.14.

Quite simply, Derek discovered that Golden Plovers were regularly spaced, so once he found one nest and had a feel for the density of the birds, he could rapidly rule out 'cold' ground and home in on areas likely to have nests. It sounds so easy, but it was a fundamentally important breakthrough at the time. In his paper, he lists mean distances between nests on two of his study areas over 13 years, and in an exceptional compilation of the literature gives breeding densities for 78 areas, beginning with Dartmoor and ending with Fetlar. The great majority of assessments were based on his and my father's observations.

Six pages cover what he termed 'Breeding Dispersion', a compelling account of what he considered to govern nest spacing and territoriality in these birds, with cross

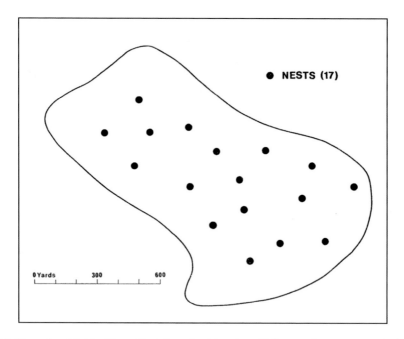

Figure 11.14. Dispersion of Golden Plover (*Pluvialis apricaria*) nests on Mallerstang limestone grasslands, Yorkshire in 1974. (From Ratcliffe [36])

references to his work on Ravens and Peregrine[41] and an 'in press' paper by Ian Newton on the Sparrowhawk (*Accipter nisus*) (which unusually he did not list in the References). Ian went on to become the foremost authority on the Sparrowhawk and its population biology (Fig. 15.2)[42]. His book *Bird Populations*[43] opens with:

> "This book is about bird numbers, and about why these numbers vary in the way they do, from year to year or from place to place. It is therefore concerned with the various factors that limit bird numbers: with the role of food supplies and other resources, of competitors, predators, parasites and pathogens, and of various human impacts."

In the ensuing 523 pages, Ian masterfully weaves the findings of his own and hundreds of others' studies to unravel the intricacies of his subject. He closes[43] with what could appropriately have featured as part of Derek's epitaph: "In an environmentally conscious society, therefore, the study of wild bird populations is likely to remain a scientific necessity for long into the future, and also a continuing source of fascination and pleasure for ornithologists."

Birds of prey – an ecological jigsaw puzzle

Derek adored maps. Everywhere in Derek's car there were 'New Popular Edition One-Inch Maps' of the Ordnance Survey. Pale yellow, with red borders, these cloth one-inch to the mile maps were on seats, on the floor, in the glove compartment, and stashed in loose piles in the boot. Derek devoured maps, and it did not take me long to understand why. Each day, before a field outing, maps were produced and areas invisibly circled with the wave of a biro. Routes were plotted, never involving backtracking, and a softly spoken commentary listed what we hoped to see.

Derek acknowledged in *The Peregrine Falcon*[24,44] "the anonymous men of the Ordnance Survey, without whose dedicated labours in the field we should all be bereft of our most basic tool. I thank them for making field studies possible and for giving enormous pleasure besides."

What began as schoolboy quests[45] evolved into the backbone of a ground-breaking raptor survey and monitoring methodology[1,10,23-25,41,44,46-54]. Derek was heavily influenced in particular by Ernest Blezard (Fig. 1.9), who tutored him in field methods and encouraged him particularly with his early publications[55 and see 2,10,23,24,56]. In each district with Ravens and Peregrine Falcons, Derek amassed what was known about nest sites— past and present—and their tenure by breeders or non-breeders. Abandoned and seemingly little-used sites were especially challenging, for days might be spent checking out what Derek called 'duds'. But how important that he did this, for to be sure of absence and nesting failure is one of the toughest jobs for a fieldworker, and to achieve this on a large scale demands unstinting patience, energy, and obdurate stubbornness (see Greenwood and Crick[4] and Hardey *et al.*[57] which is dedicated to Derek).

Covering the ground

Derek had all these attributes, and far more, and probably walked and scrambled over a greater expanse of the British uplands than anyone else known to science. In fact, I doubt if any other single person walked over as much upland terrain. Mountain Munro baggers cover great distances, but often with their eyes to the ground and along prescribed routes. For Derek this was anathema—tracks and paths were avoided, except on a bicycle—and truly vast expanses were walked and memorised. He amassed a large collection of coffee-table landscape photography books and relished the challenge of picking out a picture at random, working out its location, and what it had by way of plants and animals. What a talent to have – the ability to reach into the land and see, know, and understand its rich tapestry. And what a gift! Derek had a knowledge of which areas held certain birds, and how these changed over the years – an insight into the workings of nature borne out of decades of first-hand encounters manifested later in beautifully crafted writing.

In his monographs[23,24,44] and wider writing on upland birds[10,25,53,54,58], Derek provided exhaustive detail at the regional level on status and success of territories. The data are exceptional and best appreciated when you see some of the maps derived from them (Fig. 11.15).

In the tables of his books he compiled data on nest-site use, timing of nesting, clutch size, fledging success, territory occupation, and many other facets, typically organised by region in Britain and Ireland. If Derek had only published his monographs with these data, and made no other contribution, he would still have been regarded as an outstanding field ornithologist.

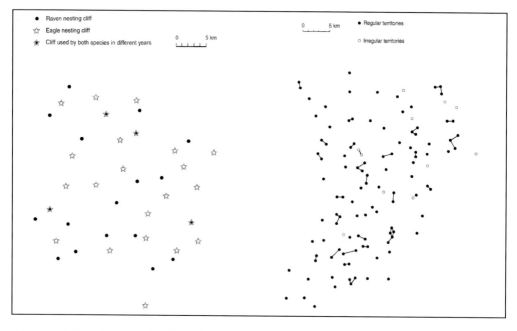

Figure 11.15. Examples of breeding dispersion of the Raven (*Corvus corax*) and Golden Eagle (*Aquila chrysaetos*). The left panel shows the breeding dispersion of Ravens and Golden Eagles in part of Wester Ross, and the right panel shows the same for Ravens in the Lake District. (From [23])

What governs numbers?

In each of his books on birds, and virtually all of his papers on raptors, Derek agonised over what governed numbers and their spatial and temporal variability. His remark at the end of the section on 'Mechanism of territorial spacing' in *The Raven* (Fig. 11.16)[23] is telling: "Until there is more definitive evidence on this topic, it is best to say nothing further. This is another field in which circular thinking develops." This came after a *cri de coeur* on the preceding page: "Food supply in a bird such as this is extremely difficult to measure accurately and this leads to some fairly large assumptions based on rather superficial evidence." Understanding patterns in numbers was at the root of his research on birds of prey, for his international reputation was first forged through his revelations about why birds were inexplicably absent from some areas, and faring poorly over many.

In *The Peregrine Falcon* (Fig. 14.6)[24,44] and *The Raven* (Fig. 11.16)[23] we are given rich insights to these matters, which form the heart of

The Raven

DEREK RATCLIFFE

Figure 11.16. Derek Ratcliffe's (1997) monograph *The Raven*[23]. This was Derek's favourite bird that he studied for over 50 years in many parts of Britain.

208

his narrative. The Raven (Fig. 13.4) gave him particular fulfilment for he was so respectful of the intelligence of the birds (ending his monograph with a chapter on the topic). I do not think Derek ever conducted an ecological experiment, so it is interesting that he closed his book with: "Many of the time-honoured tales of Ravens are the purest whimsy that say far more about their human inventors than about the bird. Only further careful experimentation of a rigorous, scientific kind is likely to throw more light on the subject of Raven intelligence."

In his work on the Golden Plover[36] you sense Derek had his greatest intellectual and fieldwork challenges, for this was the bird that so embodies the wild uplands and gives up its secrets so reluctantly (Fig. 11.10). The Peregrine (Fig. 14.5) excited him and brought him to national and international prominence as a scientist[5] first, and later as a conservationist. But the Raven (Figs. 11.17 & 13.4) was his favourite: "Perhaps in our modern times, we should see the Raven as a creature of different and good omen, which – by its survival or disappearance – signals equally the fate of the wilder places of our islands and the richness of their fauna and flora."[23].

Figure 11.17. Raven (*Corvus corax*) eggs in a nest in the Moffat area of southern Scotland, 1961. This nesting site was one of Derek's favourite Raven sites that he regularly visited and monitored over 50 years. Photo: Derek Ratcliffe.

Birds of the far north – northern Fennoscandia

"I have thus attempted to fill what appears to be a gap in information about this region of northern Europe, but trust that my attempt to write about a land to which I am but an outside visitor will not appear preposterous… However, it is still a tonic to those from battered Britain to wander far and wide amidst scenes where the effects of human hand are so little evident. We are grateful to have seen Lapland whilst it is still largely unspoiled wilderness, a magic region which has repeatedly drawn us back." From *Lapland. A Natural History* by Derek Ratcliffe[59] (Fig. 11.18).

It was Derek's dream to take off in the spring to be in the untouched wilds of northern Scandinavia[2], and in 1991 he realised it, making trips each year except one until 2004. In *Bird Life of Mountain and Upland*[1] there are many references to the overriding influences of land use on the habitats and birds. Indeed, that book was organised around these, describing in turn the ecology and behaviour of the birds of 'The sheep-walks', 'The grouse moors', and 'The deer forests', before moving onto 'The flows', 'The maritime hills' and 'The high tops'. So imagine Derek's unbridled joy at being able to spend weeks in the untamed far northern landscapes indulging in the pursuit of nesting birds, supported by Jeannette (Fig. 17.2), his wife and acknowledged expert nest finder, who could work out where waders' nests and chicks were by carefully watching the adults' eyes as they alarmed.

Ingvar Byrkjedal[3] describes Derek's original contributions to Scandinavian ornithology, to which I add three wider ones. First, *Lapland*[59] provides us with an important photographic inventory of habitats used by birds[60], with descriptions to match enlivened by an eye familiar with some of the more modified variants in Britain, and therefore perceptively appreciative of the floral richness in Scandinavia. Second, the

**LAPLAND
A Natural History**

DEREK RATCLIFFE

Figure 11.18. Derek Ratcliffe's (2005) masterly book *Lapland: A Natural History* based on 14 expeditions with Jeannette Ratcliffe from 1990 to 2004 (missing only 2000). The book documents and illustrates[see 60] the wide range of habitats in Lapland and the ecology and biogeography of its birds and plants, and discusses wildlife conservation. The book was published soon after Derek's death in May 2005.

historical accounts of the naturalists working there provide a valuable chronology of botanical and zoological endeavours. In each of his books Derek paid tribute to earlier workers, and here the narrative is all the more valuable for many of us unfamiliar with some of the more obscure studies. Third, the comprehensive inventories on bird (and other animal) species and details of their conservation status, phenology, and breeding habits form an important scientific record, and one which has already been mined[30].

Tucked away at the back of the book, in the tightly typed Appendix 2, is an important essay on 'Wader Breeding Systems'. Derek found these beguiling, with variants in tendencies to be monogamous, polyandrous, or polygamous, and reversed roles in mating displays, incubation, and care of chicks. It is an interesting account of 26 species, with the conspicuousness of some species contrasting with the cryptic appearance and habits of others being put forward to explain some differences. We long-debated the issues covered. In the end Derek, like so many other researchers trying to explain the diversity of habits, commented[59]: "Here, again, it appears that much of the divergence in behaviour is almost random, around a core pattern, and that there is no consistent correlation between flushing distance and either cryptic appearance or nest concealment."

Derek would have been delighted that the report *Conservation Status of Birds of Prey and Owls in Norway* by Oddvar Heggøy and Ingar Jostein Øien[61] paid homage to his work, for this is one of the first such national overviews of raptors published in Europe.

Bird conservation

Derek was one of the principal architects of modern-day bird conservation in Britain, but came to it late in his ornithological career. His early studies barely mention conservation, and it was only in the aftermath of his early discoveries about pesticide impacts[47-51,62,63, and see 5] that we get wider mention of conservation concerns. As he was working as the Scientific Assessor leading the compilation of sites under *A Nature Conservation Review*[64,65] (Fig. 19.4), which began in 1966, he came to see and understand population declines attributable to key habitat losses, changes, and fragmentation, food shortages, persecution, and pesticides and other pollutants[e.g. 66].

A Nature Conservation Review (NCR)

Working closely with John Parslow, Tony Prater, and George Atkinson-Willes, Derek had to find the best means of conserving birds through site safeguard. It was challenging work not least because expectations were high, and scrutiny was intense, with birds belonging to the only faunal group comprehensively covered by protective legislation[64]. Nestling in the NCR[67] between sections on 'Mammals' (compiled largely by Derek, with a specialist contribution from Bob Stebbings on bats) and 'Reptiles and Fish' (written by Ian Prestt (Fig. 20.1), far better known for his work on birds, and from 1975 Director of the Royal Society for the Protection of Birds (RSPB)) we find 16 pages setting out the rationale for a network of protected areas for breeding birds first, and then passage migrants, and autumn and winter populations.

Breeding populations of bird species were ranked according to abundance (date stamped at 1973), starting with those with populations smaller than nine pairs (Honey Buzzard (*Pernis apivorus*), Marsh Harrier (*Circus aeruginosus*), Montagu's Harrier (*Circus pygargus*), Osprey (*Pandion haliaetus*), Goshawk (*Accipter gentilis*)), and ending with the commonest (Chaffinch (*Fringila coelebs*), Yellowhammer (*Emberzia citrinella*), House Sparrow (*Passer domesticus*)). For each species the NCR sought a representative sample of protected sites for their populations, with a desire to have a greater proportion of rarer birds' populations within grade 1 and 2 NCR sites. Of the 15 species with breeding populations of less than 100 pairs, six had at least 50% of their populations in these sites. Intriguingly, if we look at these named raptors today, with the exception of Montagu's Harrier, their national populations are massively greater: 46, 320-380, 12-16, 168-224, and 280-430 pairs, respectively, in the 2006-10 period[57]. Of the commoner birds (with breeding populations of more than 10,000 pairs), some of the seabirds had at least 50% of their populations in NCR sites (Gannet (*Morus bassanus*), Storm Petrel (*Hydrobates pelagicus*), Manx Shearwater (*Puffinus puffinus*), Fulmar (*Fulmarus glacialis*), Kittiwake (*Rissa tridactyla*), Razorbill (*Alca torda*), Guillemot (*Uria aalge*), Puffin (*Fratercula arctica*)). Only one other species in this class of abundance had so much of its habitat contained within NCR sites—the Ptarmigan—on account of so much of its montane habitat being included in the NCR sites for botanical reasons.

For some species, such as the then rare Red Kite (*Milvus milvus*) (fewer than 99 pairs in 1973; during 2010-12 at least 1,258 breeding pairs recorded[57]), composite sites were identified to embrace nesting and feeding habitats. For the wintering, passage, and migratory birds, mainly waders and wildfowl, sites were ranked according to peak counts, with the section concluding[64] that: "If the key sites listed in the *Review* are adequately safeguarded, this will go a long way towards meeting the needs of a national policy for wildfowl conservation; additional arrangements may still be needed, however, to provide some measure of protection in other areas." This holds firm today, and interestingly Derek told me that the clause beginning with "additional arrangements" caused a lot of consternation in Government circles for it suggested further action was needed beyond having a representative suite of protected areas, which of course was, and still is, the case.

Derek visited most of the sites (volume 2 of the NCR (Fig. 19.4) listed a total of 735 grade 1 and 2 sites for all habitat, floristic, and faunal features, each regarded as of national importance), and corresponded directly with specialists who had worked them. Several names frequent the correspondence: Bill Bourne, Stanley Cramp, Desmond Nethersole-Thompson, and David Saunders, as well as scores of Nature Conservancy colleagues. Each would receive letters or memos with questions on the veracity of data or alternative information sources, and Derek was assiduous in replying to every comment or remark. Whilst the NCR primarily sought to represent the best habitat formations in Britain[see 67], it set an international standard for statutory sites for birds. As Derek wrote towards the end of the NCR Volume 1[64], its production "is a means to the end and not an end in itself. Its declared objective is only a proximate goal and the final purpose will be fulfilled only if and when adequate safeguards have been achieved for as many as possible of the nationally important sites."

In the concluding section on breeding-bird conservation, Derek commented[64] "The future of bird populations in Britain is closely bound up with trends in land-use. Increasing simplification is now apparent within the agriculture ecosystem complex, through the steady elimination of all competitors for living space, to give maximum production by the crop species; this may be expected to continue in the lowlands, at least… It is nevertheless clear that adverse pressures on bird life can only increase." This has proved correct[68], and it is striking to note how references in the NCR birds section to wetland drainage, spread of intensive sheep grazing, the 'improvement' of marginal hill ground, and prevalence of toxic chemicals still have resonance, though the last of these is not now cited as a concern, and climate change—not mentioned in the NCR—is now a dominating worry.

The NCR is a masterpiece of conservation philosophy[67]. No wonder both Councils of the Natural Environment Research Council and Nature Conservancy Council paid special tribute to Derek in the NCR's Preface "for the talent and dedication shown in carrying out his duties as Scientific Assessor for the review." In time, this paved the way for a major programme of Sites of Special Scientific Interest notification[69] (Fig. 20.3) and the classification of Special Protection Areas under the European Commission (EC) Birds Directive, as well as the establishment of some new National Nature Reserves.

Raptor re-introductions, forestry, and persecution

Beyond his leadership of the NCR, as the NCC's Chief Scientist, Derek led some ambitious bird conservation programmes, working especially closely with the RSPB[9,69]. I highlight three contributions here. First, his leadership, with colleagues, of the reintroduction programmes of White-tailed Eagles (or Sea Eagles: *Haliaeetus albicilla*) (Fig. 11.19), with a large-scale release programme begun on Rum in 1975[e.g. 70,71] , and Red Kites, with two release programmes in the Chiltern Hills, Oxfordshire, and the Black Isle, N. Scotland, both begun in 1989[e.g. 72]. Several NCC colleagues worked closely with Derek on these, and J Morton Boyd, John Love, Derek Langslow, Mike Pienkowski, and Colin Galbraith deserve special mention.

Figure 11.19. White-tailed Eagle (Sea Eagle: *Haliaeetus albicilla*) off Askøy, near Bergen, 2013. Photo: Arild Breistøl

Recently, Ian Newton reminded me of the origins of both programmes. The idea for another Sea Eagle attempt, following the early Fair Isle attempt by George Waterston with just four birds[71], came on a car journey with Derek from Edinburgh to Moffat to look at Sparrowhawks and Peregrines. Ian suggested another reintroduction attempt, and Derek encouraged him to produce a proposal which could go to the

Scottish Committee on Birds, which met periodically in St. Andrews House, Edinburgh. The Committee was set up to allow key bird issues in Scotland to be discussed among stakeholders, including Government Departments, agencies, and NGOs, notably RSPB, and was chaired by Vero Wynne-Edwards. The proposal was approved, and Derek and Morton Boyd were determined that the birds should be released on Rum, a National Nature Reserve, in order to reduce any criticism from crofting or agricultural interests, with RSPB supporting the programme later. The Red Kite programme proposal came from Mike Pienkowski (NCC Senior Ornithologist) and Ian Newton, following a visit to Wales to meet with Peter Davis and Peter Davies, experts on the Welsh kite population, which had increased slowly to around 50 pairs but was not faring well. The possibility of using continental birds for release was then discussed, and the programme went ahead as a joint NCC-RSPB venture in 1989 with the release of 10 birds from Sweden and one reared from a rescued egg in Wales (in the pilot year, two of the birds were killed by illegal poisoning).

The second area of note here is that Derek's determinedly strategic direction of the NCC in combating afforestation of the uplands and peatlands of Britain[73] was exceptionally brave[9,34,35,69,74]. Derek wrote much of *Nature Conservation and Afforestation in Britain*[73] (Fig. 20.4) with the cover bearing his evocative photo of 'the advancing tide of new forest'[25] engulfing the uplands of Kirkcudbrightshire (Fig. 22.1). Some of his later writings increasingly raged against the desecration of wild land by forestry incursions[1,10,23,25,33,44,53,58,75,76]. His conviction to tackle this head on was borne directly from first-hand contact with losses of spacious landscapes he had grown up with[10,25,53]; his last book, published posthumously, devoted a whole chapter to afforestation[25].

Finally, having documented so incisively the impacts of pesticides on Peregrines, Derek increasingly commented on the impacts of persecution on raptors[1,23,25,52-54,58,76]. With time, his longer-term perspectives on changes are becoming more valuable for studies of raptor–grouse–habitat associations [e.g. 77] and considerations of prospects for Golden Eagle conservation in South Scotland[78].

Derek ended his last book[25] with a polemic on 'game preservation' – he had had enough, buoyed by his experiences decades earlier with Norman Moore (Figs. 19.3 & 19.7) and contemporaries battling the pesticides' vested interests. He foresaw hallmarks of a further struggle. He increasingly spoke of the RSPB[69] being the only organisation in Britain which could engineer real changes, and would have relished reading Mark Avery's *Fighting for Birds*[79]. Derek may have been right, and we shall see what the future holds. But I know many of my colleagues hold dear to his closing line in *Galloway and the Borders*[25]: "If they wish to avoid a land ruined for wildlife, as well as much larger social and economic problems, it is up to concerned people to raise their voices and put pressure on the politicians to take more realistic action."

All told, Derek's contributions to field ornithology and bird conservation are exceptional, and whilst honours and formal recognition were sparse, the respect of his peers was immense and enduring[5,7,8]. Rather than closing here, I want to give a sense of what it was like being in the field with Derek as a youngster. It is our children and students who will take up the torch for conservation, and I hope the following essay gives a flavour of Derek's influence on a very young ornithologist.

Early sightings

Eleven years old in 1969, I am looking for Derek in the North-West Highlands. In the depths of Strath Dionard, flanked by the hulking Cranstackie ridge and Cnoc a'Mhadaidh ramparts, I am alone. A slew of rocky outcrops, boulders, peaty knolls, and pools support the sparsest of life. It is a desolate place, with variously exposed ancient pine stumps betraying a formerly more vibrant land (e.g. Fig. 4.31). Millennia ago, before the fleeting incursion of trees, the ice relentlessly ground down the rock, chiselling and grinding away at the ancient Lewisian gneiss base gradually exhumed over time. House-sized rocks, now strewn in chaos, were dumped by the ice. It is piercingly cold and wet, and I am shivering. It seems an awful place, intimidatingly bereft of life, rarely warmed by the sun, and limited in colour to hues of brown and grey. There are just occasional bird calls, snatched by the gusting wind, but the deep impression is one of emptiness – nothing really other than a wildly hostile, unyielding, and hungry landscape. I look towards Farrmheall, a whaleback of a hill, and see the tiny road etched across its face – four miles (6.5 km) away I can see the faintest of movements. How strange – the only signs of life seem to be tiny metallic specs traversing the hill, and from where I am watching they seem set to collide. Peering, I see they differ in size, some moving fast, others really slow, and many stuttering – but they do not crash into one another but instead pass by, with the same numbers from left and right. In this place of raw antiquity it is the road that I watch. Along it the drivers and their kin will have given scant thought to what is below them in the glen, instead they are scurrying to Durness or Rhiconich.

And what of Derek? Where is he? Weeks before he had written to my parents to say he would come, and today is when he is due. I am told he is never late[e.g.80], and have been sent to meet him. The eldest of six children, I am tasked with bringing Derek to the family hut (Fig. 11.20). Perched by the river, with just a small window facing into

Figure 11.20. The Nethersole-Thompson family (25 May 1969) outside the hut they subsisted in for six weeks each spring between 1964 and 1982. From left to right the children are Patrick, Richard†, Eamonn, Maimie, Katharine, and Bruin (Des). Maimie and Desmond Nethersole-Thompson are behind the children. Photo: Derek Ratcliffe

215

a dark peat bank, it has a rickety door opening unto the north. Inside there is a small cupboard, bench, square table and chair, single canvas-clad bed, and a two-ring gas stove and cylinder. Measuring no more than ten feet wide and twelve feet deep (~3 m x 3.6 m), it is our home for six weeks each year. Eight of us subsist in it, often spending three or four days at a time cooped together – talking, crying, laughing, shouting, but often silent. The river is our constant companion, and the creaking woodwork shielding us is our friend. We know every nail, knot, and warp in the planks. We have become acutely sensitive to the elements around us and the countenance of rock is bewilderingly diverse. We see all manner of imagery in the grey crags, and talk about it.

No wonder I am scanning for Derek, for I am promised a trip with him. I am afraid he will not appear. For more than an hour I have been looking far out towards Carn Leacach, hoping to see some movement. And then I spy him, much closer than anticipated, bounding towards me. I get a wave and am struck by his direct, straight line of walking towards me. He wears a green beret, green cotton jacket, v-necked sweater, grey-white trousers tucked neatly into rather petite mountain boots, and has a slate-grey canvas rucksack with a protruding tripod. And as he comes to me he grabs my hand in a firm handshake, never a hug, and delightedly tells me he has found a Golden Plover's nest. Then he asks me how I am, how things are at school, and how we are faring with the Greenshanks, to which I reply "alright", "bad", and "quite well". Here is how Derek described that part of his day in his notebook[31]:

> "25 May 1969. As I crossed the rugged gneiss country between Gualin and the Strath Dionard fishing hut, a Golden Plover flew away from about 60 yards ahead. After a long search I found the nest with 4 eggs on a small peat ridge between a bare gneiss slab and a depression with *Campylopus atrovirens* and *Sphagnum compactum*."

Greenshanking

I take Derek to the hut (Fig. 11.20) where there is great excitement at his arrival. Sometimes for weeks on end we see no strangers. We mostly want news of football, and shortly after we got to the hut that year we heard that Celtic had beaten Rangers 4-0 in the Scottish Cup final in front of 132,000 dervishes. But it was the home internationals we wanted to know about, for Scotland played England at Wembley on 10 May, and then Cyprus in a 'friendly' on the 17th, and we needed the scores. Derek had no idea, having no interest in football or sport (we heard a week later that we lost the former 1-4, which was pretty crushing, and won the friendly 8-0). Even my father listened intently for news of the football, or the 'fitba' as Derek teased much later. But with the most important question unanswered most of the tribe scampered.

Interactions between Derek and my father spanned the gamut of emotions, and there was always an excited edge to a meeting after a while apart. I cannot recall how the initial conversation went, but within a minute or so of arriving at the hut Derek was explaining how he found the Golden Plover's nest by searching. Not taken in by this, my father muttered "It's no dammed use searching, you have to sit and watch." Derek softly and carefully explained that he had seen the incubating bird flit at some distance, but his host was having none of it, insisting that you simply had to have patience and to sit and watch the bird back to be sure of where it had its nest. "But I found the darned nest", was Derek's retort, at which point my mother moved the conversation on amiably, as she so often did.

Frankly, their exchanges could be combustible. Derek was loved by my family, and my parents held him in deep regard and affection. After what seemed like an eternally long catch-up my father was by now bubbling with excitement at the day ahead. Three days earlier at 22:45, with my youngest brother Eamonn aged just six and a half, he had found a Greenshank's nest (e.g. Fig. 17.7) a mile and a half (2 km) from the hut. Most nests were found in the evening, sometimes as late as midnight, following a nest exchange between the pair (the other occurring early in the morning). This had been a tough nest to find; my parents wrote later in Greenshanks[19]: "Maimie met us on our way back and could hear Eamonn chattering from a long way off. Although delighted with his success, it was two years before he went greenshanking again!" This was my father's 28th Greenshank nest found in Sutherland, but much more significantly was his 199th since he started studying them in the 1920s. The 200th nest beckoned, and Derek was on hand to help.

In the late afternoon we headed in to the head of the glen. As recalled in Greenshanks (Fig. 11.21) by my father[19], "On 10 May, eight-year-old Richard and I located a pair three miles from the hut; on the 13th Patrick and I heard one of them calling beside the river. Derek Ratcliffe had joined us in camp, and on the 25th he, Bruin, and Patrick went with me to search for this 200th nest." It was a striking sight – my large-framed father, aged 61, shambling in his tawny duffel coat and festooned with two pairs of binoculars and a shoulder piece-bag, with the nimble 39-year-old Derek immediately in tow on a tight footpath. For half a mile this path bore our party, a skilfully constructed footpath which for decades had withstood fishermen and stalkers' garron ponies. But beyond the burn flowing out from Coire Duail there was a near-impenetrable quagmire which extended two miles (3 km) to Loch Dionard. Crossing the rickety bridge high over the burn, Derek and I were off, squelching as fast as we could to the aptly named Eamonn's Greenshank nest.

My father had provided such a good description of where the nest had been found that by the time he caught up with us, Derek had his tripod and camera set up. When found, the nest had been shrouded in darkness, but now we had the first chance to see the bird in

Greenshanks

Desmond and Maimie
NETHERSOLE-THOMPSON

Figure 11.21. Desmond and Maimie Nethersole-Thompson's monograph on Greenshanks[19] based on over 60 years of observations including 15 years in their study area (Fig. 11.20). The book is dedicated to four people including Derek Ratcliffe "who first told us about our greenshanks" in north-west Sutherland in 1957, and includes a chapter by Derek on the breeding habitat of the Greenshank in Scotland[29].

its glory sitting tightly on four eggs. But no, just as the duffel-coated maestro (as Derek later delighted in calling my father) appeared Derek moved in too fast, and the bird jumped before a picture could be taken. Worse still, my father had not seen it, but by God he heard it scream on taking off. Words were exchanged, with Derek feebly complaining that he had not got close enough to get a picture. I honestly cannot recall the maestro's response, but words were uttered which resembled those I had heard when my father raged at speeches over the wireless made by the then leader of the Conservative party, Edward Heath. Volleys of furious utterings followed Derek and I as we headed deeper into the glen.

By around 17:00 we reached the site of the elusive 200[th.] In *Greenshanks*[(19)] the scene is set: "Bruin and Derek sat close to the river; Patrick and I went uphill to cover a complex of quartzite screes. For over three hours we had no joy but, in the evening, Patrick saw an eagle circling the corrie and disappearing into a cloud. Shortly after 20:00 we saw Derek and Bruin searching for a golden plover's nest on the river flats. At 20:25 a greenshank arrived and began violent *chipping*, apparently from the far side of the ridge above. We allowed it plenty of time and then started to search. Soon a greenshank was screaming overhead. Derek found a couple of unlined scrapes close to where we had heard the *chipping*."

What is not detailed is an almighty set-to between the duo. Derek had grown bored with sitting by the river – he hated being still for more than an hour, and had his sights on checking a Golden Eagle's nest. Excitedly, I encouraged him, and we waded the river and headed for an abandoned ruin. Looking directly south-west into towering cliffs, we watched in awe as a tiny eaglet was fed by its parent, which had just landed heavily onto the nest with what looked like a Mountain Hare (*Lepus timidus*). In the pre-gloaming silence we took Derek's telescope in turns to spy the mighty eagle and its chick. The eyrie was massive, and teetered on a thin ledge three hundred feet (90 m) above the loch. We were jubilant, and on returning to our original Greenshank sentry we sat barely five minutes before hearing a Golden Plover calling. Derek was sure it was close to a nest, so we went in to search (as my father and Patrick watched us from afar), but had no success.

At around 21:30 we met up with our compatriots, by this time searching amongst the boot-ripping screes for the 200th nest. A simple question from the maestro was our undoing – had we seen where the bird had flown in two hours ago, and again at half past eight? "No", replied Derek, "nothing was happening so we went off to check the eagle." It transpired we would have had the most perfect view of the homing bird, which had flown in but desisted from exchanging several times. My father was incandescent, and soon bellowing. On reflection it seems strange that in one of the most remote and wild mountainscapes in Britain, late into the evening and well beyond a tranquil sunset, we bore witness to a powder keg of emotions. In the midst of shudderingly spluttered expletives spewing forth Derek caught one phrase which he often repeated much later, when we failed to find a nest through collective failure, "You should be court-martialled for abandoning your posts!"

We were truly chastened, and away from the angry duffel coat, Derek mused heavily before sighing to me, "Your Pa seems a bit cross". I have no idea what I said then, but had it been now I might have retorted, "Well quite old son, we've only just messed things up for the old boy, and now we're for it!" Frankly, it was a pretty hellish trudge back through the bog to the hut, which we reached just after midnight.

With understated succinctness, Derek concluded his diary entry for 25 May[31] with:

> "We tried to watch the change over of the next pair of Greenshank, just below Loch Dionard, but the non-sitter flew into dead ground, and we missed the exact place, though there was a scrape at about the approximate place… Nearby, we found the pluckings of a recently killed Greenshank. The probable killer was revealed when a female Sparrowhawk cruised along the glen, evidently on the hunt again (which probably originated from Strathbeg, 1.5 miles away). The pair we had been watching had re-mated. We went on to scan a golden eagle feeding its chick."

Strangely, I have no memory at all of finding the remains of the Greenshank or of the Sparrowhawk, which would have been my first sighting in the Strath. Instead, my vivid recollection is of a heavily built sergeant major (he had been a Captain in the War) roaring in disdain. Three days later, the 200th nest was found, with *Greenshanks*[19] describing the nest "with four small roundish eggs, heavily blotched with red at their blunter ends." And yet, I wonder what the tightly crouching greenshank on its nest must have made of the cacophony of the raging duffel coat flaying and gesticulating at Derek and me – for we were unknowingly just 20 yards (18 m) from the bird on its clutch. Nine years later, on 4 June 1978, my sister Maimie and late brother Richard found the 300th nest, just yards from the site of the 200th nest.

Figure 11.22. Desmond Nethersole-Thompson with sons Patrick and Bruin inspecting a Greenshank's nest in north-west Sutherland, 29 May 1969. Photo: Derek Ratcliffe

Three days later we found a Greenshank's nest in what is now called the 'Derek-Bruin' territory, still occupied most years. It was Derek's first find of a nest following an evening watch for the exchange, and we were thrilled to flush the bird off its nest. The following day my father had to see it, and buoyed by Derek's great find, the pair of them forded the river and trudged through saturated heath and bog to reach the nest an hour and a half later. This time the bird sat sufficiently tightly for Derek to take some pictures, before it jumped, and after we weighed the eggs, he took a picture of the three of us by the nest (Fig. 11.22).

Restless again, by the late evening we were on the boulder-dominated Cranstackie summit searching for Dotterel (Fig. 11.3) and Golden Plover (Fig. 11.10) on its long southward ridge dropping gradually to Conamheall, where we cut down from the now mist-drenched tops into the glen and back to the family hut. We saw nothing of note, and with a handshake Derek was off. For a schoolboy thirsty for wild encounters with nature these were the best of times, and I longed for many more adventures together.

Looking for Wood Sandpipers

On 27th May, we had travelled to a special loch near Tongue, to look for nesting Wood Sandpiper (*Tringa glareola*) (Fig. 17.9), then one of our rarest birds with possibly only three pairs breeding in Britain. Derek recorded in his notes[31] that he found the area "to have considerable bird interest otherwise – 200-300 black-headed gulls [*Chroicocephalus ridibundus*], greenshank, redshank [*Tringa totanus*], snipe [*Gallinago gallinago*], dunlin [*Calidris alpina*], golden plover, curlew, lapwing, wigeon [*Anas penelope*], black throated diver [*Gavia arctica*]." He was so impressed that seven years later it became a grade 1 Nature Conservation Review (NCR) site[65], and it still has Wood Sandpipers.

On that day late in May we searched for the elusive wader but had no success. Within a month I was back with my father, enduring two wretched midge-infested evenings looking for the nest. And we found it, and later my father closed *Highland Birds*[21] with an acclimation of our success: "With thumping heart and shaking knees I had to walk away. The Great Bog of Sutherland had been so kind to me!" Derek was thrilled when he heard the news. We had been searching in the wrong terrain, and for years afterwards Derek would ask me to describe precisely how we had tracked down the nest with three eggs. My father was more to the point than I on one occasion: "It was quite simple really. We sat down, had a cigar to get rid of the damned midges, waited for the exchange, and then watched where the returning bird landed. You see an awful lot more when you sit and watch!" Cigars, incidentally, were regular issue for us to suppress midges in June evenings; Derek never smoked.

The Clo Mor - reaching out for eggs

Some four miles east of Cape Wrath are some of the tallest sea cliffs on mainland Britain, the Clo Mor (Fig. 14.1), reaching up over 210 m above the sea. On 28 May Derek and I reached the cliffs, having taken the ferry and lighthouse-bound minibus, and then walked northwards from Inshore over the bare Sgribhis Bheinn (371 m) plateau. I had been there the previous year with Derek and my father, when Derek recorded[31]:

"June 8, 1968, with DNT [Desmond Nethersole-Thompson] and Bruin on Sgribhis Bheinn where a dotterel was found nesting in 1967. A quick look at Clo Mor showed that there had been no decrease in Fulmars, Kittiwakes and Guillemots since 1957, but I was not near the best Puffin slopes and could not judge their success. Bruin picked up a rather weathered Golden Eagle feather on the top of Sgribhis Bheinn."

It was (and still is!) a terrifying place for everywhere there were spent and a few unspent shells, for the area was used for gunnery practice by naval and air forces, with aircraft regularly dropping massive thousand-pound bombs. A few years previously one woman had part of her hip blown away when she stooped to pick up an unexploded shell. Craters, pits, and all manner of pock marks littered the land as we picked our way to the cliff edge. What a place, dominated by the massive Torridonian Sandstone precipice of the Clo Mor. Sheer cliffs and steep, lushly vegetated slopes marked out the land, and the stench of seabird guano was gut wrenching. Some years later Derek wrote in the NCR[65]:

"There is here an immense seabird breeding station. The colony of puffins may perhaps have once approached that of St Kilda in size, but it appears to have recently been greatly reduced and now numbers only a few tens of thousands of pairs. The populations of Guillemots, Razorbills, Fulmars and Kittiwakes are among the biggest of these species in Britain, though the difficulties of counting are such that reliable figures are not available. Until recently Golden Eagles had here a coastal mainland nesting place and there were two pairs of Peregrines. Great Skuas are colonising the moorland."

The Golden Eagle pair abandoned the site around 1969, possibly because of the bombardments, but Great Skuas (*Stercorarius skua*) have since increased in number and range.

Derek describes our mission as follows in his notebook[31]:

"Bruin and I descended the geo at 300733 to reach the seabirds at the bottom and collect some eggs for chemical analysis… in a litter of blocks filling the bed of the chasm, we found the heaped bodies of Puffins, numbering about two dozen, and very evidently killed by a Fox."

Unroped, we slithered down the ravine into the tumult of the seabird city. Derek just below me, periodically reached out to stop me tumbling, occasionally offering a "be careful" and "watch, that rock's unstable". It was terrifying, but towards the bottom, among the Kittiwakes, the main ordeal began, for we had to collect eggs. Inch by inch I crept along slimy ledges to reach out for them. Perched in clusters, the deeply clad nests mostly had clutches of two, beautifully speckled and variably creamy coloured. Roughly the size of small golf balls, the eggs were stuffed into my cotton windcheater pockets now smeared in mess. Some cracked as I worked my way back to Derek's outstretched hand, before I would go out again to reach out for yet more, all the time palming the rock with my back to the heavy sea-swell below. Bending was hardest, delicately dipping sideways to grab an egg, and then ever so slowly rising to place my cargo in a pocket.

We must have collected twenty or so eggs, and as Derek packed them into square cardboard eggboxes, perched on a large scree boulder, my legs turned to jelly. I shook uncontrollably, and Derek realised we had taken a risk too far. But youngsters are resilient, and soon I was emboldened to go out for more, but Derek was having none of it. We had got what we needed and began our ascent, me above just in case I fell, picking our way for hand and foot holds, aching as we reached the top and increasingly spat at by Fulmars. Of course the mission was vital to Derek's central ground-breaking research on egg breakage in raptors and other birds, and his paper published in the *Journal of Applied Ecology* the following year[63] was cited in 2013 as one of the 100 most influential papers published in 100 years of British Ecological Society journals[6,81]. Kittiwakes, incidentally, showed no significant changes in eggshell thickness since 1950, though recent research has shown increases in levels of various chemical contaminants in their eggs[e.g. 82].

On your way

It was Derek who discovered the glen so good for Greenshanks that my father began his study there on 7 May 1964. Derek first made a visit on 15 May 1957, when it got just four lines in his notebook[31], including: "Golden Plover were sparsely distributed on Farmheall and the surrounding moors; the summit of this hill is possible dotterel ground." Three days later he had much more joy in the glen. "Greenshanks were scattered over the area, feeding singly at the lochs, and I had the good luck to flush a bird from its nest at a few yards range…" On 21 May he "cycled along the fishing track up Strath Dionard to reach Foinaven and disturbed probably at least three Greenshanks along the course of the river… I looked at the high corries on the northeast side of Foinaven, which appeared to be perfect Snow Bunting habitat, but saw nothing of the bird". That was good enough for my father, who uprooted us all each spring to spend marvellously unique times in pursuit of these birds (Fig. 11.20). In time these special days gave rise to *Greenshanks* (Fig. 11.21)[19] and *Waders: their breeding, haunts and watchers*[83].

In Search of Nature[10] describes Derek's first meeting with my father, in winter 1960, in which he remarks: "Desmond and I hit it off right away, although I knew he was out of favour with the Scottish Establishment." On several occasions Derek, and later the renowned ecologists Adam Watson and J. Morton Boyd, were told it would not help their careers to be associated with my father. He was a former egg collector, with left-leaning political tendencies, and was loathed by some prominent and influential Highland landowners. Derek and my father delighted in telling me how they would arrange to meet at the Nature Conservancy (NC) offices without senior officers finding out. As all incoming mail was opened, 'date stamped', and placed in pigeon holes which others could see, they had to make covert plans. My father came up with the ruse of writing Derek under the *nom de plume* of 'The Reverend John Smith', signing off 'Yours reverently'. In different NC offices throughout Scotland Derek would arrive to letters from his minister, 'looking forward to holding communion with you' (Fig. 11.23). It worked!

When I got news I was to join the Nature Conservancy Council in 1985 I received a letter from Derek (Fig. 11.24) which gave a sense of what lay in store: "It is in many ways a frustrating and infuriating organisation, but it is the only one with the power to do anything comprehensive for wildlife in Britain, and it will be what you and your

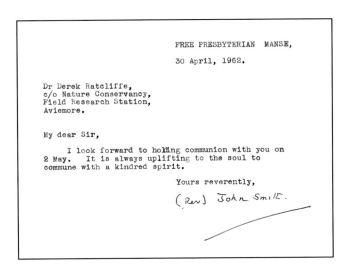

FREE PRESBYTERIAN MANSE,

30 April, 1962.

Dr Derek Ratcliffe,
c/o Nature Conservancy,
Field Research Station,
Aviemore.

My dear Sir,

I look forward to holding communion with you on
2 May. It is always uplifting to the soul to
commune with a kindred spirit.

Yours reverently,

(Rev) John Smith.

Figure 11.23. Copy of a letter sent by the 'Reverend John Smith' to Derek Ratcliffe, 30 April 1962.

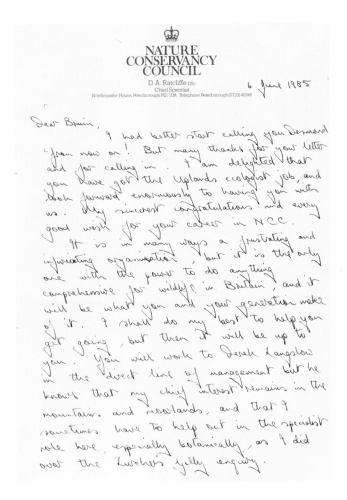

Figure 11.24. Copy of a letter from Derek Ratcliffe to Des (Bruin) Thompson, 6 June 1985.

generation make of it." The NCC lasted only another six years, with its unpopularity in Scotland, and in particular its opposition to afforestation, a root cause of its demise[70,84]. Derek played a key role in making it so unpopular[9,35,70,84], and the irony is not lost on me that Richard Lindsay, myself, and others were advised several times to have nothing to do with Derek after he had retired. We ignored this advice, and along with many colleagues benefitted massively from Derek's sustained interest and contributions to our work[e.g. 30,38,54,57,58].

Derek and I often spoke about my father and his influence on us both. During our last conversation Derek remarked that his favourite passage was at the end of the Preface to *The Snow Bunting*[17] (Fig. 11.25), where reflecting on the birds studied he wrote: "For this is their story just as much as it is ours; and to it, long ago, I had freely given my most precious possession – my youth."

Derek too had given of his youth in search of nature[10]. Only after his death, some weeks after we spoke, did I hold his copy of *The Snow Bunting*[17] in which my father had penned an inscription in 1966. It read: "To Derek, who is making history. Lift your eyes from the ground and look up to the stars, for Brother, you are on your way." Indeed he was.

Figure 11.25. Desmond Nethersole-Thompson's classic book on *The Snow Bunting*[17] and its status, ecology, and population biology. Derek Ratcliffe contributed a detailed account[27] of its habitat in Scotland. Derek was particularly attached to Desmond's Preface "For this is their story just as much as it is ours; and to it, long ago, I had freely given my most precious possession – my youth."

Acknowledgements

I am deeply indebted to John Birks, Arild Breistøl, Terry Burke, Ingvar Byrkjedal, Alan Fielding, Paul Haworth, Richard Lindsay, Ian Newton, Jeannette Ratcliffe, Steve Redpath, Chris Rollie, David Stroud, Bill Sutherland, Dawn and Pat Thompson, Phil Whitfield, and Jeremy Wilson for providing me with comments and material for this chapter. I have drawn heavily from Derek's unpublished field notebooks and correspondence. I am very grateful to Cathy Jenks for substantial editorial help.

References

(1) Ratcliffe, D.A. (1990) *Bird Life of Mountain and Upland.* Cambridge University Press, Cambridge.

(2) Birks, H.J.B and Birks, H.H. (2015) Derek Ratcliffe – botanist and plant ecologist. In: *Nature's Conscience – The Life and Legacy of Derek Ratcliffe* (eds. D.B.A. Thompson, H.H. Birks & H.J.B. Birks). This volume, Chapter 4.

(3) Byrkjedal, I. (2015) A thousand nest record cards - from Derek Ratcliffe to the University Museum of Bergen. In: *Nature's Conscience – The Life and Legacy of Derek Ratcliffe* (eds. D.B.A. Thompson, H.H. Birks & H.J.B. Birks). This volume, Chapter 17.

(4) Greenwood, J.J.D & Crick, H.P.F. (2015) "It seemed like a dream come true": Derek Ratcliffe and the Peregrine surveys. In: *Nature's Conscience – The Life and Legacy of Derek Ratcliffe* (eds. D.B.A. Thompson, H.H. Birks & H.J.B. Birks). This volume, Chapter 14.

(5) Newton, I. (2015) Pesticides and birds of prey – the breakthrough. In: *Nature's Conscience – The Life and Legacy of Derek Ratcliffe* (eds. D.B.A. Thompson, H.H. Birks & H.J.B. Birks). This volume, Chapter 15.

(6) Rollie, C. (2015) In Galloway and the Borders – in search of an enduring youth. In: *Nature's Conscience – The Life and Legacy of Derek Ratcliffe* (eds. D.B.A. Thompson, H.H. Birks & H.J.B. Birks). This volume, Chapter 13.

(7) Anon (1993) BOU Godman-Salvin Medal Citation. Derek Ratcliffe. *Ibis*, **133**, 329-330.

(8) Newton, I. (2006) Derek Almey Ratcliffe 1929-2005. *Ibis*, **148**, 392-394.

(9) Stroud, D.A., Reed, T.M., Pienkowski, M.W. & Lindsay, R.A. (2015) The Flow Country: battles fought, war won, organisation lost. In: *Nature's Conscience – The Life and Legacy of Derek Ratcliffe* (eds. D.B.A. Thompson, H.H. Birks & H.J.B. Birks). This volume, Chapter 23.

(10) Ratcliffe, D.A. (2000) *In Search of Nature.* Peregrine Books, Leeds.

(11) Coward, T.A. (1943) *The Birds of the British Isles and their Eggs* (7th edition). Frederick Warne, London.

(12) Barkham, P. (2006). The egg snatchers. *The Guardian.* 11 December. http://www.theguardian.com/environment/2006/dec/11/g2.ruralaffairs (accessed April 2014)

(13) Braid, M. (1994). Egg society denies aiding nest thefts. An obscure group named after a Victorian clergyman is accused of acting as a front for illegal collectors who damage rare species. *The Independent.* 2 October. http://www.independent.co.uk/news/uk/home-news/egg-society-denies-aiding-nest-thefts-an-obscure-group-named-after-a-victorian-clergyman-is-accused-of-acting-as-a-front-for-illegal-collectors-who-damage-rare-species-1440402.html (accessed April 2014)
Lovegrove, R. (2007) *Silent Fields.* Oxford University Press, Oxford.

(14)   Kiff, L.F. (1989) Oology: From hobby to science. *Living Bird Quarterly*, **8**, 8-15.
       Kiff, L.F (2005) History, present status, and future prospects of avian eggshell
       collections in North America. *The Auk*, **122**, 994-999.

(15)   Winkler, K. (2005) Bird Collections: development and use of a scientific
       resource. *The Auk*, **122**, 966-971.

(16)   Hauber, M. E. (2014) *The Book of Eggs. A life-size guide to the eggs of six hundred of
       the world's bird species.* University of Chicago Press, Chicago.

(17)   Nethersole-Thompson, D. (1966) *The Snow Bunting.* Oliver & Boyd, Edinburgh.

(18)   Nethersole-Thompson, D. (1973) *The Dotterel.* Collins, London.

(19)   Nethersole-Thompson, D. & Nethersole-Thompson, M. (1979) *Greenshanks.*
       Poyser, Berkhamsted.

(20)   Cole, A.C. & Trobe, W.M. (2011) *The Egg Collectors of Great Britain and Ireland. An
       Update* (2nd edition). Peregrine Books, Leeds.

(21)   Nethersole-Thompson, D. (1974). *Highland Birds* (2nd edition). Highlands and
       Islands Development Board, Inverness.

(22)   Bukaciński, D. & Bukacińska, M. (1997) Production of erythristic eggs by the
       Black-Headed Gull in Poland. *Willson Bulletin*, **109**, 177-182.
       Hays, H. & Parkes, K.C. (1993) Erythristic eggs in the Common tern. *Journal of
       Field Ornithology*, **64**, 341-345.

(23)   Ratcliffe, D.A. (1997) *The Raven.* Poyser, London.

(24)   Ratcliffe, D.A. (1980) *The Peregrine Falcon.* Poyser, Calton.

(25)   Ratcliffe, D.A. (2007) *Galloway and the Borders.* Collins, London.

(26)   Ratcliffe, D.A. (1973) The Dotterel as a breeding bird in England. In: *The Dotterel*
       (by D. Nethersole-Thompson), pp. 190-197. Collins, London.

(27)   Ratcliffe, D.A. (1966) The habitat of the snow bunting in Scotland. In: *The Snow
       Bunting* (by D. Nethersole-Thompson), pp. 153-165. Oliver and Boyd, Edinburgh.

(28)   Ratcliffe, D.A. (1973) Breeding habitat of the Dotterel in Britain. In: *The Dotterel*
       (by D. Nethersole-Thompson), pp. 153-173. Collins, London.

(29)   Ratcliffe, D.A. (1979) The breeding habitat of the Greenshank in Scotland. In:
       Greenshanks (by D. Nethersole-Thompson & M. Nethersole-Thompson), pp. 185-
       192. Poyser, Berkhamsted.

(30)   Thompson, D.B.A., Kålås, J.A. & Byrkjedal, I. (2012) Arctic-alpine mountain
       birds in northern Europe: contrasts between specialists and generalists. In: *Birds
       and Habitat: Relationships in Changing Landscapes.* (ed. R.J. Fuller), pp. 237-252.
       Cambridge University Press, Cambridge.

(31)   Ratcliffe, D.A. (1956-2005) Unpublished Field Notes. Held by Jeannette Ratcliffe.

(32)   Mitchell, J. (2015) National Service and beyond. In: *Nature's Conscience – The Life
       and Legacy of Derek Ratcliffe* (eds. D.B.A. Thompson, H.H. Birks & H.J.B. Birks).
       This volume, Chapter 2.

(33)   Ratcliffe, D.A. & Thompson, D.B.A. (1988) The British Uplands: their ecological
       character and international significance. In: *Ecological Change in the Uplands* (eds.
       M.B. Usher & D.B.A. Thompson), pp. 9-36. Blackwell Scientific Publications,
       Oxford.

(34) Lindsay, R.A., Charman, D.J., Everingham, F., O'Reilly, R.M., Palmer, M.A., Rowell, T.A., Stroud, D.A. (eds. D.A. Ratcliffe & P.H. Oswald) (1988) *The Flow Country – The Peatlands of Caithness and Sutherland.* 174 pp. Nature Conservancy Council, Peterborough.

(35) Lindsay, R. (2015) A letter to Derek Ratcliffe. In: *Nature's Conscience – The Life and Legacy of Derek Ratcliffe* (eds. D.B.A. Thompson, H.H. Birks & H.J.B. Birks). This volume, Chapter 24.

(36) Ratcliffe, D.A. (1976) Observations on the breeding of the Golden Plover in Great Britain. *Bird Study*, **23**, 63-116.

(37) Byrkjedal, I. & Thompson, D.B.A. (1998) *Tundra Plovers.* Academic Press (Poyser), London.

(38) Ratcliffe, D.A. (1998) Foreword. In: *Tundra Plovers: the Eurasian, Pacific and American Golden Plovers and Grey Plover* (by I. Byrkjedal & D.B.A. Thompson), pp xix-xxi. Academic Press (Poyser), London.

(39) Nethersole-Thompson, C. & Nethersole-Thompson, D. (1939) Some observations on the sexual-life and breeding biology of the Southern Golden Plover (*Charadrius apricarius*) as observed in Inverness-shire. Handwritten, unpublished two-volume MS.

(40) Nethersole-Thompson, D. & Nethersole-Thompson, C. (1961) The breeding behaviour of the British Golden Plover. In: *The Birds of the British Isles, Volume 10* (by D.A. Bannerman), pp. 206-214. Oliver & Boyd, Edinburgh.

(41) Ratcliffe, D.A. (1962) Breeding density in the Peregrine *Falco peregrinus* and Raven *Corvus corax. Ibis*, **104**, 13-39.

(42) Newton, I. (1986) *The Sparrowhawk.* Poyser, Calton.

(43) Newton, I. (2013) *Bird Populations.* Collins, London.

(44) Ratcliffe, D.A. (1993) *The Peregrine Falcon* (2nd edition). Poyser, London.

(45) Ratcliffe, D.A. (1947) Personal observations on some local birds. *The Carliol*, **XXII**, 428-437. (Reprinted in this volume as Chapter 3).
Ratcliffe, D.A. (1949) Magpies nesting in rocks. *North Western Naturalist*, **3**, 129.
Birks, H.J.B. & Birks, H.H. (2015) Derek Ratcliffe – early days in pursuit of nature. In: *Nature's Conscience – The Life and Legacy of Derek Ratcliffe* (eds. D.B.A. Thompson, H.H. Birks & H.J.B. Birks). This volume, Chapter 1.

(46) Ratcliffe, D.A. (1963) The status of the Peregrine in Great Britain. *Bird Study*, **10**, 56-90.

(47) Ratcliffe, D.A. (1965) The Peregrine situation in Great Britain 1963-64. *Bird Study*, **12**, 66-82.

(48) Ratcliffe, D.A. (1966) The present status of the peregrine in Britain. *Falconer*, **46**, 249-250.

(49) Ratcliffe, D.A. (1967) The Peregrine situation in Great Britain 1965-66. *Bird Study*, **14**, 238-246.

(50) Ratcliffe, D.A. (1969) Population trends of the Peregrine Falcon in Great Britain. *Peregrine Falcon Populations: Their Biology and Decline* (ed. J.J. Hickey), pp. 239-269. University of Wisconsin Press, Madison.

(51) Ratcliffe, D.A. (1972) The Peregrine population of Great-Britain in 1971. *Bird Study*, **19**, 117-156.
Ratcliffe, D.A. (1973) Studies of the recent breeding success of the Peregrine, *Falco peregrinus. Journal of Reproductive Fertility*, **19**, 377-389.
Ratcliffe, D.A. (1984) The Peregrine breeding population of the United Kingdom in 1981. *Bird Study*, **31**, 1-18.
Ratcliffe, D.A. (1988) The Madison conference and research on peregrines. *Peregrine Falcon Populations. Their Management and Recovery* (eds. T.J. Cade, J.H. Enderson, C.G. Thelander & C.M. White), pp. 17-20. The Peregrine Fund, Boise.

(52) Ratcliffe, D.A. (1988) The Peregrine population of Great Britain and Ireland. In: *Peregrine Falcon Populations. Their Management and Recovery* (eds. T.J. Cade, J.H. Enderson, C.G. Thelander & C.M. White), pp. 147-157. The Peregrine Fund, Boise.

(53) Ratcliffe, D.A. (2002) *Lakeland.* HarperCollins, London.

(54) Ratcliffe, D.A. (2003) The peregrine saga. In: *Birds of Prey in a Changing Environment* (eds. D.B.A. Thompson, S. Redpath, A.H. Fielding, M. Marquiss & C.A. Galbraith), pp. 91-98. The Stationary Office, Edinburgh.

(55) Ratcliffe, D.A. (1958) Broken eggs in Peregrine eyries. *British Birds*, **51,** 23-26.
Ratcliffe, D.A. (1960) Broken eggs in the nests of Sparrowhawk and Golden Eagle. *British Birds*, **53**, 128-131.

(56) Ratcliffe, D.A. (1996) Ernest Blezard (1902-1970). Lakeland wildlife. *Transactions of the Carlisle Natural History Society*, **12**, 127-132.

(57) Hardey, J., Crick, H.P., Wernham, C., Riley, H.T., Etheridge, B. & Thompson, D.B.A. (2013) *Raptors: A Field Guide for Surveys and Monitoring* (3rd edition). The Stationery Office, Edinburgh.

(58) Ratcliffe, D.A. (2003) Foreword. In: *Birds of Prey in a Changing Environment* (eds. D.B.A. Thompson, S. Redpath, A.H. Fielding, M. Marquiss & C.A. Galbraith), pp. xix-xx. The Stationary Office, Edinburgh.

(59) Ratcliffe, D.A. (2005) *Lapland: A Natural History.* Poyser, London.

(60) Ratcliffe, D.A. (2015) Lapland images. In: *Nature's Conscience – The Life and Legacy of Derek Ratcliffe* (eds. D.B.A. Thompson, H.H. Birks & H.J.B. Birks). This volume, Chapter 29.

(61) Heggøy, H. & Øien, I.J. (2014) *Conservation Status of Birds of Prey and Owls in Norway: 2014 Report.* 129 pp. NOF/Birdlife Norway. Report 1-2014.

(62) Ratcliffe, D.A. (1965) Organo-chlorine residues in some raptor and corvid eggs from northern Britain. *British Birds*, **58**, 65-81.
Ratcliffe, D.A. (1967) Decrease in eggshell weight in certain birds of prey. *Nature*, **215**, 208-210.

(63) Ratcliffe, D.A. (1970) Changes attributable to pesticides in egg breakage frequency and eggshell thickness in some British birds. *Journal of Applied Ecology*, **7**, 67-115.

(64) Ratcliffe, D.A. (ed.) (1977) *A Nature Conservation Review, Volume 1.* Cambridge University Press, Cambridge.

(65)   Ratcliffe, D.A. (ed.) (1977) *A Nature Conservation Review, Volume 2*. Cambridge University Press, Cambridge.

(66)   Ratcliffe, D.A. (1971) Criteria for selection of nature reserves. *Advancement of Science*, **27**, 294-296.
Ratcliffe, D.A. (1976) Thoughts towards a philosophy of nature conservation. *Biological Conservation*, **9**, 45-53. (Reprinted in this volume as Chapter 26).
Ratcliffe, D.A. (1977) Nature conservation - aims, methods and achievements. *Proceedings of the Royal Society of London B-Biological Sciences*, **197**, 11-29.
Ratcliffe, D.A. (1977) Uplands and birds - an outline. *Bird Study*, **24**, 140-158.

(67)   Thompson, D.B.A., Sutherland, W. & Birks, H.J.B. (2015) Nature conservation and the Nature Conservation Review – a new philosophical framework. In: *Nature's Conscience – The Life and Legacy of Derek Ratcliffe* (eds. D.B.A. Thompson, H.H. Birks & H.J.B. Birks). This volume, Chapter 19.

(68)   Fuller, R.J. (ed.) (2012) *Birds and Habitat: Relationships in Changing Landscapes*. Cambridge University Press, Cambridge.
Wilson, J.D., Evans, A.D. & Grice, P.V. (2009) *Bird Conservation and Agriculture*. Cambridge University Press, Cambridge.

(69)   Housden, S. (2015) Fighting for wildlife – from the inside. In: *Nature's Conscience – The Life and Legacy of Derek Ratcliffe* (eds. D.B.A. Thompson, H.H. Birks & H.J.B. Birks). This volume, Chapter 20.

(70)   Marren, P. (2002) *Nature Conservation*. HarperCollins, London.

(71)   Bainbridge, I.P., Evans, R.J., Broad, C.H., Crooke, C.H., Duffy, K., Green, R.E., Love, J.A. & Mudge, G.P. (2003) Re-introduction of White-tailed eagles (*Haliaeetus albicilla*) to Scotland. In: *Birds of Prey in a Changing Environment* (eds. D.B.A. Thompson, S.M. Redpath, A. Fielding, M. Marquiss & C.A. Galbraith), pp. 393-416. The Stationery Office, Edinburgh.

(72)   Carter, I., Cross, A.V., Douse, A., Duffy, K., Etheridge, B., Grice, P.V., Newbery, D.C., Orr-Ewing, D.C., O'Toole, L., Simpson, D. & Snell, N. (2003) Re-introduction and conservation of the red kite (*Milvus milvus*) in Britain: current threats and prospects for future range expansion. In: *Birds of Prey in a Changing Environment* (eds. D.B.A. Thompson, S.M. Redpath, A. Fielding, M. Marquiss & C.A. Galbraith), pp. 407-416. The Stationery Office, Edinburgh.

(73)   Nature Conservancy Council (1986). *Nature Conservation and Afforestation in Britain*. 108 pp. Nature Conservancy Council, Peterborough.
Wilson, J.D., Anderson, R., Bailey, S., Chetcuti, J., Cowie, N. R., Hancock, M.H., Quine, C.P., Russell, N., Stephen, L. & Thompson, D.B.A. (2014) Modelling edge effects of mature forest plantations on peatland waders informs landscape-scale conservation. *Journal of Applied Ecology*, **51**, 204–213.

(74)   Stroud, D.A., Reed, T.M., Pienkowski, M.W. & Lindsay, R.A. (eds. D.A. Ratcliffe & P.H. Oswald) (1987) *Birds, Bogs and Forestry - The Peatlands of Caithness, and Sutherland*. 121 pp. Nature Conservancy Council, Peterborough.

(75)   Ratcliffe, D.A. (1986) The effects of afforestation on the wildlife of open habitats. In: *Trees and Wildlife in the Scottish Uplands* (ed. D. Jenkins), pp. 46-54. Institute of Terrestrial Ecology, Huntingdon.

Ratcliffe, D.A. (1988) The British upland scene. In: *NCC Research in the Uplands* (eds. D.B.A. Thompson, S. Whyte & P.H. Oswald), pp. 7-15. Nature Conservancy Council, Peterborough.

Ratcliffe, D.A. (1989) An uncertain future for official nature conservation. *British Wildlife*, **1**, 89-91.

Ratcliffe, D.A. (1990) Upland birds and their conservation. *British Wildlife*, **2**, 1-12. (Reprinted in this volume as Chapter 18).

Ratcliffe, D.A. (1995) The government's response to the European Union Habitats and Species Directive. *British Wildlife*, **6**, 307-309.

(76)   Ratcliffe, D.A. (1988) Human impacts on the environment in relation to the history and biological future of the Peregrine. In: *Peregrine Falcon Populations. Their Management and Recovery* (eds. T.J. Cade, J.H. Enderson, C.G. Thelander & C.M. White), pp. 813-820. The Peregrine Fund, Boise.

(77)   Redpath, S.M. & Thirgood, S.J. (1997) *Birds of Prey and Red Grouse.* The Stationery Office, London.

(78)   Fielding, A.H. & Haworth, P.F. (2014) *Golden eagles in the south of Scotland: an overview.* Scottish Natural Heritage Commissioned Report, Battleby.

(79)   Avery, M. (2012) *Fighting for Birds: 25 years in Nature Conservation.* Pelagic Publishing, Exeter.

(80)   Balharry, D. (2015) North-West Highland reminiscences. In: *Nature's Conscience – The Life and Legacy of Derek Ratcliffe* (eds. D.B.A. Thompson, H.H. Birks & H.J.B. Birks). This volume, Chapter 12.

(81)   Tew, T. (2013) Ratcliffe, D.A. (1970) Changes attributable to pesticides in egg breakage frequency and eggshell thickness in some British birds, Journal of Applied Ecology. In: *100 Influential Papers Published in 100 years of the British Ecological Society Journals* (eds. P.J. Grubb & J. Whittaker), p. 43. British Ecological Society, London.

(82)   Braune, B.M. (2007) Temporal trends of organochlorines and mercury in seabird eggs from the Canadian Arctic, 1975-2003. *Environmental Pollution*, **148**, 599-613. Coulson, J.C. (2011) *The Kittiwake.* Poyser, London.

(83)   Nethersole-Thompson, D. & Nethersole-Thompson, M. (1986) *Waders: Their Breeding Haunts and Watchers.* Poyser, Calton.

(84)   Radcliffe (sic), D. (1989) The end of British nature conservation? *New Scientist*, **9 September**, 75-76.

12. North-West Highland reminiscences

Dick Balharry

It was my good fortune and privilege to be appointed warden of Britain's first National Nature Reserve, Beinn Eighe (Fig. 12.1), in 1962. Anancaun Field Station at Kinlochewe was our home and base for this special reserve lying at the east end of Loch Maree in Wester Ross. Anancaun also had a laboratory and hostel offering self-catering for ap-

Figure 12.1. Beinn Eighe National Nature Reserve, Wester Ross, 1969. Photo: John Birks

proximately ten people. With its distinctive location at the heart of a magisterially wild mountain landscape (Fig. 12.2) the reserve attracted many eminent scientists and their students. They worked on a gamut of ecological, entomological, mycological, geological, palaeoecological, and geomorphological topics—many highly specialised—and the great majority were smitten with the scree-draped landscapes with their spangling native pinewoods on the lower reaches. One person, a quietly spoken, modest, and rather erudite natural scientist, stood out – as much for his expert knowledge as for his obsessive fascination for wildlife.

Figure 12.2. Slioch, Loch Maree, and Scots Pine (*Pinus sylvestris*) trees on the southern shore of the loch. 1969. Photo: John Birks

Since boyhood my preferred classroom has been the great outdoors and now I had a uniquely rich wealth of teachers living next door. Over the 12 years I spent on the Reserve the visitors intrigued me. We would parry questions and robustly debate their work and wider matters. They were refreshingly demanding, with a succession of when?, why?, how?, and what? questions, sorely testing my ability to give sound, reasonable, and satisfying responses. All of this engendered in me a keenly forged desire to learn – something I have never lost.

In April 1963, I met Derek Ratcliffe, then the Nature Conservancy's (NC) Senior Scientific Officer (having been promoted to the post five years previously). He was based in Edinburgh (transferring six months later to the newly formed Monks Wood Experimental Station near Huntingdon, where he joined the Woodland Research Section and greatly contributed to the work of the Toxic Chemicals and Wildlife Research Team led by Norman Moore (Fig. 19.3)). This was the month that Winston Churchill became the first honorary citizen of the US, and the film *Lawrence of Arabia* won an Academy Award

– all far away from birds of prey and mountain vegetation, the specialist subjects of my illustrious visitor. Derek arrived at the reserve with his colleague and friend, Jim Lockie[1], the NC's Senior Zoologist (Fig. 12.3). Jim went on to become a highly respected lecturer in conservation science at Edinburgh University, co-author of the important book *Ecology and Land Use in Upland Scotland*[2] published in 1969, and a fine carpenter and wood turner.

Figure 12.3. Derek Ratcliffe (left) and Jim Lockie (right) on fieldwork in the North-West Highlands, 1963. Photographer unknown but reproduced with permission from Dick Balharry and Jim Lockie

We had three days to explore and survey Golden Eagle (*Aquila chrysaetos*) and Peregrine (*Falco peregrinus*) (Fig. 14.5) territories over the vast expanse of wild mountainous terrain that engulfed the reserve. Derek spent the two previous years master-minding national surveys of peregrines, revealing just how dire their plight was[3]. Together, he and Jim were at the heart of landmark work unravelling the fortunes of Highland raptors[4,5], with Jim specialising on the diet and distribution of eagles[6]. Of the several hundred people who came to stay next door to us at Anancaun, none was more welcome than these two. And being with them provided me with a unique training experience I have valued constantly over the past fifty years. On mountain treks we mapped territories, and with great effort found the eyries (often checking alternatives many miles apart), recorded breeding success, and determined their diets. There were some intriguing surprises – we would trudge mile after mile seeing very little, on occasion flushing a Greenshank (*Tringa nebularia*) (Figs. 11.21, 11.22 & 17.8) or Golden Plover (*Pluvialis apricaria*) (Figs. 11.10 & 11.13), yet behold – in the eagle nests we came upon the remains of Water Voles (*Arvicola amphibius*), whole nests of Meadow Pipits (*Anthus pratensis*) (plucked from the ground by a presumably desperately hungry predator), Cuckoo (*Cuculus canorus*), Red Grouse (*Lagopus lagopus scotticus*), Ptarmigan (*Lagopus muta*), and virtually every other upland bird and mammal in the region.

We must have covered 30+ miles (50+ km) daily, constantly on the move and eyeing the sky and mountain flanks and ridges for movement. It was exhausting, but exhilarating. On one memorable (and unusually cloudless) day the following April, Derek and I hitched a lift on a boat, taking us westwards across Loch Maree (now frequented by Sea Eagles (*Haliaeetus albicilla*) (Fig. 11.19) – a pipedream back then). Decanted on the north shore, we steadily hauled up through mature native Pedunculate Oak (*Quercus robur*), Alder (*Alnus glutinosa*), Downy Birch (*Betula pubescens*), and Ash (*Fraxinus excelsior*) woodlands – most of them showing absolutely no signs of natural regeneration, having been grazed and browsed heavily by Red Deer (*Cervus elaphus*). There followed a salutary lesson in the ravages of deer and other 'extractive land-uses' on what I had, until then, thought of as wild, pristine land. Starting with the shallow and eroding peat, in parts with protruding fossil pine stumps (Fig. 4.31), and then pointing to sheltered ravines, the few fenced woods, and beyond heaths, grasslands, and rocky ledges, Derek dissected the landscape, and with the forensic skill of a deft pathologist, he took me through the many signs of mal-use and mis-management which had reduced what we stood in to depauperate remnants of former glories. It was sobering, for I, and many before, loved this landscape and felt proud of it. Yet, in the space of an hour or so I came to realise the full horror or what had gone before – and was on-going. Yes, there is a uniquely special wildness to the North-West Highland landscape so boldly dominated by rock, peat, and water (Figs. 12.1 & 12.2). But what a landscape we *could* have. For the rest of my life I have endeavoured to make the Highlands a better place – and to awaken people's often closed minds to what has, and is, happening around them. And the light switch was thrown by nature's finest tutor.

Later, on gaining a considerable height (having meandered up through a treacherous ravine, for Derek always scaled mountains through these to look for rare and interesting plants in places free of grazing[(7)]), we rested. Beyond, in every direction, we feasted on a panorama of grandeur. There were glorious colours, dominated by hues of brown, and again I listened to the soft voice this time describing the origins of the massifs, corries, towering ramparts, and myriad bejewelled bog pools.

Finding eagles was our goal, and, having moved on, a wind- and ice-shattered precipitous cliff that for centuries has been the ancestral home of eagles reared up to confront us. After eye-watering scans of each ledge for new eyries, without success, our thoughts turned to breeding failure. Dumping our rucksacks we sat in the cool shade of the cliff and continued the search – by now forlorn. Deer and a few wild goats were eagerly grazing vegetation surrendered by snowmelt under the warm sunshine. Great boulders, some far larger than houses, which had long since parted company from the precipitous rock face above us, were utterly dominant. But as an antidote to the physical heavyweight of all this we notched the distant piping of a Greenshank (Fig. 11.22) far below, and nearby the agitated chatter of a Ring Ouzel (*Turdus torquatus*) – we were close to its nest. We were in a special place – relishing a close companionship of quietness with few words; something you share with kindred souls rarely and preciously.

We scanned the vast scree fields, rocky battlements, and ever changing skies high above us. And there, far distant in the pale blue of the heavens, we caught a dark speck

– a Golden Eagle (Fig. 12.4). With eyes glued to binoculars we watched, enthralled by a spectacular, aerobatic repertoire of gliding, swooping, soaring, and plummeting at heights varying from an estimated 3,000 to 4,000 feet (900-1,200 m) above us, and getting nearer. The eagle's golden mantle reflected sunlight as she wheeled in tighter turns. Suspended motionless directly above us, her head dipped as if trying to penetrate the dark shadowy depths below. Then, suddenly and dramatically, she closed her wings and fell. She must have dropped over 2,000 feet (600 m) before her wings eased open, with the resistance to the rushing air loudly adding to the drama we were witnessing. WHOOSH! Now only 200 feet (60 m) above us, legs unfolded and feathers dancing as the air

Figure 12.4. Stages in the life of a Golden Eagle (*Aquila chrysaetos*), 1978. The deformed chick in the lower right picture is an unusual occurrence and its deformities may have been related to the impacts of dieldrin and aldrin which were then used in sheep dip. Photos: Dick Balharry

whipped around them, her massive wings opened still further breaking her meteoric descent. Then, at around just 100 feet (30 m) above us, she swerved and swung up with outstretched feet to pitch on a nearby ledge. Regaining balance from her forward momentum she paused momentarily to gaze around, and then tottered on to her eyrie under an overhanging rock. We had missed it! We exchanged glances, amazed she had not seen us. Her attention was riveted to the eyrie, and she had been oblivious to the two of us in the deep shadow. Now she was giving her undivided attention to nest arranging, presumably with one or two pale eggs, and we crept out of sight. Three months later an eaglet fledged and flew from the eyrie – and it is just remotely possible that he or she still lives!

Derek became my mentor, and more than that. His patience, tolerance, and ability to teach in the field were remarkable. Always positive in the field, his explanations of where to look for a particular plant or bird were unswervingly accurate. As a Greenshank 'chipped' in alarm or 'tewed' when making contact with a mate, or a Peregrine (Fig. 14.5) voiced its displeasure, Derek matched the most riveting observations of animal behaviour with clear interpretations of what was unfolding. Over time I have accompanied many other naturalists in the mountains, but none have come near to matching Derek's knowledge and explanations.

And so, to April 1966, on a day when Derek was expected at around 6 pm (he was always on time – sometimes early, and never late!). I climbed Beinn Eighe to look for rare Snow Buntings (*Plectrophenax nivalis*) which just occasionally nested there. On my way down, having had no joy, I caught sight of Derek's white Triumph Vitesse car turning off the main road that led down to Anancaun. I had with me some plant specimens taken from the tops, and with curiosity on my mind, I popped by our garden to collect a further sample – of an exotic nursery alpine I had bought a few weeks earlier. I placed it in a bag with the other vascular plants and mosses and stuffed it into my rucksack. A few minutes later I found Derek in the house, devouring tea and pancakes, and chatting with Adeline, my wife.

Soon, Derek was asking where I had been and what I had seen. Disappointed to hear about the Snow Buntings (it was early yet for them), his attention turned to my enthusiasm over some plants I had found and needed identifying. Derek's smile reflected his continuing zest for learning, sharing, and explaining. After a short study of each specimen, all now neatly arranged on a nearby table, he gave a fascinating description of each of the habitats and locales of where I had found each plant, along with its English and Latin names. His account was perfect. However, one plant was left to the last, and it was set aside. Now what will he say about the intruder, I wondered. He then moved it, followed by "and you never got this on Beinn Eighe did you – this is native to the Himalaya but might be available in alpine nurseries in this country!" What I had thought would be a real test was easy for his encyclopaedic knowledge of Scotland's native flora and vegetation[7]. He was gentle with me despite my 'smart Alec' tease, and brushed aside my apologies explaining in some detail how it was so obvious to him. It was quite brilliant, and I loved him for being so direct and honest.

His erudite writings are a life legacy of huge importance. How I wish our country's leaders would heed the wise words which close his classic monograph on the Peregrine (Fig. 14.6)[8].

"The Peregrine is a species too entangled with human affairs to remain untouched by the further onslaughts on our natural environment that surely lie ahead. If, as has so often been said, it is a key species that acts as a barometer of ecosystem health, then its fortunes should be a matter of widespread concern. More particularly, those to whom the Peregrine is a source of inspiration and wonder have a special duty of vigilance, and a willingness to do battle with the future philistines who care nothing for the beauty of wild nature. It will be their responsibility to ensure that it survives, not just for aesthetic, scientific and other value, but in its own right as one of the most spectacular inhabitants of our planet."

For Peregrine you can read any of our wild, native species. Penning this reminiscence has reminded me of Derek's warmth, humility, and extraordinary scholarship.

References

(1)   Anderson, T.R. (2013) *The Life of David Lack – Father of Evolutionary Ecology*. Oxford University Press, Oxford.

(2)   McVean, D.N. & Lockie, J.D. (1969) *Ecology and Land Use in Upland Scotland*. Edinburgh University Press, Edinburgh.

(3)   Greenwood, J. & Crick, H.Q.P. (2015) "It seemed like a dream come true": Derek Ratcliffe and the Peregrine surveys. In: *Nature's Conscience – The Life and Legacy of Derek Ratcliffe* (eds. D.B.A. Thompson, H.H. Birks & H.H.B. Birks). This volume, Chapter 14.

(4)   Lockie, J.D. & Ratcliffe, D.A. (1964) Insecticides and Scottish Golden Eagles. *British Birds,* **57**, 89-102.

(5)   Lockie, J.D., Ratcliffe, D.A. & Balharry, R. (1969) Breeding success and organochlorine residues in Golden Eagles in west Scotland. *Journal of Applied Ecology,* **6**, 381-389.

(6)   Lockie, J.D. (1964) The breeding density of the Golden Eagle and Fox in relation to food supply in Wester Ross, Scotland. *Scottish Naturalist,* **71**, 67-77.

(7)   Birks, H.J.B. & Birks, H.H. (2015) Derek Ratcliffe – botanist and plant ecologist. In: *Nature's Conscience – The Life and Legacy of Derek Ratcliffe* (eds. D.B.A. Thompson, H.H. Birks & H.J.B. Birks). This volume, Chapter 4.

(8)   Ratcliffe, D.A. (1980) *The Peregrine Falcon* (1st edition). Poyser, Calton. Ratcliffe, D.A. (1993) *The Peregrine Falcon* (2nd edition). Poyser, London.

13. In Galloway and the Borders - in search of an enduring youth

Chris J. Rollie

Introduction

Derek Ratcliffe was something of a hero of mine since I came upon his writings as an undergraduate in the late 1970s. I first met him almost thirty years ago in Galloway. I was a rather self-conscious apprentice to his great friend, and my mentor, the late Dick Roxburgh (Fig. 13.1), then a retired miner and well-known raptor enthusiast. Dick and I were on the peregrine trail when we bumped into Derek. I stayed very much in the background as the two of them quietly exchanged news of their beloved hill birds. Soon after that, I started corresponding with Derek, and we quickly became close friends, each year spending the happiest and most fulfilling of days in the field in Galloway.

As we learn earlier in this book, Derek first came to Galloway (Fig. 13.2) as a sixteen year old, in 1946, fired by his great mentor Ernest Blezard (Fig. 1.9), and some other remarkable naturalists[1,2]. He was so impressed that he returned year after year, missing only one year in the next 59! He stayed with various shepherds, where he was fed, in his words, "like a fighting cock", and where he grew to admire and respect the ways and lore of the hill folk[2]. In this way, over the years, he came to know just about every significant crag and ravine in Gal-

Figure 13.1. Dick Roxburgh, a passionate Peregrine (*Falco peregrinus*) enthusiast looking at a Peregrine's ground nest in east Ayrshire, 1988. Photo: Derek Ratcliffe

Figure 13.2. The fine granite crags of the Clints of Dromore, Galloway, a favourite haunt of Derek Ratcliffe since 1946 and of Peregrines (*Falco peregrinus*) and Ravens (*Corvus corax*), 1990. Photo: Derek Ratcliffe

loway (Fig. 1.5), together with Dumfriesshire, the Borders, Lakeland, the Northern Pennines, Snowdonia, and Northumberland (Figs. 1.6 & 5.1)[2,3]. In fact, it is perhaps unlikely that any other person has ever had such a comprehensive knowledge of these upland areas, whilst his early work with the Nature Conservancy also allowed him to explore much of the Scottish Highlands[2-4].

Peregrines and their recovery

Through his work on Peregrines (*Falco peregrinus*) and Ravens (*Corvus corax*) he became a fearless and expert climber, scrambling to dangerous ledges in the loneliest of places[1-4]. He was an unashamed admirer of the aesthetic beauty and variety of birds' eggs, but always in their rightful place – the nest[4]. He soon came to recognise and describe consistencies in the characteristics of typical clutches from several different areas, and he could track the fortunes of females over the years by their signature clutch colour markings. I worked with Derek after he made the link between organochlorines and eggshell thinning, ultimately leading to changes in the use of DDT and other pesticides[5,6]. In 2013, Tom Tew[7] in *100 Influential Papers Published in 100 years of the British Ecological Society Journals* writes of Derek's classic 1970 paper[8]

> "The publication of *Silent Spring* in 1962 first raised public concern over pesticides but it was the rigorous work of Derek Ratcliffe throughout the 1960s, culminating in this paper in 1970, that provided the evidence

that changed the policy, and thus changed the world. ... Ratcliffe was forging the science of evidence-based environmentalism. His science shifted national policy. National concerns in the UK linked with those in the US became an international campaign. The European Union banned dieldrin from agricultural use in 1981 and DDT in 1986."[7]

The recovery of the Peregrine population (Fig. 14.5) is one of the most celebrated successes in conservation[9], described by Adams[10] as "arguably the most important scientific contribution yet to nature conservation in Britain"[11]. Derek maintained his effort in the field to track the increasing distribution and overall number of breeding pairs[9]. The population eventually expanded beyond the capacity of big crags to deliver discrete territories, with small crags and even ground sites being used in some areas (Fig. 13.3). The use of man-made structures also increased – I showed Derek a new site on old colliery winding gear in Ayrshire only three weeks before he died. He wanted to see

Figure 13.3. Three Peregrine (*Falco peregrinus*) eggs in a ground nest in Peeblesshire, 1971. Photo: Derek Ratcliffe

any such unusual sites for himself, and to photograph them in his own distinctive way – with his Pentax or Olympus camera using Kodachrome 25 or 64 film, mounted on a tripod.

Days looking for Ravens

Perhaps Derek's favourite bird, and certainly mine, was that great character, the Raven (Fig. 13.4). Derek adored and admired in equal measure its form, character, aerobatics, intelligence, vocal repertoire, and haunts[4]. For him, Ravens epitomised the wild country that he loved so much, and they were always welcome companions in these places. He was impressed by the folklore associated with this bird around the world, and combined this and a wealth of biological information to produce a classic monograph on the species[12] (Fig. 11.16). He visited over 500 nesting places at least once (Fig. 11.17), and followed some of these in each of fifty years! As no other bird, he marvelled at the variety in eggshell colouration, and whereas I have only seen one clutch of the extremely rare erythristic eggs, Derek saw several[4]. He was an ardent follower of the remarkable 20th century recovery of Ravens and recorded their return as nesters in several English counties.

However, it was in his favourite Southern Uplands that he was to witness first-hand such a remarkable transformation in their fortunes (Figs. 1.5, 1.6 & 5.1). Through the 1950s and 1960s he became intimately familiar with just about all the known territories, though during that time he estimated that 40-50% of them were robbed annually. Whilst the population in Lakeland increased slightly between 1960 and 1990, numbers in southern Scotland and Northumberland fell drastically during the earlier part of that

Figure 13.4. Raven (*Corvus corax*), central Wales, 2008. Photo: Tony Cross

period, and Derek, Mick Marquiss, and Ian Newton linked this largely to blanket conifer afforestation (Fig. 22.1)[13]. Although dieldrin in sheep dip had significantly manifested itself in the fortunes of Golden Eagles (*Aquila chrysaetos*) (Fig. 12.4) in the early 1960s, at that time Derek found only low residues in eight Raven eggs, including four from the Southern Uplands, and, after dieldrin was banned, his sample of ten eggs from the Lake District in 1970 showed only traces of the chemical. On the other hand, the removal of sheep for afforestation over huge areas in Galloway and Dumfriesshire, in particular, supplied compelling evidence of desertion of territories in the most affected areas, and the population declined to a low point in 1980[14].

Remarkably, within the next ten years, the fortunes of Ravens took a turn for the better and they were becoming the excited talk of 'hill men' in south-west Scotland. Encouraged by Dick Roxburgh (Fig. 13.1), I wrote to Derek in 1988 to relate some personal experiences with Ravens and to mention some of the old places where they had returned to breed. Raptor group colleagues had already been talking of a repeat region-wide breeding survey, but Derek's enthusiastic encouragement sealed the affair. A survey in 1989 was repeated in 1994, by which time the breeding population in southern Scotland (including the coast) was 67 pairs, 19 of them in trees. A third survey of the same area in 1999 found 127 pairs, 40 of them using trees[15]. By this time, of course, not only had most of the old crag haunts been reoccupied, but new ones had been adopted and tree sites were increasing annually. While the replacement of sheep carrion by deer, and in some areas goats, was part of the improving picture in the maturing conifer forests, the reduction of direct persecution and illegal poisoning on sheep walks was also having an effect and these marvellous birds were flourishing once more.

Figure 13.5. Derek Ratcliffe, Donald Watson, and Dick Roxburgh on a visit to some Raven (*Corvus corax*) sites in late March 1995, Galloway. Photo: Chris Rollie

Together with the recovery of Peregrines[6,9], the spread of Ravens towards the end of the 20th century and since brought a warm glow to the old guard of birders, who had witnessed such horrors at the hands of the unholy trinity of pesticides, persecution, and blanket afforestation. Before, the croak and cronk of the Raven had to be sought out in those special remote places, or along the wild coastal cliffs (Fig. 4.20), but now increasingly they could be heard elsewhere, indeed anywhere, and how we all smiled to hear them. A picture (Fig. 13.5) taken in late March 1995, on a visit to some Raven sites with Derek, Donald Watson, and Dick Roxburgh, in some way captures the moment; I just wish I had taken more! The nest itself was in pines near the foot of Cairnsmore of Deugh (Carsphairn). Years later, another image of Derek at a Peregrine's nest captures a special moment – a first glimpse of an attractive clutch in an easily accessible site (Fig. 13.6).

In search of nesting waders

Fired by historic accounts of a significant breeding Dotterel (*Charadrius morinellus*) (Figs. 11.3 & 11.5) population on the high Lakeland fells in former times, Derek spent several youthful summers in pursuit of nests in this home territory[2], but it was not until 1952 in the Grampians that he found his first nest[2]. He had covered some likely tops in Galloway in the summer of 1949, but saw none, though was somewhat compensated by coming across the Azure Hawker dragonfly (*Aeshna caerulea*) (Fig. 1.8), which had never

Figure 13.6. Derek Ratcliffe at a Peregrine (*Falco peregrinus*) nest with three eggs, at an easily accessible site in Galloway, 2003. Photo: Chris Rollie

been recorded south of the Highlands before[1,2]. He loved the central Galloway hill area (Figs. 1.4 & 1.5), which he felt held much of the character of Sutherland, but summer sojourns in 1951, 1952, 1961, 1965, and 1971 brought him no Dotterel, despite the seeming suitability of several tops. His Peregrine work of 1960-62 brought him into contact with Desmond Nethersole-Thompson (Fig. 11.22) and Donald Watson (Fig. 13.7), and fired on by the former, in 1964 Derek encouraged Donald to intensify the search of his adopted home in Galloway, particularly after any eggs would have hatched, but not to leave it too late either! The following year he accompanied Donald on a search of some suitable tops, but without success. In 1967, though, Donald did find a nest with two eggs, which Derek thought to be the first really authentic 20th century breeding record in Galloway. Although the exciting secret was kept by Desmond Nethersole-Thompson and Derek, word leaked locally and even reached the ears of less interested folks in the corridors of the Nature Conservancy in Edinburgh, causing some embarrassment to Derek,

Figure 13.7. Joan and Donald Watson, October 1990, close friends of Derek Ratcliffe who lived in Dalry, Galloway. Donald was a notable painter of wildlife and landscapes (see Fig. 13.8) and Joan was a keen butterfly enthusiast. Photo: Derek Ratcliffe

who had so kept the faith. His view was always that such sensitive breeding birds should be protected from "people who would never dream of doing a bit of hunting off their own bat... [but who would] ...come running hell for leather as soon as they are given a hot tip!" Derek held an identical view about rare and endangered plants such as the Killarney Fern (*Trichomanes speciosum*) (Fig. 4.27) and Oblong Woodsia (*Woodsia ilvensis*) (Figs. 4.12 & 9.4)[3] In the case of the 1967 Dotterel, fortunately both chicks fledged and the wild Galloway hills settled again to their own birds and select devotees.

Another Galloway nest (three eggs) was found by a school party in 1971, but this failed and robbery was suspected. On 1 June 1975 Derek and Donald were back on the tops, armed with a long dragging rope in a throwback to the eggers' methods of the old days[4]. Although illegal and frowned upon now, in the hands of experts it was perfectly acceptable back then. Anyway, their efforts yielded rich reward when a male came off three eggs just ahead of the rope. The nest was beautifully situated in moss between two flat stones and superbly captured in Derek's classic photograph (Fig. 13.8: also Figure 182 in ref. 15). Donald was back on 27 June, by which time there were three healthy chicks, and his brief sketches on the day were worked up into the evocative and characteristic picture that has since become a celebrated limited edition print (Fig. 13.9). This time the secret was kept and all three chicks fledged.

Encouraged by both of these dear friends, I have made near annual pilgrimages to the high Galloway tops, and have been lucky enough to find two breeding attempts, both successful, in 1998 (three chicks; with Duncan Orr-Ewing) and 2008 (two chicks;

Figure 13.8. Male Dotterel (*Charadrius morinellus*) incubating a clutch of three, Galloway, 1 June 1975. Photo: Derek Ratcliffe

Figure 13.9. The male Dotterel in Figure 13.8 with a brood of three chicks on 27 June 1975. From a painting by Donald Watson

with George Christie), the latter providing an important record for the new breeding birds atlas[16]. More often, of course, I have been unsuccessful and alone, but always compensated by the special solitude of those places and the thoughts of those who had gone before in search of this elusive bird.

Derek was extremely modest, but he would not shy away from telling you that on several occasions he found five or six or even seven Golden Plover (*Pluvialis apricaria*) (Fig. 11.13) nests in one day[4]. This is some feat, and it is revealing that, of all his many achievements, he savoured such successes in the field amongst his very highest – though in listening, one could sense his frustration as darkness fell and he had equalled but not beaten his record! Nesting waders were a great passion, and he was an ardent and persistent nest finder (as was Jeannette Ratcliffe (Fig. 17.2)), with Lapland providing compelling haunts in recent years for this obsession and their yearning for unspoilt wilderness[4,17,18] (Fig. 11.18).

> "On the whole, Lapland does not have high densities of birds, except for certain hot-spots, mainly on the coast. But it is the challenging wilderness and the difficult birds that I find captivating. The freedom to roam is a great boon, and I recapture my youth (or something of it) up there in exploring the wilds, even though we hardly ever penetrate more than about a mile from the road." (Derek Ratcliffe letter of 6 March 2004)

However, whaups (Curlews (*Numenius arquata*)) with their evocative calls and splendid eggs were, I think, his favourite wader, and he and Jeannette spent countless hours in their camper-van watching these fine birds on their breeding grounds in Galloway. Over the years, he recorded a worrying decline in their numbers, reflected in most other parts of the UK, but he never lost the thrill of finding a new nest. On 1 May 2005, Derek and I were joined by Bob Stakim on a visit to Airds Moss, a large expanse of blanket bog in Ayrshire and a great place for breeding waders. As we approached the Moss, a whaup got up from quite nearby, and we resolved to seek the nest if the bird rose again on our return. After an hour or so of birdwatching and botanising—Derek found *Racomitrium lanuginosum* moss there less than 200 m above sea level—we returned whence we came and once again, the whaup rose. Derek stayed on the track as Bob and I splurged across extremely boggy ground to reach the spot, whereupon finding the nest with four eggs (Fig. 13.10), Derek expectantly hurried over to join us. The three of us gazed down on the clutch before meeting eyes to share in the unspoken delight at the scene. Derek, who had spent many youthful summers in Norfolk[1,2], characteristically summed up our feelings with a quiet "booootiful!" He must have seen hundreds, perhaps over a thousand, of such nests before, and yet he greeted each new find with the same enthusiasm and wonder[4].

Figure 13.10. A "bootiful" whaup (Curlew (*Numenius arquata*)) clutch on Airds Moss, Ayrshire, 1 May 2005. Photo: Derek Ratcliffe

Wider issues – plants and trees

It is this remarkable fieldcraft and ongoing dedication to his interest that elevated Derek to a position of esteem and admiration in ornithology[4]. Arguably, Derek and Ian Newton are held in higher regard by Britain's raptor workers than anyone else since the 1940s, and indeed this standing is worldwide. But Derek was a remarkable all-rounder – an eminent botanist, entomologist, and herpetologist even. Plants, as we see elsewhere, took him to all parts of Britain and beyond[3], but the uplands always called loudest. In 1956 in the Moffat Hills (Fig. 5.1), he was first to discover Alpine Foxtail (*Alopecurus magellanicus*) (Fig. 5.4) south of the Scottish Highlands, and three years later he found more on Cross Fell in the Pennines[19]. He discovered the rare intermediate-fen moss *Hamatocaulis vernicosus* in Dalveen Pass, and the montane Broad-bordered White Underwing moth (*Anarta melanopa*) in the Southern Uplands.

Two things were completely unnecessary when in the field with Derek – a camera and a field guide – any field guide! His eyes were everywhere, and he found keen interest wherever his gaze led him – upwards and ahead for birds, on the ground for plants and insects, and all around for natural form and landscapes, of which he was an expert photographer[3]. Each year there would be a special extra interest, and he took me with him into new worlds of natural history as we paddled in burns looking for *Radula voluta* (a rare liverwort) (Fig. 4.4), or following the progress of the acid-sensitive *Lobaria pulmonaria*, a huge lichen that grows on the alkaline bark of Ash (*Fraxinus excelsior*). Some years ago at my suggestion, a colleague wrote to Derek asking if he would write a Foreword for the Dumfries & Galloway Local Biodiversity Action Plan. He did,

Figure 13.11. View towards the Clints of Dromore, Galloway (*top*) and away from them to the extensive conifer plantations (*bottom*), 2004. Photos: Derek Ratcliffe

and in addition sent page after page of detailed notes on every taxon in that award-winning document. That he could have done so for quite possibly as much as half of these plans speaks loudly for his remarkable knowledge and total commitment to nature.

But all was not rosy. When it came to conifers, Derek became animatedly angry. He detested conifers and the utter ruination they inflicted on previously open, spacious wild landscapes. Whilst he liked being in native stands of Scots Pine (*Pinus sylvestris*) (Fig. 21.4) and Juniper (*Juniperus communis*), he abhorred the geometric and relatively sterile forests of exotic conifers, particularly Sitka Spruce (*Picea sitchensis*) and Lodge-pole Pine (*Pinus contorta*), which seemed to spread like a pernicious cancer snuffing out the life and vitality of the land (Figs. 13.11, 21.1 & 22.1). We read elsewhere about his battles with forests – and foresters[20,21]. In the thick of it, his last resort solution was designation of the best areas, and when the conifers threatened his cherished Cauldron of the Dungeon in Galloway, he encouraged the designation of the Silver Flowe (Fig. 1.7) as a National Nature Reserve (NNR)[1,7], being the only significant well-developed series of bogs with concentric pools south of the 'Flow Country' of Caithness and Sutherland, a term which he himself coined. If he had much to say in print on afforestation, he had much more to say in the field, and he described in considerable detail how he encountered stern opposition, sometimes from surprising quarters, in his drive to protect our rich biodiversity from this horror[15,20,22].

Shortly after his retirement, and following the government's long overdue removal of tax-break incentives[20] to the super-rich and pension funds to finance the creation of blanket conifer forests over some of the most important bird and botanical areas in Europe, the new initiative of Regional Indicative Forest Strategies (RIFSs) emerged. On the face of it, the idea was a good one in that environmental, agricultural, and other interests would identify priority areas and local authorities were charged with undertaking a sieve-mapping exercise whereby preferred, potential, and sensitive zones were identified to prospective foresters. The theory seemed fine, but in Dumfries and Galloway at least, the RIFS was simply ignored by the forest industry and was never properly adopted by the Forestry Commission (FC), who were the grant-giving and approval authority for new planting.

Derek saw through this from the outset and seethed further as the tax-break incentives were in large part simply replaced by higher direct grants towards afforestation, and forestry rolled on to the further detriment of open country birds and other wildlife. In his *Bird Life of Mountain and Upland* (Fig. 11.7)[22] he estimated that over 5,000 pairs of Curlew were lost directly to afforestation in the Southern Uplands. Throughout the 1990s, as a Royal Society for the Protection of Birds (RSPB) Conservation Officer I struggled to oppose further threats to the suite of special moorland birds, including Curlew (Fig. 13.10), Golden Plover (Fig. 11.10), and even Golden Eagle (Fig. 12.4). Meanwhile conifers continued to be planted on deep peat, which was as much sacrilege to us then as it is to just about everyone nowadays. Derek and I visited various threatened places and places already 'lost' to conifers and talked at great length about the continuing nonsense of it all. It was in some way cathartic for us both to concur on just how wrong it all was. He was a diligent correspondent (Figs. 11.24 & 27.1)[4,23], of course, and his letters from home in the south confirmed his visible outrage in the field during spring visits.

> "I have always regarded them (RIFSs) as a near confidence trick to support business as usual in forestry advance. You need to look at not just the proportion of Galloway under conifers, but the proportion of plantable hill land, which must surely now exceed 50%. It makes a nonsense of any concept of "reasonable balance" for this open-ended expansion to continue. But then the FC has always refused to interpret this as applying to the proportion of land under plantation, and has sought instead to understand it as their feeble cosmetic gestures to forest design and conservation needs within the planted areas." (letter of 23 November 1994)

Two weeks later, on 9 December 1994, Derek wrote:

> "These foresters make me mad. They try to sell the RIFSs on the grounds that this is a means of sharing out the cake and achieving a balance on the ground. To then say that they are "only indicative", as an excuse for cheering on every application that comes up, is to me a gross deception and shows that they are merely using this as a crafty device for maintaining business as usual."

In the months leading up to his sudden death, he was determined to tell the story as he saw it in his *Galloway and the Borders* (Fig. 27.4)[15] book in Collins's New Naturalist series. Indeed, in his concluding two chapters, respectively *Afforestation* and *Conservation and the Future*, he has done this passionately, but honestly and with a clarity, serenity even, that can only come from the hand of a true master of his subject. He conveys calmly the losses he had witnessed to the native flora and fauna of these areas, and with it the sense of outrage that we should all feel at these. At the same time he sounded a clarion call to alert readers to the continuing threats of afforestation, wind farms, and persecution of raptors on grouse moors, pointing out that it was up to concerned people to raise their voices and put pressure on the politicians to take more reasonable action.

The 'sporting' types

Derek always saw the protection of large numbers of Red Grouse (*Lagopus lagopus scoticus*) and other game in order for people to take pleasure in shooting them as an affront to nature and something of a peculiarly British absurdity[4]. But he saw the continuing illegal persecution of Hen Harriers (*Circus cyaneus*) and other raptors as "a disgrace but nobody seems able or willing to do anything about it" (letter of 15 June 2000). He feared that the conservation side had been hoodwinked into the Joint Raptor Study (JRS) (or 'Langholm Project') and "were in great danger of falling in with the shooters' propaganda that grouse management is perfection for other wildlife conservation in the uplands." (letter of 16 May 1998). In fact, he was more interested in the Langholm demonstration of what he already knew: that the increase in raptors following protection demonstrated that they were being routinely killed on grouse moors elsewhere. He was desperate to ensure that the increases in Ravens, Peregrines, and Hen Harriers following protection during the JRS, were not allowed to fall to the old ways following the conclusion of the project, and he wrote as much to senior conservation figures at the time.

With Hen Harrier and Peregrine populations tumbling on and around grouse moors following the publication of the JRS (in 1998), he was determined to speak out in his *Galloway and the Borders* (Chapter 10 on Conservation)[15]

> "I think it is time to carry at least the war of words into their camp. ****** has just sent me a press cutting with the news that your senior law officers have ruled gamekeeper prosecutions out of order, when the evidence against them has been obtained without access consent. I thought free access to moorland in Scotland was now enshrined in law." (letter of 18 August 2004)

Derek, of course, knew that there were many different aspects to the law, but like many he felt deeply aggrieved that incontrovertible evidence of illegal raptor killing was at times going unpunished and indeed sometimes not even getting to court. He was determined to speak out in his Galloway book[15], and did.

> "By the time I have done, I shall have enlarged my circle of enemies appreciably – but perhaps the internal editors at Collins will cry foul first!" (letter of 18 August 2004)

Mercifully, the editors did not, and, in addition to the remarkable yet characteristic wealth of factual information on Galloway and the Borders[15], we are left with Derek's sincere and heartfelt views on both the attractions of, and problems encountered by, its native wildlife and its true followers. As such the book has been remarkably well received by a widespread readership, impressed at once by its information and the intelligent yet endearingly simple clarity Derek again achieved in his writing, to say nothing of his wonderful photographs and those of his talented friends[3].

Sadly, he submitted the book's draft only a few days before he died and so he never got to see the final result. However, having already provided much preparatory information, Des Thompson, myself, and others were determined to support Hugh Brazier as editor, and, given the reception of the book, I feel sure that Derek would have been very pleased with the result. I am just as sure that he would have written another classic by now had he still been alive! He told John Birks soon before he died that his next planned book was to be on the Northern Pennines or the Pennines as a whole or perhaps the Yorkshire Dales. And he had spoken with Des Thompson about joining forces on a book on the Flow Country of Caithness and Sutherland.

Derek's last visit

Derek disliked blind conformity, but strategic conformity even more so. He was disgusted when vested interests, power, and privilege conspired to destroy the nation's priceless natural heritage at the cost of the taxpayer[20], and in retirement he spoke out more loudly against environmental damage[24]. He was delighted when Penguin republished Freud's last book *Civilization and its Discontents*[25], which he felt brought a fairly accurate generic view to the way our society behaves in relation to such matters. Throughout, he retained a strong, dry humour and I will never forget his ability to mimic regional accents as he related one tale or another.

In late April 2005, sixteen years after Derek retired, Des Thompson, other senior Scottish Natural Heritage (SNH) staff, and I were privileged to hear him encourage SNH towards better management of the Cairnsmore of Fleet NNR (Fig. 13.12), which he had known since 1947 and which he had been instrumental in designating. We listened intently as he calmly and cogently covered his ground, the gist of which was that there were quite enough examples of overgrazing in the Southern Uplands without having to demonstrate this on a National Nature Reserve! Following this, SNH took 300 sheep off the site.

The previous year, we retraced some of Derek's earliest steps in Galloway[1,2], and the following extract from his letter of 5 May 2004 gives a remarkable insight into the place he reserved in his heart for his favourite haunts (Figs. 13.2 & 1.5), and his determination to succeed.

> "It was great to see some old haunts again. Climbing once again to the peregrine eyrie at Dromore was a great tonic, and even seeing the birds sailing about the Big Gairy. I was delighted to be able to photograph again the scene from the Laggans across to the Cauldron - 49 years after my original pictures. It seemed odd to meet hikers and cyclists in those places, which were virtually trackless when I first knew them. Seeing the place again, it could have been only last week when I waded out into Loch Dee to avoid the "lane" of the combined Laggans; and I had the strange sensation that my intervening life of 58 years had somehow evaporated! I still have little regrets about some events - such as that, after making that long trek to the top of the Loch Dungeon corrie, I did not have time to descend to search for the Peregrines that I was sure were somewhere below. I found them two years later."

Figure 13.12. Visit to Cairnsmore of Fleet National Nature Reserve, late April 2005. From left to right: Geoff Shaw, Des Thompson, Chris Rollie, Rob Soutar, Derek Ratcliffe, Kevin Carter, and Andrew Bielinski. Photo: Chris Miles

Let me conclude with a personal reflection on this remarkable enthusiasm for the natural world. Only twice or thrice in my life have I met with a certain glint in the eye of someone who reminds me of something I have lost from my youth but so long to find again. Derek had it, hinting at a sense of wonder he had in absolute and undiminished measure since his childhood. When the big knocker on my door sounded each spring, and I opened the door to find Derek, I met with the warm smile and expectant eyes that heralded more golden days in the field. He could not wait to get started and rarely wanted the day to end, characteristically looking around in the fading light and calmly saying "I suppose we'd better be getting back then." He recalled that the conciseness of his early notes reflected the tiredness he usually felt at the end of exhausting yet massively rewarding long days in the field. Derek's diary entry for 17 April 1960 at the Clints of Dromore (Figs. 13.2 & 13.11) captures the mood:

> "I ended the day at the Clints of Dromore and made for the west end of the crags. One peregrine flew out, closely followed by the other. Both circled over and began to call as I approached. They had three good eggs in the old raven nest, which I found had been scraped out earlier on. The hen was very noisy but only as I was departing from the crags did she and the male attack the ravens, which were hanging about their own part of the crags. The only kill I found was a homer. A ring ouzel piped from the Clints in the fading light."

References

(1) Birks, H.J.B., Thompson, D.B.A. & Birks, H.H. (2015) Derek Ratcliffe – early days in pursuit of nature. In: *Nature's Conscience – The Life and Legacy of Derek Ratcliffe* (eds. D.B.A. Thompson, H.H. Birks & H.J.B. Birks). This volume, Chapter 1.

(2) Ratcliffe, D.A. (2000) *In Search of Nature*. Peregrine Books, Leeds.

(3) Birks, H.J.B. & Birks, H.H. (2015) Derek Ratcliffe – botanist and plant ecologist. In: *Nature's Conscience – The Life and Legacy of Derek Ratcliffe* (eds. D.B.A. Thompson, H.H. Birks & H.J.B. Birks). This volume, Chapter 4.

(4) Thompson, D.B.A. (2015) Contributions to ornithology – in search of nesting birds. In: *Nature's Conscience – The Life and Legacy of Derek Ratcliffe* (eds. D.B.A. Thompson, H.H. Birks & H.J.B. Birks). This volume, Chapter 11.

(5) Newton, I. (2015) Pesticides and birds of prey – the breakthrough. In: *Nature's Conscience – The Life and Legacy of Derek Ratcliffe* (eds. D.B.A. Thompson, H.H. Birks & H.J.B. Birks). This volume, Chapter 15.

(6) Ratcliffe, D.A. (1980) *The Peregrine Falcon*. Poyser, Calton.

(7) Tew, T. (2013) Ratcliffe, D.A. (1970) Changes attributable to pesticides in egg breakage frequency and eggshell thickness in some British birds, Journal of Applied Ecology. In: *100 Influential Papers Published in 100 years of the British Ecological Society Journals* (eds. P.J. Grubb & J. Whittaker), p. 43. British Ecological Society, London.

(8) Ratcliffe, D.A. (1970) Changes attributable to pesticides in egg breakage frequency and eggshell thickness in some British birds. *Journal of Applied Ecology*, **7**, 67-115.

(9) Greenwood, J. & Crick, H.Q.P. (2015) "It seemed like a dream come true": Derek Ratcliffe and the Peregrine surveys. In: *Nature's Conscience – The Life and Legacy of Derek Ratcliffe* (eds. D.B.A. Thompson, H.H. Birks & H.J.B. Birks). This volume, Chapter 14.

(10) Adams, W.M. (1986) *Nature's Place: Conservation Sites and Countryside Change*. Allen and Unwin, London.

(11) Evans, D. (1992) *A History of Nature Conservation in Britain* (2nd edition). Routledge, London and New York.

(12) Ratcliffe, D.A. (1997) *The Raven*. Poyser, London.

(13) Marquiss, M., Newton, I. & Ratcliffe, D.A. (1978). The decline of the raven *Corvus corax* in relation to afforestation in southern Scotland and northern England. *Journal of Applied Ecology*, **15**, 129-44.

(14) Mearns, R. (1983). The status of the raven in southern Scotland and Northumbria. *Scottish Birds*, **12**, 211-18.

(15) Ratcliffe, D.A. (2007) *Galloway and the Borders*. Collins, London.

(16) Balmer, D., Gillings, S., Caffrey, B., Swann, R., Downie, I. & Fuller, R. (2013) *Bird Atlas 2007-11: The breeding and wintering birds of Britain and Ireland*. BTO Books, Thetford.

(17) Ratcliffe, D.A. (2005) *Lapland: A Natural History*. Poyser, London.

(18) Byrkjedal, I. (2015) A thousand nest cards – from Derek Ratcliffe to the University Museum of Bergen. In: *Nature's Conscience – The Life and Legacy of Derek Ratcliffe* (eds. D.B.A. Thompson, H.H. Birks & H.J.B. Birks). This volume, Chapter 17.

(19) Corner, R.W.M. (2015) Derek Ratcliffe and plant-hunting in southern Scotland and northern England. In: *Nature's Conscience – The Life and Legacy of Derek Ratcliffe* (eds. D.B.A. Thompson, H.H. Birks & H.J.B. Birks). This volume, Chapter 5.

(20) Stroud, D., Reed, T., Pienkowski, M. & Lindsay, R. (2015) The Flow Country: battles fought, war won, organisation lost. In: *Nature's Conscience – The Life and Legacy of Derek Ratcliffe* (eds. D.B.A. Thompson, H.H. Birks & H.J.B. Birks). This volume, Chapter 23.

(21) Kirby, K.J. (2015) Battling forestry and building consensus: woodland conservation post-1949. In: *Nature's Conscience – The Life and Legacy of Derek Ratcliffe* (eds. D.B.A. Thompson, H.H. Birks & H.J.B. Birks). This volume, Chapter 21.
Housden, S. (2015) Fighting for wildlife – from the inside. In: *Nature's Conscience – The Life and Legacy of Derek Ratcliffe* (eds. D.B.A. Thompson, H.H. Birks & H.J.B. Birks). This volume, Chapter 20.

(22) Ratcliffe, D.A. (1990) *Bird Life of Mountain and Upland*. Cambridge University Press, Cambridge.

(23) Marren, P. (2015) Derek Ratcliffe and I: A correspondence. In: *Nature's Conscience – The Life and Legacy of Derek Ratcliffe* (eds. D.B.A. Thompson, H.H. Birks & H.J.B. Birks). This volume, Chapter 27.

(24) Radcliffe (sic), D.A. (1989) The end of British nature conservation? *New Scientist*, **9 September**, 75-76.

(25) Freud, S. (2004) *Civilization and its Discontents*. Penguin Great Ideas, London.

14. "It seemed like a dream come true" – Derek Ratcliffe and the Peregrine surveys

Jeremy J.D. Greenwood and Humphrey Q.P. Crick

How it all began

The story of how Derek Ratcliffe led British birdwatchers in one of their most influential pieces of survey work begins simply[1]:

> "In 1960 pigeon fanciers in South Wales alleged increasingly serious depredation by Peregrines on homing pigeons and petitioned the Home Office (then responsible for bird protection law) to remove legal protection so that falcon numbers could be 'controlled'. The Home Office asked the Nature Conservancy for facts on numbers of Peregrines and their prey, and since these were unavailable, Director-General Max Nicholson asked the British Trust for Ornithology to obtain them."

This led to a series of six censuses of the British Peregrine (*Falco peregrinus*) population, which provided key evidence of the environmental impact of organochlorine pesticides, eventually leading to restrictions and bans on the use of DDT and the cyclodienes, and ultimately to the proof that the controls were effective.

Writing fifty-two years after the beginning of the first survey, Derek wrote[2]

> "It was the field data obtained by a large number of voluntary helpers which gave the British Trust for Ornithology's Peregrine Enquiry of 1961-62 the lead in pointing the way to the critical scientific studies of cause and effect. The efforts became truly international, giving rise to global sharing of knowledge of these birds."

Our account of this triumph of conservation science is based not just on the publications in the bibliography but also on the instructions issued to the fieldworkers (Appendices 14.1 & 14.2), material in the British Trust for Ornithology (BTO) archives,

Humphrey Crick's recollections of working with Derek on the 1991 and 2002 surveys, and the recollections of some of Derek's closest fieldwork collaborators.

Faltering first steps

The first mention of the Peregrine Enquiry in BTO papers is of a decision not to undertake it:

> "The Trust had been approached by the Nature Conservancy to run an enquiry if agreement could be reached with the racing pigeon interests. It was suggested that the organisers be I.J. Ferguson-Lees and D. A. Ratcliffe. Since this request, the racing pigeon interests had disclaimed their spokesman. It was agreed that no action should be taken unless a further request was received" (Scientific Advisory Committee (SAC) of the BTO, 12 March 1960).

Although this decision was confirmed by BTO Council on the same day as the SAC, it was quickly reversed: the Council minutes for 30 April 1960 record that "following a further request from the Nature Conservancy, this survey would now take place."

The BTO was, at that time, involved in a number of studies to do with the impact of pesticides on birds, and, given its small size at the time, a survey of Peregrines may have seemed unimportant. It is true that, in his paper reporting on the survey[3], Ratcliffe wrote

> "Yet, by the mid-1950s it was evident [e.g. Ferguson-Lees, 1957[4]] that several southern districts depleted by war-time persecution showed only a partial recovery to the pre-war level of population. By the time the present enquiry was launched in 1961, there were clear signs of decrease in nesting populations in southern England [e.g. Treleaven, 1961[5]], and very few young were being reared by the remaining pairs. In north Wales, northern England and southern Scotland low nesting success became prevalent and was associated with the frequent breakage or disappearance of eggs, and the evidence indicated that these were eaten or otherwise destroyed by the owners themselves [Ratcliffe, 1958[6]]."

It is certainly possible that Derek had concerns about the state of the Peregrine population as early as spring 1960 but he was not present at the SAC meetings and there is no reason why such concerns should have been widespread at that time. After all, Ferguson-Lees' earlier survey[7] had shown a remarkable increase in the population after the war and in 1957 he wrote[4] that "the picture as a whole suggests little alteration over the last seven years", which could have led to a general complacency. Furthermore, Derek's 1958 paper in *British Birds*[6], first mentioning broken eggs in Peregrine eyries, said nothing about low nesting success being prevalent: further, it made no suggestion that the breakage of eggs was an indication of general problems for the species. Indeed, we have found no references to the signs of population reductions in southern England being apparent as early as March 1960.

But if the SAC did not regard the Peregrine survey as important, the Nature Conservancy (NC) obviously did, either because the survey had a high political profile and was therefore a good opportunity to demonstrate to Whitehall just what the volunteer movement could deliver (a matter that Max Nicholson (Fig. 19.2) was always keen on) or because Derek had already begun to suspect that all was not well with the Peregrine population. Whatever the reason, the suggestion at the March SAC meeting that Derek could help organise the survey as part of his professional duties must surely have originated with the NC. Ferguson-Lees was an obvious choice for organiser, given his previous work on the species and the contacts he had established with potential sources of information; he was also a member of the SAC (and soon to be a member of BTO Council). Derek was a much less obvious choice for, although he had been studying Peregrines and other upland birds in various areas since 1945[1,8-10], his only peer-reviewed publication on Peregrines was his 1958 *British Birds* paper[6]. But he and his work were already well known within the NC, for whom he had been working on the 'Highland Vegetation Survey' since 1956[11]. Although Derek's colleague Norman Moore (Fig. 19.3) (who had been appointed as Head of the newly established Toxic Chemicals and Wildlife Section of the Conservancy in 1960[12]), was a member of the SAC, he was not present at the March meeting so we think that, rather than Derek's name being brought up at the meeting, the NC had already offered his help when it asked BTO to undertake the survey. "The upshot was that I ran the Peregrine enquiry as my job. I could hardly believe my good luck – it seemed like a dream come true."[1]. In the event, the NC went even further, also contributing half the costs of the BTO employing an Assistant Secretary to help organise the Peregrine survey and the embryonic Common Bird Census, through a contract to the value of £2,212.

Whatever the origin of Derek's involvement in the BTO Peregrine surveys, it was key to their success. He was willing to use all the available information, whether from birdwatchers, gamekeepers, or egg collectors, and he was able to persuade all sorts of people to provide this information. Those who worked with him, either in the field or through correspondence, speak of his immense practical knowledge (which allowed him to understand the difficulties of fieldworkers and to interpret the sometimes scanty observations that they were able to provide), his generosity in sharing information, and his extraordinary memory of places and events.

Drawing together existing information and a team of helpers

Peregrines are faithful to traditional nesting sites, so the first step was to compile an inventory of these from Ferguson-Lees' survey[7], Derek's own notebooks, and their many contacts[1,3,13]. This allowed fieldwork to be focused on those areas where Peregrines had bred in the past. In regions for which there was little existing information, such as much of the Highlands and Islands of Scotland, fieldworkers searched likely localities on the basis of suitable-looking crags revealed on Ordnance Survey maps at an appropriate distance from known pairs (using the knowledge that nesting Peregrines are usually spaced out at regular intervals)[10]. Letters were sent "to anybody and everybody we think may be able to help" on 1 June 1960, explaining the reasons for the survey, the importance of collaboration of all those who knew about Peregrines, and the impartiality of the BTO.

This last point was important as it was felt that contributors needed to be reassured that their information would be treated in strict confidence and would not be used against the interests of the people supplying the data. Further helpers were recruited through an announcement in the September 1960 issue of *Bird Study*, which was repeated in both the December 1960 and March 1961 issues and in a slightly different form in *British Birds* in March 1961, with a reminder as a footnote to the paper by Treleaven[5] in the April issue. The minutes of the SAC December 1960 meeting refer to a "provision for making small grants to encourage helpers to visit the remoter areas" but this was not referred to in the announcements and it is not clear whether such grants were ever made. The minutes refer also to a letter being prepared for publication in the press, but no copy of this seems to have survived.

The need for professional fieldworkers

Despite the efforts to recruit helpers, it was reported to the SAC in December 1960 that there were still large gaps in planned coverage, especially in western Scotland, Ireland, and parts of Wales. Derek was able to persuade his employers that he needed to undertake much fieldwork, allowing him to apply his long experience with Peregrines in their remote haunts[8-10]. With his NC colleague and friend, Ian Prestt (Fig. 20.1), who also provided assistance in the office (e.g. the Peregrine 1961 July progress report, held in BTO archives), Derek covered his "old stamping grounds in north Wales" and "worked the Scottish Highlands, travelling in the Dormobile for an energetic ten weeks, searching crags where peregrines had nested or might do so."[1] (Fig. 14.1). David Wilson, the BTO's Secretary, who was responsible for the Trust's professional management, fortunately also had the personal experience and enthusiasm to make a substantial contribution to the fieldwork[1,14]. K.D. Smith, the Assistant Secretary, with decades of field experience in Southern Rhodesia and Eritrea[15], also contributed greatly to the fieldwork in both years.

Eventually, over 170 people assisted the enquiry – by visiting nesting places themselves, gathering records from others, or providing information about previous nesting distribution[3]. For its time, and given the nature and remoteness of much of the terrain covered, this was a remarkable army of volunteers.

Geographical scope

The survey was to cover the whole of Great Britain and its nearby islands. As in all subsequent surveys, the Isle of Man was included and the Channel Islands excluded. It was intended to include Ireland but there proved to be too few observers there. In a paper to the SAC in December 1961, after the first year's work, Derek suggested that the plan to cover Ireland fully in 1962 should be dropped, "as this would occupy the organisers for the whole Peregrine season, and even then the complete census would probably not be achieved". His argument that it would be better to concentrate on getting good coverage in Great Britain, with perhaps a few sample areas in Ireland ("to find out whether the decline had set in there") was accepted, though in the event it proved impossible to get enough useful information for Ireland even on a sample basis.

Figure 14.1. Two of the many awe-inspiring Peregrine (*Falco peregrinus*) sites that Derek Ratcliffe visited and surveyed by himself in 1961 or 1962 as part of the BTO's Peregrine Enquiry. The Clo Mor, near Cape Wrath, Sutherland, 1973 (*left*) and Ramasaig Cliff, Isle of Skye, 1992 (*right*). Photos: John Birks

The need for two years' work

It has sometimes been asserted that the survey was extended to 1962 because the results in 1961 were so dramatic as to be almost unbelievable unless confirmed. This is not true. It is clear from committee minutes and from the announcements of the survey during 1960 and 1961 that it was always intended that the fieldwork would extend over two years. The original plan had been to use 1962 to fill the gaps remaining from 1961. In a paper to the December 1961 meeting of the SAC, however, Derek argued that it would be better to repeat the survey in the areas that had been covered in 1961 because "only in this way can the scale and rate of any continuation of the decline be measured" and "as the population is at present in the state of flux it would not in any case be justifiable to add together the results of two lots of different districts in different years to give a composite figure of population for all districts for one year". The committee, which included the outstanding statistician J.A. Nelder[16], rejected this argument on the grounds that a decrease of as much as 30% would be needed to give statistically sound results and that it was important to achieve complete coverage over the two years in order to compare the results with any later survey. Although the decrease between the two years turned out to be so great that it may well have been statistically significant had Derek's proposal been accepted, the committee decision was justified by the results of the work that was done: it provided both good coverage of the whole country and a clear indication of continuing decline.

Aims and methods

It is not possible to count non-breeding Peregrines precisely, so the 1961 survey followed Ferguson-Lees' lead and focused on the size of the breeding population. It aimed to discover both the number of birds and how many of them bred successfully. Information on food was gathered at the request of the NC[3]. Previous detailed studies[17] had shown that each pair of Peregrines appears to hold a breeding territory, which contains one to several nesting cliffs. In making the inventory, the territory (equivalent to a breeding pair) was thus the basic unit for census work, and the nesting cliffs were grouped accordingly[3]. In this account, we follow Derek's usage of the term 'territory' for the area containing all the nesting places of a breeding pair, though we accept that because Peregrines may not defend the whole of that area against conspecifics (the territory in the strict sense) it may be better to use the term 'nesting range' [18,19]. Derek later stated that territories were included in his assessments of the results of the surveys if they appeared to be occupied during spring and early summer, except if the birds were present but not proved to nest in a locality where breeding was previously unknown; such birds were counted only as prospectors within the nonbreeding population[20]. Presumably it was more difficult to do this in the first survey than in later ones because less information was then available about previous use of the territories.

The survey recorded the following for each territory: whether Peregrines were present and breeding, clutch and brood size, whether young flew successfully, the causes of a nesting failure, any other information relevant to breeding biology, and species taken as prey. Extensive instructions and a recording sheet were provided (Appendices 14.1 & 14.2). It is difficult to get instructions for collaborative surveys right first time and, though the 1961-62 instructions were carefully crafted, based on Derek's long experience, they were not perfect. They did not mention, for example, the desirability of making at least three visits to a territory so that late nesting birds are not missed. This also enables one to distinguish non-breeding territory-holders from pairs that fail early, and single birds holding a territory from birds that have lost a mate. Nor was it explained that pairs that fail may move to another site for their replacement clutch, so one has to guard against counting them as two pairs. Because breeding failures were so frequent at this time, such difficulties were particularly great[20].

Discovery of the pesticide connection

Early information

As soon as fieldwork began, it was clear that something was wrong[1,20]. Many territories known to be have been occupied in years gone by were now unoccupied or held only non-breeding pairs or single birds; some pairs that produced eggs failed later. Indeed, one gets the impression from Derek's accounts[1,3,20] that reports of populations being in decline in the late 1950s in southern England and parts of Wales came in while the network of observers for 1961 was being set up. Certainly, Treleaven's April 1961 paper[5] indicated that the population in Cornwall had more or less recovered from severe wartime persecution by 1955 but thereafter had decreased sharply, with few young being produced by the remaining pairs. As editor of *British Birds*, Ferguson-Lees must have seen the paper at least weeks and perhaps months before it was published – he must have known something was wrong!

Pointing the finger at pesticides

There was sufficient evidence of the constancy of Peregrine populations in the historical past that it was not possible to dismiss the emerging decline in the late 1950s as merely a short-term variation. Derek reported the apparent collapse of the Peregrine population in the south to Stanley Cramp, chair of the BTO SAC, halfway through the 1961 field season. Cramp was also chair of the BTO-RSPB (Royal Society for the Protection of Birds) Committee on Toxic Chemicals, which produced its first report that year[21] and he suggested that the new organochlorine insecticides used in agriculture were responsible[1].

The interim results

On 6 July 1961, Derek circulated a report to Cramp, to the BTO president, to five senior officers of the NC, and to his fellow organisers and professional fieldworkers. It is not clear whether other members of the SAC saw this report: there was a discussion about it at the SAC meeting on 11 July but the minutes record only the decline in population, whereas the report itself was more wide-ranging:

> "in view of the 1961 findings the emphasis has clearly shifted and, without pre-judging the … issue, we are now regarding the decline of the Peregrine population as a conservation problem and considering the possible causes. This is particularly so since the most feasible suggestion is that the Peregrine is yet another victim of the toxic chemicals which are at present playing havoc with our wildlife.... Other possibilities will be discussed in a further report which I am preparing… Suggestions for further action will be made therein. The toxic chemical idea will be explored with Dr Moore but until at least good circumstantial evidence is obtained, this explanation of the decline should not be made in any public statement, except as one possibility among others."

A further report was written for the December SAC, confirming that a huge decline in population had taken place and remarking, in relation to the Peregrine's legal status, that "it seems quite likely that it is rapidly becoming a question of conserving a dwindling if not disappearing species." Despite the temptation that there must have been to plunge directly into the issue of toxic chemicals, Derek and the committee stuck to the original plan to use 1962 to complete the basic information on the size of breeding population. As the minutes recorded,

> "It was not felt that special investigations into the causes of the decline would be profitable as the population was too small to carry out tests and bodies were not likely to be found."

Further publicity

The importance that was now accorded to the Peregrine survey is shown by there being three further notices about the survey in *Bird Study* during 1961, briefly reporting on the coverage and preliminary results obtained (including the apparent massive decline in the population), appealing for outstanding information for 1961 to be sent in, and asking for further help in 1962. There was a further appeal for help in *Bird Study* in March 1962, both to cover areas that had not been covered in 1961 and to repeat observations that had been made that year "in order to find out whether the decline has continued, halted or even been reversed".

The March appeal also said that an interim report would be sent out to participants "shortly". We have been unable to trace a copy of this report but it may be that it was the three-page report that was published in *Bird Study* in June, which provided an extensive summary of the results of the 1961 work. It had a table summarising the results and their geographical pattern but it was steadfastly factual: there were no remarks about the magnitude of the population decline being extraordinary or alarming; there were no suggestions as to the possible causes. A press release issued about this report was equally bland. There was clearly some debate, however, as to whether to make any public statements about the possibility that toxic chemicals were involved, for Sheail[22] records that: "Plans to publish a report on the 1961 survey were abandoned by the BTO until more information was available" and what appears to be a copy of this report, entitled 'The Peregrine Enquiry 1961', is held in the BTO archives. Its content is similar to that of the final report of the 1961-62 survey[3], including the reasons for supposing that the population decline had been caused by toxic agrochemicals. Marked "Bird Study" and "PRINTERS COPY", this document clearly got close to being published.

The full results for 1961-62

Establishing the baseline: what was the population in earlier years?

Derek's 1963 paper[3] (Fig. 14.2) is replete with detail and background information, important for a full understanding of the survey results and their significance. He began by reviewing the distribution, habitat, and densities of peregrines breeding in Britain before turning to what he could determine about past population changes. The provision of such important detail was characteristic of the way in which Derek wrote papers, though modern editors are reluctant to allow authors the space to do so.

Population declines evident in 1961-62

Derek knew of 718 territories, of which 60% and 68% were visited in 1961 and 1962, respectively – remarkably good coverage given the remoteness of many of the nesting sites (Fig. 14.1) and the comparatively small number of observers then available. The results were unequivocal: "By 1961, two-fifths of the pre-war population had evidently disappeared ... in 1962 only half the known territories were occupied."[3]

The survey produced much data on the breeding productivity of the remaining Peregrines and, in comparison with the slender evidence from earlier in the century, these suggested that output had declined.

Possible causes of the decline

In his 1963 paper[3] Derek devoted 6½ pages to a detailed and masterly analysis of the possible causes of the decline that the survey had revealed. He reviewed the possible effects of climate change, decreased food supplies, persecution, disease, and agricultural toxic chemicals. It was a brilliant scientific exposition, bearing the hallmark of an outstanding but understated knowledge of Peregrines across the country. His conclusions not only withstood criticism from the spokesmen of the agrochemical industry but have also withstood the test of time[23].

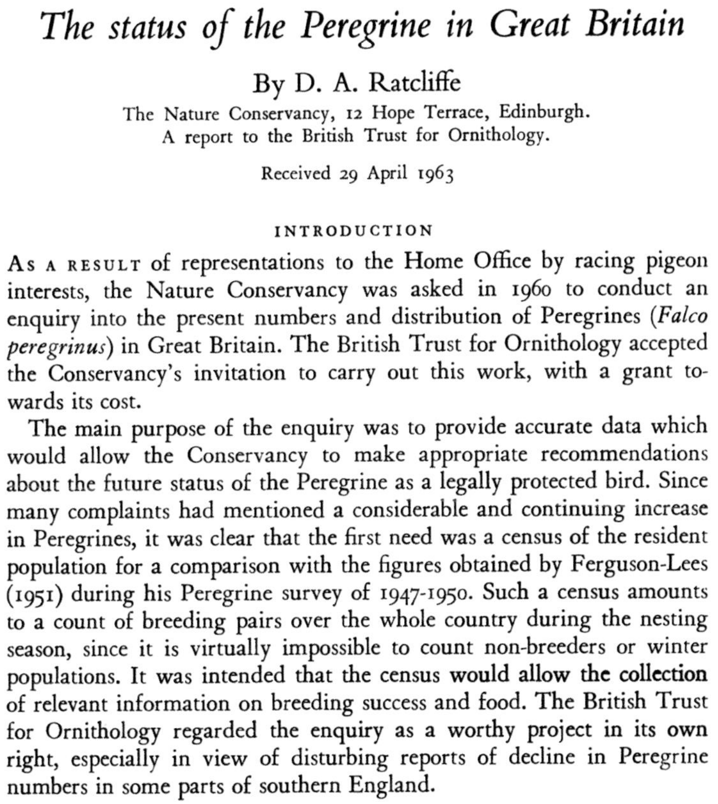

The status of the Peregrine in Great Britain

By D. A. Ratcliffe

The Nature Conservancy, 12 Hope Terrace, Edinburgh.
A report to the British Trust for Ornithology.

Received 29 April 1963

INTRODUCTION

As a result of representations to the Home Office by racing pigeon interests, the Nature Conservancy was asked in 1960 to conduct an enquiry into the present numbers and distribution of Peregrines (*Falco peregrinus*) in Great Britain. The British Trust for Ornithology accepted the Conservancy's invitation to carry out this work, with a grant towards its cost.

The main purpose of the enquiry was to provide accurate data which would allow the Conservancy to make appropriate recommendations about the future status of the Peregrine as a legally protected bird. Since many complaints had mentioned a considerable and continuing increase in Peregrines, it was clear that the first need was a census of the resident population for a comparison with the figures obtained by Ferguson-Lees (1951) during his Peregrine survey of 1947-1950. Such a census amounts to a count of breeding pairs over the whole country during the nesting season, since it is virtually impossible to count non-breeders or winter populations. It was intended that the census would allow the collection of relevant information on breeding success and food. The British Trust for Ornithology regarded the enquiry as a worthy project in its own right, especially in view of disturbing reports of decline in Peregrine numbers in some parts of southern England.

Figure 14.2. Derek Ratcliffe's classic paper of 1963 in *Bird Study* on The status of the Peregrine in Great Britain[3] in which he presented the results of the 1961 and 1962 Peregrine enquiries

Derek referred to the first two reports of the BTO-RSPB Committee on Toxic Chemicals[21,24] and other evidence that showed that birds and other wildlife had been found to be poisoned by toxic chemicals in Britain, from the 1950s onwards. Residues had been found not just in birds apparently poisoned by these chemicals but also in road kills – and many of these were Peregrine prey species. He could point to the recent report that traces of pesticides and their derivatives had been found in an addled Peregrine egg, the only one analysed in Britain thus far[25], noting that the egg came from Scotland, where levels of contamination were likely to be lower than in the south. He suggested, for the first time in print, that the frequent breakage of Peregrine eggs reported in recent years[6] was an effect of pesticide contamination, noting evidence of such effects in domestic fowl.

The clinching argument rested on the data that he had assembled through the survey[3]:

> "The wave-like spread northwards of decline coincides closely with the pattern of use of organic pesticides, both geographically and in time. These substances first came into general use from about 1945 onwards… Since 1950 there has been an ever-growing use of newer, highly poisonous chemicals… Such pesticides were used first and most extensively in the main arable farming and fruit growing districts of south-eastern England, the Home Counties and the Midlands, and these have remained the chief centres of use. But more recently, and particularly through the frequent dressing of seed by seedsmen, these chemicals have become used over the greater part of Britain where arable farming is practised."

Nearly nine pages of the paper were devoted to reviewing the food of Peregrines, partly based on information obtained during the survey, to address the concerns about homing pigeons (*Columba livia*) (the original cause of the survey) and Red Grouse (*Lagopus lagopus scoticus*) (as grouse moor management was associated with much illegal persecution of moorland raptors).

Derek concluded that the number of domestic pigeons being killed by British Peregrines at that time amounted to substantially less than 1% of the total population of homing pigeons. Interestingly, later studies concluded that Peregrines account for 3-4% of the mortality of homing pigeons, though at least 70% of the pigeons taken had already become feral[26].

He concluded that only a small proportion of the available Red Grouse population fell victim to Peregrines. Even now, more than five decades later, the impact of Peregrines on Red Grouse populations is not clear, probably because it varies from place to place and from time to time [20,27].

Developments in the 1960s

The results become known

The reduction in the Peregrine population revealed by the 1961 survey must have been obvious to many of the participants. Such was the drama unfolding that discussions regarding the survey results in the BTO's SAC and elsewhere meant that the results would soon become public. During the winter, the RSPB and the Scottish Home Office requested (and were granted) access to the data to help with negotiations with falconers (SAC minutes, December 1961 and April 1962). The results were enough to convince the Home Office that maximum legal protection for the Peregrine should be maintained indefinitely[22].

The BTO and RSPB jointly organised a conference on birds of prey in Cambridge in March 1963. This was reported briefly in *Bird Study* in the same month and in more detail (with two of the papers in full) in April in *British Birds*[28]. In the summer, *Bird Notes*[29] presented a detailed account of the proceedings. A wide range of parties participated in the conference – naturalists, conservationists, falconers, landowners, sportsmen, gamekeepers, pigeon-fanciers, etc. Reflecting on the conference in *Bird Notes*[29], Michael Woodford (Honorary Secretary of the British Falconers Club) wrote:

> "It was not long before all differences of opinion had been forgotten in the face of the enormity and seriousness of the problem confronting us. Those who had come convinced of the importance of the depredations of gamekeepers and egg collectors quickly realised that these inroads into the stocks of raptors are insignificant compared with the slaughter being occasioned by the use of toxic chemicals on the land."

The pigeon-fanciers were equally convinced: an article starting on the front page of *The Racing Pigeon* for 9 March stated that there was every possibility of the Peregrine soon being wiped out and that, while some pigeon fanciers might feel this to be desirable, the majority disagree, "some very strongly".

International evidence

Although other countries did not have the capacity to mount censuses on the scale that Derek had conducted in Britain, similar losses of Peregrine populations, accompanied by similar suspicions as to the cause, were reported from many other countries[20,23]. Having read Derek's 1963 paper[3] and having begun to think that some of his own observations on the impact of insecticides on birdlife might be being replicated on the broader scale, Joe Hickey (Fig. 14.3) conducted an investigation of Peregrine breeding in the eastern United States in 1964 and found

Figure 14.3. Joe Hickey (1907–93), one of America's leading ornithologists whose work on Peregrines (*Falco peregrinus*) in the United States in 1964 was inspired by Derek Ratcliffe's 1963 paper[3] and who in turn contributed to the idea of measuring eggshell thickness over time using historical collections[34,35].

complete breeding failure[22], even though he thought there were about 300 breeding pairs before 1942[30]. He convened an important international meeting on the species in 1965, bringing together much expertise and further raising the profile of the issues[31]. Derek's paper[32] set the results and interpretation of the 1961-62 survey in a broader context and looked forward:

> "If the use of organochlorine pesticides ... diminishes substantially and is matched by a synchronous recovery in the Peregrine population, circumstantial evidence will be complete."

Enlisting the aid of egg collectors

When Derek first published his 1958 paper[6] on Peregrines breaking their own eggs he suggested that this might be why some were being eaten by the parent birds. Niko Tinbergen pointed out to him that if the eggs had been broken accidentally then they would probably eat them anyway. Derek began to wonder whether the eggs were being broken because their shells had become thinner and, after the international conference, he circulated a draft paper on the subject[23]. Joe Hickey (Fig. 14.3) and Desmond Nethersole-Thompson (Fig. 11.22) pointed out that this idea could be tested by the examination of eggs in museums and private collections. Nethersole-Thompson, a former egg collector, "poured his tremendous energy into opening the doors of the underworld", putting Derek into contact with collectors who allowed him access to illegal collections[33]. On the basis of a massive sample of historical collections Derek made a critically important discovery. The thickness of eggshells had decreased on average by about 20%, beginning in 1947, coinciding with the onset of exposure of British Peregrines to DDT[34,35]. Further such work on Peregrines and other species, combined with laboratory experiments, confirmed a causal connection. It is important not to forget, however, that Derek concluded[1] that

> "the dramatic 'crash' of the British falcon population from 1956-63 was largely the result of these acute toxic affects [of cyclodienes]. No doubt DDT (and perhaps lindane) contributed to the decline through sub-lethal effects, but the bird had lived with these pesticides without declining."

Ian Newton[23] discusses the wider implications of this work, the impact of Derek's classic *Nature* paper[34], and his other major contributions on the impact of pesticides on Peregrines[35,36].

Further surveys in the 1960s

In order to track further changes, Derek asked some of those who had contributed to the survey to continue providing information in subsequent years[37-39]. Over 40 people did so – enough to reveal the broad pattern. However, the sample was haphazard, with a tendency for people to visit territories that were occupied in 1961-62 rather than those that had been abandoned by then. Furthermore, in a rare failure to foresee potential problems arising during volunteer-based surveys, Derek appears not to have foreseen that some observers did not appreciate the importance of distinguishing between 'no observations made' and 'observations made but nothing to report'. It was only in 1965 that Derek requested mildly: "it is a great help if observers, in submitting nil returns for their areas, will list one by one the deserted territories which were examined." This meant that particular care had to be taken in interpreting the earlier results.

Even with those caveats, it appeared that the decline continued in 1963 but stabilised in 1964–67, with regional variations – including a slight recovery in northern regions, following the imposition of restrictions on the use of cyclodiene pesticides in 1962 and further restrictions in 1964. In his 1965 paper[37], Derek was able to add further details to the arguments that he had presented in 1963[3] that the chief reason for the losses in the Peregrine population was the effect of such poisons.

Four more surveys

Continued monitoring

Derek's work on Peregrines during the 1960s was given a great boost when he joined the Toxic Chemicals and Wildlife Section at Monks Wood in 1963. There he was also able to work with people working on small raptors, notably Ian Prestt[40] (Fig. 20.1) (later to become Director General of the RSPB, and one of Derek's closest friends[41]) and others[1,23]. A person of lesser enthusiasm and dedication might have been deflected from organising further Peregrine surveys given new responsibilities – being put in charge of a review of National Nature Reserve acquisitions in 1966 (published in 1977 as the two volume *A Nature Conservation Review,* and edited by Derek[42,43]), and being appointed Deputy Director (Science) of the Nature Conservancy in 1970 (moving to office-based work in London) and by becoming Chief Scientist of the Nature Conservancy Council (NCC) in 1973[1,11]. But not Derek, for he organised surveys in 1971 and 1981, and co-organised another in 1991, two years after his retirement.

Subsequent surveys

By the end of the 1960s, the Peregrine had become a *cause célèbre* because of its decline in many parts of the world, apparently resulting from the use of pesticides. It was therefore thought appropriate to conduct a full census in 1971, not only to establish the exact status of the bird but as a basis for a review of its conservation needs, not least because it was seen as a valuable ecological indicator. Presumably the same applied in 1981, especially as there were indications of significant changes in the population[33,39].

By 1991, although the BTO proposed another survey, some argued that there was no need for another census, because the species was obviously 'out of danger' and resources could be better directed elsewhere. This was a very short-sighted argument against the continued monitoring of a key indicator that was not only at the top of a number of food chains, but also representative of a number of habitats (notably upland and cliff-laden coastal habitats) and regions (outside central and southern England) that were otherwise relatively poorly covered by other monitoring programmes. In fact, the 1981 survey had suggested that the recovery was possibly patchy, so up-to-date information was needed to determine whether further conservation action was needed in some areas. Furthermore, there was renewed pressure from pigeon-racing and game-keeping interests for relaxation of the protection of birds of prey because of their recovery and spread into lowland areas where they were beginning to nest in quarries and man-made structures. Given that the Peregrine recovery was a major conservation success, it was also considered important to document it fully, so the 1991 survey went ahead.

By 2001, it was routinely accepted that government and conservation agencies needed up-to-date figures on Peregrines because the UK supported 12-14% of the European population[44]. However, the outbreak of Foot-and-Mouth disease in the UK, and the resultant restrictions imposed on access to the countryside, meant that it became impossible to carry out the survey in 2001, so it was postponed until 2002[18].

During the 1991 and 2002 surveys, Derek shared his lifetime's collection of Peregrine data to help ensure that the BTO planned and analysed the survey most effectively. During the analysis of the 1991 survey, Humphrey Crick, the BTO organiser of the survey, went through the results site-by-site with Derek, referring to some enormous paper spreadsheets that Derek had created over the years. These held the summary information for each site for each year, entered as data had come in from national surveys, from Derek's own observations, and from observations by his many loyal and trusted correspondents[8]. Derek and Humphrey were thus able to nail down whether a site was new, or simply a new position within an existing territory, or even a budding-off from a previous group of alternative sites to form a new territory. Sometimes the record was, confusingly, a different name and grid location for a pre-existing site; sometimes the grid references had been recorded wrongly and the location was clearly unsuitable (e.g. in the middle of an arable field). They would then consult Derek's huge collection of OS maps[10] to find the likely site, aided by the error usually being the transposition of eastings and northings. They interpreted the observations of the birds, to fit into the standard notation that Derek had established over the years. After the 2002 survey the data from all the surveys was computerised, both to safeguard them and to allow easier analysis in future. Derek spent several days working closely with Rachel Coombes at BTO headquarters to iron out ambiguities in the original data sheets, thus producing a definitive set of data for the Peregrine going back over 50 years. This is a uniquely rich data set for a raptor.

More recent findings

The population breeding in Great Britain in 1971 had increased to over 50% of its pre-war numbers and in 1981 to nearly 90% – and to clearly over 100% in some regions[45]. Thereafter, the national population considerably exceeded the estimate for the 1930s[18,46] (Fig. 14.4).

Where did these additional birds fit in? In some areas at least, the density of the breeding population rose, both through more frequent occupation of territories that had previously been used only occasionally, and through the splitting of territories into two or even three. The extent of the land occupied also increased, with Peregrines using sites never known to have been occupied before, often on small cliffs, quarries,

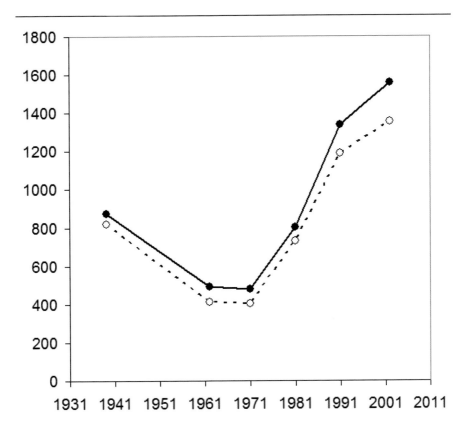

Figure 14.4. Estimated numbers of occupied territories (solid line and solid symbols) of Peregrines (*Falco peregrinus*) in the United Kingdom and Isle of Man and notional pairs (dashed line and open symbols). Some territories appear to be occupied by only a single bird. "Notional pairs" are based on the assumption that half of those territories were in fact occupied by pairs, so that the number of notional pairs is the number of pairs occupying territories minus half the number of territories apparently occupied by just a single bird. The figure is derived from data from the BTO's consolidated Peregrine data set and figures from Ratcliffe[20,45] and from Crick & Ratcliffe[46].

buildings (Fig. 14.5), rocky banks, and even on the ground (Figs. 13.3 & 13.6)[8]. Derek frequently commented that the recovery was "remarkable and quite unexpected at first."

Conclusions

The Peregrine survey of 1961–62 provided the most striking evidence available in the 1960s on the effects of toxic chemicals on wildlife. Prestt & Ratcliffe[47], in their review of the effects of organochlorine insecticides on European birdlife, remarked, it was "only in Britain that sufficiently detailed information on the population of certain bird species is available to show the results these effects (both legal and chronic poisoning) have had on wild populations." Yet no-one in 1960 appears to have thought that a survey of Peregrines had a part to play in the investigations of toxic chemicals – it was, indeed, "a most fortunate accident that the British Trust for Ornithology carried out a survey on the Peregrine Falcon at a time when that species was at its lowest ebb"[12].

Figure 14.5. A Peregrine Falcon (*Falco peregrinus*) in the centre of Bergen, 2011. Peregrines have shown an amazing population recovery in Norway during the last 10–20 years. The Peregrine's recent colonisation of urban habitats in many European cities indicates its considerable adaptability. Its current success is a direct result of Derek Ratcliffes's classic studies on the causes of the decline of the Peregrine in Britain in the 1950s–1960s discussed in this chapter and in Newton[23]. Photo: Kristian Henriksen.

In one of his last papers on Peregrines, 'The peregrine saga'[48], Derek remarks

> "The peregrine has thus shown itself to be a robust and resilient species, capable of living in almost any part of Britain. It has bounced back while many birds of lowland and especially farmland habitats have appeared to be much more sensitive to changes in land use and with bleaker long-term prospects. How ironic if the peregrine proved to be one of the toughest survivors, better able than most species to cope with the environmental vicissitudes of the 21st century."

The Peregrine surveys are a supreme example of the value of collaboration between amateurs and professionals in ornithology (especially when they share a passion for the object of the investigation), between researchers and policymakers, and between voluntary and the statutory organisations. It is likely that Derek, having started his ornithological career as a skilled amateur with a strong background of working with his local natural history societies[1,9], already recognised the value of a close working relationship between the voluntary and statutory sectors. The encouragement provided by Max Nicholson (Fig. 19.2) at the NC gave the firm footing with which to develop this relationship to the benefit of all. The involvement of volunteer fieldworkers allowed surveys to be conducted on a nationwide scale, which was crucial for identifying the problem and its causes. Formal studies aimed at finding out whether pesticide applications had deleterious effects on birds and other non-target species in the 1950s were on far too fine a scale to reveal anything. In the later years, the expertise and training provided by the specialist Raptor Study Groups[49] and the expertise in data curation and analysis at the BTO took forward the national survey process begun by Derek in 1960.

Derek was key to the success of the surveys. His deep knowledge of the species was hugely important for planning the fieldwork, instructing fieldworkers, interpreting the observations, and revealing the causes of the population changes. His success as a survey organiser also rested on his clear respect for the skills, knowledge, and experience of volunteer fieldworkers and his ability to build their trust and gain their respect. Derek was trusted as much for his integrity as a scientist as for his skills, knowledge, experience, and stamina in the field. He visited many of the leading Peregrine enthusiasts annually. During the preparation of this chapter we have received letters from several, who speak of his enthusiasm, his boundless energy, his helpfulness, his understanding of the difficulties involved in fieldwork, and his avid hand-written correspondence – with letters often written after long days in the field[8,10,11,50].

The building of trust was particularly important for the Peregrine research, where so many of those studying the species are unwilling to share, let alone publish, their information because they think that secrecy is the best way protect their birds from persecution. Even Derek sometimes had difficulty persuading people that the value of their data was seriously reduced if they did not provide all the information the survey required. He and his colleagues spent many hours trying to remove ambiguity and imprecision from databases because a few fieldworkers were reluctant to supply full information. Fortunately, he was generally able to persuade people to co-operate: had he been less persuasive, the Peregrine surveys might have failed and the world would have been so much slower to learn of the insidious environmental effects of agrochemicals.

Another element of Derek's success was that he was willing and able to draw on sources of help other than the birdwatchers, including those traditionally seen as enemies of the Peregrine, even those whose activities were sometimes outside the law.

In any long-term investigation, it is crucial to maintain a good database to record the observations carefully. Derek did this, and began long before computers were available. His paper records were so well organised that they were readily transferred to the BTO computer at the time of the 2002 survey.

Finally, we must mention Derek's ability not only to weigh up arguments with meticulous care, but to present the results with great clarity and objectivity. This was as important for the reception of his work by fellow scientists and decision-makers as for the wider audience, many of whom came to be great fans of his writing[51].

Derek was awarded the BTOs Bernard Tucker Medal in 1964 for his outstanding contribution to the scientific work of the Trust (and that merely honoured the first of the five surveys!). The definitive data set for the Peregrine, going back over 50 years, is truly a legacy of incomparable value to the world of conservation – as is the largely thriving population of Peregrines in the nation's skies, a joy that Derek shared with us all (Fig. 14.6).

The Peregrine Falcon

SECOND EDITION

Figure 14.6. Derek Ratcliffe's 1993 classic monograph on *The Peregrine Falcon* (second edition)[20] in which he documents very many aspects of the ecology, behaviour, breeding, migration, population biology and trends, status, and conservation of the Peregrine (*Falco peregrinus*), particularly in Great Britain

DEREK RATCLIFFE

Acknowledgements

We thank Peter Lack and Jan Toomer for much work in extracting relevant material from the BTO archives. For a variety of help we also thank Leo Batten, Ian Carter, Brian Etheridge, James Ferguson-Lees, Geoff Horne, Alan Lauder, Norman Moore, Ian Newton, Chris Rollie, Patrick Stirling-Aird, Sophie Wilcox (Alexander Librarian), Jim Wells, Chris Wilson, David Wilson, and many BTO staff (Rob Fuller, Liz Humphries, John Marchant, Carole Showell, and Chris Wernham).

References

(1)   Ratcliffe, D.A. (2000) *In Search of Nature*. Peregrine Books, Leeds.

(2)   Ratcliffe, D.A. (2003) Foreword. In: *Birds of Prey in a Changing Environment* (eds. D.B.A. Thompson, S. Redpath, A.H. Fielding, M. Marquiss & C.A. Galbraith), pp. xix-xx. The Stationary Office, Edinburgh.

(3)   Ratcliffe, D.A. (1963) The status of the Peregrine in Great Britain. *Bird Study*, **10**, 56-90.

(4)   Ferguson-Lees, I.J. (1957) Peregrine Falcon (*Falco peregrinus*). In: The Rarer Birds of Prey. Their present status in the British Isles (various authors). *British Birds,* **50**, 149-55.

(5)   Treleaven, R.B. (1961) Notes on the Peregrine in Cornwall. *British Birds*, **54**, 136-142.

(6)   Ratcliffe, D.A. (1958) Broken eggs in Peregrine eyries. *British Birds*, **51**, 23-26.

(7)   Ferguson-Lees, I.J. (1951) The Peregrine population of Britain. *Bird Notes*, **24**, 200-205, 309-314.

(8)   Rollie, C.J. (2015) In Galloway and the Borders – in search of an enduring youth. In: *Nature's Conscience – The Life and Legacy of Derek Ratcliffe* (eds. D.B.A. Thompson, H.H. Birks & H.J.B. Birks). This volume, Chapter 13.

(9)   Birks, H.J.B., Thompson, D.B.A. & Birks, H.H. (2015) Derek Ratcliffe – early days in pursuit of nature. In: *Nature's Conscience – The Life and Legacy of Derek Ratcliffe* (eds. D.B.A. Thompson, H.H. Birks & H.J.B. Birks). This volume, Chapter 13.

(10)   Thompson, D.B.A. (2015) Contributions to field ornithology – in search of nesting birds. In: *Nature's Conscience – The Life and Legacy of Derek Ratcliffe* (eds. D.B.A. Thompson, H.H. Birks & H.J.B. Birks). This volume, Chapter 11.

(11)   Birks, H.J.B. & Birks, H.H. (2015) Derek Ratcliffe – botanist and plant ecologist. In: *Nature's Conscience – The Life and Legacy of Derek Ratcliffe* (eds. D.B.A. Thompson, H.H. Birks & H.J.B. Birks). This volume, Chapter 4.

(12)   Moore N.W. (1987) *The Bird of Time. The Science and Politics of Nature Conservation.* Cambridge University Press, Cambridge.

(13)   I.J. Ferguson-Lees, personal communication.

(14)   David Wilson, personal communication.

(15)   Ash, J.S. & Monk, J.F. (1974) K.D. Smith. *Ibis*, **116**, 235 -236.

(16)   Greenwood, J.J.D. (2012) John Nelder: statistics, birdwatching and the Hastings Rarities. *British Birds*, **105**, 733-737.

(17)   Ratcliffe, D.A. (1962) Breeding density in the Peregrine *Falco peregrinus* and Raven *Corvus corax*. *Ibis*, **104**, 13-39.

(18)   Banks, A.N., Crick, H.Q.P., Coombes, R., Benn, S., Ratcliffe, D.A. & Humphries, E.M. (2010) The breeding status of Peregrine Falcons *Falco peregrinus* in the United Kingdom and Isle of Man in 2002. *Bird Study,* **57**, 421-36.

(19) Hardey J., Crick H., Wernham C., Riley, H, Etheridge, B. & Thompson, D. (2013) *Raptors. A Field Guide for Surveys and Monitoring* (3rd edition). The Stationery Office, Edinburgh.

(20) Ratcliffe, D.A. (1993) *The Peregrine Falcon* (2nd edition). Poyser, London.

(21) Cramp, S. & Conder, P. (1961) *Report No. 1 of the B.T.O.-R.S.P.B. Committee on Toxic Chemicals. The deaths of Birds and Mammals connected with Toxic Chemicals in the first half of 1960.* RSPB, London.

(22) Sheail, J. (1985) *Pesticides and Nature Conservation. The British Experience 1950-1975.* Clarendon Press, Oxford.

(23) Newton, I. (2015) Pesticides and birds of prey – the breakthrough. In: *Nature's Conscience – The Life and Legacy of Derek Ratcliffe* (eds. D.B.A. Thompson, H.H. Birks & H.J.B. Birks). This volume, Chapter 15.

(24) Cramp, S., Conder, P.J. & Ash J.S. (1962) *Deaths of Birds and Mammals from Toxic Chemicals.* Royal Society for the Protection of Birds, London.

(25) Moore, N.W. & Ratcliffe, D.A. (1962) Chlorinated hydrocarbon residues in the egg of a peregrine falcon (*Falco peregrinus*) from Perthshire. *Bird Study*, **9**, 242-244.

(26) Shawyer, C. R., Clarke, R. & Dixon, N. (2000) A study into raptor predation of domestic pigeons *Columba livia*. Department of the Environment, Transport and the Regions, London.
Shawyer, C.R., Clarke, R & Dixon, N. (2003) Causes of racing pigeon (*Columba livia*) losses, including predation by raptors, in the United Kingdom. In: *Birds of Prey in a Changing Environment* (eds. D.B.A. Thompson, S.M. Redpath, A.H. Fielding, M. Marquiss & C.A. Galbraith). pp. 263-267. The Stationery Office, Edinburgh.

(27) Redpath, S.M. & Thirgood, S.J. (1997) *Birds of Prey and Red Grouse.* The Stationery Office, London.
UK Raptor Working Group. (2000) *Report of the UK Raptor Working Group.* DETR, Bristol & JNCC, Peterborough.
Watson, A. & Moss, R. (2008) *Grouse.* Collins, London.

(28) Anon. (1963) *British Birds*, **56**.

(29) Anon. (1963) *Bird Notes*, **30**, 205-219.

(30) Hickey, J.J. & Anderson, D.W. (1969) The Peregrine Falcon: life history and population literature. In: *Peregrine Falcon Populations: Their Biology and Decline* (ed. J.J. Hickey), pp. 3-42. University of Wisconsin Press, Madison.
Hickey, J.J. (1942) Eastern population of the Duck Hawk. *Auk*, **59**, 176-204.

(31) Hickey, J.J. (ed.) (1969) *Peregrine Falcon Populations: Their Biology and Decline.* University of Wisconsin Press, Madison.

(32) Ratcliffe, D.A. (1969) Population trends of the Peregrine Falcon in Great Britain. In: *Peregrine Falcon Populations: Their Biology and Decline* (ed. J.J. Hickey), pp. 239-269. University of Wisconsin Press, Madison.

(33) Ratcliffe, D.A. (1980) *The Peregrine Falcon.* Poyser, Calton.

(34) Ratcliffe, D.A. (1967) Decrease in eggshell weight in certain birds of prey. *Nature*, **215**, 208-210.

(35) Ratcliffe, D.A. (1970) Changes attributable to pesticides in egg breakage frequency and eggshell thickness in some British birds. *Journal of Applied Ecology*, **7**, 67-115.

(36) Ratcliffe, D.A. (1965) Organo-chlorine residues in some raptor and corvid eggs from northern Britain. *British Birds*, **58**, 65-81.

(37) Ratcliffe, D.A. (1965) The Peregrine situation in Great Britain 1963-64. *Bird Study*, **12**, 66-82.

(38) Ratcliffe, D.A. (1967) The Peregrine situation in Great Britain 1965-66. *Bird Study*, **14**, 238-246.

(39) Ratcliffe, D.A. (1972) The Peregrine population of Great Britain in 1971. *Bird Study*, **19**, 117-156.

(40) Prestt, I. (1965) An enquiry into the recent breeding status of some smaller birds of prey and crows in Britain. *Bird Study*, **12**, 196-221.

(41) Housden, S. (2015) Fighting for wildlife – from the inside. In: *Nature's Conscience – The Life and Legacy of Derek Ratcliffe* (eds. D.B.A. Thompson, H.H. Birks & H.J.B. Birks). This volume, Chapter 20.

(42) Ratcliffe, D.A. (ed.) (1977) *A Nature Conservation Review, Volumes 1 and 2*. Cambridge University Press, Cambridge.

(43) Thompson, D.B.A., Sutherland, W. & Birks, H.J.B. (2015) Nature conservation and the Nature Conservation Review – a new philosophical framework. In: *Nature's Conscience – The Life and Legacy of Derek Ratcliffe* (eds. D.B.A. Thompson, H.H. Birks & H.J.B. Birks). This volume, Chapter 19.

(44) Greenwood J.J.D., Crick, H.Q.P. & Bainbridge I.P. (2003) Numbers and international importance of raptors and owls in Britain and Europe. In: *Birds of Prey in a Changing Environment* (eds. D.B.A. Thompson, S. Redpath, A.H. Fielding, M. Marquiss & C.A. Galbraith), pp. 25-49.The Stationery Office, Edinburgh.

(45) Ratcliffe, D.A. (1984) The Peregrine breeding population of the United Kingdom in 1981. *Bird Study*, **31**, 1-18.
Ratcliffe, D.A. (1988) The Peregrine population of Great Britain and Ireland. In: *Peregrine Falcon Populations. Their Management and Recovery* (eds. T.J. Cade, J.H. Enderson, C.G. Thelander & C.M. White), pp. 147-157. The Peregrine Fund, Boise.

(46) Crick, H.Q.P. & Ratcliffe, D.A. (1995) The Peregrine *Falco peregrinus* breeding population of the United Kingdom in 1991. *Bird Study*, **42**, 1-19.

(47) Prestt, I. & Ratcliffe, D.A. (1972) Effects of organochlorine insecticides on European birdlife. In: *Proceedings of 15th International Ornithological Congress* (ed. K.H. Voous), pp. 486-513. Brill, Lieden.

(48) Ratcliffe, D.A. (2003) The peregrine saga. In: *Birds of Prey in a Changing Environment* (eds. D.B.A. Thompson, S. Redpath, A.H. Fielding, M. Marquiss & C.A. Galbraith), pp. 91-98. The Stationary Office, Edinburgh.

(49) Etheridge, B., Riley, H.T., Wernham, C.V., Holling, M. & Stevenson, A. (2013) *Scottish Raptor Monitoring Scheme Report 2011*. Scottish Raptor Study Groups: Inverness.

(50) Marren, P. (2015) Derek and I: A correspondence. In: *Nature's Conscience – The Life and Legacy of Derek Ratcliffe* (eds. D.B.A. Thompson, H.H. Birks & H.J.B. Birks). This volume, Chapter 27.

(51) Lawton, J. (2015) Foreword. In: *Nature's Conscience – The Life and Legacy of Derek Ratcliffe* (eds. D.B.A. Thompson, H.H. Birks & H.J.B. Birks). This volume.

Appendix 14.1: Instructions for the 1961-62 survey

BRITISH TRUST FOR ORNITHOLOGY

PEREGRINE ENQUIRY 1967

Notes on Questionnaire

A. Census

The main purpose of the enquiry is to find out the number of breeding pairs of Peregrines in Britain (and, if possible, Ireland as well) and to show, by comparison with previous records, whether this number has changed in recent years. It is being organised by Dr. D. A. Ratcliffe and I. J. Ferguson-Lees, assisted by K. D. Smith.

A pair of Peregrines can only be proved to breed when their nest with eggs or young is actually seen. If a regularly occupied nesting place is visited and one or both birds are about but no nest can be seen, relevant particulars should be given. It may be that the nest is inaccessible though clearly indicated by the birds' behaviour; that eggs have yet to be laid; or that the eggs or young have been taken or destroyed. In the last two cases, the birds' behaviour will be inconclusive and only one of the pair may be present. If neither of the pair can be found at a regular haunt it may also be that the time is too early for eggs or that the nest has failed, but, in addition, it may mean that one or both have been destroyed; that the birds are nesting at an alternative crag; that the birds are present in the territory but not attempting to nest; or that the territory is completely deserted.

If no bird is to be seen at a favourite nesting crag, search should be made for castings and pluckings or kills under old eyries and on perching places, as the place may (for one of the above reasons) be being used only as a roost at the time. Such traces may, however, appear at a crag when the nest is at an alternative cliff. Peregrines are tight sitters when incubation is advanced and may easily escape detection at this stage.

In short, for each Peregrine territory the observer should try to find out

> (a) whether Peregrines have actually nested (i.e. laid eggs) and with what success;

(b) whether Peregrines have been present during the breeding season but without nesting;

(c) whether Peregrines are completely missing.

When a pair of Peregrines lays eggs but the nest later fails, the reason for failure should be stated if known with certainty. Evidence in recent years has shown that many nests have failed when there has been no suspicion of human interference, and failure should not be put down to egg-collecting, shooting, etc., without good reason. In particular, careful watch should be kept for traces of broken eggs in or below the eyrie, and any such signs noted. Eggs are particularly liable to disappear one by one during incubation.

The limits of the census area should be accurately defined, using boundaries which may be traced on the 1" O.S. map. It would be appreciated if the exact location of nesting crags could be given, and the use of O.S. grid references is by far the best way of avoiding confusion in this respect. All such details will be treated as strictly confidential and will not be made available to anyone but the two organisers and the few officials of the Trust who are closely connected with the enquiry.

B. **Non-breeding birds**

It frequently happens that when both occupants of an eyrie are in sight, a third bird appears on the scene, only to disappear later. These instances should be noted, together with the reaction of the occupants towards the intruder.

It is also desirable to know whether, as seems probable, settled pairs of Peregrines stay in their territories throughout the year, using their nesting crags or other rocks as roosts; or whether they move away to other areas. Out of the nesting season Peregrines may spend the whole day farther afield, returning only to their roosts towards dusk, but castings and traces of kills will usually be found at these roosts. Information is thus also needed about the distribution of the species during autumn and winter, and about the presence of non-breeding birds during nesting time.

C. **Food**

Peregrines are more often seen in pursuit of prey than actually making a "kill". Such chases should be recorded, but it should not be presumed that they will be successful. Peregrines often appear to pursue birds without pressing home their attack and then finally abandon the chase, evidently because they do not intend to kill; this particularly happens as a displacement activity when they are disturbed at the eyrie.

Prey remains are most usually to be found as pluckings or dismembered bodies on prominent buttresses, blocks, pinnacles, etc., around the eyrie when there are eggs, and on the eyrie when there are young. If there is any shadow of doubt about identity of the victim, the remains should be sent, with details, to Dr. D. A. Ratcliffe. Kills found away from the nesting crags should be disregarded, unless they are undoubtedly known to be the work of Peregrines, as they may have been made by other predators. Whenever possible, the numbers of separate individuals of each prey species should be given, though this may at times be difficult or even impossible. If homer rings are found at eyries it is important to record the date stamped on the ring.

Any other relevant information not covered by the questionnaires would be welcomed, and all questionnaires should be returned to Dr. D. A. Ratcliffe, c/o British Trust for Ornithology' 2 King Edward Street, Oxford, before the end of October 1961.

Appendix 14.2: The 1961-62 recording form - summary

Page one of the form had boxes for:

1.   Observer's name and address

2.   Census area: (a) county or counties, (b) exact limits of area covered

3.   How many pairs of Peregrines were proved to breed in the census area (i.e. how many eyries were known to contain eggs or young)?

4.   How many pairs were only suspected of breeding (i.e. both birds seen at some time during the nesting season, but no nest located)?

5.   How many pairs were known to breed in the census area in previous years?

6.   How many pairs known to breed in previous years were: (a) represented by only a single bird or (b) apparently completely missing?

Page two of the form ("Details of nesting places and eyries") *had columns for recording observations* (including potential repeat visits to sites). These were:

1.   Name of locality and OS grid reference (alternative crags of the same pair should be included)

2.   Date of visit

3.   Nest contents (eggs/young)

4.   Number of young reared to flying stage

5.   Cause of unsuccessful breeding

6.   Other observations if no nest found (birds seen or absent, any evidence for breeding)

7.   Whether occupied regularly in previous years (dates if possible)

8.   General description of site with position of eyrie on cliff (distance from top and bottom) and type of rock

Page three of the form had boxes for:

1.   Non-breeding birds - Please give details (dates should always be given) of

(a) extra birds seen about an occupied eyrie

(b) unpaired birds habitually frequenting certain places not known as nesting haunts

(c) any records of juvenile birds

2.   Food

(a) Observations of hunts by Peregrines, stating place, date and time of day, species chased, whether successful (kill actually seen) or unsuccessful

(b) Observations of prey remains (see notes), stating place (including whether a nesting haunt or not), date, species of bird and numbers of individuals (when possible); unidentified or doubtful feathers and remains of kills should be collected, labelled as above and sent to the organisers

15. Pesticides and birds of prey - the breakthrough

Ian Newton

Introduction

No-one who was familiar only with the earlier research of Derek Ratcliffe – mainly botanical[1] – would have guessed that he would come to be a key player in assessing the impacts of pesticides on birds. Derek is now widely known for his pioneering work on organochlorine pesticides, and as the discoverer of shell thinning. Yet his involvement came largely through his life-long love of the Peregrine Falcon (*Falco peregrinus*) (Fig. 14.5) in the wild[2] rather than of biochemistry or agriculture, as chronicled in detail in his classic book on the species[3].

Organochlorines (or chlorinated hydrocarbons) formed the first major group of synthetic pesticides to be introduced into widespread agricultural use as insecticides during the 1940s and 1950s, not only in Britain but also over much of the world. They were found to have devastating impacts on birds and mammals, especially in some species of predators. Derek played such a crucial role in marshalling the early evidence against these chemicals that it is hard to imagine how the story would have unfolded without his persistent interest, involvement, and dedication.

The organochlorines included the famous insecticide DDT, which was used during the Second World War to control arthropod parasites of humans, thus controlling the spread of typhus and other arthropod-borne diseases. The problems began in the late 1940s when DDT and a related compound, gamma-BHC (or lindane), came into wider use in the countryside to combat insect pests of farm crops and mosquitoes and other insect-vectors of human diseases. While extremely toxic to insects, these chemicals were relatively harmless to birds and mammals (apart from cats which proved sensitive to DDT). In a bird or mammal body, DDT is rapidly converted to its metabolite DDE, and it is this compound which is most often detected in body tissues. In the late 1950s, another group of organochlorine chemicals, the cyclodienes, were introduced for similar purposes. These included aldrin, dieldrin, and heptachlor epoxide, which were very effective as insecticides, but turned out to be far more poisonous than DDT to mammals and birds. Within the animal body, aldrin is rapidly metabolised to dieldrin, which is often denoted as HEOD.

Several characteristics combined to make these chemicals effective as pesticides, but environmentally problematic. First, they were chemically extremely stable, and could last unchanged for months, even years, in the environment. Second, they were highly fat-soluble, so could accumulate in animal bodies, and readily pass from prey to predator. Predators could thereby obtain a toxic dose through accumulating a series of lower sub-lethal doses from the various prey animals they ate. Third, the stability of these chemicals enabled them to spread widely in air or water currents, or in animal bodies, reaching areas hundreds of kilometres from where they were manufactured or applied. This became shockingly apparent in the 1960s when DDE residues were detected in the bodies of penguins and other seabirds of the Southern Ocean[4].

Another group of organochlorines had been produced since the 1930s, but in the 1960s were also discovered to be widespread in the environment. They were the poly-chlorinated biphenyls (PCBs), industrial chemicals used widely in plastics, lubricants, and insulating materials. Because these compounds were chemically similar to the organochlorine pesticides, fears were raised that they may also be having adverse effects on animal life. All this knowledge was accumulated over a number of years. First though, let us step back and look at how Derek Ratcliffe encountered and tackled some of the problems.

Early Days

The Peregrine surveys 1961 and 1962

From Derek's perspective, the story began in 1960 when complaints from pigeon fanciers that Peregrines were increasing and eating their birds reached a new crescendo, especially in the mining valleys of south Wales which had long been a stronghold of 'the fancy'. A petition sent to the Home Office requested the removal of legal protection from the Peregrine, so that falcons could be killed to reduce the losses of homing pigeons. Eventually, the British Trust for Ornithology (BTO) was asked to provide up-to-date information on the species, and Derek was invited to become the organiser of a national survey[5]. Many people became involved, and in the spring of 1961 an attempt was made to check as many of the known nesting sites as possible to assess occupancy, breeding success, and food. The pigeon fanciers had claimed that Peregrines were increasing, but some ornithologists had noted local declines, for example in Cornwall[6].

In fact, the 1961 survey revealed that the Peregrine was in dire trouble over much of the country. It had almost disappeared from southern England and parts of Wales, had much declined in northern England and southern Scotland, and locally also in the northern parts of Scotland. Overall, nearly half the known territories appeared deserted, many for the first time on record. Some of the remaining territories were occupied by single birds, and in those occupied by pairs, breeding success was poor[5]. A repeat, but fuller, survey in 1962 revealed that the situation had worsened. Hitherto, in the absence of human persecution, Peregrine populations had remained remarkably stable, and many of the territories now deserted were formerly known to have been occupied year after year[3,5].

The emerging picture was in marked contrast to that painted by the pigeon fanciers, whose request for a change in the legal status of the species was denied. The focus switched instead to finding the cause of this unprecedented and rapid decline in Peregrine numbers[5].

Causes of the Peregrine crash

Several potential causes, such as human persecution, prey collapse, and disease, were rapidly ruled out, and attention focused on a different issue. During 1956-1960, thousands of birds of various species were found dead and dying in recently-sown cereal fields across Britain. This occurred mainly in spring, where the grains had been dressed with some newly-released pesticides, the cyclodiene compounds. The aim was to protect the sown grains against insect attack, reducing the losses for farmers. But it turned out that these pesticides were also extremely toxic to birds and mammals, killing many that fed on treated grains spilled on the soil surface. The birds usually died in convulsions, yet were otherwise in good condition, and chemical analyses revealed the presence of HEOD residues in their body tissues.

Affected species included not only seed eaters, such as finches, buntings, sparrows, corvids, pigeons, and game birds, but also raptors, such as the Sparrowhawk (*Accipiter nisus*) and the Kestrel (*Falco tinnunculus*), which fed on the dying birds. They also included various owls and many Red Foxes (*Vulpes vulpes*). The many thousands of birds found dead around arable land were assumed to form a tiny proportion of the total killed, and the situation can be exemplified by an account from an informant from Tunstall in Norfolk: "The place is like a battlefield. My keeper has found innumerable corpses, including masses of small birds … this slaughter … is going on all around here and quite apart from the game, the destruction of wildlife is quite pitiful". Records of this unprecedented mortality were collected by the BTO, the Royal Society for the Protection of Birds (RSPB), and (from 1963) the Game Research Association, and published in two influential reports edited mainly by Stanley Cramp[7,8]. It seemed that, for a number of wild bird species, these new seed dressings had become a serious mortality factor over large parts of Britain. Could the same phenomenon have affected Peregrines, which were much less common, and less easily noticed? In fact, a few Peregrine carcasses were found around this time, but their significance was not appreciated, and they were not examined.

We can assume that many seed-eating birds died away from the fields, and others that had obtained only sub-lethal doses would have survived – but for a time carried the poison in their bodies. Some of these contaminated prey individuals could have been killed and eaten by Peregrines and other predators away from arable land. The notion that Peregrines could obtain residues in this way was soon settled by Derek, when he obtained addled eggs from a Peregrine eyrie in Glen Almond in Perthshire in 1961. One was analysed and found to contain small amounts of HEOD (from aldrin and dieldrin), DDE (from DDT), heptachlor epoxide, and gamma BHC. This finding proved, at once, that a Peregrine nesting in hill country far distant from arable land could accumulate organochlorine residues through feeding on contaminated prey[5].

Other circumstantial evidence pointed to the notion that organochlorines could have been associated with the crash in Peregrine numbers. The decline in their breeding numbers had been most marked in or near arable districts, and least marked in areas such as the Scottish Highlands, further removed from arable land. In addition, the population crash had coincided in time with the widespread introduction of cyclodienes in agriculture.

In the face of the evidence on wild bird deaths, the Government's Advisory Committee on Pesticides and other Toxic Chemicals recommended, in July 1961, that a voluntary ban be placed on the use of cyclodienes for spring-sown cereal dressings. The risk was judged to be greater from spring than autumn sowings, but nevertheless the autumn use of cyclodienes was restricted to districts where cereals were at greatest risk from Wheat Bulb Fly (*Delia coarctata*) larvae (which hatch in the soil and attack the young plants). The following spring (1962) there was clearly a marked reduction in bird deaths around cereal fields, compared with previous years. Nevertheless, the downward trend in Peregrine numbers continued for at least two more years, and eggs collected from 13 eyries in 1963 were all found to contain various organochlorine residues. Moreover, a male Peregrine found dead on its nest on Lundy Island off the Devon coast, in June 1963, proved to have in its fresh liver 70 ppm DDE, 4.0 ppm HEOD, 1.5 ppm heptachlor epoxide, and 2.0 ppm BHC. These combined levels were considered by some to form a lethal dose, lending weight to the suspicion that enhanced mortality could have been a major factor in the population crash.

The Peregrine survey in 1964[5] revealed no further decline in numbers – providing the first encouraging sign after the ban of cyclodienes from 1962 on spring-sown cereals. From then on, nest surveys and the collection of addled eggs for analysis were undertaken annually by volunteers, enabling the population trends to be monitored in relation to trends on organochlorine levels.

Eggshell thinning

For some years, beginning before the population crash, Derek had been obsessively puzzled by the appearance of broken eggs in Peregrine eyries. He and others had witnessed Peregrines eating their own broken eggs[9]. In mid 1966, he prepared a note on egg breaking and circulated it to friends for comment. He considered a number of explanations for the phenomenon, including a decrease in eggshell thickness – for which he had no evidence. Two of the readers, Desmond Nethersole-Thompson (Fig. 11.22) (working in the Scottish Highlands) and Joseph Hickey (Fig. 14.3) (in the USA), encouraged Derek to check this possibility by comparing recent with earlier eggs available in museums and private collections. With enthusiastic help from Desmond (a former egg-collector), who revealed in confidence the names and addresses of egg collectors he had known in the past, Derek set about this daunting task. As shell weight was likely to vary with the size of the egg, as well as the thickness of the shell, Derek devised an index of relative shell weight, assessed as actual weight (mg)/length x breadth (mm) (i.e. size). This value was based on three measurements that could be readily obtained from precious shells in collections without damaging them. It was subsequently adopted widely, and became known as 'The Ratcliffe index'. As well as Peregrines, Derek examined eggs of other species, and found reduced shell indices in the Sparrowhawk (17%), Merlin (*Falco columbarius*) (13%), Golden Eagle (*Aquila chrysaetos*), (10%), Hobby (*Falco subbuteo*) (5%), and Kestrel (5%) among the raptors, and also in Shag (*Phalacrocorax aristotelis*) (12%),

Rook (*Corvus frugilegus*) (5%), and Carrion Crow (*Corvus corone*) (5%). On the other hand, no evidence of significant shell thinning emerged for Buzzard (*Buteo buteo*), Raven (*Corvus corax*), Guillemot (*Uria aalge*), Razorbill (*Alca torda*), Kittiwake (*Rissa tridactyla*), Black-headed Gull (*Chroicocephalus ridibundus*), Golden Plover (*Pluvialis apricaria*), or Greenshank (*Tringa nebularia*). Among the group showing thinning, accurate dating of the change was possible only for the Sparrowhawk. In the other species, either the degree of thinning was too small or samples were too few to date the change precisely, although it seemed to have occurred sometime between 1946 and 1952. This was around the time that DDT and gamma-BHC came into wide agricultural use, but clearly pre-dated the introduction of the cyclodienes. Derek wondered if these other less toxic organochlorines could be responsible. Prior to this period, shell indices had been remarkably constant for these various species, in some extending back into the 19th century.

Derek's paper describing shell thinning in the Peregrine and others was published in *Nature*[10], followed three years later by a much more detailed assessment, extending to a wider range of species, in the *Journal of Applied Ecology*[11]. Both papers quickly became what would now be called 'citation classics', stimulating much further work on eggshells around the world. His pioneering findings were thus replicated in region after region, wherever organochlorine pesticides had been used.

While DDT did not come into widespread farm-use in Britain until 1948, military stockpiles flooded onto the market after the war ended in 1945, and found broad-scale use in domestic, horticultural, and veterinary applications.

> "As early as March 1946 the Racing Pigeon magazine carried an advertisement for a DDT formulation suitable for controlling ectoparasites on homers. So the most likely route from a DDT pack to a Peregrine was marvellously simple and direct: the dusted homers carried it straight there on their bodies"[3].

During his visits to Peregrine eyries, Derek collected any pigeon rings present, and kept them in sealed containers along with details of date and site. Some of these rings were later analysed for organochlorines. Most gave a blank result, but two rings yielded minute traces of DDT and DDE, one from Galloway in 1947 and the other from Snowdonia in 1956. In at least the latter, the residue could have come from an agricultural source.

Further evidence on the start of DDT/DDE contamination in Peregrines was provided by David Peakall, who analysed solvent rinsings from Peregrine eggs collected over the critical period. Three clutches collected in 1933, 1936, and 1946 showed no trace of residues, but a second clutch for 1946 contained traces of DDE. Four out of five clutches taken in 1947 from various localities also contained DDE; and eight further clutches taken in 1948-1952 all contained DDE[12]. It thus emerged that DDE contamination first appeared in Peregrine eggs during the years 1946-1948, matching the start of shell thinning in this species.

Population recovery

The use of aldrin and dieldrin as seed dressings continued on a reduced scale until it was finally banned in 1975, a time when less formal restrictions were also placed on DDT. All the restrictions on organochlorines in Britain were 'voluntary', until European Commission (EC) regulations in 1979 made them mandatory. All remaining uses of cyclodiene pesticides were ended in 1981, and DDT was banned the following year, except for emergency use on cutworms. The uses of the offending organochlorines in Britain had therefore been progressively reduced over a period of more than 20 years, rather than as a one-off ban as in some other countries. In a total of 550 Peregrine eggs from 449 clutches analysed during 1963-1986, only one egg, from the central Highlands in 1984, had no detectable DDE, and only 6% of all eggs had no detectable HEOD[13]. Residues were still found in Peregrine and other raptor eggs until the end of the century when the programme ended, a testimony to the persistence of these chemicals in the natural environment.

From the low point in 1963-1964, the recovery of Peregrine numbers took place steadily over the next 30 years or so[5]. It was first evident in the north and west, in areas where the birds were least affected, and then gradually spread south and east, with the areas from which the birds had totally disappeared being the last to be re-colonised. In terms of numbers, recovery was virtually complete by 1985, but in many areas numbers exceeded their 1930-1939 base-line levels, and re-colonisation of the south-east was still incomplete until well into the 1990s. Some coastal sites in the north and west also remained unoccupied (Fig. 14.1), with contamination of the marine environment with organochlorines (including PCBs) suggested as a continuing problem. The overall recovery of the Peregrine population was associated with a progressive reduction in residue levels in eggs, and with improved shell thickness and productivity[1,13]. These events thus added to the body of evidence that organochlorines were the major cause of this entire phenomenon.

Even Golden Eagles (Fig. 12.4), living all their lives in hill country away from arable land, did not escape organochlorines, and showed shell thinning. For a time, DDT, gamma-BHC, and then dieldrin were used in dips to kill insect parasites on the skin and wool of sheep. It transpired that these chemicals were absorbed through the skin into the flesh of the sheep. Golden Eagles, feeding on sheep carrion, were found to be contaminated by all these chemicals which appeared in their eggs along with other organochlorines[14]. But it is not known to what extent organochlorines affected either the eagles or the many people in Britain who ate sheep meat at the time. This study, in which Derek was also involved, gave further concern about the organochlorines[14].

Despite every effort by the agricultural and agro-chemical lobbies to discredit the evidence, pressure to phase out the organochlorines gradually mounted. Arising from Derek Ratcliffe's pioneering start[3], and the publication of Rachel Carson's *Silent Spring*[15] in 1962, concern against the organochlorines soon became global, and the recovery of raptor populations became a *cause célèbre* of the growing conservation movement[5,16].

Other Developments

During the early years of his research, Derek was based at Monks Wood Experimental Station near Huntingdon, in the Pesticides and Toxic Chemicals group headed by Norman Moore (Fig. 19.3). The Station was established partly in response to the farmland bird deaths that had occurred in the 1950s, and from 1963 a programme was set up to analyse the carcasses and eggs of birds. Initially a wide range of species was examined, drawn from terrestrial, freshwater, and marine habitats. Contamination with organochlorines proved almost universal, with the greatest levels in predators (results later summarised[17]). Thereafter, analyses were concentrated on the carcasses of dead raptors and fish-eating birds provided by members of the public, together with the eggs of selected species, such as Peregrine, Golden Eagle, Sparrowhawk, and Gannet (*Morus bassanus*). This programme provided a means to follow trends in residue levels over the years in various vulnerable species[18]. It is unfortunate that it began only after the main period of cyclodiene use was over, and after the population crashes had occurred, but it nevertheless continued to yield some Sparrowhawks and Peregrines with lethal HEOD levels into the mid 1970s. Residues of HEOD and DDE continued to be found at reducing levels in birds of prey for several further decades, a testimony to the persistence of these chemicals in the natural environment.

More on eggshell thinning

The publication of Derek's first paper[10] on shell thinning stimulated a flurry of similar work elsewhere. In North America, Hickey and Anderson[19] showed the existence of shell thinning in Peregrines there also dated to the late 1940s. They went on to demonstrate the same phenomenon in at least twelve other raptors, and nine species of other birds. The proposed role of organochlorines in eggshell thinning was subsequently confirmed by experiments on captive birds[20-22]. While DDT/DDE caused shell thinning, this was not so for gamma-BHC, or for any other organochlorine pesticides or PCBs. In the American Kestrel (*Falco sparverius*), the correlative relationship between the DDE concentration in the egg and the degree of shell thinning was the same in experimentally dosed captive birds as in wild ones[23]. This not only validated the experimental testing, but also showed that DDE on its own could cause the effect.

By the 1960s it was clear that Sparrowhawks had declined catastrophically in most parts of Britain, impressions confirmed for this and other raptors in a survey organised by Ian Prestt (Fig. 20.1), also working from Monks Wood[24]. I was given the opportunity to work on Sparrowhawks in 1971, initially in south-west Scotland where reasonable numbers remained, but later covering other areas. Within a few years, Derek had become Chief Scientist in the Nature Conservancy Council, based in London. This position gave him little time for research, but he encouraged me to understand more of the pesticide impacts on Sparrowhawks and to gain greater information on shell thinning. We spent occasional days in the field together which involved checking Peregrine nest sites, but also (for me) long and helpful discussions. Within each clutch Derek had treated each egg as statistically independent, yet my work in south Scotland (with Jim Bogan of the Glasgow Veterinary School) had shown that eggs from the same clutch (laid by the same female) had very similar shell indices and organochlorine contents[25]. This meant that each egg could not be considered statistically independent from others in the same clutch. But it also meant that single eggs could be considered as representative, in these respects, of the entire clutch from which they came. So from then on, in graphs and statistical analyses, I used average values for each clutch, regardless of the number of eggs obtained and analysed. Using this procedure on the eggs that Derek had examined greatly reduced the number of data points, and it was clear that much larger samples of eggs were needed if we were to gain a fuller picture of the patterns of shell thinning across the country, and if the dates of shell thinning in different species were to be determined more precisely.

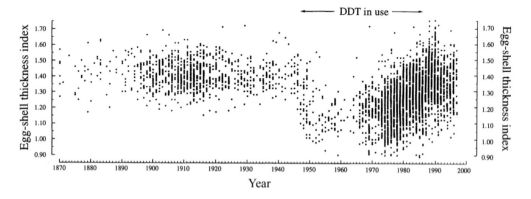

Figure 15.1. Shell thickness indices of the British Sparrowhawk (*Accipiter nisus*) 1870-1997 in Britain soon after which the research programme came to an end. Shells became thin abruptly from 1947, following the widespread introduction of DDT in agriculture, and recovered from the 1970s, following progressive restrictions in the use of the chemical, which was banned altogether from 1981. Each spot represents the mean shell index of a clutch (or part-clutch), and more than 2000 clutches are represented from all regions of Britain. Shell index was measured as shell weight (mg)/shell length x breadth (mm). (Extended from Newton[25]).

Derek generously gave me all his data on eggshells, together with the names and addresses of egg collectors (in confidence) who had been helpful. From these people, and my correspondence and meetings with Desmond Nethersole-Thompson (Fig. 11.22), I gained other contacts, and also visited all the main provincial museums in Britain that held egg collections to weigh and measure the eggs of Sparrowhawk, Peregrine, Merlin, and other raptors. At that time, most of the egg collectors I met were educated professional people, and not a single one denied me access to his collection, including recently taken specimens! By 1990, I had sampled eggs from more than 2,000 Sparrowhawk clutches (Figs. 15.1 & 15.2), drawn from every county in Britain, and had greatly added to the data for Peregrines, Merlins, and other raptors. The data for these various species confirmed that, among the samples available, the first thinned eggshells appeared in 1946 for Peregrine, in 1947 for Sparrowhawk, and in 1949 for Merlin, with more in subsequent years[13,26,27]. These were

The SPARROWHAWK

IAN NEWTON

Figure 15.2. *The Sparrowhawk* monograph[25] where Chapter 24 (Effects of pesticides) discusses in detail the impacts of pesticides on Sparrowhawk (*Accipiter nisus*) populations between 1947 and 1982 in Britain and elsewhere in Europe.

the post-war years over which DDT first became widely used in Britain, and increasingly so on farmland. This did not alter Derek's conclusions in any significant way, but it strengthened them with larger samples, and gave more precision to the timing, which was itself an important part of the evidence implicating DDT.

In correlative analyses, no organochlorine other than DDE was correlated with shell indices, unless that compound was itself correlated with DDE. We obtained no independent evidence that the other organochlorines (HEOD, BHC, or PCBs) could have caused shell thinning. This, again, had been suspected by Derek, and confirmed in experimental studies. On the other hand, we gained significant correlations, in several species, between the eggshell index (reflecting shell thinning) and the concentration of DDE within the eggs (assumed to reflect the level in the female that laid the egg). Meanwhile, in North America, Peakall and Kiff[28] had assembled all the available data on Peregrine shell-thinning across the world. They found that all populations showing at least 17% shell thinning had declined (some to extinction), while all those showing less than 17% shell thinning had maintained their numbers (Fig. 15.3). This suggested that, at high levels, DDT/DDE could cause sufficient shell thinning to produce population decline, but it did not exclude the additional involvement of cyclodienes in the declines.

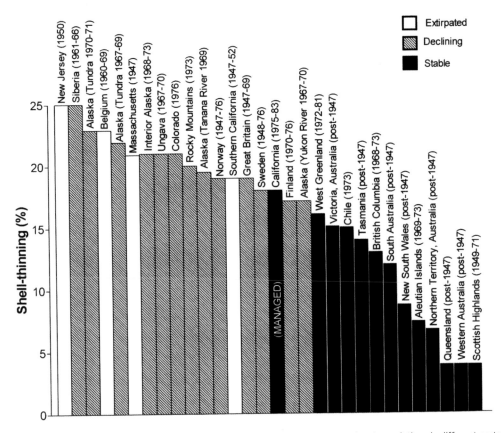

Figure 15.3. Shell thinning and population trend in Peregrine Falcon (*Falco peregrinus*) populations in different parts of the world. All populations showing more than 17% shell thinning (associated with a mean level of 15-20 ppm DDE in fresh egg content) declined, some to the point of extinction. In the one exception, extra eggs and young were added by biologists to maintain numbers (from Peakall & Kiff[28]).

An average of 17% shell thinning thus emerged as critical to population persistence, associated with an average of 15-20 ppm DDE in the wet weight of egg content. These were average figures applicable at the level of populations and did not apply rigidly to individual eggs. Approximately the same mean level of shell thinning was also associated with population declines in other raptor species[21]. The fact that, in many Peregrine and other raptor populations, decline was more rapid than expected on DDT alone presumably arose because mortality was enhanced to varying degrees by HEOD poisoning.

Organochlorine routes to harmful effects

Two modes of action of organochlorines on raptor populations could therefore be identified (Fig. 15.4), with DDE acting primarily to reduce reproductive rate, and HEOD to increase mortality. It seemed that the relative importance of these two mechanisms differed in different regions, according to patterns of organochlorine usage. DDT acting alone was expected to cause, at most, a slow decline in adult numbers, whereas HEOD, by killing full-grown birds, acted much more rapidly to reduce numbers. As subsequent experimental work revealed, DDE could also kill birds, but only at exceptionally high levels. In North America, where DDT was used in huge amounts relative to aldrin and dieldrin, shell thinning seemed of greater significance, and Peregrine population declines tended to be slow, whereas in Britain and other parts of Europe, aldrin and dieldrin were of greater significance, and declines were more rapid, occurring in Britain within 3-5 years of the introduction of these compounds.

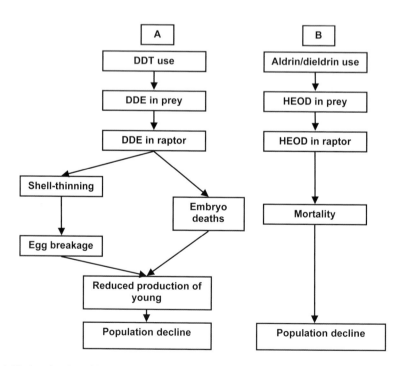

Figure 15.4. Modes of action of DDE (from the insecticide DDT) (A) and HEOD (from aldrin and dieldrin) (B) on raptor populations. (From Newton[26]).

Arguments over the relative roles of DDT and HEOD

In summing up a conference on Peregrines in the US, Ian Nisbet[29] suggested that North American researchers may have greatly under-estimated the role of the cyclodienes in the decline of Peregrines, and that the British conclusions were nearer the truth. In the published proceedings, two papers appeared denying this and suggesting that the Brits were wrong[30]. In discussing this controversy in his book on the Peregrine[3], Derek gave four main strands of circumstantial evidence in support of the importance of cyclodiene involvement in Britain:

1. Peregrines over much of Britain had endured ten years of shell thinning (1947-56) without showing population decline, and some populations even recovered from wartime persecution during this period.

2. The population crash followed the introduction of cyclodienes as seed dressings, and spread rapidly as their use expanded. Pigeons and other prey species were contaminated with these dressings, and while many died, others remained available as contaminated prey.

3. The decline of Peregrine breeding numbers was so abrupt that it could not have occurred due to reproductive failure alone, but must have involved additional mortality.

4. The crash halted after the first restrictions on cyclodienes as spring seed-dressings in 1962 and 1964, whereas the use of DDT was little affected until later restrictions recommended by the Advisory Committee from 1969.

The same points could be made for Sparrowhawks, and in addition Sparrowhawks figured among the widespread kills of farmland birds evident in the late 1950s. After the period of heaviest cyclodiene use, some of the Sparrowhawk carcasses sent to Monks Wood and other laboratories for analysis were found to have lethal levels of HEOD in their livers. Such poisoned specimens continued to arrive until the mid 1970s, when cyclodienes were banned altogether from their main use. Moreover, the recovery of Sparrowhawk numbers in east-central England followed closely the reduction in geometric mean HEOD levels in fresh carcass livers below 1 ppm (Fig. 15.5), but showed no relationship with DDE levels.

Species variations in sensitivity

Some kinds of birds proved more sensitive to DDT/DDE than others. For any given concentration of DDE in their eggs, raptors and pelicans showed the greatest degree of shell thinning, and gulls and gallinaceous birds the least. Raptors and pelicans thus emerged as particularly vulnerable to DDE, partly because their position high in food-chains led them to accumulate large amounts, but also because of their high physiological sensitivity[21]. The greatest degree of shell thinning recorded in any species involved the Brown Pelican (*Pelecanus occidentalis*) in California, which was contaminated by the effluent from a DDT factory. On Anacapa Island off Los Angeles, a mere two chicks arose from 1,272 nesting attempts in 1969. Virtually all the eggs collapsed on laying, and the shells were, on average, 50% thinner than normal[31]. This species was the most sensitive to DDE of all those studied, an average of 3 ppm in the content of fresh eggs being

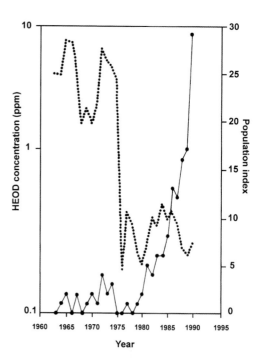

Figure 15.5. Trend in geometric mean HEOD levels (dotted line) in the livers of Sparrowhawks (*Accipiter nisus*) found dead in eastern England in relation to an index of population level in the same area (solid line). HEOD is the chemical residue derived from the insecticides aldrin and dieldrin and the population index is based on the number of carcasses received for analysis. As aldrin and dieldrin were removed from use around 1975, HEOD residues in Sparrowhawk bodies declined, and bird numbers recovered. (From Newton[44]).

associated with nearly total breeding failure at the population level[32]. The European species of pelicans may be similarly sensitive, but I know of no information to refute or support this.

Another general finding was that, among raptors, species that mainly ate birds declined more rapidly and to a greater extent than those that fed mainly upon mammals. Years later, an explanation for this difference emerged, namely that birds are less able to metabolise and excrete organochlorines than are mammals, so birds tend to accumulate these chemicals to greater level in their bodies[33]. So, bird-eating raptors were much more likely to accumulate lethal levels from their prey than were mammal eaters, such as the Kestrel, and thereby suffered greater mortality and shell thinning.

The bird feeders also top longer food-chains than do the mammal feeders, giving more opportunities for residues to concentrate. The relationship between vulnerability and feeding habits was shown repeatedly in many studies in different regions[21], but perhaps most vividly in a forest area in the north-western United States. This study involved a single experimental spraying of DDT (at 0.8 kg per ha) conducted in 1974, two years after the chemical had been banned from general use in the United States. In insectivorous American Kestrels, residues in blood plasma peaked one year after the spraying, with a mean value of 0.78 ppm. In comparison, residues in three species of accipiters, ranked in ascending order of proportion of birds in the diet, were 2.6 times higher in Goshawk (*Accipiter gentilis*), 3.8 times higher in Cooper's Hawk (*A. cooperii*), and 6.1 times higher in Sharp-shinned Hawk (*A. striatus*). The last species had almost disappeared from the area two years after the spraying[34]. It is the ecological equivalent of the Eurasian Sparrowhawk.

Turning the tide

Owing to their environmental impacts, and contamination of the human food-chain, the use of these chemicals was reduced progressively in Britain from 1962, but as indicated above, it was not until the early 1980s that their use was effectively eliminated here (under EC influence). As in the Peregrine, from the mid 1960s to the mid 1990s, shell thickness, breeding success, survival, and population levels of other affected species gradually recovered, enabling them to re-colonise areas from which they had been extirpated. Peregrines (Figs. 13.3, 13.6, 14.4 & 14.5) and Sparrowhawks (Fig. 15.5) had fully re-occupied their former range by the mid 1990s[3,5,35,36]. All of these improvements were associated with reductions in the residues of organochlorine chemicals in eggs and tissues (Fig. 15.6). By the mid 1990s the numbers of Peregrines, Sparrowhawks, and other raptors in Britain were higher than at any previous time during the 20th century, the intervening period having also seen big reductions in the direct human persecution of these birds. The recovery was remarkable and striking (Fig. 14.4).

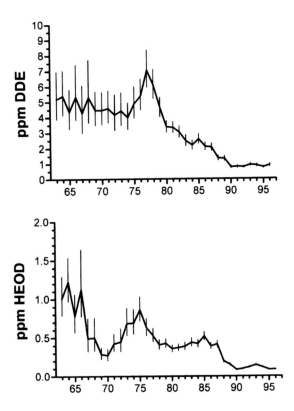

Figure 15.6. Trends in the levels of DDE and HEOD in the livers of Sparrowhawks (*Accipiter nisus*) sampled over the period 1963-1997, soon after which the research programme came to an end. DDE is derived from DDT, and HEOD from aldrin and dieldrin. The three-year moving geometric mean levels (with geometric standard errors) show a progressive decline over the period shown, following successive restrictions in the use of such pesticides. From Newton et al.[45], based on analyses at Monks Wood Experimental Station.

Subsequent Pesticide Problems

While the organochlorines affected bird populations through having direct effects on the reproduction and mortality of individuals, most other pesticides have affected birds indirectly, through destroying the organisms that form their food. This is the main way in which modern pesticides affect bird populations. This takes us outwith the scope of this chapter, but the problems are now well recognised – and sobering[37,38]. Most insecticides kill many kinds of invertebrates (not only insects); some fungicides kill some invertebrates as well as removing the fungal food-supplies of others; and herbicides can remove the food plants of other insects as well as the seeds eaten by granivorous birds. While pesticides continue to be used at current scales, it is unlikely that bird-food supplies on farmland will ever reach the levels prevailing in pre-pesticide days. So, it is not surprising that, over recent decades, many small bird species on farmland have declined markedly, some by more than a staggering 90% in Britain[39].

Apart from the organochlorines, the main types of pesticides applied against arthropod pests since the 1950s include the organophosphates, carbamates, pyrethroids, and, most recently, the neonicotinoids. These latter chemicals are similar to nicotin, the natural insecticide found in tobacco leaves. They were developed as neurotoxins during the 1990s but have come into widespread use only in more recent years. It is too soon to assess their full effects on biodiversity, but they are extremely toxic to a wide range of insects. They are also systemic, being taken into plants and killing any insects which suck the sap or eat the leaves. Particular concerns have been expressed over their potential effects on bees and other pollinators. Neonicotinoids have been found in nectar and pollen, but only at extremely low levels, and as yet the evidence for colony-level effects is unconvincing, although they undoubtedly influence key aspects of bee behaviour. They have nevertheless have been banned temporarily from several countries, including Britain and Ireland to allow time for further evidence to be obtained. They are not cumulative in the same way as the organochlorines, and are less persistent, but they can last more than a month in bright sunlight, and up to several years in darker situations, washing from the soil into watercourses. They are not especially toxic to mammals and probably not to birds so, as with many other pesticides, their main impacts are likely to result from their effects on lower organisms that form the food of birds.

In addition to the general depression of insects and other bird-food supplies on farmland, three other chemically-induced problems have developed in recent decades. These include the: (1) deliberate and illegal use of selected pesticides to kill birds of prey (achieved by applying the concentrate to meat baits, such as Rabbit (*Oryctolagus cuniculus*) carcasses, laid out to attract raptors and other scavengers); (2) use of second-generation rodenticides which can cause secondary mortality of rodent predators such as the Barn Owl (*Tyto alba*) and Red Kite (*Milvus milvus*); and (3) the use of veterinary drugs, such as anthelmintics in cattle, which have caused massive declines in the 'dung fauna' in Britain. Alarmingly, since the mid 1990s, a much bigger veterinary problem has developed in South Asia where diclophenac and other non-steroidal anti-inflammatory drugs administered to cattle have caused the collapse of vulture populations. Until these drugs came on the scene, vultures in India numbered in the tens of millions, with the White-backed Vulture (*Gyps bengalensis*) considered the most numerous large raptor on earth. However, it was reduced within 15 years to less than 1% of its former level[40-42].

Unfortunately, diclophenac has recently been approved for outside veterinary use in Europe, thereby posing a threat to European vultures too.

The Ratcliffe Philosophy

His work on pesticide impacts forced Derek into uncomfortably, and at times unpleasant, close contact with government agriculturalists and industrial chemists. Years later, he wrote bitterly of this experience, and of the tactics used by the 'pesticide apologists'. In his Peregrine book (Fig. 14.6)[3], he wrote as follows:

> "The scientific campaign would have achieved little without a great deal of exacting committee work in which a few people patiently presented the evidence and argued the issues over and over again with a largely unsympathetic and, at times, hostile majority. In Britain, the brunt of this wearisome task of convincing the unwilling fell on Norman Moore, formerly head of the Toxic Chemicals and Wildlife Section of Monks Wood Experimental Station. . . . . It was not an easy time. Some of us had our first experience of scientists playing politics, and we learned how vicious a vested interest under pressure can be. It was clearly in many people's interests, one way or another, to believe that the wildlife conservationists were talking nonsense, and they left no stone unturned in trying to establish this. Every new paper with more evidence was dissected and gone over minutely, to see what flaws could be found. Some of the toughest opposition came, not surprisingly, from the agrochemical industry's own scientists, but certain members of the Government's agricultural establishment were well to the fore. Tactics at times resembled those of the courtroom rather than the scientific debating chamber and the 'smear technique' was openly used. There were tedious arguments over the nature of proof and the validity of circumstantial evidence. The attempts to deny effects of pesticides on wild raptors descended now and then in obscurantism."

Eventually the balance of informed opinion shifted, and over most of the western world governments accepted the evidence of environmental hazards posed by organochlorine pesticides, but often after a long struggle against industry and other vested interests in which the tactics discussed above were used to their full[43]. Governments either banned organochlorines outright or phased them out; the EC eventually instituted a mandatory ban. The results of these actions were reflected in the progressive recovery of Peregrine and other raptor populations in almost every country where declines had been reported. Meanwhile, like cigarette manufacturers, pesticide companies found a ready market for their products in the developing world – but that is another story.

All of this deeply affected Derek, and in his career he progressively developed a rather pessimistic attitude to the prospects for conservation in the face of an ever expanding and demanding human population.

> "Although I dislike having to use such an analogy, it seems to me that

nature conservation is comparable to being on the weaker side in a long drawn-out war, in which the other side has overwhelmingly superior forces and must eventually and inevitably win. Certain positions may be held and even small re-advances made locally, but on the whole the line of the defenders is gradually beaten back. While the other side's overall plan of campaign is obvious enough, it may be difficult to know where the next attack will occur and in what strength. In this situation, the defenders' strategy must be one for minimising losses overall and maintaining maximum tactical flexibility to repel new advances. So it is with nature conservation. Having won a particular battle, we have to shift the weight of our defence or counter-attack to another part of the front where pressure is heavier, but we can never assume safely that there will be no renewal of attack at the site of recent victory."[3].

Sadly, the history of pesticide and drug development over the past half-century illustrates this principle well.

On a fine day, while seated and eating sandwiches overlooking a mountain landscape in Galloway, our discussion turned to scientific accolades, and how scientists, on generally poor salaries, are recognised for important research. Derek commented to the effect that he cared little for honours and medals, but that his main reward in life was to gain the respect of those he most respected. Well, he certainly achieved that and far more, not only for all his outstanding science but also for his scientific and personal integrity.

References

(1)   Birks, H.J.B. & Birks, H.H. (2015) Derek Ratcliffe – botanist and plant ecologist. In: *Nature's Conscience – The Life and Legacy of Derek Ratcliffe* (eds. D.B.A. Thompson, H.H. Birks & H.J.B. Birks). This volume, Chapter 4.

(2)   Birks, H.J.B., Thompson, D.B.A. & Birks, H.H. (2015) Derek Ratcliffe – early days in pursuit of nature. In: *Nature's Conscience – The Life and Legacy of Derek Ratcliffe* (eds. D.B.A. Thompson, H.H. Birks & H.J.B. Birks). This volume, Chapter 1.
Thompson, D.B.A. (2015) Contributions to field ornithology – in search of nesting birds. In: *Nature's Conscience – The Life and Legacy of Derek Ratcliffe* (eds. D.B.A. Thompson, H.H. Birks & H.J.B. Birks). This volume, Chapter 11.

(3)   Ratcliffe, D.A. (1993) *The Peregrine Falcon* (2nd edition). Poyser, London.

(4)   George, J.L. & Frear, D.E.H. (1966) Pesticides in the Antarctic. *Journal of Applied Ecology Supplement*, 3, 155-167.

(5)   Greenwood, J.J.D. & Crick, H.Q.P. (2015) "It seemed like a dream come true": Derek Ratcliffe and the Peregrine surveys. In: *Nature's Conscience – The Life and Legacy of Derek Ratcliffe* (eds. D.B.A. Thompson, H.H. Birks & H.J.B. Birks). This volume, Chapter 14.

(6)   Treleaven, R.B. (1961) Notes on the Peregrine in Cornwall. *British Birds*, **54**, 136-142.

(7)   Cramp, S. & Conder, P.J. (1961) The deaths of birds and mammals connected with toxic chemicals in the first half of 1960. *Report no 1 of the BTO-RSPB Committee on Toxic Chemicals*. RSPB, Sandy.

(8)   Cramp, S., Conder, P.J. & Ash, J.S. (1962) *Deaths of Birds and Mammals from Toxic Chemicals, January-June 1961*. RSPB, Sandy.

(9)   Ratcliffe, D.A. (1958). Broken eggs in Peregrine eyries. *British Birds*, **51**, 23-26.

(10)   Ratcliffe, D.A. (1967) Decrease in eggshell weight in certain birds of prey. *Nature*, **215**, 208-210.

(11)   Ratcliffe, D.A. (1970) Changes attributable to pesticides in egg breakage frequency and eggshell thickness in some British birds. *Journal of Applied Ecology*, **7**, 67-107.

(12)   Peakall, D.B., Reynolds, L.M. & French, M.C. (1976) DDE in eggs of the Peregrine Falcon. *Bird Study*, **23**, 183-186.

(13)   Newton, I., Bogan, J.A. & Haas, M.B. (1989) Organochlorines and mercury in the eggs of British Peregrines. *Ibis*, **131**, 355-376.

(14)   Lockie, J.D., Ratcliffe, D.A. & Balharry, R. (1969) Breeding success and dieldrin contamination of Golden Eagles in West Scotland. *Journal of Applied Ecology*, **6**, 381-389.
        Balharry, R. (2015) North-West Highland reminiscences. In: *Nature's Conscience – The Life and Legacy of Derek Ratcliffe* (eds. D.B.A. Thompson, H.H. Birks & H.J.B. Birks). This volume, Chapter 12.

(15)   Carson, R. (1962) *Silent Spring*. Houghton Mifflin, Boston.

(16)   Rollie, C.J. (2015) In Galloway and the Borders – in search of an enduring youth. In: *Nature's Conscience – The Life and Legacy of Derek Ratcliffe* (eds. D.B.A. Thompson, H.H. Birks & H.J.B. Birks). This volume, Chapter 13.

(17)   Prestt, I. & Ratcliffe, D.A. (1972) Effects of organochlorine insecticides on European birdlife. *Proceedings of 15th International Ornithological Congress* (ed. K. H. Voous), pp. 486-513. Brill, Lieden.

(18)   Cooke, A.S., Bell, A.A. & Haas, M.B. (1982) *Predatory birds, pesticides and pollution*. Institute of Terrestrial Ecology, NERC, Cambridge.

(19)   Hickey, J.J. & Anderson, D.W. (1968) Chlorinated hydrocarbons and eggshell changes in raptorial and fish-eating birds. *Science*, **162**, 271-273.

(20)   Cooke, A.S. (1973) Shell-thinning in avian eggs by environmental pollutants. *Environmental Pollution*, **4**, 85-152.

(21)   Newton, I. (1979) *Population Ecology of Raptors*. Poyser, Berkhamsted.

(22)   Risebrough, R.W. (1986) Pesticides and bird populations. *Current Ornithology*, **3**, 397-427.

(23)   Lincer, J.L. (1975) DDE-induced eggshell-thinning in the American Kestrel: a comparison of the field situation and laboratory results. *Journal of Applied Ecology*, **12**, 781-793.

(24)   Prestt, I. (1965) An enquiry into the recent breeding status of some of the smaller birds of prey and crows in Britain. *Bird Study*, **12**, 196-221.

(25)   Newton, I. & Bogan, J.A. (1978) The role of different organochlorine compounds in the breeding of British Sparrowhawks. *Journal of Applied Ecology*, **15**, 105-116.

(26)   Newton, I. (1986) *The Sparrowhawk*. Poyser, Calton.

(27)   Newton, I., Bogan, J.A., Meek, E. & Little, B. (1982) Organochlorine compounds and shell-thinning in British Merlins. *Ibis*, **124**, 328-335.

(28)   Peakall, D.B. & Kiff, L. F. (1988) DDE contamination in Peregrines and American Kestrels and its effects on reproduction. In: *Peregrine Falcon Populations. Their Management and Recovery* (eds. T.J. Cade, J.H. Enderson, C.G. Thelander & C.M. White), pp. 337-350. The Peregrine Fund, Boise.

(29)   Nisbet, I.C.T. (1988) The relative importance of DDE and dieldrin in the decline of Peregrine Falcon populations. In: *Peregrine Falcon Populations. Their Management and Recovery* (eds. T.J. Cade, J.H. Enderson, C.G. Thelander & C.M. White), pp. 351-375. The Peregrine Fund, Boise.

(30)   Cade, T.J., Enderson, J.H., Thelander, C.G. & White, C.M. (eds.) (1988) *Peregrine Falcon Populations: Their Management and Recovery*. The Peregrine Fund, Boise.

(31)   Risebrough, R.W., Sibley, F.C. & Kirven, M.N. (1971) Reproductive failure of the Brown Pelican on Anacapa Island in 1969. *American Birds*, **25**, 8-9.

(32)   Blus, L.J. (1982) Further interpretation of the relation of organochlorine residues in Brown Pelican eggs to reproductive success. *Environmental Pollution*, **28**, 15-33.

(33)   Walker, C.H. (1983) Pesticides and birds - mechanisms of selective toxicity. *Agriculture, Ecosystems and Environment*, **9**, 211-226.

(34)   Henny, C.J. (1977) Birds of prey, DDT, and Tussock Moths in Pacific Northwest. *Transactions of the North American Wildlife and Natural Resources Conference*, **42**, 397-411.

(35)   Crick, H.Q.P. & Ratcliffe, D.A. (1995) The Peregrine *Falco peregrinus* breeding population of the United Kingdom in 1991. *Bird Study*, **42**, 1-19.

(36)   Newton, I. & Haas, M.B. (1984) The return of the Sparrowhawk. *British Birds*, **77**, 47-70.

(37)   Newton, I. (2004) The recent declines of farmland bird populations in Britain: an appraisal of causal factors and conservation actions. *Ibis*, **146**, 579-600.

(38)   Potts, G.R. (2012) *Partridges*. Collins, London.

(39)   Gregory, R.D., Noble, D.G. & Custance, J. (2004) The state of play of farmland birds: population trends and population status of lowland farmland birds in the United Kingdom. *Ibis*, **146** (Suppl. 2), 1-13.

(40)   Pain, D.J., Bowden, C.G.R., Cunningham, A.A., *et al.* (2008) The race to prevent the extinction of South Asian vultures. *Bird Conservation International*, **18**, s30-s84.

(41)   Green, R.E, Newton, I., Shultz, S., Cunningham, A.A., Gilbert, M., *et al.* (2004) Diclofenac poisoning as a cause of vulture population declines across the Indian subcontinent. *Journal of Applied Ecology*, **41**, 793–800.

(42)   Newton, I. (2013) Vultures and drugs. *British Birds*, **106**, 58-59.

(43)   Oreskes, N. & Conway, E.M. (2010) *Merchants of Doubt – How a handful of scientists obscured the truth on issues from tobacco smoke to global warming*. Bloomsbury, New York.

(44)   Newton, I. (1988) Determination of critical pollutant levels in wild populations, with examples from organochlorine pesticides in birds of prey. *Environmental Pollution*, **55**, 229-40.

(45)   Newton, I., Dale, L., Finnie, J.K., Freestone, P., Wright, J., Wyatt, C. & Wyllie, I. (1997/98) *Wildlife and Pollution Annual Report*. Report No. 285. Joint Nature Conservation Committee, Peterborough.

16. Fouling our nest

Elspeth Huxley

Reprint of Huxley, E. (1964)
Fouling our nest.
Punch, **November 25**, 806-807.

Fouling Our Nest

WILD LIFE in Britain is threatened from two directions. On the one hand, we're fouling our nest with our social and industrial excreta — residues of pesticides, effluent of factories, radioactive fall-out, oil discharge from tankers, exhaust fumes from road vehicles, discarded vehicles (6,000 cars just dumped last year), and all the other unattractive by-products of humanity's industrial activities. In the second place we're changing, distorting and destroying the habitat of our surviving wild birds and beasts not only by taking land for buildings and roads, flooding it with reservoirs and covering it with pylons, though there is plenty of that too, but by the mere dispersal of ourselves. Each man kills the thing he loves, and mobs of humans murder solitude.

To glance first at the nest-fouling. Pesticides are now suspect, and much more care is taken to test them and control their use. But while we may, or may not, be able to deal with their residues in our own systems, we can't stop them harming insects, plants and birds.

By every post the Nature Conservancy's laboratories near Huntingdon receive dead birds, whose fat is extracted from the breast muscles and liver to be analysed. Residues of the organochlorines are frequently found. Among aquatic birds, herons have the most, grebes next and moorhens very little; among land birds, sparrow-hawks the most, owls rather less, woodpigeons almost nil. Always it's the predators that have the highest poisonous residues. The reason is the food-chain. Fish caught seventy miles out to sea contain dieldrin which must have been washed down from the residues of sprays into the rivers, and have passed through a whole series of plants and animals. The eggs and corpses of shags, guillemots, kittiwakes, puffins, gulls and oyster-catchers found addled or dead off St. Abb's Head had up to 8.9 parts per million of organo-chlorine residues in their fat or yolk which they, in turn, can have derived only from their fishy diet.

At each link in the food-chain, the concentration rises; the higher the position of the animal, the more poison it gets. Ground beetles resident in soil sprayed with dieldrin and DDT lay on their backs twitching for up to forty-eight hours, thus tempting skylarks, who gobbled up too many and died. (Death of a lark: "although it lacked muscular co-ordination and could not fly or stand, it continued to beat its wings and clutch with its toes while lying on its side.") It's always the predator at the top of the food-chain who's most vulnerable. A little of what you fancy does you good, but a lot of nothing else does you in.

ELSPETH HUXLEY
explores high-pressure food production methods and the price we pay for them

Most British birds of prey are declining in numbers, especially peregrine falcons, kites, sparrow-hawks and golden eagles, because they're failing to breed. Every single predator's egg so far examined in the Conservancy's laboratories has contained pesticide residues. Up to 1939, about 650 pairs of peregrines bred regularly in Britain. During the war they were severely hammered in order to protect carrier pigeons, but when it was over they were themselves protected, and their numbers built up again. In 1955, a new decline set in, and in 1962 only 68 pairs hatched their young. By now only a very few isolated pairs of peregrines remain in England and Wales, and most of these fail to breed. A few survive in Scotland but here, too, they are laying smaller clutches and hatching fewer chicks.

All this has coincided with the spread of pesticides. Organochlorine residues have been found in the eggs. This isn't cast-iron proof, but as circumstantial evidence it could scarcely be stronger. "The contamination of the peregrine population is now demonstrated beyond doubt," affirms Mr. D. A. Ratcliffe, who organised a survey conducted by the British Trust for Ornithology, "by the finding of residues of dieldrin, heptachlor, BRC and DDT in every one of 12 eggs from 11 different eyries. A peregrine found dead on Lundy Island contained 78 ppm of total chlorinated hydrocarbon in its liver" —

a more than lethal dose. Sparrow-hawks and buzzards are also sitting on infertile eggs. Sheep dips and sprays are generally blamed and that's one reason why, from 1965, dieldrin, aldrin and heptachlor are to be banned.

Once Britain was almost wholly covered in forest and that's when our bird population evolved. Of our 50 major land species, about 40 are still basically woodland birds. Now we're down to less than 5 per cent of forest, the lowest proportion in Europe and one of the lowest in the world. The birds have taken to the hedgerows. They're all right there, but if the hedgerows go, they won't be; they're unlikely to adapt themselves to barley prairies, or to nest in electric fences, feedlots and barbed wire. Chaffinches, blackbirds, thrushes, wrens, robins, tits, goldfinches, all would go. We might keep some partridges, lapwings, skylarks and corn buntings, and most waterfowl; otherwise we'd be reduced to pigeons, starlings and sparrows, with some crows and jackdaws thrown in.

Are the hedgerows seriously threatened? Yes, they are. We have an estimated 616,000 miles of hedge covering about half a million acres, and containing a lot of trees. Most hedges were planted between 100 and 150 years ago, but about one-third are older, and there's one at Charlton, in Wiltshire, mentioned in a deed of AD 861.

The economic usefulness of hedges is over. The high cost of labour, massive farm machinery, electric fences, the need to exploit every acre, all these combine to make the hedge not merely useless, but a liability. So they're being bulldozed out intentionally, and accidentally damaged by the growing practice of burning straw instead of baling it. Between one-tenth and one-fifth of the hedges have gone over the past 20 years. The fathers of the present generation of farmers often paid their men a shilling for every hedgerow sapling they spared. Now hedging has been mechanised and pretty soon there'll be no more hedgerow trees. The Nature Conservancy made a sample survey in the east Midlands and found that for every 10 miles of hedge that existed in 1947, only 4 miles remained in 1964. "If it wasn't for the shooting," the sampler

    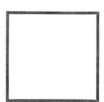

said, "in that area there'd be no hedges left at all. Sporting farmers keep them to shelter game birds and offer nesting places. And the Belvoir hunt have preserved all their fences." The paradox that it's the men who want to kill animals who keep them alive is, anyway in this instance, quite true.

If a hedge isn't bulldozed, then it's mechanically clipped and sprayed. Naturalists believe that butterfly populations have fallen mainly because so many of the hedgerow wildflowers they live on have disappeared. The loss of charlock, cornflowers, poppies, wild geranium, meadowsweet, many docks and thistles, nettles, may not worry farmers, but those insects who lived on and bred in them diminish, and so affect the birds who ate them — another food-chain. "Those hedges and ponds, roadside verges and railway embankments which survive are a national asset," says Dr. Norman Moore, "and should be preserved." But they're not. Over 1,000 farm ponds have been filled in.

If Hardy's native were to return today to Egdon Heath in Dorset, instead of a solitary, ochred reddleman trudging across the sombre wastes beside a horse-drawn van, he'd find bus routes and housing estates, War Department installations and the Forestry Commission's dripping conifers. The actual heathland, the "unenclosed wild," has shrunk from 75,000 acres in 1811 to about 25,000 acres today, and been chopped into over 100 bits and pieces. Soon the returning native will find no heath at all; big forestry and building schemes are brewing for most of the surviving patches. Five varieties of vascular plant, the black game and the natterjack toad have gone. On the other hand, fallow, roe and sika deer have been added, and of course a lot of conifers. A century ago, the Dartford warbler was to be found from Norfolk down to Cornwall; today an estimated 425 pairs survive in Dorset and Hampshire, and that's all. The sand lizard and the smooth snake are getting scarce and the Dorset heath has been driven into corners by the Forestry Commission, and needs protection if it's to survive.

Most herbicides sprayed on hedges and roadside verges don't persist as organo-chlorides do, and so don't directly harm birds and insects, but they do make drastic changes in the habitat. Along Akeman Street in Gloucestershire, an old Roman road, 12 years' annual spraying of the verges has knocked out nettles, thistles, docks and broad-leaved weeds like hedge-parsley, cow parsnip and hogweed, and all the coarse, tufty grasses like cocksfoot and tall oat-grass. In their place have come smaller plants with finer leaves, like the fescues and meadow-grasses (Poas), that don't grow nearly so tall. Some wildflowers have vanished, but not all; ladies' bedstraw, toadflax, blue scabious, white milk vetch, campion and speedwell survive and primroses, violets and aconites aren't affected because they flower before spraying time. There's no doubt that spraying tidies up the verges, giving them a lawn-like look well suited to the modern roadside picnic with its folding tables and chairs, crockery and paper napkins. Not much comfort there for insects or for birds and bumblebees. Chemicals narrow the range and reduce the biological potential of plant communities—more and more of less and less.

17. A thousand nest cards - from Derek Ratcliffe to the University Museum of Bergen

Ingvar Byrkjedal

I first met Derek Ratcliffe at John and Hilary Birks' home in Bergen in May 1990. Derek (Fig. 17.1) and his wife Jeannette (Fig. 17.2) had arrived in Bergen to begin their first of fourteen annual trips to northern Scandinavia to study birds. I was invited to meet them because I had done some field work on waders in the interior of Finnmark and might be able to give advice on some areas of possible interest. Derek's was a well-known name to me, not only from his classic publications, such as his book *The Peregrine Falcon* (Fig. 14.6)[1], but also his superb efforts in unravelling the impacts of DDT on raptors[2]. As a young student working on a thesis on the golden plover in the 1970s, I came upon Derek's extensive Golden Plover (*Pluvialis apricaria*) paper in *Bird Study* (Fig. 11.9)[3] – a paper that remained the base-line study of the species for at least twenty years. A dog-eared and almost worn-out reprint copy testifies to my frequent use of it.

Figure 17.1. Derek Ratcliffe examining a Crane (*Grus grus*) nest in a patterned bog near Allioja, northern Finland, 1994. Photo: Derek Ratcliffe

Figure 17.2. Jeannette Ratcliffe on Finnmarksvidda, Norway, 1993. Photo: Derek Ratcliffe

For me, the meeting was very interesting and pleasant. It did not take long for the talk to turn to breeding waders, a favourite subject of both of us. Derek, in his quiet, low-spoken, and modest way, soon revealed that he was a person with first-hand knowledge of these birds. His deep field-based experiences extended far beyond birds, and when I left, I knew I had met someone truly remarkable. Unfortunately, this was the only time I came to meet him, but the occasion turned into a correspondence which lasted until his death, and I was thrilled he wrote the Foreword for my book with Des Thompson on *Tundra Plovers* (Fig. 11.11)[4]. That first summer Derek and Jeannette completed a very successful northern Scandinavian trip, not least due to their extraordinary talent for finding nests. In the autumn an extensive and well-written report arrived on my desk, giving a summary of Derek's field notes from the trip.

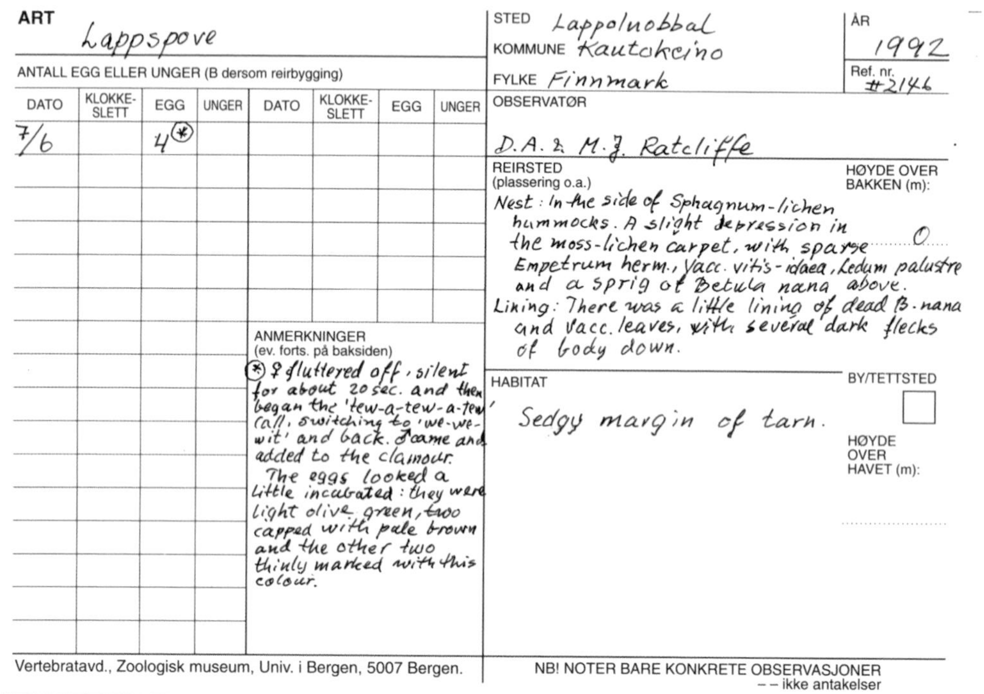

ART				STED	*Lappoluobbal*		ÅR
Lappspove				KOMMUNE	*Kautokeino*		*1992*
ANTALL EGG ELLER UNGER (B dersom reirbygging)				FYLKE	*Finnmark*		Ref. nr. *#2146*

DATO	KLOKKE-SLETT	EGG	UNGER	DATO	KLOKKE-SLETT	EGG	UNGER
7/6		*4* ⊛					

OBSERVATØR

D.A. & M.J. Ratcliffe

REIRSTED (plassering o.a.)

HØYDE OVER BAKKEN (m):

Nest: In the side of Sphagnum-lichen hummocks. A slight depression in the moss-lichen carpet, with sparse Empetrum herm., Vacc. vitis-idaea, Ledum palustre and a sprig of Betula nana above. *O.*
Lining: There was a little lining of dead B. nana and Vacc. leaves, with several dark flecks of body down.

ANMERKNINGER (ev. forts. på baksiden)

⊛ ♀ fluttered off, silent for about 20 sec. and then began the 'tew-a-tew-a-tew' call, switching to 'we-we-wit' and back. ♂ came and added to the clamour. The eggs looked a little incubated: they were light olive green, two capped with pale brown and the other two thinly marked with this colour.

HABITAT

BY/TETTSTED ☐

Sedgy margin of tarn.

HØYDE OVER HAVET (m):

Vertebratavd., Zoologisk museum, Univ. i Bergen, 5007 Bergen.

NB! NOTER BARE KONKRETE OBSERVASJONER
– – ikke antakelser

Figure 17.3. A sample nest card for Bar-tailed Godwit (*Limosa lapponica*) completed with information provided by Derek and Jeannette Ratcliffe.

Some years earlier a nest record scheme had begun at the University Museum of Bergen. The detailed descriptions found in Derek's report were just right for this archive, and with Derek's permission the nest record information found its way to the nest cards (Fig. 17.3). The contact with Derek continued as he made summer trips annually more or less along the same route, driving north through Sweden, into northernmost parts of Finland, and then entering Norway near Kautokeino and continuing to the Varangerfjord all the way north to Vardø. And each trip gave rise to a detailed report, with more nest cards for us to fill in. The reports were a joy to read, conveying not only a wealth of information on birds and plants, but also a vivid sense of being there. Cold, grey days with rain or sleet, warm sunny days with hordes of mosquitoes, tension as promising observations of a Broad-billed Sandpiper (*Limicola falcinellus*) were about to be made, excitement at the discovery of a Dusky Redshank (*Tringa erythropus*) (Fig. 17.4) nest – the reader is there, experiencing all of this and much more.

Figure 17.4. Spotted (Dusky) Redshank (*Tringa erythropus*), July 2011. Derek was particularly successful at finding nests of this elusive bird. Photo: Kåre Kyllingstad

The North Scandinavian summer trips made the basis for Derek's beautifully produced book *Lapland: A Natural History* (Fig. 11.18), published by Poyser posthumously[5]. This was his penultimate book, which he sadly just missed seeing (remarkably, as soon as he had finished work on this one, he penned *Galloway and the Borders* (Fig. 27.4) for the New Naturalist series which was published two years later[6]). I wish he had published his field reports as they are far too enjoyable and far too important to be lost.

The reports on the fourteen summer trips Derek and Jeannette made to northern Scandinavia supplied the University Museum of Bergen with more than 1000 nest cards, 1158 to be exact. The majority of the nest cards (70%) relate to Norwegian material, but 19% and 11% of the cards are from information gathered in Finland and Sweden, respectively. The cards represent altogether 80 species, an overview of which is given in Table 17.1.

Table 17.1. Nest card information extracted from Derek Ratcliffe's annual reports from his Fennoscandian tours, 1990-2004 (except 2000, when no trip was made). The cards are kept in the archives of the University Museum of Bergen.

Species	Number of nest cards
Willow Grouse *Lagopus lagopus*	7
Ptarmigan *Lagopus muta*	3
Capercaillie *Tetrao urogallus*	2
Whooper Swan *Cygnus cygnus*	9
Teal *Anas crecca*	2
Eider *Somateria mollissima*	1
Long-tailed Duck *Clangula hyemalis*	1
Goldeneye *Bucephala clangula*	4
Smew *Mergus albellus*	1
Red-throated Diver *Gavia stellata*	4
Black-throated Diver *Gavia arctica*	12
White-tailed Eagle *Haliaeetus albicilla* (Fig. 11.19)	2
Hen Harrier *Circus cyaneus*	1
Rough-legged Buzzard *Buteo lagopus*	17
Merlin *Falco columbarius*	7
Gyr Falcon *Falco rusticolus*	4
Peregrine Falcon *Falco peregrinus* (Fig. 14.5)	4
Crane *Grus grus* (Fig. 17.1)	2
Oystercatcher *Haematopus ostralegus*	42
Northern Lapwing *Vanellus vanellus*	7
Golden Plover *Pluvialis apricaria* (Figs. 11.10 & 11.13)	34
Ringed Plover *Charadrius hiaticula*	75
Little Ringed Plover *Charadrius dubius*	1
Dotterel *Charadrius morinellus* (Fig. 11.5)	26
Jack Snipe *Lymnocryptes minimus*	4
Great Snipe *Gallinago media*	1
Snipe *Gallinago gallinago*	4
Bar-tailed Godwit *Limosa lapponica* (Fig. 17.10)	4
Whimbrel *Numenius phaeopus* (Fig. 17.5)	31
Curlew *Numenius arquata* (Fig. 13.10)	3
Spotted (Dusky) Redshank *Tringa erythropus* (Figs. 17.4 & 17.7)	20
Redshank *Tringa totanus*	21
Greenshank *Tringa nebularia* (Fig. 17.8)	7
Wood Sandpiper *Tringa glareola* (Fig. 17.9)	37
Common Sandpiper *Actitis hypoleucos*	7
Turnstone *Arenaria interpres*	41
Little Stint *Calidris minuta* (Fig. 17.11)	5
Temminck's Stint *Calidris temminckii*	52
Purple Sandpiper *Calidris maritima*	8

Species	Number of nest cards
Dunlin *Calidris alpina*	21
Broad-billed Sandpiper *Limicola falcinellus* (Fig. 17.6)	15
Ruff *Philomachus pugnax*	32
Red-necked Phalarope *Phalaropus lobatus*	13
Common Gull *Larus canus*	43
Great Black-backed Gull *Larus marinus*	7
Arctic Tern *Sterna paradisaea*	86
Arctic Skua *Stercorarius parasiticus*	47
Long-tailed Skua *Stercorarius longicaudus*	17
Hawk Owl *Surnia ulula*	1
Great Spotted Woodpecker *Dendrocopos major*	2
Great Grey Shrike *Lanius excubitor*	2
Magpie *Pica pica*	3
Hooded Crow *Corvus cornix*	4
Raven *Corvus corax* (Figs. 11.17 & 13.4)	39
Siberian Tit *Poecile cinctus*	3
Skylark *Alauda arvensis*	1
Shorelark *Eremophila alpestris*	13
Willow Warbler *Phylloscopus trochilus*	12
Fieldfare *Turdus pilaris*	60
Redwing *Turdus iliacus*	26
Song Thrush *Turdus philomelos*	4
Mistle Thrush *Turdus viscivorus*	1
Robin *Erithacus rubecula*	1
Bluethroat *Luscinia svecica*	16
Redstart *Phoenicurus phoenicurus*	6
Whinchat *Saxicola rubetra*	1
Wheatear *Oenanthe oenanthe*	8
Spotted Flycatcher *Muscicapa striata*	6
Pied Flycatcher *Ficedula hypoleuca*	2
White Wagtail *Motacilla alba alba*	4
Yellow Wagtail *Motacilla flava*	16
Meadow Pipit *Anthus pratensis*	57
Red-throated Pipit *Anthus cervinus*	6
Brambling *Fringilla montifringilla*	25
Arctic Redpoll *Carduelis hornemanni*	1
Redpoll *Carduelis flammea*	9
Pine Grosbeak *Pinicola enucleator*	1
Reed Bunting *Emberiza schoeniclus*	3
Lapland Bunting *Calcarius lapponicus*	21
Snow Bunting *Plectrophenax nivalis*	10
Sum NEST CARDS	1158
Sum SPECIES	80

With their 25 species, the waders are particularly heavily represented in the material. Derek and Jeannette do not seem to have missed any of these breeding in the region they visited. Admittedly, these species are well represented in that fauna, and the nests of some, such as the Whimbrel (*Numenius phaeopus*) (Fig. 17.5), can be fairly easy to find. But there is no doubt that waders were among those birds especially looked for, and this is particularly the case with the elusive, little known and difficult-to-find species. There are some very impressive finds here. Stumbling upon a nest of Broad-billed Sandpiper (Fig. 17.6) is difficult enough, but finding 15 nests is rich testament to real expertise. And 20 nests of Dusky Redshank (Fig. 17.7) (Derek's preferred name for the Spotted Redshank, *Tringa erythropus*) is no less a feat. Other notoriously difficult waders represented in the list are Greenshank (*Tringa nebularia*) (Fig. 17.8), Jack Snipe (*Lymnocryptes minimus*), Wood Sandpiper (*Tringa glareola*) (Fig. 17.9), with 37 nests found, and Bar-tailed Godwit (*Limosa lapponica*) (Fig. 17.10). Those of us who have attempted to find nests of Yellow Wagtail (*Motacilla flava*) will be impressed by the 16 nests found!

Figure 17.5. Nest of a Whimbrel (*Numenius phaeopus*) in open sub-alpine Birch woodland, Tärnaby, northern Sweden, June 2001. Photo: Derek Ratcliffe

Figure 17.6. Nest of a Broad-billed Sandpiper (*Limicola falcinellus*), northern Norway, June 2006. Photo: Terje Lislevand

Figure 17.7. Nest of a Spotted (Dusky) Redshank (*Tringa erythropus*) in a mixture of lichen and pine needles, Enontekiö, northern Finland, June 1991. Photo: Derek Ratcliffe

Figure 17.8. Nest of a Greenshank (*Tringa nebularia*) in a patch of pine needles in open Scots Pine woodland, Enontekiö, northern Finland, June 2002. Photo: Derek Ratcliffe

Figure 17.9. Wood Sandpiper (*Tringa glareola*) incubating in an old Fieldfare (*Turdus pilaris*) nest, 2.5 m up a small Scots Pine tree, Enontekiö, northern Finland, June 2001. Most Wood Sandpipers nest on the ground. Photo: Derek Ratcliffe

Figure 17.10. Bar-tailed Godwit (*Limosa lapponica*), Finnmark, northern Norway, June 1995. Photo: Terje Lislevand

Nest cards can be used for a number of research purposes, including the calculation of nest loss. Provided the same nests are visited more than once, nest loss can be calculated from the number of days nests have been observed 'exposed' to predators, etc., by an algorithm referred to as 'Mayfield's method'. Due to short stays in the various localities, Derek provided few repeated observations of the same nests; only 6% of the nests were visited more than once. But he did do something more unusual - he visited some of the old nests again in the following year. In doing this, he found that a number of species, including ground-nesters such as waders, every now and then re-use their previous year's nest scrape. This is an interesting observation, indicating that waders may be more fussy about their choice of nest site than we tend to think. In most wader species males make several nest scrapes at the time of pairing up, which are paraded to their mate, who finally chooses one. Scrapes re-used may perhaps be particularly attractive ones, and it would be very interesting to try to find out more about the factors important in their selection. Interestingly, Derek discussed this many times with his ornithological mentor Desmond Nethersole-Thompson (Fig. 11.22) who reminded Derek that the faithfulness to previous years' nest scrapes was much appreciated by egg collectors! But what Derek could not understand was why nest predators, such as Red Foxes (*Vulpes vulpes*) and Ravens (*Corvus corax*) (Fig. 13.4), could not tap into this habit. At least we now know that the tendency to return to scrapes occurs much less frequently when a wader's clutch is predated in the previous year.

Being a top botanist[7], Derek described in detail not only the plant communities surrounding each nest, but also the material used in nest construction. I doubt there are more detailed nest and habitat descriptions in any nest record scheme than those made by Derek and Jeannette, primarily of waders' but also of a few other species' nests. Derek was brutally honest in describing what he saw, for instance leading to the recording of two Brambling (*Fringilla montifringilla*) nests built of toilet paper – definitely detracting from the aesthetics of the usually beautiful birch-bark nests of this species.

There is no doubt that Derek knew his birds exceptionally well. These days, when biologists do research to understand the laws of nature by means of complex mathematical models, remote sensing, and genetic laboratory techniques, one has a feeling that they sometimes seem to forget the animals or plants they are studying. The modern techniques are important, of course, leading to great achievements; and we cannot do without them. But one must never forget that there is no substitute for the raw and intimate study of wild animals and plants in their favoured haunts. Derek's writings and conversations bore witness to this magnificently.

Figure 17.11. Little Stint (*Calidris minuta*) with young, Finnmark, northern Norway, July 2005. Photo: Terje Lislevand

References

(1)   Ratcliffe, D.A. (1980) *The Peregrine Falcon* (1st edition). Poyser, Calton.
        Ratcliffe, D.A. (1993) *The Peregrine Falcon* (2nd edition). Poyser, London.

(2)   Ratcliffe, D.A. (1967) Decrease in eggshell weight in certain birds of prey. *Nature,* **215**, 208-210.

(3)   Ratcliffe, D.A. (1976) Observations on the breeding of the Golden Plover in Great Britain. *Bird Study,* **23**, 63-116.

(4)   Byrkjedal, I. & Thompson, D.B.A. (1998) *Tundra Plovers: The Eurasian, Pacific, and American Golden Plovers and Grey Plover.* Poyser, London.

(5)   Ratcliffe, D.A. (2005) *Lapland: A Natural History.* Poyser, London.

(6)   Ratcliffe, D.A. (2007) *Galloway and the Borders.* Collins, London.

(7)   Birks, H.J.B. & Birks, H.H. (2015) Derek Ratcliffe – botanist and plant ecologist. In: *Nature's Conscience – The Life and Legacy of Derek Ratcliffe* (eds. D.B.A. Thompson, H.H. Birks & H.J.B. Birks). This volume, Chapter 4.

18. Upland birds and their conservation

Derek Ratcliffe

Reprint of Ratcliffe, D.A. (1990) Upland birds and their conservation. *British Wildlife,* **2**, 1-12.

Upland Birds and their Conservation

D A Ratcliffe

The term 'upland' is conveniently broad for the generality of high land in Britain – mountain, hill and fell, all connoting ground of some altitude and often pronounced relief. Yet definitions based on some arbitrary elevation above sea level are unsatisfactory, for the farther north one goes, the lower the altitude at which ground of upland character is found. Montane-type heaths occur almost at sea level in the far north of Scotland and its islands, where extreme windiness virtually extinguishes the tree line.

While we are considering in this article mainly land above or beyond the climatic limits for arable farming, most hill regions also have a transitional zone of marginal land now capable of cultivation under modern techniques, and here, the 'uplands' include this marginal ground, along with low-level bogs (peat-mosses).

The birds

The uplands represent a generally harsh environment, characterised by a cold, wet and windy climate and generally poor, infertile soils, giving a low carrying capacity for animals, both domestic and wild. Their bird fauna is thus somewhat limited, in numbers of both species and individuals. I have listed as upland 67 out of the total 230 or more British breeding species (Table 1). The main importance of the uplands for birds is as a breeding area between March and July, since the majority of species leave for more congenial lowland quarters by the end of summer and do not return until the worst of winter is past. Nearly all the invertebrate feeders depart, and the year-round residents tend to be predators, scavengers and vegetarians. Few new species appear on the hills in the autumn and most of these are only passing through.

The composition of our upland wildlife, both

1

British Wildlife

Table 1 Data on breeding birds of the British uplands

SPECIES	1	2	3	4	5	6	7	8	9	10	11	12	13	14	15	16
Black-throated Diver	□	□	■	□	□	■	■	□	□	□	□	3	D	U	■	■
Red-throated Diver	□	■	■	□	□	■	■	□	□	□	□	4	S		■	■
Mallard	■	□	□	□	■	■	□	□	■	P	#	6	S		□	□
Teal	■	□	□	□	■	■	□	□	□	P	□	4	S		□	□
Wigeon	□	□	■	□	■	■	■	□	□	□	□	3	S		□	□
Common Scoter	□	□	■	□	□	■	■	□	□	□	□	2	S		□	■
Red-breasted Merganser	□	□	■	□	■	■	□	□	□	□	□	4	I	P	□	□
Goosander	□	□	■	□	■	■	□	□	■	□	□	4	I	P	□	□
Greylag Goose	□	□	■	□	□	■	□	□	□	□	■	3	I	P	□	□
White-tailed Eagle	□	■	■	□	□	■	■	□	□	■	■	1	I	R	■	■
Golden Eagle	□	■	■	#	□	□	■	□	□	■	■	3	D	F	■	■
Buzzard	■	■	□	□	■	□	□	□	□	□	□	4	S		□	□
Red Kite	□	□	■	□	□	□	□	□	□	■	■	2	I	P	■	■
Hen Harrier	□	□	■	□	■	□	■	□	■	P	#	3	D	FA	■	■
Peregrine	□	■	■	#	■	□	■	□	□	□	■	3	I	P	■	■
Merlin	□	■	■	□	■	□	■	□	□	■	#	3	D	FA	■	■
Kestrel	■	■	□	□	■	□	□	□	□	□	□	5	S		□	□
Red Grouse	□	□	■	#	■	□	□	□	□	P	□	6	D	FA	□	□
Ptarmigan	□	□	□	■	■	□	□	□	□	□	■	5	S		□	□
Black Grouse	□	□	■	□	■	□	□	□	□	□	■	5	D	A	□	□
Oystercatcher	■	■	■	□	■	■	■	□	□	□	□	5	I	A	□	□
Lapwing	■	□	□	□	■	□	□	□	□	□	□	6	D	A	□	□
Ringed Plover	■	■	□	□	■	□	□	□	□	□	■	4	S		□	□
Golden Plover	□	□	■	□	■	□	□	□	□	□	#	5	D	FA	■	■
Dotterel	□	□	□	■	■	□	□	□	□	□	□	3	I	C	■	■
Snipe	■	□	□	#	■	□	□	□	□	□	□	5	D	AF	□	□
Curlew	■	□	□	□	■	□	□	□	□	P	□	5	D	AF	□	□
Whimbrel	□	■	□	□	■	□	□	□	□	□	□	3	I	C	#	■
Wood Sandpiper	□	□	□	□	□	■	□	□	□	□	□	1	E		■	■
Common Sandpiper	□	■	■	#	■	□	■	□	□	□	□	5	S		□	□
Redshank	■	■	□	□	■	□	■	□	□	□	□	5	S		□	□
Greenshank	□	□	■	□	■	□	□	□	□	■	□	4	D	F	#	■
Temminck's Stint	□	□	□	□	■	□	□	□	□	□	□	1	E		#	#
Purple Sandpiper	□	□	□	□	■	□	□	□	□	□	□	1	E		#	#
Dunlin	□	■	■	□	■	□	□	□	□	■	□	4	D	F	#	□
Ruff	□	■	■	□	■	□	□	□	□	□	□	1	E		■	■
Red-necked Phalarope	□	■	■	□	■	□	□	□	□	□	□	2	D	U	■	■
Great Skua	□	■	■	□	■	□	□	□	□	□	□	4	I	P	□	□
Arctic Skua	□	■	■	□	■	□	□	□	□	□	□	4	I	P	□	□
Great Black-backed Gull	■	■	□	□	■	□	□	□	□	□	□	5	S		□	□
Lesser Black-backed Gull	■	■	□	□	■	□	□	□	□	□	□	5	S		□	□
Herring Gull	■	■	□	□	■	□	□	■	□	□	□	6	D	U	□	□
Common Gull	□	■	■	□	■	□	■	□	□	□	□	5	S		□	□
Black-headed Gull	■	□	□	□	■	□	□	□	□	□	□	6	S		□	□
Stock Dove	■	□	□	□	■	□	■	■	□	□	■	5	S		□	□
Cuckoo	■	□	□	□	■	□	■	□	□	P	□	5	S		□	□
Snowy Owl	□	□	□	■	□	□	□	□	□	□	■	1	E		■	■
Short-eared Owl	□	□	■	□	■	□	□	□	■	P	#	4	S		■	■
Nightjar	■	□	□	□	■	□	■	■	□	P	□	4	D	U	■	■
Skylark	■	□	□	#	■	□	□	□	□	□	□	7	S		□	□
Shore Lark	□	□	□	■	□	□	□	□	□	□	□	1	E		□	■
Raven	■	■	■	□	■	□	■	□	■	■	■	4	D	FA	□	□
Carrion/Hooded Crow	■	■	□	□	■	□	□	□	□	■	■	6	S		□	□
Jackdaw	■	■	□	□	■	□	□	■	□	□	■	6	S		□	□
Chough	□	■	■	□	□	□	■	□	□	□	■	3	S		□	□
Wren	■	■	□	#	■	□	■	□	■	■	■	7	S		□	□
Dipper	■	□	■	□	■	□	■	□	□	□	■	5	S		□	□
Ring Ouzel	□	□	■	#	■	□	■	■	□	□	□	5	D	FU	□	□
Wheatear	■	■	□	#	■	□	□	□	□	■	□	5	D	F	□	□
Stonechat	■	■	□	□	■	□	□	□	■	P	□	5	D	A	□	□
Whinchat	■	□	□	□	■	□	□	□	■	P	□	5	S		□	□
Meadow Pipit	■	■	□	#	■	□	■	■	□	P	□	7	S		□	□
Pied Wagtail	■	■	□	□	■	□	□	■	□	□	□	6	S		□	□
Grey Wagtail	■	□	□	□	■	□	■	□	□	□	□	5	S	U	□	□
Twite	□	■	■	□	■	□	□	□	□	■	□	5	S		□	□
Snow Bunting	□	□	□	■	■	□	□	■	□	□	■	2	I	C	□	■
Lapland Bunting	□	□	□	■	□	□	□	□	□	□	□	1	E			■
Total 67 species	29	28	32	9	53	22	34	21	26	24	18				17	22

2

Key to table on breeding birds of the British uplands

1 **Widespread:** a wide-breeding distribution outside the uplands
2 **Coastal:** major breeding occurrences in coastal habitats
3 **Sub-montane:** mainly upland and/or northern in Briatin
4 **Montane:** breeding only above the potential tree-line. # denotes regular nesting within the montane zone
5 **Heaths and grasslands:** the predominant dry ground habitats
6 **Open waters:** lakes, tarns, pools, rivers and streams
7 **Acidic bogs:** raised and blanket bogs, and associated poor fens
8 **Cliffs and screes:** rock ledges and crevices, mainly as nesting sites
9 **Marginal land:** mainly enclosed rough grasslands
10 **Trees/woodland:** some association with these for nesting; P=occurrence in young plantations or clear fells
11 **Year-round resident:** # denotes species which sometimes winter on lower moors or around the edges of upland massifs
12 **Population size** (in seven classes): 1=1-9 pairs 2=10-99 pairs 3=100-999 pairs 4=1,000-9,999 pairs 5=10,000-99,999 pairs 6=100,000-999,999 pairs 7=1,000,000 pairs upwards
13 **Status:** S=stable, though within the limits of normal fluctuations I=increasing D=decreasing Refers, as far as information allows, to upland populations
14 **Reasons for change:** A=agricultural improvements F=afforestation P=protection and conservation C=climatic influence U=uncertain
15 **EC Birds Directive:** listed species requiring special conservation measures; # denotes additional migratory species qualifying for such measures
16 **Schedule 1:** species on Schedule 1 of the Wildlife and Countryside Act 1981

plant and animal, can best be understood through an historical perspective, going right back to the last Ice Age, when nearly all our present northern and western uplands were largely buried under permanent ice and snow. The subsequent northward migration of zones of tundra, steppe, scrub and, finally, forest, as the ice melted over thousands of years, redistributed the flora and fauna while Britain and mainland Europe were still a continuous land mass. Northern, treeless habitats with their plants and animals eventually became isolated on the upper levels of the higher mountains and extinguished altogether by the spread of forest across the lower hills, except where the ground remained too wet or rocky for trees to grow. This restriction of their habitat caused once widespread birds such as the Ptarmigan to become relict in distribution, in the same way as many arctic-alpine plants. The migratory birds of similar northern and montane distribution, such as Dotterel and Snow Bunting, are better described as 'fringe' species which respond to the highly localised occurrence of suitable habitat.

The forests had no sooner reached their greatest post-glacial extent than early humans began their onslaught upon them – a process of destruction which expanded until, at the Roman occupation, Britain was already substantially de-

nuded of its tree cover. Clearance continued until, by 1900, only 5% of this country was still covered by woodland, and many upland districts supported only a few scattered fragments. The hill ground formerly under trees was used as grazing range – for cattle, goats, and later predominantly sheep, though the Victorians converted large areas into preserves for Red Deer and Red Grouse. Repeated moor-burning helped to prevent forest regeneration. The upshot was that many birds which formerly belonged to open woodland and forest edge or treeless peat bog were provided with a vast increase in habitat. The dwarf-shrub heaths (especially of Heather) and grasslands of the former forest zone represented a biotic and sub-montane derivative to which open-ground species readily adapted. This remains, in fact, together with the even more modified rough pastures of the marginal land, the most productive of upland habitats in terms of variety and abundance of birds.

Our uplands can be divided into six main types, though these merge and overlap to some extent:

SHEEPWALKS Most hill country carries some sheep but the areas which most bear the imprint of centuries of sheep management, in their prevailing grassiness and loss of dwarf-shrub heath, are from the southern uplands southwards.

GROUSE MOORS The gentle contouring and drier climate of many eastern uplands, from Wales northwards, has favoured management for Red Grouse and the dwarf shrubs, notably Heather, which are its staple food.

DEER FORESTS The remoter and often rugged mountains of the Scottish Highlands have been managed as range for Red Deer, which can cope with the harsh climate and poor soils, and provide sporting revenue besides.

PEAT BOGS OR FLOWS These occur on the waterlogged ground of low-lying and almost flat northern moorlands, and higher plateaux, where deep layers of acidic peat have formed over thousands of years. They may be managed for sheep, grouse or deer but their carrying capacity is low. The most extensive areas are in east Sutherland and Caithness – the Flow Country.

HIGH TOPS Although part of massifs managed as sheepwalk, grouse moor or deer forest, the montane or alpine zone, lying above the potential (climatic) tree line, is sufficiently distinctive to be regarded as a separate category. This zone is best represented in the Highlands, and descends to low levels in the far north.

MARITIME HILLS The western and northern seaboard, especially of Scotland, has low hills and moorlands with distinctive features deriving from the proximity to the sea.

Together with the less developed coastlands, our uplands are the last wild places on any significant scale in Britain, with extensive areas of semi-natural vegetation composed of native plants. Indeed, some of the remoter Scottish hills have appreciable areas of natural habitat: fell-fields, snow-beds, peat bogs, lakes, cliffs and screes, virtually unmodified by human activity. The uplands are not only the habitat of a distinctively northern or montane element of the European bird fauna, but also provide major niches for many species widespread in various lowland habitats. These last include an important group of predators, but also passerines and waders.

The conservation importance of the uplands for birds is thus not only in holding a distinctive biogeographical element confined to these sub-montane and montane habitats, but also in supporting major population segments of more widespread species. Taking a still wider, international view, the birds of the British uplands are important for the following features:

Southern outposts of distinctive boreal, sub-arctic and arctic biotopes and bird communities. These include the high tops with Ptarmigan, Dotterel and Snow Bunting; the northern flows with Greenshank, Golden Plover, Dunlin, Arctic Skua, Black- and Red-throated Divers, Common Gull, Common Scoter, Wigeon and Greylag Goose; and maritime hills with Great and Arctic Skuas, Whimbrel, Red-necked Phalarope and Red-throated Diver.

Uniquely British biotopes and bird communities, notably heather-dominated moorland with Red Grouse, Merlin, Hen Harrier, Short-eared Owl, Golden Plover, Ring Ouzel and Stonechat; but also treeless deer forest with Golden Eagle, Greenshank and Black-throated Diver; and sheepwalks with Raven, Peregrine, Buzzard, Curlew and Lapwing.

Species of highly restricted or disjunct world distribution, especially Great Skua, Red Kite, Twite and Chough.

The unusually high breeding density and/or large population of some species, compared with most countries, e.g. Ptarmigan, Red Grouse, Golden Plover, Peregrine and Golden Eagle.

The geographical divergence into southern insular forms of northern species such as Willow Grouse, Golden Plover, Dunlin; and the ecological adaptation of open-forest-tundra species such

Greenshank, a local wader confined to the Highlands, where it nests mainly on treeless moorland and has recently lost ground to afforestation.

Kevin Carlson/Nature Photographers

4

A view of Fleet Forest fom the White Top of Culreoch looking to Black Craig showing the advancing tide of blanket conifer forests across the Galloway hills. If left to the foresters there would be no end to this transformation until they ran out of plantable land.

as Greenshank and Wood Sandpiper to treeless habitats.

Occurrence of migratory species, whose total range is shared with other countries.

Conservation objectives

The overall aim is to minimise further loss of upland habitats and decline of associated bird species, but with special emphasis on the safeguard of internationally important features. Both national and international needs could be met by a strategy which aimed, within each upland region of Britain, to:

1 Maintain or increase the species diversity of bird assemblages characteristic of natural and semi-natural habitats. Where practicable, the natural spread of species should be encouraged, by removing known resistances; and the disappearance of established species prevented through appropriate management. Deliberate reintroduction of lost species is allowable, but with each case considered on its own merits.

2 Maintain populations and breeding densities of all species legally protected during the breeding season, though within the limits of normal fluctuations. Declining species may require remedial management, based on knowledge of their ecology.

3 Protect and encourage species on Schedule 1 of the Wildlife and Countryside Act 1981 (22 of the listed upland species in Table 1), especially the rare and endangered ones.

4 Ensure that the control of Schedule 2 Part II species (those which may be killed or taken by authorised persons at all times), and the issue of any licences to kill otherwise protected species, is based on well-substantiated cases and achieved by legal methods.

Before dealing with the measures for achieving these goals, it is necessary to examine those aspects of land use and other human activity which have caused loss and damage to upland habitats and their birds in the past, and which will continue to do so unless appropriate counter-action is taken.

Conservation problems

Since 1940, about 30% of the British uplands have suffered deterioration or loss in nature conservation terms, mainly through intensification of land use. The main impacts have been:

AGRICULTURE 'Reclamation' of moorland to cre-

5

Derek Ratcliffe

The sheepwalks of the Pennines, showing marginal land passing to unenclosed hill grassland on Penyghent. The limestone of this district means that the land is able to support high numbers of both sheep, such as these Swaledales, and birds.

ate additional enclosed farmland has continued and, with modern techniques and machinery, has driven back the moorland edge to quite high levels in some districts. While the extension of improved pastures may enhance the food value of upland for some species, such as the Lapwing, it causes a permanent loss of nesting habitat for Red and Black Grouse, Golden Plover, Dunlin, Hen Harrier and Short-eared Owl. The widespread improvement of the often rush-infested rough grasslands of the marginal land has had a disastrous impact on populations of Lapwings, Curlews, Redshanks and Snipe, though Oystercatchers have increased locally.

Centuries of grazing and associated moorburning have all but eradicated heather moorland in the main sheep areas. Uniform, species-poor acidic grassland, often heavily invaded by bracken on dry ground, is the less interesting replacement, and there has been accompanying soil erosion and scree formation in some areas. This has continued since 1940 through an agri-cultural policy which encourages hill farmers, by three forms of subsidy including headage payments, to pack as many sheep as possible onto their grazings. While this at least ensured a heavy sheep and lamb mortality, and a resulting carrion supply which supported high breeding densities of Ravens, Buzzards and, more locally, Golden Eagles, even this benefit has faded. Modern improvements in sheep husbandry have steadily reduced mortality, to the point where some Raven populations are showing symptoms of decline. The disappearance of heather has seen the abandonment of many grouse moors, and the decline of other birds such as Merlin, Golden Plover and Stonechat.

AFFORESTATION By far the largest and most serious loss of open hill ground has been by the large-scale planting of conifers (one million hectares), mostly since 1940. Blanket afforestation by the Forestry Commission and private forestry companies has transformed whole moorland landscapes in districts such as the southern Cheviots, Eskdalemuir, Galloway, Knapdale and Kintyre. An upland bird fauna has been replaced on a parallel scale by one of woodland, causing a significant reduction in the Great Britain populations of Curlew, Golden Plover, Dunlin, Greenshank, Snipe, Red Grouse, Ring Ouzel and Wheatear; and more local declines in Merlin, Golden Eagle, Buzzard and Raven.

Some upland birds such as Short-eared Owl, Hen Harrier, Black Grouse, Whinchat, Tree Pipit and, locally, Nightjar, benefit from the first 10-15 years of new forest, before the young trees close into dense thickets. But this is a largely temporary gain. Subsequent forest re-planting, after clear-felling at 30-50 years, briefly restores a bird community in which woodland edge or glade species are better represented than those of open ground. Once the forests are established, the net effect is thus of substantial loss of upland bird populations.

There has been much debate over how much this matters, and of the benefits of increase in woodland birds, including once rare species such as Goshawk, Crossbill and Siskin. Most wildlife conservationists feel that the blanketing of our uplands with conifers has gone quite far enough, and were especially outraged by the foresters' ruthless onslaught on the great peatlands of the Flow Country, with their outstanding bird interest.

OTHER ACTIVITIES These are more localised in their effect. Water supply and hydro-electric projects cause disturbance and often permanent flooding of valley floors, but may attract aquatic birds. Mining and quarrying also provide nesting sites for various cliff-breeders in due course. Various recreational activities have been an increasing source of disturbance. In a few especially popular hiking areas there is evidence of decline in Golden Plover numbers, while rock climbing causes some failures among cliff-nesters. Multiplying hill roads and all-terrain vehicles open up the hills, ski developments often promote increased summer access to the high tops, and hang-gliding is a local nuisance; but their more serious effects are on the wilderness character of the uplands.

Grouse preservation conserves heather moorland, but is still accompanied by widespread, illegal and unacceptable slaughter of protected predators, which greatly restricts their national distribution and numbers. Unintentional disturbance by fishermen has an adverse effect on the breeding of various aquatic and riparian birds. The now unlawful 'sport' of egg-collecting

continues to cause concern in regard to rarer species, and the unlicensed taking of young raptors is another perennial problem.

The movement of most species away from the uplands at the end of the summer exposes them to the risk of adverse habitat change or other threats in their autumn and winter quarters. Those resorting to lowland or coastal haunts in this country face a range of problems, while for the full migrants events outside Britain pose still greater uncertainty.

The final and now most threatening of all aspects of human impact are the more indirect – the various forms of environmental pollution. We had a foretaste of these in the organochlorine insecticide episode, when the breeding success and/or numbers of certain upland raptors (notably Peregrine and Golden Eagle) far from sources of use were markedly depressed. After a prolonged battle with agro-chemical interests there were phased withdrawals of the harmful pesticides and good recovery of the affected species followed. That problem has not entirely passed, and there are worries that the Merlin may also be a victim of such effects.

Of still greater concern is pollution by gaseous emissions, largely from burning of fossil fuels, which are causing widespread acidification of waters and soils, and the still more alarming trend to global warming. Even if some of the less apocalyptic predictions about the 'greenhouse effect' come true, the results for wildlife and habitat in Britain could be more serious than all the other human impacts put together. They could gradually negate much of what has been achieved in the conservation of our wildlife in general, and so they demand overriding attention in the overall conservation strategy.

Conservation measures

SPECIALLY PROTECTED AREAS The surest means of protecting wildlife is by conferring legal status on land for that purpose, so that it becomes the primary objective of management. Upland nature reserves established by the Nature Conservancy Council, Royal Society for the Protection of Birds, local authorities, local trusts and others are an important contribution, totalling 106,680ha. The national network of Sites of Special Scientific Interest established by the NCC

7

is another major arm of the protected-area strategy, though a less certain measure because of its legal flaws and the frequent subordination of wildlife management to the owner or occupier's main purposes. The overall total of designated areas, including SSSIs, covers about 750,000ha or 11% of the remaining area of uplands.

For birds in general, all these protected areas work best for highly aggregated species, since a few sites can then encompass a large part of the population. Many species of upland birds have a well-dispersed distribution, so that this measure is less effective for them, and especially for the larger predators, each pair of which may need a territory of several hundred or thousand hectares. For these, nature reserves and other special areas can contain only a small fraction of their total populations. Nevertheless, the various categories of protected area make an important contribution to the conservation of rarer species such as Dotterel, Snow Bunting, Purple Sandpiper, Wood Sandpiper, Red-necked Phalarope, and Great and Arctic Skuas.

The Dotterel is a summer visitor to the high tops, mainly in the Highlands. It is a fringe northern bird which could be affected by global warming.

The nine upland National Parks of England and Wales cover 705,605ha of uncultivated hill ground, though this area includes a substantial part of the designated areas already mentioned. Although they give only limited control over agricultural improvements and afforestation damaging to bird life, these Parks afford some degree of protection against adverse change. In combination with the reserves and SSSIs, they support significant population segments of widespread species such as Peregrine, Raven, Buzzard, Red Grouse, Curlew, Golden Plover, Dunlin, Common Sandpiper, Ring Ouzel, Wheatear, Dipper, Skylark, Meadow Pipit and Grey Wagtail. Scotland has no National Parks and its National Scenic Areas are an irrelevant substitute as regards wildlife conservation measures.

Protected areas properly fulfil their purpose only if they are appropriately managed, by deliberate manipulation of habitats and species, according to the insights of ecological research. Shortage of funds has led to some neglect in this field, though there are reserves where a policy of minimum intervention is best. Deliberate re-introduction of species is often controversial, but had general support in the case of the White-

Kevin Carlson/Nature Photographers

A view of the high montane fell-fields of the Cairngorms in June, resting haunts of Ptarmigan, Dotterel and Snow Bunting, where snow fields linger through the summer.

tailed Eagle, a spectacular long-lost bird unlikely to have made its own way back here. The island reserve of Rhum was chosen as an especially suitable launching place for this venture, which has succeeded in restoring the bird as a breeding species to Britain.

THE WIDER COUNTRYSIDE Even if all upland birds could be adequately protected within designated areas, the larger part of the populations of most species would still be at risk in the wider countryside beyond. For these, other, broader measures affecting land-use changes are needed. The endless preaching at the various land-development interests which are continuing to erode the remaining areas of natural and semi-natural habitat has clearly had very limited success. They become more amenable when there is the option of paying them compensation for desisting, or when there is the threat of legislation which will make life more difficult.

Farming is gradually and painfully having to accept the fact of agricultural over-production and land which is surplus to needs. The principle of paying farmers to manage land in traditional ways which maintain wildlife and scenic values

is finding increasing acceptance. The Environmentally Sensitive Areas located in upland areas mostly include marginal land, rather than open hills, and their effectiveness in achieving conservation objectives is still unknown. A more sharply focused scheme to restore heather moorland by reducing sheep numbers has been worked out between the NCC, National Trust and tenant farmers in the central Lake District. While it is not in an area with much interest for moorland birds, it may serve as a model for other schemes elsewhere, and the Government grant-aid for a programme of heather restoration is to be welcomed, even if the boosting of grouse shooting is the main reason behind it.

The giving of grant-aid for the largely futile cutting of moorland drains has happily ceased. There is, however, still a variety of taxpayer support for individual attempts at hill-land improvement and reclamation which will continue in many a desperate attempt at survival, though they amount to economic nonsense. It is high time that the Government grasped the nettle of wholesale decline in the economics of hill-farming, and produced a comprehensive package in which public money – in the present threefold form of direct grant-aid and subsidy, tax reliefs and price support – was deployed in ways which

9

gave hill farmers a decent income but avoided further erosion of wildlife interest. How far it is possible to restore lost wildlife interest remains to be seen.

Forestry is a still more intractable issue. The only way to prevent it causing further losses of upland birds is to stop planting more trees on the uplands. The self-serving arguments that afforestation is only putting back what has been lost, that it creates a richer habitat, and that it diversifies the uplands, will not wash. An industry so heavily reliant on public funds has to be under much tighter public control which takes account of the other interests in the countryside affected by afforestation. The Government must end the cosy system whereby the forestry industry almost holds a licence to print its own money.

The present *modus operandi* of the Forestry Commission, and its back-scratching relationship with the private forestry sector, is at the heart of the problem. When the Government pronounces on forestry matters, it is the Commission that has written the words. We are presented with a 'policy' which is no more than a formula for an open-ended advance of alien conifer plantations across the uplands, according to a land market loaded in favour of forestry interests. Even in the National Parks there have been the most intense battles to prevent intrusive planting in sensitive areas, and the influential forestry lobby is working hard to loosen the resistance of the one bulwark that has obstructed them – the common lands of England and Wales. While the removal of tax reliefs for private afforestation in March 1988 dealt a serious blow to this sector, the forestry lobby seeks to restore its fortunes, and has recently won management grants which will increase public funding to a ridiculous level.

The only effective solution appears to be to remove from the Forestry Commission much of the decision-making responsibility on the location of the new forests, by placing this under planning control, and insisting that the EC requirement for environmental impact assessment is applied to all planting proposals above 25ha. In addition, the Commission should be instructed to heed the National Audit Office strictures on the economics of afforestation, and apply strict cost/benefit criteria to all new plant-

ing, whether by its own enterprise or through approval and grant-aid to the private sector. There are already positive measures to promote the afforestation of lowland farmland, surplus to agricultural requirements, where the trees would grow well and could even produce an environmental benefit. It would be far more preferable to switch financial support from upland forestry to these.

While improvements to the existing forests for wildlife should certainly be encouraged, there should be a clear understanding that this is a quite separate issue, which does not give further excuse for continuing with upland afforestation. Control over forestry in National Parks, Areas of Outstanding Natural Beauty and National Scenic Areas must become much stricter, and common lands must not be allowed to become foresters' stamping grounds.

Other development issues will have to be handled – as before – by planning control, but with the added need for environmental impact assessment over proposals significant to wildlife and scenic beauty. Such developments need to be foreseen in structure plans, and there should be a presumption against approval for proposals sought *ad hoc* outside these plans. This applies especially to developments concerning water resources, energy, mineral extraction and quarrying (including peat), buildings, transport, recreation and defence. Objectors need to challenge the justifications behind proposals, especially those involving public funds, and to identify precisely whose interests are being served. Developments that are allowed to proceed should have been rigorously and fairly scrutinised, to determine the balance of public interest involved, and within overall policies that have considered these issues strategically and according to safeguards intended to minimise adverse effects. The publicity and educational work on environmental awareness must not only continue but be improved. The sooner that basic principles of ecology and conservation are built into the school curriculum the better.

The Wildlife and Countryside Act 1981 includes previous legislation on bird protection against unlawful killing and taking, with special penalties for species on Schedule 1 (protected also against wilful disturbance and unlicensed

Britain has one of the largest European populations of the Golden Eagle, but it is slowly losing ground to blanket afforestation in its Scottish haunts.

photography at the nest). While this contains rather than prevents deliberate harmful interference, it is a very necessary component of the available conservation measures.

International measures

It is important to honour obligations to international conservation measures, and especially those concerning migratory species. Britain is a signatory to several relevant treaties or conventions. The Birds Directive of the EC requires member states to take measures to protect specially listed species and regularly occurring migrants not on the list (see Table 1). The required measures include the setting up of Special Protection Areas to safeguard habitats and the NCC has recently prepared for the UK Government a comprehensive list of areas deserving this status. Britain has the main or only EC populations of at least 20 upland species. The Bern and Bonn Conventions carry similar obligations for signatory states to protect, respectively, important wildlife habitats and migratory species, while the Ramsar Convention deals with the conservation of wetlands, and thereby includes major upland bird habitats such as peat bogs and open waters – tarns, lakes and streams. The World Heritage Convention requires nomination of 'cultural and natural properties' considered to be of 'outstanding universal value' against a set of carefully defined criteria. The Cairngorms area and the Flow Country are regarded by many conservationists as strong candidates qualifying for nomination as such 'natural properties'.

These measures give the potential for a considerable reinforcement of the national conservation programme. Out of 40 SPAs and 44 Ramsar sites notified by the UK, 4 and 8, respectively, are upland. At least another 37 upland SPAs are proposed. It is, however, unfortunate that the Government shows perennial suspicion of these obligations and some reluctance to meeting them with appropriate action. There was, indeed, open hostility to EC proposals for a new Habitats Directive, and, although this has been modulated, it seems to be more for reasons of political diplomacy than from any real change of heart. Fears of constraints to development and the profits of commerce lie behind the lip service paid to environmental concern Nothing better reveals our Government's real attitudes to nature

Derek Ratcliffe

The rugged granite uplands of Galloway with plantations below. These are the haunts of Golden Eagle, Peregrine and Raven.

conservation than this foot-dragging over internationally required action.

The biggest challenge facing all nations is the need for urgent and meaningful action on atmospheric pollution, to combat acidification and global warming. Our Prime Minister has shown a clear appreciation of the problems, but we want deeds and not words, plus a willingness to forget petty jingoisms and work in real international cooperation for the good of the world.

References

Cramp, S, & Simmons, K E L 1977-88 *Handbook of the Birds of Europe, the Middle East and North Africa. The Birds of the Western Palearctic.* Vols I-V. Oxford University Press
Fuller, R J 1982 *Bird Habitats in Britain.* Poyser, Calton
Marchant, J H, Hudson, R, Carter, S P, & Whittington, P 1990 *Population Trends in British Breeding Birds.* British Trust for Ornithology, Tring
NCC 1984 *Nature Conservation in Great Britain.* NCC, London
NCC 1986 *Nature Conservation and Afforestation in Britain.* NCC, Peterborough
Nethersole-Thompson, D, & Nethersole-Thompson 1986 *Waders, their Breeding Haunts and Watchers.* Poyser, Calton
Sharrock, J T R 1976 *The Atlas of Breeding Birds in Britain and Ireland.* British Trust for Ornithology, Tring
Stroud, D A, Mudge, G P, & Pienkowski, M W 1990 *Protecting Internationally Important Bird Sites.* A review of the EEC Special Protection Area network in Great Britain. NCC, Peterborough
Tompkins, S 1989 *Forestry in Crisis. The Battle for the Hills.* Helm, London
Usher, M B, & Thompson, D B A 1988 *Ecological Change in the Uplands* (British Ecological Society special publication no. 7). Blackwell Scientific, Oxford

Dr Derek Ratcliffe was the Nature Conservancy Council's Chief Scientist before his retirement in 1989. His book *Bird Life of Mountain and Upland* is to be published by Cambridge University Press this autumn.

THE CONSERVATIONIST –
protecting nature

19. Nature conservation and the Nature Conservation Review – a novel philosophical framework

Des Thompson, William J. Sutherland, and John Birks

A beginning

On Thursday 29 April 1948 something important happened for nature conservation in Britain. In the House of Commons, the Lord President of the Privy Council and Leader of the House, The Right Honourable Herbert Morrison MP (later Baron Morrison of Lambeth), responded to a question from Mr (later Sir) Edward Keeling MP asking "...whether he will now make a statement about the Reports on the Conservation of Nature in England and Wales, Command Paper 7122, and Scotland, Command Paper 7235, Part II?"[1]

The Lord President replied:

> "The Government have decided to accept in principle the recommen-
> dations of these two Reports calling for the establishment of a Nature
> Conservation Board and a Biological Service under the auspices of the
> Agricultural Research Council. The Board and the Service will cover
> Great Britain as a whole, but there will be a special committee super-
> vising the Scottish Division of the Service on the lines recommended
> by the Scottish Wild Life Conservation Committee. Part of the facilities
> serving Great Britain as a whole will also be located in Scotland. I
> should make it clear that the Government are not necessarily commit-
> ted to the scale of expenditure mentioned in these Reports and that it
> will in any case take some years before it is possible to work up to the
> full scale of operations envisaged in them."

And with that, Britain's statutory nature conservation movement took its first real steps. Derek Ratcliffe played a key role in the ensuing decades, but as Herbert Morrison rose to his feet in the House of Commons, Derek, a first-year undergraduate at the University of Sheffield[2], was back at his lectures having returned from an eleven-day exhilarating field trek in Galloway. His diary entry for 19 April 1948, entitled 'Return Home', lists territories checked: one Golden Eagle (*Aquila chrysaetos*), 16 Raven (*Corvus corax*), six Buzzard (*Buteo buteo*), and 11 Peregrine (*Falco peregrinus*), with a total of 22 nest contents ascertained. The Tenth of April 1948 at Craignelder was a special day with Derek's first sighting of nesting Golden Eagles[3-6]. Approaching an old nest from below, he describes: "Not a thing moved and there was dead silence, until at last I clapped my hands. For a second nothing happened and then a huge form rose and flung itself from the nest. I heaved a sigh of relief for now I knew that at last an ambition was fulfilled – a Galloway eagle's eyrie."[7]. Returning south on the train from Newton Stewart, he wrote: "From the train I saw again the desolate fortresses of Cairnsmore Forest. Near Cullendoch an old Black Grouse [*Tetrao tetrix*] flew level with the train for quite a distance. I gazed across the Shaw Hill and pictured the Peregrine sitting on her eggs and then the train left the wilds." [7].

At the beginning of the trip, having parked his bicycle below the Clints of Dromore (Figs. 13.2 & 13.10) before setting off for the hill, he rather prophetically fell into conversation with an elderly shepherd who advised him: "Ye'll no be going to spiel the rocks – for there's places ye can get into that ye canna get oot o' again"[3]. Derek was indeed off to spiel (climb). Remote and distant from government policy making at the time, his field insights would prove invaluable when, almost eight years later, in January 1956, he would join the Nature Conservancy[2] and play a fundamentally important role in shaping the philosophy and practice of nature conservation in Britain.

In this chapter we trace the early post-war work in Britain that went into developing nature conservation and its philosophy as we know it today. We reflect on the importance of the ensuing framework governing the importance of nature conservation sites – guided by what are often referred to as the 'Ratcliffe criteria' given in *A Nature Conservation Review*[8,9]. We have tried not to litter the text with references, and acknowledge that this narrative presents our own personal interpretation of events. We have drawn particularly on Stamp[10], Sheail[11,12], Ratcliffe[3,8,13,14], Adams[15,16], Moore[17], Evans[18], Smout[19,20], Marren[21], and Avery[22].

Early days for nature conservation

It is remarkable that in the immediate aftermath of the Second World War the UK Government, under Prime Minister Clement Attlee, put in place a new movement for nature conservation. The economy was exhausted, the country mired in debt, and rationing restricted food, fuel, clothing, and even soap. Yet the country wanted, and needed, a far better protected countryside. As Dudley Stamp explains in *Nature Conservation in Britain*[10] there was a "great coming together of activities". Ultimately it was pressure on land that drove the movement, with new space needed for industrial development, housing, agriculture, and forestry – much of which had to be sensitive to the needs of rural communities and amenities.

But something else had been stirring in the nation's consciousness – nature was in decline. If we went back just to the late 19th century we would have seen once extensive areas of natural habitat already reduced to mere fragments of heavily drained fens, marshes, and peatland plains, slivers of woodland, heaths burdened by heavy sheep grazing, and sprawling towns and villages on the coast, especially around river mouths and along the larger rivers. In rural parts, in glens and valleys, and by lochs, there would have been villages and hamlets, and on the open hill fresh signs of scattered settlements abandoned in the face of the 'clearances' for sheep. Rivers would often have been filthy, and on some days the air would have been wretchedly smog-ridden near some of the larger cities and towns. In the uplands, far beyond the upper reaches of cultivation, great swathes of the landscape would have borne witness to decades, in parts centuries, of tree felling, burning, and heavy grazing pressures, and large mammalian and bird predators would then have been largely absent through scrupulously effective 'management'.

Of course, there were positive aspects to this, with a rich and varied wildlife associated with a diversity of lowland habitats embracing downs, heathland, farmland and meadows, arable, myriad hedgerows, and scrubby woodland juxtaposed with heath, bogs, and grassland. Over large tracts of the uplands sheep numbers were low, and many large sporting estates had few, if any, sheep. For much of our wildlife, the uplands were the last stronghold for predators formerly much more widespread, such as Wildcat (*Felis silvestris*), Pine Marten (*Martes martes*), and Golden Eagle.

Nature conservation had slow beginnings, and the early steps were motivated by the need to protect birds from being shot – with their feathers playing a decisive part. The destruction of birds for plumes for Victorian ladies' hats triggered the first legislation (Sea Birds Preservation Act 1869[19]), on account of the killing of Kittiwakes (*Rissa tridactyla*) and Great Crested Grebes (*Podiceps cristatus*) for their feathers, and later the Wild Birds Protection Act 1880[19] came into force. The numbers of birds shot prior to the act were phenomenal – 107,250 seabirds shot in just four months, with up to 11,000 shot by eight people in just a week[19]. The Society for the Protection of Birds, formed in 1889 and composed largely of women, was determined to discourage both the killing of birds for feathers and the wearing of feathers. Such was their success that the Society received its Royal Charter in 1904, with one of the most revered zoologists of the time, Alfred Newton, exerting considerable support and influence. Fired by his horror at the extermination of the last Great Auk (*Penguinus impennis*) in Iceland in 1844 (he subsequently mounted his own expedition to see if any others had persisted), Newton addressed the British Association in 1868, decrying that "Fair and innocent as the snowy plumes may appear on a lady's hat, I must tell the wearer the truth – she bears the murderer's brand on her forehead."[11].

Much of the concern for nature was about species, most notably birds. Heightened awareness of habitat destruction arose a decade later, spurred by the voracious appetite of agriculture and forestry for 'unproductive' land. And it is here that the banker and entomologist Nathaniel Charles Rothschild (father of Miriam – another scientist and conservationist) came to the fore as arguably the first pioneer of nature conservation as we now know it today – establishing the UK's first nature reserve through purchasing Wicken Fen in 1899 and Woodwalton Fen in 1910. He established the Society for the Promotion of Nature Reserves (SPNR, later becoming the Royal Society of Wildlife Trusts) in May 1912, and in 1916 produced for the Board of Agriculture a schedule of 251 proposed reserves – some of the best wildlife sites in the UK. Tragically, suffering from encephalitis, Rothschild took his own life in 1923, aged 46, and it has been argued that this fundamentally stalled the progress of nature conservation until the 1940s[23]. But at least we had here the beginnings of a portfolio of sites for nature conservation, and ever since then the movement has ultimately been motivated by a desire to secure sites to protect them from development or other losses. Nature conservation has since grown into an ecologically, politically, and economically complex discipline, with hardened conservationists standing by the first principle of securing the best of nature. Three pillars of nature conservation emerged – propping up protected species, protected areas, and the 'wider countryside'[10,19,21].

The 1930s saw growing public concern about the countryside with increased demand for public access, memorably marked by the mass trespass on Kinder Scout in 1932, and a desire to protect its natural beauty. The latter came to a head in 1936, following the Forestry Commission's afforestation of Ennerdale and its purchase of Dunnerdale and Eskdale in the Lake District. This elicited strong opposition from the Council for the Protection of Rural England and a list of some 13,000 petitioners led by the Archbishop of York[24]. Politically, these clashes increased support for the establishment of National Parks. Local nature conservation organisations, what we now call Wildlife Trusts, sprang up under the auspices of the SPNR, the first in Norfolk in 1926, then the Pembrokeshire Bird Protection Society in 1938, Yorkshire in 1948, followed by Lincolnshire, Leicestershire, Cambridgeshire, and many more beyond (there are now 45 in the UK, one in the Isle of Man, and another in the Channel Isles). Attention was being drawn to dramatic changes wrought on the land, and prominent people spoke out about losses of wildlife and the diminution of scenic beauty in many of our wilder places.

By the beginning of the Second World War there were growing complaints and articles published about losses of nature. The Forestry Commission paved the way for wide-scale afforestation[25], and large areas were being taken over for military purposes and agriculture (ironically, some of the military training areas, such as Salisbury Plain, have since become important sanctuaries for nesting birds such as Stone Curlew (*Burhinus oedicnemus*), with around 12% of the breeding population on the Plain). The extensive felling of mature woods, ploughing of ancient grasslands, and the development of large areas for airfields and various commodities angered the founders of the environmental movement.

In 1941 the SPNR held a conference which led to the formation of the Nature Reserves Investigations Committee. This published several reports, and in 1943 published *Nature Conservation in Great Britain*[26] (a second edition appeared two years later[27]), a fundamentally important forerunner to what were to be the foundations for today's nature conservation[10,14,28]. W.T. Calman in Fife wrote a letter[29] to *The Spectator* in 1943 succinctly describing its importance: "This little pamphlet (price 6d.) provides an excellent outline of the aims and methods of Nature Conservation which deserves the attention of all interested in the subject." That letter was a response to a widely overlooked but fundamentally important article[30] by Arthur Tansley (Fig. 19.1) in *The Spectator*, in which he set out a lucid argument for nature conservation. Tansley had chaired the British Ecological Society's Nature Reserves Committee, formed in 1943. He wrote:

> "The first object of nature-preservation is maintenance for the people at large of the beauty and interest of characteristic British scenery. It is widely felt that the public should be allowed freer access to important

Figure 19.1. Sir Arthur Tansley, Co. Wicklow 1949. Photograph taken by Eric Hultén and reproduced by Harry God-win in his account of Tansley's life and career in the *Biographical Memoirs of Fellows of the Royal Society* (1957). Reproduced by permission of Peter Iredale.

areas of scenery and increased facilities to visit them. That is the primary purpose of the proposal to form 'National Parks' in the widest sense. A second object is the preservation of our natural fauna and flora, not only because our native plants and animals interest a large number of people and are often beautiful, but because their close study is a fascinating branch of biology which can play an important part in certain aspects of a wider education and is of direct value in improving forestry and the pastoral side of agriculture. The conservation of as much as possible of our wild life as a whole – plants and animals alike – should have wider appeal. To countrymen and to town-dwellers who love the country this is an essential part of their environment, and its gradual destruction or degradation represent an irreparable loss."

Here we have reference to two fundamentals of the emerging nature conservation movement – the creation of National Parks, and the appeal of nature and importance of conserving it. Tansley[30] ended his essay with prescience:

"What we really need is a central Government authority comparable with the American 'Fish and Wild Life Service' of the U.S. Depart-ment of the Interior, but including plants as well as animals – it is

335

quite essential that their interdependence should be recognised. Under such an authority all National Reserves to which the necessary legislation would apply would be scheduled. Individual Parks and Reserves would have to be managed by special committees, and both the central authority and the local committees would have to be assured of adequate ecological advice."

Four years later, Tansley wrote a second article[31], again in *The Spectator*, this time reflecting on two important Government reports that would define the face of nature conservation in Britain. He commented: "It will be seen that the functions of the National Parks and of the National Nature Reserves would be distinctly different. The parks are intended primarily for public enjoyment; the reserves for preserving representative samples of wild life and for increase of knowledge about them."

Finding good sites for nature – Command papers 7122 and 7235

During 1943-1947 there was significant work by committees and individuals culminating in two extraordinary official reports, which very much lived up to Tansley's[30] appeal. *Conservation of Nature in England and Wales*[32] and *Report of the Committee on National Parks and Conservation of Nature in Scotland*[33] set out the philosophy for caring for nature and wild places. Breath-taking in their vision, clarity, and sense of purpose, these reports prescribed **the** national strategy for nature conservation. These were the reports that Herbert Morrison responded to in Parliament in the following year. And thirty years later, *A Nature Conservation Review* (NCR)[8,9] began with a reiteration of their importance:

> "These documents presented the basic philosophy that the practice of nature conservation in Britain should centre around the safeguarding of a fairly large number of key areas adequately representing all major types of natural and semi-natural vegetation, with their characteristic assemblages of plants and animals, and habitat conditions, of climate, topography, rocks and soils, and biotic influences."

It was clear – to protect nature you had to identify the best, the most threatened, and the most representative examples, and then safeguard them. How easy to state this, but how challenging to enact it. Beckoning were National Nature Reserves (NNRs) and the national series of notified Sites of Special Scientific Interest (SSSIs) in Britain, and Areas of Special Scientific Interest (ASSIs) in Northern Ireland. But a massive amount of work was needed first to raise the importance of nature, and what was befalling it.

Importantly, the justification for Government action, and what was done, arose arguably mainly from the need to set aside or protect some representative areas of the countryside as a resource principally for scientific endeavour and education. Hence, there emerged a desire for a close relationship between the administrative structures for nature conservation and the existing research councils. Growing out of this was a dominant focus on the acquisition of a series of nature reserves and recognition of sites that had 'special scientific interest'. This was more a policy for conserving certain places for the particular purposes of science rather than a policy to protect nature.

Some pioneering heroes of nature conservation in Britain

A wonderfully talented group of people worked at this, many of them ecologists bringing conservation science to the fore for the first time. Sir Julian Huxley and Charles Elton had outstanding influences on ecological thinking. Huxley was quite brilliant in making the connections between the needs to protect nature in specific areas and to research and understand nature; he had, after all, long advocated the central importance of science in, and for, government. Some other champions for nature and strategic land planning emerged at this time, with Lord Justice Scott, Lord Reith, R.S. (later Lord) Hudson, John Dower, Dudley Stamp, Sir Arthur Hobhouse, and Sir J. Douglas Ramsay playing defining roles.

But two utterly different people between them largely moulded nature conservation as we now know it. The aforementioned Arthur George Tansley (later Sir) (1871-1955) (Fig. 19.1) was a truly pioneering plant ecologist, publishing his *tour de force* in 1939 *The British Islands and Their Vegetation*[34]. He was founder President of the British Ecological Society (1913-1915, and the only person to serve a second term, 1938-1939; WJS is the current President), first President of the Council for the Promotion of Field Studies (now the Field Studies Council, currently chaired by DBAT), the founding editor of the *Journal of Ecology,* founder of the journal *New Phytologist,* and the deviser with Roy Clapham (Fig. 4.2) of the 'ecosystem' concept[2,3,35]. His academic accomplishments were numerous[35], and he had an exceptional international reach through his work. He was described by Ratcliffe[14] as the "foremost thinker of those who launched the post-war conservation movement" and published an elegant book on the subject in 1945, *Our Heritage of Wild Nature*[36], a forerunner to Cmd. 7122[32]. What is not so well known about Tansley is his close relationship with the psychologist Sigmund Freud (whose obituary he wrote for the Royal Society in 1941) and which undoubtedly influenced his philosophical beliefs in the value of nature[35]. In 1920 he published a popular introduction to psychology *The New Psychology and its Relation to Life*[37], introducing the ideas of Freud and Carl Jung, and he never lost his fascination in this field. Derek Ratcliffe became fascinated in human behaviour and psychology after reading this book as a student in Sheffield where his teacher was Roy Clapham[2], a former student and colleague of Tansley. It is tempting to see some of Jung's views on the 'collective unconscious' (memories and ideas inherited from ancestors) in Tansley's writings on the importance of nature and the damage wrought on it. He was a brilliant academic, writer, and philosopher, and in possession of an extraordinarily clear and incisive mind on what mattered most for nature[35].

Our other pioneer was small, cockney-spoken, intelligent, innovative, organisationally supremely efficient, and highly energetic. He was Edward Max Nicholson (1904-2003) (Fig. 19.2), and if Tansley devised the plans for nature conservation, it was Nicholson who brilliantly steered its new course. He founded the British Trust for Ornithology in 1932 (becoming its Chair in 1947) through his passion for co-operative bird-watching, which he described in *The Art of Bird-Watching*[38]. He sustained a massive interest in birds throughout his life, and was editor of *British Birds* (1951-1960), President of the Royal Society for the Protection of Birds (RSPB) (1989-1995), and one of the editors of the monumental nine volumes *Birds of the Western Palearctic* (published between 1977 and 1994[39]). Writing the foreword for the last volume, he closed with:

"Despite all the troubles it has entailed, the warmth and respect with which ornithologists have welcomed it has made the enterprise eminently worthwhile". His pamphlet *A National Plan for Great Britain*[40] ultimately paved the way for what is now the British think-tank, 'The Policy Studies Institute'. During the Second World War, having just joined the Civil Service in 1940, he took charge of organising Atlantic shipping operations and convoys (often undertaken in unimaginably treacherous conditions), played a key role in the invasion of Europe by Operation Overlord, and worked closely with Winston Churchill. Described as a 'maverick figure' in the civil service, he exerted much influence over Government policy[41]. He went on to form the World Wildlife Fund for Nature (WWF) (with Sir Peter Scott, Guy Mountford, and Victor Stolan), and played a key role in the creation of the International Institute for Environment and Development (which led to the formation of the United Nations Environment Programme (UNEP), and the introduction of the term 'sustainable development') and the *ENDS Report* (an influential journal on environmental policy). With Sir Julian Huxley (then Director General of UNESCO, the UN scientific and educational organisation) he formed in 1947–1948 what is now the International Union for Conservation of Nature (IUCN). In his later years he developed a keen interest in urban ecology, helping establish Britain's first urban ecology park, and died aged 98 in April 2003. One of his greatest trump cards in the nature conservation story was a close working relationship with Herbert Morrison, for Max was his private secretary in the Attlee administration[41].

Figure 19.2. Max Nicholson (1904-2003) was influential in founding the Nature Conservancy and becoming its Director-General 1951-1965. He was a strong supporter of Derek Ratcliffe and his various projects early in his career including the Peregrine enquiries[79], the Highland Vegetation Survey[2], and the botanical survey of Upper Teesdale[2]. Max was an active ornithologist and chair of the British Trust for Ornithology (1947-1949), environmentalist, and author of many books including *The System – The misgovernment of modern Britain* (1967) and *The Environmental Revolution* (1970). Photo: Biel J. Perelló, The Albufera International Biodiversity Group.

The Government machinery hard at work

In one sense it was the argument over where industry should expand beyond London and Birmingham in the 1940s that provided the stimulus for Government to act. In 1938 Sir Montague Barlow was appointed to chair the Royal Commission on the Distribution of the Industrial Population, reporting in January 1940. As Stamp[10] put it crisply, it was "a complex document with majority and minority reports and various notes of reservation". And no wonder, for the report probed the fundamental question of where developments should go. Farmland was being lost to industry whilst other industrial areas were being abandoned. In response to this, in October 1941, the Government set up a Committee on Land Utilisation in Rural Areas under Lord Justice Scott. It had to consider conditions that would govern "building and other constructional developments in country areas consistently with the maintenance of agriculture…". In effect, this had to advise on where development should occur. It reported in August 1942, and in many ways was the blueprint for what was to come. Through Stamp's direct influence as Vice-Chair and drafter, it set out a rationale for "National and Regional Parks and other open spaces" primarily for public recreation, and the establishment of 'Nature Reservations'.

It advised that "The Central Planning Authority, in conjunction with the appropriate Scientific Societies, should prepare details of areas desired as nature reserves (including geological parks) and take the necessary steps for their reservation and control – which must be strict if rare species are to be safeguarded"[10]. Here, we find language with a resonance of nature conservation today.

In due course and heavily influenced by the Scott Report, the Agriculture Act 1947 set out a new ethos for farming, and the Town and Country Planning Act 1947 made planning compulsory across the whole country. But what of nature? The Government determined that further thinking was needed on some key matters. John Dower was asked to chair a committee to look in detail at National Parks in England and Wales, and Sir J. Douglas Ramsay was asked to do the same for Scotland, with its separate legislation. Both reported in 1945, with Dower's published in May 1945[42], shortly before his untimely death, setting out the philosophy governing the need for National Parks. Dower recommended the creation of a 'Wild Life Conservation Council', as 'a permanent organ of Government'. The Ramsay Committee report[33] recommended the creation of five National Parks amounting to just over 480,000 hectares of high quality landscapes in Scotland.

Now matters were moving at speed. In August, the Government set up The National Parks Committee (England and Wales) chaired by Sir Arthur Hobhouse, and two special committees: one dealing with footpaths and access (under Hobhouse); and the second with the grand title of 'The Wild Life Conservation Special Committee' concerned with England and Wales, chaired by Sir Julian Huxley, with Sir Arthur Tansley as one of the Vice-Chairs, and several eminent scientists as members. In Scotland, Edinburgh University's naturalist Professor James Ritchie chaired a Committee considering similar matters.

The emergence of nature conservation in statute

In July 1947, Huxley's Committee reported to the Minister of Town and Country Planning[43], setting out the need for a nature conservation body. Much of the leadership behind this came from Arthur Tansley (Fig. 19.1) – Huxley having moved to UNESCO. Crucially, it set out a lengthy list of proposed nature reserves, and the modern rationale for nature conservation, with a heavy emphasis on ecological science. The Ritchie Committee reported to the Secretary of State for Scotland[33]. It accepted the scientific rationale for conserving nature, agreed that there should be a Great Britain Nature Conservation Board, and provided a list of proposed Nature Reserves in Scotland[33].

Swiftly, a Nature Conservancy Board (NCB) and a Biological Service was formed in 1948, responsible to the Agricultural Research Council. Max Nicholson (Fig. 19.2) played a decisive role here, for he persuaded Herbert Morrison, as Lord President of the Privy Council, to set up the Nature Conservancy (NC). It was established as a separate body under the aegis of a committee of the Privy Council by Royal Charter of 23 March 1949. It derived its statutory powers from the National Parks and Access to the Countryside Act 1949[44]. Hence, it could own or lease NNRs, enter into a nature reserve agreement whereby the landowner, lessee, or occupier would allow the Conservancy to carry out a management programme for nature conservation and their property, and the Act granted the Conservancy powers to acquire land by compulsion, to lease or enter into a management agreement with the land owner (in order to properly maintain a reserve), and to formulate bye-laws for the protection of each reserve.

The Huxley and Ritchie Committees recommended a list of proposed nature reserves where wildlife would be studied and protected, the creation of SSSIs for areas outside the statutory reserves, the undertaking of survey and experimental work, a series of institutes of terrestrial ecology, and the setting up of an official biological service to establish and maintain the reserves, to carry out the necessary research, and to advise on nature conservation generally. Accordingly, the Nature Conservancy's functions were "to provide scientific advice on the conservation and control of the natural flora and fauna of Great Britain; to establish, maintain and manage nature reserves in Great Britain, including the maintenance of physical features of scientific interest; and to organise and develop the research and scientific services related thereto"[44].

What did not happen, however, was the merging of work to connect National Parks with nature conservation. Instead, what has often been articulated as the 'great divide' emerged, with Ratcliffe[14] commenting that "It was a distinction made in no other country in the world where there are official countryside conservation programmes, and one lost on the British public at large." Academic ecologists and scientists advanced thinking on ecology and nature conservation. Separately, the National Parks, wider access, and recreational interests were pursued by those who enjoyed walking and scenic beauty. With hindsight, there was extraordinarily little connection between the two. Politically, this chimed with no appetite for, and indeed some vested resistance to, merging land ownership and management too heavily with state-led ambitions for conserving nature. As Ratcliffe[14] put it "…the more innocuous-sounding and 'scientific' nature conservation enterprise was allowed a much more solid foundation of executive powers." To this day, many people, even those closely connected with the environmental movement, are perplexed at the reach and influence of the scientific interests of habitats, species, and other natural features, in contrast to the little cognisance given to landscape, amenity, and scenic features to which so many more people can relate.

Tansley, Huxley, and their peers, with huge tactical support from Nicholson, won through to give us the statutory basis we have today. However, it should be noted that Tansley, in particular, wholly understood and articulated the interdependence between nature and wider countryside scenic interests and enjoyment[36].

All of this happened in immediate post-war Britain. The compelling historian and writer Correlli Barnett wrote the trilogy on the 'Pride and Fall' of British power in the 20th century. In *The Lost Victory. British Dreams, British Realities 1945-1950*[45], he argued that in the aftermath of the Second World War Britain lost major opportunities to modernise as an industrial power. Rather than investing in industry and infrastructure, Barnett argued that Britain invested its post-war loans into the Welfare State, with the 'liberal establishment' ultimately responsible for this. In his 514 page tome there is no mention of 'environment' or of 'nature', and 'agriculture' gets just three mentions. It is sobering to think what might have happened had this so-called liberalism not prevailed, and a more utilitarian ethos taken hold. In the ensuing decades, nature conservation faced many onslaughts from the latter.

The Nature Conservancy and Nature Conservancy Council

In 1949 life began for the Nature Conservancy, headed by a Director-General appointed by the Lord President of the Council (up to 1965), and by the Secretary of State for Education and Science (thereafter). In addition to creating SSSIs, the Nature Conservancy established a number of stations to undertake survey and experimental work early on at Merlewood in the Lake District and Furzebrook on the Isle of Purbeck. The largest was at Monks Wood in Huntingdonshire, while the most northerly was the Hill of Brathens – all homes to gifted ecologists. Arthur Tansley (Fig. 19.1) was its first Chair (retiring in 1953, and dying two years later), and Captain Cyril Diver its first Director-General (succeeded three years later by Max Nicholson (Fig. 19.2), who served until 1966). The Conservancy's first governing body included some of our finest scientists, including E.B. Ford, Charles Elton, and W.H. Pearsall.

Through the 1950s and 1960s the Nature Conservancy built up an enviable reputation, recognised as authoritative around the world. Max Nicholson's feisty intellect made him a forceful adversary and clever strategist. In 1965 the Nature Conservancy became part of a new research council, the Natural Environment Research Council (NERC). The government's responsibility for nature conservation was transferred from the Lord President of the Council to the Secretary of State for Education and Science, but the Conservancy's responsibilities for establishing and managing reserves and carrying out research remained virtually unchanged. In 1973 the 'split' occurred. The Nature Conservancy was abolished and replaced by the Nature Conservancy Council (NCC). Established by the Nature Conservancy Council Act, the NCC was as a grant-aided body, financed by and responsible to the Department of the Environment. Still responsible for establishing, maintaining, and managing NNRs, providing advice and disseminating knowledge about nature conservation, and commissioning or supporting research relevant to nature conservation, it lost its direct research functions.

'The Split'

This was a turbulent time for UK nature conservation, described well by Sheail[11,12] and Adams[15]. Certain aspects of the so-called 'split' of the Nature Conservancy had resonance straddling three decades right up to the demise of the NCC, and wore heavily on the influence of science in nature conservation. When Prime Minister Edward Heath (later Sir) came to power on 19 June 1970, he promised his party conference that autumn "a quiet revolution" which would foster individual effort and take government out of the market place[46]. He wanted the formation of larger departments, clearer lines of accountability, and increased efficiency in decision making. Critically, the reviews that followed included one on Government Research and Development, an area of activity that had grown rapidly in the 1960s in recognition of Labour Leader Harold Wilson's (later Baron Wilson of Rievaulx) October 1 1963 Labour Party Conference speech labelled the "white heat of the technological revolution" driver of economic success. The Research Councils, in particular came to early attention in Heath's administration because of the anomalous position of the Agricultural Research Council (ARC) and the ways in which fundamental research was in the purview of the ARC, whereas applied research sat firmly with Ministry experimental farms. A typical Westminster "turf war" was emerging over whether the functions of the ARC should be controlled by "Agriculture" or by "Science".

The leading force arguing for change was Victor Rothschild, the 3rd Baron Rothschild, a physiologist by training and zoologist in early career at Cambridge. He headed Heath's Central Policy Review Staff, known as 'The Think Tank' (1971-74). Brother to entomologist Miriam (after whom WJS's professorial chair at Cambridge is named) and son of Charles, who has featured earlier in our account, he worked on a review published as the 'Rothschild Report' of 1971, *The Organisation and Management of Government Research and Development*. Accepted by Heath's Secretary of State for Education and Science, Margaret Thatcher (later Baroness Thatcher of Kesteven), this provided a new principle – that applied research and application should be done on a customer-contractor basis.

This had a profound impact on the organisation of nature conservation in Britain. First, half of the Research Council's financial resources were to be allocated to the 'customer' departments and agencies so that they could purchase the necessary research, and second, 'customer' departments and bodies were to appoint 'Chief Scientists' to ensure they had the understanding and skill to commission scientific research. The Nature Conservancy succumbed to this principle; it was abolished, with its research stations and most of its scientific staff passed to the newly formed Institute for Terrestrial Ecology under the aegis of the NERC.

The successor body, the NCC, took on the advisory functions of the old Nature Conservancy alongside work to acquire nature reserves and identify sites of special scientific interest. The link between NNRs and scientific investigation was sorely weakened and there was a new separation introduced between many science practitioners in the research institute of NERC and their policy colleagues on the staff of the NCC. The new market-based language and structures encouraged a more utilitarian approach to government research with an expectation that research should deliver 'products'. The upshot was that it became far harder to secure the funds needed to meet the challenge set out so boldly and properly in the 1940s.

And in the midst of this we find Derek Ratcliffe, appointed as 'Chief Scientist' of the NCC. He had with him a small team that would grow over the years into the 'Chief Scientist Directorate', but in its early days Derek and colleagues sorely felt the absence of the large cadre of former colleagues.

The Nature Conservation Review – the underpinning framework

And it is here that we come to consider Derek's pivotal contribution to nature conservation, which straddled 'the split'. The Nature Conservation Review (NCR) was initiated in 1965 to re-appraise candidate sites for an expansion of the NNR series. Derek was put in charge of this and appointed Scientific Advisor to the Nature Conservancy's NCR (initially called Research Acquisition and Management Review). He oversaw an ambitious programme of field survey and analysis of existing data. He and colleagues rapidly realised that many high quality sites had been missed from the Huxley and Ritchie Committees' lists, and that, as he put it[13]:

"… the rate of attrition of wildlife and habitat through human impact had accelerated markedly since 1947. There was thus an urgent sense of need to justify the protection of a much larger number and extent of key sites so as to ensure the survival of an adequate proportion of this fast-dwindling heritage of nature. The previous standards of judgement in reserve selection were not in question, but a more closely argued rationale for a substantial expansion seemed desirable. The urge to try to identify some natural or absolute criteria for prescribing the choice of sites was strong, much as the original systematists such as Linnaeus sought 'natural' principles of classification."

In 1963 Derek had joined the Nature Conservancy's Monks Wood Toxic Chemicals and Wildlife Division[2,3] led by Norman Moore (Fig. 19.3), and began a close working relationship with Norman, which first gave rise to the breakthrough on DDT and cyclodiene insecticide impacts on birds of prey and other wildlife[17,47], and later developed the early thinking on nature conservation criteria[17]. Many people overlook the importance of Norman's original work in this latter area, for example during 1975-1979 he led the development of early guidelines for the selection of Sites of Special Scientific Interest (SSSI) (Fig. 20.3)[48]. A large team worked with Derek to create the NCR, and he was meticulously careful to acknowledge their many contributions and those of a much wider span of contacts in universities, NGOs, and government bodies[8].

Figure 19.3. Norman Moore, one of the most influential figures in nature conservation in Britain during the second half of the 20th century and a very close colleague and friend of Derek Ratcliffe. He worked in the Nature Conservancy (later the Nature Conservancy Council) from 1953 to 1983. He played a major part in the preparation of *A Nature Conservation Review*. The Great Stack, Handa Island, 1967. Photo: the Moore family, reproduced with permission of Peter Moore.

343

At last, published in 1977 (Fig. 19.4), twelve years in the making, with a sixteen-line Foreword signed rather scruffily by Shirley Williams (later Baroness Williams of Crosby) and Peter Shore (later Baron Shore of Stepney), respectively the Secretaries of State for Environment, and for Education and Science, this was a monumentally important scientific and operational publication. It provided the definitive framework for comparing sites and evaluating their importance[8,9]. It was a triumph, and all the better as it was supported a year earlier by Derek's exquisitely drafted set of 'Thoughts towards a philosophy of nature conservation'[49]. Derek ended his memoir *In Search of Nature*[3] with his appointment to, as he put it 'master-mind' this review of NNRs, and to vet personally as much of it as possible.

Quite aside from the wonderful opportunities this gave him to explore further reaches of Britain, it presented a uniquely difficult challenge, which Derek described in his characteristically understated way[3]:

> "I realised the Conservancy was likely to have to justify new proposals in a rather more rigorous way than in the past, and so worked out a detailed rationale with which to support the list. This involved spelling out the selection process, and especially the criteria for evaluation of the importance of candidate sites. This was new ground, for the earlier

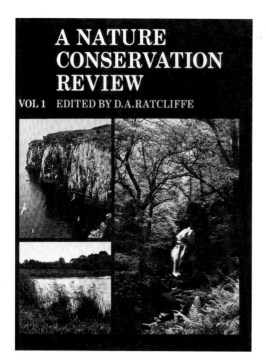

Figure 19.4. *A Nature Conservation Review*[8,9] edited (and largely written) by Derek Ratcliffe in conjunction with the Chief Scientist Team of the Nature Conservancy Council. The first volume presents a masterly review of the assessment and selection of 'key sites', of the ecological variation of the seven major habitat types in Britain, and of the conservation of the flora and fauna in Britain. The second volume presents detailed site accounts for the 735 'key sites' within six of the major habitat types using the criteria presented in the first volume. It provided a new and thorough perspective on the aims, philosophy, and methodology for conservation planning and remains of great international importance.

documents prescribing the needs for a National Nature Reserve series had taken much of this process for granted, as the best judgements of experienced naturalists and ecologists. It was the beginning of nature conservation evaluation, which now has quite a large literature."

Indeed, and as one of the first major overviews of conservation evaluation internationally revealed[50], Derek pioneered world-leading criteria for conservation evaluation.

The two NCR volumes are a joy to hold and read. We have quarried them on many occasions – the first volume outlines the rationale[8], and the second lists and details the 735 sites which deserved protection as NNRs[9]. John and Hilary Birks assisted with the selection of botanical sites and wrote several of the upland, peatland, and woodland site descriptions. We have all spent many days in the field discussing the rationale that Derek arrived at for selecting sites and judging their importance. The NCR volumes are extraordinarily well illustrated and written[2] – beautifully and so deftly articulated that many colleagues have commented how difficult it is to summarise further what is written. Chapters 2 and 3 of the first volume[8], outlining the rationale of the review and the ecological background to site selection, are in the space of 21 large two-column pages some of the most elegantly crafted passages of the conservation science literature in Britain. Virtually devoid of references, and beguilingly simple in its exposition on fundamentally complex concepts, you are taken on a defining tour of why nature matters.

In the spirit of Cmd. 7122[32], the challenge was to embrace the variety of interests we find in nature, and to set out the values associated with priorities for protection. Ten criteria emerged (Table 19.1), which have come to be known as the 'Ratcliffe criteria'. By applying these, Derek and colleagues arrived at their list of sites. They then had to devise a national series of these, according to broad habitat types. They chose seven: coastlands; woodlands; lowland grasslands, heaths and scrub; open waters; peatlands; upland grasslands and heaths; and artificial ecosystems. For each of these types (except artificial ecosystems) there was an objective to select a series of sites adequately representing the national range of variation in the following ecological features: climatic (local and regional gradients); physiographic (biological features associated with major variations in landforms); edaphic (associations with major variations in physical and chemical properties of soils and their parent materials); and anthropogenic (associations with major variations in land management). The ensuing sites were graded 1–4, with 1* denoting international importance and 4 lower, regional importance, but still rated as SSSI.

This was difficult work, and Derek occasionally betrayed a sense of frustration over the process[8, p.14]: "The issues involved are complex, and discussion is not made easier by the semantic confusion which has arisen over a long period through the habitually loose use of terms in ecology and nature conservation; these terms themselves now have such breadth of application that that are often virtually meaningless, and require further qualification." Derek ended his commentary on the rationale by commenting that[8]: "The results cannot be validated by reference to any absolute standards or economic base, but must be judged more broadly in terms of their eventual long-term contribution to nature conservation."

Table 19.1. The ten criteria for site assessment and selection given by Ratcliffe[8].

Criteria	Description
Size (extent)	Larger sites tend to have greater diversity of features
Diversity	Numbers of communities and species, and range of variation
Naturalness	Ecosystems and habitats least influenced by people
Rarity	Rare communities, habitats, or groups of species
Fragility	Sensitivity of habitats, communities, and species to environmental change
Typicalness	'Living museums', and typical/commonplace in field of ecological variation
Recorded history	Use for scientific study, and long-term records
Position in an ecological/ geographical unit	Number of characteristic formations, communities, and species of a district
Potential value	Through management or natural changes, potential to develop a greater nature conservation interest
Intrinsic appeal	The more popular groups of species, notably birds

One important spin-off from the NCR exercise was the increasing realisation that there was an urgent need for an up-to-date workable classification of British vegetation types in conservation evaluation and management as Tansley's[34] two-volume synthesis was not adequate for these purposes. This realisation by Derek Ratcliffe and Donald Pigott led to the NCC funding the National Vegetation Classification (NVC) (1975-2000)[2] and the production of the monumental five volumes[51] that present the results of the NVC (with HJBB as one of the authors). The NVC has since proved its worth in many aspects of conservation evaluation, basic description, ecological studies, and management [e.g. 2,25,52]

Beyond the Nature Conservation Review

The benchmark was in place for selecting NNRs and judging and comparing the importance of sites. *Nature Conservation in Great Britain*[53] (Fig. 19.5), published by the NCC in 1984, re-stated the ethos for statutory conservation as: "The primary objective of nature conservation is to ensure that the national heritage of wild flora and fauna and geological and physiographic features remains as large and diverse as possible so that society may use and appreciate its value to the fullest extent." Written largely by Derek, this placed site safeguard as the cornerstone of conservation. SSSI notification became the principal statutory means of achieving this (under the Wildlife and Countryside Act 1981). The SSSI designation was applied to all NNRs and to all those deserving such status as listed in the NCR. In March 1989 the *Guidelines for Selection of Biological SSSIs* (Fig. 20.3) were published[48], with Sir William Wilkinson (Figs. 19.6 & 11.8), Chair of the NCC, recording in his Foreword that the guidelines set out "more fully the general principles upon which the NCC bases its determination of 'special interest' in regard to biological SSSIs". Again, Derek oversaw the production of these, working closely with Philip Oswald and other colleagues in his

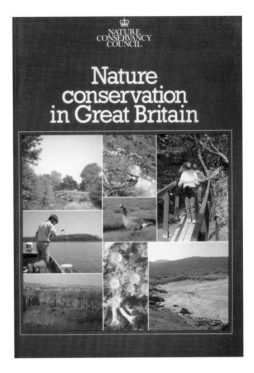

Figure 19.5. *Nature Conservation in Great Britain*[53], largely written by Derek Ratcliffe and the Chief Scientist Team of the Nature Conservancy Council, was the NCC contribution to the UK's response to the World Conservation Strategy. It is a detailed review and national strategy that recognises 'cultural values' as the principal purpose of nature conservation.

Chief Scientist Directorate to craft the 288-page document. DBAT worked with Derek and David Horsfield on the upland habitat guidelines, and saw first-hand how Derek could weave words to meet the essence of Cmd. 7122 and the NCR. It was one of the last publications from the NCC, and has endured since (in December 2013 the JNCC published a revision of the rationale governing SSSI selection[54]).

The European Commission Birds Directive

In 1979 the European Commission (EC) adopted the Council Directive on the Conservation of Wild Birds (79/409/EEC)[55]. Usually referred to as the 'Birds Directive', this provides for the protection, management, and control of all species of naturally occurring wild birds in the European territory of Member States. In particular, it requires Member States to identify areas (Special Protection Areas, SPAs) to be given special protection for the rare or vulnerable species listed in Annex I (Article 4.1), for regularly occurring migratory species (Article 4.2), and for the protection of wetlands, especially wetlands of international importance. Guidelines prepared to assist the selection of SPAs in the UK were derived in part from the NCR criteria. The process involves two stages: Stage 1 identifies areas which are likely to qualify for SPA status; and Stage 2 judgements are used to select the most suitable areas by number and size for SPA classification[56]. Terms such as 'naturalness' and 'history of occupancy' hark back directly to the NCR (Table 19.1). The UK has 270 classified SPAs covering 2.75 million hectares (as at 5 July 2013)[57].

Figure 19.6. Sir William Wilkinson (1912-1996), Chair of the Nature Conservancy Council 1983-1991, and President of the British Trust for Ornithology 1993-1996. The INCA card he is holding is from the Industry and Nature Conservation Association. He strengthened the influence of the Nature Conservancy Council in the 1980s and steered it through the very demanding times of the Flow Country afforestation struggle[59]. 1989. Photo: reproduced by permission of Kate Wilkinson.

The end of the Nature Conservancy Council

On 11 July 1989 the dismemberment of the NCC was announced by the Secretaries of State for the Environment and Scotland (and shortly after for Wales)[58]. In 1991, the principal functions of the NCC in England were vested in English Nature (EN) (and in October 2006 as Natural England when EN, the Countryside Commission, and the Rural Development Service merged). Separate bodies were set up for Wales (Countryside Council for Wales, which merged the NCC with the Countryside Commission, later becoming Natural Resources Wales in April 2013 following a merger with Forestry Commission Wales) and Scotland (NCC Scotland). The Joint Nature Conservation Committee (JNCC) was set up to deal with UK-wide and international conservation issues. In 1992 Scottish Natural Heritage (SNH) was formed out of NCC Scotland and the Countryside Commission for Scotland[21].

The European Commission Habitats Directive

The Council Directive 92/43/EEC on the Conservation of natural habitats and of wild fauna and flora, known as the EC Habitats Directive, was adopted in 1992[55]. Through this the EU meets its obligations under the Bern Convention, and it applies to the UK and its Overseas Territory of Gibraltar. The main aim of the Directive is to promote the maintenance of biodiversity by requiring Member States to take measures to maintain or restore natural habitats and wild species, listed on the Annexes to the Directive, at a favourable conservation status. Special Areas of Conservation (SACs) are strictly protected sites designated under the Directive, with Article 3 of the Directive requiring the establishment of a European network of important high-quality conservation sites making a significant contribution to conserving the 189 habitat types and 788 species identified in Annexes I and II of the Directive. Of these, 78 habitats and 43 species are embraced by the Directive in the UK[59]. The NCR criteria, and indeed the NCR sites, were crucially important in determining the selection of candidate SACs[60]. Derek Ratcliffe took an especially keen interest in the UK Government's adoption of the Directive[61] and was determined to ensure the eventual suite of SACs was adequate. As of 14 February 2014 the UK has 615 SACs, which together with 33 Sites of Community Importance and four candidate SACs, amount to just over 8 million hectares[59].

A wider international perspective

Writing from an international perspective about *A Nature Conservation Review*[8,9] in 2011, Griffiths and Vogiatzakis[62; p. 569] note that

> "There is no generally accepted scheme for establishing conservation priorities, partly as a result of the complexity and variety of life itself but also because of limited resources of time and money and the need to prioritize. The criteria established by Ratcliffe in the *Nature Conservation Review in Britain* in the 1970s retain their currency and have been developed and adopted by the International Union for Conservation of Nature (IUCN). However, the application of the criteria is piecemeal and, in many parts of the world the pressure for development is so intense that it is difficult to apply strict conservation criteria that do not also take into account human welfare. Furthermore, the information required to implement the criteria established by Ratcliffe often does not exist, and time-consuming and expensive fieldwork may be required to make good the information gaps if the system is to be applied rigorously and effectively."

The NCR criteria[8] have, however, remained in place, bolstered by further knowledge of habitats and species, and they influenced the selection in Europe of Special Protected Areas (SPAs) under the EC Birds Directive (1979), and Special Areas for Conservation (SACs) under the EC Habitats Directive 1991[63]. Most conservationists working 'on the ground' are still rooted in the NCR, and many can quote the majority of the ten Ratcliffe criteria (Table 19.1).

Where next?

Inevitably, with the passage of time, we can reflect on what was done and what might have been done differently. The nature conservation scene is much more complex now, and the terms 'biodiversity', 'ecosystem services', and 'ecosystem approach' are prevalent (e.g. UKNEA 2011 Synthesis[64], with the main report running to 1,465 pages). Biodiversity strategies have been published for the UK, and most recently for Scotland[65].

The global academic and practitioner interest in identifying priority species, sites, habitats, and ecosystems has developed from the fundamental principles identified in the Nature Conservation Review[8,9]. The upsurge in knowledge and awareness of nature is phenomenal, with magnificent inventories now available to the public (the National Biodiversity Network holds more than 90 million records). Atlases of plants and animals at the local and national scales grow in number and detail (the latest atlas of breeding and wintering birds in Britain and Ireland[66] is a *tour de force*; the first breeding bird atlas was published by Lord & Munns[67], and the first national atlas of breeding birds by Sharrock[68]). The *New Atlas of the British Flora*[69] and the *Atlas of British and Irish Bryophytes*[69] are similarly major achievements in biological recording in Britain and Ireland by devoted botanists, professional and non-professional. There is a healthy growth in the membership of specialist bodies concerned with nature, and the media coverage of wildlife is evolving into one of the real highlights of TV, radio, and other outlets.

But there are concerns. The skills and knowledge base in nature is diminishing in schools and universities, with many students graduating in ecological science without having spent much more than a couple of days in the field. There is a risk aversion to carrying out fieldwork, especially with youngsters[70]. Many ecological reports are now impenetrable, with earlier attention to detail with scientific names now given over to overwhelming detail on statutory matters and facts and figures wholly divorced from giving the reader a sense of what has been worked on. The language associated with reports on nature can be oppressive, with the 'ecosystems' mantra at times quite awful to read. That said, there has been a wonderfully refreshing upsurge in nature and landscape writing with some supremely talented writers coming to the fore in the popular media[e.g. 71] with outstanding and highly readable books [e.g. 21,22,72].

If we have one criticism of what has been done by the statutory nature conservation movement, in particular, but conservation practitioners more widely, it is that collectively they have not widely recorded in detail the many thousands of management interventions put in place annually to protect or improve nature. Derek himself recognised this problem. This issue of failing to monitor solutions was identified well over a decade ago[73] and a range of developments since then have made it easier for practitioners to document and use research. These include a website devoted to conservation evidence, a journal *Conservation Evidence* for practitioners to document results without the usual scientific demands for extensive literature reviews, and systematic reviews (see www.ConservationEvidence.com) and synopses that collate the evidence – those published so far are on bees[74], birds[75], amphibians[76], and farmland conservation[77]. In practice, research still concentrates on the changes in status and threats rather than the means of retaining or enhancing biodiversity.

Repeatedly since the publication of Cmd. 7122[32] the nature conservation movement has been pressed to provide evidence on threats to nature, and what might be gained through action [e.g. 78], and often this has not been addressed through detailed and appropriate monitoring or reporting[e.g. 79]. This is curious considering the initial developments and emphasis on research we describe in this chapter. One of the objectives for the establishment of NNRs was to encourage research, but in practice the aims of conservation and the requirements of research often conflict, so researchers often seek research sites elsewhere. Reserve wardens usually lack the time, encouragement, and scientific skills to monitor impacts so the massive potential for learning is lost. Derek's

Figure 19.7. Three 'greats' of nature conservation in Britain who were very influential in Derek Ratcliffe's lifetime work in the Nature Conservancy and Nature Conservancy Council (NCC). Max Nicholson (left), Sir William Wilkinson (centre), and Norman Moore (right). June, 1993. Photo: unknown photographer, reproduced by permission of Dick Seamons.

classic work on pesticides showed how dramatic the impact of monitoring could be on public policy[47,80] and yet well-structured monitoring is still patchy[79]. The good components include the rigorous programme of site condition monitoring, at least for protected areas, and reported by the JNCC (which has also reported recently on habitats and species of EC interest in the UK, and the latest UK contribution to the Convention on Biological Diversity [81]).

Will a new doctrine emerge to overtake the current approach to nature conservation and protected areas? We think not in the immediate future so long as it is understood that the best way of securing a better future for nature is within protected areas. As long as nature continues to be squeezed out this is unlikely to change. The great post-war efforts of Arthur Tansley, Max Nicholson, and their peers, and later by Derek Ratcliffe, Norman Moore, William Wilkinson, and their colleagues, still stand strong in the face of all manner of pressures (Fig. 19.7). And any scrutiny of this which is minded to be critical and dismissive must first ask what could have been done better, and with more lasting impact? Nature as we know and love it is not a commodity that can be bought and sold. It is a phenomenon of the Earth which is irreplaceable and uniquely important to people largely for what it is rather than what it can do; and it motivates us through its attractions, diversity, and workings. Derek understood that, was moved by the beauty of nature (Fig. 19.8), and fought tooth and nail to save it. We are in his debt.

Figure 19.8. Pasqueflower (*Pulsatilla vulgaris; Anemone pulsatilla*), Cambridgeshire, 1975. The Pasqueflower represented to Derek what *A Nature Conservation Review*[8,9] was trying to achieve, as this beautiful rare and local plant of chalk and limestone grasslands is severely threatened by destruction of these habitats. Photo: Derek Ratcliffe

Acknowledgements

We are grateful to the following for information, comments, or advice: Roddy Fairley, Colin Galbraith, John Hopkins, David Horsfield, Clive Mitchell, Iain Macdonald, Peter Marren, Peter Moore, Ian Newton, Robin Payne, David Stroud, and the late Malcolm Vincent. We thank Cathy Jenks for her skilled editorial help.

References

(1) Hansard (1948) House of Commons Debate, 29 April 1948. Hansard, vol. 450 cc 600-1.

(2) Birks, H.J.B. & Birks, H.H. (2015) Derek Ratcliffe – botanist and plant ecologist. In: *Nature's Conscience – The Life and Legacy of Derek Ratcliffe* (eds. D.B.A. Thompson, H.H. Birks & H.J.B. Birks). This volume, Chapter 4.

(3) Ratcliffe, D.A. (2000) *In Search of Nature*. Peregrine Books, Leeds.

(4) Rollie, C. (2015) In Galloway and the Borders – in search of an enduring youth. In: *Nature's Conscience – The Life and Legacy of Derek Ratcliffe* (eds. D.B.A. Thompson, H.H. Birks & H.J.B. Birks). This volume, Chapter 13.

(5) Birks, H.J.B., Thompson, D.B.A. & Birks, H.H. (2015) Derek Ratcliffe – early days in pursuit of nature. In: *Nature's Conscience – The Life and Legacy of Derek Ratcliffe* (eds. D.B.A. Thompson, H.H. Birks & H.J.B. Birks). This volume, Chapter 1.

(6) Ratcliffe, D.A. (2007) *Galloway and the Borders*. Collins, London.

(7) Ratcliffe, D.A. (1948) Records of Fell Outings. Unpublished, handwritten diary.

(8) Ratcliffe, D.A. (ed.) (1977) *A Nature Conservation Review*. Volume 1. Cambridge University Press, Cambridge.

(9) Ratcliffe, D.A. (ed.) (1977) *A Nature Conservation Review. Volume 2*. Cambridge University Press, Cambridge.

(10) Stamp, D. (1969) *Nature Conservation in Great Britain*. Collins, London.

(11) Sheail, J. (1976) *Nature in Trust. The history of nature conservation in Britain*. Blackie, Glasgow.

(12) Sheail, J. (1998) *Nature Conservation in Britain. The formative years*. The Stationery Office, London.

(13) Ratcliffe, D.A. (1986) Selection of important areas for wildlife conservation in Great Britain: the Nature Conservancy Council's approach. In: *Wildlife Conservation Evaluation* (ed. M.B. Usher), pp. 135-160. Chapman & Hall, London.

(14) Ratcliffe, D.A. (2003) *A history of nature conservation in Great Britain*. (unpublished manuscript). Held by the British Trust for Ornithology, Thetford.

(15) Adams, W.M. (1986) *Nature's Place: Conservation sites and countryside change*. Allen & Unwin, London.

(16) Adams, W.M. (2003) *Future nature. A vision for conservation*. Earthscan, London.

(17) Moore, N.W. (1987) *The Bird of Time. The Science and Politics of Nature Conservation*. Cambridge University Press, Cambridge.

(18) Evans, D. (1997) *A History of Nature Conservation in Britain* (2nd edition). Routledge, Abingdon.

(19) Smout, T.C. (2000) *Nature Contested. Environmental History in Scotland and Northern England Since 1600.* Edinburgh University Press, Edinburgh.

(20) Smout, T.C. (2009) *Exploring Environmental History: Selected Essays.* Edinburgh University Press, Edinburgh.

(21) Marren, P. (2002) *Nature Conservation.* HarperCollins, London.

(22) Avery, M. (2012) *Fighting for Birds. 25 years in nature conservation.* Pelagic Publishing, Exeter.

(23) Rothschild, M. & Marren, P. (1997) *Rothschild's Reserves. Time and fragile nature.* Balaban, Philadelphia.

(24) Symonds, H.H. (1936) Afforestation in the Lake District – A Reply to the Forestry Commission's White Paper of 26th August 1936. J.M. Dent and Sons. London.

(25) Kirby, K.J. (2015) Battling forestry and building consensus: woodland conservation post-1949. In: *Nature's Conscience – The Life and Legacy of Derek Ratcliffe* (eds. D.B.A. Thompson, H.H. Birks & H.J.B. Birks). This volume, Chapter 21.

(26) Nature Reserves Investigation Committee (1943) *Nature Conservation in Britain.* NRIC.

(27) Nature Reserves Investigation Committee (1945) *Nature Conservation in Britain.* NRIC.

(28) Smith, G.F.H. (1947) Nature protection in Great Britain. *Nature,* **160**, 457-459.

(29) Calman, W.T. (1943) Nature Reserves. *The Spectator,* **10 June**, 12.

(30) Tansley, A.G. (1943) Nature Reserves. *The Spectator,* **3 June**, 7-8.

(31) Tansley, A.G. (1947) Saving wildlife. *The Spectator,* **31 July**, 9-10.

(32) Cmd. 7122 (1947) *Conservation of Nature in England and Wales.* Command 7122. HMSO, London.

(33) Cmd. 7235 (1947) *Report of the Committee on National Parks and Conservation of Nature in Scotland.* The Ramsay Report. Command 7235. HMSO, London.

(34) Tansley, A.G. (1939) *The British Islands and their Vegetation. Volumes 1 & 2.* Cambridge University Press, Cambridge.

(35) Ayres, P.G. (2012) *Shaping Ecology: The Life of Arthur Tansley.* Wiley-Blackwell, Chichester.

(36) Tansley, A.G. (1945) *Our Heritage of Wild Nature: A Plea for Organised Nature Conservation.* Cambridge University Press, Cambridge.

(37) Tansley, A.G. (1920) *The New Psychology and its Relation to Life.* George Allen & Unwin, London.

(38) Nicholson, E.M. (1931) *The Art of Bird-Watching: A Practical Guide to Field Observation.* Witherby, London.

(39) Cramp, S. & Perrins, C.M. (eds.) (1978-1984) *Handbook of the Birds of Europe, Middle East, and North Africa. The Birds of the Western Palearctic.* 9 volumes. Oxford University Press, Oxford.

(40) Nicholson, E.M. (1931) *A National Plan for Great Britain.* Supplement in the Weekend Review of 14 February 1931.

(41) Morgan, K.O. (1984) *Labour in Power 1945-1951.* Oxford University Press, Oxford.

(42) Cmd. 6628 (1945) *National Parks in England and Wales*. Command 6628. The Dower Report. HMSO, London.

(43) Cmd. 7121 (1947) *Report of the National Parks Committee*. Command 7121. The Huxley Report. HMSO, London.

(44) Royal Charter (23 March 1949) constituted the Nature Conservancy. Further powers and duties were set out in the National Parks and Access to the Countryside Act 1949. UK Government, Westminster.
http://www.legislation.gov.uk/ukpga/Geo6/12-13-14/97

(45) Barnett, C. (1995) *The Lost Victory. British Dreams, British Realities 1945-1950*. Macmillan, London.

(46) Anon (2005) Sir Edward Heath. Obituary. *The Telegraph*, **18 July**, 2005.

(47) Newton, I. (2015) Pesticides and birds of prey – the breakthrough. In: *Nature's Conscience – The Life and Legacy of Derek Ratcliffe* (eds. D.B.A. Thompson, H.H. Birks & H.J.B. Birks). This volume, Chapter 15.

(48) Nature Conservancy Council (1989) *Guidelines for Selection of Biological SSSIs*. 288 pp. Nature Conservancy Council, Peterborough.

(49) Ratcliffe, D.A. (1976) Thoughts towards a philosophy of nature conservation. *Biological Conservation*, **9**, 45-53. (Reprinted as Chapter 26 in this volume).

(50) Usher, M.B. (ed.) (1986) *Wildlife Conservation Evaluation*. Chapman and Hall, London.

(51) Rodwell, J.S. (ed.) (1991-2000) *British Plant Communities 1-5*. Cambridge University Press, Cambridge.

(52) Averis, A.M., Averis, A.B.G., Birks, H.J.B., Horsfield, D., Thompson, D.B.A. & Yeo, M.J.M. (2004) *An Illustrated Guide to British Upland Vegetation*. Joint Nature Conservation Committee, Peterborough.
Newton, A.C. & Humphrey, J.W. (1997) Forest management for biodiversity: Perspectives on the policy context and current initiatives. In: *Biodiversity in Scotland: Status, Trends, and Initiatives* (eds. L.V. Fleming, A.C. Newton, J.A. Vickery & M.B. Usher), pp. 179-197. The Stationery Office, Edinburgh.
Peterken, G. (2013) *Meadows*. British Wildlife Publishing, Gillingham.
Proctor, M.C.F. (2013) *Vegetation of Britain and Ireland*. Collins, London.
Savill, P.S., Perrins, C.M., Kirby, K.J. & Fisher, N. (eds.) (2010) *Wytham Woods – Oxford's Ecological Laboratory*. Oxford University Press, Oxford.
Welch, D. (2013) The floristics of contrasting grazed-down Scottish moorland sites initially dominated by heather (*Calluna vulgaris*). *New Journal of Botany*, **3**, 169-177.

(53) Nature Conservancy Council (1984) *Nature Conservation in Great Britain*. 112 pp. Nature Conservancy Council, Shrewsbury.

(54) Bainbridge, I., Brown, A., Burnett, N., Corbett, P., Cork, C., Ferris, R., Howe, M., Maddock, A., Mountford, E. & Pritchard, S. (eds.) (2013) *Guidelines for Selection of Biological SSSIs. Part 1: Rationale, Operational Approach and Criteria for Site Selection*. Joint Nature Conservation Committee, Peterborough.
http://jncc.defra.gov.uk/pdf/SSSI%20Guidelines%20Part%201%20PUBLICATION%20FINAL_Dec2013(2).pdf

(55) Bridgewater, P. (2015) National and global biodiversity politics and legalities – some reflections. In: *Nature's Conscience – The Life and Legacy of Derek Ratcliffe* (eds. D.B.A. Thompson, H.H. Birks & H.J.B. Birks). This volume, Chapter 25.

(56) JNCC (2014) SPA Selection Guidelines. http://jncc.defra.gov.uk/page-1405

(57) JNCC (2014) Classified and potential Special Protection Areas in the UK. http://jncc.defra.gov.uk/page-1399

(58) Radcliffe (sic), D. (1989) The end of British nature conservation? *New Scientist*, **9 September**, 75-76.
Stroud, D.A., Reed, T.M., Pienkowski, M.W. & Lindsay, R.A. (2015) The Flow Country: battles fought, war won, organisation lost. In: *Nature's Conscience – The Life and Legacy of Derek Ratcliffe* (eds. D.B.A. Thompson, H.H. Birks & H.J.B. Birks). This volume, Chapter 23.

(59) JNCC (2014) *Special Areas of Conservation*. http://jncc.defra.gov.uk/page-23

(60) JNCC (1997) *The Habitats Directive: Selection of Special Areas of Conservation in the UK*. JNCC Report No. 270. JNCC, Peterborough. Updated at: http://jncc.defra.gov.uk/page-1457

(61) Ratcliffe, D.A. (1995) The government's response to the European Union Habitats and Species Directive. *British Wildlife,* **6,** 307-309.

(62) Griffiths, G.H. & Vogiatzakis, I. (2011) Habitat approaches to nature conservation. In: *The Sage Handbook of Biogeography* (eds. A.C. Millington, M.A. Blumler & U. Schickhoff). pp. 562-571. Sage, Los Angeles.

(63) Council of Europe (1992) http://ec.europa.eu/environment/nature/legislation/habitatsdirective/index_en.htm (accessed April 2014)

(64) UKNEA (2011) *The UK National Ecosystem Assessment. Synthesis of Key Findings*. UNEP-WCMC, Cambridge.

(65) Anon (2013) *2020 Challenge for Scotland's Biodiversity. A Strategy for the conservation and enhancement of biodiversity in Scotland*. Scottish Government, Edinburgh.

(66) Balmer, D., Gillings, S., Caffrey, B., Swann, B., Downie, I. & Fuller, R. (2013) *Bird Atlas 2007-11: The Breeding and Wintering Birds of Britain and Ireland*. British Trust for Ornithology, Thetford.

(67) Lord, J. & Munns, D.J. (1970) *Atlas of Breeding Birds in the West Midlands*. Collins, London.

(68) Sharrock, J.T.R. (1976) *The Atlas of Breeding Birds in Britain and Ireland*. Poyser, Berkhamsted.

(69) Preston, C.D., Pearman, D.A. & Dines, T.D. (eds.) (2002) *New Atlas of the British and Irish Flora*. Oxford University Press, Oxford.
Blockeel, T.L., Bosanquet, S.D.S., Hill, M.O. & Preston, C.D. (2014) *Atlas of British and Irish Bryophytes*. Pisces Publishing, Newbury.

(70) Field Studies Council (2014) *Reaching into the outside. Where next for field studies and outdoor learning providers?* Field Studies Council, Preston Montford.

(71) Barkham, P. (2013) What we have loved, others will love. *The Guardian*, **10 August**, 34-35.
Macfarlane, R. (2013) The best B&B. *The Guardian Review*, **28 December**, 13.

(72) Barkham, P. (2010) *The Butterfly Isles. A Summer in Search of Our Emperors and Admirals*. Granta, London.
Barkham, P. (2013) *Badgerlands: The Twilight World of Britain's Most Enigmatic Animal*. Granta, London.
Birkhead, T.M., Wimpenny, J. & Montgomerie, B. (2014) *Ten Thousand Birds. Ornithology since Darwin*. Princeton University Press, Princeton.
Cocker, M. (2007) *Crow Country*. Jonathan Cape, London.
Dee, T. (2013) *Four Fields*. Jonathan Cape, London.
Laing, O. (2011) *To the River: A Journey Beneath the Surface*. Canongate, Edinburgh.
Mabey, R. (2005) *Nature Cure*. Chatto & Windus, London.
Macfarlane, R. (2007) *The Wild Places*. Granta, London.
Macfarlane, R. (2012) *The Old Ways. A Journey on Foot.* Viking, New York.
Macfarlane, R. (2013) New words on the wild. *Nature*, **498**, 166-167.

(73) Sutherland, W.J. (2000). *The Conservation Handbook*. Blackwell Scientific Publications, Oxford.
Sutherland, W.J., Pullin, A.S., Dolman, P.M. & Knight, T.M. (2004) The need for evidence-based conservation. *Trends in Ecology & Evolution*, **19**, 305-308.

(74) Dicks, L.J., Showler, D.A. & Sutherland, W.J. (2010) *Bee conservation: evidence for the effectiveness of interventions*. Pelagic Publishing, Exeter.

(75) Williams, D.R. Pople, R.G., Showler, D.A., Dicks, L.V., Child, M.F., zu Ermgassen, E.K.H.J. & Sutherland, W.J. (2013) *Bird Conservation - evidence for the effects of interventions*. Pelagic Publishing, Exeter.

(76) Smith, R.K. & Sutherland, W.J. (2014) *Amphibian Conservation: evidence for effectiveness of interventions*. Pelagic Publishing, Exeter.

(77) Dicks, L.V., Ashpole, J.E., Danhardt, J., James, K., Jönsson, A., Randall, N., Showler, D.A., Smith, R.K., Turpie, S., Williams, D. & Sutherland, W.J. (2013) *Farmland Conservation Synopsis*. Pelagic Publishing, Exeter.

(78) Housden, S. (2015) Fighting for wildlife – from the inside. In: *Nature's Conscience – The Life and Legacy of Derek Ratcliffe* (eds. D.B.A. Thompson, H.H. Birks & H.J.B. Birks). This volume, Chapter 20.

(79) Haughland, D.L., Hero, J.-M., Schieck, J., Castley, J.G., Boutin, S., Sólymos, P., Lawson, B.E., Holloway, G. & Magnusson, W.E. (2010) Planning forwards: biodiversity research and monitoring systems for better management. *Trends in Ecology & Evolution*, **25**, 199-200.
Lindenmayer, D.B. & Likens, G.E. (2010) Improving ecological monitoring. *Trends in Ecology & Evolution*, **25**, 200-201.
Lindenmayer, D.B., Likens, G.E., Haywood, A. & Miezis, L. (2011) Adaptive monitoring in the real world: proof of concept. *Trends in Ecology & Evolution*, **26**, 641-646.
Magurran, A.E., Baillie, S.R., Buckland, S.T., Dick, J.McP., Elston, D.A., Scott, E.M., Smith, R.I., Somerfield, P.J. & Watt, A.D. (2010). Long-term datasets in biodiversity research and monitoring: assessing change in ecological communities through time. *Trends in Ecology & Evolution*, **23**, 574-582.
McDonald-Madden, E., Baxter, P.W.J., Fuller, R.A., Martin, T.G., Game, E.T., Montambault, J. & Possingham, H.P. (2010) Monitoring does not always count. *Trends in Ecology & Evolution*, **25**, 547-550.

Nichols, J.D. & Williams, B.K. (2006) Monitoring for conservation. *Trends in Ecology & Evolution*, **21**, 668-677.

(80) Greenwood, J.J.D. & Crick, H.Q.P. (2015) "It seemed like a dream come true"–Derek Ratcliffe and the Peregrine surveys. In: *Nature's Conscience – The Life and Legacy of Derek Ratcliffe* (eds. D.B.A. Thompson, H.H. Birks & H.J.B. Birks). This volume, Chapter 14.

(81) JNCC (2014) Website reports on UK nature conservation: UK wide monitoring of protected areas: http://jncc.defra.gov.uk/page-3520; and protected areas and habitats and species of EC interest in the UK: http://jncc.defra.gov.uk/page-4060; and 5th report to the Convention on Biological Diversity: http://jncc.defra.gov.uk/page-6569

20. Fighting for wildlife - from the inside

Stuart Housden

One hot summer.....

The summer of 1976 was the hottest recorded in central England in more than three hundred years, and is still quoted as the benchmark for subsequent heat waves. Reservoirs were almost empty and hosepipe bans were in force. In July that year I joined the Royal Society for the Protection of Birds (RSPB), moving from London to the rather clubbable atmosphere at the RSPB's headquarters—still known as 'The Lodge'—in Sandy. Here, on a green and sandy ridge in Bedfordshire, about 80 staff ran the UK's largest wildlife charity. The atmosphere was a mix of academic and school staff room with a dash of colonial administration for good measure. I knew my birds, had a fair understanding of ecology, and could campaign and make a nuisance of myself. After all, it was only 18 months since I had been a leader in the National Union of Students. I was part of a 'new generation' group of staff recruited following a freeze on posts which had endured for 3 years due to the prevailing, dire economic situation.

But my new colleagues did not inhabit a 'sleepy hollow'. They were convinced of the need to protect more of Britain for birds, stop the misuse of agricultural pesticides, and see far more weight given to the environment by politicians and decision makers. Our internal debates were often furious – lunchtimes became heated as the arguments raged back and forth over whether to buy more reserves or devote more resources to research and policy advocacy. But despite these internal tensions the staff were unflinchingly loyal and devoted to the cause of growing the RSPB, and were utterly convinced the organisation had much to offer, both in Britain, and overseas with our partners in the International Council for Bird Protection (later becoming BirdLife International).

Much of my time was spent on the road meeting raptor enthusiasts and supporting networks of informed volunteers concerned at the illegal killing of birds or the theft of their eggs. I participated in many 'dawn raids', witnessing first-hand the freezers full of dead buzzards, owls, falcons, and even Golden Eagles (*Aquila chrysaetos*) held by would-be taxidermists. Collections of eggs and egg-collecting paraphernalia became a familiar sight – as on occasion did the unwelcome threats of violence.

Eggs and egg collectors

In 1975 Ian Prestt (Fig. 20.1) became our Director General (the DG, as the RSPB's Chief Executive Officer was known then), having been the Deputy Director of the Nature Conservancy Council (NCC) in the previous year, and before that having Cabinet Office and Department of Environment experience. Based at Monks Wood, Ian and Derek Ratcliffe were close friends and colleagues[1]. Derek was Chief Scientist in the NCC, having been appointed in 1970, and latterly in all but name became the second-in-command – and the driving conscience of that organisation. Their collaboration went back a long way: Derek mentored Ian when he studied Grey Herons (*Ardea cinerea*), and they worked together to unravel the impacts of organochlorine pesticides, such as DDT, on food chains and wildlife, particularly birds of prey in Britain. They monitored the decline of the Sparrowhawk (*Accipiter nisus*) and the Peregrine Falcon (*Falco peregrinus*) as the insidious effects of persistent pesticides

Figure 20.1. Ian Prestt (1929–1995) past Director General of the Royal Society for the Protection of Birds (RSPB) and a close scientific colleague and personal friend of Derek Ratcliffe. Reproduced with permission of the RSPB

took hold. Derek's painstaking work had shown how the eggshells of raptors were thinned, so that eggs broke in the nest[2]. Together, they provided much of the scientific case that persuaded a reluctant farming lobby, and the then Ministry for Agriculture, Fisheries and Food (MAFF), to take steps to limit the use of, and finally ban, these chemicals. During this period Ian saw the supreme importance of science in persuading Government to act, but was just as inspired to make sure that the RSPB should harness public opinion to demand action. Derek masterminded the former, and Ian jumped at the chance to lead the RSPB into battle on the latter.

Derek was a regular visitor to The Lodge at this time. He and Ian would talk strategy and tactics and agree who would do what. But it was Derek's knowledge of egg collectors, from his pesticide work[2,3], that first led me to speak with him. I was an Investigations Officer tasked with combating wildlife crime. The egg collectors were still a serious threat to rarer species, particularly birds like Osprey (*Pandion haliaetus*), Hobby (*Falco subbuteo*), Peregrine Falcon, and Red-backed Shrike (*Lanius collurio*). A genteel war was being conducted between the RSPB and the 'old school' collectors. These were often retired school masters, men of the cloth, or country doctors, who saw themselves as serious oologists – not mere collectors. Indeed, some of them had, in confidence, allowed Derek access to their collections so he could measure eggshell thickness in eggs taken in pre-DDT times[2,3,4]. He never broke these confidences but was helpful in suggesting areas where collectors operated, or the sites which collectors frequented. Such intelligence helped us target our meagre resources to best effect – the Lake District and south-west Scotland for Peregrines, and some favoured parts of Breckland for Woodlarks (*Lullula arborea*) and Red-backed Shrikes. I was struck by Derek's intimate knowledge of these places and their birds; much later, of course, he would write about them in great detail[1,5].

Wetlands and peatlands

My role changed in 1978 as the RSPB grew concerned at the loss of wetlands, particularly in England, and the inadequate number of Sites of Special Scientific Interest (SSSIs), which offered some protection. Many of the best areas were hopelessly unprotected. At the time, MAFF had a policy of grant-aiding, at substantial intervention rates, the drainage of meadows, fenland, saltmarshes, and seasonally flooded areas to bring them into intensive agricultural use. This was an incentive to destroy and undermine conservation interests. We devised a two-pronged strategy to tackle this – identify the best areas so that they might be notified as SSSIs, and challenge the economic basis of MAFF's decision-making process funded by the taxpayer.

First, we had to enlist the advice of the NCC, and its Chief Scientist would be essential to this. Farmers, so-called 'Internal Drainage Boards', and MAFF were convinced that converting wetlands to intensive production was in the national interest – whatever the economic or environmental costs. And the legislation protecting SSSIs from agricultural and drainage operations was very weak. NCC had few powers at its disposal to intervene, but we hatched a plan to combine forces.

Persuading the NCC to take a robust stance, and alongside the RSPB and other non-governmental organisation (NGOs), challenging Government policy, was key to changing this. Derek compared notes with us and argued that NCC's advice to Government should be based on sound science and be independent of political influence from MAFF or the National Farmers' Union (NFU). He was determinedly convinced that it was for Government to balance the interests of conservation with private economic gain – and NCC should give clear and evidence-based advice, even if it was unpopular with powerful vested interests. But what was so clever was that Derek had the nous to engineer a situation where the NGOs could be far more effective than agency staff in persuading Ministers, other politicians, and senior officials to act. Ministers and their mandarins had little time for government agencies complaining about conservation policy and practice; but an NGO publicly rebuking a Minister and his, or rarely her, Department was altogether different – hundreds of letters, and strident magazine or even newspaper columns had great effect. Derek would load the bullets, and we would fire the shots. For the first time we also began to challenge MAFF's economic case for investment in drainage schemes to bring land into intensive production, as at Gedney Drove End on the Wash and Amberley Wild Brooks in Sussex (Fig. 20.2). Shifting the debate to the wise use of the Government's cash made this a completely different ball game and eventually the

Figure 20.2. Amberley Wild Brooks (also known as Amberley Wildbrooks), west Sussex, is an internationally important wetland for birds, dragonflies, wetland and aquatic plants, and other biota. It is a Site of Special Scientific Interest and an Important Plant Area and is part of the Arun Valley Special Protection Area which is a Ramsar Wetland Site[6]. It is managed as a Nature Reserve by the Sussex Wildlife Trust and the Royal Society for the Protection of Birds. Photo: Dave Spicer

cost/benefit appraisals were amended so that the true costs were revealed. Again, Derek was quietly helpful as he reported on the discomfort within MAFF at the Treasury's hard questioning about those sponsoring these drainage schemes.

Protected sites – early days for SSSIs

During the late 1970s Derek had co-ordinated the production of the scientific site selection criteria used by the NCC to identify areas that should be declared as SSSI. At the time, NCC had a duty to notify areas which in its opinion met the criteria (it was much later, in 1989, that the SSSI selection guidelines were published[7]) (Fig. 20.3). This was a highly important principle not lost on the RSPB – or the NCC's scientific staff. It meant that science determined what was important in a conservation context, and the evidence from surveys and other data were used to assess whether a site qualified for protection, all based on common, nationally agreed criteria.

This meant that nationally the most important sites were identified and designated as SSSIs which then offered them some, but not complete protection. The political and economic judgements as to what should happen if they were threatened by development or in need of improvement were hotly debated, involving Ministers when important issues determining where the national interest lay. The beauty of this system and its value to conservation was that it was pretty difficult to fudge matters and ignore key sites. But it was not fool-proof and civil servants in London, Edinburgh, and Cardiff often tried to circumvent the process and prevent sites being notified as SSSIs in the first place.

One case stands out, and I believe without Derek's intervention the area today would be cloaked by a blanket of Sitka Spruce (*Picea sitchensis*). In the late 1970s and all through the 1980s forestry expansion, led by the State-funded Forestry Commission (FC), took hold of large swathes of the uplands, particularly in North Wales, parts of Northern England, but especially in Scotland. At its peak over 20,000 hectares each year were being afforested, with only a token eye glancing at the impact on rivers and water chemistry[8], and losses of habitats and species such as Golden Plover (*Pluvialis apricaria*) and Dunlin (*Calidris alpina*)[9].

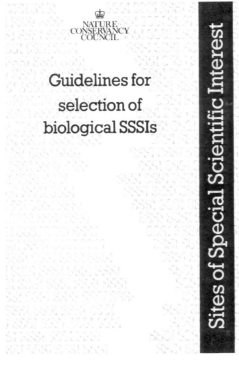

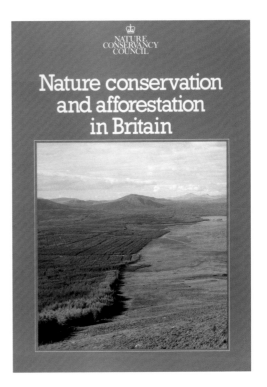

Figure 20.3. *Guidelines for Selection of Biological SSSIs* (1989) Nature Conservancy Council. This publication, masterminded by Derek Ratcliffe, provided a clear basis for scientific reasons determining what is important in a nature conservation context and was a turning point in the protection of Britain's nature

Figure 20.4. *Nature Conservation and Afforestation in Britain* (1986) Nature Conservancy Council. This publication, largely co-ordinated and written by Derek Ratcliffe, highlighted the adverse effects afforestation was having on wildlife in the uplands of Britain

In 1986 I received a call from my colleague David Minns based in our Edinburgh HQ. He had heard that there were plans to plant thousands of acres of new forestry on the Isle of Bute in the Firth of Clyde. This sizeable island was renowned for its breeding Golden Eagle, Peregrine, and Merlin (*Falco columbarius*), and had some nice waders, Ring Ouzel (*Turdus torquatus*), Black Grouse (*Tetrao tetrix*), and Twite (*Carduelis flavirostris*). It was a diverse and rich locality with a high density of scarce species. And it was unprotected.

Taking the NCC's SSSI criteria we ran a check against available information and quickly realised that the main upland block on the island handsomely qualified for SSSI status – both on its species diversity as well as its richness of raptors. The case was quickly made and presented to the NCC with a request for rapid action given the imminent threat. The case was referred to an able scientist, Mike Pienkowski, the NCC's senior ornithologist, who soon realised the importance of the area. His recommendation to notify the site was forwarded to the NCC's Scottish HQ in Edinburgh. There, matters took a political course – senior staff instantly realised the political sensitivities involved and sought further clarification. Their Advisory Committee for Scotland became involved and questioned the need to progress with the site, not least its potential to annoy powerful vested interests should the NCC press ahead. When brought to Derek's attention, simple advice was given: "Gentlemen, we do not have the luxury of not proceeding, our legal instrument and the law of the land make it a duty of the organisation to use the powers available to it." The designation proceeded, and although ploughing and ground preparation had commenced, much of the Isle of Bute's uplands got protected as a SSSI (the North End of Bute SSSI, covering 934 hectares) and to this day the area remains of great importance.

Similar arguments occurred in North Wales, the Scottish Borders, the Galloway Hills, and, of course, across the Flow Country of Caithness and Sutherland[9]. The role NCC played in correctly identifying places where forestry would adversely impact key wildlife sites in the Uplands (Fig. 20.4)[10] increasingly irritated the then Scottish establishment in particular who were very warm to the arguments in favour of the new forestry advanced by the Edinburgh-based FC. The seeds of the break-up of the NCC were sown in these land-use arguments[11,12].

The EC Birds Directive

During 1978 it became increasingly apparent that the European Commission (EC) would pass a Directive to protect wild birds across the Union, with a particular emphasis on securing the protection of important sites, as well as preventing the destruction of birds and unregulated hunting. Many of the draft provisions had been modelled on the UK's Protection of Birds Act 1954, which had been largely drafted and promoted by the RSPB. Indeed RSPB staff, particularly Alistair Gammell our International officer, were actively helping the Commission with scientific information and building support for the draft Directive across the then European Economic Community (EEC), frequently working with our partners in other European countries, and beyond. The Directive was duly passed on 2 April 1979 as Directive 79/409/EEC[13], and is now the ECs oldest piece of nature legislation[6]. The RSPB had opened a dialogue with the then Department of Environment (DoE), well before the Directive was agreed, to ensure that UK Ministers were fully aware of the opportunity to protect migratory species – 'our' birds, as they undertook long journeys across the continent to their African wintering quarters. Indeed, I remember taking a call from Denis Howell MP—the Environment Minister (1974-79, and famously made Minister for Droughts in 1976, then Minister for Floods, and finally Minister for Snow in 1978-79)—who asked me which species were most important to protect from spring shooting as he did not think he could persuade the French Government to protect everything on 'our' list. He was calling from just outside the negotiating room at the time! I think Skylark (*Alauda arvensis*), Lapwing (*Vanellus vanellus*), Song Thrush (*Turdus philomelos*), and a few other species were protected as a result!

Mrs Thatcher arrives at Number 10 Downing Street

Once the Directive was adopted, the work to transpose this measure into UK law commenced. There was a new Government in power, Mrs Thatcher (later Baroness Thatcher of Kesteven) having entered office on 4 May 1979. Outside No. 10 Downing Street, she quoted from the *Prayer of St Francis*, uttering: "Where there is discord, may we bring harmony... And where there is despair, may we bring hope."[14] For nature conservation, this was ominous. She had appointed Michael Heseltine (later Baron Heseltine of Thenford) as her Secretary of State for Environment, with a team that included Tom King (now Baron King of Bridgwater, who succeeded Mr Heseltine in 1983) as Minister of State, and Hector Monro (later Baron Monro of Langholm) as the Junior Minister. At the outset things looked bright, and Mr Heseltine refers in his memoirs[15] to one of his first acts in his new Department being to summon the most important figure in nature conservation – Ian Prestt, with an RSPB membership fast approaching half a million.

Discussions with the NCC, over the species elements of the Directive, and how to tackle any consequential changes to domestic legislation, were relatively straightforward – even if the NCC was not as onside as we wished over the task of removing some species, particularly the 'shore' waders from the 'hunting' schedule. But the area of real opportunity was presented by Articles 3 and 4 of the Directive, which required the identification and protection of Special Protection Areas (SPAs) for Annex 1 (the most threatened) species and migratory species. Article 3 required special measures to avoid the loss and deterioration of habitat across the general countryside, to protect the range and numbers of birds.

We argued to the NCC that this was the opportunity to underpin the whole network of SSSIs across Britain with proper protection against changes in farming and forestry practices, as well as being a material fact when planning decisions were taken.

These days we take it for granted that drainage, the ploughing of moorlands, or afforestation of SSSIs are subject to controls and discussion. But back then, SSSIs were pretty much fair game, and many were being damaged through inappropriate uses despite their being recognised as the finest areas for wildlife in Britain. One only has to look at the treasure trove documented in *A Nature Conservation Review* (NCR)[16,17], the bible of our best sites, to appreciate how much was at stake.

A cautious NCC

The NCC was initially cautious. Conversations with DoE civil servants and Ministers had made it clear that in their view, around 25-30 SPAs would suffice to meet the demands of the Directive and most of these would either be existing National Nature Reserves or RSPB nature reserves. No new protection was considered necessary for the great bulk of SSSIs, not even for those listed in the NCR[17].

A strong consortium of NGOs rallied to try and persuade the Government, and ultimately Parliament, that if wildlife in Britain was to be protected then all SSSIs should have statutory measures preventing their destruction. However, it was essential that the NCC did not give cover to the Government by endorsing their limited proposals as being adequate to meet the requirements of the Directive.

And here, the close friendship and trust between Derek Ratcliffe and Ian Prestt came to be crucial. Derek regularly called in to The Lodge to brief Ian on the state of play within NCC. Derek shared our view that the Directive provided a major opportunity to modernise British legislation, and that the SSSI series as a whole should be seen as a national resource for future generations – not as a series of sites with an 'academic' interest for a few. Despite his advice and the unified views of the major NGOs, from the Wildlife Trusts, World Wildlife Fund (from 1986, the World Wide Fund for Nature) and RSPB, and learned societies, the NCC remained cautious in not wanting to upset its new Ministers. Indeed at a meeting of the full Council in early 1980, the NCC resolved to accept that the 25-30 SPAs approach suggested by DOE was adequate, and this would form the basis of its advice to Government.

I supported Ian Prestt at the Council meeting of the NCC—unusually, a small delegation of NGO leaders had been allowed to present the case for greater SSSI protection to the Council—but our advocacy was unsuccessful. I remember waiting outside the meeting with the great and good from across the NGOs, only to be called in to hear the fateful decision.

A blow, but later triumph

It was a major blow, and would allow DoE Ministers to claim publically they were acting with the advice and support of their statutory scientific and conservation advisers. Unless this could be overturned, the chances of providing real protection of all SSSIs were fading fast.

In discussion with Derek and others within NCC it became apparent that new survey data were being gathered that would show that the 'voluntary' approach to SSSI protection, which Government favoured, was in serious disarray. Many landowners and farmers were simply not 'voluntarily' looking after these sites. Quite the opposite – a serious level of damage was occurring across the country. Derek and his team worked at a furious pace to quantify the damage, gathering the key evidence needed to persuade the NCC Council and Ministers at the DoE to look afresh at the issue.

Peter Marren's New Naturalist volume *Nature Conservation*[11] describes this period very well. He quotes Norman Moore (Fig. 19.3), the NCCs Chief Advisory Officer, reporting in 1980 that eight percent of all SSSIs had suffered damage during the past twelve months, with the main causes being agricultural 'improvement' and the 'cessation of traditional practices'. Other key publications emerged around then, not least Marion Shoard's *The Theft of the Countryside*[18], Richard Mabey's *The Common Ground*[19], and a superb article in *New Scientist*[20] by David Goode (Derek's Deputy since 1976) which set out a whole range of examples of destruction to SSSIs, as did *Nature Conservation in Great Britain*[21].

All of this was rapidly seized upon by the NGO community and we used it to generate much media coverage demanding action in the weeks afterwards. The draft Wildlife and Countryside Bill, which was the legislation the Government intended to introduce to enact the Birds Directive (and other conservation and access measures), was being introduced to the House of Lords. A coalition of peers had expressed keen support, and one—a young Labour peer, Lord Peter Melchett (Fig. 20.5)—was to play a pivotal role in the debates over the coming year. Seizing upon the report from NCC's science team he asked the NCC to attend a meeting in the Jubilee Room in the House of Lords.

Here were gathered the Liberal peer Lord Beaumont (coordinator of the Green Alliance, 1978-80) and the Tory life peer Baron Chelwood (a staunch supporter of the RSPB and former Council member of the NCC; he famously later in life moved an amendment in the House of Lords to have the Community Charge, or Poll Tax as it is better known, varied by income).

Figure 20.5. Lord Peter Melchett, a persuasive Labour peer who played a major role in the introduction of the Wildlife and Countryside Bill 1980 leading to its Royal Assent on 30 October 1981. He was former chair of Wildlife Link and Executive Director of Greenpeace until 2001. Photo: Matthew Usher (www.edp24.co.uk)

Attending were Sir Ralph Verney, recently appointed Chairman of the NCC, many Council members, and the newly formed and emboldened Wildlife and Countryside Link (originally Wildlife Link) – a strong and rapidly becoming effective alliance of NGOs. It was a momentous occasion, with the debate well informed and passionate. How could NCC's own science be ignored? NCC had a duty to protect and conserve Britain's special sites and wildlife, and clearly the voluntary protection upon which the Government depended was seriously failing. Many of the Wildlife and Countryside Link members joined the debate, having brilliantly rehearsed arguments playing to different members' specialisms.

The upshot was a U-turn. In October 1980 the NCC Council listened in awe to a broadside from Lord Melchett, arguing that Ministerial orders and 'reciprocal notification' should be given to all SSSIs, effectively meaning that a contract would be drawn up between every SSSI owner and the NCC to oversee management[11]. The Council agreed, and essentially laid the bones of what we still have for SSSIs – formal agreements with owners and managers over SSSIs, with compensation for income lost. It was a sublime triumph for conservation evidence, and for forthright and disciplined advocacy. And it was justice for nature.

Just a month later, on 25 November 1980, the Wildlife and Countryside Bill was introduced, and because of congested business in the Commons, received its first reading in the House of Lords. Here, there was massive and intense interest in the Bill – over the weeks of debate 1,120 amendments were tabled (a record for the Lords), reduced to 560 for the Lords Committee stage, which occupied 13 sitting days[22]. I was then the Parliamentary Officer for the RSPB and worked closely with MPs and peers in Westminster providing many hundreds of pages of rapidly typed briefings and draft amendments. The most crucial amendment, drafted by Tim Sands of the Royal Society for Nature Conservation (RSNC) and myself, sought 'reciprocal notification' and placed a duty on NCC to advise owners and occupiers of land designated as a SSSI of the importance of the land and activities which would damage that interest, and in return requiring, for the first time in law, owners to consult the NCC in advance before undertaking any such activity. This was tabled by Lord Buxton of Alsa, a wildlife champion famed for introducing the Anglia TV *Survival* wildlife series (and later resigning from the NCC Council over its proposed dismemberment), and Lord Onslow, the 7th Earl of Onslow, who was a member of the Joint Committee on Human Rights until his death, and who famously once decried in the House of Lords that: "one hundred years ago, the Church was in favour of fox hunting and against buggery. Now it is in favour of buggery and against fox hunting." The amendment failed – by just two votes. There was intense political horse-trading. Peter Melchett reminds me that there was a deal in the Lords, involving the Government Chief Whip (Lord Dernham), the Labour Chief Whip (Baroness Llewelyn-Davies of Hastoe, the first woman to take charge of the whip's office in either of the Parliamentary houses), and Peter, which allowed the Bill to progress through the Lords on condition that the Government introduced amendments in the Commons to safeguard SSSIs.

The Bill was introduced in the House of Commons, on 27 April 1981, and the second reading debate was introduced by Mr Heseltine, who subsequently during the protracted Committee stage had to go to the Cabinet to secure support for reciprocal notification, such was the force of the argument from the other Parties during the Committee stage, which jeopardised the passage of the Bill. Critical amendments were tabled and accepted, not least requiring landowners to give advance notice of any 'potentially damaging operation' of an SSSI. Section 28, as it became, provided for the crucial protection of SSSIs by enacting reciprocal notification. On 30 October 1981 the Wildlife and Countryside Act[23] came into being. Tam Dalyell MP (Fig. 20.6) (later Sir Tam Dalyell) was a key member of the Committee and his knowledge of Parliamentary procedures and his extraordinary ability to speak knowledgeably and at great length about species or wildlife habitats, was a crucial weapon that helped swing the day, as he recounts vividly in his memoir[24].

Figure 20.6. Sir Tam Dalyell, Labour MP for West Lothian (1962-1983) and Linlithgow (1983-2005). He campaigned tirelessly on issues such as the Lockerbie bombing, the sinking of the *General Belgrano*, the first Gulf War, and the 2003 invasion of Iraq and was a passionate advocate for scientific and conservation matters in Parliament[24]. Photo: Edinburgh Book Festival

A new advocacy wins through for nature

In many ways this was the birth of informed and advocacy-led nature conservation. Tim Sands and I were privileged to have been able to draft the amendments eventually used by Government as the basis for Section 28 of the Act. We were able to address the criticism from the farming and landowning communities that they were simply not aware of a site's importance, so damaging it was an accident. By changing the law, we changed this: now they had to advise the NCC of any potentially damaging operation. The passage of the Act was hugely influential in modernising conservation legislation and it was a huge team effort involving many NGOs, politicians, and novel uses of campaigning media that harnessed the support from grass-roots members of the various NGOs.

But we were set on the path to success by the timely and authoritative work by Derek and his devoted team, providing the hard and convincing evidence that voluntary conservation efforts were failing Britain's special places and wildlife. This work required considerable determination and personal courage. Without that evidence it would have been extremely hard to build the case that led to defeats of the Government in a Conservative dominated House of Lords, or a momentum for change that had stood unchallenged since the 1940s, i.e. that farming and forestry were run in a manner that did not damage the countryside or the wildlife it supports. If this argument had been won in 1949 when the legislation was passed establishing SSSIs, National Parks (in England and Wales), and the forerunner of the NCC, our countryside would be far richer in wildlife today.

Conversely, I often I wonder what Britain would look like if we had not won the day in 1981. The continued loss of SSSIs would have left the nation impoverished. Of course, had we failed to rally and marshal the evidence, I doubt that we would have had more than fractions of our wildlife sites intact. And for that, I thank Derek Ratcliffe, his colleagues, and some remarkable individuals who rose to the fight for nature and defied party whips and vested interests.

References

(1)   Ratcliffe, D.A. (2000) *In Search of Nature*. Peregrine Books, Leeds.

(2)   Newton, I. (2015) Pesticides and birds of prey – the breakthrough. In: *Nature's Conscience – The Life and Legacy of Derek Ratcliffe* (eds. D.B.A. Thompson, H.H. Birks & H.J.B. Birks). This volume, Chapter 15.

(3)   Ratcliffe, D.A. (1970) Changes attributable to pesticides in egg breakage frequency and eggshell thickness in some British birds. *Journal of Applied Ecology*, **7**, 67-115.

(4)   Rarcliffe, D.A. (1967) Decrease in eggshell weight in certain birds of prey. *Nature*, **215**, 208-210.

(5)   Ratcliffe, D.A. (1980) *The Peregrine Falcon*. Poyser, Calton.
       Ratcliffe, D.A. (1990) *Bird Life of Mountain and Upland*. Cambridge University Press, Cambridge.
       Ratcliffe, D.A. (1993) *The Peregrine Falcon* (2nd edition). Poyser, London.
       Ratcliffe, D.A. (1997) *The Raven*. Poyser, London.
       Ratcliffe, D.A. (2002) *Lakeland*. HarperCollins, London.

Ratcliffe, D.A. (2007) *Galloway and the Borders*. Collins, London.

(6)   Bridgewater, P. (2015) National and global biodiversity politics and legalities – some reflections. In: *Nature's Conscience – The Life and Legacy of Derek Ratcliffe* (eds. D.B.A. Thompson, H.H. Birks & H.J.B. Birks). This volume, Chapter 25.

(7)   Nature Conservancy Council (1989) *Guidelines for Selection of Biological SSSIs*. 288 pp. Nature Conservancy Council, Peterborough.

(8)   Battarbee, R.W. (2015) Forestry, 'acid rain', and the acidification of lakes. In: *Nature's Conscience – The Life and Legacy of Derek Ratcliffe* (eds. D.B.A. Thompson, H.H. Birks & H.J.B. Birks). This volume, Chapter 22.

(9)   Stroud, D. A., Reed, T.M., Pienkowski, M.W. & Lindsay, R.A. (2015). The Flow Country: battles fought, war won, organisation lost. In: *Nature's Conscience – The Life and Legacy of Derek Ratcliffe* (eds. D.B.A. Thompson, H.H. Birks & H.J.B. Birks). This volume, Chapter 23.

(10)   Nature Conservancy Council (1986) *Nature Conservation and Afforestation in Britain*. 108 pp. Nature Conservancy Council, Peterborough.

(11)   Marren, P. (2002). *Nature Conservation*. HarperCollins, London.

(12)   Radcliffe (sic), D. (1989) The end of British nature conservation? *New Scientist*, **9 September**, 75-76.

(13)   http://ec.europa.eu/environment/nature/legislation/birdsdirective/index_en.htm

(14)   Thatcher, M. (1993) *The Downing Street Years*. HarperCollins, London. Thatcher, M. (1995) *The Path to Power*. HarperCollins, London.

(15)   Heseltine, M. (2001) *Life in the Jungle: My Autobiography*. Coronet, London.

(16)   Ratcliffe, D.A. (ed.) (1977). *A Nature Conservation Review, Volumes 1 and 2*. Cambridge University Press. Cambridge.

(17)   Thompson, D.B.A., Sutherland, W.J. & Birks, H.J.B. (2015) Nature conservation and the Nature Conservation Review – a new philosophical framework. In: *Nature's Conscience – The Life and Legacy of Derek Ratcliffe* (eds. D.B.A. Thompson, H.H. Birks & H.J.B. Birks). This volume, Chapter 19.

(18)   Shoard, M. (1980). *The Theft of the Countryside*. Temple Smith, London.

(19)   Mabey, Richard (1980). *The Common Ground. A place for nature in Britain's future*. Hutchinson and NCC, London.

(20)   Goode, D. (1981). The threat to wildlife habitats. *New Scientist,* **22 January 1981**, 219-223

(21)   Nature Conservancy Council (1984) *Nature Conservation in Great Britain*. 112 pp. Nature Conservancy Council, Shrewsbury.

(22)   Cherry, G.E. & Rogers, A. (1996) *Rural Change and Planning. England and Wales in the Twentieth Century*. Chapman and Hall, London.

(23)   http://jncc.defra.gov.uk/page-1377

(24)   Dalyell, T. (2011). *The Importance of Being Awkward. The Autobiography of Tom Dalyell*. Birlinn, Edinburgh.

21. Battling forestry and building consensus: woodland conservation post-1949

Keith Kirby

Introduction

The template for much modern conservation in Britain is the landscape of the late nineteenth and early twentieth century; a landscape of open heaths, coppices, flower-rich meadows, and heather moors. This was the countryside experienced by the founding fathers and mothers of conservation. It was prior to the major period of urban expansion and industrialisation of agriculture and followed the 1870 agricultural depression, when much arable land reverted to grass. Large parts of the landscape could then perhaps be more easily seen as 'natural', or at least semi-natural[1]. There had been some broad-scale planting of conifers in the nineteenth century, particularly around reservoirs, such as Thirlmere in the Lake District, and on Scottish estates. However, the great blankets of Lodgepole Pine (*Pinus contorta*) and Sitka Spruce (*Picea sitchensis*), that Derek Ratcliffe so despised, had yet to unfold across the lowland and upland heaths and bogs (Figs. 21.1 & 22.1)[2].

What is now recognised as ancient woodland[3] formed only a small part of the land-use pattern – about 2-3% of the land surface. Indeed, total woodland cover was only about 4-5% in 1900. Much of the broadleaved woodland was still managed (just) as coppice. Grazing on commons and in former royal forests such as Epping was still widespread, thereby maintaining the wood-pasture tradition. All this changed dramatically in the decades that followed the Second World War[4,5].

Derek Ratcliffe and those with whom he worked during the critical period from the mid-1960s through to the mid-1980s laid the foundations on which subsequent woodland conservation has been based. New ways of defining and characterising the woodland cover were developed and a system for evaluating and selecting sites was published. Our woods were put into a broader European perspective. However, the situation has changed and there needs to be a 'paradigm shift' in terms of how we approach woodland conservation in the twenty-first century.

Figure 21.1. Extensive forestry plantation below the steep west side of the Cauldron of the Dungeon, Galloway, 1982. Photo: Derek Ratcliffe

Defining and characterising British woodland

When the Nature Conservancy (NC) was established, the main description of semi-natural woodland was that given by Tansley[6]. He identified the broad patterns of variation from beechwoods in southern England to Scottish pinewoods. However, much of the variation was left largely undifferentiated as various forms of oak woodland. There was a need for a major survey and evaluation of this resource.

A national woodland survey was initiated by the NC in the 1960s by Dick Steele[7]. The results fed into the selection of Sites of Special Scientific Interest (SSSI), and formed the pool from which were selected those to be included as of at least national importance in the Nature Conservation Review (NCR)[1]. The NCR also included discussion of species associated with woodland, including the first list of woodland plant species, used subsequently in site survey and evaluation. The 234 woodland sites in the NCR cover the broad spectrum of differences between woods in the south-east and the north-west, but again the breakdown was into a few, essentially Tansleyan, types, based on the major tree species (Beech (*Fagus sylvatica*), Pine (*Pinus sylvestris*), Oak (*Quercus* spp.), etc.).

Alternative ways of dealing with the variation in semi-natural woodland were developed in the 1970s. Bob Bunce[8] used the 1960's national woodland survey results to pioneer an approach to woodland classification based on random sampling from a representative sample of woods. Oliver Rackham and George Peterken separately built on Tansley's use of the tree and shrub layer to define a wide range of stand types to characterise woods (see Peterken[9] and Rackham[5] for descriptions of their woodland types). These classifications, particularly Peterken's Stand Type system, were used within the

Nature Conservancy Council (NCC) to help identify important sites. They had, however, the drawback that they were independent of the systems adopted for other habitats and of those used on the continent. The development of the National Vegetation Classification (NVC), for which Derek Ratcliffe was a major champion[10], helped to bridge these gaps. After all, Derek and Donald McVean had earlier carried out extensive surveys using a novel phytosociological approach in the 1950s and 1960s in Scotland[10,11]. The woodland section of the NVC, the first of the NVC volumes, was published in 1991[12] and, despite some legitimate criticisms, has since provided a robust framework for woodland vegetation description[13].

The combination of the NVC and the canopy-type categories of Rackham[5] and Peterken[9] established that there remains a surprising diversity – even in tiny scraps of surviving semi-natural woodland. This reflects the strong north-south temperature and east-west rainfall gradients across Britain superimposed on a very varied range of soils. The patterns of variation, particularly in the woodland fauna, are also heavily influenced by differences in woodland structures created by centuries of woodland management[5]. The challenge, then, was to accommodate this range of variation within the emerging SSSI system.

The protected site system and its limitations for woodland conservation

Many of the woods included in the NCR, or otherwise brought into the SSSI system, had long been well-known to naturalists. In the SSSI guidelines[14] Derek Ratcliffe wrote that

> "An inherited knowledge of the best places to find and collect rare and local species developed during Victorian times and became part of a common fund of knowledge amongst naturalists.... When, in 1915, Charles Rothschild compiled a list of desirable nature reserves.... he drew on the opinions of many leading figures throughout the country. Thirty-two years later the listings of the Society's Nature Reserves Investigation Committee ...represented the distillation of collective knowledge from a large body of informed opinion. A similar sifting was applied to the choice of SSSIs when these became a statutory category."

The woodland surveys carried out from the 1960s onward, but particularly during the early 1980s, allowed for a more systematic assessment of which sites should be brought into the SSSI system. The ten NCR evaluation 'criteria', from size and diversity to intrinsic appeal, set out by Ratcliffe[1] were converted into more-or-less elaborate scoring procedures[15,16]. The number and extent of woodland SSSIs increased, and, following the 1981 Wildlife and Countryside Act[17], they received more protection against gross habitat destruction through clearance or conversion to non-native conifer plantations.

Despite this increase, woodland remained less well represented within the SSSI system than most other habitats, particularly in England where the bulk of the semi-natural woodland survived[18]. High-quality woodland is not so scarce that almost every site can (and should) be notified – as with many grassland types. Neither is it concentrated mainly in large blocks, such that relatively few sites are needed to bring in the bulk of the resource, as with many upland habitats. The native pinewoods provide a test of this idea: unlike most broadleaved woods they occur mostly as large blocks and more than eighty per cent of the then known resource was within the SSSI system by the mid-1980s.

There would have needed to be a massive increase in woodland field surveys and in the number of broadleaved woods within the SSSI system to have brought the coverage up to that for other habitats, at a time when other habitats appeared to be under more threat. So, during the 1980s, George Peterken embarked on a different approach. This involved close working with the Forestry Commission (FC) to develop policies and guidance that would favour conservation management across the whole ancient and semi-natural woodland resource, not just the minority that was within the SSSI series[3,19-24].

This promotion of woodland conservation beyond the SSSI system was consistent with the hierarchical approach to conservation that had been proposed in *Nature Conservation in Great Britain* (p.83)[25]. The ancient woodland inventory also became a model that was adopted for other habitats. However, at the time, the approach sat somewhat uncomfortably with others in the Nature Conservancy Council, effectively being led by Derek, who were at 'daggers drawn' with the FC over questions of afforestation of the upland moors and particularly the bogs of Caithness and Sutherland[26-28].

The European significance of British woods

During the period when Derek Ratcliffe was Chief Scientist, the role of the European Commission, later the EU, became increasingly significant. Initially, this was as a driver of farm intensification, in the guise of the Common Agricultural Policy (the CAP, which began in 1962 although the UK was not a member until 1972). It later became a source of agri-environment grants (including co-funding much forestry planting) which became a major influence on nature conservation priorities. In the NCR and the SSSI guidelines the elements of British woodland identified as important in an international context were:

- oceanic assemblages of ferns, bryophytes, and lichens (Fig. 21.2), a particular interest of Derek's[29-31]

- mature semi-natural wood-pasture with its populations of veteran trees (Fig. 21.3)

- outlying/edge-of-range occurrences of continental types such the native pine woods (Fig. 21.4)

- localised abundance of species such as Ash (*Fraxinus excelsior*) (Fig. 21.5)[32], Holly (*Ilex aquifolium*), or Bluebell (*Hyacinthoides non-scripta*) (Fig. 21.6) that particularly thrive in Britain because of our oceanic climate or because there is less competition from more continental species.

The EU Habitats and Species Directive, brought in during 1992[33], later included, as Annex 1 habitats; western oakwoods with their Atlantic cryptogam assemblages (Fig. 21.2); native pine (Fig. 21.4) and beechwoods (Figs. 21.7 & 21.8) as edge-of-range Continental types; and ash-dominant woods on limestone representing an extreme form of the

Figure 21.2. Oceanic woodland on steep boulder-strewn slopes with abundant Atlantic bryophytes, lichens, and ferns. Coed-y-Rhygen, Gwynedd, May 2005. Photo: Derek Ratcliffe (this is the last photo that Derek took)

Tilio-Acerion community (Fig. 21.5)[32,34]. Wood-pasture (Fig. 21.3) and sites important for veteran trees were not recognised as such, but in the selection of woodland Special Areas of Conservation, the conservation agencies gave strong weight to 'old growth' features so that the most important wood-pastures received recognition and protection, such as in the New Forest, Windsor Great Park, Sherwood Forest, and Staverton Park (Fig. 21.3).

Building consensus

Many of the forestry/conservation sector debates were hampered by the failure of one party or another to accept that there were and still are three issues which are discrete and not alternatives:

a) the conservation of ancient and semi-natural woodland, which is where much of our woodland wildlife has survived until now

b) the best ways to encourage rich wildlife communities in the new woods that have been created or developed naturally, particularly those formed over the last 60 years

c) most contentiously from the forestry sector's perspective, new afforestation must be steered away from valuable open habitats.

This last matter has been less of an issue in recent decades than it was during the 1970s

Figure 21.3. Wood-pasture with veteran Pedunculate Oak (*Quercus robur*) trees and abundant Holly (*Ilex aquifolium*). Staverton Park, Suffolk, 1975. Photo: John Birks

Figure 21.4. Native Scots Pine (*Pinus sylvestris*) woods, Abernethy, Strathspey, eastern Scottish Highlands, 1972. Photo: John Birks

Figure 21.5. Ash (*Fraxinus excelsior*)-dominated woodland, Popes Wood, Cotswold Common and Beechwoods National Nature Reserve, Gloucestershire, 1975. Photo: Derek Ratcliffe

Figure 21.6. Bluebell (*Hyacinthoides non-scripta*) glades in the Castramont Woods, Kirkcudbrightshire, May 1982. Photo: Derek Ratcliffe

Figure 21.7. Beech (*Fagus sylvatica*) wood on chalk near Royston (Therfield) Heath, Hertfordshire, 1974. Photo: John Birks

Figure 21.8. Tall Beech (*Fagus sylvatica*) trees in Popes Wood, Gloucestershire, July 1975. Photo: Derek Ratcliffe

and 1980s because of a general reduction in forestry activity, but, with a revival of interest in woodland creation for energy purposes, and for climate change adaptation, it is coming back into focus[35].

Progress has been made on all of these matters, as reflected in a wealth of guidelines[36] now available on different aspects, not just of nature conservation, but also soil conservation, landscape, historic environment, etc. Information on where there are sensitive sites is more comprehensive and widely available, for example in England through 'Nature on the Map'[37]. Policies have also been developed for the restoration of semi-natural woodland and open habitats damaged under past forestry policies[38,39]

In general there is much more common cause now between the forestry and conservation sectors in facing future conservation and land-use challenges. In Wales, the FC and Countryside Council for Wales have been merged as part of a new environmental body—Natural Resources Wales—since April 2013. The future arrangements for the conservation agencies and the FC in the other countries are also under review.

This does not, unfortunately, mean that woodland conservation in the twenty-first century is assured: some old and many new challenges remain to be faced. Institutions may merge, but the differences of view amongst staff with different backgrounds may still remain!

Future directions and challenges for woodland conservation

Conservation philosophy needs to adapt to a changing environment

The area of broadleaved woodland has increased over the last sixty years, as has the area of woodland within protected areas. However, many species groups (woodland birds, open-glade butterflies, larger moths, woodland plants) have declined in richness. The causes are varied and differ for different groups and woodland types[4,7].

While there has been a net increase in woodland composed of native trees and shrubs, areas of rich ancient woodland have been lost[e.g. 19], while the gains have been of young woodland of lower nature conservation value. Lack of or changing management of such sites means that the extent of open woodland and areas of dense young growth on which many woodland species depend are less than they were[40]. Continued, and in places increased, grazing discourages regeneration, simplifies woodland structures, and removes vulnerable species. In the uplands this is particularly by sheep, but also across most of the country by the spread of deer[41]. Changes in the conditions around the sites, for example the loss of hedges, scattered trees, and scrub in the countryside between woods, lead to increased isolation of species within woods[42]. Intensification of farming has increased negative edge effects such as spray and fertiliser drift into woods[43]. The effects of aerial pollution are a concern, notably acidification in the 1980s, but more recently the build-up of nitrogen in forest soils from diffuse pollution, even though, to date, there is only limited evidence for significant effects on the woodland vegetation[44]. Finally, climate change will impact on our woods[45], not just through changes in the average rainfall or temperature, but also through the frequency of extreme events, such as the 1976 drought or the 1987 storm[46,47], which leave their mark on woods for decades to come.

Faced with these threats we should conserve some areas as in the past. However, if we persist in using the state of woods as they were in the nineteenth century as our main conservation template we are almost bound to fail. Conservation will get squeezed into smaller and smaller areas, because of the demands of other land-uses; at the same time the areas that are allocated to conservation will become less suitable for current assemblages because of fragmentation effects and climate change.

In England, the Lawton Review stressed the need for better managed sites, but also for more sites, bigger sites, and with better connections between them[18]. There has been much discussion and modelling of forest habitat networks[48-50]. If this approach is to be taken seriously it means not just basing conservation practice on what can be achieved in the best woodland sites. Instead, it means looking positively at the contribution of secondary woods and scrub, of short-rotation coppice, and productive conifer plantations that exist now or are likely to be created in the landscape. And it means looking at the conservation of 'woodland species' in non-woodland habitats and *vice-versa*. Spruce plantations and secondary woods on enriched farmland will never assume the importance of ancient broadleaved woods, so our conservation management for these needs to build on what they can provide while also meeting other objectives; we should not try to turn them into something they cannot be.

Native versus non-native species and use of local provenance

Is it logical to continue to treat Sycamore (*Acer pseudoplatanus*) (and Beech (Fig. 21.9) in northern Britain beyond its original native range) as invasive aliens[51]? Should their spread, where it occurs, be seen as simply the latest stage in the cultural evolution of our woods under a changing environment? If we accept some 'non-native' species (as in

Figure 21.9. Old Beech (*Fagus sylvatica*) trees outside their native UK range, Knockman Wood, Galloway, 2004. Photo: Derek Ratcliffe

practice happens, even on many nature reserves) what others, such as Rhododendron (Fig. 6.17)[30], should be the focus of control measures, and where? Why has apparently more conservation rhetoric and effort been put into Sycamore control than into Grey Squirrel (*Sciurus carolinensis*) control? Management of species should be based more on their impact on conservation objectives and less on their origin and method of arrival into Britain.

Attitudes to 'genetic integrity' of species and populations may need to be reviewed[52]. Local populations of plants and animals are in some cases genetically distinct from those elsewhere in Britain or on the Continent. This may reflect genetic adaptation to local conditions, but in other cases it may simply be the outcome of genetic drift resulting from the small size of many habitat patches and species populations. Even if species have adapted to local conditions will this still be appropriate under future climate change scenarios? Should we, for example, be introducing more southerly provenances of native trees as a small part of the mixtures used in planting new woods?

Pests and diseases

Pests and diseases did not feature strongly in most woodland conservation thinking in the period 1960 to 1990, with a few exceptions, such as Dutch Elm Disease. The pressures on sites were seen to come largely from direct human action, particularly land-use change. There may even have been an element of smugness in the conservation sector, which saw pests and diseases as threats that could be serious for monoculture plantations of conifers, but somehow would not be significant in ancient semi-natural woods.

Since 2000 this has changed. There has been a sharp increase in the incidence of new (to Britain) tree pests and diseases, including Oak Processionary Moth (*Thaumetopoea processionea*), Red Band Needle Blight (*Dothistroma septosporum*) (affecting both native and introduced pine species), acute oak decline, and recently ash dieback[53,54]. Do we simply allow the woods to respond as they can to such outbreaks, or try to control their impact via silvicultural means and biosecurity measures to reduce spread? In what situations might we accept more intensive control measures (if available) such as pesticide or fungicide treatments? If a high degree of tree mortality is expected should we actively introduce alternative disease-resistant species to potentially vulnerable sites?

Letting nature take its course

The cultural nature of our landscape has become widely appreciated over the last fifty years and forms the basis for conservation intervention where past farming or forestry practice has been withdrawn. However, in the last decade a case has been made for leaving some areas to natural development, by reducing intervention as much as possible[55-57]. On a smaller scale this has long been practised, largely for research purposes in reserves such as Lady Park Wood[58,59], but more recent proposals involve whole landscapes. This approach cannot be a substitute for more active conservation management, but it does have a place as part of future land-use options, even in parts of lowland England.

Conclusions

The strength of the conservation movement in the period 1960-1990 was that it was at the cutting edge of scientific understanding of the issues, and successfully turned that understanding into action for nature. Sometimes this was through confrontation, as in the battles over afforestation led by Derek Ratcliffe; in other cases through building consensus as with George Peterken's work on ancient woodland conservation. Over the last two decades thinking has been consolidated in policy and practice. Woodland and woodland species are now better protected. There is a lot more conservation taking place on the ground; and conservation activity is more widely spread amongst organisations and individuals than in the past.

As the old threats were addressed, however, so new ones have emerged. The challenges for woodland conservation ahead are different from those faced in the past, but no less serious. We are in a period of transition, when we can see that some of the old conservation philosophy is no longer so relevant, but what is to replace it is still unclear. Devolution means that Scotland, Wales, and England are developing their own slightly different approaches to conservation. Attempts at UK-wide reviews and approaches have become more difficult, not least because they lack social or political legitimacy.

We are as much in need now, as then, of the sort of intellectual leadership and conviction shown by staff of the NC and NCC during the critical period of 1960-1990. So long as we have government conservation agencies, we should expect them to provide similar clear and sound advice. If at times this is unpalatable or difficult for other sectors to accept then so be it.

Acknowledgements

The views (and any errors) in this paper are mine, but my thanks go to George Peterken, Duncan Stone, and Kate Holl for helpful comments on earlier drafts.

References

(1)   Ratcliffe, D.A. (ed.) (1977) *A Nature Conservation Review. Volumes 1 and 2*. Cambridge University Press, Cambridge.

(2)   Foot, D. (2010) *Woods and People: Putting Forestry on the Map*. The History Press, Stroud.

(3)   Peterken, G.F. (1977) Habitat conservation priorities in British and European woodlands. *Biological Conservation*, **11**, 223-236.

(4)   Hopkins, J. & Kirby, K.J. (2007) Ecological change in British broadleaved woodland since 1947. *Ibis (supplement)*, **149**, 29-40.

(5)   Rackham, O. (2003) *Ancient Woodland: Its History, Vegetation and Uses in England* (revised edition). Castlepoint Press, Dalbeattie, Scotland.

(6)   Tansley, A.G. (1949) *The British Islands and Their Vegetation*. Cambridge University Press, Cambridge.

(7)   Kirby, K.J., Smart, S.M., Black, H.J., Bunce, R.G.H., Corney, P.M. & Smithers, R. J. (2005) *Long-term ecological changes in British woodland (1971-2001)*. English Nature Research Report 653, Sheffield.

(8)   Bunce, R.G.H. (1982) *A Field Key for Classifying British Woodland Vegetation*. Institute of Terrestrial Ecology, Cambridge.

(9)   Peterken, G.F. (1993) *Wodland Conservation and Management* (2nd edition). Chapman and Hall, London.

(10)   Birks, H.J.B. & Birks, H.H. (2015) Derek Ratcliffe – botanist and plant ecologist. In: *Nature's Conscience – The Life and Legacy of Derek Ratcliffe* (eds. D.B.A. Thompson, H.H. Birks & H.J.B. Birks). This volume, Chapter 4.

(11)   McVean, D.N. & Ratcliffe, D.A. (1962) *Plant Communities of the Scottish Highlands*. HMSO, London.

(12)   Rodwell, J.S. (ed.) (1991) *British Plant Communities: 1 Woodlands and Scrub*. Cambridge University Press, Cambridge.

(13)   Goldberg, E.A. (2003) *National vegetation classification - ten years of experience of using the woodland section*. Research Report 335, Joint Nature Conservation Committee, Peterborough.

(14)   Nature Conservancy Council (1989) *Guidelines for Selection of Biological SSSIs*. 288 pp. Nature Conservancy Council, Peterborough.

(15)   Goodfellow, S. & Peterken, G.F. (1981) A method for survey and assessment of woodland or nature conservation using maps and species lists: the example of Norfolk woodlands, *Biological Conservation*, **21**, 177-195.

(16)   Kirby, K.J. (1993) Assessing nature conservation values in British woodland, *Arboricultural Journal*, **17**, 253-276.

(17)   Housden, S. (2015) Fighting for wildlife – from the inside. In: *Nature's Conscience – The Life and Legacy of Derek Ratcliffe* (eds. D.B.A. Thompson, H.H. Birks & H.J.B. Birks). This volume, Chapter 20.

(18)   Lawton, J. (2010) *Making Space for Nature: A Review of England's Wildlife Sites and Ecological Network*. DEFRA, London.

(19)   Spencer, J.W. & Kirby, K.J. (1992) An inventory of ancient woodland for England and Wales. *Biological Conservation*, **62**, 77-93.

(20)   Roberts, A.J., Russell, C., Walker, G.J. & Kirby, K.J. (1992) Regional variation in the origin, extent and composition of Scottish woodland. *Botanical Journal of Scotland*, **46**, 167-189.

(21)   Goldberg, E.A., Kirby, K.J., Hall, J.E. & Latham, J. (2007) The ancient woodland concept as a practical conservation tool in Great Britain. *Journal of Nature Conservation*, **15**, 109-119.

(22)   Goldberg, E.A., Peterken, G.F. & Kirby, K.J. (2011) Origin and evolution of the Ancient Woodland Inventory. *British Wildlife*, **23**, 90-96.

(23)   Forestry Commission (1985) *The Policy for Broadleaved Woodland*. Forestry Commission, Edinburgh.

(24)   Forestry Commission (1994) *The Management of Semi-Natural Woodland: Guides 1-8*. Forestry Commission, Edinburgh.

(25) Nature Conservancy Council (1984) *Nature Conservation in Great Britain.* 112 pp. Nature Conservancy Council, Shrewsbury.

(26) Nature Conservancy Council (1986) *Nature Conservation and Afforestation in Britain.* 108 pp. Nature Conservancy Council, Peterborough.

(27) Tomkins, S. (1989) *Forestry in Crisis: The Battle for the Hills.* Christopher Helm, London.

(28) Stroud, D.A., Reed, T.M., Pienkowski, M.W., & Lindsay, R.A. (2015) The Flow Country: battles fought, war won, organisation lost. In: *Nature's Conscience – The Life and Legacy of Derek Ratcliffe* (eds. D.B.A. Thompson, H.H. Birks & H.J.B. Birks). This volume, Chapter 23.

(29) Ratcliffe, D.A. (1968) An ecological account of Atlantic bryophytes in the British Isles. *New Phytologist,* **67**, 365-439.

(30) Long, D.G. & Rothero, G.P. (2015) Bryology in the Highlands and Islands of Scotland. In: *Nature's Conscience – The Life and Legacy of Derek Ratcliffe* (eds. D.B.A. Thompson, H.H. Birks & H.J.B. Birks). This volume, Chapter 6.

(31) Preston, C.D. (2015) Derek Ratcliffe and the Atlantic bryophytes of Britain and Ireland. In: *Nature's Conscience – The Life and Legacy of Derek Ratcliffe* (eds. D.B.A. Thompson, H.H. Birks & H.J.B. Birks). This volume, Chapter 7.

(32) Peterken, G.F. (2013) Ash – an ecological portrait. *British Wildlife,* **24**, 235-242.

(33) European Commission (1992) *Directive on the conservation of natural habitats and wild fauna and flora: the habitats directive, 92/43/EEC.* European Commission, Brussels.

(34) Rodwell, J.S. & Dring, J. (2001) *European Significance of British Woodland Types.* English Nature Research Report 460. English Nature, Peterborough.

(35) Kirby, K.J., Reid, C.M. & Green, R. (2011) More trees without the trouble. *Quarterly Journal of Forestry,* **105**, 295-301.

(36) http://www.forestry.gov.uk/ukfs (accessed March 2013).

(37) http://www.natureonthemap.naturalengland.org.uk/map.aspx?m=sssi (accessed March 2013).

(38) http://www.forestry.gov.uk/england-openhabitats (accessed March 2013).

(39) http://www.forestry.gov.uk/keepersoftime (accessed March 2013).

(40) Kirby, K.J. (2009) Effect of the shift from coppice to high forest in English Woods on the woodland flora. In: *Woodland Cultures in Time and Space* (eds. E. Saratsi, M. Burgi, E. Johann, K.J. Kirby, D. Moreno & C. Watkins). pp. 155-162. Embryo Publications, Athens.

(41) Fuller, R.J. & Gill, R. (2001) Ecological impacts of deer in British woodland. *Forestry,* **74**, 193-299.

(42) Bailey, S. (2007) Increasing connectivity in fragmented landscapes: an investigation of evidence for biodiversity gain in woodlands. *Forest Ecology and Management,* **238**, 7-23.

(43) Gove, B., Power, S.A., Buckley, G.P. & Ghazoul, J. (2007) Effects of herbicide spray drift and fertilizer overspread on selected species of woodland ground flora: comparison between short-term and long-term impact assessments and field surveys. *Journal of Applied Ecology, 44*, 374-384.

(44) Verheyen, K., Baeten, L., De Frenne, P., Bernhard-Romermann, M., Brunet, J., Cornelis, J., Decoq, G., Dierschke, H., Eriksson, O., Hedl, R., Heinken, T., Hermy, M., Hommel, P., Kirby, K.J., Naaf, T., Peterken, G.F., Petrik, P., Pfadenhauer, J., van Calster, H., Walther, G.-R., Wulf, M. & Verstraeten, G. (2012) Driving factors behind the eutrophication signal in understorey plant communities of deciduous temperate forests. *Journal of Ecology, 100*, 352-365.

(45) Kirby, K.J., Quine, C.P. & Brown, N.D. (2009) The adaptation of UK forests and woodlands to climate change. In: *Combating Climate Change: A Role for UK Forests* (eds. D.J. Read, P.H. Freer-Smith, J.T.L. Morison, N. Hanly, C.C. West & P. Snowdon). pp. 164-179. The Stationery Office, Edinburgh.

(46) Kirby, K.J. & Buckley, G.P. (1994) *Ecological Responses to the 1987 Great Storm in the Woods of South-East England*. English Nature Science 23, English Nature, Peterborough.

(47) Peterken, G.F. & Mountford, E.P. (1996) Effects of drought on beech in Lady Park Wood, an unmanaged mixed deciduous woodland. *Forestry, 69*, 125-136.

(48) Peterken, G.F., Baldock, D. & Hampson, A. (1995) *A Forest Habitat Network for Scotland*. SNH Research Report 29, Scottish Natural Heritage, Edinburgh.

(49) Latham, J. (2006) Forest habitat networks for Wales. *Quarterly Journal of Forestry, 100*, 280-284.

(50) Watts, K., Ray, D., Quine, C.P., Humphrey, J.W. & Griffiths, M. (2007) *Evaluating Biodiversity in Fragmented Landscapes: Applications of Landscape Ecology Tools*. Information Note, Forestry Commission, Edinburgh.

(51) Natural England (2009) *Guidance on Dealing with the Changing Distribution of Tree Species*. Technical Information Note TIN053, Natural England, Sheffield.

(52) Kirby, K.J. (2013) Tree species and provenance choice in high-value nature conservation sites. *Quarterly Journal of Forestry, 107*, 223-227.

(53) Kirby, K.J., Perry, S.C. & Brodie-James, T. (2010) Possible implications of new tree diseases for nature conservation. *Quarterly Journal of Forestry, 104*, 77-84.

(54) http://www.forestry.gov.uk/pestsanddiseases (accessed March 2013).

(55) Vera, F.W.M. (2000) *Grazing Ecology and Forest History*. CABI, Wallingford.

(56) Taylor, P. (2005) *Beyond Conservation: A Wildland Strategy*. Earthscan and BANC, London.

(57) Hodder, K.H., Buckland, P.C., Kirby, K.J. & Bullock, J.M. (2009) Can the pre-Neolithic provide suitable models for re-wilding the landscape in Britain? *British Wildlife, 20* (supplement), 4-15.

(58) Peterken, G.F. (2000) *Natural Reserves in English Woodland*. English Nature Research Report 384, English Nature, Peterborough.

(59) Peterken, G.F. & Mountford, E.P. (2005) Natural woodland reserves – 69 years of trying at Lady Park Wood Reserve. *British Wildlife, 17*, 7-16.

22. Forestry, 'acid rain', and the acidification of lakes

Richard W. Battarbee

Introduction

In the aftermath of the Second World War, concerned about the perceived strategic need for a national timber resource and problems of rural unemployment, Britain embarked on a massive programme of upland afforestation. Large tracts of moorland were acquired by the UK Forestry Commission and planted with exotic conifers, principally Sitka Spruce (*Picea sitchensis*) and Lodgepole Pine (*Pinus contorta*), tree species imported from western North America capable of growing quickly in wet, acidic environments. As the forests grew, concern also grew about the scale of landscape transformation that was taking place and the extent to which moorland wildlife habitat was being lost. Derek Ratcliffe, in particular, was critical of the extent and nature of the afforestation in Galloway as evidenced by the thoughtful and comprehensive chapter on 'Afforestation' in his *Galloway and the Borders* New Naturalist book in which he maintained that afforestation "has over-stepped the boundaries of acceptability by a fairly wide margin" ([1] p. 283) (Figs. 22.1 & 22.2).

In 1981 students taking the University College London MSc in Conservation course carried out a group research project in and around the Galloway forests to explore the impact of afforestation on wildlife. They could find very little of biological interest in the forested areas, especially in areas where the canopy had already closed, and, partly to express their frustration and disappointment, it was decided to title their report 'The afforestation of the Uplands: the botanical interest in the areas left unplanted'! It documented the flora of the land along the forest firebreaks and the unplanted margins of the forest abutting steep land and alongside stream and lake shores and made recommendations about the need for extensive buffer strips in riparian areas to leave space for wildlife[2].

However, concerns about afforestation not only focussed on the loss of moorland

Figure 22.1. Extensive forestry plantation: Fleet Forest, Galloway, 1984. Photo: Derek Ratcliffe

habitat but also on the potential effect of forestry on freshwaters. In Galloway and indeed in other upland parts of the UK subject to afforestation, a decline in salmon and trout populations in streams and lakes had been observed coinciding with the period of rapid afforestation during the 1960s and 1970s. Trees planted too close to streams and lake shores caused shading, aerial spraying of fertilisers on the forest was often carried out in a manner not always following best practice, a problem compounded where trees were planted too close to watercourses, and ploughing to drain the wet peaty soils was sometimes conducted with little regard to their vulnerability to erosion. Too often drains were drawn too steeply and were easily scoured by storm runoff causing gully erosion and the mass transport of soil and sediment into streams and lakes leading to loss or disturbance of trout spawning sites. Clear evidence of the erosion caused by injudicious ploughing and drainage is provided by records of rapidly increased accumulation rates in the sediments of lakes with afforested catchments in comparison to those with moorland catchments[3].

Although poor land- and forest-management practices were doubtless responsible for damaging fish populations, there was another, much more contentious accusation: that afforestation was partly or even wholly to blame for streams and lakes becoming acidified. In the early 1980s the UK Government and the UK nationalised power company, the Central Electricity Generating Board (CEGB), were reluctant to admit that acidic gas emissions from power stations could be the cause of the acidification problem that was being widely recognised in upland areas of Britain, including Galloway, and they were eager to point out that land-use change might be an alternative explanation. The need to understand the 'forest effect', as it was called, and the respective roles of afforestation and acid rain in explaining surface water acidification consequently

Figure 22.2. Cauldron of the Dungeon and Loch Dee from the White Laggan 1955 (treeless) and 2004 (afforested). Photos: Derek Ratcliffe

became a research priority of national and international importance and one that pitted the Forestry Commission against the CEGB. It was an issue that Derek Ratcliffe became especially interested in not least because there was an apparent association between the decline in Dipper (*Cinclus cinclus*) numbers and acidification[4], and that Dippers were less abundant in afforested streams (Juliet Vickery, personal communication in [1]).

Evaluating competing hypotheses for surface water acidification using a palaeoecological approach

The observation that afforested sites were characterised by more acidic waters than those flowing from otherwise very similar moorland streams[5] indicated a 'forest effect' but did not demonstrate necessarily an 'acid-rain effect' at either moorland or afforested sites. One of the first priorities in the acid-rain debate was to establish whether the acidic waters draining non-afforested sites were indeed acidified relatively recently as suggested from the survey of Galloway lakes and streams by Dick Wright and Arne Henriksen[6] who visited the region from Norway in 1979 seeking to demonstrate that 'acid rain' was not just a Scandinavian problem.

In the early 1980s when Roger Flower and I, with funding from the CEGB, began work on the Galloway lochs this was our first principal objective. We evaluated the forest hypothesis by comparing lakes with and without afforested catchments using evidence for their respective acidification histories based on diatom analysis of ^{210}Pb-dated sediment cores. We chose the Round Loch of Glenhead (RLGH) as the site with a non-afforested, moorland catchment and Loch Grannoch as the afforested comparison site where a high proportion of the catchment had been planted with conifers. Our results quite quickly and conclusively showed that the moorland site (RLGH) had become significantly more acidic since the mid 19th century and that the afforested site began to become more acidic in the early 20th century, many decades before its catchment was afforested[7]. The results strongly indicated that the acidification at both sites was the result of acid deposition, not afforestation, a conclusion supported by later diatom data of a similar nature from other sites in the UK[8,9]. It was also underpinned by data from the sediment records showing the presence and increasing concentration of air pollutants, especially heavy metals and fly-ash particles, occurring concomitantly with the evidence for acidification[10,11].

Roger Flower's later diatom analysis of a core from Loch Dee (Fig. 22.3)[8], the site photographed by Derek Ratcliffe in 1955 and 2004 designed to show the landscape impact of afforestation in Galloway (Fig. 22.2), very clearly illustrates that acidification began towards the end of the 19th century well before the start of catchment planting shown in the lower photograph. The diatom diagram shows a rapid loss of the planktonic diatom *Cyclotella comensis* at the end of the 19th century and the more gradual loss through the 20th century of *Achnanthes microcephala*, a benthic taxon, abundant in water of circumneutral to alkaline pH but intolerant of acidic conditions.

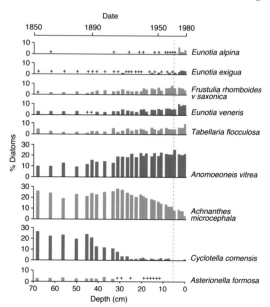

Figure 22.3. Diatom diagram from Loch Dee showing that catchment afforestation (dashed vertical line) in the 1970s came well after the loch started to be acidified in the late 19th century as shown by the rapid loss of *Cyclotella comensis* from about 1890 (modified from Flower et al.[8])

Empirical evidence for the 'forest effect'

Despite this conclusive evidence for acid deposition as the principal cause of surface water acidification in Galloway and other regions, the empirical evidence for an additional 'forest effect' was very strong. The question was whether the effect was as a result of the forest growth itself, for example through the uptake of base cations from soils and alterations in evapotranspiration and runoff hydrology, or through the effect of the forest canopy trapping air pollutants from the atmosphere, a process often termed the 'scavenging effect'.

Although a number of earlier studies had shown evidence of pollutant interception by forest canopies, it was the pioneering work of Ron Harriman and Brian Morrison of the Freshwaters Fishery Laboratory in Pitlochry that provided direct evidence of its impact on freshwaters. In the late 1970s they established a network of chemical and biological monitoring stations draining moorland and afforested headwater streams in the Loch Ard Forest in the Trossachs area of Scotland[5] and compared the chemistry of stream water from the various catchments with the chemistry of precipitation. They showed that precipitation chemistry was exceptionally acidic (pH = 4.43) with a high non-marine (i.e. pollutant) sulphate concentration, especially when air masses had crossed industrial regions to the south and east, but that on any sampling day the forest streams were more acid than adjacent moorland streams. Overall the forest streams had lower pH (Fig. 22.4) and higher concentrations of toxic labile aluminium than the moorland streams, few or no brown trout, and were almost entirely lacking in mayfly nymphs. The effect was shown to be more severe with older forest and with increased percentage of forest cover in the catchment. They attributed the difference between the moorland and afforested streams to the ability of the conifer canopies to collect air pollutants but did not rule out the role of base-cation uptake as an additional factor.

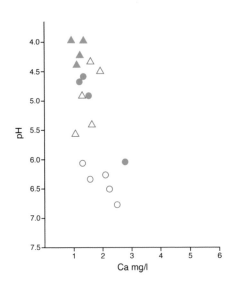

Figure 22.4. Comparison of pH for streams with moorland (brown symbols) and afforested (green symbols) streams in the Loch Ard Forest, Scotland in relation to calcium (Ca) concentration and flow (triangles = high flow; circles = low flow) (modified from Harriman & Morrison[5])

A similar study[12] was conducted later in Wales using data from afforested and moorland headwater streams of the River Tywi flowing into Llyn Brianne, a large drinking-water reservoir in South Wales. The moorland–afforestation comparison generated results very similar to those of the Scottish study, especially with respect to the lower pH and/or higher labile aluminium concentrations in afforested streams, and their lack of brown trout populations. These conclusions were further reinforced by a regional survey of Welsh streams with and without afforested catchments[13].

The 'scavenging' process

Although the evidence for a 'forest effect' remained incontrovertible and pollutant interception by the forest canopy the most likely overall mechanism, the detailed processes
involved remained largely unresolved until a seminal study at a research site in Kielder
Forest, Northumberland by David Fowler and his colleagues at the Institute for Terrestrial Ecology in Penicuik[14]. Unlike a number of previous studies, Fowler and colleagues
took into account differences between the deposition processes for particles and for pollutant gases to leaf surfaces, and carried out field experiments to compare deposition
processes between pollutants both onto forest canopies and onto moorland vegetation
at a range of elevations.

    Their results showed there were substantial differences between the rates of
deposition of pollutant gases to leaf surfaces, depending on their chemical reactivity
with the surfaces themselves. The deposition of individual aerosol particles and cloud-
water droplets were strongly dependent on particle size, with larger cloud-water
droplets being deposited much more efficiently than individual aerosol particles. Cloud-
water droplets were collected especially efficiently by the forest canopy due to its aero-
dynamically rough surface enhancing turbulent diffusion processes, in contrast to the
smoother surfaces of moorland vegetation.

    The study also showed the importance of elevation. The condensation level in
Britain that leads to cloud-droplet formation occurs over high ground typically over 300
m. As aerosols in polluted air contained high concentrations of sulphate and nitrate,
forests at high elevation covered for long periods by clouds substantially enhance pollutant deposition. Fowler et al.[14] argued that "for land above 600 m, which is in cloud
for typically 2000 hours per year in western Britain, cloud-water deposition may increase

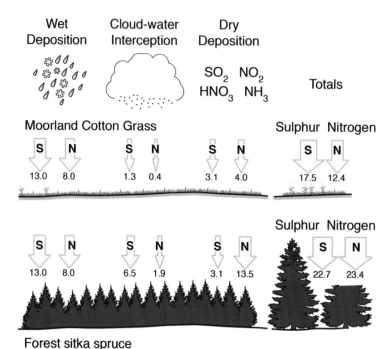

Figure 22.5. Summary of
atmospheric pollutant in-
puts at the Kielder Forest
study site at 300 m elevation and with 1500 mm
rain. Units are kilograms
per hectare per year (modified from Fowler et al.[14])

precipitation by about 12% and may add up to 40% of additional solutes to the wet deposition, because the concentrations of the major ions in orographic cloud water exceed those in rain water by a factor of between 2 and 3".

Fowler et al.[14] summarised their results (Fig. 22.5) by showing a comparison between all pollutants and their mode of deposition for afforested and moorland vegetation. The presence of 15 m high trees was estimated to increase annual inputs of sulphur and nitrogen from the atmosphere by 30% and 90%, respectively[14].

Evidence from process modelling

The size of the 'scavenging effect' revealed by Fowler et al.'s study[14] demonstrated clearly why streams draining high elevation conifer plantations in regions with high concentrations of air pollutants could be considerably more acidic than adjacent moorland streams. It did not, and was not designed, however, to address the importance of scavenging in comparison with processes directly related to forest growth. The extent to which conifer plantations could cause surface water acidification through forest-growth processes in the absence of acid deposition and associated pollutant scavenging remained an important question.

Jack Cosby, Alan Jenkins, and co-workers[15] argued that the most effective way to address this issue was through process modelling. They used the Model of Acidification of Groundwater in Catchments (MAGIC)[16], a model that simulates changes in the size of the pool of exchangeable base cations in the soil in response to changes in pollutant deposition and to changes in the biological uptake or release of ions by vegetation. As input and output fluxes change in the model, the chemical equilibria between soil and soil solution change and thereby determine changes in the chemistry of surface waters draining the soil.

In this study the model was applied to two afforested catchments in the Loch Ard Forest and the model was modified by including terms for ion uptake by the growing forest, dry deposition to the moorland surface prior to planting, increased deposition from 1950 until 1965 to take account of the increasing 'scavenging effect' from forest planting to canopy closure, and a continuously variable runoff to represent evapotranspiration changes in response to the water demand of the growing forest[15]. The model was then run with three alternative scenarios, first with no acid deposition but with forest growth, second with acid deposition but with no forest growth; and finally with acid deposition and forest growth combined.

The results of the simulation are shown in Figure 22.6. For the first scenario of afforestation in the absence of acid deposition, the model indicated a small decrease in alkalinity and a slight increase in hydrogen ion concentration following planting in 1950. For the second scenario of acid deposition in the absence of forestry, alkalinity decreased gradually from the middle of the 19th century and then more rapidly in the post-war period. In this case hydrogen ion concentration followed a reciprocal trend driven by the prescribed increase in sulphur emissions in the model. When both acid deposition and afforestation were included as drivers in the model, the third scenario, there were major changes in alkalinity and hydrogen ion concentration exceeding the sum of their separate effects. Jenkins et al. explained that this "acidification intensifies as the increased sulphate input from the canopy filtering far exceeds the forest uptake requirement".

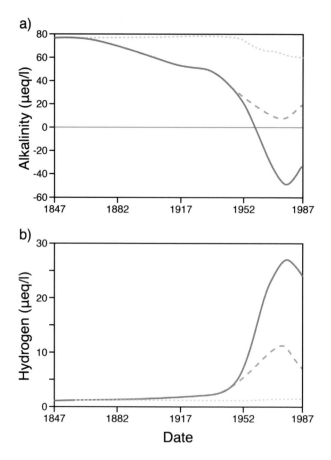

Figure 22.6 (a) Simulated stream-water alkalinity and (b) hydrogen ion concentration for three alternative scenarios: (i) forest growth in the absence of acid deposition (dotted line); (ii) acid deposition in the absence of forest growth (dashed line); and (iii) acid deposition and forest growth combined (continuous line) (from Jenkins et al.[15]).

They also observed from the model output that afforestation resulted not only in stream acidification but also in soil acidification caused by a marked decrease in the percentage base saturation following planting[15].

Palaeoecological evidence for the 'forest effect'

At about the same time as these experimental and modelling studies were being carried out, the University College London Palaeoecological Research Unit (now the Environmental Change Research Centre) designed a palaeolimnological study within the Surface Water Acidification Project[17] to test the forest-growth hypothesis[18]. We selected lakes in Scotland with and without afforested catchments situated in areas of high and low acid deposition and proposed first, that if scavenging was the dominant process, the afforested site in the high deposition area should be more strongly acidified than the afforested site in the low deposition area, and second that if base-cation uptake and related forest-growth factors were important the afforested site in the low deposition area should be acidified more strongly than the moorland site in the same area.

The sites we chose were Loch Chon (afforested) and Loch Tinker (moorland) in the Trossachs, a high acid deposition area, and Loch Doilet (afforested) and Lochan Dubh (moorland) in the Ardnamurchan area of western Scotland, a low acid deposition area. At each site we obtained sediment cores, dated them using ^{210}Pb-dating, analysed them for heavy metals and fly-ash particles to indicate their historic exposure to acid deposition, and carried out pH reconstruction using a diatom-pH transfer function[19].

The results (Fig. 22.7) show that all four of the lakes had acidified, consistent with their exposure to acid deposition over the last century, but for Loch Chon, the afforested site in the high deposition area, the rate of acidification accelerated after afforestation. For Loch Doilet, in the low deposition area, on the other hand, the rate of acidification after afforestation was not significantly different from the adjacent moorland site, Lochan Dubh. Although using lakes to conduct natural experiments in this way can be problematical as all natural lakes have their own individuality, the results of the study nevertheless strongly favoured the 'scavenging effect' over the forest-growth hypothesis, consistent with all other lines of evidence.

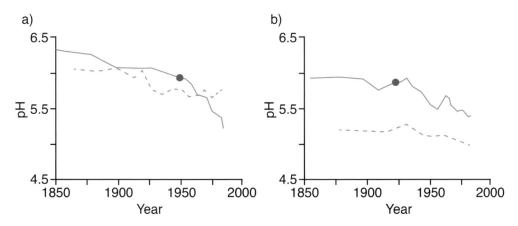

Figure 22.7. Inferred pH against time for (a) Loch Chon (solid line) and Loch Tinker (dotted line) in a high acid deposition area of Scotland, and (b) Loch Doilet (solid line) and Lochan Dubh (dotted line) in a relatively low acid deposition area of Scotland. The date of afforestation at Loch Chon and Loch Doilet is shown by a closed circle (from Kreiser et al.[18])

Forest and water guidelines and the 'critical loads' approach

Concern for the potential damage of forestry to freshwaters in the UK Uplands in the mid 1980s led to the publication by the Forestry Commission in 1988 of guidelines to improve forestry procedures and protect water quality[20]. This first edition was published before the relationship between acid deposition and forestry was fully established. Consequently, a second edition was published in 1991[21] following a expert-led review meeting jointly organised by the Forestry Commission and the Department of the Environment in Darlington in June 1990[22]. The review considered all the processes by which surface waters might become acidified as a result of afforestation and concluded that the 'scavenging effect' was the most important, especially in catchments exposed to high cloud-droplet impaction. The report made three principal recommendations: that the 'critical loads' approach[23] should be used to assess where new planting could be allowed to take place; that further measurements and monitoring in afforested catchments should be undertaken to improve acid deposition estimates in high rainfall areas; and that the newly established UK Acid Waters Monitoring Network (UK AWMN: now the UK Upland Waters Monitoring Network (uwmn.defra.gov.uk)) should be used to monitor afforested sites in order to assess the effects of reduced deposition in forested areas on biological systems over the long term.

The 'critical loads' approach, as applied to freshwaters, refers to a method of calculating how much acid deposition a water body can neutralise without causing biological change. In the case of afforestation the second edition of the Forestry Commission's Forests and Water Guidelines[21] set out procedures based on this approach to prevent new tree planting in sensitive catchments where the scavenging effect of the forest at maturity was likely to cause critical-load exceedance and thereby likely to damage freshwater plants and animals. The subsequent edition of the guidelines[24] added that if the total acid deposition was predicted to exceed the critical load, approval of a planting grant or restocking plan would be unlikely until reductions in pollutant emissions occurred, or in the case of restocking, the area of closed canopy, conifer forest above 300 m elevation was reduced to <30% of the catchment. The 'critical loads approach' as applied to forestry continues to be refined[25] but it remains the principal measure used by the Forestry Commission to protect surface waters from further acidification[26].

Recovery from acidification

The introduction of planting guidelines to avoid surface water acidification came far too late to prevent problems arising across the UK Uplands, but as a result of reductions in the emissions of acid gases from fossil fuel combustion over the last 25 years[27], acidified lakes and streams, including those with afforested catchments, are beginning to recover[28]. A central question is whether afforested sites have recovered to the same extent and in the same way as non-afforested sites. Analysis of data from long-term monitoring sites in the UK including Llyn Brianne[29], the Loch Ard Forest streams[30] and the AWMN sites[31] comparing trends between afforested and non-afforested sites have provided consistent evidence.

Although trends at afforested sites can be expected to be quite complex and site specific, reflecting between-site differences in catchment land-use history, the proportion of catchment planted, and the times of felling and re-planting[30], all long-term datasets have demonstrated that afforested sites are recovering at a similar rate to moorland sites. However, they also show that afforested streams today remain more acidic than moorland ones mainly because they were more acidified and had higher labile aluminium concentrations at the start of the recovery period[29,30]. Afforested sites, moreover, may be more prone to 'acid episodes' following stormy weather due to the scavenging of sea-salt aerosols by the forest canopy. Although sea-salts are not acidic, sodium and magnesium ions are exchanged for acidity and aluminium in organic soils generating highly acidic stream flow that can be very damaging to aquatic animals, especially fish. This effect can be severe on the west coast of Britain where precipitation may contain a high sea-salt concentration. Such events can be extremely harmful to salmonid fish if they occur at times of hatching, fry development, and smelting.

The results from sites in the AWMN provide supporting evidence from other regions of the UK[32] for these findings. Of the 22 sites in the AWMN five have afforested or partially afforested catchments. Three of these sites (Afon Hafren, Loch Grannoch, Loch Chon) are paired with nearby moorland sites (Afon Gwy, Round Loch of Glenhead, Loch Tinker, respectively) with each pair sharing similar catchment soils and bedrock and exposed to similar acid deposition loads. The comparisons between sites in the analysis showed that in each case the afforested site has had higher concentrations of non-marine sulphate, nitrate, and chloride and lower pH throughout the period of monitoring than its respective partner, and that both afforested and non-afforested sites were recovering chemically in a similar way. The data also show some degree of convergence taking place for some pairs, such as the Round Loch of Glenhead and Loch Grannoch (Fig. 22.8) indicating more rapid change taking place in the historically more acidified afforested sites that have benefited from both the reduction in acid deposition and, albeit to a lesser extent, from a decrease in scavenging as mature forest has been felled and replanted[cf. 33].

The similar trends between sites (e.g. Fig. 22.8) provide further evidence that the scavenging process (described above) is the dominant one contributing to the 'forest effect' as the recovery at both afforested and moorland sites is strongly related to the decline in air pollution. Little or no improvement would be expected over this time period at afforested sites if forest-growth processes were the dominant reason for acidification.

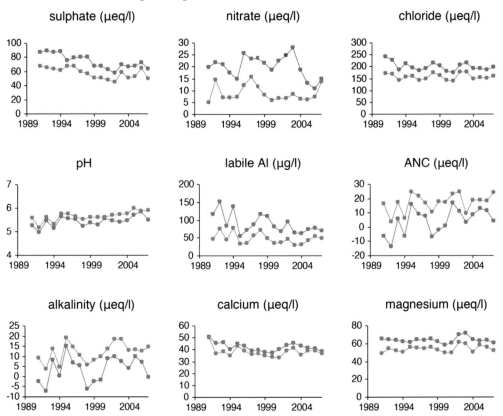

Figure 22.8. Comparison of mean annual chemistry time-series for a range of water chemistry determinands at the moorland site of the Round Loch of Glenhead (brown) and the paired afforested site of Loch Grannoch (green) in Galloway, south-west Scotland. Al = aluminium, ANC = Acid Neutralising Capacity (from Kernan et al.[32])

Prospects for the future

In recognition of the problems associated with conifer plantations in the UK uplands there has been a change in forestry policy. Today, improved landscape design and the promotion of biodiversity have, in addition to timber production, become central objectives. Older forests previously dominated by single tree species and even-aged stands are being converted to forests with more open space, a higher proportion of native broad-leaf trees, an increased variety of conifer species, and a broader range of tree ages (T.R. Nisbet, personal communication). Lowering the proportion of closed canopy forest at any given time in the planting-felling cycle is thereby designed to decrease overall pollutant scavenging and further reduce acidification pressure on streams and lakes.

The new policy also includes the opening up of stream sides and the creation of riparian buffer zones planted with native woodland species. According to Broadmeadow and Nisbet[34] the removal of heavy shading improves freshwater and riparian habitats and can increase fish numbers. Plans for Loch Grannoch in Galloway, for example, seek to lower the tree-line below 300 m, partly to reduce the pollutant 'scavenging effect' but also to improve foraging habitat for raptors. Significant areas of native broad-leaved woodland will be planted to form riparian buffer zones along the main inflowing streams. The net effect of these changes will be to reduce the proportion of conifer cover from 64% in the 1980s to 29% by 2050[32].

In an attempt to assess the effectiveness of these policies, Helliwell and colleagues[35] used the dynamic model MAGIC described above to simulate their impact on surface water chemistry over the next century. As Jenkins et al.[15] had previously done, the key processes controlling pollutant scavenging, catchment runoff, and removal of base cations through forest harvesting were incorporated into the model and the model was run using the Forestry Commission plans for afforested sites.

Results from the model experiments showed a continued recovery at afforested sites similar to the recovery predicted for moorland sites driven by reductions in atmospheric deposition (by 2020) and decreased scavenging by coniferous forests. Over the longer term (until 2100) the effect of afforestation on soil and surface water base-status varied between sites with some sites showing a decrease in base saturation and some a slight increase indicating that the proposed effects of forest removal in the plans were small in promoting recovery from acidification in comparison to the effect of reducing acid deposition.

Although these model projections are very instructive they do not necessarily describe what might happen in reality. In particular there is much uncertainty about the future behaviour of nitrogen in soils. The potential release of nitrogen, mainly as nitrate, into streams depends on the extent to which concentrations in soils have built up over decades of air pollution, its rate of uptake by trees and removal in harvested timber, and the amounts released into the atmosphere by denitrification. Models differ in their projections but in the worst case some show that soils may in future become saturated by nitrogen, even under conditions of decreasing N deposition. If and when soils become saturated, nitrate will be leached into streams, potentially limiting or even reversing recovery from acidification.

Uncertainty also surrounds the potential impact of climate change on recovery success as changes in temperature and precipitation control many of the processes operating in soil and water systems. A specific concern is the possibility that increased storminess especially in the west of Britain will lead to increasing interception of sea-salts by forest canopies as pointed out above. If there is an increase in the frequency and intensity of sea-salt laden storms, acid stream-water episodes damaging to fish may not be fully abated by the expected reduction in air pollutants[36].

Given the extent to which lakes and streams in Galloway have begun to recover and given that the emphasis of afforestation policy in Galloway and other upland regions of the UK has shifted to take account of water quality and biodiversity issues, Derek Ratcliffe may well today have a somewhat more benign view of upland forestry than when he wrote his chapter on afforestation in 2004-2005[1]. However, despite showing signs of improvement many streams and lakes remain chronically acidified and a return to more favourable pre-acid deposition conditions seems very unlikely as the legacy of past air pollution lingers and new pressures in the future, especially from climate change, seem unavoidable. For afforested sites especially, the combination of these forces together with the influence of new planting regimes and land-management practices will in all probability drive freshwaters towards entirely new ecosystem structures[37]. A programme of continued research on the potential interactions between forest growth, the mobility and uptake of legacy pollutants, and climate change, supported by long-term monitoring in order to track changes in both terrestrial and freshwater biodiversity over the next forest planting and felling cycle is called for – a programme that Derek Ratcliffe would almost certainly espouse.

Acknowledgements

I should like to thank John Birks, Chris Evans, Roger Flower, David Fowler, Alan Jenkins, Rachel Helliwell, Iain Malcolm, Don Monteith, and Tom Nisbet for helpful comments, Miles Irving for drawing the figures, and Cathy Jenks for help with editing and formatting.

References

(1)   Ratcliffe, D.A. (2007) *Galloway and the Borders*. Collins, London.
(2)   UCL Conservation Course (1981) The afforestation of the Uplands: the botanical interest in the areas left unplanted. *Discussion Papers in Conservation, No 35*. 88 pp. University College London.
(3)   Battarbee, R.W., Appleby, P.G., Odell, K. & Flower, R.J. (1985) Pb-210 dating of Scottish lake sediments, afforestation and accelerated soil erosion. *Earth Surface Processes and Landforms*, **10**, 137-142.
(4)   Ormerod, S.J., Allinson, N., Hudson, D. & Tyler, S.J. (1986) The distribution of breeding dippers (*Cinclus cinclus* (L), Aves) in relation to stream acidity in Upland Wales. *Freshwater Biology*, **16**, 501-507.
(5)   Harriman, R. & Morrison, B.R.S. (1982) Ecology of streams draining forested and non-forested catchments in an area of central Scotland subject to acid deposition. *Hydrobiologia*, **88**, 252-263

(6)   Wright, R.F. & Henriksen, A. (1980) *Regional Survey of Lakes and Streams in South-western Scotland, April 1979.* 63 pp. SNSF Project Internal Report 72/80. Oslo.

(7)   Flower, R.J. & Battarbee, R.W. (1983) Diatom evidence for recent acidification of two Scottish lochs. *Nature,* **305**, 130-133.

(8)   Flower, R.J., Battarbee, R.W. & Appleby, P.G. (1987) The recent palaeolimnology of acid lakes in Galloway, south-west Scotland: Diatom analysis, pH trends, and the role of afforestation. *Journal of Ecology,* **75**, 797-823.

(9)   Battarbee, R.W. *et al.* (1988) Lake acidification in the United Kingdom 1800-1986: Evidence from analysis of lake sediments. 68 pp. ENSIS Ltd, London.

(10)   Battarbee, R.W., Flower, R.J., Stevenson, A.C. & Rippey, B. (1985) Lake acidification in Galloway - a palaeoecological test of computing hypotheses. *Nature,* **314**, 350-352.

(11)   Battarbee, R.W. *et al.* (1989) Causes of lake acidification in Galloway, south-west Scotland: a palaeoecological evaluation of the relative roles of atmospheric contamination and catchment change for two acidified sites with non-afforested catchments. *Journal of Ecology,* **77**, 651-672.

(12)   Stoner, J.H., Gee, A.S. & Wade, K.R. (1984) The effects of acidification on the ecology of streams in the Upper Tywi catchment in West Wales. *Environmental Pollution,* **35**, 125-157.

(13)   Ormerod, S.J., Donald, A.P. & Brown, S.J. (1989) The influence of plantation forestry on the pH and aluminium concentration of upland Welsh streams: a re-examination. *Environmental Pollution,* **62**, 47-62.

(14)   Fowler, D., Cape, J.N. & Unsworth, M.H. (1989) Deposition of atmospheric pollutants on forests. *Philosophical Transactions of the Royal Society of London B,* **324**, 247-265.

(15)   Jenkins, A., Cosby, B.J., Ferrier, R.C., Walker, T.A.B. & Miller, J.D. (1990) Modelling stream acidification in afforested catchments: an assessment of the relative effects of acid deposition and afforestation. *Journal of Hydrology,* **120**, 163-181.

(16)   Cosby, B.J., Hornberger, G.M., Galloway, J.N. & Wright, R.F. (1985) Modeling the effects of acid deposition: assessment of a lumped parameter model of soil-water and streamwater chemistry. *Water Resources Research,* **21**, 51-63.

(17)   Mason, B.J. (1990) *The Surface Waters Acidification Programme.* Cambridge University Press, Cambridge.

(18)   Kreiser, A.M., Appleby, P.G., Natkanski, J., Rippey, B. & Battarbee, R.W. (1990) Afforestation and lake acidification: a comparison of four sites in Scotland. *Philosophical Transactions of the Royal Society London B,* **327**, 377-383.

(19)   Birks, H.J.B., Line, J.M., Juggins, S., Stevenson, A.C. & ter Braak, C.J.F. (1990) Diatoms and pH reconstruction. *Philosophical Transactions of the Royal Society London B,* **327**, 263-278.

(20)   Forestry Commission (1988) *Forests & Water Guidelines.* 24 pp. Edinburgh.

(21)   Forestry Commission (1991) *Forests & Water Guidelines* (2nd edition). 24 pp. London.

(22) Nisbet, T.R. (1990) *Forests and Surface Water Acidification*. 16 pp. Forestry Commission, Edinburgh.

(23) Nilsson, J. & Grennfelt, P. (1988) *Critical Loads for Sulphur and Nitrogen*. Miljørapport 15, Nordic Council of Ministers, Copenhagen.

(24) Forestry Commission (2003) *Forests & Water Guidelines* (4th edition). 66 pp. Forestry Commission, Edinburgh.
http://www.biodiversity.ru/programs/ecoservices/library/functions/water/doc/Forestry_Comission_2003.pdf

(25) Forestry Commission (2011) *Forests and Water. UK Forestry Standard Guidelines*. 80 pp. Forestry Commission, Edinburgh.
http://www.forestry.gov.uk/pdf/FCGL007.pdf/$file/FCGL007.pdf
http://www.forestry.gov.uk/pdf/fcgl002.pdf/$FILE/fcgl002.pdf

(26) Nisbet, T.R. & Evans, C.E. (2013) *Forestry Commission Research Note: Forestry and Surface Water Acidification*.
http://www.confor.org.uk/Upload/Documents/14_acidification_research_note_consultation_jan2013.pdf

(27) Centre for Ecology & Hydrology (2012) *RoTAP. Review of Transboundary Air Pollution: Acidification, Eutrophication, Ground Level Ozone and Heavy Metals in the UK*. 292 pp. NERC, Edinburgh.

(28) Curtis, C.J., Battarbee, R.W., Monteith, D. & Shilland, E. (eds.) (2014) Threats to UK Upland Waters. *Ecological Indicators*, **37**, 267-430.

(29) Ormerod, S.J. & Durance, I. (2009) Restoration and recovery from acidification in upland Welsh streams over 25 years. *Journal of Applied Ecology*, **46**, 164-174.

(30) Malcolm, I.A., Gibbins, C.N., Fryer, R.J., Keay, J., Telzlaff, D. & Soulsby, C. (2014) The influence of forestry on acidification and recovery: Insights from long-term hydrochemical and invertebrate data. *Ecological Indicators*, **37**, 317-329.

(31) Monteith, D.T., Evans, C.D., Henrys, P.A., Simpson, G.L. & Malcolm, I.A. (2014) Trends in the hydrochemistry of acid-sensitive surface waters in the UK 1988–2008. *Ecological Indicators*, **37**, 287-303.

(32) Kernan, M., Battarbee, R.W., Curtis, C.J., Monteith, D.T. & Shilland, E.M. (2010) *UK Acid Waters Monitoring Network 20 Year Interpretative Report*. ENSIS Ltd, University College London.

(33) Neal, C., Robinson, M., Reynolds, B., Neal, M., Rowland, P., Grant, S., Norris, D., Williams, B., Sleep, D. & Lawlor, A. (2010) Hydrology and water quality of the headwaters of the River Severn: Stream acidity recovery and interactions with plantation forestry under an improving pollution climate. *Science of the Total Environment*, **408**, 5035-5051.

(34) Broadmeadow, S. & Nisbet, T.R. (2004) The effects of riparian forest management on the freshwater environment: a literature review of best management practice. *Hydrology and Earth System Sciences*, **8**, 286-305.

(35) Helliwell, R.C., Aherne, J., Nisbet, T.R., MacDougall, G., Broadmeadow, S., Sample, J., Jackson-Blake, L. & Doughty, R. (2014) Modelling the long-term response of stream water chemistry to forestry in Galloway, Southwest Scotland. *Ecological Indicators*, **37**, 396-411.

(36)   Dunford, R.W., Donoghue, D.N.M. & Burt, T.P. (2012) Forest land cover contin-ues to exacerbate freshwater acidification despite decline in sulphate emissions. *Environmental Pollution,* **167**, 58-69.

(37)   Curtis, C.J., Battarbee, R.W., Monteith, D. & Shilland, E. (2014) The future of upland water ecosystems of the UK in the 21st Century: a synthesis. *Ecological Indicators,* **37**, 412-430.

23. The Flow Country: battles fought, war won, organisation lost

David Stroud, Tim Reed, Mike Pienkowski, and Richard Lindsay

"I had never seen such a desolate landscape. It far eclipsed Galloway and other Highland areas I visited. The sheer size of these great flat bogs (flows) was so daunting. From Morven northwards almost to the sea, 25 miles distant, lay a continuous sweep of low, gently undulating moor covered with bog. It was bisected by the Thurso and Wick railway, but this did little to detract from its appearance of wilderness. Away out in the middle of these flows, miles from the nearest road, there was a great feeling of solitude. … there was a distinct similarity to the loneliness of the Arctic tundra and its birdlife. I did not foresee then that one of nature conservation's more desperate battles would be fought over these greatest of our boglands in the 1980s."

Derek Ratcliffe writing about his first visit to the Flow Country of Caithness and Sutherland in May 1958 (p. 205 *In Search of Nature*)[1]

Introduction

Whilst much of Britain's post-glacial landscape eventually became wooded to a natural tree-line[2], the pattern of vegetation development in the uplands and the far north was more varied. By Neolithic times, extensive tracts of open treeless peatland had begun to form, for example across parts of the Southern Pennines[3]. Subsequent millennia saw the progressive development of further open moorland landscapes in the uplands through direct forest clearances and latterly the consequences of intensive sheep grazing[2]. In the cool, oceanic post-glacial climate of northern and western Scotland, peatland development blanketed uplands and lowlands alike[2]. These areas had always been

Figure 23.1. Winter view looking west across the Flow Country towards Ben Griam Mor, Ben Griam Beg, and Ben Loyal from Knockfin Heights, Caithness. The extensive areas of bog pools of different sizes are characteristic of the Flow Country of Caithness and Sutherland, 1986. Photo: Steve Moore

largely treeless[2,4], and as a result, specialised assemblages of animals and plants had developed in association with these open blanket-mire landscapes[5] as well as the unique cultural landscapes of managed Heather (*Calluna vulgaris*) moorland[6]. The term 'upland' in this context thus also embraces the ecologically related moorlands and peatlands formed at lower elevations in the far north and west of Britain (including the Flow Country of Caithness and Sutherland).

These upland landscapes (Fig. 23.1), their historical development, and their internationally important fauna and flora, were captivatingly described by Derek Ratcliffe in his 1990 book *Bird Life of Mountain and Upland*[7], an account which synthesised a life-time of experience. There is, however, a sad irony in the fact that by the time this volume was published, such areas had already undergone one of the most extensive of land-use changes and ecological transformations experienced by 20th century Britain. In the north of Scotland it had led to, in Derek's words "the most massive single loss of important wildlife habitat in Britain since the Second World War"[8].

These dramatic changes were caused by widespread and large-scale afforestation of monoculture plantations mainly consisting of non-native conifer trees (Figs. 21.1 & 22.1), stimulated by a combination of government policy and financial incentives. The state's promotion of upland afforestation was driven by differing motivations during the course of the 20th century. Initially, following the alarms of the First World War and the effects of the German submarine blockade, there was perceived to be a national strategic need for pit-props. In later years, and particularly after the Second World War, this strategic requirement was increasingly replaced by a range of economic drivers and incentives[9].

Until the Second World War the Forestry Commission (FC) had avoided planting on deep peat, even experimentally, but the development of efficient tractor units during the war and the invention of the Cuthbertson plough just after the war led the FC to begin a series of planting trials on deep peat in northern Scotland using new tree species, most notably Lodgepole Pine (*Pinus contorta*) from North America[10]. By the 1970s, this combination of tractor unit, double-mouldboard plough, and Lodgepole Pine was being used widely on deep peat, but as late as 1978 the Nature Conservancy Council (NCC) was being assured by FC District Officers that planting was only likely "on the margins of deep peat areas".

Although having been reassured at a Hill Land Use Discussion Group held in Caithness in 1978 that widespread afforestation of the Flow Country would be techni-cally impossible for the foreseeable future, the NCC's Chief Scientist Team (CST) nonetheless began an extensive programme of scientific survey in the area starting the following year, beginning in Caithness as part of NCC NW Scotland Region's develop-ment of a conservation strategy for Caithness. The resulting identification of several peatland sites meriting notification as Sites of Special Scientific Interest (SSSI) in Caith-ness subsequently led to a reluctance at various levels of decision-making in NCC Scot-land to consider further peatland notifications in the adjacent district of Sutherland – or indeed anywhere else in Scotland. The CST survey teams thus focused on gathering further information about the largely-unexplored interior of Caithness and Sutherland, particularly about the peatlands and the birdlife, without any strong expectation of further sites being added to the rather meagre list of peatland or ornithological SSSIs and National Nature Reserves (NNRs) which existed at the time in the two districts. Meanwhile the Royal Society for the Protection of Birds (RSPB) was undertaking paral-lel bird surveys in central and west Sutherland.

In the early 1980s, however, the rate and extent of new afforestation across the uplands of Britain increased markedly, stimulated by ever-improving technologies for the deep ploughing of peat, together with new silvicultural techniques involving use of mixed plantings where a fast-establishing nurse species such as Lodgepole Pine facili-tated establishment of more commercially attractive species such as Sitka Spruce (*Picea sitchensis*) (Fig. 23.2). This technically-driven expansion was artificially accelerated by a

Figure 23.2. Forestry deep ploughing of wet blanket-bog in Caithness, looking north towards Lochan Croc nan Lair, 1987. Photo: Steve Moore

grant- and tax-regime which meant that such afforestation offered investors substantial tax advantages and large sums at an extremely good and largely tax-free rate of return, whether or not useable trees were subsequently produced. Through his love of, and extensive time spent in, the uplands of Britain[1], Derek had direct experience of the ecological consequences resulting from this post-war wave of extensive afforestation, documenting in particular the consequences for Ravens (*Corvax corax*) (Fig. 13.4)[11], Golden Eagles (*Aquila chrysaetos*) (Fig. 12.4)[12] and upland flora[13].

In 1980, Derek had drafted and presented the NCC's evidence[14] to the, then newly established, House of Lords Select Committee on Science & Technology. This addressed not only loss of peatlands and uplands to new afforestation, but also nature conservation concerns arising from the conversion and loss of lowland woodlands[15]. The Committee subsequently "expressed concern" about the risks inherent in monocultural plantations. It recommended that forests should be diversified as soon as possible both in age and composition and that special plots should be maintained to monitor changes in soil fertility and the influence of afforestation on wildlife and other environmental features[16]. These conclusions rather missed the key point. There was a clear argument that much new forestry was ecologically damaging to important environments and fundamentally inappropriate in some of the landscapes where it was now occurring.

The Government's response in 1982 concentrated nearly exclusively on issues of lowland forestry, although "endors[ing] the recommendation that close attention should be paid to advance forest planning to harmonise the location and design of new forests with other interests"[17].

By the mid 1980s the sheer extent of the impacts resulting from new forestry was, however, becoming one of the most pressing nature conservation issues in Britain. Derek had long been working on a major document summarising the current extent and trends in new afforestation, reviewing the range of forestry practices, their implications for nature conservation, and documenting the scale of environmental losses being reporting by the NCC's specialists and others[18].

Pro-afforestation interests on the NCC's Council in the late 1970s and early 1980s meant that early attempts by Derek to get this policy document adopted ran into the sand. For its adoption as organisational policy there would need to have been an unacceptable dilution of the proposed stance. Rather than accept such changes, Derek withdrew the report at that time.

The report was eventually published by the NCC in June 1986[9] under the Chairmanship of William Wilkinson (who was subsequently knighted in 1989) (Figs. 19.6 & 11.8). In his Introduction to *Nature Conservation and Afforestation in Britain*[9] (Fig. 20.4), William Wilkinson noted that the NCC's views on the relationship between nature conservation and forestry

> "…were expressed briefly in 1980 in evidence to the Sherfield Committee on *Scientific aspects of forestry* (House of Lords 1980). The Committee's Report has led to an improvement in conservation prospects for existing broadleaved woodlands…
>
> Over new afforestation, however, we continue to be very concerned. Several recent cases of conflict between forestry and nature conservation interests on important wildlife areas and the portents for continuing losses to wildlife and physical features have convinced NCC that it now has to make its views widely known, so that nature conservation needs in relation to afforestation are understood and recognised. Much has been said in the last ten years or so about the case for further afforestation, but there is no adequate statement about the relationship between afforestation and nature conservation. This paper aims to provide such a statement." (pp. 4-5)

The words "that it now has to make its views widely known" are key, but also in some senses ground-breaking and brave. The NCC was a government agency. It had the statutory right to disagree publicly with Government. However, Government was its funding source and the members of its governing council were appointed by Government – so it did not lightly exercise that right. In a move which particularly angered the Ministry of Agriculture, the NCC had previously questioned Ministry of Agriculture economics in the case of, firstly, Amberley Wildbrooks (Fig. 20.2)[18] and then of Gedney Drove End[19]. The NCC Chairman at the time, Sir Ralph Verney, had subsequently experienced an abrupt termination of his appointment after Gedney Drove End. Nevertheless, some would say that afforestation, in particular the Flow Country issue, was the first occasion that the NCC openly and publicly questioned UK Government policy – and within two years the government had announced the abolition of the NCC[19,20]. In common with normal practice amongst Government bodies (and those lobbying them), discussions about afforestation and the Flow Country had been held without publicity for several years – at both local and national levels. It was because these discussions got nowhere that the NCC, reluctantly, decided to go public. This decision, and in particular the launch of *Birds, Bogs and Forestry*[8], were not a surprise to other parties (as those parties implied at the time); rather, it was the logical—indeed the only—next step when all avenues of discussion within the Government system had failed.

In passing, it is worth noting that nowhere in *Nature Conservation and Afforestation in Britain*[9] (Fig. 20.4) is there any record of Derek's leading role as its editor and main author[see also 21]. The document is simply credited to the organisation as a whole in perhaps a classic case of the observation by Harry S Truman (amongst others) that "It is amazing what you can accomplish if you do not care who gets the credit."

The Flow Country Controversy

Introduction

There was a growing number of major conflicts over new afforestation in upland Britain in the 1980s[15,18,22,23], notably massive and highly damaging new afforestation across sites such as the Berwyns[19,24] in mid Wales, Creag Meagaidh[19] in the central Highlands, and on Islay[19], which were attracting considerable concern and attention[25,26], while many other sites, such as Mindork Moss in Dumfries and Galloway, were silently overwhelmed by this wave of expansion. However, issues were rapidly coming to a head in northern Scotland, seen by forestry interests as 'the final frontier'[27]. Steadily moving closer and closer to centre stage in this story was the destruction of extensive blanket bogs of Caithness and Sutherland – the largest example of a primeval ecosystem in Britain (Figs. 23.1, 24.3 & 24.4). Concern was not limited to conservationists. Elected Councillors from the by now heavily-forested Dumfries & Galloway Region (where trees on many sites were now reaching a mature stage – Figs. 21.1 & 22.1) tried to warn their fellow Councillors in Highland Region of the socio-economic problems of blanket afforestation, but were rebuffed, reporting back sadly that the Highland Councillors seemed intent on not learning from the experience and mistakes of others.

Whilst peatland losses in Caithness and Sutherland had been one of the examples highlighted in *Nature Conservation and Afforestation in Britain*[9], the rapidity of losses everywhere was giving an increasingly extreme sense of urgency. "Environment and amenity bodies were caught unawares by the speed in which aggressive forestry companies were buying up land"[19].

The key drivers for new afforestation were two types of support from the public purse. First, there were generous rates of grant aid to cover the direct costs of plantation establishment. These had been introduced by the first Margaret Thatcher administration through an amendment to the 1967 Forestry Act[28] with the intention of stimulating the private forestry sector. Second, there was the potential to offset remaining establishment costs against other tax liabilities. Such tax-offset potential had existed for several decades and had been established originally in the 1950s to aid capital works on country estates. However, it only started to be exploited on a large scale in a forestry context from the early 1980s. Lean & Rosie[29] described the process as follows:

"So when, for example, Sir Austin Bide, honorary president of Glaxo Holdings, brought 532 acres of land at Stennieswater in the Scottish Borders for £158,000 last March, he was making a very sound investment indeed. The cost of creating a forest on Sir Austin's plot is likely to be about £215,000. So on paper, he will pay a total £373,000 for the land and its development. But in return he will get a grant of £53,000 from the Forestry Commission and (assuming he pays the top rate of tax) £129,000 in tax relief – a total cost to the public purse of £182,000. So, one way or another, about half of his forestry investment will be at the cost of the public.

Generous though this seems, many investors do even better. […] Timothy Colman should recoup 70% of his costs in the Flow Country. And Lady Porter, that scourge of wasteful public spending, will do even better out of the public purse. Assuming again that she pays the top rate of tax, she should receive a cool £511,000 in tax relief and grants – just less than 70% of her investment – from a grateful nation for planting trees in this unique area.

If the people who planted the forests were to hold on to them until they were felled, the taxman would get them in the end, for under Schedule D they would have to pay tax on the profit from the timber. This they generally avoid. Instead they sell the plantations, usually after about 10 years, when the trees – now a dense, dark, prickly thicket – are worth up to £2,700 an acre. It is estimated that some end up with a return rate of up to 33.5% a year on their original investment – which means that the investment has almost doubled in value in two years. It is a remarkable way of turning otherwise taxable income into tax-free capital.

The only thing that is not tax-free is the cost of the land; but many investors take out special forestry loans to pay for the land, with interest only payments – and the interest, too, can be offset against tax."

This represented remarkably easy money for investors – particularly those paying the highest rates of tax. "The Thatcherite boom combined with a favourable tax regime to make forestry attractive to newly-rich investors, whilst generous public finance, a key force driving afforestation, was also available"[27]. In Caithness and Sutherland, extensive land holdings were acquired by a forestry company called Fountain Forestry which accumulated 40,000 ha between 1980 and 1986[30]. It then developed and marketed a package of investment services which involved selling-on this land for the creation of new plantations. With clever marketing, some investors probably genuinely believed that they were doing something of environmental benefit (as well as benefiting themselves financially in huge measure), rather than enabling something profoundly damaging to the environment in their name – as several high-profile celebrities were later to find to their cost.

In the summer of 1984 the extent of actual and planned peatland afforestation in Caithness and Sutherland (Figs. 23.3 & 23.4) was already causing an increasing degree of alarm at the NCC and RSPB local level. Meanwhile the CST survey teams were beginning to feel that as fast as they surveyed sites they were vanishing beneath the forestry plough. By the autumn of 1984, Roy Dennis, RSPB Highland Officer, "alarmed at the rate of commercial tree planting on peatlands in Sutherland and Caithness" had written to the NCC NW Regional Office proposing that four important bird sites be notified as SSSI immediately, emphasising the urgency with the comment that "[t]here is no time to spare"[31]. Notification was, however, a slow process even to obtain agreement that the organisational wheels should start turning, and in this case it was also hampered by the sense that further SSSI proposals would not be welcomed in certain quarters.

The full scale of the developing problem became clear, however, in early 1985 with the circulation of an internal but widely distributed report by NCC's Assistant Regional Officer for Sutherland, Stewart Angus (published in 1987[32]). This brought together previously scattered information on actual and proposed forestry plans, together with future projections. As a result of this report, together with continued pressure from the RSPB to act, a case was assembled by CST and regional staff for the notification of 11 new SSSI peatland sites in Sutherland which were considered to hold some of the best remaining peatland habitat and supported substantial breeding wader populations. Some of these sites were huge, barely on a scale seen before, but were ultimately approved by NCC's Scottish Advisory Committee.

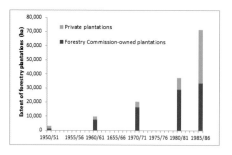

Figure 23.3. Increase in the extent and type of ownership of forest plantations in Caithness and Sutherland between 1950/51 and 1985/86. These were the best estimates presented at the launch of *Birds, Bogs and Forestry*[8] in July 1987.

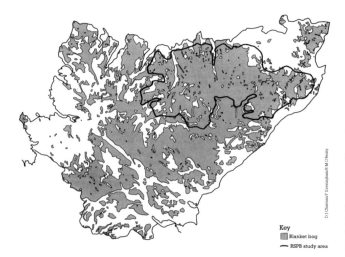

Figure 23.4. The indicative extent of relatively deep peat soils in the Flow Country of Caithness and Sutherland (from Lindsay et al. 1988[5]) covering an area of 401,375 ha. The extent of the more limited 'RSPB study area'[36] of 184,300 ha is largely in Caithness. For a detailed description of the peat-soil mapping process, see Lindsay et al. (1988)[5].

While an important step forward from the 'no more peatland sites' policy, the notification of these new sites could only be a stop-gap measure. As the NCC's Annual Report for 1985–1986[33] observed:

> "If notified, [the new sites] would bring about 23% of the total blanket bog [of Caithness and Sutherland] under statutory protection. However, the rate of afforestation is such that one of the proposed sites, Borralan, has already been almost completely destroyed by deep ploughing prior to planting and two others have been significantly damaged. This all occurred between the initial survey and the final selection of sites of SSSI status. … the scale of private afforestation in Sutherland and Caithness is beyond the scope of existing protective mechanisms…"

At this time, therefore—in early 1986—the NCC was faced with five substantive tasks:

- to document and establish the scientific case for the importance of the peatlands, the conservation interests present, and the extent of recent losses;

- to establish the global significance of the peatlands as a context for conservation advocacy;

- in the first instance, to obtain means of influencing the decisions concerning new afforestation proposals *before* they were approved, given that most of these were occurring outwith Sites of Special Scientific Interest (SSSIs) and thus beyond the NCC's primary statutory locus;

- then, to protect as much of the remaining undamaged peatlands as possible through either notification as SSSIs or by other means;

- and ultimately, to address the fundamental driver of new afforestation – a system of financial incentives (notably tax relief) which was massively stimulating new upland afforestation.

Others have reviewed various aspects of the Flow Country controversy and its aftermath[19,27,34,35]. We consider here how NCC, and particularly Derek Ratcliffe, addressed these five challenges. A chronology of the key events in this controversy is summarised in Table 23.1 in the Appendix.

Establishing the scientific case

Definitions and delineation

Initial concerns over forestry in northern Scotland had been directed towards a core area of the flattest blanket bogs in Caithness – typically so-called 'patterned mires' with extensive pool systems at the centre of peat masses (Figs. 23.1, 24.3 & 24.4). The advocacy of the RSPB (particularly in its publication *Forestry in the Flow Country: The Threat to Birds* in July 1985[36]) had until this point focused on this core area (Fig. 23.4) of some 184,300 ha[30]. The later RSPB publication *Forestry in the Flows of Caithness and*

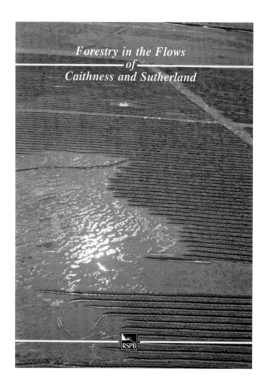

Figure 23.5. *Forestry in the Flows of Caithness and Sutherland*[30], presented not only the ornithological importance of the RSPB study area but also an analysis of the economics of afforestation in the Flow Country. The cover dramatically shows forestry ploughing right to the margins of an area of patterned bog.

Sutherland[30] (Fig. 23.5) widened its discussion to "prime blanket peatland", namely the Flow Country of Caithness and Sutherland.

It was very soon apparent that important peatlands were distributed far beyond this core area. In a memorandum[37] outlining the key elements of the NCC case, Derek argued instead for the defence of a far larger area of concern:

> "Attempting to delineate flow ground[1] as distinct from the moorland as a whole is a highly artificial procedure, and the Flow Country should be regarded as the whole of Sutherland and Caithness east of a line N – S through Strathnaver to Rogart station, excepting enclosed agricultural land. It is described in the Vegetation of Scotland[38] (ed. J. Burnett) p. 442 and the NCR[39], Vol I, p. 277 as a moorland complex covering c. 2,500 km², and we should maintain our view of this larger area as that under discussion."

That memo was for staff of his own Chief Scientist Directorate (CSD – as the CST had by then become), but a week later he issued a further "aide-memoire on where we stand"[37] to CSD colleagues. This stated that:

> "There is still a problem over definition of the area which we seek to defend against further afforestation. There is the feeling that the area defined by the RSPB and used by SHQ[2] in discussions with SDD [Scottish Development Department] is inadequate and there is no reason for NCC, with its wider remit, to feel bound by this."

---

1. i.e. dubh lochan complexes or patterned mires

2. NCC's Scottish Headquarters - at senior levels, more sympathetic of afforestation

Derek's clear view of the importance of the *whole* of the Caithness and Sutherland peatland landscapes was strongly supported by the NCC's Chair William Wilkinson (see below).

Terminology was important too. The initial public debate used the term 'the Flow Country' to refer to the more limited RSPB area, but to avoid presentational confusion, the NCC consistently referred to the issue as relating to 'the peatlands of Caithness and Sutherland' to make unambiguous their wider concerns. However, by the time of publication of the NCC's major review of the peatland's ecology in 1988[5], the term was being increasingly applied to the wider area, with the title *The Flow Country – The Peatlands of Caithness and Sutherland* being careful to reinforce this.

Ultimately, this wider definition of the area of nature conservation concern was of immense tactical significance, with forestry interests now becoming more willing to engage in dialogue concerning the more restricted area of Caithness and east Sutherland, once the NCC had broadened the geographical scope of the argument. In some delicate discussions, the CSD ornithology team explained the logic of working on a larger area to their RSPB colleagues, who then undertook to refer to their own smaller area as a sample where they had undertaken most studies ('RSPB study area'[30]), and to revert to the larger area as the full region under consideration.

Birds, Bogs and Forestry and *The Flow Country*

As discussed earlier, the NCC had organised Upland Bird Surveys in Caithness and Sutherland since 1979, whilst the RSPB had undertaken parallel surveys in Caithness between 1980 and 1986. Together they had surveyed 77 extensive sites – several in more than one year. Alongside these ornithological surveys and following pilot studies in 1978, a major programme of peatland survey had also been undertaken by the NCC in seven field seasons between 1980 and 1986. Further information and evaluations were available from separate NCC surveys of rivers and freshwater lochs.

The ornithological studies had been the first extensive surveys of upland birds in Britain. As well as collecting information on breeding densities, they had explored the implications of aspects of breeding biology for survey methodologies[40]. By 1985, however, a comprehensive report summarising all the surveys was urgently needed to document the surveys and to characterise these peatland bird communities in a UK context.

In parallel with the survey work, the need for the NCC to go public on the matter was becoming clear. This would need a decision by its Council. NCC's Chair (William Wilkinson) and senior management asked the four of us to prepare a presentation for the meeting of Council on 14 October 1986. By chance, this happened to be, in part, a joint meeting with the Countryside Commission for Scotland (CCS) at their headquarters at Battleby, near Perth. In addition, two events occurred prior to this meeting which were to have important consequences for the final outcome of the meeting. First, during the summer Peter Tilbrook, NCC NW Scotland Regional Officer, and Stephen Ward, from NCC Scotland HQ (SHQ), had organised a flight for the Chair over the Flow Country to see the scale of the issue for himself. One of us acted as 'tour guide' during the flight, but quite frankly needed to say very little because the scenery spoke for itself. William Wilkinson was visibly shocked by what passed beneath us, mile upon mile of serried plough lines broken only by stream-courses and small islands of unploughed patterned bogs and their pools (Figs. 23.6 & 23.7). Second, in September 1986 the International Mire Conservation Group (IMCG) held a 10-day field symposium in northern Scotland, specifically to visit the Flow Country peatlands and see the issue of afforestation for

Figure 23.6. Aerial view of forestry ditches dug into a large area of patterned bog within the Flow Country of Caithness and Sutherland. Note the extensive areas of forestry plantations in the background almost as far as the eye can see. 1987. Photo: Mike Pienkowski

Figure 23.7. Low aerial view showing an 'island' remnant of patterned bog in the Flow Country of Caithness and Sutherland within a sea of recently planted forestry. 1987. Photo: Mike Pienkowski

themselves. Today a well-established international force for peatland conservation, in 1986 IMCG was a fledgling international network consisting of leading peatland conservation specialists from Canada, USA, Ireland, Finland, Sweden, UK, Germany, and Austria, with one of us its first Chair. This was their second-ever field symposium. It was part-funded by the NCC on the initiative of Derek Ratcliffe and Derek Langslow, and it was accompanied by a BBC Radio 4 journalist. Radio 4 subsequently devoted an entire programme to the IMCG's travels through the Flow Country.

Two of us who attended the Council meeting and made a joint presentation were so concerned about the importance of this presentation at a venue which we had not previously used that we adopted an extreme belt-and-braces approach. The presentation was therefore carried north as a slide presentation (we were in pre-computer-projection days), backed up by a version on overhead projection sheets, and an ultimate backup (in case of total electrical failure) on huge sheets of paper! CCS joined the NCC Council for the presentation, before withdrawing to leave the Council to decide its position. As they left, they generously commented that the CCS had missed the importance of the area and wished the NCC well in defending it.

The NCC's subsequent debate was fairly heated for that forum, with senior SHQ officers essentially opposed to the proposals developed by the CSD in consultation with local officers, but Council members were generally supportive. During the debate, the Chair was able to speak with complete conviction because of what he had witnessed on his Flow Country flight, and we were able to back up questions about the true international significance of the area thanks to the unequivocal collective statement about the area made by the IMCG. Perhaps most importantly of all, Derek's quiet but firm interventions as Chief Scientist both validated his staff's conclusions and answered technical objections. These interventions included both the compatibility of conservation protection (but not of afforestation) with existing land-uses and an answer to the Director for Scotland's view that moving from the RSPB boundary to a more comprehensive framework (see above) would undermine the NCC's credibility. Derek pointed out that the change in circumstances more than justified this, as the FC had said previously that it had never been their intention to plant on the flows.

The Council agreed that:

a. The scientific evidence established the unique nature of the whole area and the impracticability of subdividing it.

b. The NCC's objective should be to prevent any loss or fragmentation of the interest and every effort must be made to secure the area.

c. The NCC was not committed to the RSPB boundary and Director Scotland should go back to the Technical Group [of the Scottish Office] and attempt to safeguard as much as possible.

d. In view of the need to make decisions at short notice, a small group from Council would convene to advise as appropriate.

Whilst the original survey and reporting timetabling had envisaged production of a technical ornithological report followed by a technical peatland ecosystem report, through mid-1986 and at the Council meeting it became clear that the NCC instead urgently needed a high-profile publication which would present the totality of the conservation argument against peatland afforestation in Caithness and Sutherland. Consequently the technical ornithological report metamorphosed, and Derek guided this metamorphosis into what was to become *Birds, Bogs and Forestry*[8] (Fig. 23.8), an account not just of the ornithological survey work but incorporating the other key elements of the NCC's case. *Birds, Bogs and Forestry*[8] was written by the four of us and edited by Derek and our NCC colleague Philip Oswald. Whilst leaving the drafting of the report to his staff, Derek repeatedly provided detailed editorial input as the report developed, in particular shaping its structure as well as contributing sections outlining effects of afforestation on bird communities and addressing the lack of compensatory gain with the establishment of different bird communities in the new plantations.

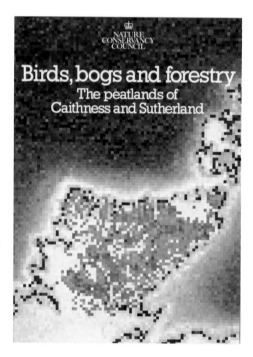

Figure 23.8. *Birds, bogs and forestry*[8] was the first publication by the Nature Conservancy Council about the Flow Country of Caithness and Sutherland and its ornithological and ecological importance, nationally and internationally. It was launched on 23 July 1987.

The report's production was also aided by clear direction from the very top. William Wilkinson, immediately after the October 1986 Council meeting, specified that "[t]his work has the highest priority of any other within NCC including renotification [of SSSIs required under new legislation] and individuals having the necessary skills need to be identified and put on notice even if not immediately required."

By November 1986, an initial draft of the overview report had been produced and was widely circulated for peer review to national peatland and ornithological experts, and for comment and input by other NCC staff. In early 1987, an advanced draft was supplied to the Chief Scientist of the Department of the Environment (DoE), whom Derek had kept informed of the process and who had been periodically briefing Ministers. Sir Martin Holdgate responded supportively, and with about a page of helpful suggestions on wording and structuring points.

The eventual launch of *Birds, Bogs and Forestry* (Fig. 23.8) by the NCC was thus the conclusion of a long process of consultation and technical review, both within and outside government, such that the issue was not a surprise to other interests, despite claims that the report had been "kept under wraps to date"[41]. The launch was a high profile event at the Institution of Civil Engineers in London on 23 July 1987. With a sensitive political awareness, the NCC's Chair, supported by the authors, Derek, Great Britain Headquarters staff involved, the Senior Press Officer, and many local staff involved, had originally been keen to launch the publication in Scotland and preferably in Caithness or Sutherland – close to the area of concern. That desire was strongly vetoed by John Francis, ex-Scottish Office and then NCC's Director for Scotland as well as by others in

NCC's Scottish Headquarters. The predictable outcome was that much of the media commentary focused on the English location of the launch venue and what that implied, rather than addressing the key message of the report. Many Scottish MPs were invited to the launch. Robert MacLennan (MP for Caithness and Sutherland and now Baron MacLennan of Rogart) was, however, apoplectic with rage at the perceived insult and did not attend (Alan Vittery, personal communication). MacLennan famously described the NCC scientific claims as "preposterous"[19]. He considered that the "forests were a godsend and the NCC seemed bent on 'sterilising' the land, just like the Highland Clearances of evil memory" [19]. Furthermore, several interests came to the launch with prepared statements that tended to attribute contents to the report which were not in fact included in it, although this did not necessarily prevent their comments from being reported.

The NCC Chair's presentation[42] was uncompromising:

> "… This is a very special place in the world. It is because it is still unique, despite the damage already suffered, the 'balanced' solution, normally so sensible, cannot in this case be right. There are occasions when "absolutes" must prevail. We all see the need to look after Westminster Abbey, St Peter's, Venice, the Taj Mahal, and revile those who blew up the Parthenon. We are right to give such consideration to these man-created masterpieces of civilisation. Do the masterpieces of God and nature deserve anything less?

> During recent years great concern has been expressed about loss of wildlife habitat in Britain and indeed world-wide, for example tropical rain forests. Many of these losses took place before nature conservation and certainly the legislation to support it was conceived. The destruction of the forests in mediaeval times and earlier, the almost total loss of the fens in the 17th and 18th centuries, the wartime and post-war inroads into the coastlands, lowland heaths, chalk grasslands, and old hay meadows mostly occurred in response to perceived national needs or because adequate knowledge existed. Here too nothing illegal has been done, but the area of the Caithness and Sutherland peatlands already lost to forestry represents perhaps the most massive loss of important wildlife habitat in Britain since the Second World War. As from today the situation is different; the picture and issues are clear; any further losses will be deliberate."

NCC's second major report *The Flow Country*[5] (Fig. 23.9) took longer to prepare[21], being based on detailed field surveys spanning several years of survey and covering the whole of the peatland area within Caithness and Sutherland. In all, 399 sites were surveyed in detail, many sites only accessible for survey by walking in from the nearest road and camping for two or three days (Figs. 24.5 & 24.6[21]). With the working title *Tundra Britain* – it was a technically much more complex (and larger) report than *Birds, Bogs and Forestry*[8] and included the first-ever assessment of the global extent of blanket bog, compiled painstakingly by correspondence with peatland experts worldwide in the days before instant communication by email was possible.

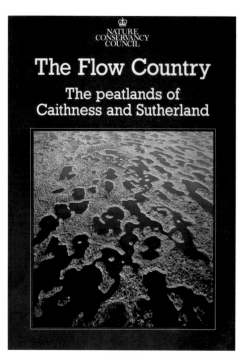

NATURE CONSERVANCY COUNCIL

The Flow Country

The peatlands of Caithness and Sutherland

Figure 23.9. *The Flow Country*[5] presented the first detailed vegetational and ecological accounts of the patterned bogs in the Flow Country, the international importance of these bogs, and an analysis of the global extent of blanket bog. It was launched in May 1988.

In parallel with the preparation of this new overview report, liaison continued at regional, Scottish, and UK levels with interested departments and agencies (see below). It is worth highlighting at this point that the NCC became a pivotal focus of information in these ongoing discussions because it had embraced the emerging technology of computer mapping or GIS (geographic information systems). It had quickly become evident early in the Flow Country case that the critical questions all hinged on the overlap of interests. The distribution of peat, the distribution of high-quality peatlands, the pattern of breeding wader distributions, the areas approved for forestry planting, and the distribution of high-quality agricultural land – all overlapped in a variety of ways. Our initial attempts to synthesise these various interests consisted of large acetate overlays, each representing a different feature of interest. More overlays were required to cater for the ever-expanding range of maps, until around 23 acetate sheets were lying one on top of the other, rendering interpretation of the overlapping interests virtually impossible. The need for information about the way in which these sectoral interests overlapped was obvious, and so it was decided that a novel approach was required.

As part of an evaluation process looking at the utility of computer mapping within the NCC coordinated by Chris Goodie, it was agreed that Doric Computer Systems would convert all the acetate maps into digital format and then use Arc/Info GIS to assist with overlay analysis (Fig. 23.10). Derek Ratcliffe and Derek Langslow both strongly supported this transition to new technology. They could see that the whole tenor of the debate was suffering increasingly from what could reasonably, under the circumstances, be termed 'the fog of war'. What was needed was clarity of information about the way in which the various land-use interests and natural features were distributed and overlapped across Caithness and Sutherland. Such clarity would help to cut through some of the wilder and more questionable claims being made by various interest groups and enable a more measured discussion to be had based on agreed facts.

From this point on, thanks to the willingness of other parties to provide maps for digital conversion, the NCC was able to provide detailed figures about existing conditions, map any combination of sectoral interests, and even model possible future scenarios in a way which no other participant in the debate was able to do. If a working group, or a Minister, required the definitive figures concerning some combination of overlapping interests, the NCC was able to produce the figures almost immediately, thereby helping to emphasise and enhance NCC's reputation as a source of factual

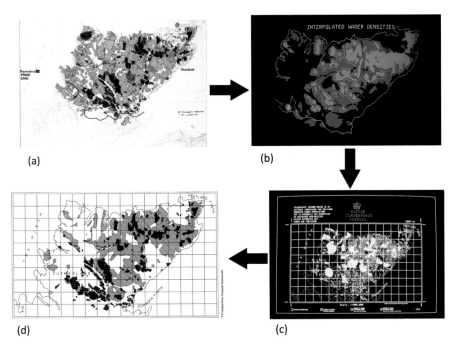

Figure 23.10. Composite image showing the progression of data handling for the Flow Country, beginning with original acetate maps (a), then digitising data (wader densities) (b), then GIS collation of data (more than 30 datasets displayed) (c), and final GIS analysis to show the extent of high-value conservation ground within the plantable zone of Caithness and Sutherland (d). Images: NCC & Doric Computer Systems Ltd

scientific information on which all parties could rely – precisely the sort of reputation which Derek Ratcliffe had sought to foster throughout his working life within the Nature Conservancy and the NCC.

Much of the information that was ultimately published in *The Flow Country* in 1988[5]—including information on international contexts—had been compiled in 1986 by the CSD's peatland survey and ornithological teams as part of NCC's overall case. The additional powers of analysis and display provided by the Arc/Info GIS tools meant that this information could now be distributed and queried much more readily. In various formats, therefore, the case was developed for presentation internally to the NCC's Council and subsequently in various external fora including the Scottish Office's Departmental Group on the Countryside, and ultimately the Highland Regional Council's Working Group.

Establishing the global significance

From the outset it had been clear that establishing the *global* significance of the Caithness and Sutherland peatlands would be a crucial element in advocating its protection with Government. William Wilkinson saw the critical importance of such international validation of the NCC's case and directed that "[t]he exact status of the international importance of the area needs to be established. This should be supervised and authenticated personally by Dr Ratcliffe"[43]. In response, Derek encouraged his teams to use their professional networks of international contacts to raise the profile of the issue.

The ornithological case was presented at international meetings[44], whilst support for the peatland context had come from the field symposium of the IMCG. The IMCG's assessment of the Flow Country as "unique and of global importance" and "one of the world's outstanding ecosystems" was vital. Indeed, the wide international expertise within IMCG was crucial in supporting the NCC's claim that the Caithness and Sutherland peatlands were "...possibly the largest single expanse of blanket bog in the world..."[5,45]. John Birks co-ordinated a letter by several peatland ecologists and palaeoecologists to *The Times* (14 March 1988) that drew attention to the Flow Country and its global importance.

Of great significance was a letter[46] from Jeffrey McNeely, then Director of the International Union for the Conservation of Nature (IUCN) Programme and Policy Division to Dick Steele, NCC's Director General and also an IUCN Regional Councillor.

> "Over the past months, the importance of the Flow Country of Caithness and Sutherland has been brought to the attention of IUCN by a number of organisations. I am therefore writing to express IUCN's support for the Nature Conservancy Council report on the region "Birds, Bogs and Forestry: the Peatlands of Caithness and Sutherland", especially the strong recommendations for comprehensive conservation action over a wide area.

> As you will note [...] IUCN fully supports the recommendations detailed in the draft report. Furthermore, given the immense significance of the site, both as a unique example of this peatland ecosystem, and as a breeding habitat for a bird community of international importance, I would urge you to consider nominating the Flow Country as the first British wetland listed under the World Heritage Convention.[3]"

Further validation came from DoE's Chief Scientist Sir Martin Holdgate, who in 1988 was to become the IUCN's Director General. As the case developed, Holdgate was called on to review the NCC's scientific case[4]. In doing so, he was able to contribute important information about the extent and floristics of patterned blanket mires in southern Chile and Argentina, particularly Tierra del Fuego – from his earlier times with the Falkland Islands Dependencies Survey.

And of course, Derek's extensive personal knowledge of European peatlands was also important in establishing contexts:

> "The only comparable European blanket bog systems are already extensively or wholly degraded by erosion (Stainmore, Pennines), afforestation (Irthing North Tyne moors, Cheviots; Wigtownshire Flows), or peat cutting (Bog of Erris, Co. Mayo)."[37]

---

3. This call was stressed further in a Resolution (17/63) of the 17th General Assembly of the IUCN in Costa Rica (January 1987).
4. Receiving a detailed briefing from the CSD team on 27 February 1987 and following this up with further questions to Derek Ratcliffe.

Influencing new afforestation proposals

At the time, there was no mechanism through which the NCC could influence proposals for new afforestation outside SSSIs. This amounted to 85–90% of the total area. The NCC's immediate concern was thus to obtain some means of influencing decisions regarding this area whilst the wider issue of the extent of statutorily protected peatland remained unresolved.

Between October 1981 and October 1985 the NCC had been consulted by the FC on just 9.4% (41 of 435) Forestry Grant Scheme applications, the approval process for new private forestry[47].

Through 1986, debate, and high-level communication between the NCC and the FC, concerned the urgent need for the NCC to influence the FC's decision-making process beyond SSSIs. The issue also extended to non-SSSI areas of importance in the public ownership of FC itself.

In a September 1986 press release[48], the RSPB's Director General Ian Prestt (Fig. 20.1):

> "condemned as meaningless the Forestry Commission's consultation procedures designed to protect the outstanding wildlife of the Scottish flow country.
>
> I am appalled to learn of large new areas of Forestry Commission land in Caithness and Sutherland fenced and ploughed for planting with conifers next to SSSIs. [...] The Forestry Commission knows of the great concern over wildlife in this unique area. We regard this new ploughing as a provocative act. They have had these landholdings for a number of years and knowing the concern of conservationists we would expect them to consult widely before sending in the ploughs. [...] This completely disregards the Forestry Commission's statutory obligations to balance the interests of forestry with those of nature conservation.
>
> We are requesting an urgent meeting with these ministers to discuss proper consultation mechanisms between the Forestry Commission and the NCC..."

(See Figs. 23.2 & 23.5-23.7 for examples of this "provocative act".)

In February 1987, following Chair-level communications between the NCC and the FC, full consultation on all new forestry grant applications was finally agreed. This, at long last, gave the NCC a formal locus to make representations concerning all new proposals.

Protecting peatlands: establishing SSSIs

In the 1980s, the only policy mechanism that would allow the NCC to constrain afforestation was for areas to be notified as SSSIs[5] – although even that mechanism had loopholes which could be, and often were, exploited[18]. International designations[49]

---

5. Although Section 29(1) of the 1981 Wildlife & Countryside Act (WCA) did, and does, allow the Secretary of State to make an order giving protection to "any land ... for the purpose of ... complying with an international obligation."

such as Special Protection Areas (SPAs) under the European Union (EU) Birds Directive, listing of Wetlands of International Importance under the Ramsar Convention, and indeed the World Heritage Site listing proposed by IUCN would all require areas to be notified first as SSSIs. Indeed, most of the few Ramsar sites and SPAs designated until the late 1980s had been restricted to state-owned National Nature Reserves or other well-protected areas.

Whilst the NCC had the statutory authority to notify SSSIs in its own right[6], as noted earlier, the issue for the NCC was simply that notification on the scale required to protect the peatlands would be unprecedented in scale. An enhanced programme of notification on the scale required would represent a major *de facto* constraint to future land-use change which had potentially substantial employment and socio-economic consequences.

Prior to taking detailed proposals to Ministers, William Wilkinson wanted clarity on the options. He summarised his view[43] of the NCC's strategy following the first major presentation to the NCC's Council on 14 October 1986:

"Objectives

1. To try and protect as much as is scientifically justifiable of this unique site preferably as one large block, or in as large blocks as possible, if as would seem, a patchwork of smallish SSSIs would be significantly less effective. The reasons for this are:

   i. The site would seem to justify it.

   ii. From an optical point of view one needs to be seen to have tried.

   iii. To gain more negotiating room.

The difficulties would seem to be in three areas.

   i. The legal framework appears inadequate.

   ii. Largely because of the tax regime, the land values are particularly inflated.

   iii. The sheer logistical problems of carrying out normal notification procedures on this scale.

As a first step therefore we need, through the appropriate channels, to present as good and as well costed a case as possible for special measures on the part of Government, to act upon as <u>Ministers</u> think fit.

Procedures to be undertaken

2. If, as I am told, normal SSSI procedures are totally impractical either for scientific, logistical or political reasons or a combination of factors, this needs to be established lucidly and in detail.

---

6. Under WCA Section 28

3. The boundaries of the whole site (or of a number of large sites) needs to be determined. In particular, outlying areas which are not fully up to standard and where loss would not affect other areas which were important, should be eliminated."

As NCC staff wrestled with possible site-protection mechanisms, senior-level inter-departmental discussions developed through the Scottish Office's Departmental Group on the Countryside. This brought together all the concerned land-use agencies, including the NCC, the FC, the Countryside Commission for Scotland (CCS), the Crofting Commission (CC), the Highland and Islands Development Board (HIDB), and the Scottish Office's own Department for Agriculture and Fisheries for Scotland (DAFS).

Different aspects of the issue impacted on each of these bodies. For example, 'tax relief forestry' was so financially profitable to individuals that there were now also schemes being proposed for agricultural land. Any policy changes with regard to the peatlands might also have consequences for small, local woodland schemes being promoted to crofters, whilst the FC and HIDB were keen to encourage the development of the forest industry as part of regional economic regeneration.

A full meeting of the Departmental Group took place on 18 December 1986 with Derek presenting the NCC's scientific case. In the subsequent discussion, the CCS suggested it might be appropriate for the FC to seek a directive for the Secretary of State for Scotland to withhold planting grants in Caithness and Sutherland, initially for a limited period but subject to review. This prompted a good deal of discussion on the statutory locus of FC and Ministers.

The NCC's Director for Scotland, John Francis, then outlined the statutory obligations under which the NCC worked and that to proceed with formal notification of individual SSSIs would be an extremely protracted process with major resource implications. The HIDB expressed disquiet at such a potential landscape-scale designation, especially the implications for the local economy in a resource-poor region. Similarly, DAFS indicated they would not support a complete ban, as they were anxious to promote farm forestry in the area.

One of the issues raised at the meeting was NCC's requirements under Section 37 (S.37) of the Countryside Act of 1968[50], which states that "In the exercise of their functions … [the NCC is] to have due regard to the needs of agriculture and forestry and to the economic and social interests of rural areas." Whilst the clause was used at that meeting in an obvious and rather clumsy attempt to undermine the NCC's position, Derek had previously focused on this obligation as an important part of the NCC's case. In an internal minute to his staff[37] he had stressed that:

"There is no loss to the nation or even to the local socio-economic scene if no more trees are planted. Forestry is uneconomic here and would never be considered were it not for the high rate of subsidy and profit margins guaranteed by the tax arrangement for private forestry. The only loss is to one private company which is exploiting unsatisfactory rules. The level of public subsidy could be more effectively used to support employment in other ways.

(We say this to comply with our duty under S.37 of the 1968 Act.)"

A few days later, he had developed the argument further[51]:

> "There is no doubt that there is a strong economic case to be made against further afforestation in the Flow Country. My view is that we should make this case as showing compliance with our duty under 'S.37', but we need to do it very circumspectly. Our approach should be to demonstrate that we have thought about the economic and social implications of "no more trees" in the two districts and to show, as far as possible, that to transfer support from forestry to existing land uses (grazing, sport, fishing) would be more beneficial to the local population. As part of this argument it would be proper to show that the case for public support of forestry has been questioned by others (Ramblers[26] etc.) and that our own studies show these doubts to be justified."

The 18 December 1986 Departmental Group meeting concluded with acknowledgement that the NCC's Chair "had instructed [NCC's] Director General to conduct negotiations at departmental level and that to a very large extent these considerations would pre-empt discussion in this Group in the short-term."

Many subsequent meetings of this kind were attended by the CSD specialists, working with colleagues from NCC's Scottish Headquarters. It must be remembered that, at this time, the NCC was a Great Britain body and that this was long before parliamentary and government devolution to Scotland. Nevertheless, some Scottish HQ staff clearly felt greater affinity with the Scottish Office than with their employer. Given that the NCC Scottish Director was acting under instructions from the NCC Council against his own preference, there were inevitable tensions. Whilst Derek was not a natural in respect of organisational procedures, he knew how to deploy such procedures effectively, especially to shield his staff from unreasoned attacks – actions which Derek himself rarely commented on but which were well known and much appreciated by his staff[21].

The functional end of the controversy came in January 1988 with a decision from Malcolm Rifkind, then the Secretary of State for Scotland (and now Sir Malcolm Rifkind, Member of Parliament for Kensington), to protect half the extent of the Caithness and Sutherland peatlands[52]:

> "We seek to achieve two legitimate objectives: to meet the ecological criteria, which we have done on a scientific basis, and at the same time, take account of the livelihood of those who live in that part of Scotland and who have a legitimate interest with regard to their livelihood and the work opportunities that are available to them."

Described as 'a judgement of Solomon' there was disappointment as to future implications. A *Daily Telegraph* editorial article[53] well captured typical feelings within the conservation community:

> ### "Half a cheer for Rifkind
>
> Mr Malcolm Rifkind, the Scottish Secretary deserves half a cheer for his decision to create a 430,000-acre site of special scientific interest in the

unique and barren Flow Country of Caithness and Sutherland. Mr William Wilkinson, the Nature Conservancy Council's chairman dubbed it a step in the right direction. But it still yields too much to those with indefensible vested interests, and allows the further spread of conifer planting which is destroying primæval peat bog with its wading birds, diminishing one of Britain's scarce and thus precious empty landscapes, and possibly putting salmon and trout fisheries at risk – all to provide tax breaks for absentee millionaires.

…

The Scottish Secretary has been half persuaded that tree-planting is a praiseworthy form of private enterprise which creates jobs in a thinly populated area. The argument is dubious at best and has fallen foul of the National Audit Office; […] An area with immense recreational potential and natural beauty is still at risk of being despoiled at the taxpayer's expense."

Tackling tax-break forestry

The NCC had a particular challenge in addressing the grant and taxation anomalies which drove the destructive and largely unproductive afforestation. This was because, at the time, it was not really expected for a government agency with duties in conservation to make economic arguments, despite statutory responsibilities to have regard to such matters, and the reaction to NCC's actions in the Gedney Drove End case[19], as discussed earlier, had been both swift and brutal.

Derek was keen to make sure that the NCC's analyses in this area were sound, and recruited, as an afforestation specialist, a former Forestry Commission officer (Rob Soutar) who was already unhappy about the FC's grant policies. He worked closely with the NCC's economist, Mark Felton. Similarly, the RSPB had analysts available and made reference to this material in their publications[30]. The NCC certainly did not shrink from deploying the financial argument in its discussions within Government. Several environmental journalists were becoming interested and concerned at the issue, and raised the profile[e.g. 29]. One of us found himself (with Derek's tacit approval) in an unusually hard-hitting interview for the normally gentle and poetic BBC Radio 4 programme 'The Countryside in Winter' which was broadcast on Christmas Day 1987, finding himself 'trapped' by the interviewer into admitting that this destruction of a national treasure was essentially for the financial benefit for rich people.

Throughout, the RSPB maintained a very high public profile for the issue. Drawing lessons from Des Wilson's highly effective campaigning tactics with respect to removing lead from petrol and other issues[54], Ian Bainbridge and David Minns very effectively ensured a weekly drip-feed of media stories typically including the tag of 'out-of-control forestry' thereby constantly reinforcing the view that forestry in northern Scotland had little strategic direction. Additionally, they worked with sympathetic MPs to produce regular Parliamentary Questions unpicking taxation arrangements and related issues. Following embarrassment caused by inconsistent and sometimes contradictory responses, the Forestry Commission eventually dedicated a single staff member to co-ordinate all draft replies to Flow Country/forestry Parliamentary Questions. Indeed so great was the media frenzy which had by now developed that it was even felt across the Atlantic. *Animal Kingdom*, the magazine produced by the Bronx Zoo and widely-read throughout the USA, devoted almost an entire issue to the Flow Country conflict[55].

The major solution to the underlying problem came from an unexpected quarter. In December 1986, two months after the NCC Council's decision to fight for the Flow Country, the National Audit Office (NAO) reported on the Forestry Commission. The NAO noted a difficulty in assessing the Forestry Commission's performance due to its unusual accounting systems, the very low real rates of return from its investment, and "as regards the private forestry sector, where new investment is stimulated by grants and tax incentives, NAO have some doubts about the national economic benefits derived from the support being made available"[56]. These were damning words, bearing in mind the extremely moderate language normal then in such reports.

The end for tax-break forestry came abruptly on 15 March 1988 in the spring Budget, when the Chancellor, Nigel Lawson (now Baron Lawson of Blaby), announced to a packed House of Commons:

> "I accept that the tax system should recognise the special characteristics of forestry, where there can be anything up to 100 years between the costs of planting and the income from selling the felled timber. But the present system cannot be justified. It enables top rate taxpayers in particular to shelter other income from tax, by setting it against expenditure on forestry, while the proceeds from any eventual sale are almost tax free.
>
> The time has come to bring it to an end. … It is, perhaps, a measure of the absurdity of the present system that the total exemption of commercial woodlands from tax will, in time, actually increase tax revenues by over £10 million a year.
>
> […] The net effect of these changes will be to end an unacceptable form of tax shelter; to simplify the tax system, abolishing the archaic schedule B in its entirety; and to enable the Government to secure its forestry objectives with proper regard for the environment, including a better balance between broad-leaved trees and conifers."[57]

What happened next …

More strategic approaches to planning new afforestation

In August 1987, the Highland Regional Council (HRC) established a Working Party to develop a land-use strategy for Caithness and Sutherland, with inputs from all the relevant government agencies. The Working Party met six times between then and January 1989 when the Strategy was finally and formally adopted.

It was a major task for the NCC to ensure that the final Strategy dealt accurately with the issues at stake. The story of this Strategy is for elsewhere, but a detailed commentary by Derek[58] on the final draft gives a flavour of the issues the NCC faced (and also, in point 2, his clear view on the critical importance of context (see above) and scale):

> "1. The report contains evidence of bias against nature conservation amounting to prejudice. The forestry case and arguments are taken almost entirely at face value and subject to little scrutiny, whereas the nature conservation case and arguments are dissected and questioned in fine detail, in a consistently destructive way. [...]
>
> These are not acceptable tactics. HRC are entitled to say for socio-economic reasons they are not disposed to accept all that NCC wants, but they should not subject our case to a biased attack.
>
> 2. HRC are bound to approach the whole issue in a parochial manner which fails to take account of the GB or even the Scottish interest as a whole. On this basis, of course they find (6.34) that the social and economic effects of forestry are beneficial. This contrasts with the NAO report of 1986[56], which found that forestry in the far north of Scotland caused a loss to the national economy, and produced a handful of jobs at high public cost. From their detached stance they were able to say that the best means of subsidising employment in this region was not necessarily through investment on the <u>land</u> in any way. HRC are naturally going to applaud any nationally uneconomic activity which puts millions of pounds into Caithness & Sutherland with no further questions asked.
>
> 3. The repeated criticism that NCC has not met its duty under S.37 (e.g. [para] 6.31). No guidance has ever been given on how NCC should interpret this duty (nor how other departments should interpret their reciprocal duty). It is certainly not required that NCC should make statements about this duty every time it produces a technical report on a conservation issue. NCC has taken note of the NAO report as an authoritative statement of the socio-economic value of forestry in the region, which seems to leave little further to be said. But in the interest of local employment NCC also put in its own paper (Felton & Soutar) on afforestation in the region. Chairman NCC also wrote to the Secretary of State for Scotland on 15 June 1987, informing him of NCC's views in its S.37 duty in regard to the Flow Country issues."

In the month before the Strategy was finally agreed by the Regional Council, much work centred on ensuring that the NCC could join the consensus rather than submit a minority report. The NCC Chair's public reaction was "Some gains for nature conservation but less than we wished for."[59]

In the years that followed, and stimulated by the controversies of the mid-1980s, new afforestation in Scotland progressively came under more strategic direction. Initially this was through the production of Indicative Forestry Strategies for each of the Scottish Regions[60]. These, without prejudging other planning processes, broadly indicated areas of high environmental interest where there would likely be conflicts if new afforestation were to occur. The intention was to direct new afforestation into less sensitive areas – exactly the sort of approach which had been so lacking in the Flow Country.

Policies within the Forestry Commission have also since changed markedly[15,23]. Recent guidance[61] presents policies that have moved markedly on from the 1980s:

> "The Forestry Commission has concluded that for conservation and wider environmental reasons there should be a strong presumption against further forestry expansion on the following peatland types:
>
> - Active raised bog and degraded raised bog capable of restoration to active status.
>
> - Extensive areas (exceeding 25 ha) of active blanket bog averaging 1 m or more in depth or any associated peatland where afforestation could alter the hydrology of such areas.
>
> In future, the Forestry Commission will not approve grant applications containing proposals for new planting or new natural regeneration in these situations."

In addition, there is now a strategy in place for the re-establishment of open habitat on areas deemed to be worthy of restoration management, with the result that a number of afforested peat bog areas are now having their plantations removed and restoration management is being put in place to re-establish open bog habitat[62]. The one key un-resolved area concerns the question of whether to re-stock 2nd or even 3rd rotation plantations on peat, or whether to restore these areas to bog habitat rather than to re-stock.

Dismemberment of the NCC

On 11 July 1989, the Secretaries of State for the Environment (Nicholas Ridley) and Scotland (Malcolm Rifkind) "without any consultation, and without attempting any proper costings or drafting of proposed legislation, announced the dismemberment of NCC (Fig. 23.11) into three independent country agencies."[20,63]

NCC's principled and robust stance in defence of the Flow Country has been widely acknowledged as "the trigger for the Council's dismemberment"[19,20,34,64]. The ultimate consequence of that organisational change is for others to document, but with respect to forestry, Sir William Wilkinson noted in his introduction to NCC's final annual report[63] that:

Figure 23.11. Removing the Nature Conservancy Council sign from Northminster House, Peterborough, and replacing it with the name of the new country agency, English Nature, 1989. Photo: Richard Lindsay

"Afforestation too remains a problem in the uplands, though little by little a more sympathetic approach is detectable. The Scottish Office's policy of urging the Regions to draw up indicative forestry strategies is greatly to be commended and should be extended to England and Wales."

One of us reflected with Sir William shortly before his death in April 1996 as to whether the NCC had been right to take on the battle, even though we always knew that there would be a risk to the organisation. We concluded: how could UK exhort South American countries to save the Amazon, if UK could not conserve the Flow Country – and what was the point of a conservation organisation that did not fight for such a uniquely important area?

Designations

In Caithness and Sutherland, following the Secretary of State's 1988 announcement, the focus of NCC work moved to the identification, boundary delineation, and notification of SSSIs. In summer 1988, the NCC established a Caithness and Sutherland Peatland Conservation Project, with a dedicated project team working largely out of NCC's Golspie Office. The Team's final report[65] recorded:

"Now that the complete suite of SSSIs to arise from the project has been notified or approved for notification, […] the total area of 'new' peatland SSSIs will be 120,652 ha. Together with an estimated 40,000 ha of peatland lying in pre-1989 SSSIs, the total area of peatland in Caithness and Sutherland to be notified is some 92% of that which in 1988 the Secretary of State for Scotland recognised might be thus safeguarded." (see Figure 23.12).

The task for the Project Team had been immense, involving 24 people. Although in 1988 the work was projected to take 62.5 staff years over five years, by the end it had utilised 50.75 staff years, over seven years[65] – not including large continuing inputs from CSD and other GBHQ staff. As well as the central notification programme, the team had started important public awareness and education activities, completed further vegetation surveys, and launched a Peatland Management Scheme in 1991 to maintain condition of notified areas.

Following completion of the SSSI notification programme, the way was then clear for formal international designations. In February 1999, the combined SSSI extent was classified as a Special Protection Area (SPA) under the EC Birds Directive (of 145,516.75 ha) and as a Ramsar Site of 143,502.79 ha. Designation as a 143,538.7 ha Special Area of Conservation under the Habitats Directive followed in March 2005. However, 28 years after IUCN first called for its listing as a World Heritage Site, the Flow Country still remains on the 'tentative list' of such potential UK sites (Fig. 23.13).

For a while, the Flow Country peatlands held the distinction of being the UK's largest statutorily protected site. It has ceded that honour following designation of the more extensive North Pennine Moors and Cairngorms Massif SPAs, and a marine SPA over twice the size in the Outer Thames Estuary.

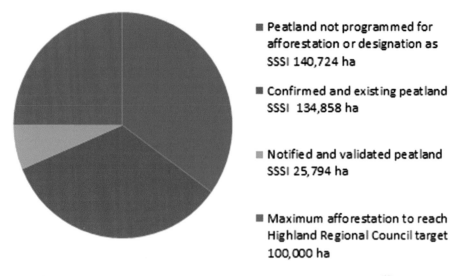

- Peatland not programmed for afforestation or designation as SSSI 140,724 ha

- Confirmed and existing peatland SSSI 134,858 ha

- Notified and validated peatland SSSI 25,794 ha

- Maximum afforestation to reach Highland Regional Council target 100,000 ha

Figure 23.12. The Caithness and Sutherland peatland resource as at 31 March 1996[65].

Peatland restoration: tackling the damage

Following the RSPB's acquisition in 1995 of their reserve at Forsinard, which included areas of plantations as well as undamaged peatland, pioneering work has been undertaken to restore the damage. This was made possible through two major EU-funded LIFE projects[66], one in 1994-98 and another in 2000-06. To date, 1,774 ha of conifer plantations have been felled, as well as 158 km of hill drains and 42 km of forest drains blocked with a total 11,128 dams to restore water-tables. Following the LIFE projects, acquisition of open land and plantation adjacent to the reserve has continued on a more local scale with a further 367 ha of plantation and 2,050 ha of open ground acquired for restoration. This is pioneering work, the monitoring of which will help further to refine the techniques used for their potential wider application.

Scientific understanding of afforestation impacts on peatlands

Since the 1980s there has been considerable research to better understand the multiple impacts of peatland afforestation summarised in *Birds, Bogs and Forestry*[8]. We cannot explore this here, other than to note that most recent research on many aspects vindicates the NCC's concerns in the 1980s.

In particular, the NCC's research showed significant 'edge effects' of new afforestation where bird nesting densities were depressed close to new plantations[67]. This results in impacts on bird populations over significantly larger areas than those immediately lost to forestry and was an element of the NCC's case – although there were problems in the early analysis and the concept was highly criticised in some quarters. Most recent research[68], following 25 years of plantation maturation in the Flow Country, has supported NCC's concerns and found "reduced occupancy [of Dunlin (*Calidris alpina*) and Golden Plover (*Pluvialis apricaria*) (Fig.11.10)] within several hundred metres from forest edges". These edge effects are now one of the many drivers for peatland restoration (above) in the area.

Meanwhile new evidence and understanding in the field of peatland hydrology have brought about something of a paradigm shift in the way that peat-bog systems are thought to function. Hugh Ingram's translation of the seminal Russian work *Water Movement in Mirelands*[69], together with his 'Ground Water Mound Theory'[70], brought the realisation that peat bogs function as single hydrological entities and thus allocating the margins to planting while leaving the pool systems for wildlife was not a viable conservation option. Forestry research also highlighted the degree to which the peat-bog surface dries, cracks, and subsides beneath a plantation forest, causing deep drying and major morphological changes to the bog system[71].

The future

One of the more significant outcomes from the EU LIFE-funded Peatlands Project (see above) was the development of a Management Strategy for the period 2005-2015[72]. This was developed with wide stakeholder and community input, and addresses issues such as the need for strategic development of the renewable energy industry – issues entirely new since the 1980s.

> "…the peatlands have suffered over the last decades from policy shifts, varied standards of stewardship, and uncertainties. This Strategy is the first time that a clear, shared vision for the future has been attempted. It is a vision for a future where land uses complement rather than compete with each other."[73]

Most recently, through the stimulus of the IUCN UK Peatland Programme, the Scottish Parliament has enthusiastically endorsed the principle of peatland restoration for the ecosystem services provided by such systems, and the Scottish Government has announced the allocation of £15 million to support the restoration of Scotland's peatlands[74].

Figure 23.13. Bog pools, Blar nam Faioleag NNR, Caithness, 1986. Photo: Richard Lindsay

Final comments

Lowe et al.[24] reviewed the earlier conflict between forestry and conservation interests in the Berwyn range of mid Wales. They noted how, in inter-agency discussions on land-use:

> "it is evident the Forestry Commission [FC], WOAD [Welsh Office Agriculture Department] and ADAS [Agricultural Development and Advisory Service] regarded the designation of an SSSI as essentially contestable. As Lofthouse[75] emphasised:
>
> "I have observed that when FC, WOAD/ADAS and NCC officers meet together the FC's view on what land is plantable is not questioned. WOAD/ADAS opinion as to what is or is not improvable agriculturally is accepted. Yet NCC views on what land should be notified as SSSI seems to be more critically examined by the other two." "

This was very much our impression in much of the intra-governmental debate regarding the future of the Flow Country. Derek's seminal publication *Nature Conservation in Great Britain*[76] had concluded:

> "Nature conservation has in the past sometimes conducted its business on too apologetic and timid a note. Such a tendency to submissive posture is a recipe for retaining a low peck-order position in the league of land and resource use interests. If nature conservation is to gain the acceptance it deserves as a relevant concern for the whole of society, its practioners all have to behave as if it really matters. Conservationists must argue their interests and their cases with a firmness and conviction which stem from a visible belief in and commitment to the things they talk about. ... And for all those who affirm the importance of nature conservation, the challenge will be to turn opportunity and intention into achievement. Posterity will judge all of us by deeds and not words."

That the NCC—under the leadership of Sir William Wilkinson (Fig. 19.6) and the scientific leadership of Derek Ratcliffe—was prepared to act with such conviction was a significant change to the *status quo* (which then expected nature conservation interests 'to be seen but not heard') and a challenge to establishment interests. Ultimately the case had positive outcomes for both forestry and conservation. "In terms of the scale of the area concerned and in respect of the longer term consequences, there have been few more significant conservation battles in the UK"[27]. It was a conflict that could not be avoided.

Acknowledgements

We acknowledge and thank the many other NCC staff instrumental in developing and supporting the case against afforestation of the Flow Country. These included Stewart Angus, Lesley Cranna, Mark Felton, Terry Keatinge, Derek Langslow, Ian Mitchell, Alan Mowle, Philip Oswald, Margaret Palmer, Mary Palmer, Alison Rush, Malcolm Rush,

Dick Seamons, Kristin Scott, Rob Soutar, Des Thompson, Peter Tilbrook, Martin Tither, Steven Ward, and Sir William Wilkinson – the NCC's inspirational Chair.

We also thank the very many others who contributed to the development of the NCC's case acknowledged by Stroud *et al.*[8] and Lindsay *et al.*[5]. Thanks also to Julia Newth for helping source publications and to Alan Vittery for information about the launch of *Birds, Bogs and Forestry*[8].

References

(1) Ratcliffe, D.A. (2000) *In Search of Nature*. Peregrine Books, Leeds.

(2) Birks, H.J.B. (1988) Long-term ecological change in the British uplands. In: *Ecological Change in the Uplands* (eds. M.B. Usher and D.B.A. Thompson), pp. 37-56. Blackwell Scientific Publications, Oxford.

(3) Tallis, J.H. (1964) The pre-peat vegetation of the southern Pennines. *New Phytologist*, **63**, 363-373.

(4) Peglar, S.M. (1979) A radiocarbon-dated pollen diagram from Loch of Winless, Caithness, north-east Scotland. *New Phytologist*, **82**, 245-263.
Charman, D.J. (1994) Late-glacial and Holocene vegetation history of the Flow Country, northern Scotland. *New Phytologist*, **127**, 155-168.

(5) Lindsay, R.A., Charman, D.J., Everingham, F., O'Reilly, R.M., Palmer, M.A., Rowell, T.A., Stroud, D.A. (eds. D.A. Ratcliffe & P.H. Oswald) (1988) *The Flow Country – The Peatlands of Caithness and Sutherland*. 174 pp. Nature Conservancy Council, Peterborough.

(6) Thompson, D.B.A., Hester, A.J. & Usher, M.B. (1995) *Heaths and Moorland: Cultural Landscapes*. Scottish Natural Heritage, Edinburgh.

(7) Ratcliffe, D.A. (1990) *Bird Life of Mountain and Upland*. Cambridge University Press, Cambridge.

(8) Stroud, D.A., Reed, T.M., Pienkowski, M.W. & Lindsay, R.A. (eds. D.A. Ratcliffe & P.H. Oswald) (1987) *Birds, Bogs and Forestry - The Peatlands of Caithness and Sutherland*. 121 pp. Nature Conservancy Council, Peterborough.

(9) Nature Conservancy Council (1986) *Nature Conservation and Afforestation in Britain*. 108 pp. Nature Conservancy Council, Peterborough.

(10) Wood, R.F. (1974) *Fifty Years of Forestry Research - A Review of Work Conducted and Supported by the Forestry Commission, 1920-1970*. 134 pp. HMSO, London.

(11) Marquiss, M., Newton, I. & Ratcliffe, D.A. (1978) The decline of the raven *Corvus corax* in relation to afforestation in southern Scotland and northern England. *Journal of Applied Ecology*, **15**, 129-144.

(12) Marquiss, M., Ratcliffe, D.A. & Roxburgh, R. (1985) The numbers, breeding success and diet of golden eagles in southern Scotland in relation to changes in land use. *Biological Conservation*, **34**, 121-140.

(13) Ratcliffe, D.A. (1986) The effects of afforestation on the wildlife of open habitats. In: *Trees and Wildlife in the Scottish Uplands* (ed. D. Jenkins), pp. 46-54. Institute of Terrestrial Ecology, Huntingdon.

(14) Ratcliffe, D.A. (1980) Forestry in relation to nature conservation. (Minutes of evidence, House of Lords Select Committee on Science & Technology, Sub-Committee I – Forestry.) Memorandum submitted by the Nature Conservancy Council. HMSO, London.

(15) Kirby, K.J. (2015) Battling forestry and building consensus: woodland conservation post-1949. In: *Nature's Conscience – The Life and Legacy of Derek Ratcliffe* (eds. D.B.A. Thompson, H.H. Birks & H.J.B. Birks). This volume, Chapter 21.

(16) Nature Conservancy Council (1981) *Seventh Annual Report 1 April 1980–31 March 1981*. Nature Conservancy Council, Shrewsbury.

(17) House of Lords Select Committee on Science and Technology (1982) *Scientific Aspects of Forestry. Government response to the Second Report of the Select Committee (Session 1979-90).* 7 pp. HMSO, London.

(18) Housden, S. (2015) Fighting for wildlife – from the inside. In: *Nature's Conscience – The Life and Legacy of Derek Ratcliffe* (eds. D.B.A. Thompson, H.H. Birks & H.J.B. Birks). This volume, Chapter 20.

(19) Marren, P. (2002) *Nature Conservation*. HarperCollins, London.

(20) Radcliffe (sic), D. (1989) The end of British nature conservation? *New Scientist*, **9 September**, 75-76.

(21) Lindsay, R.A. (2015) A letter to Derek Ratcliffe. In: *Nature's Conscience – The Life and Legacy of Derek Ratcliffe* (eds. D.B.A. Thompson, H.H. Birks & H.J.B. Birks). This volume, Chapter 24.

(22) Rollie, C. (2015) In Galloway and the Borders – in search of an enduring youth. In: *Nature's Conscience – The Life and Legacy of Derek Ratcliffe* (eds. D.B.A. Thompson, H.H. Birks & H.J.B. Birks). This volume, Chapter 13.

(23) Battarbee, R.W. (2015) Forestry, 'acid rain', and the acidification of lakes in Galloway, south-west Scotland. In: *Nature's Conscience – The Life and Legacy of Derek Ratcliffe* (eds. D.B.A. Thompson, H.H. Birks & H.J.B. Birks). This volume, Chapter 22.

(24) Lowe, P., Cox, G., MacEwen, M., O'Riordan, T. & Winter, M. (1986) *Countryside Conflicts. The Politics of Farming, Forestry and Conservation.* Gower, Aldershot.

(25) Grove, R. (1983) *Future for Forestry*. British Association of Nature Conservationists.

(26) Tompkins, S.C. (1986) *The Theft of the Hills: Afforestation in Scotland.* 32 pp. Ramblers Association, London.

(27) Warren, C. (2000) 'Birds, Bogs and Forestry' revisited: the significance of the Flow Country controversy. *Scottish Geographic Journal*, **116**, 315-337.

(28) http://hansard.millbanksystems.com/acts/forestry-act-1981 (accessed March 2014).

(29) Lean, G. & Rosie, G. (1988) Forests of money. *Observer Magazine*, **14 February**, 34-41.

(30) Bainbridge, I.P., Minns, D.W., Housden, S.D. & Lance, A.N. (1987) *Forestry in the Flows of Caithness and Sutherland.* 24 pp. Royal Society for the Protection of Birds, Conservation Topic Paper 18.

(31) Letter from Roy Dennis, RSPB Highland Officer, to Peter Tilbrook, Nature Conservancy Council NW Scotland Regional Officer, 20 September 1984.

(32) Angus, S. (1987) *The Peatland Habitat Resource of Sutherland and Caithness in Relation to Forestry*. Unpublished Nature Conservancy Council report.

(33) Nature Conservancy Council (1986) *Twelfth Annual Report 1 April 1985–31 March 1986*. Nature Conservancy Council, Shrewsbury.

(34) Mackay, D. (1995) *Scotland's Rural Land Use Agencies. The History and Effectiveness in Scotland of the Forestry Commission, Nature Conservancy Council, and Countryside Commission*. 227 pp. Scottish Cultural Press, Aberdeen.

(35) Sheail, J. (1998) *Nature Conservation in Britain. The Formative Years*. 282 pp. The Stationary Office, London.
Scott, M. (2008) The Flow Country revisited. *British Wildlife*, **19**, 229-239.

(36) Royal Society for the Protection of Birds (1985) *Forestry in the Flow Country – The Threat to Birds*. RSPB, Sandy.

(37) Ratcliffe, D.A. (1986) Presentation on the Flow Country. Internal NCC memorandum, 4 September 1986.

(38) Burnett, J.H. (ed.) (1964) *The Vegetation of Scotland*. Oliver Boyd, Edinburgh.

(39) Ratcliffe, D.A. (ed.) (1977) *A Nature Conservation Review, Volumes 1 and 2*. Cambridge University Press, Cambridge.

(40) Reed, T.M., Barrett, C.F., Barrett, J.C. & Langslow, D.R. (1983) Diurnal variability in the detection of Dunlin *Calidris alpina*. *Bird Study*, **30**, 244-246.
Reed, T.M., Langslow, D.R. & Symonds, F.L. (1983) Breeding waders of the Caithness Flows. *Scottish Birds*, **12**, 180-186.
Reed, T.M., Barrett, C.F., Barrett, J.C., Hayhow, S. & Minshull, B. (1985) Diurnal variability in the detection of waders on their breeding grounds. *Bird Study*, **32**, 71-74.

(41) Highland Regional Council (1987) Press Release: Not a tree more... 8 pp. 21 July 1987.

(42) Wilkinson, W. (1987) Address by the Chairman of the Nature Conservancy Council at the launch of *Birds, Bogs and Forestry* Report on 23 July 1987. 4 pp. Unpublished.

(43) Wilkinson, W. (1986) Caithness and Sutherland. Internal NCC memorandum from NCC Chairman; CH/RSJ/2556; 16 October 1986.

(44) Pienkowski, M.W., Stroud, D.A. & Reed, T.M. (1987) Problems in maintaining breeding habitat, with particular reference to peatland waders. *Wader Study Group Bulletin*, **49** Supplement: *IWRB Special Publication* 7, 95-101.

(45) Stroud, D.A. (1987). A review of some consequences of open ground afforestation for upland birds. In: *Forests for Britain: the BANC Report*, pp. 29-37. British Association of Nature Conservationists.

(46) Letter from Jeffrey McNeely, International Union for Conservation of Nature, to Richard Steele, Nature Conservancy Council, 29 January 1987.

(47) Hetherington, M. (1987) *Afforestation Consultations in North Scotland*. Interim report of a study carried out as part of an MA thesis. 12 pp. University of Sheffield, Department of Town & Regional Planning.

(48) Royal Society for the Protection of Birds (1986) Press Release: RSPB condemns further ploughing of moorland in the Flow Country. 10 September 1986.

(49) Bridgewater, P. (2015) National and global biodiversity politics and legalities – some reflections. In: *Nature's Conscience – The Life and Legacy of Derek Ratcliffe* (eds. D.B.A. Thompson, H.H. Birks & H.J.B. Birks). This volume, Chapter 25.

(50) Countryside Act (1968) http://www.legislation.gov.uk/ukpga/1968/41 (accessed March 2014).

(51) Ratcliffe, D.A. (1986) Defence of the Flow Country. Internal NCC memorandum, 26 August 1986.

(52) Hansard House of Commons, 24 February 1988, vol. 128, col. 287, *Forestry* http://hansard.millbanksystems.com/commons/1988/feb/24/forestry (accessed March 2014).

(53) *Daily Telegraph* (1988) Editorial, 26 January 1988.

(54) Wilson, D. (1984) *Pressure: the A to Z of Campaigning in Britain.* Heinemann Educational Books, London.

(55) Walter Jr., E.J. (1988) The battle to save Britain's last wilderness. *Animal Kingdom*, **91**(3), 8-40.

(56) National Audit Office (1986) *Review of Forestry Commission Objectives and Achievements.* HC 75, HMSO, London.

(57) Hansard House of Commons, 15 March 1988, vol. 129 cols. 993-1013. Nigel Lawson. Budget. At http://www.margaretthatcher.org/document/111449 (accessed March 2014).

(58) Ratcliffe, D.A. (1988) Comments on Caithness and Sutherland HRC Working party. Draft of final Report. Internal NCC memorandum, 14 August 1988.

(59) Nature Conservancy Council (1989) News Release: Statement by Chairman of NCC in response to Highland Regional Council Working Party Report. 26 January 1989.

(60) Scottish Development Department (1990) *Indicative Forest Strategies.* Scottish Development Department Circular No. 13/1990. SDD, Edinburgh. Subsequent planning documents.

(61) Patterson, G. & Anderson, R. (2000) *Forests and Peatland Habitats.* Forestry Commission Guideline Note. Forestry Commission, Edinburgh.

(62) Forestry Commission Scotland (2013) *Strategic Guide for the Conservation Management of Open Habitats on Scotland's National Forest Estate.* http://www.forestry.gov.uk/pdf/OpenHabitatsStrategy.pdf/$file/OpenHabitatsStrategy.pdf (accessed March 2014).

(63) Wilkinson, W. (1990) Chairman's Review. In: *Nature Conservancy Council 16th Report 1 April 1989-31 March 1990*. pp. 7-11. Nature Conservancy Council, Peterborough.

(64) Dalyell, T. (1989) Thistle Diary: Dismembered bodies and fishy tales. *New Scientist*, **2 September**, 79.

(65) Scottish Natural Heritage (1996) *Caithness and Sutherland Peatland Conservation Project. Thirtieth (and final) report ending 31 March 1996.* 8 pp. Internal SNH progress report, Edinburgh.

(66) http://www.lifepeatlandsproject.com (accessed March 2014).

(67) Stroud, D.A., Reed, T.M. & Harding, N.J. (1990) Do moorland breeding waders avoid plantation edges? *Bird Study,* **37**, 177-186.

(68) Wilson, J.D., Anderson, R., Bailey, S., Chetcuti, J., Cowie, N.R., Hancock, M.H., Quine, C.P., Russell, N., Stephen, L. & Thompson, D.B.A. (2014) Modelling edge effects of mature forest plantations on peatland waders informs landscape-scale conservation. *Journal of Applied Ecology,* **51**, 204–213.

(69) Ivanov, K.E. (1981) *Water Movement in Mirelands.* [English translation by A. Thompson and H.A.P. Ingram]. Academic Press, London.

(70) Ingram, H.A.P. (1982) Size and shape in raised mire ecosystems: a geophysical model. *Nature,* **297**, 300-303.

(71) Shotbolt, L., Anderson, A.R. & Townend, J. (1998) Changes to blanket bog adjoining forest plots at Bad a' Cheo, Rumster Forest, Caithness. *Forestry,* **71**, 311-324.
Anderson, A.R., Ray, D. & Pyatt, D.G. (2000) Physical and hydrological impacts of blanket bog afforestation at Bad á Cheo, Caithness: the first 5 years. *Forestry,* **73**, 467-478.
Lindsay, R.A. (2010) *Peatbogs and Carbon: A Critical Synthesis to Inform Policy Development in Oceanic Peat Bog Conservation and Restoration in the Context of Climate Change.* Commissioned Report to the Royal Society for the Protection of Birds.

(72) Scottish Natural Heritage (2005) *The Peatlands of Caithness and Sutherland. Management Strategy 2005-2015.* 52 pp.
http://www.lifepeatlandsproject.com/htm/pdf/A7.pdf (accessed March 2014).

(73) Lord Thurso, MP (2005) Foreword to Management Strategy. In: *The Peatlands of Caithness and Sutherland. Management Strategy 2005-2015.* p. 3. Scottish Natural Heritage, Edinburgh.

(74) Scottish Government (2013) Funding for peatlands.
http://news.scotland.gov.uk/News/Funding-for-peatlands-48d.aspx (accessed March 2014).

(75) Lofthouse, R.G.A. (1980) *The Berwyn Mountains area of Wales: an appraisal.* HMSO, Cardiff.

(76) Nature Conservancy Council (1984) *Nature Conservation in Great Britain.* 112 pp. Nature Conservancy Council, Shrewsbury.

(77) Thompson, D.B.A. & Lindsay, R.A. (1987) The Battle of the Bog. *New Scientist,* **8 January**, 41-45.

(78) Mabey, R. (1987) The Battle of the Bogs. *Sunday Times* colour supplement, **25 October**, 18-26.

(79) Scott, M. (1987) Sensible reports, insensitive launch, incensed Scotsmen, incidental trees. *BBC Wildlife,* **November**, 566.

(80) http://hansard.millbanksystems.com/lords/1988/feb/17/nature-conservancy-council-1 (accessed March 2014).

Appendix: Table 23.1. Chronology of key events related to the Nature Conservancy Council's (NCC) involvement in the Flow Country afforestation controversy 1970s–1989 and of external events.

Date	Events related to the NCC	External events
1970s		The Forestry Commission assures the Nature Conservancy Council that afforestation of the Flow Country would be technically impossible for the foreseeable future.
Late 1970s – early 1980s		New technical and silvicultural technologies allowed more widespread deep ploughing of peat for planting. Generous grants from the public purse under the 1967 Forestry Act to cover the direct costs of plantation establishment, and a forestry company combining these with the potential to offset remaining establishment costs against other tax liabilities, made this an extremely profitable investment (whether or not the trees grew), especially to individuals in high tax-brackets. By the early 1980s, the rate and extent of new afforestation markedly increased.
1979–1986	NCC organised Upland Bird Surveys (later Moorland Bird Study) in Caithness and Sutherland since 1979, whilst RSPB had undertaken parallel surveys in Caithness between 1980 and 1986. A major programme of peatland survey and separate NCC surveys of rivers and freshwater lochs is also undertaken by NCC.	
1985	Drafting of report by Stewart Angus (NCC Golspie) giving first overview of the extent of peatland afforestation	
1986		
June	Publication of *Nature Conservation and Afforestation in Britain* by NCC (24/6/86)[9]	
July		Department of Agriculture and Fisheries for Scotland Report on "the potential for future afforestation in the Flow County of Caithness and Sutherland"

Date	Events related to the NCC	External events
August	Derek Ratcliffe memo[37] outlining the key elements of the Flow County conservation case	Publication of *The Theft of the Hills* by The Ramblers Association and WWF[26] Inter-agency meeting at Scottish Office to discuss land-use mapping – "Caithness and Sutherland (Flow Country) Forestry Study" (14/8/86)
September	Presentation to NCC's Board of Directors on forestry economics Meeting between NCC's Chairman and Secretary of State for the Environment (Nicholas Ridley MP) with discussion of Caithness & Sutherland peatlands	Visit to Flow Country by International Mire Conservation Group RSPB write to Parliamentary Under-Secretary of State for Scotland (M. Ancram MP) calling "...for a halt to further forestry operations in the flow country until an integrated approach to the future of this area is adopted..."(10/9/86) RSPB issue Press Release condemning further ploughing of Flow Country – "countered and dismissed by a [Forestry] Commission spokesman" (10/9/86)[48]
October	NCC Council consider major paper on Flow Country : "Peatlands of Caithness and Sutherland" – first substantive discussion by Council (14/10/86)	Consideration by Technical Working Group of Scottish Office Departmental Group on the Countryside (22/10/86)
November	Draft of *Birds, Bogs and Forestry* produced and widely circulated for peer-review and comment Major internal strategy planning meeting involving key staff from NCC's NW Region, SHQ & CSD; Inverness (18-19/11/86)	
December		Consideration of NCC's case by Scottish Office Departmental Group on the Countryside (18/12/86) National Audit Office published review[56] questioning the economic justification of Forestry Commission investing further public funds in afforestation of marginal land in northern Scotland (Review of Forestry Commission Objectives and Achievements; HC 75)

Date	Events related to the NCC	External events
1987		
January		Call by IUCN[46] for Flow Country to be designated as first UK wetland under the World Heritage Convention "given the immense importance of the site..." (29/1/87)
February	Council consider scientific case for Flow Country for second time (24/2/87) Council issue Press Release confirming its unanimous view of the importance of the Flow Country (24/2/87) Feature article in *New Scientist*[77]	FC extends consultation arrangements with NCC for all grant applications for new afforestation in Caithness and Sutherland (17/2/87)
March	Flight over the peatlands by NCC's Advisory Committee on Science to view intact and destroyed patterned mires.	
June		Publication of *Forestry in the Flows of Caithness and Sutherland* by RSPB[30]
July	Publication and launch of *Birds, Bogs and Forestry*[8] in London, and call by NCC's Chair for a moratorium on future forestry planning in Caithness and Sutherland (23/7/87)	
August		Scottish Environment Minister James Douglas Hamilton asks Highland Regional Council (HRC) for its view on NCC's position by end of September. HRC establish a Working Party
September	Draft copy of *The Flow Country* sent to Scottish Development Department (10/9/87)	NCC presentations to i) Country Commission for Scotland Commissioners who were determining "its position in regard to afforestation in the flow country", and ii) Scottish Development Department (8/9/87) Highlands and Islands development Board release detailed response to *Birds, Bogs and Forestry* (30/9/88)
October		Major feature in *Sunday Times* supplement[78]

438

Date	Events related to the NCC	External events
November		Feature in *British Wildlife*[79]
1988		
February	Malcolm Rifkind MP, Secretary of State for Scotland announces protection of half the extent of the Caithness and Sutherland peatlands as SSSI (23/2/88) / Broadcast of ITV documentary 'Forestry and the Flow Country: paradise ploughed' presented by David Bellamy (9/2/88)	IUCN 17th General Assembly (Costa Rica) adopts Resolution 17/63 on International Importance of Scottish Peatlands (1-10/2/88) / Major debate in House of Lords on NCC annual report which focused significantly on Scottish afforestation issues (17/2/88) [Hansard vol. 493, col. 677-738 [80]]
March	Meeting between HRC/Scottish Development Department & NCC officials; NCC HQ (4/3/88)	Nigel Lawson announces change of tax regime in Budget[57] (15/3/88)
May	Publication and release of *The Flow Country*[5]	
November	Initiation meeting for Caithness and Sutherland Peatlands Project Team, Edinburgh (4/11/88)	HRC Caithness & Sutherland Working Party issue revised Land Use Strategy following six meetings since August 1987
1989		
January		HRC consider and agree revised Caithness and Sutherland Land Use Strategy
July	Nicholas Ridley MP, Secretary of State for the Environment, and Malcolm Rifkind MP, Secretary of State for Scotland, announce their decision to break up the NCC into its country components[19,64] (11/7/89)	

24. A letter to Derek Ratcliffe

from *Richard Lindsay*

I have three regrets concerning Derek Ratcliffe. First, in all the years I worked with Derek, I never spent a single day in the field with him. Second, I once shouted at him, quite loudly. Third, I did not come to appreciate what an amazing man he was until it was too late. Each of these regrets, while offering little that is positive in terms of my own character or powers of perception, nevertheless throws a revealing light on the kind of man he was – and 'kind' is a word which sits very naturally with my memories of Derek.

I first met Derek after David Goode brought me down from Cumbria to the Nature Conservancy Council's (NCC) Great Britain Headquarters (GBHQ) in Belgrave Square. David was then the Chief Scientist Team's (CST) Peatland Specialist. I was to work for him on a project cataloguing losses of raised bogs and also, it gradually emerged, to be his informal assistant. On the day of my arrival, David said that he would introduce me to the 'Chief Scientist', who had apparently expressed a desire to meet me. The only person with a similar-sounding title I had heard of until this point (given that this was the late-1970s) was the mysterious, shadowy head of the Russian Space Programme, known only as the 'Chief Designer'. This image was in no way dispelled when David led me into the Chief Scientist's office because sitting behind a desk was someone who exactly fitted my image of what the Chief Designer must look like – balding, side-tufted eyebrows, firm set of the mouth, but a twinkle in the eye. I half-expected his first words to be in Russian – "Welcome, comrade!" or something similar. Instead, I was greeted with: "Ah, Richard, I've been so looking forward to meeting you! Tell me, how is Glasson Moss?"

I should explain that in the previous year (the blazing-hot summer of 1976), while I had been working in the NCC's Lake District office, Glasson Moss National Nature Reserve (NNR) had suffered a catastrophic fire which burnt from July until November. Glasson lies just to the west of Carlisle and close to the Solway shore. It was one of

Derek's favourite raised bogs from his youth[1], rich in the beautiful, golden bog moss *Sphagnum pulchrum* (Fig. 24.1), and offering up an especially distinctive birdlife. Derek had heard about the fire with a mounting sense of loss as the news trickled through during the summer, and now he wanted my opinion of just how bad the damage was. I did not know anything about Derek's schoolboy affection for the place[1] so I described the bog as I had last seen it – a smoking, charred wreck with the stench of burnt peat still strong in the air over Carlisle – but I also pointed out that some areas of good bog vegetation, including areas of golden bog moss, had survived the fire entirely. Derek shook his head and said gloomily: "I think the site is probably lost. I don't think it will ever recover." I was to learn that Derek was prone to occasional prognostications of gloom and doom on conservation matters. After a mutual silence while we mourned the place, Derek rallied and asked me a series of very kindly questions about my time in the Lake District, about whether I had found somewhere to live in London, and about my planned work for David. I left the office thinking that he was a very kindly man, but I still had no clearer picture of what a Chief Scientist actually did. Based on the premise of the Chief Designer, it was probably something pretty awe-inspiring.

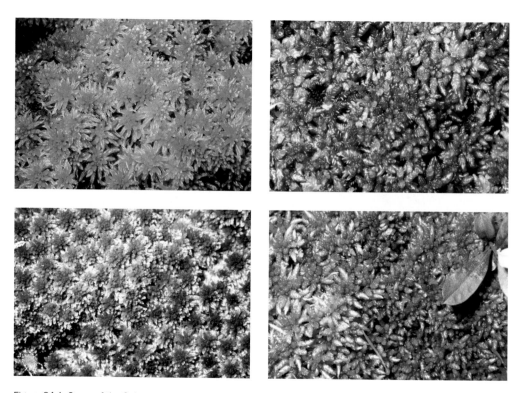

Figure 24.1. Some of the Sphagna recorded from Glasson Moss NNR, Cumbria, and also from the Flow Country of Caithness and Sutherland. *Sphagnum pulchrum*, Isle of Skye, 1968 (*top left*); *S. magellanicum*, Yorkshire, 1965 (*top right*); *S. fuscum*, Isle of Skye, 1968 (*lower left*); and *S. papillosum*, Galloway, 1966 (*lower right*). Photos: John Birks

Over the next few months in GBHQ I met Derek fairly regularly, our meeting venue generally being the tea room. Tea-breaks at Belgrave Square were eagerly anticipated, scheduled affairs, from 10:30–11:00 and 15:30–16:00. An egalitarian roster of volunteers set up the snack counter, then prepared and served tea to the rapidly-growing queue as various people emerged from their offices hidden away in the extraordinary warren of basements, attics, and ballrooms that was 19–20 Belgrave Square. The snack-bar was located in a basement room with a table around which senior staff tended to congregate, thus leading to its general description as 'the monitors' table'. 'Other ranks' tended to sit on the stools and easy chairs in the room next door. Derek and David both normally chose to sit with the 'other ranks' and so, when not serving behind the counter myself, I would find myself chatting with Derek over a cup of tea about the mysteries of *Dicranum undulatum* (*D. bergeri*) (Fig. 24.2), *Campylopus shawii* (Fig. 6.4), and different species of *Sphagnum* (Figs. 24.1 & 24.2) – at least they were mysteries to me, but Derek was elucidatory and patience itself, describing their particular 'look' in the field and the likely places to find them.

Figure 24.2. *Dicranum undulatum* (*D. bergeri*), Cheshire, 1965 (*left*) and *Sphagnum cuspidatum*, Yorkshire, 1965 (*right*). Photos: John Birks

Conservation was not doing well at the time[2], and we had several tea-time conversations about the failings of existing legislation, the losses which were occurring, and the actions – or inaction – of "those buggers" (one of Derek's very few swear words, but a favourite when he was annoyed; it was applied equally to certain politicians, landowners, farmers, big corporations, civil servants, or even colleagues). I had seen the effect of this weak legislation first hand in the Lake District – creeping behind a hedge on a narrow lane with Stuart Lane, the Assistant Regional Officer, to establish whether reports of an old flower-rich meadow being ploughed were true, then bumping into the farmer, who demanded to know what we were doing, and after explaining that we were checking on the condition of a Site of Special Scientific Interest (SSSI), being bluntly told: "Well, you'll not stop me from doing my farming!" What I did not have, which Derek by now had in abundance, was an understanding of where nature conservation sat in the pecking-order of civil service politics. He would listen patiently to my naive comments about what needed to be done, even agree with some points, and then gently steer the conversation towards things which had a realistic chance of being achieved.

Derek had amassed a huge number of field notebooks over the years[3], and so it was decided that someone should be employed to transcribe these and disseminate their contents to the operational staff in the regions. Consequently Katherine Hearne joined the contract staff (at that time consisting of myself and Sue Rowe) down in the 'basement lab' as it was known, and spent her days surrounded by banks of notebooks. Every now and then, Katherine would burst out laughing because Derek had written some wry comment in the margin, or she would exclaim in amazement and read us some extraordinary entry. That Christmas, we organised an unofficial Christmas banquet in the lab and invited as many colleagues as we could squeeze into that modest-sized room. I have what I think is an accurate memory of Derek sitting at the table, sporting a party hat from a cracker, while chatting cheerfully and amiably with his neighbours. In the only photos I have of the event, that part of the table where Derek sat is not in view, but the memory of him being there is strong, and, perhaps more importantly, it says much about him that his presence at such a somewhat anarchic, enjoyable event is entirely feasible.

During our tea-breaks, and subsequently after Derek was transferred to the Huntingdon Office, during his regular visits to Belgrave Square, he was always interested to hear what we had found on our peatland surveys. He made the effort to talk to each and every member of my small but slowly-expanding survey team. Whenever we were able to report something interesting or unusual, that slow and slightly reserved smile of his would develop, followed by questions, and then he would often chuckle with delight, or let out a deeply satisfied sigh, before congratulating whoever had been telling him about it. Derek always managed to leave the bearer of such information with the impression that he was envious and delighted, and that he doubted whether he could have achieved as much. Given that this was the 'Chief Designer' speaking, it tended to leave the recipient more than a little giddy.

At the outset of the 1980s, initially encouraged and supported by David Goode, then, after he left to become Ken Livingstone's ecology guru at the Greater London Council, supported directly by Derek, I set in train a broad-scale programme of survey across the peatlands of Britain. By now I had been given much more responsibility, and my purpose was simple enough – to identify the best remaining peatland sites before they vanished beneath the plough. Fire-brigade survey, we called it, because it was becoming increasingly evident that thousands of hectares of blanket bog were being damaged at an ever-increasing rate by drainage in the form of agricultural moor-gripping and afforestation[4]. We regarded Caithness and Sutherland as one of the key places for such survey because Derek had described the great "flow country" of these northern Scottish districts in Sir John Burnett's edited tome *The Vegetation of Scotland*[5]. Derek had first visited the area in 1958 and revisited what he called the "mysterious *terra incognita*"[1] many times in search of birds and wildness. David Goode had also shown me some of the bog systems in Caithness, emphasising that the Nature Conservancy and the NCC had only looked at a tiny fraction of what was there. Crucially, Derek was also becoming deeply alarmed about the increasingly aggressive spread of conifer forestry on to deep peat following a series of trial plantings undertaken by the Forestry Commission[4], made possible by the development of the Cuthbertson plough in the late 1940s.

We spent nearly five years surveying the enormous expanse of the Flow Country (Figs. 24.3 & 24.4), though it was not widely called that then. As time went by, however, we also found ourselves racing against the forestry ploughs. This was because the full financial opportunities of the Forestry Grant Scheme soon came to be realised by a number of clever accountants acting on behalf of those who found themselves in the super-tax bracket. The story of the battle for the Flow Country is told elsewhere in this book[2,4], but I would like to highlight one particular part played by Derek, and also ultimately by Derek Langslow (Derek's lieutenant), in this seminal conservation battle.

This particular story begins with my first real regret. In those days, surveys of the Flow Country (Fig. 24.3) were not easy undertakings. At the opposite end of the country from our London headquarters, it was a near-trackless waste, with only two main roads (for 'main', read single-track) passing northwards through the heart of the area. In many cases, the only feasible way to ac-

Figure 24.3. Low aerial view of the extensive bog pools at Shielton Bog, Caithness Flow Country. Photo: Steve Moore and Richard Lindsay

cess the peatland systems we planned to survey involved walking in from the road for a day and then camping (Fig. 24.5). There, we would subsist in the flows for three days, surveying everything around us, before breaking camp and trekking out. Sometimes the experience was simply awful, with day after day of relentless, soaking, driving rain or thick, soaking cloud (Fig. 24.6), but sometimes things were good, even extraordinary, and all the more richly memorable for that. One particular midsummer's eve amidst the Forsinard flows will stay with me forever – Common Snipe (*Gallinago gallinago*) drumming, distant Dunlin (*Calidris alpina*) trilling and hoarse-whistling, a Merlin (*Falco columbarius*) hunting below us, and a spectacular lenticular cloud capping Ben Griam Beag. That very scene was to vanish the following year, replaced by ghastly deep furrows and seedling trees, and now all we have are the memories and data sheets recording what was lost. My real regret, recalling that whole experience now, was that we should have shared these magical moments with Derek, but I did not realise it at the time.

Figure 24.4. Pool and hummock patterning on Badanloch Bogs, Sutherland Flow Country. Photo: Richard Lindsay

Every two weeks during the field season we would return to London and re-group, do our laundry, prepare the next set of field sheets, catch up with any other matters emerging during our absence, and I would usually meet up with Derek at some point, often in the tea-room. He would ask how things were going, what we had found, and I would tell him our latest news from the far north. We would discuss our findings, what we should look for, and where we were going next. Derek would become quite excited by the whole thing, but he never once suggested that he might join us. I did not expect him to because I knew that he was always desperately busy, but I realise now that Derek's diffidence probably prevented him from, as he would see it, 'imposing' on us. I can see now that some of his remarks were probably oblique suggestions that maybe he could join us, at least for a few days. If I had said: "Right Derek, I still can't identify *Campylopus shawii* to save my life, would you mind joining us for a day or two?", he might well have jumped at the chance. Alas I mistook his diffidence for business elsewhere. He was the Chief Designer: he had rockets to build! To have spent even just a couple of days with Derek in those far northern flows would, I suspect, have been quite something. Indeed I learnt much later from my uplands colleague Des Thompson, who trekked with Derek across the flows recording birdlife during fortnightly expeditions in the late 1980s, that Derek repeatedly remarked "Wouldn't it be great if Richard and his team were with us?" Sadly it just never happened.

Then we come to my less-than-honourable moment and my second regret. While we were surveying the Flow Country and, amongst other things, persuading the NCC's Scottish Advisory Committee to agree several very large new SSSIs as a stop-gap measure, the plight of this special place had become a *cause celebre*[4]. The spotlights of the media and several major non-governmental organisations (NGOs) were on us and our work.

Figure 24.5. John Riggall, Fiona Everingham, and John Ratcliffe setting off to camp and survey the Flow Country in 1981. Photo: Richard Lindsay

Figure 24.6. Sarah Garnett and Richard Lindsay at their tents while surveying the A'Mhoine peninsula, Sutherland in 1981. Photo: John Riggall

Political pressure was bearing down from a great height. We had amassed an absurdly large volume of survey data for the area. Now we needed to analyse and write up the data into a case which, as Dick Steele, then Director General of the NCC, said must be "absolutely bomb-proof" – an instruction which left me feeling physically sick with the weight of responsibility. The NCC, now with its HQ in Peterborough, had never tried to conserve two whole Scottish districts before, so our task involved acutely real and hugely daunting challenges.

David Stroud and his ornithological team had done a brilliant job in pulling together all the bird data and a summary of the peatland data for the area and in 1987 published them in *Birds, Bogs and Forestry*[6], which was enormously effective in raising the stakes concerning what was there – and thus what would knowingly be lost. But the pressure was now on to publish a more wide-ranging report which drew on the massive volume of habitat data we had, as well as for the first time identifying in detail the international importance of the area, derived from the literature and from a welter of scientific and conservation contacts throughout the world. Frankly, we were flagging and were still far behind in terms of analysis and writing. Pressure was mounting to produce this grand companion to *Birds, Bogs and Forestry* and my team, consisting at that stage of John Riggall, Terry Rowell, Fiona Everingham, Dan Charman, Fiona Burd, and Rachel O'Reilly, had been working flat out for almost a year – assembling the data, carrying out analyses on pretty rudimentary computers, and toiling as we wrote up the results. Our NCC Chairman, Sir William Wilkinson, was by now decidedly agitated about the whole affair. He had to tell ministers that the much vaunted and promised report was almost there, and that it would decisively present the compelling case for site protection. The stakes were high. The NGO sector, strong on birds, relied massively on our habitat expertise and experience[2]. It was put to us quite simply (and starkly) that no-one else could make the case. We knew that our small team stood between failure and making a difference for nature.

Physically and mentally we were by now close to the end of our tether. Early in 1988, Derek called me into his office to review where we were. When I explained the unfinished state of things he sighed, then said that perhaps he would need to take the work from us and arrange to have it finished some other way. Alas, at this point, I erupted. I shouted a number of things which I still deeply regret to this day. For the first (and last) time in my life I saw Derek genuinely angry on a personal level, actually shouting, albeit in a strangely restrained way. I yelled some more and then stormed out.

Five minutes later I was back, but before I could even open my mouth to apologise, Derek slowly, kindly, and deliberately sought to make amends for the pressure I had been put under, the fact that it had come to this, and promised that from here on he would do everything he could to help us. I could have hugged him, except we would both have been extremely embarrassed. There followed deeply-felt apologies between us, and then we hatched a plan – because we had to. Derek mobilised a number of his national and international contacts (including John and Hilary Birks in Bergen) to provide critical referees' comments and further information for the text as it came along. Derek took on the daunting job of co-editing the text as referees' commentaries poured in, often by fax. With his expert skills and judgement on birds, plants, habitats, ecosystem functions, invertebrates, and conservation, Derek came into his own. He masterfully wove the tapestry, just as he had done earlier in assembling *A Nature Conservation*

Review[7,8], and how he relished it. Des Thompson has since told me how, during their montane and Flow Country trek of June 1988, Derek and he would work on the text each evening, with Derek emerging the following morning clutching beautifully hand-written annotations and screeds of text which had to be posted to Peterborough, first class! Each night, Derek must have spent further hours shaping the text of the final chapter into a coherently persuasive conservation case. All of this allowed us to integrate the information coming in from the bird, freshwater, and peatland surveys and thus to generate a composite view of overlapping conservation value which appeared as *The Flow Country: The Peatlands of Caithness and Sutherland*[9].

To cap it all, when it came to discussing the title page, authorship, and other details, Derek suggested that those of us who had undertaken the survey, analysed the data, and written the drafts, should be the main authors. He and Philip Oswald (who meticulously proof-read and edited the entire document) would be listed as 'Editors'. And in a move so characteristic of his humility, Derek made it clear that the reference citation should explicitly give the main authors' names rather than the names of the editors, and he himself always referenced it thus[8]. On reflection, for us to have shared authorship of such a work with Derek Ratcliffe is something which I think we would all now have treasured, but at the time it just seemed like a neat solution. What an extraordinary person to work with. My third regret is that I did not realise this at the time.

Of course, Derek had his weaknesses, especially given the often politically-motivated environment in which he found himself having to work. In meetings involving aggressive but politically-astute individuals, Derek did not always shine because he was frequently left so aghast by the way that people were prepared to state something with certainty while knowing it to be a lie, but a lie which was politically acceptable to the powers above. Such behaviour often received the appellation of 'those buggers' after the meeting, but during the meeting Derek was often at a loss to know how to respond, given his own strong beliefs that truth and facts are what make a sound scientific argument and consequently a solid conservation case. At such moments (and there were some particularly sticky ones during the Flow Country story), Derek Langslow was able to deflect or neutralise these blatant and occasionally aggressive attacks with an impressive combination of factual detail and political nous, thereby turning the argument round in NCC's favour. Derek Ratcliffe, on the other hand, tended to become visibly cross and frustrated over such blatant lies, which just played into the other side's hands ('the conservation case is evidently being driven by emotional arguments', they would sneer), though he would then pursue an evidence-based argument just at the point when the decision-makers in the room did not want to get 'bogged down in detail', and it infuriated them. What they wanted was a politically acceptable way forward. What Derek Ratcliffe wanted was for everyone to understand the facts because for Derek the facts made clear what action was needed.

Derek Langslow was Derek's Assistant Chief Scientist, and a highly adept scientific administrator, manager, and committee man. They made a formidable team, and Derek Langslow, Mike Pienkowski, David Stroud, Rob Soutar, Des Thompson, Margaret Palmer, and others working in the Chief Scientist Directorate all deserve a great deal of praise for their work in this battle.

While he was no political Machiavelli, Derek Ratcliffe was nevertheless a superb strategist, as displayed by his strategically successful publications for the NCC, which include the masterful two-volume doomsday book *A Nature Conservation Review*[7,8] (the NCR), the revision of the SSSI Guidelines[10] into a robustly coherent case, and the two key NCC strategy documents, *Nature Conservation in Great Britain*[11] and *Nature Conservation and Afforestation in Britain*[12]. Uniquely for such a senior figure in the public sector (and, as David Stroud once pointed out, a characteristic shared with the Duke of Wellington), Derek saw and articulated the bigger picture without being distracted by the clutter of bureaucracy, staffing, and resourcing matters (topics which Derek Langslow administered with relish and energy). But the fundamental principle which Derek Ratcliffe encouraged, supported, and impressed on his team, and indeed the key ingredient for the icing on his own richly layered writing, is that scientific understanding of our ecosystems can only truly be attained through extensive first-hand experience in the field.

Surprisingly enough, Derek appears to have lacked confidence in his own ability to turn such understanding into scientifically-sound and practical conservation science. Just a few years before his death, Derek wrote a typically kind and heartfelt letter to my wife and me when he heard that we had suffered a sad event. I wrote back to thank him, and also to tell him that the evaluation principles which he had set out in the NCR formed a key part of what I was now teaching my students in relation to site evaluation, and that they thoroughly enjoyed practical exercises which involved using these principles. The NCR criteria[8] also continued to underpin my own conservation guidance to colleagues in other countries, who embraced them with similar enthusiasm. Derek replied to say that he was glad to hear this, but also to say that he had never really got over the criticism of these principles which he had received from someone in Institute of Terrestrial Ecology (ITE) following the NCR's launch. Even after so many years, this clearly rankled, and still led him to question whether he had produced something which was as good and scientifically-sound as it could have been.

Being Chief Scientist meant that Derek also had to run the Chief Scientist Team (CST) (later a Directorate). Thinking back on the CST, I find that I am drawn to make some comparison with the codebreakers at Bletchley Park during World War 2 – a somewhat individualistic, even eccentric, group of highly effective specialists dedicated to a common aim (and amid such experts I always felt a bit of a fraud, really). Derek managed the team to make the most of its collective strengths, and many of the publications associated with his name are, as Derek readily acknowledged, collaborative works which drew on the collective expertise of the team [e.g. 7,10–12]. His approach also meant that Derek did not 'run' the Chief Scientist Team and its meetings, but instead rather encouraged us to share ideas, support each other, and be creative in our thinking. I do not ever recall an edict coming from Derek formally instructing us to do something. His memos, often long, tended to be requests urging or encouraging us to do certain things, but generally also explaining why it was important that we did so.

The highlight of the CST year was the Research Review Meeting, during which the allocation of funding for research was discussed and (generally) decided. Given the significance of this meeting and the consequences arising from it, one might have expected it to have been a somewhat fraught event, but under Derek's guidance they became more of an inter-disciplinary brainstorming session ranging across the whole spectrum of conservation science. It was an exhausting, sometimes frustrating, but ultimately strangely exhilarating experience because, although there were inevitably winners and losers in the final allocation process, every bid was given a fair hearing and, as the day progressed, a broader picture steadily emerged, offering a view across the issues affecting the natural heritage of Britain as a whole and a sense of how each research bid fitted into this overall picture. The broader view was clearly what Derek sought and what guided him in his contributions to the discussions. Nonetheless, he also took an active interest in each and every bid, offering well-informed, valuable, and often uncomfortably penetrating observations across an astonishingly wide range of subjects.

I still miss the Chief Scientist Team, and that strong sense of common purpose. And I miss the remarkable man who led us. Both the work, and legacy, of the 'Chief Designer' have indeed proved to be pretty awe-inspiring. I feel privileged to have such vivid recollections of working with Derek Ratcliffe, and there is no question in my mind that my formative years of work, and those of many others, were shaped and immeasurably improved by working in his long and kindly shadow.

Acknowledgements

Having acknowledged Derek Ratcliffe's part in all of this, I would also like to extend my grateful thanks to all those who formed part of the Peatland Team during those eventful years. In particular, my thanks go to John Riggall, who cheerfully and calmly kept the show on the rails whenever I was flagging or failing, and to Fiona Everingham, who ensured that we never arrived on a site unannounced and that we always knew where the fuel for the stove was packed. I am enormously grateful to everyone else who, at various times, also formed part of that team during the events described here, namely Jane Smart, Bob Missin, Sara Oldfield, and Sarah Garnett in the early years, David Stroud, John Ratcliffe, Fiona Burd, and Sylvia White in the middle years, and Dan Charman, Rachel O'Rielly, Terry Rowell, and Colin Wells in the later years. Extraordinary times, extraordinary people.

References

(1)   Ratcliffe, D.A. (2000) *In Search of Nature*. Peregrine Books, Leeds.

(2)   Housden, S. (2015) Fighting for wildlife – from the inside. In: *Nature's Conscience – The Life and Legacy of Derek Ratcliffe* (eds. D.B.A. Thompson, H.H. Birks & H.J.B. Birks). This volume, Chapter 20.

(3)   Birks, H.J.B., Thompson, D.B.A. & Birks, H.H. (2015) Derek Ratcliffe – early days in pursuit of nature. In: *Nature's Conscience – The Life and Legacy of Derek Ratcliffe* (eds. D.B.A. Thompson, H.H. Birks & H.J.B. Birks). This volume, Chapter 1.
Birks, H.J.B. & Birks, H.H. (2015) Derek Ratcliffe – botanist and plant ecologist. In: *Nature's Conscience – The Life and Legacy of Derek Ratcliffe* (eds. D.B.A. Thompson, H.H. Birks & H.J.B. Birks). This volume, Chapter 4.

(4)   Stroud, D.A., Reed, T.M., Pienkowski, M.W. & Lindsay, R.A. (2015) The Flow
        Country: battles fought, war won, organisation lost. In: *Nature's Conscience – The
        Life and Legacy of Derek Ratcliffe* (eds. D.B.A. Thompson, H.H. Birks & H.J.B.
        Birks). This volume, Chapter 23.

(5)   Ratcliffe, D.A. (1964) Mires and bogs. In: *The Vegetation of Scotland* (ed. J.H. Bur-
        nett). pp. 426-478. Oliver and Boyd, Edinburgh.

(6)   Stroud, D.A., Reed, T.M., Pienkowski, M.W. & Lindsay, R.A. (eds. D.A. Ratcliffe
        & P.H. Oswald) (1987) *Birds, Bogs and Forestry. The Peatlands of Caithness, and
        Sutherland.* 121 pp. Nature Conservancy Council, Peterborough.

(7)   Ratcliffe, D.A. (ed.) (1977) *A Nature Conservation Review, Volumes 1 and 2.* Cam-
        bridge University Press, Cambridge.

(8)   Thompson, D.B.A., Sutherland, W.J. & Birks, H.J.B. (2015) Nature conservation
        and the Nature Conservation Review – a novel philosophical framework. In:
        Nature's Conscience – The Life and Legacy of Derek Ratcliffe (eds. D.B.A. Thompson,
        H.H. Birks & H.J.B. Birks). This volume, Chapter 19.

(9)   Lindsay, R.A., Charman, D.J., Everingham, F., O'Reilly, R.M., Palmer, M.A.,
        Rowell, T.A. & Stroud, D.A. (eds. D.A. Ratcliffe & P.H. Oswald) (1988) *The Flow
        Country – The Peatlands of Caithness and Sutherland.* 174 pp. Nature Conservancy
        Council, Peterborough. http://jncc.defra.gov.uk/page-4281

(10)   Nature Conservancy Council (1989) *Guidelines for Selection of Biological SSSIs.* 288
        pp. Nature Conservancy Council, Peterborough.

(11)   Nature Conservancy Council (1984) *Nature Conservation in Great Britain.* 112 pp.
        Nature Conservancy Council, Shrewsbury.

(12)   Nature Conservancy Council (1986) *Nature Conservation and Afforestation in
        Britain.* 108 pp. Nature Conservancy Council, Peterborough.

25. National and global biodiversity politics and legalities - some reflections

Peter Bridgewater

Prologue

I joined the Nature Conservancy Council (NCC) in 1989 as its last formally appointed Chief Scientist, following in the footsteps of Derek Ratcliffe's long and impressive tenure. It was a hard act to follow, but having arrived in the UK from Australia I remember well the warm welcome my family received from Derek and his wife Jeannette (Fig. 17.2). We stayed with them for a short period, and were taken out, all still jet lagged, to the Ouse Washes (Fig. 25.1) as a sighting of a Spoonbill (*Platalea leucorodia*) was possible. This was a rapid and real introduction to Derek's enthusiasm for nature, especially birds.

We formally overlapped for around six weeks, and during that time I grew to understand Derek's approach to work, his deep and abiding commitment to nature conservation, his loyalty to his colleagues, and, above all, the deep hurt he felt about what he saw as the unnecessary changes in 1972, when the Rothschild Report gave rise to the Government's 'split' of the former Nature Conservancy (NC) into research (Institute of Terrestrial Ecology) and an operational conservation body – the Nature Conservancy Council (NCC). For me, such fears came to pass rapidly, for in the first week following Derek's departure, the Government announced its intention to disband the NCC, with new country conservation agencies being established, and 'my' Chief Scientist Directorate facing a very unsure and uncertain future[1].

While the circumstances led me to return to a very good job offer in Australia I do believe the Government's move was, in theory, the correct one, but very poorly handled. The proposals in Scotland and Wales were sensible, resulting in strong bodies (Countryside Council for Wales (CCW) and Scottish Natural Heritage (SNH)) being established which dealt with nature conservation across a wide canvas. However, even there, while Wales was off to a good start, in Scotland, the situation was less satisfactory, with a further year elapsing before Scottish Natural Heritage was properly established. In

Figure 25.1. The Ouse Washes at Sutton Gault. Photo: Richard Humphrey (www.geograph.org.uk)

England, the situation was least satisfactory, with the landscape conservation functions remaining with a weakened Countryside Commission, and species, habitat, and geo-conservation being left to a truncated English Nature. It was not until 2004 that this situation was finally resolved with the creation of Natural England (NE), paralleling the responsibilities and scope of the CCW and SNH. And most challenging of all was the creation of a GB (now UK) body, the Joint Nature Conservation Committee (JNCC) with responsibilities for maintaining GB (and now UK) standards and leading on international matters. At the time of writing I was chairing the JNCC, and so have had an opportunity to reflect hard on what has worked—and not worked—for conservation.

But this story is being played out further as I write, with the CCW now being combined with the Forestry Commission (FC) and Environment Agency (EA) functions as a new agency Natural Resources Wales, and a review is in progress between the EA and NE in England, with the future of Forestry activities in England remaining ambiguous. By late 2014 this has been clarified by a decision that EA and NE will work closely together, but not actually fuse, and the FC functions remain much as before. That the 'good idea' of 1989 is still being played out (and remains unresolved) is partly political in nature, and partly an inability of those supporting conservation to speak with a strong and united enough voice to influence appropriate change at a political level.

I know that Derek Ratcliffe was firmly convinced this dismemberment of the NCC was another tragic step on the path of devaluing nature conservation and its role in

British society[1]. In that I fear he may have been right, but alas it is not limited to the UK! I try to outline here the story of how biodiversity became more central in policy and science, yet paradoxically less well looked after by the global community. The narrative could begin in many times and places, but I chose my starting line in Stockholm – forty years ago.

The 1970s: the dawning of environmental awareness

Since 1970, European Conservation Year, the world has witnessed great changes in our understanding and perceptions of the environment. Prior to then, very few governments had separate Departments or Ministers dealing with the environment. At national and international levels the environment was simply part of other activities. At the United Nations (UN) level, the UN Educational, Scientific and Cultural Organization (UNESCO) was dealing with the environment through its science sector; the Food and Agriculture Organization (FAO) had many programmes dealing with natural resources; and the UN Development Programme (UNDP) took little notice of the environment as it was tasked with development. As for the UN Secretariat, it had almost no cognisance of the natural environment; focusing instead on the socio-economic environment, which was what the global community appeared to want.

With hindsight, the 1960s were a time of environmental awakening, especially with regard to the ways in which human society was using dangerous chemicals to 'protect' species on which we depended from depredations of others. One of the consequences is well documented – the accumulation at the top of food chains of organochlorines used in pesticides, resulting in dramatic drops in populations of birds of prey. Derek's work on the Peregrine Falcon (*Falco peregrinus*), so well known, was part of the unravelling of this story[2-4].

In 1972, partly in response to these issues, but also as a reaction to increasing concerns for the environment across western nations, a major UN Conference on The Human Environment was held in Stockholm, Sweden[5]. This Stockholm Conference, as it came to be known, established the United Nations Environment Programme (UNEP) as an environmental presence for the first time in the UN system. The Conference made strides in developing legal protocols for environmental protection, building on activities in the previous two years of the decade.

In the previous year, the first of the global conventions dealing with environmental issues was born in Ramsar, Iran, as governments, non-governmental organisations, and UNESCO sought to establish a global focus on maintaining wetlands to ensure the survival of migratory waterfowl. This was to be achieved through the establishment of the Convention on Wetlands of International Importance especially for Waterfowl, better known by its shorter title of Ramsar Convention[6]. Although this Convention was signed into being in 1971, it had taken the best part of a decade to reach that point, and it remained un-ratified until 1975. After that time its pace of acceptance became faster.

Even earlier, in 1968, UNESCO had held a key conference on the Biosphere, which gave rise to its Man and Biosphere programme[7]. Within UNESCO the results of the Biosphere conference in 1971 had begun to be realised with the earliest Biosphere Reserves being declared. This continues today through the development and expansion of the World Network of Biosphere Reserves. Synchronously, the Convention on the

Protection of the World's Natural and Cultural Heritage (World Heritage Convention[8]) began to inscribe sites on the World Heritage List.

And so, by the mid-1970s there were in place opportunities under three arrangements to recognise special natural places of global significance, and to provide them with appropriate national management and conservation (often wrongly ascribed as 'protection'), according to the rules and procedures of each international programme or convention. Besides the place-based conventions two others with a species focus were established in the 1970s: the Convention on International Trade in Endangered Species (CITES)[9]; and the Bonn Convention on Migratory Species (CMS)[10]. By the end of the decade, five conventions dealing with biodiversity were born, even though the concept of, and indeed the term, 'biodiversity', was still in gestation.

The 1980s: a period of consolidation

The Stockholm meeting also marked the beginning of a discussion on the principles for international legal frameworks for environmental protection. That process was reviewed in 1982 at a gathering in Montevideo, which produced a programme for development and a review of environmental law.

On the science side, perhaps the most exciting development was the elaboration of the concept of biological diversity as encompassing all levels of the biological hierarchy - from genes to landscapes and seascapes, and embracing species, habitats, and ecological communities. This concept (perhaps most eloquently elaborated through the US Office of Technology Assessment (OTA)[11]) gave rise to the word 'biodiversity' in 1986, as a contraction of biological diversity, and spawned much discussion and deliberation internationally towards an international convention. Yet, although the concept was novel and exciting, discussions on forming the Convention tended to be at the level of dealing with threatened species, or threatened ecosystems, rather than at the more holistic level which the concept provided. Those discussions continued, many would say interminably, through to the next decade – indeed they are still with us as we try to unravel the complexities of our living world.

In 1983, the UN established the World Commission on Environment and Development (WCED), chaired by Gro Harlem Brundtland who had been Prime Minister of Norway, and was again, as the commission published its findings in 1987.

The key output from this Commission was the still widely-cited report *Our Common*

Figure 25.2. The 'Brundtland Report', 1987.

Future[12], frequently referred to as the 'Brundtland Report' (Fig. 25.2). This report set out very clearly the frame in which the discussions should proceed (WCED 1987), and the Chairman's Foreword commented:

> "The environment does not exist as a sphere separate from human actions, ambitions, and needs, and attempts to defend it in isolation from human concerns have given the very word "environment" a connotation of naivety in some political circles. The word "development" has also been narrowed by some into a very limited focus, along the lines of "what poor nations should do to become richer.", and thus again is automatically dismissed by many in the international arena as being a concern of specialists, of those involved in questions of "development assistance".

> But the "environment" is where we all live; and "development" is what we all do in attempting to improve our lot within that abode. The two are inseparable."

1989 in the UK, however, brought for many an unwelcome shock, in the form of break-up for the GB Nature Conservancy Council[1]. Almost twenty years earlier, the then Nature Conservancy, founded in 1949, had been stripped of its research support functions, which became the Institute for Terrestrial Ecology (ITE), leaving the Nature Conservancy Council, as it became, with the Chief Scientist Directorate (formerly the Chief Scientist Team), headed by Derek Ratcliffe. That Directorate, while not actively engaged in research, became an interface between the ITE and the management directorates of the NCC.

As I mentioned earlier, dividing NCC functions was not necessarily a bad thing, yet the clumsy way in which it proceeded led to a marked slowdown in the effective delivery of nature conservation in Great Britain for the best part of a decade. It was indeed ironic that while nature conservation, or conservation and management of biodiversity, was being given a considerable boost internationally, in the UK poor management and governance resulted in a lessening in effective understanding and delivery of biodiversity conservation[1].

The 1990s: action, at last?

The 'Brundtland Report' led to the UN World Conference on Environment and Development (WCED), otherwise known as the 'Earth Summit' and 'Rio Conference', in Rio de Janeiro in 1992[13]. Twenty years after Stockholm, and with concern about the environment in all aspects growing rapidly, the Rio Conference was upbeat and the pace of its achievements remarkable. A remarkable number of governments participated (172), with 108 represented by heads of state or government. There were 2,400 representatives of NGOs, and 17,000 people attended the parallel NGO Forum! At its close, the Conference Secretary General, Maurice Strong, hailed the Summit a "historic moment for humanity." The Earth Summit agreed two legally binding Agreements of truly global significance: the UN Convention on Biological Diversity (UNCBD)[14] and the UN Framework Convention on Climate Change (UNFCCC)[15]. It also gave birth to a third key document, the United Nations Convention to Combat Desertification (UNCCD)[16], ratified in 1994. In addition, the following were published: *Rio Declaration on Environment and Development*[17]; *Agenda 21*[18]; and *Forest Principles*[19]. The three Conventions (UNCBD, UNCCD, and UNFCCC – now popularly known as the Rio conventions) had rather wide scope, changing the tendency of the previous decades to negotiate and agree rather narrow and sectoral conventions. *Agenda 21* is a 300-page document providing codified ways to manage the environment in the 21st century. For those involved in nature conservation, the CBD seemed a final recognition by governments of the importance of their work. Why, even DDT was finally banned in 1992 under European Commision (EC) regulations ("except for emergency use against cutworms"). And yet by the decade's end a disappointing report card would be waiting.

The WCED established the Commission on Sustainable Development (CSD)[20], a body managed by the UN Secretariat in New York. It aimed to cover the spectrum of activities relating to sustainable development, and meets annually. Disappointingly, the CSD has not produced any radical new thinking on sustainable development generally and certainly none with regard to conservation.

Individual activities under the various established and new Conventions proceeded apace through the 1990s, including the adoption by the CBD of a programme on inland waters[21] – which includes lake and river systems. Within the UN system as a whole, and in its programmes, key thinking underlying Integrated Water Resources Management (IWRM)[22] — a key conservation and management issue — remained separate. Even within organisations, e.g. UNESCO, the existence of two programmes from the era of the 1970s, the International Hydrological Programme (IHP)[23] and the Man and Biosphere Programme (MAB)[7], continue to have separate governing bodies, and often duplicate effort and work. Promotion of an 'ecotone's activity', very much focussed on rivers, and a programme on ecohydrology are tending to blur that separation, and highlight the value of an integrated approach.

But perhaps the 'water community' and the 'ecosystem' community failing to make effective common cause distinguishes the 1990s in a poor light, with policy actions and activities proceeding in separate areas of research, development, and implementation, despite the adoption of the IWRM paradigm in 1977. That the IWRM could be agreed in 1977, and yet still be discussed (rather than being implemented) in 2010, is a condemnation of international processes.

Five years on from Rio, in 1997, a much smaller gathering was held under the general title of Rio+5[24]. Sombrely, this meeting was much less upbeat than the 1992 gathering. It reported a lack of progress on the entire set of key issues discussed during the Earth Summit. Also in 1997, the UN Secretary General, Kofi Annan, issued a report entitled *Renewing the United Nations*[25], which, among other things, took up the question of global governance, including environmental governance.

In 1998, the World Bank, UNEP, and National Aeronautics and Space Administration (NASA) produced a joint scientific report entitled *Protecting our Planet Securing Our Future*[26]. For the first time, a report examined environmental governance from the viewpoint of its necessary scientific underpinnings. Also in 1998, a UN Task Force on Environment and Human Settlements[27] was established to examine governance issues linking environmental issues and human settlements. The Task Force, again for the first time, linked areas that had hitherto been treated as quite separate – and that were actually quite inseparable!

A new century – but little has changed

In the first decade of the 21st century perhaps the most significant development was the holding of the third global meeting on environment and development in 2002 in Johannesburg, South Africa. That meeting, called the World Summit on Sustainable Development (WSSD)[28], generated less hype than the Rio meeting had in 1992, yet was still strong on hyperbole. No new conventions were born, but some ambitious targets were created. Most notably, the target to reduce the rate of loss of biodiversity by 2010, and the implicit admission that the establishment of the CBD 10 years earlier had yet to show any meaningful change in attitudes and outcomes. That target was subsequently endorsed by the CBD itself later that year. A real problem in all these global meetings is that the excitement of the moment, and the need to finish by tight deadlines, means that targets are agreed, without thought for implementation, monitoring, or measuring success. And so it goes.

A particularly noteworthy target agreed at WSSD was to establish a network of marine protected areas by 2012. Some progress has been made in delivering that target globally, although patchily. In the UK there have been two important developments in 2012. First, in the waters around the Scottish coast, a selection of Nature Conservation Marine Protected Areas (MPAs) has been undertaken using a science-led approach, while at the same time the selection process has incorporated opportunities for stakeholders to feed in to the development of the network. These interests extend beyond Scotland, and include UK and non-UK users of Scotland's sea. Moving forward, all users of the Scottish marine environment will have an important role to play in developing the management of proposed MPAs. Full details of this activity are discussed elsewhere[29].

The second important development was a stakeholder-led project in predominately English inshore waters and English, Welsh, and Northern Irish off-shore waters to attempt a balance between fisheries, renewable energy (wind farms), off-shore exploration and extraction, and conservation. Key to the success of this endeavour was to be the identification and establishment of a series of Marine Conservation Zones (MCZs). Historically, designation processes have begun with nature conservation bodies such as Natural England and the Joint Nature Conservation Committee providing the Government with advice on where sites should be designated. This advice would be followed by a Public Consultation to allow the public to comment on the proposals. However, the Government recognised the valuable knowledge and experience sea-users and interest groups have of the marine environment, and judged it important to consider the social and economic impacts that MCZs might have. It therefore included, in the Marine and Coastal Access Act, provision for stakeholders to be involved in making the initial recommendations for MCZs. In September 2011, recommendations were submitted to government for a number of Marine Conservation Zones (MCZs)[30]. These recommendations came from groups of sea-users and those with an interest in the sea through a series of discussions and negotiations. Natural England and JNCC, as the Government's advisers on the natural environment, reviewed these recommendations and submitted advice to Government on the science behind these recommendations and the quality of the ecological data. At the time of writing the government is developing a public consultation process on this issue. I am sure that Derek would have been pleased to see progress, albeit slow, in an area he was quietly stewarding over two decades ago.

But another issue has been brewing in the first decade of this century – international environmental governance. In 2000 an important meeting was held in Malmö, Sweden – the first UNEP Global Ministerial Environment Forum (GMEF)[31]. It was a milestone in bringing together the world's Ministers for the Environment to discuss the key issues, especially the issues of environmental governance. Such a gathering brought to one table all the cultural complexities of the world's countries and their political systems.

In 2001, the UNEP Governing Council began to examine the possibilities of establishing new measures for international environmental governance. This initiative sought to create a new 'landscape' of environmental governance at the international level. Decision 21/21, February 2001 of the UNEP General Council established an Open-ended Intergovernmental Group of Ministers or Their Representatives on International Environmental Governance. This group held a number of meetings and some expert consultations. The sequence of these was:

- First Meeting, New York, April 2001

- Civil Society Consultations Nairobi, May 2001

- Expert consultations, Cambridge, United Kingdom, May 2001

- Committee of Permanent Representatives to UNEP, Nairobi, June 2001

- Second Meeting, Bonn, Germany, July 2001

- Third Meeting Algiers, Algeria, September 2001

- Fourth Meeting, Montreal, Canada, December 2001

- Fifth meeting, New York UNHQ, January 2002

- Final Meeting, Cartagena, Colombia, February 2002

These meetings established several important steps to reform international environmental governance. The Civil Society Consultations on International Environmental Governance, held in Nairobi, came up with two key conclusions.

- That UNEP should be strengthened and its responsibilities extended so as to encompass sustainable development as well as the environment; and

- The fragmented multilateral environmental agreements (MEAs) should be clustered under the strengthened UNEP. In its discussions on international environmental governance, the Committee of Permanent Representatives to UNEP arrived at a recommendation that the question of the conversion of UNEP into a United Nations specialised agency should be studied.

Finally, the Expert Consultations on International Environmental Governance made two observations. The first was that The World Summit on Sustainable Development would have to focus on the role of United Nations organisations in the context of international environmental governance, and that financing was a critical issue in this context. The second observation was that UNEP should implement its sustainable development agenda and secure support for the integration of environmental institutions.

The UN agencies have roles and mandates that are unclear and overlapping, leading to conflicting priorities and inefficiency. The only responses, so far, to the above-discussed conclusions have been the establishment of the Environment Management Group[32] (under the general management of UNEP) and the relative inactivity of the long established but relatively ineffectual Ecosystem Conservation Group[33] (also under the general purview of UNEP). These solutions have not delivered eagerly sought outcomes, but at least there is now clear potential to do so.

In fact, the above-discussed series of meetings did not unfold in a fully developmental fashion. The process peaked rather too soon at Algiers in September 2001. Since that meeting everything became vaguer and the positions of the European Union, OECD countries in general, and the G77+China, certainly became more entrenched and incompatible. Indeed, the final plan of implementation adopted at the World Summit on Sustainable Development in Johannesburg was disappointing. It largely failed to adequately address the issues raised in the above-discussed earlier meetings.

A link between these actual and potential assessments, promoting enhanced scientific monitoring capabilities, and government policy delivery, is critical, and suggests that science and human-centred values must combine to attain good governance solutions. Those based solely on science, without recognising human perceptual issues, and the need to integrate cultural imperatives, will ultimately fail. In the same measure, governance solutions based exclusively on human values, without the seasoning of scientific attributes, will also fail.

Where next?

We began this journey in Stockholm, and have ended with a welter of international meetings and 'agreements'. Much effort and dialogue have gone into all of this. But I cannot help feeling a deep sense of frustration over the unfocussed and diversionary, rather than focussed and visionary, frameworks guiding it all.

Quite simply, we have to move from sophistry and words to real action – the global community does not have the luxury to spend more time re-crafting mechanisms for governance. No, what we must have is serious and meaningful management and conservation actions – at local and national levels. And just as nature's global landscapes have become more fragmented and less resilient, so the institutional landscape has become more cluttered and replete with redundancy, duplication, and hopeless obfuscation.

So, can we move forward, and build on the aspirations of the thousands of people involved in Rio more than twenty years ago? In 2012 there was a further Rio meeting, so-called Rio+20. That meeting produced a highly disappointing 'outcome' document which was, as usual, declared a success! Yet some glimmers of hope were there – a decision to construct sustainable development targets is one. If targets can be used to energise the process, as well as provide a destination and a means of measuring how far we have travelled, this can be a turning point. Providing so-called universal membership, allowing for all the world's Ministers of the Environment to attend the UNEP Global Environment Ministerial Forum, is another. The first meeting held under that new regimen took place in February 2013.

At that meeting Governments called for the transformation of the existing

Governing Council into a UN Environment Assembly of UNEP and to build stronger links between UNEP's science-based Global Environment Outlook process and its ministerial meetings – further implementing the call by member states at the Rio+20 meeting to strengthen the science-policy interface. Yet for those involved in nature conservation the picture in detail is not so rosy – many discussions were focussed on energy, green economy, and other buzz-words hiding the business-as-usual approach.

The biggest sign of hope came not from the usual government mediated processes — which almost came close to de-railing the whole event — but an extraordinarily rich series of side-events involving business, the third sector (voluntary and community organisations), and a wide range of civil society. Many new alliances and partnerships were formed, and although some will wither, many will survive and flourish. Managing the environment, especially the natural environment, is more and more becoming a task that civic society is, and must, take over from governments, which seem increasingly incapable of undertaking it. This is a message that Derek, reluctant public servant that he was, would approve of, with a glimmer of a smile, as if to say – "Well, I told you so…"

References

(1)   Radcliffe (sic), D. (1989) The end of British nature conservation? *New Scientist*, **9 September**, 75-76.

(2)   Ratcliffe, D.A. (1980) *The Peregrine Falcon*. Poyser, Calton.
        Ratcliffe, D.A. (1993) *The Peregrine Falcon* (2nd edition). Poyser, London.

(3)   Ratcliffe, D.A. (1967) Decrease in eggshell weight in certain birds of prey. *Nature*, **215**, 208-210.

(4)   Newton, I. (2015) Pesticides and birds of prey – the breakthrough. In: *Nature's Conscience – The Life and Legacy of Derek Ratcliffe* (eds. D.B.A. Thompson, H.H. Birks & H.J.B. Birks). This volume, Chapter 15.

(5)   http://www.unep.org/Documents.Multilingual/Default.asp?documentid=97 (accessed February 2013)

(6)   http://www.ramsar.org/cda/en/ramsar-about-about-ramsar/main/ramsar/1-36%5E7687_4000_0__ (accessed February 2013)

(7)   http://www.unesco.org/new/en/natural-sciences/environment/ecological-sciences/man-and-biosphere-programme/ (accessed February 2013)

(8)   http://whc.unesco.org/en/convention/ (accessed February 2013)

(9)   http://www.cites.org/eng/disc/what.php (accessed February 2013)

(10)   http://www.cms.int/about/intro.htm (accessed February 2013)

(11)   http://www.fas.org/ota/reports/8727.pdf (accessed February 2013)

(12)   http://www.un-documents.net/wced-ocf.htm (accessed February 2013)

(13)   http://www.un.org/geninfo/bp/enviro.html (accessed February 2013)

(14)   http://www.cbd.int/ (accessed February 2013)

(15)   http://unfccc.int/2860.php (accessed February 2013)

(16)   http://www.unccd.int/en/Pages/default.aspx (accessed March 2013)

(17) http://www.un.org/documents/ga/conf151/aconf15126-1annex1.htm (accessed February 2013)

(18) http://www.unep.org/Documents.Multilingual/Default.asp?documentid=52 (accessed February 2013)

(19) http://www.un.org/documents/ga/conf151/aconf15126-3annex3.htm (accessed February 2013)

(20) http://sustainabledevelopment.un.org/csd.html (accessed February 2013)

(21) http://www.cbd.int/waters/ (accessed February 2013)

(22) http://www.un.org/waterforlifedecade/iwrm.shtml (accessed February 2013)

(23) http://www.unesco.org/new/en/natural-sciences/environment/water/ihp/ (accessed February 2013)

(24) http://www.un.org/esa/earthsummit/ (accessed February 2013)

(25) http://www.mauricestrong.net/images/unreform/N9718979_English.pdf (accessed February 2013)

(26) Watson, R.T., Dixon, J.A., Hamburg, S.P., Janetos, A.C. & Moss, R.H. (eds.) (1998) *Protecting our Planet Securing our Future*. UNEP, NASA, and the World Bank.

(27) http://www.iisd.ca/journal/toepfer.html (accessed February 2013)

(28) http://www.un.org/jsummit/ (accessed February 2013)

(29) SNH and JNCC (2012) *Advice to the Scottish Government on the selection of Nature Conservation Marine Protected Areas (MPAs) for the development of the Scottish MPA network*. Scottish Natural Heritage Commissioned Report No. 547. http://jncc.defra.gov.uk/PDF/SNH%20and%20JNCC%20MPA%20network%20advice%20-%20Final%20report.pdf

(30) JNCC and Natural England (2012) *JNCC and Natural England's advice to Defra on recommended Marine Conservation Zones*. Peterborough and Sheffield. http://jncc.defra.gov.uk/PDF/120718MCZAP_JNCC_NE_MCZ%20advice_final_Executive_Summary.pdf

(31) http://www.unep.org/resources/gov/overview.asp (accessed February 2013)

(32) http://www.unemg.org/ (accessed February 2013)

(33) http://www.unep.org/documents.multilingual/default.asp?DocumentID=43&ArticleID=204&l=en (accessed February 2013)

26. Thoughts towards a philosophy of nature conservation

Derek Ratcliffe

Reprint of Ratcliffe, D.A. (1976) Thoughts towards a philosophy of nature conservation. *Biological Conservation*, **9**, 45-53.

THOUGHTS TOWARDS A PHILOSOPHY OF NATURE CONSERVATION

D. A. RATCLIFFE

Chief Scientist, The Nature Conservancy Council, 19/20 Belgrave Square,
London SW1X 8PY, Great Britain

ABSTRACT

This essay examines some basic issues underlying the philosophy of nature conservation. It distinguishes between economic and cultural reasons for conserving wildlife and its habitat, and deals largely with the latter. Nature conservation reflects and supports a spectrum of public interest ranging from deep science to simple perception, and has a rightful place in education. It is seen as an activity conducive to civilised living, through its ability to give an abiding sense of purpose, and harmony of relationships, both with environment and other people. Concern for wildlife is consistent with concern over the world-wide ills of human society, for it can help to promote a way of life in which there is greater understanding and control over the irrational and animalistic aspects of our existence. For many people it gives the foundation for a much-needed ethic. The question of whether we conserve wildlife and habitat because of its right to existence poses one of the ultimate philosophical problems, and can only be answered in terms of a personal credo.

INTENTIONS

This essay puts together in outline some of the basic issues encountered in an attempt to construct my own *credo* of nature conservation. My aim has been not only to find a rationale which validates nature conservation as an essential human activity, but also to identify fundamental difficulties and dilemmas seeming to lie beyond resolution. Since I work for an official nature conservation organisation, dependent entirely on public funds, my views are related to a sense of the social relevance and accountability of this profession. They are therefore probably not exactly the views which I should have presented had I been writing simply as a

45

Biol. Conserv. (**9**) (1976)—© Applied Science Publishers Ltd, England, 1976
Printed in Great Britain

private individual, operating under no such constraint. Nevertheless, they are personal and not official views, and necessarily offer much scope for debate and even disagreement. None of the thoughts presented is new, taken separately, and some of them have been the subject of whole books; but colleagues have been kind enough to say that they had not previously come across them assembled in the same way, and that they found this construction useful. This has encouraged me to present this essay for reflection and reference by those already versed in the concepts and practice of nature conservation who are, as I am, trying to develop and promote a philosophy of this subject.

THE SEMANTIC PROBLEM

Conservation is well on the way to becoming a meaningless word unless it is qualified. Those of us concerned with wildlife and its habitat are being forced increasingly to specify 'nature' in speaking of conservation, to avoid being misunderstood in the scope of our interest. Conservation as it has been understood and preached in the sense of avoiding the running down of the capital of global resources, has become a personal belief or even a new religion for many. It has spawned a vast literature, varying much in quality, but all with basically the same message—that man will destroy his environment and himself unless the headlong exploitation of natural resources and his own multiplication in numbers are controlled. Any thinking person is concerned about these issues, for upon them hangs the whole question of the fate of mankind. Many of us in the nature conservation field are greatly concerned about the conservation of natural resources and land use in general. We believe that the insights of biology and ecology can contribute much which is beneficial to these matters, in working out a rational policy for resource management. A major problem we thus have to face here is to decide how far our interest and involvement should pass beyond the narrower confines of nature conservation, in the limited sense, into the broader sphere of conservation as it concerns the management of resources in general. This is a matter which concerns our personal philosophies of conservation, and involves a certain range of viewpoint, but I am concerned here to look at the narrower view, and to relate it to the broader one. We can all understand the economic arguments for conservation, and those concerning human material welfare; these are topical issues on which each of us should form his or her own views. However, the field I wish to examine more deeply is that which I regard as the mainstream function in nature conservation, that is, the safeguarding of our flora and fauna (*i.e.* wildlife) with its habitats.

THE SPECTRUM OF HUMAN CONCERN

Why do we want to conserve wildlife? This is the question behind my title. Some of the reasons were presented in the original British Government White Paper, Cmd. 7122, The Conservation of Nature in England and Wales (1947), and para. 50 contains an especially lucid exposition, in spelling out the requirement for a national series of nature reserves representing an adequate range of habitats, communities and species, within which the whole gamut of scientific interest can be explored. But whilst envisaging the need for special safeguards for these most important areas, this document embraced a prospect of nature conservation covering virtually the whole country, and subsequent practice has worked towards a national approach going far beyond a series of nature reserves. The underlying purposes of nature conservation spelt out in 1947, and remaining unchanged, may be grouped into economic and cultural (educational, scientific and aesthetic/amenity).

These are inter-related aspects, and the separation is to some extent artificial. Education and research in relation to wildlife may have economic benefits as in the better management of certain species of commercial value and this may also be true of aesthetics, for example, if one reflects on the numbers of binoculars, telescopes and cameras sold to naturalists. Similarly, education can include research and research can have aesthetic rewards. The contribution of nature conservation to economics lies especially in the field of land use studies and management of wild species of importance as a crop, e.g. red deer, grouse and salmon. I think most of us would, however, agree that economic ends are not the primary aim of nature conservation. It is not these which I wish to discuss, but the range of human concern which for the want of a better term can be regarded as cultural, and is to do with matters of the senses and the spirit, as much as with the intellect.

From the education angle, either the subject of nature conservation is an end in itself, which becomes supported by this process of learning, or it is a means to some other end, served by increased knowledge of the natural world. The contribution of ecology to a liberal education is increasingly accepted, and even to people who remain unresponsive to the attractions of nature for its own sake, an understanding of natural processes and phenomena may have gains in making them more know-ledgeable and useful members of society. And what of science? The concept carries within itself the notion of advancement of knowledge, though there is a certain tendency to focus on the methods and processes which again constitute the means. But the real meaning and validity of science must lie in its ends. Science contributes to human progress, and has brought enormous benefits to the lot of mankind though it has also created its burdens and dilemmas. Beyond material and medical advancement, science has brought understanding and enlightenment, and has helped to increase happiness through improved relationships, of people to each other, as well as to their environment otherwise. There is now, however, concern that the technology of science is advancing much faster than ethical and spiritual development, so that human progress is one-sided and unsatisfactory. This idea of cultural evolution perhaps helps to identify where the ultimate value of science belongs, in that it provides intellectual challenge and reward, and continually expands our perception and comprehension of our universe and its mysteries, giving a sense of purpose and achievement to life. Scientists derive great intellectual satisfaction from their work, and it is often a large part of their whole life—even a substitute religion, again, though few recognise it in such terms, for above all, scientists prize objectivity and are mostly resistant to the thought that their emotions could influence their work. The Antarctic traveller, Cherry-Garrard, said: 'Exploration is the physical expression of the intellectual passion', and his words seem admirably to sum up the motivation of science.

After the scientists are the many people with simpler interests, who find enjoyment in the countryside and its wildlife. They range from those who like seeing attractive animals and flowers, to dedicated amateur naturalists who virtually live for their spare time interests, and who often make their own significant contribution to science as well as the professionals. This body of amateurs is a growing proportion of the population, and represents an interest which is mainly recreational and aesthetic, though these are feeble words to describe the enthusiasms of the real devotees. It is the professional nature conservationist's job to support this wide spread of cultural concern, but the problem is to strike the right balance in the face of competing claims. The first responsibility is surely to the interested public, and this accountability should, in my view, influence the distribution of effort within the total spectrum of functions and responsibilities. This is tricky ground philosophically. I do not necessarily believe in the greatest good of the greatest number, yet heed must be paid to the fact that within the ranks of the total public, professional and amateur, those with simpler tastes preponderate. There are more people who find pleasure in looking at primroses or listening to bird song than in counting chromosomes or pollen grains. Is there not therefore justification in weighting efforts in their direction? The weight of public interest does influence the biasses of professional effort—look at the prominence given to birds and wildfowl particularly, and the neglect of nearly all the major groups of invertebrates except butterflies and moths. Our actual attitudes to conservation of these groups are influenced by these differences in popularity—witness the inconsistent views on the ethics of collecting them.

There is nevertheless a feeling, by some at least, that real science and 'high-powered' research are more respectable and present more cogent claims for support —even though they are the esoteric province of a minority group. It is, unfortunately, true that the professional and amateur natural historians often have a low regard for each other and their interests, and the community at large contains many groups who are disinterested or even antagonistic to nature conservation. Obviously, nature conservation has to support all sectors of public interest, and preferably in such a way as to produce the greatest contribution all round. Moreover, when one looks at them closely, what is the real nature of the difference between the simple pleasure felt by the field naturalist and the intellectual rewards gained by the pollen analyst. Beauty is in the eye of the beholder.

THE NEED FOR A SENSE OF PURPOSE

I have pointed out that both the field naturalist and the scientist (some people, I know, are both) are ultimately concerned with aesthetics, so they may not be so very different. One may argue that the second is advancing knowledge in depth and that this is an activity on a higher plane than the mere perception of pleasing stimuli. But this involves setting one person's view of basic issues against another's and asserting that one is more valid or important. We come sooner or later to the more fundamental question of what we live for—and this involves us in one of the ultimate philosophical problems. We are here dealing with personal belief—a subject which has kept people arguing for thousands of years without getting very far. Let us say that most intelligent people have a very deep need for a sense of purpose in life. The revealed religions supplied this need but we have to accept that their power is declining, at least in Western society. Many scientists adhere to a Huxleyan view of progress as the continuing evolution of the human mind—its power and capacity—and this is often combined with some Utopian view, in the sense of a better existence for mankind. But what is the better existence—and if when we have ironed out the practical difficulties of living and the problems of society, what then is our purpose? Unless we are to postulate unknown realms of experience ahead, we must recognise that meaning and purpose must be identifiable within the lives of people living and experiencing here and now, not deferred to individuals as yet unborn or to a state that might be at some time in the future. This being so, is it valid to claim or imply that one person's sense of purpose and experience is more worthy or important than another's? I think not, but will leave the question to be pondered; which comes back to the bird watcher and the pollen analyst.

People seek their own satisfaction in life, but a growing problem is that as affluence and leisure increase, and the difficulty of actually making a living declines, an increasing number of people appear to have little left to live for, and do not know how to fill their lives. Psychiatrists have to deal increasingly with this problem of the 'existential vacuum'. Many people have found that the world of natural history can provide an abiding sense of purpose from the infinity of experience and interest which it offers. This does not mean that it provides of itself a solution to the meaning of life in an intellectual sense, but that its endless variety absorbs the mental energy and at some deeper level conveys an inner satisfaction, perhaps connected in part with a primitive sense of relationship with wilderness. It is one way, among others, of enriching the mental life to the point where the question of meaning does not intrude, because existence is too full and absorbing. In this sense, nature conservation may play its most important role, of promoting the greater happiness of mankind. Practising conservationists help in this by providing or maintaining the medium wherein people can develop and pursue their interests, be these large or small, trivial or profound. Their effectiveness in fulfilling this role is judged first in terms of success in maintaining the national capital of wildlife and habitat, to be studied and enjoyed at whatever level is desired. They also promote this use of the resource by guiding latent interest which may need only a little fertilisation. I do not mean that everyone should be turned into scientists, but simply shown the way to an appreciation of the world of nature, so that they can find their own level. To me, it seems entirely correct for the professional conservationists to act as leaders in public taste here, for this is expressing the courage of their convictions. So I hope no one would disagree that one of the most important tasks is to promote the growth of the nature-minded public, through educational work in nature conservation and natural history. For the larger our public following, the more power to our elbow. And if some still protest that it is wrong to mould public opinion in this way, I point out that there is more than a fair share of propaganda and seduction in the reverse direction. The public themselves will be the best judge of our actions, for confidence tricks do not usually fool people for long.

MAN, THE DOMINANT ANIMAL, AND HIS RELATIONS WITH NATURE

Some of the impatience and antagonism which many people feel towards the nature conservation movement stems from the sense that the interest of wildlife is being put before that of human beings. The DDT issue has been sharply defined in these terms by some and it then becomes easy to argue that a cranky minority is promoting measures which amplify the problems of feeding undernourished millions and saving them from disease. Is there not also something incongruous and unbalanced in an excessive concern for wildlife, when so much is wrong with mankind? Whether it is the hideous degradation of outright war, the plight of the Third World or the socio-economic ills of the so-called advanced nations, there seem to be so many more desperate problems around the world. Preoccupation with the future of animals and plants can seem quite trivial by comparison, if it cannot be related in some way to urgent human needs.

All this, however, really involves too simplistic a view. Any reduction in the misfortunes of mankind can only be, at best, a slow process, and much will depend on large-scale changes in attitudes of mind. I believe it was Aldous Huxley who saw the advancement of mankind as 'getting rid of the animal in us'. This seems very apposite. Selfishness, aggression, territorialism and the urge to fecundity are tools forged on the anvil of natural selection, and have made *Homo sapiens* what he is. But does he need them any longer? Would not the world be a better place if they could be sublimated or at least controlled, and their place taken by rational thought? An ecologist can see the global problems as a complex whole, an interaction of many factors, in which none can be looked at entirely on its own. He is familiar with the dependence of an animal population on the balance between birthrate and deathrate, as influenced by disease, food supply, predation, intra-specific strife, stress and homeostatic mechanisms. The human situation is analogous, but the inexorable laws which regulate animal populations cause untold misery and suffering when they work on *Homo sapiens*.

It seems to me that unless more people can understand and accept that resources are limited and that unfettered instinctual drives do not promote civilised living, there is little hope of an appreciable improvement in the overall human condition. The world of Nature can show us the problems, and what our lot will be if we do not learn the lessons and find our own solutions. We have conquered this world, but if we could give up our attempts to vanquish it completely, and learn to treat its remnants with respect, or preferably affection, there would be a sign that we have begun to come to terms with ourselves. When we can give up our attempts to exploit still further our dwindling capital of wildlife and its habitat, and learn to cherish it instead, it will mean that we have begun to transcend our instincts, and to justify our scientific name.

The role of flowers in human affairs gives hope. A lot of land, effort and money goes to the cultivation and distribution of flowers, whose value is largely non-material and often quite ephemeral. Flowers represent both spiritual values, through their symbolic power, and aesthetic values, through their intrinsic beauty. The remarkable thing is that this goes unquestioned and, except under the direst circumstances, is an accepted part of human life. During the last war, many flower gardens in Britain were converted to vegetable plots, but soon reverted again when the pressing need had passed. So that here is a considerable use of natural resources devoted simply to the feeding of the mind. And if cultivated plants can be invested so universally with such deep value, why not wild plants—and wild animals? It is surely only one step further to extend this sense of immaterial value to wildlife in general, as part of the cherished inheritance of a civilised society, held in trusteeship by one generation for those to come.

It will be clear that I have been talking about nature conservation as an exercise in human benefit in some form. The final question is whether or not we also conserve nature for its own sake. Those who affirm this view believe that wildlife has a right to exist and that we should act accordingly. This view is philosophically impregnable, involving a personal view of fundamental issues which an individual is entitled to hold. I respect it as such (and almost certainly in fact subscribe to it at an irrational level) but do not myself believe in it as a rational tenet with which to argue the case for nature conservation, especially against the hard-headed materialists who often form the opposing side. It tends to be applied rather more strongly to animals than plants (and especially higher animals) which suggests that anthropomorphism, with its projections and identifications, is involved, at least in some degree. Even my private inclination to champion this ethic has become tempered by my inability to find any supporting pointers in the natural world itself, outside human attitudes about it. For the unmistakable message of evolution is, surely, that no creature has a right to exist, either as an individual or a species. Some people believe that maintaining the diversity of the world ecosystem is the ultimate goal of nature conservation. This is perhaps only a more sophisticated variation on the previous theme, for it again leads to the question of whether the world eco-system has some mystical value in its own right, or whether its value lies in its use to man.

I will confess to a certain ambivalence and doubt in my own mind on this issue, which seems to me perhaps the most difficult of all in the philosophy of nature conservation. But one can, from the human purpose angle, still wish to preserve wildlife and wilderness just as fervently as those who take the non-Darwinian view of rights to existence. I would do so acknowledging that this is because I and others enjoy these things and that they have become part of our way of life. They are an essential part of our total environment, spiritual and material, and to many people have become virtually a psychological necessity. We wish to preserve them because we have transcended the animals and plants themselves, and bestow our feelings upon them. It is easy to be misunderstood in talking about this, and I am of course discussing abstract rationalisations which are remote from the feelings we experience about these things. But I think it important to be aware of hidden attitudes here, for they influence the way we react to certain situations, particularly when faced with decisions about which comes first, wildlife or human beings. A great many people have a tacit belief that animals have a right to exist, and it is as well to realise this, since it may affect the level of discussion. This is not the same as, though it merges with, the humane view of animal welfare, in the situations where animals are made to serve the needs of mankind. Both views are the expression of a *credo* which embraces, in Schweitzer's phrase, 'a reverence for life'.

A FINAL REFLECTION

Some may in fact wonder what is the point of looking into the philosophy of nature conservation at all. We all know more or less what has to be done in our work, so why not get on with it, and leave the airy-fairy ideas, which are meaningless to most people anyway. It does seem to me, however, that unless the practitioners in nature conservation understand why they practise this art—for it is an art as well as a science—they have no rational basis for their views and actions. And in this field it is vital to be seen to have the courage of one's convictions. For the nature conserva-tionist often has to argue his cause and engage in dialectical exchanges with highly intelligent people. It is then as well to be aware of the underlying philosophical issues, even if they can be glossed over or forgotten for most of the time. And I do believe that any person should enquire as deeply as they can into what they do and why they do it—not to let it become an obsession, obviously, but in a genuine spirit of scientific enquiry.

Yet, when all is said and done, this analysis of motives and attitudes has a kind of aridity, for nature conservation and its meaning penetrates far beyond the rational and conscious into the emotional and unconscious. It touches the roots of human nature and is ultimately to do with being and feeling. To go further in understanding is a metaphysical problem, and we can only attempt to appreciate what it means for each of us personally. The magic of the natural world beckons and challenges, and lures the receptive soul ever onwards but, like the Holy Grail, it is never finally found and possessed. And this is its fascination.

THE COMMUNICATOR –

landscape art and correspondence

27. Derek And I: A correspondence

Peter Marren

One of the peculiar pleasures of writing is that you can form friendships based almost entirely on correspondence. The medium of letters is as strong and binding as talk and it has the obvious advantage of being more lasting. As others in this volume have pointed out, Derek Ratcliffe was a great letter writer (Fig. 27.1). At formal meetings he often said the bare minimum, but in letters the true Derek appears, by turns passionate, wry, critical, and wise, often full of wicked gossip, sometimes scornful and angry, and nearly always generous and great-hearted. I was not fortunate enough to spend much time with him in the field, not that I could have kept up in any case. Derek had terrific stamina both as a walker and a writer. Once he sent me a five-page, hand-written letter after walking all day on the fell, and it was probably not the only one he completed that night.

Although I knew him on and off for twenty years, it was only after Derek retired as Chief Scientist of the Nature Conservancy Council (NCC) in 1989 that we started to correspond regularly. He appreciated being kept in touch with the exciting events of that time when the NCC was being broken up into three fractious 'country agencies'. He enjoyed corresponding with people with whom he saw eye-to-eye, without regard to rank or station. Over the next dozen years we kept in fairly constant touch, mainly about books that he or I were writing. In telling the story of our literary friendship here, in which I quote extensively from his letters, I hope any reader who may not have known him will receive a sense of what Derek Ratcliffe was like, and why he was revered.

I first met him in 1972 when he came to deliver a lecture to the MSc Conservation Course at University College London, where I was a student. Actually 'met' is probably the wrong word. In conservation circles Derek was already a star. Everyone on the course knew who he was and what he did. We had recently spent a week at Monks Wood where we were given a crash course in pesticides research, including Derek's immortal work on the Peregrine (*Falco peregrinus*). In addition I had written an essay about Upper

Teesdale and the part played by Derek in the doomed struggle to prevent the area from being drowned by a reservoir. He was a biological celebrity, and we were prepared to treat him as such. Yet his lecture, about the still unpublished Nature Conservation Review, lacked the starry glitter we expected. He talked in a monotone and patiently answered the deliberately provocative questions from our more histrionic students. I think he arrived and left wearing his trademark green beret. To be honest, I remember being a bit disappointed.

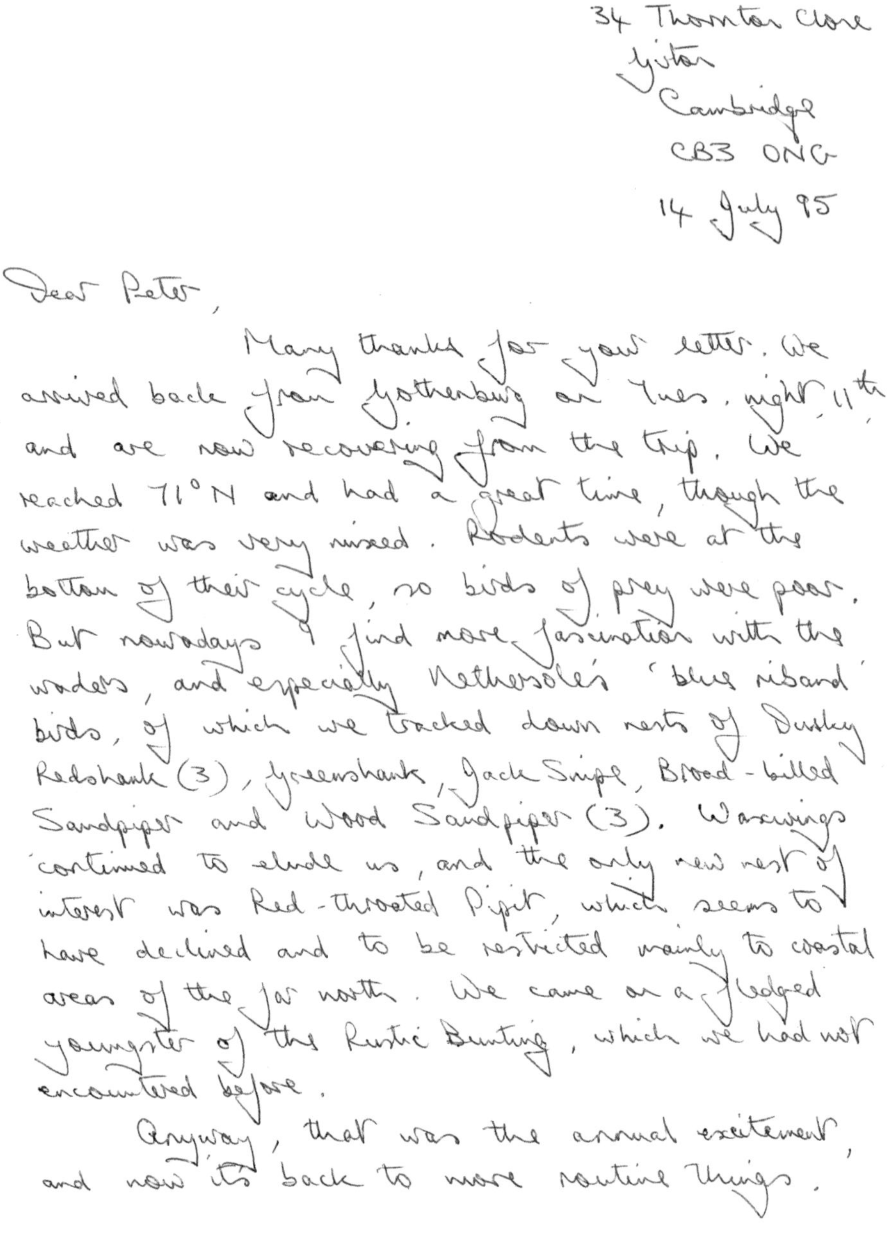

34 Thornton Close
Girton
Cambridge
CB3 0NG

14 July 95

Dear Peter,

Many thanks for your letter. We arrived back from Gothenburg on Tues. night 11th and are now recovering from the trip. We reached 71°N and had a great time, though the weather was very mixed. Rodents were at the bottom of their cycle, so birds of prey were poor. But nowadays I find more fascination with the waders, and especially Nethersole's 'blue riband' birds, of which we tracked down nests of Dusky Redshank (3), Greenshank, Jack Snipe, Broad-billed Sandpiper and Wood Sandpiper (3). Waxwings continued to elude us, and the only new nest of interest was Red-throated Pipit, which seems to have declined and to be restricted mainly to coastal areas of the far north. We came on a fledged youngster of the Rustic Bunting, which we had not encountered before.

Anyway, that was the annual excitement, and now it's back to more routine things.

Figure 27.1. A hand-written letter from Derek Ratcliffe to Peter Marren written on 14 July 1995 outlining recent nest finds by Jeannette Ratcliffe and Derek from their Lapland trip.

After that I do not remember our paths crossing again until one spring day about ten years later when he visited the Muir of Dinnet, a National Nature Reserve, in northeast Scotland. By that time I was the local man in the NCC, known as an ARO or Assistant Regional Officer and so a rather distant colleague of Derek's. The Muir of Dinnet was privately owned, and, although it was a nature reserve, the laird could still do more or less what he liked with it. Ingeniously we had agreed to divide the reserve into 'land-use zones'. The forest zone was where the laird wished to plant trees, the grazing zone where he pastured his cows, and the Strict Conservation zone the bit where he had no current plans. Derek's visit coincided with a new drain snaking through part of the Strict Reserve Zone. I remember being slightly surprised, and shamed, by Derek's reaction: "This sort of thing shouldn't happen on a National Nature Reserve". Of course he was right. We had become so used to sucking up to landowners on pragmatic grounds that we were in danger of losing our grip on what might be called ecological reality. To rub in the point, Derek spotted a Greenshank (*Tringa nebularia*) fly up from the heath. It was, as far as I remember, the only Greenshank I saw there in seven years.

In 1984 the NCC published a document called *Nature Conservation in Great Britain* (NCGB)[1]. It weighed the pros and cons of forty years of nature conservation, revealed the losses of natural habitats, and asserted with a new boldness that nature is, or should be, of concern to everyone and not just scientists and landowners. Conservationists, it proclaimed, must have the courage of their convictions. This was quite a radical message for a government body at that time, at the start of Margaret Thatcher's second term. It was out of kilter with what the civil service called the 'current thinking'. The author of NCGB was, of course, Derek Ratcliffe. No one else would have said it in quite that way.

For my own part, I felt a bit out of kilter with NCGB. It was convincing in its diagnosis and praiseworthy in its outspokenness but I thought the style was too stodgy for the document to have much chance of being read widely. Puffed up with self-importance as the NCC's new 'author-editor', and no doubt wanting to draw attention to myself, I wrote a longish circular about the inherent conflict between the NCC's public image and its message. In the course of it I criticised the NCGB for its want of verbal felicity. I sent a copy to Derek, who, as I say, I hardly knew.

Probably anyone else would have dropped the thing in the bin and sent a note of rebuke to my line manager. Instead, Derek sent me a three-page, closely typed and very well-argued personal letter. Here is part of what he had to say:

> "…it is most desirable that an organization should, from time to time, stand back and take a hard, honest look at itself. And no individual should feel themselves exempt from this scrutiny, not withstanding that it may not be particularly pleasant. But the main point of such criticism is to use the greater self-awareness to find ways to improvement in the shortcomings. This is where your essay seems to me to lack balance: it is long on description of the symptoms and short on diagnosis of fundamental causes and what to do about them. In the last para you say that you do not attempt an answer – perhaps you do not want to say more or perhaps you don't know."

In its honesty, frankness, and intelligence, this seems to me to be quintessential Derek – as was his willingness to debate on equal terms with an underling. He was critical of my piece, rightly drawing attention to its naivety and lack of anything positive to say, "although it will no doubt delight iconoclasts". But beyond that I felt I had made a friend, someone else bored and frustrated by faint-heart bureaucratic obstruction, and one who encouraged attempts at original thought even if, as in this case, they might not be all that well thought out.

In the same letter, Derek was blunt and unsparing about the failings of his own organization: "You rightly identify the civil service influence as one of the main factors in our often feeble stance, and the conflicting messages that come from above. But there is more to it than that and I think the key can be found in comparing ourselves collectively, and through the role of individuals, with the Ministry of Agriculture, Fisheries and Food (MAFF), Department of Agriculture and Fisheries (Scotland) (DAFS) or the Forestry Commission (FC). They too are civil servants – still more so – but almost to the last man they pursue the interests of their departments with an almost messianic zeal. Why the difference? Quite simply, the NCC, and the Nature Conservancy (NC) before it, has always had a monumental inferiority complex about itself and its worth to society. We behave as though we accept without question that our rightful place is at the bottom of the peck order, and the result is that we are pecked hard by everybody else to keep us right down there." "What this outfit [the NCC] needs", he concluded, "is decisions and actions, preferably fast. I see the closest analogy to nature conservation, albeit an unpleasant one, with warfare. The similarities are various, but one is that if you hesitate too long the enemy are pouring over the top, and you've had it."

I think Derek found it easier to marshal his thoughts on paper. Not that he was exactly a slouch in debate. I did not witness the battles he had with his fellow directors in the 1980s over the Flow Country of Caithness and Sutherland[2], Creag Meagaidh[3], and other places threatened with blanket afforestation. But I did once see him stand up to the angry, spluttering MP for Caithness, an action which took some courage, and answer him point by point, quietly and politely, but with unanswerable logic. He knew the subject inside out, and it gave him a confidence that belied his personal diffidence.

Derek hated the sort of me-first, materialistic society that the Thatcher Government was building. He saw the Tories as the friend of the landowners, farmers, and foresters who at that time seemed to be doing their best to destroy Britain's natural places and using public money to do it. He believed that Mrs Thatcher had eroded the idea of public service and the sanctity of knowledge to create "a new age of Philistinism". Though he doubted Labour's commitment to rural affairs, he clung to a belief that nature conservation was more easily achieved in a climate "of planning and regulation, modest state ownership of land and resources, and a belief in social justice". He once told me he had never been to an agricultural show in his life: "In the NCC it always seemed *de rigueur* to regard them as occasions to go and suck up to the farmers". Derek was not a great advocate of the arts of sucking up. Personally I did not share all of Derek's social diagnosis. I think there is much to be said in favour of private property and the freedom of choice. But from the perspective of nature conservation, the 1970s and 1980s had been, you had to admit, a pretty rubbish time. It was only later that conservation and sustainability became politically respectable. In the days when Derek was Chief Scientist nature conservation was a real struggle[2,4].

The New Naturalists

It was a long-standing ambition of mine to write a history of the New Naturalist library[5], the famous cutting-edge books published by Collins. The series, now nearly seventy years old, represented a British tradition of natural history that seemed then to be in decline. The advances of ecology, evolutionary biology, and animal behaviour provided field study with new insights, and should have invigorated natural history. Derek's own work was a living illustration of the advantages of the fusion of field observation and analytical science. But it did not seem to work out like that. For most people natural history had dwindled into recording and twitching. When I was writing the book, back in 1994, the post-war vision of nature and its conservation looked like a golden age. I wanted to write a book about it using the books themselves as the anchor. My idea was to forge a historical narrative from a fusion of bibliography, biography, and science. In this, Derek was a kind of mentor for we had talked about the New Naturalist series at length while walking over the ruined moonscape of Thorne Moors in 1992, and in the bar afterwards. While the milling machines turned the living peat into compost, we sat on a pile of cut turfs and reminisced about the founding fathers of nature conservation.

Derek had met many of the first generation of New Naturalists authors, who were also among the leading lights of the early days of nature conservation in Britain. He shared the same childhood stamping grounds near Carlisle as the author of the first book, E.B. Ford of *Butterflies*[6]. And he had met Professor Ford across an interview table "where he fixed me with a penetrating stare and fired staccato questions". A chilly encounter, then, and the picture of the smiling Ford in my book "was undoubtedly more benign than the figure I remember". As for W.H. Pearsall, though Derek regarded *Mountains and Moorlands*[7], or at least the botanical part of it, "as a sort of Bible", he was less starry-eyed about its author. He never forgave Pearsall for trying to get the floristic tables removed from the monograph on Scottish vegetation, which Derek had written with Donald McVean[8,9]. "Pearsall was not the least interested in vegetation classification," he recalled with a touch of bitterness. "He was originally a chemist and his interest was largely in processes". He was also a keen train-spotter, which seemed a bit suspicious. I think Derek saw in Pearsall the epitome of academic pretentiousness that he always found annoying. "Part of his appeal to his acolytes was his 'lifemanship' style. He had a great capacity for making *ex cathedra* pronouncements and making other people into supplicants for knowledge at the feet of the master. I once heard him, in an NCC group discussion, talk to Vero Wynne-Edwards as though he was a first-year student! He was said to come out with outrageous statements to see the effect they had on listeners, but I am sure he came to believe some of his more fanciful ideas." This sort of thing is honey for a writer although not all of Derek's remarks are as printable.

He reserved his greatest admiration for field men, among whom Ernest Blezard (Fig. 1.9), natural history curator at Tullie House Museum in Carlisle and Derek's close friend and mentor[10,11], was the first. Blezard was to have edited the New Naturalist book on the Lake District from a small team of authors but it was never completed, a common fate of multiple-authored books (the photographs taken for it by J.A. Jenson, said Derek, were "breathtakingly good"). Though Blezard was ready to write the whole book himself, the contract was offered to Pearsall instead. This was probably a mistake.

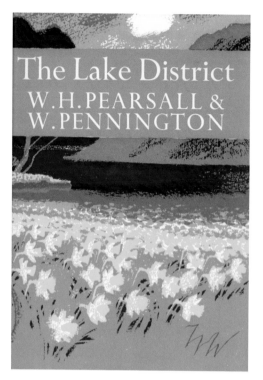

Figure 27.2. W.H. Pearsall and W. Pennington (1973) *The Lake District*, in the New Naturalist series, a book that Derek Ratcliffe wrote two sections of and regarded as a very good book.

When Pearsall died in 1964, it was found that he had burned the manuscript, presumably feeling that it was not among his best work. The eventual book was 'completed' (Fig. 27.2), that is to say rewritten practically from scratch, by Winifred Pennington (Tutin)[12]. Derek considered she did a very good job, certainly "far more erudite than the Carlisle team could have produced" though "Ernest Blezard would have written in a livelier way about the wildlife".

Derek urged me to include something about another scientist he admired, Gordon Manley, whose dedication to meteorology was such that he used to hole up inside a wooden hut on the top of Great Dun Fell during winter gales and blizzards. Derek admired that kind of thing[9,11,13]. Manley "seemed an admirable character who believed in contact with his subject", and his book, *Climate and the British Scene*[14], "was very helpful when I was a research student and trying to relate vegetation to climate" (Fig. 27.3).

Of all the New Naturalist authors, his greatest friend was probably Desmond Nethersole-Thompson (Fig. 11.21). I wish I could find the notes I made as Derek recalled with such obvious pleasure the days those two had spent in the field tracking down the nests of waders and raptors. Nethersole-Thompson, a natural rebel, a blunt, courageous and sometimes outrageous man, was a rich source of anecdote. When you heard Derek talking about an old friend like this you realised what a terrific raconteur he was. Derek had an unusually precise memory (as any reader of his memoir *In Search of Nature*[10] will know). He was also a good mimic, especially of regional accents. He admired naturalists like Nethersole-Thompson for their extraordinary field skills and their intimate knowledge. I think he also admired his rugged integrity and scorn of any 'side'. They must have appeared an odd couple, the one neat and slight, the other bearded and baggy, as they tramped the moors, but they were birds of a feather. The relationship was an important one for the history of ornithology, for it was Nethersole-Thompson who first suggested that Derek should look at egg collections for evidence of shell-thinning in Peregrines[15]. It is fitting that this memoir should be co-edited by Des the Second, who, like his father before him, became one of Derek's closest friends and soulmates.

As E.B. Ford (a great hater) used to say, "You can't like everyone". Derek strongly disliked people that, in his view, had sold nature short by one of their drivelling compromises, or puffed themselves up far beyond their abilities. After he retired, Derek's annual expeditions to Fennoscandia with Jeannette gave him a happy excuse for not attending meetings of the '49 Club, where (mostly) retired NCC folk meet in unspoiled nooks of the country to recall the old days. "I would find [the meetings] somewhat daunting, especially as I believe they attract a few people who I would be happier never to see again". I never discovered who he meant though I could hazard a guess.

Derek Ratcliffe joined the New Naturalist editorial board in 1993. This was a lucky break for me as it brought Derek into discussions about a special volume to celebrate the half-centenary of the series in 1995. The proposal had been on the table for some time, Derek told me. "It seems there was some notion (not previously put to me) that I might be persuaded to do it. They had been dithering mightily over the volume, in view of the proposed timetable, and it has now assumed some urgency. I proposed a synopsis to keep them quiet and try to stimulate some action…I declined [to write it] for various

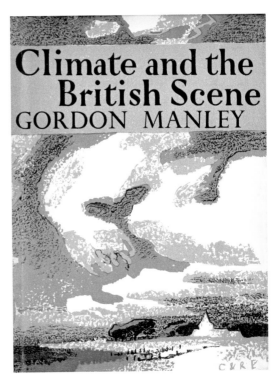

Figure 27.3. Gordon Manley (1952) *Climate and the British Scene*, in the New Naturalist series, a book that Derek Ratcliffe greatly valued and admired.

reasons – not least commitments to other writings – but said I knew just the person for the job! Of course you should write the book according to your own inclinations." He added some good and perceptive advice about Collins as publishers which I will not repeat here.

This was generous of him, and of course it offered an unexpected opportunity to write about the series as I wished. Derek, not unnaturally, became my editor; I should perhaps explain that in an arrangement unique in the publishing world, the New Naturalists are vetted by one of a board of five scientific editors who are expected to offer encouragement and advice as required, as well as to commission new titles. The book went swimmingly well and I like to think that, having picked his brains about the basic structure, and his memory of every New Naturalist author he had met, Derek was left with very little to do except read the text with due appreciation and murmur occasional advice. Yet one of the joys of working with him was the flow of hand-written letters that arrived by return of post and were invariably full of goodies. Here are just a few of the shrewd, sharp and amusing anecdotes he sent me.

> "Going back to the recent trend in ecology and the FRS thing, it is noteworthy that some of those now regarded as the great pundits, and who tend to be modellers, theoreticians and population dynamics types (e.g. Maynard Smith, Robert May, John Harper), have not appeared in the NN [New Naturalist series]. The modern scientists are personified by

Ian Newton and Sam Berry who are still able to communicate with the hoi polloi."

"F.F.D. [Frank Fraser Darling] also took refuge in the Home Counties where he lived in a minor mansion house and drove around in a vintage Bentley (or Rolls Royce): so I understand. D.N-T [Desmond Nethersole-Thompson] used to snort that his flat feet got him out of military service…. Somewhere in the second edition of *The Highlands and Islands*[16] is a reference by F.F.D. to himself as 'the senior author' which, I think, says something about Darling."

"[Kenneth] Mellanby jumped at the opportunity to write [*Pesticides and Pollution*[17]] but rode on the backs of Norman [Moore] and his Toxic Chemicals team in using their information and expertise. K.M. was a great sitter-on-the-fence on some important issues and cleverly played to the agro-chemical establishment in what he wrote. He claimed later to have been one of the first to warn of the danger of global warming through CO_2 output. But [in the book] he says: 'On the other hand this may be a completely false alarm'! I think it is a very sketchy and inadequate book in some ways."

Derek was probably the busiest New Naturalist editor. In addition to my two, he was saddled with *Ireland*[18], one of the longest titles in the series, as well as *Loch Lomondside*[19] by his old friend John Mitchell[13], and several other books. He also, of course, wrote two of the books himself, both on the upland landscapes he most enjoyed, *Lakeland*[20], his tribute to the land of his youth[11], and *Galloway and the Borders*[21], which he finished shortly before his sudden death, and, published posthumously, included a short tribute to Derek by Des Thompson (Fig. 27.4).

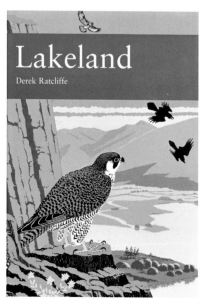
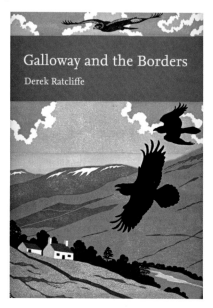

Figure 27.4. *Lakeland* (2002) and *Galloway and the Borders* (2007), Derek Ratcliffe's two books in the New Naturalist series.

Writing about Nature Conservation

After *The New Naturalists*[5] Derek and I showed one another bits of various books and reports we were doing, and talked about publishers, although he was more use to me than I should think I was to him. He brought quite a lot to *Britain's Rare Flowers*[22], especially his unrivalled knowledge of rare mountain plants and ferns. I wish now I had made more of Derek's lifelong quest for the Killarney Fern (*Trichomanes speciosum*)[9,10]. He liked to do these things thoroughly and, perhaps with the possible exception of Fred Rumsey at the Natural History Museum, had probably explored along with his friends John and Hilary Birks[9,23] more caves, chasms, and waterfalls looking for this most elusive and beautiful of ferns than anyone else. He once treated me to a slide display of Killarney Fern, telling me how he had photographed the same plant twenty years apart and found that nothing had changed: it could have been the same photograph: "It just sits there." Killarney Fern travels in one of life's very slow lanes, but there is something romantic about Derek's passion that would make a wonderful botanical short story, if there was such a thing[9].

He was also writing his memoir, *In Search of Nature*[10], about his days in the hills. I had little to do with that except to write a couple of reviews when it came out. I wrote congratulating him on having kept all his field notebooks. "Actually", he replied, "I wrote most of it out of my head, and had only occasionally to refer to notebooks. I have an extremely clear memory of much of my earlier years in the field, perhaps because they gave me so much pleasure. I used to day-dream about them during boring committee meetings when the talk seemed so far from reality. I could see the places and wildlife quite vividly, but realized most of the others were discussing complete abstractions. Anyway, I hope like-minded people will enjoy the book, and am glad to have done it." It is possible that a book of mine might have influenced his choice of publisher. Jim Whitaker of the appropriately named Peregrine Books had recently published my little book about the Observer's Books[24]. He made a decent job of it and the relationship had been a happy one. Possibly Derek was attracted by the word Peregrine, though he was not, in general, a superstitious man.

With the events of the 1980s, and the dismemberment of the NCC in particular, fresh in his mind[25], Derek had also written a long account of the agonies of trying to conserve nature in a system seemingly dedicated to its destruction. I read the entire manuscript in an early draft. It was, I recall, a rather bitter, polemical book, rigorous and damning in its analysis but requiring stamina to read through. It might have swung along better if Derek had pointed the finger at influential people rather than policies and institutions, but he was ever fearful about libelling anyone (and he might also have had a Bennite thing about "polishies, not pershonalities"). So, apart from bashing a few out-and-out enemies like Nicholas Ridley, he stuck to issues and processes. Even so, he was anxious about its harsh tone and "prolixity". The text was no tougher to read than the average issue of *Ecos*, but such things date quickly and sell poorly. Sadly no publisher was prepared to lose money over it and it remains an unpublished manuscript.

Writing about nature conservation in practice is curiously dispiriting. Derek mentioned how much he looked forward to his annual trips to the frozen north of Lapland[26] – "probably they are a form of escapism, when I leave the awful problems of UK conservation behind, as well as the gruesome events of the world in general, and return to some straightforward field natural history." Perhaps we all need escape mechanisms of some kind. I try not to take anything too seriously. Others take to golf or spend their weekends grimly polishing the car.

Derek proved a true friend once again after I embarked on an ill-advised project to pick holes in my former employer, English Nature (EN), on behalf of the World Wide Fund for Nature (WWF). This forgotten episode was a minor civil war which broke out after EN had refused to designate Orton Brick Pits as an SSSI, although they qualified on the grounds of being full of Crested Newts (*Triturus cristatus*)[27]. At the time there were anxieties about English Nature's performance as a public watchdog, and rumours that at least some of the National Nature Reserves (NNRs) were about to be privatised. In NCGB, Derek had pointed to the NNRs as the one tangible achievement in thirty years of official nature conservation. I found the business of ratting on my former colleagues strangely embittering as I worked myself up into a boiling hatred of the betrayals and compromises of recent years. Unfortunately most of my rhetorical flourishes were jettisoned by WWF, who published it anonymously, as though I was running scared. Still, we did get a Parliamentary enquiry out of it.

In the circumstances, Derek's letter of support was something I clung to with tears in my eyes. He probably did not agree with everything I said but he supported the principle of a top-level inquiry into recent goings-on, and even wrote to the minister to say so. Whether or not by coincidence both of us were invited at around this time to put our names forward for vacancies on English Nature's Council. And both our applications were summarily rejected without an interview. It may have been that we failed to qualify for a post needing "five years of relevant expertise, two of which should be in farming, landowning or forestry." In my case the whole affair could have been treated as a joke, but Derek regretted that he had given them "the chance of dishing me out a snub". "So there it is" he remarked, "confirmation of *persona non grata* status. It leaves me still less inclined to maintain silence about EN…"

In terms of the sheer weight of correspondence, the most significant of my collaborations with Derek was my second New Naturalist, *Nature Conservation*[3], for which he was once again editor and *confidante*. It may be thought that I was an odd choice for author, but I knew a lot about it and the publishers and editorial board had confidence in me. Senior conservation bureaucrats were two a penny but many of them were very busy, and some found it difficult to use words that everyone can understand. However the financial incentives for writing a New Naturalist were so feeble that even I turned it down at first. Later I convinced myself that such a book might sell reasonably well and that HarperCollins would then reprint huge quantities of the paperback edition and make me rich. Derek was encouraging: "I am sure the NN Board would jump at any offer by you to do a conservation number. The title lies in the perspective list at each meeting, but no one has any suggestions on it – probably there is still a vague hope you may be tempted…" Modesty forbids the rest of the quotation,

Derek had decided ideas about how to write the book that went beyond an editor's normal role. "I hope that somewhere near the beginning you will say what it was all supposed to be for", he wrote earnestly. "Somewhere, I hope you will try to assess what it all achieved. This seems to me the thing that is sadly lacking from all the other writings on nature conservation." He thought most writers on this subject had been "too gentlemanly". They "avoid saying a single word which could possibly upset anyone, and this political correctness introduces a leaden note to their writings, however elegant the language." Since he had read *Muzzled Watchdogs*[28], my fiery report on the conservation agencies, I was surprised that Derek felt it necessary to warn me about over-gentlemanly conduct. There was another obvious difficulty: "The trouble is that if I start offering further suggestions, these will tend to being it closer to what I have!"

My plan was to get the draft down on paper quickly and then tinker with it. I banged on with the book in the early months of 2001 and duly sent Derek several very rough chapters for editorial comment and guidance. I remember feeling rather anxious about his reply. Writing a coherent text of around 100,000 words is hard work. My previous books of this length had grown wings and flown gloriously along on a thermal of literary delight. This one, though, was more like a trudge through wet sand and one feared that some of the mud might spatter onto the reader. I think it did. Unusually, Derek's reply was typed. Though he considered what he had seen as "quite a *tour de force*", and said reasonably positive things about its general thrust, he made two overall points about the book. First, there was not enough of what he saw as 'the level of reality', that is, the impact of modern life on nature in the field – as opposed to the impact of words on bored officials in urban offices. The trouble, as he admitted, is that the conservation literature is overwhelmingly about bureaucratic processes, not about natural history.

His second point was even less easy to remedy: "I think, also, that along with this tendency, you have experienced the same difficulty that I found with my still unpublished book: that in being honest, it is hardly possible to avoid giving an overall impression of a rather depressing story of conservation performance and results. This may be the truth, but it will not be particularly palatable to many, and may lead to charges of being negative or jaundiced."

I wrote in the margin: "nothing to be done". I did, however, adopt his suggestion of brightening up a fairly gloomy chapter on nature reserves by taking examples of the very best ones [he had suggested some] and writing glowingly about them in a knocked-on section titled 'Places of peace, havens of delight'. I sensed that Derek did not like the book much. Indeed I found out later that he had written a note to the Collins folk to say he had found it disappointing and warned them to anticipate ructions later on. He reported that I had written a gloomy and pessimistic book, which appears in the minutes as "humourless", although that is not what he meant. He need not have worried on that score. The Collins editor, Myles Archibold, told me he had laughed his head off. But David Streeter, to whom Derek had shown the manuscript, feeling that he was too close to the subject to offer an entirely fair and unbiased judgment, evidently concurred with him that "too many of your apples have maggots in them".

I doubt whether Derek's organic apples would have been much more wholesome than mine. Bitter experience and a tendency to brood had engrained in him a pessimistic view of human nature. Look, for example, at this:

> "So much of the action [on the contemporary conservation scene] seems to have fallen into the hands of those who, for whatever reason, have betrayed most of the things that I believe it all stood for. When you look around the field, there appears to be only a handful of people in influential places who are not in some way corrupted by anxieties about, or aspirations for, number one. Blair seems a good role model for the rest."

Having got that off his chest, Derek seemed to cheer up. He lent me dozens of his beautiful slides. He said he enjoyed the chapter on woodlands and the unflattering things I had said about foresters: "I like the way you convey their assertive self-righteousness with a God-given right to plant trees wherever they choose." I had done what I could to improve the 'level of reality' and bring the wildlife upfront, and relegating the droning herds of conservationists to the background. In a sense I felt I was writing this book for him. From the start I had intended to dedicate it to Derek. But he could not possibly have read such a book without thinking about the one he would have done, and I think that coloured his view of it. He took the dedication in his stride: "What else can I do but accept? Thank you very much."

I was less concerned about the book's quality, in which I have an imperishable faith, than with its sales. On my behalf Derek tried to persuade the Collins editor to increase the print-run, but "it seems impossible to shift him". New Naturalist print-runs, it appeared, were set in stone by divine agency and no amount of appeals, tears, and threats could budge them. It was quite impossible to sway anyone on this point since no one, it seemed, had any responsibility. Like bank overdrafts, how a book is marketed is determined by computer algorithms built into a silicon chip. I doubt whether human beings are involved at all.

The New Naturalist team held a 60th birthday party in 2005 although I was unable to come, being away in Spain watching bustards (Otididae). Derek was there, however, and by all accounts he was in fine form, having finished his latest book, *Galloway and the Borders*[21] – and looking forward to his latest trip to Lapland with Jeannette. The last letter I had from him was all about books. He referred to his *Lakeland* book[20] (to which I had contributed a couple of pages on fungi) as a labour of love that he felt he owed to his early mentors. He had also finished his book about Lapland[29] "and felt a little apprehensive at its reception – the possibility of a Brit presuming to pronounce on their land may not be taken too kindly by some Nordics... Excuse this writing – done at a rickety table".

Derek's never-slack literary productiveness was actually accelerating during his last two years. He certainly used his experience.

He phoned me a week or two before his trip to Lapland to thank me for his copy of the new edition of *The New Naturalists*[30]. He talked about some of the birds he hoped to see. He hoped to photograph a Waxwing (*Bombycilla garrulus*) nest and there were several of Nethersole-Thompson's 'blue-ribbon' birds whose nests he was hopeful of finding. He sounded tired and seemed to have difficulty saying goodbye. But it was only in retrospect, when he died in his sleep on the way to the North Sea ferry, that his last call sounded any alarm bells.

And now he has gone and there will be no more letters. As the poet said, "the owl of Minerva spreads its wings only with the gathering of the dusk"; in other words, it is only at the end of things that they turn into a story. Derek's busy life-story is chronicled in papers, books, journals[31], reports[e.g. 2], and letters (Fig. 27.1). A written record like that is the raw stuff of biography, and in his case, of the history of nature conservation in Britain. I look forward to watching his memory grow.

References

(1)   Nature Conservancy Council (1984) *Nature Conservation in Great Britain*. 112 pp. Nature Conservancy Council, Peterborough.

(2)   Stroud, D.A., Reed, T.M., Pienkowski, M.W. & Lindsay, R.A. (eds. D.A. Ratcliffe & P.H. Oswald) (1987) *Birds, Bogs and Forestry - The Peatlands of Caithness, and Sutherland*. 121 pp. Nature Conservancy Council, Peterborough.

(3)   Marren, P. (2002) *Nature Conservation*. HarperCollins, London.

(4)   Housden, S. (2015) Fighting for wildlife – from the inside. In: *Nature's Conscience – The Life and Legacy of Derek Ratcliffe* (eds. D.B.A. Thompson, H.H. Birks & H.J.B. Birks). This volume, Chapter 20.
Kirby, K.J. (2015) Battling forestry and building consensus: woodland conservation post-1949. In: *Nature's Conscience – The Life and Legacy of Derek Ratcliffe* (eds. D.B.A. Thompson, H.H. Birks & H.J.B. Birks). This volume, Chapter 21.

(5)   Marren, P. (1995) *The New Naturalists*. HarperCollins, London.

(6)   Ford, E.B. (1945) *Butterflies*. Collins, London.

(7)   Pearsall, W.H. (1950) *Mountains and Moorlands*. Collins, London.

(8)   McVean, D. & Ratcliffe, D.A. (1962) *Plant Communities of the Scottish Highlands*. Her Majesty's Stationery Office, London.

(9)   Birks, H.J.B. & Birks, H.H. (2015) Derek Ratcliffe – botanist and plant ecologist. In: *Nature's Conscience – The Life and Legacy of Derek Ratcliffe* (eds. D.B.A. Thompson, H.H. Birks & H.J.B. Birks). This volume, Chapter 4.

(10)   Ratcliffe, D.A. (2000) *In Search of Nature*. Peregrine Books, Leeds.

(11)   Birks, H.J.B., Thompson, D.B.A. & Birks, H.H. (2015) Derek Ratcliffe – early days in pursuit of nature. In: *Nature's Conscience – The Life and Legacy of Derek Ratcliffe* (eds. D.B.A. Thompson, H.H. Birks & H.J.B. Birks). This volume, Chapter 1

(12)   Pearsall, W.H. & Pennington, W. (1973) *The Lake District*. Collins, London.

(13)   Mitchell, J. (2015) National Service and beyond. In: *Nature's Conscience – The Life and Legacy of Derek Ratcliffe* (eds. D.B.A. Thompson, H.H. Birks & H.J.B. Birks). This volume, Chapter 2.

(14)   Manley, G. (1952) *Climate and the British Scene*. Collins, London.

(15)   Newton, I. (2015) Pesticides and birds of prey – the breakthrough. In: *Nature's Conscience – The Life and Legacy of Derek Ratcliffe* (eds. D.B.A. Thompson, H.H. Birks & H.J.B. Birks). This volume, Chapter 15.

(16)   Darling, F.F. & Boyd, J.M. (1964) *The Highlands and Islands*. Collins, London.

(17)   Mellanby, K. (1967) *Pesticides and Pollution*. Collins, London.

(18)   Cabot, D. (1999) *Ireland*. HarperCollins, London.

(19)   Mitchell, J. (2001) *Loch Lomondside*. HarperCollins, London.

(20)   Ratcliffe, D.A. (2002) *Lakeland*. HarperCollins, London.

(21)   Ratcliffe, D.A. (2007) *Galloway and the Borders*. Collins, London.

(22)   Marren, P. (1999) *Britain's Rare Flowers*. Poyser, London.

(23)   Ratcliffe, D.A., Birks, H.J.B. & Birks, H.H. (1993) The ecology and conservation of the Killarney Fern (*Trichomanes speciosum* Willd.) in Britain and Ireland. *Biological Conservation*, **66**, 231-247.

(24)   Marren, P. & Carter, J. (1999) *The Observer's Book of Observer Books*. Peregrine Books, Leeds.

(25)   Radcliffe (sic), D. (1989) The end of British nature conservation? *New Scientist*, **9 September**, 75-76.

(26)   Byrkjedal, I. (2015) A thousand nest cards – from Derek Ratcliffe to the University Museum of Bergen. In: *Nature's Conscience – The Life and Legacy of Derek Ratcliffe* (eds. D.B.A. Thompson, H.H. Birks & H.J.B. Birks). This volume, Chapter 17.

(27)   Edwards, R. (1998) On stony ground. *New Scientist*, **24 January 1998**, 18-19.

(28)   WWF-UK (1997) *A Muzzled Watchdog? Is English Nature protecting wildlife?* WWF-UK Report, Godalming.

(29)   Ratcliffe, D.A. (2005) *Lapland: A Natural History*. Poyser, London.

(30)   Marren, P. (2005) *The New Naturalists* (2nd edition). Collins, London.

(31)   Jenks, C. (2015) Bibliography of Derek Ratcliffe. In: *Nature's Conscience – The Life and Legacy of Derek Ratcliffe* (eds. D.B.A. Thompson, H.H. Birks & H.J.B. Birks). This volume.

28. Landscape, art, and nature

Will Williams and David Bellamy

Introduction

In the first part of this chapter Will Williams discusses Derek Ratcliffe's love of nature and wildness, how Derek tried to capture this in his writings, photography, and art, and how he combined his rigorous scientific approach with his appreciation of the inherent value of wildlife and wild landscapes. In the second part, David Bellamy explores further the links between landscape, nature, and art.

Nature, art, and conservation

Nature was in Derek's soul. He felt its presence. He experienced that contact and that thrill of seeing a species new to him and of seeing 'old friends' again. He was moved by nature's beauty and wildness. He was inspired to paint watercolours of the Pennines, Yorkshire, and Lakeland but only those that visited his home in Cambridge had the opportunity to see and appreciate these. Art, photography, and literature became so important to him in later life as it was the best way that he could maintain that essential contact with nature.

Derek's career centred on the conservation of nature[1]. His dedication, motivation, and commitment were firmly grounded in his interest, respect, and love of all wildlife and the landscapes which constitute nature. From an early age he used his home base near London and afterwards in Norfolk and in Carlisle to spread his wings to pursue his interests from butterflies to birds[2]. On his adventures, which were mostly self-inspired, he took every opportunity to learn from others, from all walks of life, who shared his thirst to see and understand all kinds of wildlife. He thought he was lucky in so many ways but the truth is that he was so energetic in his quest, that he made the most of and

491

even created opportunities[1]. He was one of that breed of 'new naturalists' that learnt in the field and was sufficiently disciplined to keep detailed notes that served him well throughout his career[2]. And getting around was a challenge only to be overcome through long walks, the bicycle frequently taken on the train, a motorbike, and eventually graduating to a car and land-rover[1].

Until 1947, when Derek had his first camera, he was unable to record the landscapes and wildlife that made such an impression on him. His memory and notebooks served him well though. Maybe not having a camera in the early days heightened his senses of observation, hearing, and feeling. He acknowledged the ability of artists like Peter Scott, Charles Tunnicliffe, Morton Boyd, and Donald Watson to capture so much of what he experienced. With Grant Roger, he shared the joy of botanising especially in the Cairngorms but Jean Roger with her artistic mind took him into the appreciation of beauty in nature – colour, light, and tone.

Through his early years and later as a student in Sheffield and Bangor and ultimately through his work with the Nature Conservancy and subsequently the Nature Conservancy Council, he acquired an intimate knowledge and experience of landscapes throughout the UK. Lakeland, Snowdonia, Galloway and the Borders, the Pennines, the Scottish Highlands, to name but a few, are areas that he grew so fond of. The range and variety of landscapes inspired him and he loved them all for their uniqueness, whether in their geology, geomorphology, habitats, or natural beauty. He cherished the wild parts of these landscapes and because his early experience was during and after the Second World War, he knew them before the post-war intensification of land management, infrastructure and energy developments, and urbanisation. Overgrazing of the uplands and mass afforestation of Galloway[3,4] and the Flow Country of Caithness and Sutherland[5] must have been an attack on that natural beauty that meant so much to him, like tearing the canvas of a great painting.

It was no surprise that "natural beauty" was the wording that was embodied in legislation in the late 1940s and early 1950s for the protection of nature. That was how the naturalists of that time saw landscape and wildlife and that is what has inspired so many of us to pursue careers in nature conservation. But the process of implementing the legislation became dominated by the need for scientific evidence for description, management, and policy formulation and the ultimate test was the need for hard evidence to defend sites from development at public inquiries. Derek became a master at this, combining the value of wildlife to society with rigorous science in well-crafted rational and articulated language. He had built his knowledge and scientific understanding on a foundation of appreciation for the value and our spiritual need for contact with wildlife and wild landscapes[1,3-6].

In the same way, I (Will Williams) experienced this process, developing a great love of nature in my childhood years on a Welsh upland farm and especially the adventure of discovering how geology had shaped so much. This led me to study geology and ecology at the University of Aberdeen and to my PhD research into the vegetation history of the Isle of Skye with John Birks at the University of Cambridge. That is where I also met Derek for the first time, and I continued my adventure of discovering nature and landscapes. I was to meet Derek later during his career with the Nature Conservancy Council and its daughter agencies. Being based in Scotland, I had first-hand experience of how Derek brought his knowledge and scientific understanding of nature

Figure 28.1. Bannau Sir Gaer, above Llyn y Fan Fach, Brecon Beacons National Park by Will Williams

to bear on how to describe and evaluate the importance of nature and defending nature from major threats, for example the afforestation of moorland[7,8] and, in particular, the Flow Country of Caithness and Sutherland[5]. Yes, science was fundamental in Derek's work but he also introduced the social value of nature into his commitment to defend nature from so many unsustainable uses and developments.

For Derek and probably most career conservationists, the motivation is to secure the rightful place of nature on this planet not only for all our functioning ecosystems but also for underpinning our very own existence in both functional and spiritual ways. But during Derek's time, and ever increasing, is the imbalance between man's activities and their impact on nature. There is the fundamental political belief that our future lies upon economic growth with a denial that this will continue to lead to the destruction of nature.

It is living with this and its constant personal challenge that makes our contact with nature and finding ways for expressing it so important to keep us sane. Derek took up this challenge from the very beginning and expressed it in so many ways. His watercolour paintings were clearly one way, capturing the beauty, the light on the landscape, and that 'moment' of inspiration. He was also fascinated by cloud formations. He was an extremely skilled and careful photographer of plants, bird nests, habitats, and landscapes, as shown by the many pleasing pictures in his *Lakeland*[9] and *Galloway and the Borders*[3] New Naturalist books, in his *Highland Flora* book[10], and in *A Nature Conservation Review*[11]. He excelled at black-and-white photography, especially of habitats and landscapes, as in *A Nature Conservation Review*[11] and *In Search of Nature*[1]. He

Figure 28.2. Canisp and Suilven, Torridonian outliers on the ancient Pre-Cambrian basement, Assynt by Will Williams. Reproduced by kind permission of Carol McNeill

always used a tripod and never took large numbers of pictures, only a few choice ones.

Apart from painting, my personal fulfilment has been, as Trustee of the John Muir Trust[12], to see land being restored to its natural beauty in harmony with people and I think that Derek would have loved to see more of his wild areas being restored not only in conservation management but also with a clear emphasis on restoring the health of nature – Li and Corrie Dhorcaill in Knoydart, Schiehallion, Blabheinn on Skye, Ben Nevis, Quinag in Assynt, and Sandwood Bay.

It was during my early days of painting that I met David Bellamy and this was the beginning of so many painting trips to wild and wonderful landscapes of the world – the Himalayan mountain-desert of Ladakh, the snow-capped Peruvian Andes, the wild and windswept Patagonia, pristine landscapes of Svalbard, and the vastness of the Greenland Icecap. I can so fully appreciate the love that Derek had for Lapland[13] – its landscape, skies, wilderness, and wildlife that are captured so brilliantly in his book on Lapland and in his many photographs from his fourteen trips to northern Fennoscandia. A selection of Derek's Lapland images is presented as a photo-essay in Chapter 29[14]. The images are selected to show not only the range of landscapes in Lapland but also Derek's ability to capture the beauty of Lapland, its diversity of form, habitats, and atmosphere, and the feeling of wildness that Lapland generates.

Landscape, nature, and art – an artist's view

In this second part of the chapter, David Bellamy further develops the links between landscape, nature, and art, drawing from his own work as a professional artist specialising in painting landscapes where nature thrives.

Figure 28.3. Black Mount, Moor of Rannoch by David Bellamy

It was that great champion of the natural environment, Ansel Adams, who made the point about the approach of the artist and that of the environmentalist being so close[15]. This is certainly true in the case of most landscape artists who work in the great outdoors. Having an empathy with nature is a prerequisite for producing inspirational paintings of scenery. Being brought up in the countryside, nature has always had a profound effect on my life. Now, in my seventieth year it still delights, surprises, and soothes out the wrinkles of twenty-first-century living. As a youngster, I revelled in being out in the countryside as much as possible, getting wet, muddy, torn, and tired – the hallmark of an interesting day, and over all these years little has changed.

Those of us who engage with nature will know the supreme serenity such close contact can bring, as the ills of modern living fade away in the face of natural beauty, yet sadly that modern lifestyle is often such that folk spend far less time in the great outdoors than previously. Much of the time I walk and sketch alone in the natural environment. Being alone tends to bring me even closer to nature, as there are less distractions and I feel entirely at ease staring fixedly at some effect of light falling on a plant or flower, for

Figure 28.4. Borrowdale, Lake District by David Bellamy

example, enjoying nature's spectacle sometimes through the most distorted squint imaginable. A common observation technique amongst artists is to view the subject through half-closed eyes, and with a non-artist companion this behaviour might well be uncomfortable for both parties. Alone, however, I can indulge happily in these harmless machinations, observing the subject from all manner of questionable positions and viewpoints. The combination of rocks and water; the joys of following a tumbling mountain stream, for instance, are particular favourites, and this naturally leads to a closer and more enthusiastic engagement than would normally be prudent. The Lakeland sport of ghyll-climbing, when combined with sketching can, on a fine day, provide hours of enchantment in one of nature's gems.

Experiencing the subject first-hand is vital for the artist attempting to achieve an authentic and honest portrayal in whatever subject discipline, and although I mainly work up my paintings in the studio from original sketches, it is the actual process of sketching on the spot that gives the greatest pleasure and reward, even in less-than-perfect conditions. The challenge of painting when the watercolour washes instantly freeze on the paper, or when spindrift is being hurled across a beautiful composition by ferocious winds, can trigger a tremendous sense of achievement, even when this results in a most disagreeable artistic mess. Still, some of my best paintings have resulted from the most dire original sketches. This engagement with raw nature can at times seem like some kind of masochistic pleasure, yet it is always rewarding, and often memorable.

My landscape preferences have always been the wilder, untamed regions of mountain, Arctic, and desert, where the very chaos of such places tends to present even greater challenges for the landscape artist. One difficulty I seek perhaps more than others is the effect of fleeting light on such features as crags, rocks, water, trees, and so on, a much more interesting aspect than steady, perpetual light that can produce a boring image. Light, of course, is a vital, yet much ignored aspect of nature, profoundly affecting how we see the natural scene as an artist or non-artist. Chasing the light, where much of the scene is perhaps wreathed in an intense dullness, presents one of the greatest challenges to the artist, especially when accompanied by light mist or other atmospheric effects, where one is unsure if they are looking at a mountain peak or a cloud, or whether the abyss falls a few feet or several thousand. Natural beauty, when cloaked in such mystery is both spiritually and emotionally uplifting.

Figure 28.5. Dungeon Ghyll, Lake District by David Bellamy

Down the centuries, art has continually held the power to influence others, from the lowliest peasant to the most powerful in the land. In modern times the trend has been to move away from the natural environment, despite the gallant efforts of those dedicated souls, like Derek, who commit much of their time to studying or defending nature. There seems to be much less time now to 'stand and stare,' even though this is vital to our well-being. Children are no longer encouraged to run wild in nature, roaming the woods, fields, rivers, and commons in search of adventure[16]. In the British Isles, we are blessed with a rich variety of ever-changing landscapes, yet much of this natural beauty remains unknown to a large section of the population. Highlighting these places through the medium of painting has always provided great satisfaction, but in later years this has become an essential aspect of my work, given that our landscapes are now under such enormous threats from developments. In a materialistic society, we need to be reminded of our close relationship with nature and the earth, and art has the power, or at least can go some way, to achieving this goal, whether in teaching children to paint landscapes, or in exhibitions. This is increasingly becoming more important when we see the threats now facing our countryside. No longer is it exclusively a Third World problem whereby vast areas are being sacrificed for the benefit of corporate greed. If in some way my art can influence others and highlight the value of what we stand to lose, whether a wide landscape or just a grain of sand, then it will have achieved my aim.

References

(1)   Ratcliffe, D.A. (2000) *In Search of Nature*. Peregrine Books, Leeds.

(2)   Birks, H.J.B., Thompson, D.B.A. & Birks, H.H. (2015) Derek Ratcliffe – early days in pursuit of nature. In: *Nature's Conscience – The Life and Legacy of Derek Ratcliffe* (eds. D.B.A. Thompson, H.H. Birks & H.J.B. Birks). This volume, Chapter 1.

(3)   Ratcliffe, D.A. (2007) *Galloway and the Borders*. Collins, London.

(4)   Rollie, C.J. (2015) In Galloway and the Borders – in search of an enduring youth. In: *Nature's Conscience – The Life and Legacy of Derek Ratcliffe* (eds. D.B.A. Thompson, H.H. Birks & H.J.B. Birks). This volume, Chapter 13.

(5)   Stroud, D.A., Reed, T.M., Pienkowski, M.W. & Lindsay, R.A. (eds. D.A. Ratcliffe & P.H. Oswald) (1987) *Birds, Bogs and Forestry - The Peatlands of Caithness and Sutherland*. 121 pp. Nature Conservancy Council, Peterborough.
Lindsay, R.A., Charman, D.J., Everingham, F., O'Reilly, R.M., Palmer, M.A., Rowell, T.A. & Stroud, D.A. (eds. D.A. Ratcliffe & P.H. Oswald) (1988) *The Flow Country – The Peatlands of Caithness and Sutherland*. 174 pp. Nature Conservancy Council, Peterborough.
Lindsay, R.A. (2015) A letter to Derek Ratcliffe. In: *Nature's Conscience – The Life and Legacy of Derek Ratcliffe* (eds. D.B.A. Thompson, H.H. Birks & H.J.B. Birks). This volume, Chapter 24.
Battarbee, R.W. (2015) Forestry, 'acid rain', and the acidification of lakes. In: *Nature's Conscience – The Life and Legacy of Derek Ratcliffe* (eds. D.B.A. Thompson, H.H. Birks & H.J.B. Birks). This volume, Chapter 22.

(6)   Ratcliffe, D.A. (1990) *Bird Life of Mountain and Upland.* Cambridge University Press, Cambridge.

7)   Ratcliffe, D.A. (1986) The effects of afforestation on the wildlife of open habitats. In: *Trees and Wildlife in the Scottish Uplands* (ed. D. Jenkins), pp. 46-54. Institute of Terrestrial Ecology, Huntingdon.

(8)   Nature Conservancy Council (1986) *Nature Conservation and Afforestation in Britain.* 108 pp. Nature Conservancy Council, Peterborough.

(9)   Ratcliffe, D.A. (2002) *Lakeland.* HarperCollins, London.

(10)   Ratcliffe, D.A. (1977) *Highland Flora.* Highlands and Islands Development Board, Inverness.

(11)   Ratcliffe, D.A. (ed.) (1977) *A Nature Conservation Review, volumes 1 & 2.* Cambridge University Press, Cambridge.

(12)   John Muir Trust *Our Essential Wildness.* http://www.jmt.org/vision.asp (accessed March 2013).

(13)   Ratcliffe, D.A. (2005) *Lapland: A Natural History.* Poyser, London

(14)   Ratcliffe, D.A. (2015) Lapland images. In: *Nature's Conscience – The Life and Legacy of Derek Ratcliffe* (eds. D.B.A. Thompson, H.H. Birks & H.J.B. Birks). This volume, Chapter 29.

(15)   Adams, A. (1975) *The Role of the Artist in Conservation.* The Horace M. Albright conservation lecture. http://cnr.berkeley.edu/site/lectures/albright/1975.php (accessed March 2013).

(16)   Louv, R. (2010) *Last Child in the Woods.* Atlantic Books, London.

29. Lapland images

Derek Ratcliffe

Compiled by *Hilary and John Birks*

In his retirement Derek Ratcliffe rekindled his strong spirit of adventure, exploration, and discovery and returned to his first love of birds by organising annual expeditions with his wife Jeannette (Fig. 17.2) to arctic Fennoscandia to find and study rare waders and other birds in near-pristine conditions (Fig. 17.1). He wrote a wide-ranging and wonderfully illustrated book[1] on many aspects of the natural history, ornithology, botany, and ecology of Lapland based on their fourteen expeditions to arctic Fennoscandia. Some of Derek's striking images of Lapland landscapes and habitats are reproduced in this photo-essay to illustrate his great skill as a landscape photographer and his ability to communicate through photographs. We have grouped the images into 1) boreal forests, 2) mires, 3) rivers and lakes, 4) coastal areas, 5), tundra, and 6) other habitats. We have provided captions for the images based primarily on the text in Derek's book *Lapland – A Natural History* (Fig. 11.18)[1]. Details of the bird nests found by Derek and Jeannette in Lapland are discussed by Ingvar Byrkjedal in his chapter in this volume[2]. Terminology of vegetation zones follows Moen[3].

Boreal forests

Figure 29.1. Characteristic middle-boreal forest of Scots Pine (*Pinus sylvestris*), Norway Spruce (*Picea abies*), and Downy Birch (*Betula pubescens*) north of Vilhelmino, northern Sweden, 1992

Figure 29.2. Well-grown Scots Pine (*Pinus sylvestris*) trees with a compact growth form near the limit of *Pinus sylvestris* in the northern-boreal zone, Enontekiö, northern Finland, 1991

Figure 29.3. Ungrazed ground-layer dominated by *Cladina* lichen in open middle-boreal Scots Pine (*Pinus sylvestris*) woods, near Folldal, Rondane, central Norway, 1984

Figure 29.4. *Cladina stellaris* (white) with *Cladonia rangiferina* (grey), two of the most important lichens as Reindeer (*Rangifer tarandus*) food, in a middle-boreal Scots Pine (*Pinus sylvestris*) wood, Sogndal, western Norway, 1992

Figure 29.5. Northern-boreal open woodland of Downy Birch (*Betula pubescens*) by the Akkajaure reservoir with the mountains of the Stora-Sjöfallet National Park in the distance, northern Sweden, 1993

Figure 29.6. Northern-boreal sub-alpine Downy Birch (*Betula pubescens*) woods in Lyngen Fjord, Troms, northern Norway, 1990

Figure 29.7. A colourful mix of normal purple and pale-flowered forms of Wood Cranesbill (*Geranium sylvaticum*) with tall Rosebay Willowherb (*Chamerion angustifolium*) in a meadow beside a northern-boreal Birch (*Betula* spp.) woodland, near Masugnsbyn, northern Sweden, 2002

Figure 29.8. A meadow dominated by Globeflower (*Trollius europaeus*) on base-rich soil within a northern-boreal sub-alpine Birch (*Betula* spp.) wood, near Tärnaby, northern Sweden, 2002

Mires

Figure 29.9. Profusely flowering Cloudberry (*Rubus chamaemorus*) on an ombrotrophic tundra bog near Kvalnes, north Varanger, Finnmark, northern Norway, 1995. Cloudberries (molte or multe) are commonly collected to make into a dessert served with cream or, in Finland, for making into a liqueur (Lakka)

Figure 29.10. Abundant Hare's-tail Cottongrass (*Eriophorum vaginatum*) on an ombrotrophic bog colonised by Scots Pine (*Pinus sylvestris*) trees in Swedish Lapland, 1992

Figure 29.11. An aapa mire with extensive flarks (open water) in the middle-boreal zone near Storuman, northern Sweden, 2003

Figure 29.12. An extensive aapa mire with few, widely-spaced strings and extensive open-water flarks with floating mats of sedge- and moss-dominated vegetation, in the middle-boreal zone, near Storuman, northern Sweden, 2001

Figure 29.13. Willow (mainly *Salix glauca*) scrub and abundant Kingcups (*Caltha palustris*) in moss-dominated springs at the edge of a large aapa mire and fen in the middle-boreal zone near Avvakko, northern Sweden, 2003

Rivers and lakes

Figure 29.14. A slow-flowing river running through middle-boreal Scots Pine–Downy Birch (*Pinus sylvestris–Betula pubescens*) forest. The river is fringed by rafts of Bogbean (*Menyanthes trifoliata*) and the alluvial banks are covered by Willow (*Salix* spp.) and Dwarf Birch (*Betula nana*) scrub, Svappavaara, northern Sweden, 1997

Figure 29.15. Middle-boreal Spruce (*Picea abies*) forest with Scots Pine (*Pinus sylvestris*) and Downy Birch (*Betula pubescens*) along a fast-flowing river, Gardsjön, near Slussfors, northern Sweden, 1991

Figure 29.16. A 'brown water' dystrophic lake among middle-boreal forest bogs at Tårrajauer, near Jokkmokk, northern Sweden, 1995

Coastal areas

Figure 29.17. Tanafjord and the mountains north of Vestertana, north Norway with a sandy shore with Lyme Grass (*Leymus arenarius*) and Sea Pea (*Lathyrus maritimus*), 2002

Figure 29.18. The north-west coast of northern Norway at Kvænangsfjell looking to Spildra Island, Troms. In the foreground there is shallow blanket-bog, a characteristic mire type in extreme oceanic areas, 1990

Figure 29.19. Coastal habitats at Birkenstrand, Finnmark, northern Norway, 1990

Figure 29.20. Hammingberg, a remote fishing village on the Finnmark coast of the Barents Sea, northern Norway, 1994

Figure 29.21. Coastal heath dominated by Mountain Avens (*Dryas octopetala*) growing on dolomitic limestone and extending down to high-tide level, Porsanger Fjord, north of Borselv, Finnmark, northern Norway, 2001

Figure 29.22. An extensive stand of Northern Birdseye Primrose (*Primula nutans*) in a salt-marsh by Porsanger Fjord, near Borselv, Finnmark, northern Norway, 1999

Figure 29.23. A spectacular show of Moss Campion (*Silene acaulis*) growing amidst Crowberry (*Empetrum nigrum*) in coastal heath besides the Barents Sea at Vardø, Varanger Peninsula, northern Norway, 1995

Tundra

Figure 29.24. A low-alpine tundra landscape mosaic with open fell-fields in wind-exposed areas and snowfields in sheltered areas on Hangalacærro, Kongsfjordfjell, Varanger Peninsula, northern Norway, 1990

Figure 29.25. A typical low-alpine tundra landscape on Saltfjell (700 m elevation) at the Arctic Circle, with extensive fell-fields, northern Norway, 1990

Figure 29.26. Patterned ground of stone nets in the low- and mid-alpine fell-field tundra at 400 m elevation on Gurrojokskaidde, Ifjordfjell, Finnmark, northern Norway, 2003

Other habitats

Figure 29.27. A herd of Reindeer (*Rangifer tarandus*) grazing an area of abandoned meadows in the middle-boreal zone near Slagnäs, northern Sweden, 2002

Figure 29.28. The lichen *Parmelia centrifuga* showing radial growth on a boulder in open Scots Pine (*Pinus sylvestris*) woodland in the middle-boreal zone, Lule Lappmark, northern Sweden, 1997

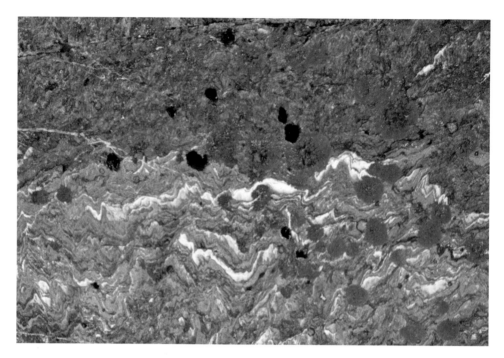

Figure 29.29. Lichens *Xanthoria elegans* (orange) and *Umbilicaria* sp. (black) on coastal dolomitic limestone along the Porsanger Fjord, north of Borselv, northern Norway, 2001

References

(1)   Ratciffe, D.A. (2005) *Lapland: A Natural History*. Poyser, London.

(2)   Byrkjedal, I. (2015) A thousand nest cards – from Derek Ratcliffe to the University Museum of Bergen. In: *Nature's Conscience – The Life and Legacy of Derek Ratcliffe* (eds. D.B.A. Thompson, H.H. Birks & H.J.B. Birks). This volume, Chapter 17.

(3)   Moen. A. (1998) *National Atlas of Norway: Vegetation*. Norwegian Mapping Authority, Hønefoss.

30. Introduction: A reminiscence

Derek A. Ratcliffe

Reprint of Ratcliffe, D.A. (1980) Introduction:
A reminiscence. In: *The Peregrine Falcon.*
Poyser, Calton, pp. 24-28.

When, as a small boy, I first became interested in birds, my imagination was fired by the pictures of a fierce-looking and beautiful bird of prey which the books said was rare, nesting only on the most formidable cliffs, and surpassing all other birds in its powers of flight. The descriptions and colour plates of the bird's eggs, said to be regarded by collectors as one of the greatest prizes on account of their exceptional variety and beauty of colouring, was enough to whet the appetite of any bird's-nesting boy. My father borrowed for me from the adults' library other books written by the great field naturalists and photographers of an earlier generation, and the vivid accounts of their experiences in the wild places of Britain conjured up a romantic vision of the Peregrine and its country. The local museum had one of the most skilfully presented exhibitions of birds in the whole country and was a most appealing place. I used to pore over the mounted specimens in their habitat settings, and was especially captivated by the Peregrines – wonderful creatures which had once graced the hill country not far away.

One day, my father took me to see the museum curator who was known to guard in his inner sanctum a magnificent egg collection which he would unlock and show on request. I gazed in fascination at these treasures, but above all at the drawer with its series of clutches of large, rich red eggs, mottled and blotched so variously that hardly two were exactly alike. I marvelled at the prowess of the god-like beings who had so evidently come to terms with my bird, and then the curator, by a casual remark, made it apparent that he was himself one of these supermen who could track down and reach the eyries of the Peregrine Falcon among the Lakeland fells. From then onwards, I knew there would be no rest for me until I too was on intimate terms with this beguiling bird.

517

During two holidays with my parents in the Lake District, I saw something of the country wherein Peregrines were said to live and nest, but gained little enlightenment. My parents were not fell-goers and our walks were confined to the roads and well-worn lower tracks, whilst I was too young to be allowed off alone. The difficulties and dangers in my future quest seemed, if anything, to increase; there were so many cliffs, and the most likely looking, often viewed through mist and rain, were horribly steep and tall. As I grew older I became more venturesome in the range of exploration around home, and with a friend hunted the farmland and woods, the lonely peat mosses and the great flat expanses of saltmarsh bordering the Solway, in search of birds and their nests. My pocket money went on bus fares and maps, and I invested in Bartholomew's one inch sheet of the Lake District. It was fascinating to pore over this and make plans, and my eagerness to penetrate the fell country finally overcame parental anxieties and objections.

Some pioneering trips to Lakeland, in search of nesting Buzzards, planned largely on the basis of likely-looking woods on the maps, were successful and encouraged me to think of tackling the birds of the crags. During the autumn of that year, 1944, I did some prospecting among the fells, for information about the whereabouts of Peregrines was difficult to come by. The bird books themselves were extremely reticent about naming nesting places, though a few supposedly deserted haunts were mentioned. When, on subsequent visits with specimens to my hero, the curator, I raised the question of Peregrines nesting on particular cliffs, the replies were so guarded as to be discouraging – 'Oh, they have done' or 'they could do'. I took to reading through more general works on the hill country, by mountaineers, walkers and others with no more than a casual interest in birds, and here I began to pick up clues from passing mentions of the mountain birds. A few writers had, however, taken a deeper interest in the fell creatures. I found great inspiration in an essay from the pen of Canon Rawnsley, 'After the Ravens in Skiddaw Forest' – a tale beautifully told in the full and gracious prose of its author's time, but remaining fresh and vivid to this day; it is, to me, one of the gems of Lakeland literature.

My prospecting trips produced at least one certain Raven nesting place, and the following February saw me after the Ravens myself, armed with a couple of sixty foot hemp plough-lines bought at a local ironmonger's. By the end of March I had found three Raven nests with eggs and triumphantly climbed to the easiest of them. The Raven cliffs included one of my main Peregrine hopes mentioned in two of my books, but when April came in I still had not located any falcons. I decided to try first a certain Westmorland crag figured in several books and mentioned by one as a Peregrine haunt. On the 21st of the month, an early train set me off at a country station nearest to my mountain destination, and I could not cover the intervening seven miles fast enough. Midday saw me at the crest of the crag facing down the head of a long dale to spacious plains beyond. Following the level crag top, I scanned the ledges below. A Buzzard's skirl was followed by an unfamiliar chattering call, and there high over the dale was what I judged to be a Peregrine tiercel stooping at a pair of these hawks. The Buzzards departed and the falcon planed down to a rock high on the fell above. Much encouraged, I continued to follow the crag edge, peering tensely down each face. At one point a recently killed Fieldfare lay near the edge and when I looked over there was a sudden movement as a blue-grey form flung itself from a ledge and out over the screes below. My gaze turned quickly from the fleeing falcon to the rock below where, on a grassy shelf, lay three beautiful eggs, reddish brown mottled with white.

The intensity of excitement at such moments is perhaps something reserved for youth, but then the young tend to have simple ambitions which can be achieved in a wholly fulfilling way. It was certainly the impetuosity of youth which set me clambering down that sheer wall to reach the eyrie. And there at last was the marvellous bird in life, cruising up and down for me to admire, and filling the dale with its strident chatter. I was at one with the gods and it was a very happy if weary schoolboy who boarded the northward-bound train that day. There have been many red-letter days in my life as a field naturalist, but none to eclipse this one.

This was beginner's luck, but it held. A week later I crept along a ledge in the Lake fells and looked down to a shelf only eight feet below to where an oblivious Peregrine brooded her hatching eggs, and in June I climbed to an old Raven eyrie in which three fine eyasses glared out from amidst a gory shambles of pigeon remains. That autumn and winter I did more prospecting, read more books and bought more maps, over which I pored for hours on end, laying plans for the following spring. When the Easter holidays came I made for pastures new and spent ten days exploring the Galloway hills, which in 1946 were as gloriously wild and untrodden a stretch of upland as any in the British Isles.

By now I had the fever, and have never really shaken it off. During every year since then I have managed to be among Peregrines at nesting time. Each spring saw me roaming the Lakeland fells, but I was drawn even more strongly to the quieter hills of the Southern Uplands, where there was the additional satisfaction of prospecting unknown ground, and working out the distribution of Peregrines and Ravens for myself. In Moffatdale and Galloway I stayed with kindly and hospitable shepherd folk in their lonely homes deep in the Peregrine country, and there spent some of the best days of my life. After long and exhausting treks, I returned each night to marvellous suppers and good talk. There was then a struggle to write up the field notes before sleep finally won. The Southern Uplands had a degree of solitude then, and forestry had only the odd foothold here and there. For some years cars were few, and although the shepherds could be seen assiduously going their rounds, I seldom met anyone else on the hills during my April visits.

Galloway, especially, was a magic country to which I returned every year with renewed enthusiasm. It was then a vast sheep walk, the last grouse moors virtually abandoned, and tourism a thing hardly worth mentioning. Few roads or even recognisable footpaths penetrated the wilderness and some of the Peregrine haunts were only to be reached by long, arduous walks. I well remember the sudden feeling of solitude when the train set me down with my bicycle at the lonely station on the moors, and I headed along the rough road across the wild and windswept uplands towards the abrupt granite crags that were always my first call. One time I passed an adder coiled in the road, as an indication of the scarcity of traffic in those days. I vividly recollect, on sunny days in April, sitting high on the hills and watching the smoke from innumerable moor fires rising into the still air at almost every point of the compass. The 'reek' from shepherds' fires was then so characteristic a feature of the scene, and the freshly burned moor had a marvellously aromatic smell as one walked over the ground. It was a land of Curlews, and as they rose and sank in graceful display flight, their liquid bubbling calls sounded far and wide over the moorlands. Now and then I slept out in the deserted cottage at Backhill of the Bush, and remember the sense of loneliness as I sat on the doorstep and watched the sun go down behind the Dungeon and Craignaw, where the granite slabs and crags took on a steely blueness as the light faded. In those days it was five miles to the next human being and the nearest road end.

As a research student, I was fortunate to live for three years in the magnificent Peregrine country of Snowdonia, and although my work was to study mountain vegetation, there were four pairs of falcons on my area to provide added attraction. During days off I tracked down most of the other Peregrine haunts in the district, and made periodic forays to the sea cliffs of Anglesey where the bird nested in contrasting habitat. A visit to the wild north-west of Sutherland in 1952 left me with the clear impression that, contrary to my expectations, there were few Peregrines among these rugged hills, and that this was, first and foremost, Golden Eagle country.

The original preoccupation with the excitements of the chase, the hunting down and reaching of nests and the sheer delight of watching and hearing these marvellous creatures, broadened gradually into a curiosity about the influences which ruled their lives. My searches began to have a more purposeful intent, though they still had to be a spare time concern. I became impressed by the apparent constancy in numbers, combined with the regularity in spacing distance between pairs, and began to wonder how this could have come about, and what it meant. Later, I started to write down my ideas and the field data, and eventually made these into a paper. Then, to my great delight, there came the opportunity to work on the Peregrine as a full time job for a couple of years, and soon I found myself involved, with many other people, in what became a cause celebre in nature conservation: the impact of the organochlorine insecticides on birds of prey. The Peregrine itself has come to symbolise one of the foremost trends of our time – the relentless domination by Man, the supreme competitor, of the rest of the living world.

And so the Peregrine story has become far more complicated than I could ever have foreseen, leading on the one hand to the deep mysteries of the physiology and biochemistry of response to pesticides, and on the other to the battleground where wildlife conservation is matched against the march of progress. My part has been that of a field naturalist trying to understand the population biology of the bird, and to direct the attention of others to more fundamental or technical issues which it was beyond my capacity or inclination to tackle. It would be less than honest of me to pretend that I was motivated other than by a wish to see my beloved bird hold its own, but I have tried hard to keep emotion out of the scientific arguments. These must stand or fall on the collection, presentation and interpretation of facts, free from wishful-thinking or hidden assumptions.

The Peregrine is, in fact, a fascinating subject for scientific study, and my attempts to understand its natural history more closely have given me much stimulation and satisfaction, though there are many deeper aspects which remain as puzzles for others to solve. Beyond this, there has been the immense pleasure of knowing so many other Peregrine enthusiasts. I owe so much to those who taught and encouraged me in my youth, to my many field companions over the years, and to the numerous other helpers and informants who have made it possible to present the Peregrine saga in more detail than would otherwise have been the case. But the greatest enjoyment, all the way through, has been the simple one of seeing these fine birds and learning of their ways in their native haunts – a country endlessly varied and magnetically beautiful.

Mortimer Batten (1923) has summed it all up for me: 'I remember in my childhood seeing or rather recognising my first Peregrine as he glided through immeasurable space among the clouds, and never in all my life can I recall having witnessed anything in Wild Nature which left an impression so indelible and so full of romance as that small black cross against the sky.'

Bibliography of Derek Ratcliffe

Banks, A.N., Crick, H.Q.P., Coombes, R., Benn, S., Ratcliffe, D.A. & Humphreys, E.M. (2010) The breeding status of Peregrine Falcons *Falco peregrinus* in the UK and Isle of Man in 2002. *Bird Study*, **57**, 421-436.

Birks, H.H., Birks, H.J.B. & Ratcliffe, D.A. (1969) *Geocalyx graveolens* (Schrad.) Nees in Kerry, a hepatic new to Ireland. *Irish Naturalists' Journal*, **16**, 204-205.

Birks, H.J.B. & Ratcliffe, D.A. (1976) *Frullania germana* (Tayl.) Tayl. ex Gottsche, Lindenb. and Nees. *Journal of Bryology*, **9**, 113.

Birks, H.J.B. & Ratcliffe, D.A. (1976) *Radula aquilegia* (Tayl.) Tayl. ex Gottsche and Lindenb. *Journal of Bryology*, **9**, 112.

Birks, H.J.B. & Ratcliffe, D.A. (1976) *Sphagnum fuscum* (Schimp.) Klingrr. *Journal of Bryology*, **9**, 118.

Birks, H.J.B. & Ratcliffe, D.A. (1976) *Sphagnum strictum* Sull. *Journal of Bryology*, **9**, 115.

Birks, H.J.B. & Ratcliffe, D.A. (1976) *Sphagnum warnstorfii* Russ. *Journal of Bryology*, **9**, 119.

Birks, H.J.B. & Ratcliffe, D.A. (1991) *Adelanthus decipiens* (Hook.) Mitt. In: *Atlas of the Bryophytes of Britain and Ireland. Volume 1. Liverworts (Hepaticae and Anthocerotae)* (eds. M.O. Hill, C.D. Preston & A.J.E. Smith), p. 62. Harley, Colchester.

Birks, H.J.B. & Ratcliffe, D.A. (1991) *Frullania teneriffae* (Webb.) Nees. In: *Atlas of the Bryophytes of Britain and Ireland. Volume 1. Liverworts (Hepaticae and Anthocerotae)* (eds. M.O. Hill, C.D. Preston & A.J.E. Smith), p. 248. Harley, Colchester.

Birks, H.J.B. & Ratcliffe, D.A. (1991) *Herbertus aduncus* (Dicks.) S.F. Gray ssp. *hutchinsiae* (Gott.) Schust. In: *Atlas of the Bryophytes of Britain and Ireland. Volume 1. Liverworts (Hepaticae and Anthocerotae)* (eds. M.O. Hill, C.D. Preston & A.J.E. Smith), p. 39. Harley, Colchester.

Birks, H.J.B. & Ratcliffe, D.A. (1991) *Herbertus stramineus* (Dum.) Trev. In: *Atlas of the Bryophytes of Britain and Ireland. Volume 1. Liverworts (Hepaticae and Anthocerotae)* (eds. M.O. Hill, C.D. Preston & A.J.E. Smith), p. 38. Harley, Colchester.

Birks, H.J.B. & Ratcliffe, D.A. (1991) *Pleurozia purpurea* Lindb. In: *Atlas of the Bryophytes of Britain and Ireland. Volume 1. Liverworts (Hepaticae and Anthocerotae)* (eds. M.O. Hill, C.D. Preston & A.J.E. Smith), p. 234. Harley, Colchester.

Birks, H.J.B. & Ratcliffe, D.A. (1991) *Radula aquilegia* (Hook. f. & Tayl.) Gott. & Lindenb. In: *Atlas of the Bryophytes of Britain and Ireland. Volume 1. Liverworts (Hepaticae and Anthocerotae)* (eds. M.O. Hill, C.D. Preston & A.J.E. Smith), p. 239. Harley, Colchester.

Birks, H.J.B., Birks, H.H. & Ratcliffe, D.A. (1969) Mountain plants on Slieve League, Co. Donegal. *Irish Naturalists' Journal*, **16**, 203-204.

Birks, H.J.B., Ratcliffe, D.A. & Goode, D.A. (1976) *Sphagnum imbricatum* Hornsch. ex Russ. *Journal of Bryology*, **9**, 114.

Crick, H.Q.P. & Ratcliffe, D.A. (1995) The Peregrine *Falco peregrinus* breeding population of the United Kingdom in 1991. *Bird Study*, **42**, 1-19.

Holyoak, D.T. & Ratcliffe, D.A. (1968) Distribution of the Raven in Britain and Ireland. *Bird Study*, **15**, 191.

Lindsay, R.A., Charman, D.J., Everingham, F., O'Reilly, R.M., Palmer, M.A., Rowell, T.A., Stroud, D.A. (eds. D.A. Ratcliffe & P.H. Oswald) (1988) *The Flow Country – The Peatlands of Caithness and Sutherland*. 174 pp. Nature Conservancy Council, Peterborough.

Lockie, J.D. & Ratcliffe, D.A. (1964) Insecticides and Scottish Golden Eagles. *British Birds*, **57**, 89-102.

Lockie, J.D., Ratcliffe, D.A. & Balharry, R. (1969) Breeding success and organo-chlorine residues in golden eagles in West Scotland. *Journal of Applied Ecology*, **6**, 381-389.

Long, D.G. & Ratcliffe, D.A. (1996) Bryophytes of Hirta, St Kilda. *Journal of Bryology*, **19**, 89-111.

Marquiss, M., Newton, I. & Ratcliffe, D.A. (1978) The decline of the raven *Corvus corax* in relation to afforestation in southern Scotland and northern England. *Journal of Applied Ecology*, **15**, 129-144.

Marquiss, M., Ratcliffe, D.A. & Roxburgh, R. (1985) The numbers, breeding success and diet of golden eagles in southern Scotland in relation to changes in land-use. *Biological Conservation*, **34**, 121-140.

McVean, D.N. & Ratcliffe, D.A. (1962) *Plant Communities of the Scottish Highlands*. Her Majesty's Stationery Office, London.

Mitchell, J. & Ratcliffe D.A.. (1999) *Woodsia alpina* (Bolton) Gray. In: *British Red Data Books 1. Vascular Plants* (ed. M.J. Wiggington). pp. 392-393. JNCC, Peterborough.

Moore, N.W. & Ratcliffe, D.A. (1962) Chlorinated hydrocarbon residues in the egg of a peregrine falcon (*Falco peregrinus*) from Perthshire. *Bird Study*, **9**, 242-244.

Morton, J.B., Boddington, D. & Ratcliffe, D.A. (1959) St Kilda wrens on Stac an Armin. *British Birds*, **52**, 392.

Nature Conservancy Council (1984) *Nature Conservation in Great Britain*. 112 pp. Nature Conservancy Council, Shrewsbury.

Nature Conservancy Council (1986) *Nature Conservation and Afforestation in Britain*. 108 pp. Nature Conservancy Council, Peterborough.

Nature Conservancy Council (1989) *Guidelines for Selection of Biological SSSIs*. 288 pp. Nature Conservancy Council, Peterborough.

Prestt, I. & Ratcliffe, D.A. (1972) Effects of organochlorine insecticides on European birdlife. In: *Proceedings of 15th International Ornithological Congress* (ed. K.H. Voous), pp. 486-513. Brill, Lieden.

Ratcliffe, D.A. (1947) Personal observations on some local birds. *The Carliol*, pp. 428-437. Carlisle Grammar School.

Ratcliffe, D.A. (1949) *Aeshna caerulea* in Kirkcubrightshire. *The Scottish Naturalist*, **61**, 175.

Ratcliffe, D.A. (1949) Magpies nesting in rocks. *North Western Naturalist*, **3**, 129.

Ratcliffe, D.A. (1954) A new flora of Cumberland, a project by Carlisle Natural History Society. *North Western Naturalist*, **3**, 135.

Ratcliffe, D.A. (1955) Cumberland dragonflies. *North Western Naturalist*, **3**, 134-135.

Ratcliffe, D.A. (1958) Notes on the Scottish flora. A limestone flora in the Ben Alder group. *Transactions of the Botanical Society of Edinburgh*, **37**, 217-219.

Ratcliffe, D.A. (1958) Broken eggs in Peregrine eyries. *British Birds*, **51**, 23-26.

Ratcliffe, D.A. (1958) The range and habitats of *Sphagnum lindbergii* Schp. in Scotland. *Transactions of the British Bryological Society* **3**, 386-391.

Ratcliffe, D.A. (1959) *Cicerbita alpina* (L.) Wallr. in Glen Callater. *Transactions of the Botanical Society of Edinburgh*, **38**, 287-289.

Ratcliffe, D.A. (1959) The mountain plants of the Moffat Hills. *Transactions of the Botanical Society of Edinburgh*, **37**, 257-271.

Ratcliffe, D.A. (1959) *Potentilla crantzii* (Crantz) Beck in the Stewartry of Kirkcudbright. *Transactions of the Botanical Society of Edinburgh*, **38**, 288-289.

Ratcliffe, D.A. (1959) The vegetation of the Carneddau, North Wales. 1. Grasslands, heaths and bogs. *Journal of Ecology*, **47**, 371-413.

Ratcliffe, D.A. (1960) Broken eggs in the nests of Sparrowhawk and Golden Eagle. *British Birds*, **53**, 128-131.

Ratcliffe, D.A. (1960) Montane plants in Ross-shire and Sutherland. *Transactions of the Botanical Society of Edinburgh*, **39**, 107-113.

Ratcliffe, D.A. (1960) The mountain flora of Lakeland. *Proceedings of the Botanical Society of the British Isles*, **4**, 1-25.

Ratcliffe, D.A. (1961) Field investigations of the BTO - The status and food of the Peregrine. *British Birds*, **54**, 131.

Ratcliffe, D.A. (1961) Notes on the Scottish flora. Mountain plants in Peeblesshire and Selkirkshire. *Transactions of the Botanical Society of Edinburgh*, **39**, 233-234.

Ratcliffe, D.A. (1962) Breeding density in the Peregrine *Falco peregrinus* and Raven *Corvus corax*. Ibis, **104**, 13-39.

Ratcliffe, D.A. (1962) The habitat of *Adelanthus unciformis* (Tayl.) Mitt. and *Jamesoniella carringtonii* (Balf.) Spr. in Ireland. *Irish Naturalists' Journal*, **14**, 38-40.

Ratcliffe, D.A. (1962) Peregrine incubating Kestrel's eggs. *British Birds*, **53**, 131-132.

Ratcliffe, D.A. (1962) *Potentilla rupestris* in East Sutherland. *Proceedings of the Botanical Society of the British Isles*, **4**, 501.

Ratcliffe, D.A. (1963) *Adelanthus decipens* (Hook.) Mitt. *Transactions of the British Bryological Society*, **4**, 506.

Ratcliffe, D.A. (1963) *Bazzania perasonii* Steph. *Transactions of the British Bryological Society*, **4**, 507.

Ratcliffe, D.A. (1963) *Hedwigia integrifolia* P. Beauv. *Transactions of the British Bryological Society*, **4**, 519.

Ratcliffe, D.A. (1963) *Jamesoniella carringtonii* (Balf.) Spruce. *Transactions of the British Bryological Society*, **4**, 508.

Ratcliffe, D.A. (1963) *Leptodontium recurvifolium* (Tayl.) Linb. *Transactions of the British Bryological Society*, **4**, 521.

Ratcliffe, D.A. (1963) *Mastigophora woodsii* (Hook.) Nees. *Transactions of the British Bryological Society*, **4**, 511.

Ratcliffe, D.A. (1963) Peregrines rearing young Kestrels. *British Birds*, **56**, 457-460.

Ratcliffe, D.A. (1963) Review: Silent Spring by Rachel Carson. *British Birds*, **56**, 222-223.

Ratcliffe, D.A. (1963) *Sphagnum lindbergii* Schimp. ex Linb. *Transactions of the British Bryological Society*, **4**, 526.

Ratcliffe, D.A. (1963) The status of the Peregrine in Great Britain. *Bird Study*, **10**, 56-90.

Ratcliffe, D.A. (1964) *Anarta melanopa* (Thunb.) (Lep: Caradrinidae) in the Southern Uplands of Scotland. *Entomologist's Monthly Magazine*, **100**, 209.

Ratcliffe, D.A. (1964) Mires and bogs. In: *The Vegetation of Scotland* (ed. J.H. Burnett), pp. 426-478. Oliver and Boyd, Edinburgh.

Ratcliffe, D.A. (1964) Montane mires and bogs. In: *The Vegetation of Scotland* (ed. J.H. Burnett), pp. 536-558. Oliver and Boyd, Edinburgh.

Ratcliffe, D.A. (1965) *Anastrophyllum donianum* (Hook.) Steph. *Transactions of the British Bryological Society*, **4**, 874.

Ratcliffe, D.A. (1965) *Anastrophyllum joergensenii* Schiffn. *Transactions of the British Bryological Society*, **4**, 875.

Ratcliffe, D.A. (1965) *Fossombronia angulosa* (Dicks.) Raddi. *Transactions of the British Bryological Society*, **4**, 876.

Ratcliffe, D.A. (1965) *Herberta adunca* auct. *Transactions of the British Bryological Society*, **4**, 878.

Ratcliffe, D.A. (1965) *Herberta hutchinsiae* (Gott.) Evans. *Transactions of the British Bryological Society*, **4**, 879.

Ratcliffe, D.A. (1965) Organo-chlorine residues in some raptor and corvid eggs from northern Britain. *British Birds*, **58**, 65-81.

Ratcliffe, D.A. (1965) The Peregrine situation in Great Britain 1963-64. *Bird Study*, **12**, 66-82.

Ratcliffe, D.A. (1965) *Scapania nimbosa* Tayl. *Transactions of the British Bryological Society*, **4**, 882.

Ratcliffe, D.A. (1965) *Scapania ornithopodioides* (With.) Waddell. *Transactions of the British Bryological Society*, **4**, 881.

Ratcliffe, D.A. (1965) Grazing in Scotland and Upland England. In: *Grazing Experiments and the Use of Grazing as a Conservation Tool* (ed. T.C.E. Wells), pp. 20-24. Symposium at Monks Wood Experimental Station, 6-7 April 1965.

Ratcliffe, D.A. (1966) *Coscinodon cribrosus* (Hedw.) Spruce. *Transactions of the British Bryological Society*, **5**, 162.

Ratcliffe, D.A. (1966) The habitat of the snow bunting in Scotland. In: *The Snow Bunting* (by D. Nethersole-Thompson), pp. 153-165. Oliver and Boyd, Edinburgh.

Ratcliffe, D.A. (1966) The present status of the peregrine in Britain. *Falconer*, **46**, 249-250.

Ratcliffe, D.A. (1967) Decrease in eggshell weight in certain birds of prey. *Nature*, **215**, 208-210.

Ratcliffe, D.A. (1967) The Peregrine situation in Great Britain 1965-66. *Bird Study*, **14**, 238-246.

Ratcliffe, D.A. (1968) An ecological account of Atlantic bryophytes in the British Isles. *New Phytologist*, **67**, 365-439.

Ratcliffe, D.A. (1969) *Hylocomium umbratum* (Hedw.) Br. Eur. *Transactions of the British Bryological Society*, **5**, 842.

Ratcliffe, D.A. (1969) *Lepidozia pinnata* (Hook.) Dum. *Transactions of the British Bryological Society*, **5**, 831.

Ratcliffe, D.A. (1969) Population trends of the Peregrine Falcon in Great Britain. In: *Peregrine Falcon Populations: Their Biology and Decline* (ed. J.J. Hickey), pp. 239-269. University of Wisconsin Press, Madison.

Ratcliffe, D.A. (1970) Changes attributable to pesticides in egg breakage frequency and eggshell thickness in some British birds. *Journal of Applied Ecology*, **7**, 67-115.

Ratcliffe, D.A. (1971) Criteria for selection of nature reserves. *Advancement of Science*, **27**, 294-296.

Ratcliffe, D.A. (1972) The Peregrine population of Great Britain in 1971. *Bird Study*, **19**, 117-156.

Ratcliffe, D.A. (1973) Breeding habitat of the dotterel in Britain. In: *The Dotterel* (by D. Nethersole-Thompson), pp. 153-173. Collins, London.

Ratcliffe, D.A. (1973) The Dotterel as a breeding bird in England. In: *The Dotterel* (by D. Nethersole-Thompson), pp. 190-197. Collins, London.

Ratcliffe, D.A. (1973) Studies of the recent breeding success of the Peregrine, *Falco peregrinus*. *Journal of Reproductive Fertility*, **19**, 377-389.

Ratcliffe, D.A. (1973) Borrowdale Woods. In: *The Lake District* (by W.H. Pearsall & W. Pennington), pp. 138-146. Collins, London.

Ratcliffe, D.A. (1973) Land use and vegetational change in Skiddaw Forest. In: *The Lake District* (by W.H. Pearsall & W. Pennington), pp. 181-183. Collins, London.

Ratcliffe, D.A. (1973) Safeguarding wild plants. In: *Wild and cultivated: A conference on horticulture and field botany* (ed. P.S. Green), pp. 18-24. Botanical Society of the British Isles, Hampton.

Ratcliffe, D.A. (1974) Ecological effects of mineral exploitation in United Kingdom and their significance to nature conservation. *Proceedings of the Royal Society of London Series A-Mathematical Physical and Engineering Sciences*, **339**, 355-372.

Ratcliffe, D.A. (1974) The Vegetation. In: *The Cairngorms – Their Natural History and Scenery* (eds. D. Nethersole-Thompson & A. Watson), pp. 42-76. Collins, London.

Ratcliffe, D.A. (1975) Humphrey Milne-Redhead 1906-1974. *Journal of Bryology*, **8**, 415-416.

Ratcliffe, D.A. (1976) Conservation of terrestrial communities. *Philosophical Transactions of the Royal Society of London Series B-Biological Sciences*, **274**, 417-435.

Ratcliffe, D.A. (1976) Observations on the breeding of the Golden Plover in Great Britain. *Bird Study*, **23**, 63-116.

Ratcliffe, D.A. (1976) Thoughts towards a philosophy of nature conservation. *Biological Conservation*, **9**, 45-53.

Ratcliffe, D.A. (1977) The conservation of important wildlife areas in Great Britain. *British Ecological Society Bulletin*, **7**, 5-11.

Ratcliffe, D.A. (1977) *Highland Flora*. Highlands and Islands Development Board, Inverness.

Ratcliffe, D.A. (1977) Nature conservation - aims, methods and achievements. *Proceedings of the Royal Society of London B-Biological Sciences*, **197**, 11-29.

Ratcliffe, D.A. (ed.) (1977) *A Nature Conservation Review, Volumes 1 and 2*. Cambridge University Press, Cambridge.

Ratcliffe, D.A. (1977) Uplands and birds - an outline. *Bird Study*, **24**, 140-158.

Ratcliffe, D.A. (1977) Wildlife resources of Great Britain. *New Scientist*, **21 July**, 158-159.

Ratcliffe, D.A. (1978) Plant communities. In: *Upper Teesdale – The Area and its Natural History* (ed. A.R. Clapham), pp. 64-87. Collins, London.

Ratcliffe, D.A. (1979) The breeding habitat of the greenshank in Scotland. In: *Greenshanks* (by D. Nethersole-Thompson & M. Nethersole-Thompson), pp. 185-192. T & AD Poyser, Berkhamsted.

Ratcliffe, D.A. (1979) The end of the large blue butterfly. *New Scientist*, **8 November**, 457-458.

Ratcliffe, D.A. (1979) The role of the Nature Conservancy Council in the conservation of rare and threatened plants in Britain. In: *Survival or Extinction. Proceedings of a conference held at the Royal Botanic Gardens Kew, September 1978* (eds. H. Synge & H. Townsend), pp. 31-35. Bentham-Moxon Trust, Kew.

Ratcliffe, D.A. (1980) *The Peregrine Falcon*. Poyser, Calton.

Ratcliffe, D.A. (1981) Introduced species in forestry and their relevance to nature conservation. *Discussion Papers in Conservation, University College London*, **30**, 32-37.

Ratcliffe, D.A. (1981) The purpose of nature conservation. *Ecos*, **2**, 8-12.

Ratcliffe, D.A. (1983) Foreword. In: *Enjoying Ornithology* (ed. R. Hickling), pp. xx-xxi. Poyser, Calton.

Ratcliffe, D.A. (1981) Why protection? *Naturopa*, **38**, 4-6.

Ratcliffe, D.A. (1984) The Peregrine breeding population of the United Kingdom in 1981. *Bird Study*, **31**, 1-18.

Ratcliffe, D.A. (1984) Post-medieval and recent changes in British vegetation - the culmination of human influence. *New Phytologist*, **98**, 73-100.

Ratcliffe, D.A. (1984) Tree-nesting by Peregrines in Britain and Ireland. *Bird Study*, **31**, 232-233.

Ratcliffe, D.A. (1985) Uplands: tomorrow is too late. *Natural World*, **15**, 30.

Ratcliffe, D.A. (1985) The way ahead: a personal view. *Natural World*, **13**, 30.

Ratcliffe, D.A. (1986) The effects of afforestation on the wildlife of open habitats. In: *Trees and Wildlife in the Scottish Uplands* (ed. D. Jenkins), pp. 46-54. Institute of Terrestrial Ecology, Huntingdon.

Ratcliffe, D.A. (1986) The need for retaining open ground habitats for wildlife. In: *Forestry's Social and Environmental Benefits and Responsibilities* (ed. R.J. Davies), pp. 32-38. Institute of Chartered Foresters, Edinburgh.

Ratcliffe, D.A. (1986) Selection of important areas for wildlife conservation in Great Britain: the Nature Conservancy Council's approach. In: *Wildlife Conservation Evaluation* (ed. M.B. Usher), pp. 135-159. Chapman & Hall, London.

Ratcliffe, D.A. (1988) The British upland scene. In: *NCC Research in the Uplands* (eds. D.B.A. Thompson, S. Whyte & P.H. Oswald), pp. 7-15. Nature Conservancy Council, Peterborough.

Ratcliffe, D.A. (1988) Human impacts on the environment in relation to the history and biological future of the peregrine. In: *Peregrine Falcon Populations. Their Management and Recovery* (eds. T.J. Cade, J.H. Enderson, C.G. Thelander & C.M. White), pp. 813-820. The Peregrine Fund, Boise.

Ratcliffe, D.A. (1988) The Madison conference and research on peregrines. In: *Peregrine Falcon Populations. Their Management and Recovery* (eds. T.J. Cade, J.H. Enderson, C.G. Thelander & C.M. White), pp. 17-20. The Peregrine Fund, Boise.

Ratcliffe, D.A. (1988) The Peregrine population of Great Britain and Ireland. In: *Peregrine Falcon Populations. Their Management and Recovery* (eds. T.J. Cade, J.H. Enderson, C.G. Thelander & C.M. White), pp. 147-157. The Peregrine Fund, Boise.

Ratcliffe, D.A. (1989) The Nature Conservancy Council 1979-1989. *Ecos*, **10**, 9-15.

Ratcliffe, D.A. (1989) An uncertain future for official nature conservation. *British Wildlife*, **1**, 89-91.

Ratcliffe, D.A. (published as Derek Radcliffe) (1989) The end of British nature conservation? *New Scientist*, **9 September**, 75-76.

Ratcliffe, D.A. (1990) *Bird Life of Mountain and Upland.* Cambridge University Press, Cambridge.

Ratcliffe, D.A. (1990) Upland birds and their conservation. *British Wildlife*, **2**, 1-12.

Ratcliffe, D.A. (1991) The mountain flora of Britain and Ireland. *British Wildlife*, **3**, 10-21.

Ratcliffe, D.A. (1991) Foreword. In: *Atlas of Bryophytes of the British Isles, Volume 1 Liverworts (Hepaticae and Anthocerotae)* (eds. M.O. Hill, C.D. Preston & A.J.E. Smith), pp. 7-8. Harley Books, Chichester.

Ratcliffe, D.A. (1992) The Backhouse *Trichomanes*. *Naturalist*, **117**, 49-50.

Ratcliffe, D.A. (1993) *The Peregrine Falcon* (Second edition). Poyser, London.

Ratcliffe, D.A. (1994) 20-20 vision. The wildlife view. *Natural World*, **42**, 14-16.

Ratcliffe, D.A. (1994) *Arabis petraea* (L.) Lam. In: *Scarce Plants in Britain* (eds. A. Stewart, D.A. Pearman & C.D. Preston), p. 51. JNCC, Peterborough.

Ratcliffe, D.A. (1994) *Carex atrata* (L.). In: *Scarce Plants in Britain* (eds. A. Stewart, D.A. Pearman & C.D. Preston), p. 76. JNCC, Peterborough.

Ratcliffe, D.A. (1994) *Carex capillaris* (L.). In: *Scarce Plants in Britain* (eds. A. Stewart, D.A. Pearman & C.D. Preston), p. 77. JNCC, Peterborough.

Ratcliffe, D.A. (1994) *Carex saxatilis* (L.). In: *Scarce Plants in Britain* (eds. A. Stewart, D.A. Pearman & C.D. Preston), p. 96. JNCC, Peterborough.

Ratcliffe, D.A. (1994) *Orthilia secunda* (L.) House. In: *Scarce Plants in Britain* (eds. A. Stewart, D.A. Pearman & C.D. Preston), p. 300. JNCC, Peterborough.

Ratcliffe, D.A. (1994) *Phleum alpinum* (L.). In: *Scarce Plants in Britain* (eds. A. Stewart, D.A. Pearman & C.D. Preston), p. 309. JNCC, Peterborough.

Ratcliffe, D.A. (1994) *Poa alpina* (L.). In: *Scarce Plants in Britain* (eds. A. Stewart, D.A. Pearman & C.D. Preston), p. 314. JNCC, Peterborough.

Ratcliffe, D.A. (1994) *Poa glauca* Vahl. In: *Scarce Plants in Britain* (eds. A. Stewart, D.A. Pearman & C.D. Preston), p. 316. JNCC, Peterborough.

Ratcliffe, D.A. (1994) *Pyrola media* Sw. In: *Scarce Plants in Britain* (eds. A. Stewart, D.A. Pearman & C.D. Preston), p. 347. JNCC, Peterborough.

Ratcliffe, D.A. (1994) *Sagina saginoides* (L.) Karsten. In: *Scarce Plants in Britain* (eds. A. Stewart, D.A. Pearman & C.D. Preston), p. 363. JNCC, Peterborough.

Ratcliffe, D.A. (1994) *Veronica alpina* (L.). In: *Scarce Plants in Britain* (eds. A. Stewart, D.A. Pearman & C.D. Preston), p. 427. JNCC, Peterborough.

Ratcliffe, D.A. (1995) The government's response to the European Union Habitats and Species Directive. *British Wildlife*, **6**, 307-309.

Ratcliffe, D.A. (1996) Ernest Blezard (1902-1970). Lakeland wildlife. *Transactions of the Carlisle Natural History Society*, **12**, 127-132.

Ratcliffe, D.A. (1996) Wildlife and its conservation in Cumbria. *Transactions of the Carlisle Natural History Society*, **12**, 89-106.

Ratcliffe, D.A. (1996) The Anglesey peregrines. In: *The Peregrine Sketchbook* (by C.F. Tunnicliffe), pp. 69-78. Excellent Press, London.

Ratcliffe, D.A. (1997) Paul Westmacott Richards, CBE (1908-1995). *Watsonia*, **21**, 413-414.

Ratcliffe, D.A. (1997) *The Raven.* Poyser, London.

Ratcliffe, D.A. (1998). Foreword. In: *Tundra Plovers: the Eurasian, Pacific and American Golden Plovers and Grey Plover* (by I. Byrkjedal and D.B.A. Thompson), pp xix-xxi Poyser/Academic Press, London.

Ratcliffe, D.A. (1998) John Grant Roger (1909-1997). *Watsonia*, **22**, 137-138.

Ratcliffe, D.A. (1999) *Oxytropis campestris* (L.) DC. In: *British Red Data Books 1. Vascular Plants* (ed. M.J. Wiggington). pp. 269-270. JNCC, Peterborough.

Ratcliffe, D.A. (2000) *In Search of Nature.* Peregrine Books, Leeds.

Ratcliffe, D.A. (2002) *Lakeland.* HarperCollins, London.

Ratcliffe, D.A. (2002) Peregrine Falcon *Falco peregrinus*. In: *The Migration Atlas. Movements of the Birds of Britain and Ireland* (eds. C. Wernham, M. Toms, J. Marchant, J. Clark, G. Siriwardena & S. Bailie), pp. 256-258. Poyser, London.

Ratcliffe, D.A. (2003) The peregrine saga. In: *Birds of Prey in a Changing Environment* (eds. D.B.A. Thompson, S. Redpath, A.H. Fielding, M. Marquiss & C.A. Galbraith), pp. 91-98. The Stationery Office, Edinburgh.

Ratcliffe, D.A. (2003). Foreword. In: *Birds of Prey in a Changing Environment* (eds. D.B.A. Thompson, S. Redpath, A.H. Fielding, M. Marquiss & C.A. Galbraith), pp. xix-xx. The Stationery Office, Edinburgh.

Ratcliffe, D.A. (2005) *Lapland: A Natural History.* T & AD Poyser, London.

Ratcliffe, D.A. (2007) *Galloway and the Borders.* Collins, London.

Ratcliffe, D.A. & Eddy, A. (1960) *Alopecurus alpinus* Sm. in Britain. *Proceedings of the Botanical Society of the British Isles*, **3**, 389-391.

Ratcliffe, D.A. & Eggeling, W.J. (1960) Report on Haaf Gruney Island, Shetlands – An ornithological and botanical survey. *Report for the year ending September 1960.* pp. 22-23. Nature Conservancy.

Ratcliffe, D.A. & McVean, D.N. (1958) Scottish vegetation survey. *Report for the year ending September 1958.* pp. 57-60. Nature Conservancy.

Ratcliffe, D.A. & Mitchell, J. (1999) *Woodsia ilvensis* (L.) R.Br. In: *British Red Data Books 1. Vascular Plants* (ed. M.J. Wiggington). p. 394. JNCC, Peterborough.

Ratcliffe, D.A. & Thompson, D.B.A. (1988) The British Uplands: their ecological character and international significance. In: *Ecological Change in the Uplands* (eds. M.B. Usher & D.B.A. Thompson), pp. 9-36. Blackwell Scientific Publications, Oxford.

Ratcliffe, D.A. & Walker, D. (1958) The Silver Flowe, Galloway, Scotland. *Journal of Ecology*, **46**, 407-445.

Ratcliffe, D.A., Parr, S., Cadbury, J., Bibby, C., Village, A., Davis, P., Everett, M., Porter, R., Taylor, K., et al. (1983) Raptor round-up. *Birds*, **9**, 24-28.

Ratcliffe, D.A., Birks, H.J.B. & Birks, H.H. (1993) The ecology and conservation of the Killarney Fern *Trichomanes speciosum* Willd in Britain and Ireland. *Biological Conservation*, **66**, 231-247.

Ratcliffe, D.A., Birks, H.J.B. & Birks, H.H. (1999) *Trichomanes speciosum* Willd. In: *British Red Data Books 1. Vascular Plants* (ed. M.J. Wiggington). p. 374. JNCC, Peterborough.

Rodwell, J.S. (ed.) Pigott, C.D., Ratcliffe, D.A., Malloch, A.J.C., Birks, H.J.B., Proctor, M.C.F., Shimwell, D.W., Huntley, J.P., Radford, E., Wiggington, M.J. & Wilkins, P. (1991a) *British Plant Communities 1. Woodlands and Scrub.* 395 pp. Cambridge University Press, Cambridge.

Rodwell, J.S. (ed.) Pigott, C.D., Ratcliffe, D.A., Malloch, A.J.C., Birks, H.J.B., Proctor, M.C.F., Shimwell, D.W., Huntley, J.P., Radford, E., Wiggington, M.J. & Wilkins, P. (1991b) *British Plant Communities 2. Mires and Heaths.* 628 pp. Cambridge University Press, Cambridge.

Rodwell, J.S. (ed.) Pigott, C.D., Ratcliffe, D.A., Malloch, A.J.C., Birks, H.J.B., Proctor, M.C.F., Shimwell, D.W., Huntley, J.P., Radford, E., Wiggington, M.J. & Wilkins, P. (1992) *British Plant Communities 3. Grasslands and Montane Communities*. 552 pp. Cambridge University Press, Cambridge.

Rodwell, J.S. (ed.) Pigott, C.D., Ratcliffe, D.A., Malloch, A.J.C., Birks, H.J.B., Proctor, M.C.F., Shimwell, D.W., Huntley, J.P., Radford, E., Wiggington, M.J. & Wilkins, P. (1995) *British Plant Communities 4. Aquatic Communities, Swamps and Tall-Herb Fens*. 283 pp. Cambridge University Press, Cambridge.

Rodwell, J.S. (ed.) Pigott, C.D., Ratcliffe, D.A., Malloch, A.J.C., Birks, H.J.B., Proctor, M.C.F., Shimwell, D.W., Huntley, J.P., Radford, E., Wiggington, M.J. & Wilkins, P. (2000) *British Plant Communities 5. Maritime Communities and Vegetation of Open Habitats*. 512 pp. Cambridge University Press, Cambridge.

Smith, J.E., Clapham, A.R. & Ratcliffe, D.A. (eds.) (1977) Scientific Aspects of Nature Conservation in Great Britain. *Proceedings of the Royal Society of London B-Biological Sciences*, **197**, 3-103.

Stroud, D.A., Reed, T.M., Pienkowski, M.W. & Lindsay, R.A. (eds. D.A. Ratcliffe & P.H. Oswald) (1987) *Birds, Bogs and Forestry – The Peatlands of Caithness, and Sutherland*. 121 pp. Nature Conservancy Council, Peterborough.

Wynne-Edwards, V.C., Morris, M.G., Pigott, C.D., Ratcliffe, D.A., Mellanby, K. & Hawksworth, D.L. (1977) General discussion. *Proceedings of the Royal Society of London B-Biological Sciences*, **197**, 97-99.

Index

Cathy Jenks and John Birks

Because Derek Ratcliffe's life was, and his legacy is, very diverse and covers, for example, mountain ecology, plant hunting, nature conservation, pesticides, and field ornithology, the book is equally diverse. Thus the index is divided into two sections: one for people, places, and topics, and the other for species (sub-divided into major species groups). Pages with illustrations of an index entry are shown in **bold**.

People, places, and topics

Species

Birds

Accipiter nisus, see Sparrowhawk
Accipter cooperii, see Hawk , Cooper's
Accipiter gentilis, see Goshawk
Accipiter striatus, Hawk, Sharp-shinned
Actitis hypoleucos, see Sandpiper, Common
Alauda arvensis, see Skylark
Alca torda, see Razorbill
Alectoris rufa, see Partridge, Red-legged
Anas crecca, see Teal
Anas penelope, see Wigeon
Anas platyrhynchos, see Mallard
Anser anser, see Goose, Greylag
Anthus cervinus, see Pipit, Red-throated
Anthus pratensis, see Pipit, Meadow
Aquila chrysaetos, see Eagle, Golden
Ardea cinerea, see Heron, Grey
Arenaria interpres, see Turnstone
Asio flammeus, see Owl, Short-eared
Athene noctua, see Owl, Little
Auk
   Great Auk (*Penguinus impennis*) 333
Blackbird (Common Blackbird: *Turdus merula*) 3, 303
Blackcap (Eurasian Blackcap: *Sylvia atricapilla*) 3
Bluethroat (*Luscinia svecica*) 309
Bombycilla garrulus, see Waxwing
Brambling (*Fringilla montifringilla*) 309, 313
Bubo scandiacus, see Owl, Snowy
Bucephala clangula, see Goldeneye
Bunting
   Corn Bunting (*Emberiza calandra*) 303
   Lapland Bunting (Lapland Longspur: *Calcarius lapponicus*) 309, 317
   Reed Bunting (Common Reed Bunting: *Emberiza schoeniclus*) 309
   Rustic Bunting (*Emberiza rustica*) 478
   Snow Bunting (*Plectrophenax nivalis*) 66, 192, 198, 222, 224, 236, 309, 317, 318, 319, 323, 324
   Buntings 283
Burhinus oedicnemus, see Curlew, Stone
Bustards (Otididae) 488
Buteo buteo, see Buzzard
Buteo lagopus, see Buzzard, Rough-legged
Buzzard
   Buzzard (Common Buzzard: *Buteo buteo*) 8, 28-30, 33, 34, 285, 303, 317, 319, 321-323, 332, 518
   Honey Buzzard (European Honey Buzzard: *Pernis apivorus*) 211
   Rough-legged Buzzard (*Buteo lagopus*) 308
   Buzzards (unspecified) 360
Calcarius lapponicus, see Bunting, Lapland
Calidris alpina, Dunlin
Calidris maritima, see Sandpiper, Purple
Calidris minuta, see Stint, Little
Calidris temminckii, see Stint, Temminck's
Capercaillie (Western Capercaillie: *Tetrao urogallus*) 308
Caprimulgus europaeus, see Nightjar
Carduelis carduelis, see Goldfinch
Carduelis flammea, see Redpoll
Carduelis flavirostris, see Twite
Carduelis hornemanni, see Redpoll, Arctic
Chaffinch (Common Chaffinch: *Fringilla coelebs*) 4, 211, 303
Charadrius dubius, see Plover, Little Ringed
Charadrius hiaticulata, see Plover, Ringed
Charadrius morinellus, see Dotterel
Chloris chloris, see Greenfinch
Chough (Red-billed Chough: *Pyrrhocorax pyrrhocorax*) 66, 317, 319
Chroicocephalus ridibundus, see Gull, Black-headed
Cinclus cinclus, see Dipper
Circus aeruginosus, see Harrier, Marsh
Circus cyaneus, see Harrier, Hen
Circus pygargus, see Harrier, Montagu's
Clangula hyemalis, see Duck, Long-tailed
Columba livia, see Pigeon, Homing
Columba oenas, see Dove, Stock
Columba palumbus, see Pigeon, Wood
Corvids 283
Corvus corax, see Raven
Corvus cornix, see Crow, Hooded
Corvus corone, see Crow, Carrion
Corvus frugilegus, see Rook
Corvus monedula, see Jackdaw
Crane (Common Crane, *Grus grus*) 305, 308
Crossbill
   Common Crossbill (Red Crossbill: *Loxia curvirostra*) 322
Crow
   Carrion Crow (*Corvus corone*) 3, 33, 193, 285, 303, 317

Northern Rockcress

Carex aquatilis, see Water Sedge

Carex atrata, see Black Sedge

Carex atrofusca, see Scorched Alpine-sedge

Carex bigelowii, see Stiff Sedge

Carex capillaris, see Hair Sedge

Carex chordorrhiza, see String Sedge

Carex lachenalii, see Hare's-foot Sedge

Carex limosa, see Bog-sedge

Carex magellanica ssp. *irrigua*, see Boreal Bog-sedge

Carex magellanica, see Tall Bog-sedge

Carex microglochin, see Bristle Sedge

Carex norvegica, see Alpine Sedge

Carex ornithopoda, see Bird's-foot Sedge

Carex pauciflora, see Few-flowered Sedge

Carex paupercula, see Boreal Bog-sedge

Carex rariflora, see Mountain Bog-sedge

Carex rupestris, see Rock Sedge

Carex saxatilis, see Russet Sedge

Carex vaginata, see Sheathed Sedge

Carex versicaria, Bladder-sedge

Cassiope hypnoides, see Matted Cassiope

Catabrosa aquatica, see Water Whorl-grass

Catacol Whitebeam (*Sorbus pseudomeinichii*) 168

Centaurea cyanus, see Cornflower

Cerastium alpinum, see Alpine Mouse-ear

Cerastium arcticum, see Arctic Mouse-ear

Cerastium cerastoides, see Starwort Mouse-ear

Cerastrium cerastoides ssp. *edmonstonii*, see Edmonston's Mouse-ear

Chamerion angustifolium, see Rosebay Willowherb

Charlock (*Sinapis arvensis*) 304

Cherleria sedoides, see Mossy Cyphel

Chestnut Rush (*Juncus castaneus*) 158, 178

Chickweed Willowherb (*Epilobium alsinifolium*) 178

Chickweed Wintergreen (*Trientalis europaea*) 179

Cicerbita alpina, see Alpine Sow-thistle

Circaea alpina, see Alpine Enchanter's Nightshade

Cirsium helenioides, see Melancholy Thistle

Cirsium spp., see Thistle

Cloudberry (*Rubus chaemomorus*) 95, 178, 183, **506**

Cochlearia micacea, see Scottish Scurvygrass

Cochlearia officinalis ssp. *alpina*, see Pyrenean Scurvygrass

Cochlearia officinalis, see Common Scurvygrass

Cochlearia pyrenaica ssp. *alpina*, see Pyrenean Scurvygrass

Cocksfoot (*Dactylis glomerata*) 304

Codonopsis, see Bonnet Bellflower

Common Juniper (prostrate) (*Juniperus communis* ssp. *nana*) 131, **135**, 178

Common Poppy (*Papaver rhoeas*) 304

Common Reed (*Phragmites australis*) 17

Common Scurvygrass (*Cochlearia officinalis*) 177

Common Toadflax (*Linaria vulgaris*) 304

Cornflower (*Centaurea cyanus*) 304

Cornus suecica, Dwarf Cornel

Cotoneaster (*Cotoneaster*) 160

"Cow Parsnip" 304

Cowberry (*Vaccinium vitis-idaea*) 179

Creeping Lady's-tresses (*Goodyera repens*) 157

Creeping Spearwort (*Ranunculus reptans*) 157

Crepis mollis, see Northern Hawk's-beard

Crowberry (*Empetrum nigrum*) 142, 179, 199, **513**

Cryptogramma crispa, see Parsley Fern

Curved Wood-rush (*Luzula arcuata*) 158, 178

Cypripedium calceolus, see Lady's-slipper

Cystopteris montana, see Mountain Bladderfern

Dactylis glomerata, see Cocksfoot

Dark-leaved Willow (*Salix myrsinifolia*) 179

Deergrass (*Trichophorum germanicum*) 142, 177

Delphinium, see Larkspur

Dense-flowered Orchid (*Neotinea maculata*) 186

Deschampsia alpina, see Alpine Hair-grass

Deschampsia cespitosa ssp. *alpina*, see Alpine Tufted Hair-grass

Deschampsia cespitosa, see Tufted Hair-grass

Diapensia (*Diapensia lapponica*) 167, 178

Diapensia lapponica, see Diapensia

Diphasiastrum alpinum, see Alpine Clubmoss

Dock (*Rumex* spp.) 304

Don's Couch-grass (*Agropyron donianum*) 178

Don's Twitch, see Don's Couch-grass

Downy Birch (*Betula pubescens*) 142, 234, **502, 504, 508, 509**

Downy Willow (*Salix lapponum*) 97, 168, **169**, 178, 184

Draba incana, see Hoary Whitlowgrass

Meconopsis cambrica, see Welsh Poppy
Melampyrum sylvaticum, see Wood Cow-wheat
Melancholy Thistle (Cirsium helenioides) 179, 182, 184
Melica nutans, see Mountain Melick
Menyanthes trifoliata, see Bogbean
Mertensia maritima, see Oysterplant
Meum athamanticum, see Spignel
Michaelmas Daisy (Aster) 160
Military Orchid (Orchis militaris) **150**
Milk-vetch (Astragalus spp.) 304
Minuartia rubella, see Alpine Sandwort
Minuartia rubella, see Mountain Sandwort
Minuartia stricta, see Bog Sandwort
Minuartia verna, see Spring Sandwort
Molinia caerulea, see Purple Moor-grass
Moneses spp., see Wintergreens
Moneses uniflora, see One-flowered Wintergreen
Moss Campion (Silene acaulis) 59, **70**, 177, 178, 186, **513**
Mossy Cyphel (Cherleria sedoides) 178, 186
Mossy Saxifrage (Saxifraga hypnoides) 178, 183
Mountain Avens (Dryas octopetala) 9, **37**, 52, **53**, 59, 95, **177**, 178, 181, 184-186, **512**
Mountain Bladder-fern (Cystopteris montana) 52, **53**, 76, 178, 182, 184
Mountain Bog-sedge (Carex rariflora) 58, 158, 178
Mountain Crowberry (Empetrum hermaphroditum) 59, 96, 177, 178
Mountain Everlasting (Antennaria dioica) 179
Mountain Heath (Phyllodoce caerulea) 178
Mountain Male-fern (Dryopteris oreades) 178
Mountain Melick (Melica nutans) 179, 184
Mountain Pansy (Viola lutea) 179, 180, 182
Mountain Sandwort (Minuartia rubella) 158, 178
Mountain Sedge, see Stiff Sedge
Mountain Sorrel (Oxyria digyna) 59, 178
Mountain Willow (Salix arbuscula) 178
Myosotis alpestris, see Alpine Forget-me-not
Myosotis stolonifera x secunda, see Pale x Creeping Forget-me-not
Myosotis stolonifera, see Pale Forget-me-not
Nardus stricta, see Mat-grass
Narrow Small-reed (Calamagrostis stricta) 94
Narthecium ossifragum, see Bog Asphodel
Neotinea maculata, see Dense-flowered Orchid

Net-leaved Willow (Salix reticulata) 52, **53**, 76, 178
Newman's Lady-fern (Athyrium flexile) 178
Northern Alpine Milk-vetch (Astragalus alpinus ssp. arcticus) **70**
Northern Bedstraw (Galium boreale) 179, 183
Northern Birdseye Primrose (Primula nutans) **512**
Northern Buckler-fern (Dryopteris expansa) 178
Northern Crowberry, see Mountain Crowberry
Northern Deergrass (Trichophorum cespitosum) 95
Northern Hawk's-beard (Crepis mollis) 168
Northern Rockcress (Cardaminopsis (Arabis) petraea) 178, 183
Northern Sedge, see Water Sedge
Northern Spike-rush (Eleocharis mamillata ssp. austriaca) 93
Norway Spruce (Picea abies) **502, 509**
Norwegian Cudwort, see Highland Cudwort
Norwegian Mugwort (Artemisia norvegica) 52, **53**, 178
Norwegian Sandwort (Arenaria norvegica) 186
Norwegian Whitlowgrass (Draba norvegica) 178
Norwegian Wintergreen (Pyrola norvegica) **71**
Oak (Quercus spp.) 372, 374
Oak Fern (Gymnocarpium dryopteris) **69**
Oblong Woodsia (Woodsia ilvensis) **55**, 59, 66, 67, 82, 92, 162, **164**, 165, 167, 171, 178, 184, 245
Oblong-leaved Hawkweed (Hieracium lingulatum) 158
One-flowered Wintergreen (Moneses uniflora) 165
Ononis reclinata, see Small Restharrow
Orchis militaris, see Military Orchid
Orthilia secunda, see Serrated Wintergreen
Oxyria digyna, see Mountain Sorrel
Oxytropis campestris, Yellow Oxytropis
Oxytropis halleri, see Purple Oxytropis
Oysterplant (Mertensia maritima) **71**
Pale Forget-me-not (Myosotis stolonifera) 179
Pale x Creeping Forget-me-not (Myosotis stolonifera x secunda) 92
Papaver rhoeas, see Common Poppy
Parsley Fern (Cryptogramma crispa) **69**, 178